# Making TEX Work

# Making TeX Work

Norman Walsh

O'Reilly & Associates, Inc.
103 Morris Street, Suite A
Sebastopol, CA  95472

**Making TEX Work**
by Norman Walsh

Copyright © 1994 O'Reilly & Associates, Inc. All rights reserved.
Printed in the United States of America.

**Editor:** Deborah Russell

**Production Editor:** Stephen Spainhour

**Printing History:**

| April 1994: | First Edition. |
| July 1994: | Minor corrections. |
| October 1994: | Minor corrections. |

This book is printed on acid-free paper with 50% recycled content, 10-15% post-consumer waste.
O'Reilly & Associates is committed to using paper with the highest recycled content available
consistent with high quality.

ISBN: 1-56592-051-1

# Table of Contents

# List of Tables

# List of Figures

# List of Examples

# *Preface*

TEX is a tool for creating professional quality, typeset pages of any kind. It is particularly good, perhaps unsurpassed, at typesetting mathematics; as a result, it is widely used in scientific writing. Some of its other features, like its ability to handle multiple languages in the same document and the fact that the content of a document (chapters, sections, equations, tables, figures, etc.) can be separated from its form (typeface, size, spacing, indentation, etc.) are making TEX more common outside of scientific and academic circles.

Designed by Donald Knuth in the late 1970s, more than a decade of refinement has gone into the program called "TEX" today. The resulting system produces publication-quality output while maintaining portability across an extremely wide range of platforms.

Remarkably, TEX is free. This fact, probably as much as any other, has contributed to the development of a complete "TEX system" by literally thousands of volunteers. TEX, the program, forms the core of this environment and is now supported by hundreds of tools.

## *Why Read This Book?*

This book is for anyone who uses TEX. Novices will need at least one other reference, because this book does not describe the nuts and bolts of writing documents with TEX in any great detail.

If you are new to TEX, there is much to learn. There are many books that describe how to use TEX. However, the focus of this book is mostly at a higher level. After digesting Chapter 1, *The Big Picture*, you should be able to proceed through the rest of the book without much difficulty even if you have never seen TEX before. So, if you are a system administrator interested in learning enough about these programs to install and test them for your users, you should be all set. If you are interested in learning how to write documents with TEX, this book will be helpful, but it will not be wholly sufficient.

Why do you need this book at all? Although many individual components of the TEX system are well documented, there has never before been a complete reference to the whole system. This book surveys the entire world of TEX software and helps you see how the various pieces are related.

A functioning TEX system is really a large collection of programs that interact in subtle ways to produce a document that, when formatted by TEX, prints the output you want. All the different interactions that take place ultimately result in less work for you, the writer, even though it may seem like more work at first. Heck, it may *be* more work at first, but in the long run, the savings are tremendous.

Many books about TEX refer the reader to a "local guide" for more information about previewing and printing documents and what facilities exist for incorporating special material into documents (like special fonts and pictures and figures). In reality, very few local guides exist.

The TEX environment is now mature and stable enough to support a more "global guide." That is what this book attempts to be. It goes into detail about previewing and printing, about incorporating other fonts, about adding pictures and figures to your documents, and about many other things overlooked by other books.

Because fonts play a ubiquitous role in typesetting, this book is also about METAFONT, the tool that Donald Knuth designed for creating fonts.

## *Scope of This Book*

Here's how the book is laid out.

**Part I:** *An Introduction to TEX.*

Chapter 1, *The Big Picture.* If you don't know anything about TEX at all, this chapter will help you get started. If you're a system adminstrator charged with the task of installing and maintaining TEX tools, you'll get enough information to do the job.

Chapter 2, *Editing.* An overview of some environments that can make working with TEX documents easier. It describes some editors that "understand" TEX, how to integrate TEX into a "programmer's editor," spellchecking, revision control, and other aspects of TEXnical editing.

Chapter 3, *Running TEX.* The mechanics of running TEX, the program. It discusses what things TEX needs to be able to run, how to start TEX, command-line options, leaving TEX, and recovery from errors.

Chapter 4, *Macro Packages*. Overview of TEX macro packages. This chapter describes how to make a format file, the major general-purpose writing packages, some special-purpose writing packages, how to make slides for presentations, and how to handle color in TEX.

**Part II**: *Elements of a Complex Document*.

Chapter 5, *Fonts*. This chapter explores the issues that need to be addressed when using fonts. Many of these issues are not particularly TEX-related, but TEX is very flexible, and it's important to understand the tradeoffs that must be made. This chapter also examines some TEX-specific issues: font selection, files that TEX needs, automatic font generation, and virtual fonts.

Chapter 6, *Pictures and Figures*. How many ways are there to include pictures and figures in a TEX document? Lots and lots of ways. This chapter examines them all.

Chapter 7, *International Considerations*. TEX is well qualified to do international typesetting. This chapter looks at the issues that are involved: representing international symbols in your input file, what TEX produces, getting the right fonts, multiple languages in the same document, and macro packages and style files that solve some of these problems. Some strategies for dealing with very difficult languages (like Japanese and Arabic) are also explored.

Chapter 8, *Printing*. What goes in has to come out. This chapter tells the what, where, why, and how of printing your documents.

Chapter 9, *Previewing*. Save paper; preview your documents before you print them.

Chapter 10, *Online Documentation*. Online documentation is becoming increasingly popular. This chapter explores different ways that both typeset and online documentation can be produced from the same set of input files.

Chapter 11, *Introducing METAFONT*. Sometimes it is necessary or desirable to create a special version of a standard TEX font. Maybe you really need the standard 10pt font at 11.3pt. This chapter will tell you how to work with existing METAFONT fonts. It *won't* tell you how to create your own fonts; that's a whole different story.

Chapter 12, *Bibliographies, Indexes, and Glossaries*. Maintaining a bibliographic database can be a great timesaver. This chapter looks at the BIBTEX program and other tools for building and using bibliographic databases. It also discusses the creation of indexes and glossaries.

**Part III**: *A Tools Overview*.

Chapter 13, *Non-commercial Environments*. Many TEX environments are freely available. This chapter describes public domain, free, and shareware versions of TEX.

Chapter 14, *Commercial Environments*. A large, complex system like TEX can be over-whelming (although I hope less so after you read this book ;-). One of the advantages of selecting a commercial implementation of TEX is that some form of customer support is usually provided. Still other commercial implementations offer features not found in any free releases. This chapter describes several commercial TEX releases.

Chapter 15, *TEX on the Macintosh*. Many issues discussed in this book apply equally to all platforms, including the Macintosh platform, but the Mac has its own special set of features. This chapter looks at some versions of TEX and other tools designed specifically for use on the Mac.

Chapter 16, *TEX Utilities*. This chapter lists many of the the utilities available in the CTAN archives and provides a brief description of what they do.

Appendix A, *Filename Extension Summary*. Lots of files can be identified by their ex-tensions. This appendix lists the extensions that are most often seen in conjunction with TEX and describes what the associated files contain.

Appendix B, *Font Samples*. Examples of many METAFONT fonts available from the CTAN archives.

Appendix C, *Resources*. A complete list of the resources described in this book.

Appendix D, *Long Examples*. This appendix contains examples (scripts, batch files, pro-grams) that seemed too long to place in the running text.

*Bibliography*. Where I learned what I know. Also, where you can look for more infor-mation about specific topics.

## *Conventions Used in This Book*

The following typographic conventions are used in this book:

| | |
|---|---|
| *Italic* | is used for filenames, directories, user commands, program names, and macro packages (except where the distinctive logo type is used). Sometimes italics are used in the traditional way for emphasis of new ideas and important concepts. |
| `Typewriter` | is used for program examples, FTP sites, TEX control sequences, and little bits of TEX syntax that appear in running text (for example, typewriter text in a reference to the LATEX picture environment is a clue that LATEX literally uses the word "picture" to identify this environment). |
| **`Typewriter Bold`** | is used in examples to show the user's actual input at the terminal. |

| | |
|---|---|
| *Typewriter Italic* | identifies text that requires a context-specific substitution. For example, *filename* in an example would be replaced by some particular filename. |
| Footnotes | are used for parenthetical remarks. Sometimes, lies are spoken to simplify the discussion, and the footnotes restore the lie to the truth.* |

Filename extensions, like ".*tex*" in *book.tex*, are shown in uppercase letters when referring to a particular type of file. For example, a TEX Font Metric or TFM file would be *somefile.tfm*. The actual extension of the file may be different (upper or lowercase, longer or shorter) depending on your operating environment.

When the shell prompt is shown in an example, it is shown as a dollar sign, $. You should imagine that this is your system's prompt, which might otherwise be %, C>, [C:\], or a dialog box.

When spaces are important in an example, the "␣" character is used to emphasize the spaces. Effective,␣isn't␣it?

In some places, I refer to specific keys that you should press. When it's important that I mean pressing particular keys and not typing something, I emphasize the keys. For instance, an example that includes Enter means that you should literally press the Enter or Return key. The sequence Ctrl-D means that you should press and hold the "Control" and "d" keys simultaneously. Control-key combinations aren't case sensitive, so you needn't press the shift key.

# *How to Get TEX*

TEX and the other programs mentioned in this book are available from a number of places. It's impossible to list all of the places where you might find any given tool, but there is one place where you will almost certainly find *every* tool: the Comprehensive TEX Archive Network (CTAN).

This network is a fully-mirrored anonymous FTP hierarchy on three continents. Always use the FTP site that is geographically closest to you. The following table lists the current members of CTAN as of July, 1993:

| Geographic Location | Site | IP Address | Top Level Directory |
|---|---|---|---|
| United States | ftp.shsu.edu | 192.92.115.10 | */tex-archive* |
| England | ftp.tex.ac.uk | 131.151.79.32 | */tex-archive* |
| Germany | ftp.uni-stuttgart.de | 129.69.8.13 | */tex-archive* |

---

*And sometimes they don't ;-)

You may also access the CTAN archives by electronic mail if you do not have FTP access. For up-to-date instructions about the mail server, send the single-line message `help` to *fileserv@shsu.edu.*

## Where Are the Files?

Every CTAN mirror site has the same well-organized directory structure. The top-level directory also contains a complete catalog of current files organized by name, date, and size. The catalogs are named *FILES.byname*, *FILES.bydate*, and *FILES.bysize*, respectively, in the top level directory. The top-level directory contains the following subdirectories:

| Directory | Description of Contents |
|---|---|
| *tools* | Archiving tools (*unzip, tar, compress,* etc.) |
| *biblio* | Tools for maintaining bibliographic databases |
| *digests* | Electronic digests (TEXhax, UKTEX, etc.) |
| *info* | Free documentation, many good guides |
| *dviware* | Printing and previewing software |
| *fonts* | Fonts for TEX |
| *graphics* | Software for working with pictures and figures |
| *help* | Online help files, etc. |
| *indexing* | Indexing and glossary building tools |
| *language* | Multi-national language support |
| *macros* | Macro packages and style files |
| *misc* | Stuff that doesn't fit in any other category |
| *support* | Tools for running and supporting TEX |
| *systems* | OS-specific programs and files |
| *web* | Sources for TEX programs (in WEB) |

The archives at `ftp.shsu.edu` and `ftp.tex.ac.uk` also support *gopher* access to the archives. The UK *gopher* supports indexed access to the archives. A World Wide Web (hypertext) interface to the archives is available from:

    http://jasper.ora.com/ctan.html

This interface includes brief descriptions of many packages and the ability to perform keyword and date searches.

## Getting Software Without FTP

The electronic alternatives to FTP, described in the section "Getting Examples From This Book" of this chapter are also viable alternatives for getting software from the CTAN archives.

In addition, there are a number of ways to get distributions through nonelectronic channels. The names and addresses of these sources are listed in Appendix C, *Resources.*

You can get many of the popular TEX distributions on diskette from the TEX Users Group (TUG). Emacs, *Ghostscript*, and other packages by the Free Software Foundation (FSF) are available on tape directly from the FSF. You may also find large bulletin board systems that support TEX (for example, Channel1 in Cambridge, MA)

## Getting Examples From This Book

All of the substantial code fragments and programs printed in this book are available online. The examples in this book are all in *Perl*, a language for easily manipulating text, files, and processes. I decided to use *Perl* simply because it is available for every platform discussed in this book. It is the only "universal" scripting language that will work under MS-DOS, OS/2, UNIX, and the Macintosh. All of the scripts in this book can be converted to a different scripting language (the various UNIX shells or something like *4DOS*'s extended batch language for MS-DOS and OS/2) if you prefer. I've tried to write the *Perl* scripts in a straightforward way so that any given task won't be too difficult.

The examples are available electronically in a number of ways: by FTP, FTPMAIL, BITFTP, and UUCP. The cheapest, fastest, and easiest ways are listed first. If you read from the top down, the first one that works is probably the best. Use FTP if you are directly on the Internet. Use FTPMAIL if you are not on the Internet but can send and receive electronic mail to Internet sites (this includes CompuServe users). Use BITFTP if you send electronic mail via BITNET. Use UUCP if none of the above work.

### NOTE

The examples were prepared using a UNIX system. If you are running UNIX, you can use them without modification. If you are running on another platform, you may need to modify these examples to correct the end-of-line markers. For example, whereas under UNIX every line ends with a line feed character (the carriage return is implicit), under DOS every line must end with explicit carriage return and line feed characters.

### FTP

To use FTP, you need a machine with direct access to the Internet. A sample session is shown below.

```
$ ftp ftp.uu.net Connected to ftp.uu.net.
220 ftp.UU.NET FTP server (Version 6.34 Oct 22 14:32:01 1992) ready.
Name (ftp.uu.net:prefect): anonymous
331 Guest login ok, send e-mail address as password.
Password: prefect@guide.com          (use your user name and host here)
230 Guest login ok, access restrictions apply.
ftp> cd /published/oreilly/nutshell/maketexwork
250 CWD command successful.
ftp> get README
200 PORT command successful.
```

```
150 Opening ASCII mode data connection for README (xxxx bytes).
226 Transfer complete.
local: README remote: README
xxxx bytes received in xxx seconds (xxx Kbytes/s)
ftp> binary        (select binary mode for compressed files)
200 Type set to I.
   (Repeat get commands for the other files.
   They are listed in the README file.)
ftp> quit 221 Goodbye.
$
```

### FTPMAIL

FTPMAIL is a mail server available to anyone who can send electronic mail to, and receive it from, Internet sites. This includes most workstations that have an email connection to the outside world and CompuServe users. You do not need to be directly on the Internet.

Send mail to *ftpmail@decwrl.dec.com*. In the message body, give the name of the anonymous FTP host and the FTP commands you want to run. The server will run anonymous FTP for you and mail the files back to you. To get a complete help file, send a message with no subject and the single word help in the body. The following is an example mail session that should get you the examples. This command sends you a listing of the files in the selected directory and the requested example files. The listing is useful if there's a later version of the examples you're interested in.

```
$ mail ftpmail@decwrl.dec.com
Subject: reply prefect@guide.com        (where you want files mailed)
connect ftp.uu.net
chdir /published/oreilly/nutshell/maketexwork
dir
get README
quit
```

A signature at the end of the message is acceptable as long as it appears after quit.

### BITFTP

BITFTP is a mail server for BITNET users. You send it electronic mail messages requesting files, and it sends you back the files by electronic mail. BITFTP currently serves only users who send it mail from nodes that are directly on BITNET, EARN, or NetNorth. BITFTP is a public service of Princeton University.

To use BITFTP, send mail containing your FTP commands to *BITFTP@PUCC*. For a complete help file, send HELP as the message body.

The following is the message body you should send to BITFTP:

```
FTP ftp.uu.net
NETDATA USER anonymous
PASS your Internet e-mail address       (not your BITNET address)
CD /published/oreilly/nutshell/maketexwork
```

```
DIR
GET README
QUIT
```

Questions about BITFTP can be directed to *MAINT@PUCC* on BITNET.

### UUCP

UUCP is standard on virtually all UNIX systems and is available for IBM-compatible PCs and Apple Macintoshes. The examples are available by UUCP via modem from UUNET; UUNET's connect-time charges apply. You can get the examples from UUNET whether you have an account or not. If you or your company has an account with UUNET, you will have a system with a direct UUCP connection to UUNET. Find that system, and type (as one line):

```
$ uucp uunet\!~/published/oreilly/nutshell/maketexwork/README \
     yourhost\!~/yourname/
```

The README file should appear some time later (up to a day or more) in the directory */usr/spool/uucppublic/yourname*. If you don't have an account, but would like one so that you can get electronic mail, contact UUNET at 703-204-8000.

If you don't have a UUNET account, you can set up a UUCP connection to UUNET in the United States using the phone number 1-900-468-7727. As of this writing, the cost is 50 cents per minute. The charges will appear on your next telephone bill. The login name is *uucp* with no password. Your entry may vary depending on your UUCP configuration.

### Gopher

If you are on the Internet, you can use the *gopher* facility to learn about online access to examples through the O'Reilly Online Information Resource. Access *gopher.ora.com* as appropriate from your site.

# Versions of TEX

The most recent versions of TEX and METAFONT are version 3.1415 and version 2.71, respectively. Version 3 of TEX introduced several new features designed to improve support for non-English languages (including the use of 8-bit input and some refinements to hyphenation control). If you use an older version of TEX, you should upgrade.

Donald Knuth has specified that TEX's version number converges to $\pi$, therefore version 3.1415 is only the fourth minor revision after version 3. The next minor revision will be version 3.14159. Similarly, METAFONT's version number converges to $e$ (2.7182818284...).

# *Implementations and Platforms*

The interface that TEX presents to the writer is very consistent. Most of the examples described in this book are applicable to every single implementation of TEX. However, TEX is not a closed system. It is possible to step outside of TEX to incorporate special elements into your document or take advantage of the special features of a particular environment. These extensions can dramatically restrict the portability of your documents.

Many of the topics covered in this book offer alternatives in those areas that are less portable. Therefore, it is natural to ask what implementations are really covered.

Before outlining which implementations are covered, let me suggest that this book will be useful even if you are using an implementation not "officially" covered here. The reality of the situation is this: many, many tools have been ported with TEX. Many of the tools mentioned in this book are available on platforms that are not specifically discussed. Time and equipment constraints prevented Amiga, Atari, NeXT, VMS, and Windows NT implementations of TEX from being specifically addressed in this edition of the book.

## *UNIX*

UNIX is probably the most common TEX platform. The emphasis in this book is on UNIX workstations running X11, producing output for PostScript and HP LaserJet printers.

*Linux* and other personal computer implementations of UNIX are not addressed specifically; however, with the successful port of X11 to *Linux*, I'm confident that every UNIX tool here can be, or has been, ported to *Linux* (and probably other PC UNIX environments).

The only implementation of the TEX program for UNIX considered in any detail is the free implementation distributed in *web2c*. This distribution is described in the section called "Web2C" in Chapter 13, *Non-commercial Environments*. Most of the other UNIX tools discussed here are also free.

## *MS-DOS*

With very few exceptions, the tools in this book are available under MS-DOS. Because PCs are very popular, a lot of effort has gone into porting UNIX tools to MS-DOS. Some packages, however, require a 386SX (or more powerful) processor. For the most part, I focus on PCs running MS-DOS only; however, Microsoft Windows and DesqView are not entirely ignored.

There are quite a few options when it comes to selecting an implementation of the TEX program under MS-DOS. Several free implementations are discussed as well as some commercial implementations. For more information about these implementations, consult Chapter 13, *Non-commercial Environments*, and Chapter 14, *Commercial Environments*.

## *OS/2*

In this book, OS/2 is treated primarily as a superset of MS-DOS. When possible, I look at OS/2-specific versions of each utility, but rely on MS-DOS as a fall-back.

Extensions to emTEX for OS/2 are explored, as are editing environments such as *epm*. The multi-threaded nature of OS/2 allows more complete porting of UNIX tools. When better ports are available for OS/2, they are discussed.

### *Macintosh*

The Macintosh is very different from the systems described above. Chapter 15, *TEX on the Macintosh*, discusses the Macintosh environment in detail.

There are four implementations of TEX for the Macintosh. Three are freely available, and one is commercial: CMacTEX is free, OzTEX and DirectTEX are shareware, and *Textures* is a commercial package from Blue Sky Research.

# *We'd Like to Hear From You*

We have tested and verified all of the information in this book to the best of our ability, but you may find that features have changed (or even that we have made mistakes!). Please let us know about any errors you find, as well as your suggestions for future editions, by writing:

O'Reilly & Associates, Inc.
103 Morris Street, Suite A
Sebastopol, CA 95472
1-800-998-9938 (in the US or Canada)
1-707-829-0515 (international/local)
1-707-829-0104 (FAX)

You can also send us messages electronically. To be put on the mailing list or request a catalog, send email to:

>  *nuts@ora.com*     (via the Internet)
>  *uunet!ora!nuts*    (via UUCP)


To ask technical questions or comment on the book, send email to:

>  *bookquestions@ora.com* (via the Internet)

# *Acknowledgments*

This book would not exist if I had not received support and encouragement from my friends and colleagues, near and far. I owe the deepest debt of gratitude to my wife, Deborah, for patience, understanding, and support as I progressed through what is easily the most all-consuming task I have ever undertaken.

The earliest draft of this book came about because my advisor at the University of Massachusetts, Eliot Moss, allowed me to tinker with the TEX installation in the Object Systems Lab and was always able to suggest ways to make it better. My friends and colleagues at UMass, Amer Diwan, Darko Stefanović, Dave Yates, Eric Brown, Erich Nahum, Jody Daniels, Joe McCarthy, Ken Magnani, Rick Hudson, and Tony Hosking, asked all the hard questions and didn't seem to mind when I used them as guinea pigs for my latest idea.

I'm indebted also to Eberhard Mattes, Geoffrey Tobin, George D. Greenwade, Peter Schmitt, Sebastian Rahtz, and Tomas Rokicki, who provided technical review comments on the materials presented here. Jim Breen and Ken Lunde offered invaluable feedback on Chapter 7.

And I'd like to thank a lot of people at O'Reilly for their help and enthusiasm; in particular, my editor, Debby Russell, offered advice, helpful criticism, and support beyond the call of duty (Debby keyed most of the index for this book as production deadlines drew near and other arrangements fell through); Chris Tong organized the raw entries into a usable index; Lenny Muellner, Donna Woonteiler, and Sheryl Avruch allowed me to work on the book when it wasn't technically my job; Stephen Spainhour copyedited it into English with the help of Leslie Chalmers and Kismet McDonough (Stephen offered helpful suggestions along the way, too); Jennifer Niederst helped me get the design right; and Chris Reilly created the figures and screen dumps. I enjoyed working with everyone at O'Reilly so much that I left UMass and joined the production department myself ;-).

Several companies provided review copies of their software while I was writing this book. I would like to thank ArborText, Blue Sky Research, Borland International, The Kinch Computer Company, LaserGo, Personal TEX, TCI Software Research, and Y&Y, for their generosity.

Finally, I'd like to thank the entire Internet TEX community. Countless thousands of questions and answers on the Net refined my understanding of how TEX works and what it can do.

# I

# *An Introduction to TEX*

Part I, *An Introduction to TEX*, introduces TEX and the tools that make up the TEX system. It describes various editing environments that simplify the job of editing TEX documents. It also discusses the mechanics of running TEX and recovery from errors, and it provides an overview of TEX macro packages and format files.

# 1

# The Big Picture

## What Is TEX?

TEX is a *typesetting system*. It is a collection of programs, files, and procedures for producing professional quality documents with minimum effort.

TEX's job is to translate the text you type into a beautiful typeset page. The key word here is "beautiful," and it is a very lofty goal.* What I mean by beautiful is that TEX, when presented with several paragraphs of plain text and left to its own devices, produces a remarkably aesthetic page. Despite the fact that TEX may have to contend with multiple fonts and mathematics, it still manages to typeset pages in which each of the following aesthetic principles hold *simultaneously:*

- The right margin is justified.

- Proper justification is achieved without letterspacing.

- Interword spacing is neither too tight nor too loose.

- The page is evenly gray.

- The baselines of multiple fonts are properly aligned.

- Hyphenation is automatic, if required, and usually correct.

- Ladders are avoided.

---

*Before I proceed, the notion of beautiful in this context needs some explanation. Several people have pointed out that the logo type used by many TEX-related programs (including TEX itself) is intrinsically ugly. These same folks argue that a sentence like "TEX is designed to typeset beautiful pages" is self-contradictory because it begins with such an ugly construction. Obviously, TEX can't *prevent* you from typesetting ugly things. But TEX can typeset beautiful things too. We at O'Reilly & Associates think that this book, typeset completely in TEX, is an excellent example.

TEX processes documents a paragraph at a time, rather than a line at a time like most other programs. Internally, TEX computes a value called *badness* for each line of the paragraph. Anything that detracts from the appearance of a line (tight or loose spacing, a hyphen, etc.) increases the badness associated with that line. Every paragraph that TEX produces is optimal in terms of the total amount of badness present. Because TEX searches for an optimal solution, changing the last word of a paragraph can affect the spacing of the first line of the paragraph. After you've gained a little bit of experience with TEX, you'll be able to override any one, or all, of the rules it uses to compute badness, but in most situations you won't want to. I will describe more of TEX's approach to text formatting and how it differs from that of word processors, desktop publishers, and other markup languages in the following sections.

TEX is not a simple program, but a set of programs, tools, fonts, and other types of files. Two programs form the core of the TEX typesetting system. One of them is TEX itself, the program that reads your input files and transforms them into typeset form. The other program is **METAFONT**, a tool for creating fonts. Producing TEX documents involves a series of steps, including editing the document, running TEX itself, and processing TEX's output in various ways.

Over the years, TEX has been made available on almost every computer platform, so it is probably available for the computer system that you use. Compiling TEX on different systems has been possible, in large part, because TEX is a text formatter and not a word processor. Unlike a word processor, TEX never deals directly with displaying text on the screen or interacting with input from the keyboard (except in a very basic way). These features of an application are typically the most difficult to port from one system to another.

Beyond the technical details that make translation from one system to another possible, Donald Knuth added an important stipulation to the free distribution of TEX: in order for any program to be called "TEX," it must pass a rigorous test suite. This means that the TEX you use behaves exactly like the TEX I use.* This feature has contributed greatly to TEX's success. It means that a large community of TEX users can transparently share documents.

# *TEX for Beginners*

If you are already familiar with TEX, you may find some of the material in this section repetitive. If so, just skim it quickly. This section will help you understand how TEX

---

*This is not a whole-truth. Implementors of TEX may make some system-dependent alterations as long as the resulting program still passes the test suite; so our TEXs may not behave *exactly* the same way. They will, however, produce identical documents given identical input (unless the input relies on system-dependent features not available in both TEXs, naturally. ;-)

interprets the things you type into your input file. When you understand the concepts discussed here, you'll be ready to write really, really simple documents in TEX.

## *Boxes and Glue*

Despite the apparent complexity of TEX's job, it uses a very simple metaphor: all typographic elements are boxes. The simplest boxes, individual characters have a set shape defined by the font they come from. There are three parameters that define a box: width, height, and depth. The distinction between height and depth is a bit subtle. When a row of characters is typeset, every character rests on an imaginary line called the *baseline*. Some characters, like the lowercase "g," descend below the baseline. The distance from the baseline to the top of a box is its height; the distance from the baseline to the bottom is its depth.

Figure 1-1 shows the character boxes formed by the Computer Modern Roman letters "g" and "h." The *x-y* distance of each box is its height and the *y-z* distance is its depth. The *reference point* of the box, marked with an *r*, is on the leftmost edge of the box where the height and depth meet. Characters that have no *descenders* (no elements that go below the baseline), have a depth of zero. TEX uses the character box metrics, but font designers are free to allow glyphs to extend outside the box (for example, at the top of the "g").

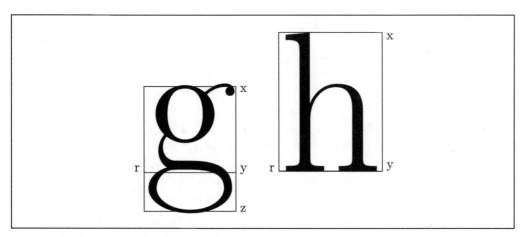

*Figure 1-1: The Letters "g" and "h" inside their boxes.*

The following paragraph demonstrates how TEX uses the metrics from the physical dimensions of each character to build word, line, and paragraph boxes.

TEX "glues" character boxes together to form words. When boxes are joined, they are always joined so their reference points are horizontally aligned as shown in Figure 1-1.*
Character-boxes (like ⊞⊟⊟⊠) are joined to form words, word-boxes (like ⊟this⊟) are joined to form lines, and line-boxes (like this) form paragraphs. TEX accomplishes the task of forming a justified paragraph by allowing the glue between words to stretch and shrink a little bit and by occasionally breaking the glue between characters to insert a hyphen. Although the rules are slightly different, TEX builds a page out of vertical boxes (paragraphs, figures, etc.) in an analogous manner.

This is a very generalized overview. In reality, a lot of subtlety is required to capture all of the nuances of typographical appearance.

## Control Sequences

A *control sequence* is a special "word" that you put in your document. These extra words are instructions for TEX, and they do not usually appear in your typeset document. Example 1-1 shows a contrived example of a TEX document that uses several control sequences.

*Example 1-1: An Example of a TEX Document*

```
\def\ora{O´Reilly \& Associates}
\font\orafont=grlg10
\parskip=\baselineskip
\parindent=0pt
\pageno=5
This book is published by \ora\ in
the \textit{Nutshell} series.
\bye
```

In most macro packages, a control sequence is a backslash followed by a sequence of letters.† TEX is case-sensitive, so the control sequence \large is different from \Large (these control sequences switch to large and very large fonts in the LATEX macro package). Control sequences end with the first non-letter, even if it isn't a space. For example, \parskip0pt is the control sequence \parskip followed by 0pt. This control sequence tells TEX to insert zero points of extra space between paragraphs.

Unless instructed otherwise (with control sequences), TEX builds rectangular paragraphs out of lines of words. Changing fonts, building tables, and typesetting mathematical equations are examples of situations in your document where TEX needs extra information.

---

*This is subtly different from saying that they are joined at the baseline. There are TEX commands which can change the position of the reference point in a box, whereas the baseline is an imaginary line that depends solely on the shape of the character.
†Technically, it's any character defined to be in the "escape" category followed by any sequence of characters defined to be in the "letter" category or a single character in the "other" category.

The number of control sequences used in a TEX document may seem overwhelming at first. Luckily, every control sequence falls into one of several categories:

**Macro control sequences**

Macro control sequences associate a name with an arbitrary string of text (including other control sequences). They are interpreted by replacing the control sequence with the text of its definition.*

Macro control sequences are the root of TEX's tremendous flexibility. By defining control sequences with meaningful names, like \chapter and \footnote, TEX can present a reasonably simple interface to the user. By redefining those control sequences, the typeset output can be modified without requiring you to retype large quantities of text.

In Example 1-1, the macro control sequence \ora is defined as a shortcut for typing "O'Reilly & Associates." This is a simple example of how a macro control sequence can be used.

**Font control sequences**

In Example 1-1, the line \font\orafont=grlg10 creates a font control sequence called \orafont. When \orafont is used, TEX will begin typesetting in the font grlg10. The name of the font, grlg10 in this case, refers to an external file that contains font metric information. Fonts are discussed in Chapter 5, *Fonts*.

**Registers**

Registers are like variables in a programming language. They hold a single value of a particular type. Many types of values can be stored: numbers (also called "count" values because they are simple counting numbers like 1, 2, 17, or -5), dimensions (also called "lengths"; they are distances like 3.5pt or 2in), boxes, glue, and token lists (an internal representation of your document used by TEX).†

If you are unfamiliar with computer programming, think of these registers as place holders. When TEX needs to save a piece of information, like how much space should be inserted between paragraphs, it stores the information in a register. When the information is needed again, in this case when TEX has finished typesetting one paragraph and is about to start another, it can retrieve that information from the register. Registers are usually given names that at least hint at how they are used. This helps people read and modify the rules that TEX uses to typeset documents.

In Example 1-1, \parskip, \baselineskip, and \parindent are dimension registers. The \pageno control sequence is a count register.

---

*Actually, macro expansion differs from pure textual replacement in a number of technical ways, but they aren't important here.

†Technically, several other kinds of values are stored this way as well, but they are less common and won't be discussed in this book at all.

There are only 256 registers of each type. The type of information (number, dimension, or token list) that a register can contain is defined when the control sequence is created. Once a variable like \parindent is created to hold a dimension, it can never hold a number or a token list.*

Registers may seem unnecessary now that you know about macro control sequences, which can store arbitrary information. However, registers differ from macro control sequences not only in the types of values they can hold, but also in the types of operations that can be performed on them. There is a TEX command called \advance, for example, that can increment the value stored in a register by an arbitrary amount. You can't \advance a macro control sequence.

### Built-in commands

A number of control sequences are built into TEX. These "primitive" operations form the basis for all higher-level functionality. There are a wide variety of control sequences of this type. Everything that can be done in TEX can be reduced to a sequence of primitive operations.

There is no way to know, simply by inspection, if a control sequence is one of the built-in sequences or not. Luckily, it doesn't matter very often; it really only matters when you are writing complex macros.

The \font control sequence in Example 1-1 is a built-in control sequence. So is \advance, mentioned above.

The number and kind of control sequences available depends upon the macro package that you are using. (Macro packages are discussed fully in Chapter 4, *Macro Packages.*) For the rest of this chapter, the default settings of Plain TEX are assumed.[†] There are other macro packages, like LATEX, Lollipop, and TEXinfo, which have different default values.

## *Special Characters*

In addition to control sequences, TEX reserves several characters for special purposes. Most of them do not occur very frequently in ordinary text, but you must be aware of them because there will be very surprising consequences if you use them incorrectly.

Table 1-1 shows all of the special characters in Plain TEX.[‡] Most of these characters are special in other macro packages as well. Font-specific characters are not reserved by TEX, but they don't produce the results you would expect when typeset in Computer

---

*Most control sequences can be redefined to hold different kinds of values, but they can never hold different kinds of values at the same time. A dimension register can be redefined to hold tokens, for example, but then it can't hold dimensions anymore (unless it is redefined again).

[†]Plain TEX is the name of a particular macro package. I selected it for the purpose of example in this chapter because it is always installed with TEX. Most of what follows in this chapter is true in other macro packages as well, but some of the details are different. See Chapter 4 for more information.

[‡]All of these special characters are configurable, but most macro packages use the Plain TEX defaults.

Modern because of the way TEX expects fonts to be laid out. Fonts are discussed in detail in Chapter 5, *Fonts.*

*Table 1-1: Special Characters in Plain TEX*

| Character | Meaning |
|:---:|:---|
| # | Used for parameter definition in macros and tables |
| $ | Toggles in and out of math mode |
| % | A comment (TEX ignores everything to the end of the line) |
| & | The column separator in tables |
| ~ | The active space (an unbreakable space) |
| _ | Marks a subscript (valid only in math mode) |
| ^ | Marks a superscript (valid only in math mode) |
| \ | Begins a control sequence |
| { | Begins a group |
| } | Ends a group |
| \| | Produces an em-dash (—) (font-specific) |
| < | Produces an upside down exclamation mark (¡) (font-specific) |
| > | Produces an upside down question mark (¿) (font-specific) |
| " | Incorrect for quoted text; use " and " instead (font-specific) |

It is best to avoid these characters until you are familiar with TEX. If you need to typeset one of these characters, Table 1-2 shows what to put in your document. You should also avoid characters outside the standard printable ASCII character set (characters with ASCII values below 32 and above 126). TEX can be configured to accept characters outside the printable ASCII range, to support non-English languages, for example, but it is not configured to do so "out of the box." Chapter 7, *International Considerations*, discusses the issues of typesetting in different languages.

*Table 1-2: How to Typeset Special Characters*

| To Get | Put This in Your Document |
|:---:|:---|
| # | \# |
| $ | \$ |
| % | \% |
| & | \& |
| " | `` |
| " | '' |
| ~ | \~{\ } |
| { | $\{$ |
| } | $\}$ |
| < | $<$ |
| > | $>$ |
| \| | $\|$ |

*Table 1-2: How to Typeset Special Characters (continued)*

| To Get | Put This in Your Document |
|--------|---------------------------|
| _ | `$\underbar{\hbox{\ }}$` |
| ˆ | `$\hat{\hbox{\ }}$` |
| \ | `$\backslash$` |

Some of the suggestions in Table 1-2 will not always produce exactly what you want. The entry for "˜" really produces a tilde accent, not a tilde character and the entries for "{" through "\" all get the actual characters from TEX's math fonts. The Computer Modern text fonts don't include these characters so it is necessary to get them from the math fonts. However, if you are using PostScript or other kinds of fonts, you may very well have curly braces, angle brackets, underscores, etc. in the font. You can access these characters directly with the \char primitive. I strongly recommend that you always define macros for this purpose, so that you can easily switch to some other method if you change fonts. Introducing \char primitives makes your document less portable. To use the \char primitive, simply put the decimal ASCII value of the character that you want to print. For example, this book is typeset with PostScript fonts that include a backslash character at position 92, so I defined \bs to print a backslash like this:

```
\def\bs{\char92\relax}
```

Using \relax after the decimal value assures that TEX won't get confused if I put a backslash in front of other digits like this \bs300dpi.

The braces "{" and "}" are a very special case. TEX uses curly braces to delimit arguments and make changes (like switching fonts) that are local to a small section of the document. These are called *grouping characters* in TEX jargon. For example, to typeset a single word in boldface, you put {\bf word} into your input file. The \bf control sequence switches to boldface type, and the curly braces localize the effect to the single word **word**. As a result, it is very important that you avoid braces (except when you use them as delimiters) and that you carefully match all opening and closing braces. One of the most common errors in TEX is to forget a closing brace.

One last special character is the blank space. For the most part, TEX doesn't care how you space your lines of text. Any space that occurs is simply a word break to TEX, and inserting multiple spaces doesn't influence how TEX typesets the line. TEX also considers the end of a line an implicit space. If you are trying to control the layout of your input text and want to break a line without introducing a space, place a comment character

(% in most macro packages) at the very end of the line. If the last character of a line is the comment character, TEX ignores the line break and all the leading spaces on the following line. This allows you to use indentation to make your input file more readable.

For example, the following lines in your input file:

```
``This                       is some ex%
        ample text.´´
```

and this line:

```
``This is some example text.´´
```

both produce:

"This is some example text."

in your typeset document.

# *Text Formatting Versus Word Processing*

For many people, writing documents with a computer implies using a word processor like *WordPerfect* or *Microsoft Word*. The word processing program controls every aspect of what you do: it's where you type your text, where you see what it will look like, where you print, and where you do everything else. Some of these environments, the so-called WYSIWYG (what-you-see-is-what-you-get) programs, attempt to show you what the printed document will actually look like *while* you edit it.*

If WYSIWYG environments are what you're used to, or what you expect, TEX's approach may seem very strange at first because TEX is a *text formatter*, not a word processor. Instead of trying to show you what your document will look like while you type, TEX expects you to do all the typing somewhere else, and then pass it a source file containing all of your text plus control sequences that tell TEX how you'd like it printed.

In *The Psychology of Everyday Things* [42], Donald Norman describes these two modes of interaction as first person and third person. First person interaction provides the user with the ability to directly manipulate the elements of a task, whether it's flying an airplane or resizing text. Third person interaction, on the other hand, occurs where the user is expected to type commands to the computer in an appropriate command language; the shell prompt is a good example of third person interaction.

Is first person interaction really better? Well, it depends. Norman writes, "Although they [WYSIWYG environments] are often easy to use, fun, and entertaining, it is often difficult to do a really good job with them." The problem which arises is that the user is required

---

*TEX pundits, and other folks who have been frustrated by the limitations of these environments, frequently refer to this as WYSIAYG—what you see is *all* you get.

to do the task, and he or she may not be very good at it. Third person systems are better when the computer program can be trusted to do a better job of the task than the user.

Is TEX really better than a word processor? Well, it depends on the task and the person doing it. TEX probably isn't better for designing one page flyers with lots of fonts and graphics (although I've done it). But for longer documents, TEX offers all of these advantages:

- TEX has a precise understanding of the rules of typesetting, so you don't have to.

- Predefined styles allow experts to extend (or bend) the rules of typesetting without burdening the user.

- Journals and magazines can achieve consistency of appearance much more reliably because the consistency is in the style files.

- TEX runs on cheap systems (old PCs with monochrome monitors and no graphics capability, for example).

- Although complex and difficult to learn, TEX offers incredibly flexible table construction tools.

- Few, if any, word processors can provide running headers and footers as flexibly as TEX. Imagine the task of writing a dictionary: the left and right hand side headers change on each page, each time a new entry is added.

- TEX offers flexible bibliography layouts.

- TEX is extensible. Its behavior can be modified by defining new commands and environments without changing the actual program.

There are some other good reasons to separate document creation from text formatting:

- Documents are portable. Because the source files are just plain text without any nonprintable characters, they can easily be copied from one system to another.

- TEX is portable. TEX runs everywhere. You can process your documents with TEX on UNIX workstations; personal computers running MS-DOS, OS/2, and Windows; IBM mainframes running VM/CMS; workstations running VAX/VMS; Macintoshes; Amigas; Ataris; and just about every other computer with a reasonable amount of memory. And the typeset output will be the same! This adds another dimension of portability to your documents.

- TEX is free. You can afford to have it on every system you use. Several sources of TEX software are listed in the preface of this book.

- TEX allows you to separate markup and output. Logical divisions in the text (chapters, sections, itemized lists, etc.) are identified by control sequences. An entirely different page layout can result from simply changing the definition of a few control sequences.

This means that the look of your documents can be changed (to fit the style guidelines of a particular journal or publisher, for example) without changing the text of your documents at all.

- Plain text files are easier to manipulate with other tools than specially encoded word processor files are. This means that you can use standard utilities on your documents: revision control, grep, shell scripts, etc. This is a less common practice in non-UNIX environments, but it is still convenient.

- You can continue to use your favorite editing tools. The extent to which you find this advantageous is dependent, naturally, on the extent to which you have a favorite editing program. Nevertheless, this can be a considerable advantage. For example, users familiar with *emacs* can continue to rely on all of the features they are used to, including interactive spellchecking, access to online services like Webster's dictionary, customized editor macros, and convenient services like reading mail.

- You get better looking output. TEX gives you far more precise control over the placement of elements on the page than most word processing programs. And TEX is very intelligent about typesetting (paragraph breaking, kerning, ligatures, etc.).

## *What About Desktop Publishing?*

Desktop publishing systems like *Ventura Publisher* and *Aldus PageMaker* are noted for their ability to incorporate multiple fonts and graphics into a document. As word processors become more sophisticated, the line between word processing and desktop publishing is becoming blurry.

This book shows you many ways that TEX can provide access to the same sophisticated features. TEX can incorporate pictures and figures in a number of ways (just take a look at the way I've wrapped text around this kiwi),* and TEX can use almost any font that another program can use—it can certainly use *all* of the popular types of fonts. Like typical word processors, desktop publishing programs force you to use a single application to create your entire document, and they lack the flexibility required to combine just the pieces that you want. All of the advantages of text formatting over word processing also apply to desktop publishing programs. I'll grant, however, that WYSIWYG environments are easier for first-time users. But that doesn't make them better, it just makes them more popular.

---

*TEX doesn't do this sort of thing automatically, but it isn't hard to do. Why the kiwi? It's on my business card...

## *What About troff?*

*troff* is the "other" text formatting system. If you've ever tried to read a UNIX reference page without formatting it first, you've seen *troff*. For a long time it was distributed as part of all UNIX systems. Now it is more likely an extra-cost option. The Free Software Foundation's *groff* processor is a free, *troff*-compatible system.

On the surface, it is easier to compare TEX and *troff* than to compare TEX to the other document preparation systems described in this chapter. In reality, the differences are subtle: TEX and *troff* have the same general paradigm; they are equally powerful to a large extent, and both have advantages and disadvantages.

*troff* is similar to TEX in many ways. Like TEX, *troff* processes a plain text file and produces a typeset document. TEX and *troff* differ in the way that formatting information is inserted into the text. TEX uses control sequences, where *troff* uses a mixture of control sequences* and "dot" commands (lines of text that begin with a period and contain typesetting commands).

Although I am inclined to say that *troff* documents are far more cryptic than TEX documents, I am certain that there are plenty of *troff* users who would disagree (strongly).

Objectively, TEX handles mathematical typesetting far better than *troff* and probably has better support for multilingual documents. The *nroff* processor, which produces plain text output from a *troff* document, at one time provided a strong argument in favor of *troff* for typesetting documents required in both typeset and plain text formats. However, the TEXinfo macro package for TEX has largely defeated that argument. In *troff*'s defense, TEXinfo is very, very different from other TEX macro packages, so it really is necessary to plan ahead and learn a very different set of macros to typeset both plain text and typeset documents with TEXinfo. Chapter 10, *Online Documentation*, discusses this issue further.

In my experience, there is more free support for TEX than *troff*. TEX is supported by a large community of users actively producing new, useful document-preparation formats, styles, and tools. In addition, TEX is more widely available than *troff*: a TEX port exists for almost every practical computer system, whereas *troff* is still mostly confined to UNIX systems (although the Free Software Foundation's *groff* package has been ported to similar systems like MS-DOS, Windows NT, and OS/2).

The following fragments show a side-by-side comparison of TEX commands, on the left, and *troff* commands, on the right:

```
\begin{figure}                      .(z
  \begin{center}                    .hl
    \hrule                          Text to be floated.
    \vspace{8pt}                    .sp
```

---

*Although it has a very different notion of what constitutes a control sequence.

```
      Text to be floated.              .ce
      \hrule                           .hl
      \caption{Example figure...}      Figure \*[fig]: Example figure...
      \vspace{8pt}                     .)z
    \end{center}
  \end{figure}
```

Both examples produce a floating figure that looks like this:

---

Text to be floated.

---

*Figure 1-2: Example figure produced by both TEX and troff .*

## What About SGML?

The Standard Generalized Markup Language (SGML) is a document description language. SGML aims to separate the content of a document from its presentation. In other words, SGML identifies the features of a document (chapter headings, paragraphs, etc.) without specifying how they are to be presented.

This means that all SGML documents must interact with a document formatter of some sort. Many people are finding that TEX is a natural choice when selecting a document formatter for their SGML environment. In fact, LATEX already provides many SGML-like commands because it was designed to separate markup from presentation. One of the specific goals of an effort (currently underway) to develop a new version of LATEX is to make SGML and LATEX work together easily, cleanly, and efficiently. For more information about the goals of this project and information about what you can do to help, please read *The LATEX3 Project* [38].

# How TEX Works

A functioning TEX system in which you are producing documents of medium size and complexity is really a collection of tools and files that are related to each other in well defined (if somewhat subtle) ways.

One of the fundamental goals of this book is to shed light on these relationships and allow you to put together a TEX system that quickly and easily does the jobs you need to accomplish.

## TEXing a Simple Document

This section briefly describes what you need to know about how TEX processes a simple document (that is, one that does not contain complex document elements like a table of contents, indexes, bibliographies, etc.). Figure 1-3 shows how the standard TEX tools fit together at the most basic level.

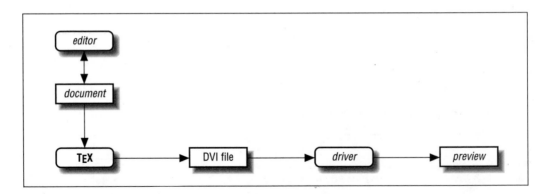

*Figure 1-3: A high-level view of TEX*

Figure 1-4 expands on Figure 1-3, showing additional tools and files that you'll often need to use.

### Editing your document

The most tangible and important part of your TEX system is your document. This is the file (or files) in which you write down what you want to typeset with TEX. In addition to the actual text, you include control sequences to describe how you want the final text to appear (size, font, justification, etc.). The section "TEX for Beginners" earlier in this chapter tells you briefly what goes into your document file.

The most common way to create a document is with an editor, which can provide you with a number of features to make typing TEX documents easier. For example, an editor can help you insert common control sequences automatically, run TEX automatically (from within the editor), and keep you from making common mistakes (like typing a left brace, but not the matching right one). These features and how they work in editors including GNU Emacs, AUC-TEX, and Multi-Edit are described in Chapter 2, *Editing*.

### Running TEX

Once you have prepared your document file, it is time to run the TEX program itself. This may not be as easy as it sounds. You need to determine the name of the TEX program at your site, to make sure all of the files TEX needs are available to it; you also need to specify the correct command-line options. Chapter 3, *Running TEX*, describes everything you need to know.

TEX may find errors in your document (places where TEX doesn't understand the instructions you used; not spelling or grammatical errors, unfortunately ;-). Chapter 3 also describes the most common errors you're likely to make and gives advice for interpreting error messages.

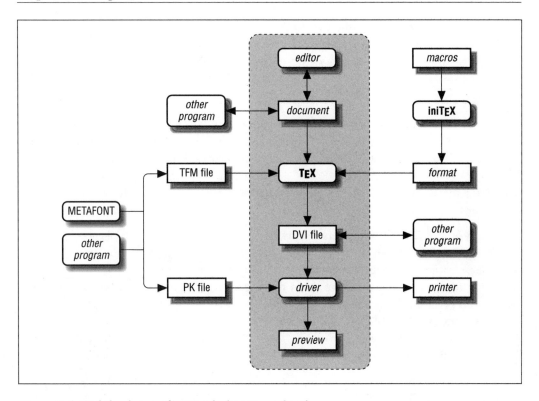

*Figure 1-4: High-level view of TEX including more detail*

If TEX is successful in formatting your document (i.e., your document doesn't contain any errors), it produces a DVI (DeVice Independent) file. The DVI file is a device-independent representation of the typeset output of your document. DVI files are transitory. Although there are a few programs that can manipulate them (to rearrange the order of the pages in the output, for example), most of the time you will immediately transform them into something else—either printed output or previewed output on the screen. (See the following section "Previewing or printing TEX documents.")

### Using macros

The control sequences that you insert in your document are defined by a macro package.*
Macro packages are collections of TEX commands (macros) that extend TEX. Macro packages are frequently stored in format files, specially compiled versions of the macro package. The iniTEX program interprets all of the control sequences in a macro package to create a format file that TEX reads when it runs.

---

*Well, actually, they're TEX primitives, are defined by a macro package, defined in a file loaded by a macro package, or defined in your document.

Many macro packages are particularly effective in implementing particular document styles or supporting particular types of writing. Two of the most common are Plain TEX and LATEX. Chapter 4, *Macro Packages*, describes Plain TEX, LATEX, and a number of other macro packages that extend the power and ease of TEX.

### Using fonts

One of TEX's strengths is its support for a myriad of predefined fonts and its ability to let you create fonts of your own. In addition to your document and the format file, when TEX runs it needs font information as well. This is provided in the form of a set of TFM (TEX Font Metric) files that tell TEX the size and shape (roughly speaking, at least) of each character, as well as some other information about how characters are related to each other.

Historically, the **METAFONT** program was the way a TEX user created fonts. Like TEX itself, **METAFONT** is about ten years old. Ten years ago, it was a unique program that was indispensible for creating the type of output TEX produces. Today there are many competing font technologies, all of them more common than **METAFONT**, and **META-FONT**'s role is diminishing. Many people use TEX today without ever using **METAFONT** at all. Nevertheless, **METAFONT** still has some importance, and we describe how to run and use it in Chapter 11, *Introducing METAFONT*. Because the standard fonts that come with TEX are still the fonts produced by **METAFONT**, it will also be mentioned elsewhere in this book.

If you are writing complex documents, you may need to learn a lot about fonts and how to define and use them. Chapter 5, *Fonts*, tells you everything you need to know, including information about the New Font Selection Scheme, a new way of describing and selecting fonts in TEX.

### Previewing or printing TEX documents

After you have produced a DVI file, as described in the section "Running TEX," later in this chapter, you run another program (generically called a DVI driver) to translate the DVI file so you can either preview or print your document. Driver programs need your DVI file and some collection of fonts (usually PK (packed) font files).* Many different kinds of fonts are described in Chapter 5.

Chapter 8, *Printing*, tells you how to print your documents and deal with the problems you may encounter using bitmapped or scalable fonts, printing pictures and figures, and other printing issues.

Often you will want to look at your document before you actually print it. Because TEX is not a WYSIWYG system,[†] you cannot do this until you have processed the DVI file. There are a number of good previewing products, including *xdvi*, *dvimswin*, and *dviscr*,

---

* Some drivers may also benefit from loading the TFM files used to create your document.

[†] *Textures* for the Mac and *Scientific Word* offer WYSIWYG-like environments, but that's not the point ;-)

that let you look at your processed document on the screen before you decide whether to print it. See Chapter 9, *Previewing*, for complete information.

## TEXing More Complex Documents

This section briefly describes how TEX processes a more complex document (that is, one that includes elements like a table of contents, indexes, bibliographies, etc.).

Many TEX formats implement sophisticated cross-referencing schemes. Cross references may sound rather esoteric, but they occur frequently. Tables of contents, figure and table numbers, indexes, and bibliographic references are all flavors of cross referencing.

Cross references make your document more complex because they require more information than is immediately available when TEX initially processes your document. For example, if you refer to a figure which occurs later in the document, TEX has no way of knowing what figure number to insert into the text at the point of the reference. These are called *forward references*.

TEX macro packages that support cross referencing overcome the difficulty of forward references by requiring you to process your document more than once. Each time your document is processed, the necessary reference information is stored into a separate file. If that file exists when you process your document, the information saved *last time* is loaded so that it is available *this time*. The practical implication of this functionality is that documents with cross references frequently have to be processed twice. Occasionally, you may have to process a document three times. This occurs when the inserted reference causes TEX to format a paragraph differently, which in turn causes TEX to change a page break.* Because most changes are incremental while revising a document, this is normally only an issue the first time you process a document.

The following sections describe the LATEX methods for constructing a table of contents, figure references, an index, and a bibliography. LATEX is used in this example because it is a very common macro package and is typical of the way macro packages provide these features. Similar mechanisms exist in most formats, except Plain TEX.

Figure 1-5 shows the relationships between many of the components described in the following sections. LATEX creates several sorts of auxiliary files depending on the kind of cross references required by your document and the style files you use. These auxiliary files may be modified (and others may be created) by other sorts of post-processing programs (like *MakeIndex* for constructing indexes or BIBTEX for constructing bibliographies). LATEX uses these auxiliary files, if they exist, to update your document when it is processed again.

---

*With extreme cleverness or extreme bad luck you can create a document which will *never* format correctly.

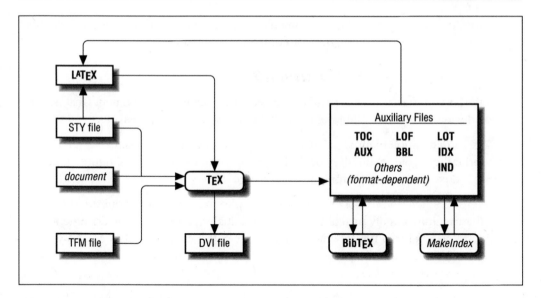

*Figure 1-5: TEXing a More Complex Document*

## Building a Table of Contents

A table of contents is the simplest form of cross reference. In LaTeX, you request a table of contents by inserting the \tableofcontents command wherever you want it to appear in your document. If you request the table of contents at the end of your document rather than the beginning, your document can be printed with only one pass through TEX.

LaTeX uses a file with the same name as your document and the extension *.toc* to hold the table of contents entries. You can control the level of detail in your table of contents by setting the \secnumdepth counter. A value of zero includes only chapters; one includes chapters and sections; two includes chapters, sections, and subsections, and so on.

The LaTeX commands \listoftables and \listoffigures perform the same functions as \tableofcontents for lists of tables and figures. They use external files with the extensions *.lot* and *.lof*, respectively. As with the table of contents, your document can be correctly formatted in one pass if the \listoftables and \listoffigures commands are placed at the end of the document.

## Figure References

Figure references are a special case of LaTeX's cross referencing mechanism. The LaTeX command \label{*string*} creates a referent. You refer to the label with the command \ref{*string*}. In normal body text, the label refers to the current section or subsection. In a figure or table environment, the label refers to that figure or table.

If your document contains no forward references (if all \label commands occur before the \ref's that refer to them) then it can be formatted in one pass. Otherwise, TEX will have to be run two or three times to make all of the references correct.

## Indexes and Glossaries

Indexes and glossaries differ from the preceding forms of reference in that they must be processed by a separate program. In general, this is true regardless of the macro package or format you use. An external program is required because indexes and glossaries must be alphabetized, and in indexes, consecutive page numbers have to be converted into ranges, and so on.

## Bibliographies

LaTeX works in conjunction with another program, called BIBTEX, to provide a flexible, convenient way to construct bibliographies. The \cite commands allows you to refer to other documents in much the same way that the \ref command allows you to refer to other portions of the same document.

You make a citation by placing the command \cite{*string*} where you wish the citation to occur. The *string* is a key that refers to the document in your bibliography database that you wish to cite. Example 1-2 is a typical entry in a bibliography database. It describes Knuth's classic book *The TEXbook* [30]. The key for this entry is "kn:texbook."

*Example 1-2: A typical bibliography database entry*

```
@Book{kn:texbook,
    author    = "Donald E. Knuth",
    title     = "The {\TeX}book",
    publisher = "Addison-Wesley",
    year      = 1989,
    edition   = "Fifteenth",
    isbn      = "0-201-13447-0"
    note      = "Paperback ISBN: 0-201-13448-9"
}
```

Each entry in the database consists of a type (book, article, magazine, etc.), a key, and a number of fields. The number and names of the fields depend on the type of entry. The database is simply a plain ASCII file containing any number of entries. You can have multiple databases.

These are the commands you use, in addition to \cite, to include a bibliography in your document:

```
% The bibliography goes here.
%
\bibliographystyle{plain}
\bibliography{textools,refbooks}
```

The \bibliographystyle command tells BIBTEX how to format the bibliography, and the \bibliography command identifies which bibliographic databases contain the citations that you have made. The "plain" style of bibliography is selected, and the *textools* and *refbooks* files contain the bibliographic information for the documents cited. Document styles can be used to alter the format of citations in your text. The default extension for bibliographic styles is *.bst*. The default extension for database files is *.bib*.

LATEX places citations and bibliography information into the *.aux* file. BIBTEX reads the *.aux* file and constructs a bibliography, which it places into a file with the extension *.bbl*, using the entries you cited and the bibliography style you selected.

## Special Things

Sometimes, producing a complex document requires the ability to interface with objects outside of TEX (pictures or figures created by high-end graphics packages, special features of a particular printer, etc.). To support this kind of communication, TEX provides a control sequence called \special. The arguments passed to the \special command are written directly to the DVI file for the DVI driver. It is the responsibility of the DVI driver to handle them. DVI drivers typically ignore \special commands that they do not recognize.

You will find \special commands of various kinds described throughout this book, particularly when discussing color typesetting in Chapter 4, *Macro Packages*, and graphics in Chapter 6, *Pictures and Figures*.

# 2

# *Editing*

This chapter describes several writing environments available for creating and modifying TEX documents. In practice, you can use almost any editing program you wish, but I'll focus on GNU emacs in this chapter. I've chosen GNU emacs for two reasons: it is a popular and very powerful editor available on many platforms (UNIX, NeXT, MS-DOS, OS/2, Macintosh, VMS, Amiga, ...), and it has the most comprehensive TEX editing environment that I've ever seen. At the end of the chapter, I'll discuss several other editors for MS-DOS and OS/2 that also have TEX editing environments.

The sole requirement for a TEX editor is that it must save files in a flat, ASCII format without any additional formatting characters or special encodings. Word processors, such as *Microsoft Word*, usually add special formatting information to your document when they save it to disk. TEX will not understand this information, so you cannot use a word processor to edit TEX documents.*

A program that allows you to edit flat ASCII files is usually called an editor (as opposed to a word processor, for example). Choosing an editor is a remarkably personal decision. Computer programmers and other people who use editors every day frequently become very attached to a particular editor. This chapter explores a number of features that an editor can provide to make editing TEX documents easier. If possible, choose an editor that offers these features. In any event, make sure you choose an editor you will be comfortable using. You'll spend a lot of time using it.

---

*Most word processors can be coerced into saving your document in plain text. If your word processor can do this, you may be able to edit TEX documents with it.

Many editors have some sort of built-in programming language. The features described in this chapter rely on modifying the behavior of the editor with its programming language. This does not mean that *you* will have to do any programming. All of the editors discussed in this chapter have TEX editing environments already available. However, if you use another editor and it doesn't have a programming language, it's unlikely that these features will be available to you.

The next section explores some helpful editor features. All of the editors in this chapter provide some or all of the features discussed, and require little or no programming on your part.

# *What Can an Editor Do?*

You will do most of your work with TEX in the editor. There are two ways that an editor can help you edit TEX documents. One is to provide typing shortcuts that are either intuitive replacements for cumbersome operations or quick ways of typing common TEX commands. The other way that an editor can help is by running TEX for you and automatically displaying the location of formatting errors in your document.

## *Quoting Automatically*

Most typewriters and many word processors use the same symbol for opening and closing quotations. You are probably used to typing the double-quote key to insert quotation marks into your text. However, if you look carefully at TEX output (or any professionally typeset document) you will notice that the opening and closing quotation marks do not look the same. The proper way to type an opening quote (") in TEX is with two single back-quotes in a row (` `). A closing quote (") is entered with two single quotes (apostrophes) in a row (´ ´). This process is tedious and error-prone since you are used to typing something else.

If you accidentally use the double quote symbol in your input, you most frequently get text that looks like "this." The exact result is actually dependent upon the font you are using. This is explained in Chapter 5, *Fonts*. Most programmable editors can change the meaning of the double-quote key to insert the correct quotation marks.

If you are interested in programming your editor to do this, you can use the following algorithm to select the correct quotation marks most of the time: if the character to the immediate left of the cursor is a space, opening brace, parenthesis, or bracket, insert opening quotes; otherwise, insert closing quotes. As a further enhancement, double quotes should be inserted immediately following a backslash.

## Matching Braces

Braces, as mentioned in Chapter 1, *The Big Picture*, are used by TEX to delimit sections of text; they appear often in TEX documents. GNU emacs, *Multi-Edit*, and *Brief* can all be programmed to highlight the matching open brace whenever you type a closing brace.

For example, if you have entered the text

```
\footnote{This is {\it not\/} the only case.}
```

and the next character that you type is ⟨}⟩, the open brace immediately following the word \footnote is highlighted, or all of the text between that brace and the current cursor position is highlighted. This feature makes it easier to find places where you have forgotten to insert a closing brace.

If you usually work in "insert" mode, you may also find it convenient to have the editor insert braces in pairs and then insert text between them. This can be accomplished in almost any editor that can be programmed, even one that isn't equipped to handle brace matching.

## Inserting Common Control Sequences

Most editors can be programmed to insert arbitrary text when a special key is pressed. This feature can be used to insert common control sequences. For example, you might have ⟨Alt-c⟩ insert the \chapter control sequence or ⟨Ctrl-e⟩ insert \begin{enumerate}.

## Running TEX Automatically

One of the nicest features that an editor can provide is the ability to run TEX automatically without leaving the editor. This is a feature that programmers demand because it allows them to run compilers directly from the editor. Editors that provide this feature usually include some mechanism for programming the editor to locate the position of errors reported by the compiler. The editor searches for error messages in the output generated by the compiler, and it positions the cursor at the location of each error. This speeds up the traditional edit/compile/debug cycle of programming. You can take advantage of these features to shorten the edit/typeset/rewrite cycle of creating a TEX document.

All of the editors discussed in this chapter can easily be adapted to run TEX in this way. If you already have a favorite editor and want to add this functionality for TEX, see the section "TEX as a Compiler" later in this chapter; it describes the process at a very general level.

# GNU Emacs

This section describes the TEX modes distributed as part of GNU emacs. Emacs is one of the most popular and most powerful editors around. Distributed by the Free Software Foundation (FSF), GNU emacs is the de facto standard editor in many UNIX environments. Recently, GNU emacs has been ported to many other platforms, including MS-DOS (*demacs*), OS/2, Macintosh, VMS, Amiga, and NeXT.

---

This section and the following section on AUC-TEX assume that you are familiar with general emacs concepts. In particular, you should be familiar with the concepts of buffers, files, regions, command keys, editing modes, and prefix arguments. If you are unfamiliar with these concepts, you can learn about them in the online help, called Info pages, for GNU emacs. Info pages should be available by pressing Ctrl-H i in emacs. You can also consult a reference to GNU emacs, such as *Learning GNU Emacs* [12] for more information.

---

Customizing some of the features of GNU emacs requires familiarity with GNU emacs lisp, which is also described in the Info pages.

## Starting TEX Mode

GNU emacs provides two similar TEX editing modes: one designed for editing Plain TEX documents (*plain-tex-mode*) and the other for editing LATEX documents (*latex-mode*). The *latex-mode* is a superset of *plain-tex-mode* that provides additional shortcut keys for some LATEX control sequences.

There are three ways to start TEX mode in GNU emacs:

| | |
|---|---|
| M-x tex-mode | Attempts to select the correct mode. |
| M-x plain-tex-mode | Always selects Plain TEX mode. |
| M-x latex-mode | Always selects LATEX mode. |

If you use `M-x tex-mode`, emacs examines the top of the buffer in order to select the appropriate mode. If the control sequences `\documentstyle` or `\begin{document}` occur near the top of the buffer, *latex-mode* is selected; otherwise, the default mode is selected. The default mode is stored in the emacs lisp variable `TeX-default-mode`.

You can also tell emacs to invoke TEX mode automatically whenever you edit a file that has a name ending in *.tex*. To do so, add the following lines to your emacs startup file, usually called *.emacs* in your home directory:*

```
(setq auto-mode-alist (append '(("\\.tex$" . tex-mode))
                               auto-mode-alist))
```

## Typing in Emacs

The emacs TEX modes change the meaning of several keys to provide features useful for editing TEX documents. These special key bindings apply only to buffers that you edit while emacs is in *plain-tex-mode* or *latex-mode*.

Automatic quotation, brace balancing in paragraphs, inserting brace pairs, skipping over unmatched braces, and closing open environments are supported.

## Running TEX Automatically

When TEX typesets your document, it produces processing and error messages. By running TEX for you, emacs can capture these messages and display them in a window. You can use this feature to help locate and correct errors.

Functions that run TEX from inside the editor rely on emacs' ability to run a subshell. Some implementations of emacs, particularly implementations for MS-DOS, which is unable to run concurrent processes, cannot use this feature. AUC-TEX, a different editing environment for GNU emacs, does allow you to use these features with MS-DOS ports of GNU emacs. (AUC-TEX is described in the next section.)

GNU emacs supports processing of both buffers and regions. These modes don't locate errors for you automatically, but they do place the output from TEX in an emacs buffer so that you can find them yourself. Chapter 3, *Running TEX*, describes how to interpret TEX output and find the location of errors.

# AUC-TEX

This section provides an overview of AUC-TEX, a powerful emacs macro package for editing LATEX documents. AUC-TEX is available on the CTAN archives in *support/auctex*. More detailed information about installing and customizing AUC-TEX can be found in the documentation distributed with the package.

AUC-TEX provides extensive support for editing TEX and LATEX documents in emacs. It provides many more features than the ordinary GNU emacs TEX modes. Although useful

---

*On file systems that don't allow filenames to begin with a period, the name frequently begins with an underscore instead.

for both Plain TEX and LATEX documents, AUC-TEX is designed with the LATEX user in mind.

AUC-TEX is *a lot* more complex than GNU emacs TEX mode. In fact, it is so complex that it may not be useful if you have a relatively slow computer.* On my machine,[†] AUC-TEX's performance leaves a lot to be desired. On the other hand, AUC-TEX is extensively configurable, and it is possible to streamline it quite a bit.

The descriptions that follow are for AUC-TEX version 8.0. The versions change frequently as new features are added. Consult the documentation which comes with AUC-TEX for a list of the new features that have been added since this book was published.

## *Starting AUC-TEX*

The instructions provided with each release of AUC-TEX describe how to build and install the software so that AUC-TEX will automatically be invoked when you edit a file with a name ending in *.tex*.

If you think AUC-TEX is already installed on your system (because the emacs Info page for it is present, for example), ask your system administrator where it is installed. One common location is */usr/local/lib/emacs/site-lisp/auctex*.

Adding the following line to your emacs startup file (typically *.emacs* in your home directory) will load AUC-TEX each time you start emacs:

```
(load-file "/path/for/auctex/tex-site.elc")
```

## *Typing in AUC-TEX*

AUC-TEX provides a large number of typing shortcuts. Many of the keystroke shortcuts are designed specifically to aid in typing LATEX documents. In addition to command keys, AUC-TEX provides another typing shortcut—command completion for LATEX control sequences with C-c TAB.

If you type a backslash followed by the beginning of a control sequence name into a buffer and then type C-c TAB, AUC-TEX completes as much of the control sequence as possible. Every time AUC-TEX adds another letter to the control sequence name, it compares the resulting name to a configurable list of LATEX control sequences. If it reaches a point where the control sequence could be continued in two different ways, it stops and displays all the possible completions. For example, there are two control sequences in standard LATEX that begin with \re: \renewcommand and \renewenvironment.

---

*That's one of the reasons that the regular GNU emacs TEX modes are described first.

[†]A 16MHz 386SX machine with only 8Mb of memory struggling to run GNU emacs under OS/2. ;-)

If you type:

\re C-c TAB

AUC-TEX will insert new because that much of the control sequence name can be deduced from the known possibilities. This changes the text in your document to:

\renew

Because AUC-TEX cannot figure out which of the possibilities you want, it displays a list of the LATEX commands that begin with \renew. You can complete the command by typing c or e and pressing C-c TAB again. If you want the \renewcommand function, type:

\renewc C-c TAB

Now, AUC-TEX will insert ommand and return to normal typing mode with the cursor positioned just after the control sequence name:

\renewcommand _

AUC-TEX has special support for LATEX sectioning commands and environments, changing fonts, commenting out sections of a document, reformatting the input text, and entering mathematics.

TEX contains a lot of support for typesetting mathematics. In that spirit, AUC-TEX provides a minor mode* for entering mathematical formulae.

In mathematics minor mode, pressing ` ' ` changes the meaning of the next character you type. The next character is interpreted as an abbreviation for a mathematical symbol or function. For example, in AUC-TEX, typing

$ C-c ~ ' a ' < ' b $

inserts

$\alpha \leq \beta$

into your document (which is typeset like this: $\alpha \leq \beta$).

Table 2-2 lists all of the abbreviations. The first column of the table displays the shortcut keys. The second and third columns show the command inserted in your document and the typeset symbol, respectively.

---

*A minor mode is a kind of editing environment provided by GNU emacs. If you are unfamiliar with minor modes, consult your emacs reference.

*Table 2-2: AUC-TEX Math Operators in Mathematics Minor-mode*

| Keys | Control Sequence | Symbol | Keys | Control Sequence | Symbol |
|------|------------------|--------|------|------------------|--------|
| `` `a `` | \alpha | $\alpha$ | `` `C-f `` | \rightarrow | $\rightarrow$ |
| `` `b `` | \beta | $\beta$ | `` `C-p `` | \uparrow | $\uparrow$ |
| `` `d `` | \delta | $\delta$ | `` `C-n `` | \downarrow | $\downarrow$ |
| `` `e `` | \epsilon | $\epsilon$ | `` `< `` | \leq | $\leq$ |
| `` `f `` | \phi | $\phi$ | `` `> `` | \geq | $\geq$ |
| `` `g `` | \gamma | $\gamma$ | `` `~ `` | \tilde | $\sim$ |
| `` `h `` | \eta | $\eta$ | `` `I `` | \infty | $\infty$ |
| `` `k `` | \kappa | $\kappa$ | `` `A `` | \forall | $\forall$ |
| `` `l `` | \lambda | $\lambda$ | `` `E `` | \exists | $\exists$ |
| `` `m `` | \mu | $\mu$ | `` `! `` | \not | $/$ |
| `` `n `` | \nu | $\nu$ | `` `i `` | \in | $\in$ |
| `` `o `` | \omega | $\omega$ | `` `* `` | \times | $\times$ |
| `` `p `` | \pi | $\pi$ | `` `. `` | \cdot | $\cdot$ |
| `` `q `` | \theta | $\theta$ | `` `@{ `` | \subset | $\subset$ |
| `` `r `` | \rho | $\rho$ | `` `@} `` | \supset | $\supset$ |
| `` `s `` | \sigma | $\sigma$ | `` `[ `` | \subseteq | $\subseteq$ |
| `` `t `` | \tau | $\tau$ | `` `] `` | \supseteq | $\supseteq$ |
| `` `v `` | \vee | $\vee$ | `` `\ `` | \backslash | $\backslash$ |
| `` `u `` | \upsilon | $\upsilon$ | `` `/ `` | \setminus | $\setminus$ |
| `` `x `` | \chi | $\chi$ | `` `+ `` | \cup | $\cup$ |
| `` `y `` | \psi | $\psi$ | `` `- `` | \cap | $\cap$ |
| `` `z `` | \zeta | $\zeta$ | `` `( `` | \langle | $\langle$ |
| `` `D `` | \Delta | $\Delta$ | `` `) `` | \rangle | $\rangle$ |
| `` `G `` | \Gamma | $\Gamma$ | `` `C-e `` | \exp | exp |
| `` `Q `` | \Theta | $\Theta$ | `` `C-s `` | \sin | sin |
| `` `L `` | \Lambda | $\Lambda$ | `` `C-c `` | \cos | cos |
| `` `Y `` | \Psi | $\Psi$ | `` `C-^ `` | \sup | sup |
| `` `P `` | \Pi | $\Pi$ | `` `C-_ `` | \inf | inf |
| `` `S `` | \Sigma | $\Sigma$ | `` `C-d `` | \det | det |
| `` `U `` | \Upsilon | $\Upsilon$ | `` `C-l `` | \lim | lim |
| `` `V `` | \Phi | $\Phi$ | `` `C-t `` | \tan | tan |
| `` `O `` | \Omega | $\Omega$ | `` `^ `` | \hat | $\hat{}$ |
| `` `C-b `` | \leftarrow | $\leftarrow$ | | | |

Additional miscellaneous commands in AUC-TEX provide automatic quotation, completion of "items" in appropriate environments (`itemize` and `enumeration` environments, for example), and insertion of brace pairs and skeletal control sequences.

## AUC-TEX Outline Mode

Outline mode is a convenient way to edit large documents. In outline mode, portions of the document that you are not editing are hidden from view. They aren't removed or deleted. Emacs indicates hidden text with ellipses.

For example, in a large document with many sections, you can use outline mode to hide all text except the section headings, and then selectively expand just the sections that you wish to edit.

## Intelligent Paragraph Reformatting

AUC-TEX understands the TEX constructions for many kinds of environments (the list environments, for example) and performs paragraph reformatting within the restrictions of these environments. AUC-TEX won't concatenate a whole series of list items together into one huge paragraph, for example.

## Multi-file Documents

It is often convenient to edit a large document in small pieces rather than in one huge file. For example, when writing a book, it is convenient to work on chapters independently and store them in different files. If you are working on a collaborative project, it may be absolutely necessary to separate the document into pieces.

The TEX \input command allows you to construct a driver file that automatically combines the individual files that make up your document when you run TEX. The driver file contains the document style options and other setup information for the whole document. Each chapter contains just the necessary text. When TEX encounters an \input command, it typesets all of the text in the specified file before continuing with the current document. Example 2-1 shows an example of a driver file.

*Example 2-1: A Simple Driver File*

```
\documentstyle[ora]{book}
\begin{document}
    \input{intro}
    \input{chap1}
    \input{chap2}
\end{document}
```

AUC-TEX provides seamless support for multi-file documents. In order to provide this support, AUC-TEX relies on the "file variables" feature of emacs, which allows you to associate editor variables with particular buffers. An editor variable is a named variable that is local to the current buffer and accessible by macro packages like AUC-TEX running under emacs. Look up file variables in your emacs reference for a more complete description. Example 2-2 shows some common local variables in AUC-TEX.

When you run TEX on a buffer, AUC-TEX looks for the editor variable `TeX-master`. If `TeX-master` is set to a filename, AUC-TEX runs TEX on that file instead of running it directly on the file you are editing. This is a tremendously useful feature because it means that you do not have to put macro definitions, document style options, and other setup information at the top of each chapter. Simply set the `TeX-master` variable in each chapter to name the driver file.

If you do not set the `TeX-master` variable, AUC-TEX will prompt you for it the first time you run a command. If the `\documentstyle` command occurs near the top of your document, AUC-TEX assumes that the current buffer *is* the master (because it contains setup information) and will not prompt you for a different master file.

Editor variables are defined by a "Local Variables" declaration at the bottom of your file. AUC-TEX inserts a Local Variables declaration automatically if it prompts you for a master file. Example 2-2 shows how local variables `TeX-master` and `TeX-command-default` can be set to *driver.tex* and `LaTeX`, respectively. Because these lines begin with a percent sign, they are considered comments by TEX and do not appear in the output. These should be the last lines in the file.

*Example 2-2: Local Variables in an Emacs Buffer*

```
% Local Variables:
% TeX-master: "driver.tex"
% TeX-command-default: "LaTeX"
% End:
```

## Running TEX

Like GNU emacs TEX mode, AUC-TEX allows you to run TEX directly from within emacs as a subshell. Running a program inside emacs creates a process. You can have only one active process for each document, plus one process for TEXing a region. If you try to run two processes on the same document, AUC-TEX will ask for permission to kill the first before running the second. AUC-TEX supports the processing of both the documents and the regions of a document.

## Finding Errors

No matter how much experience you have with TEX, some of the documents that you write will contain errors. AUC-TEX eases the burden of correcting these errors by locating them automatically in your document.

# Multi-Edit

*Multi-Edit* is an editor for the MS-DOS environment. This section describes the text-based version of *Multi-Edit*. A Windows version is in the works, and it may exist by the time you read this.

Built to be a programmer's editor, *Multi-Edit* has a number of features designed to add language-specific intelligence to the editing environment. These features (template editing, a customizable spellchecker, and configurable brace matching) can be exploited for TEX as readily as for any programming language. For several years, at least since version 5.0, *Multi-Edit* has included support for TEX.

## Setting Up TEX Support

Support for TEX is included as a language type in *Multi-Edit*. Language types are selected by filename extension; this means that you configure *Multi-Edit* to provide support for the "TEX language" whenever you edit files with the extension *.tex* (and other extensions if you choose).

Selecting the "Other/Install/Filename extensions..." menu displays a list of configured extensions. If TEX is not listed, press [Insert] to add it. You will see a screen like the one shown in Figure 2-1.

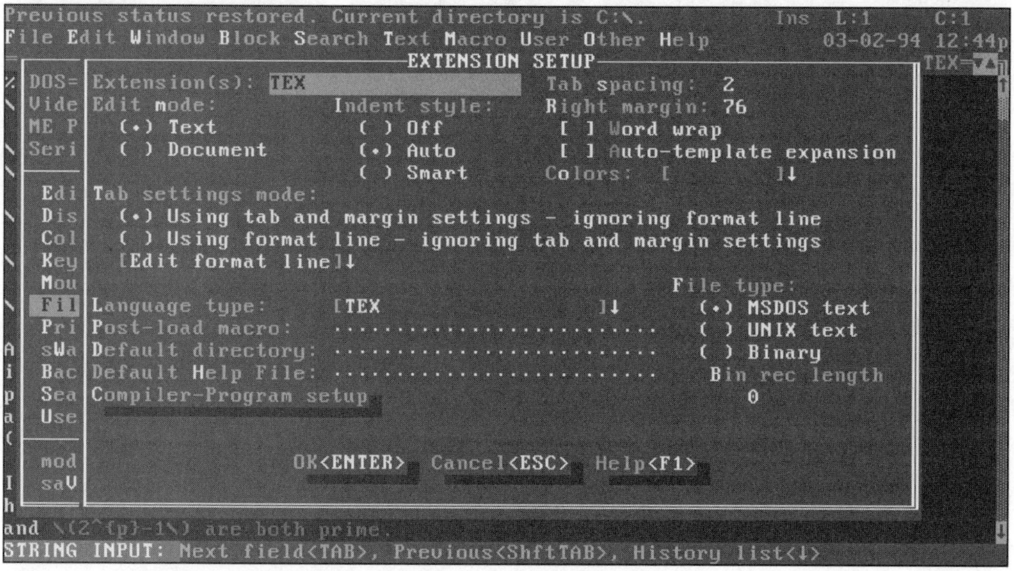

*Figure 2-1: Extension setup in Multi-Edit*

Customize the right margin, tab spacing, indent style, and colors to values that you find comfortable. The edit mode should be "text," and the tab settings should be set to "use tab and margin settings, ignore format line."

Select TEX as the language type, and add TEX as a compiler. One possible setting for TEX as a compiler (for LATEX documents, in this case) is shown in Figure 2-2.

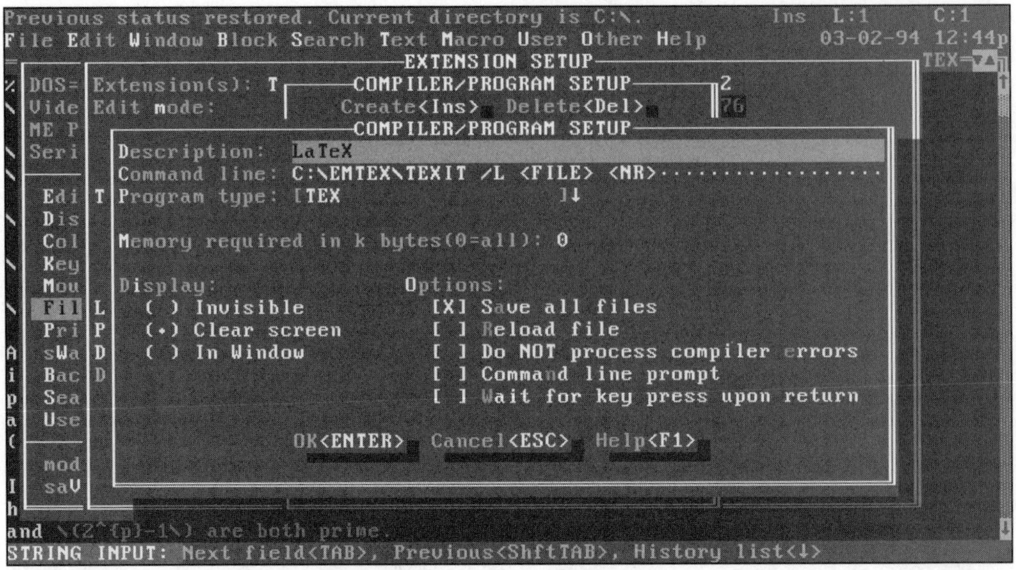

*Figure 2-2: LATEX as a compiler in Multi-Edit*

## Typing in Multi-Edit

Brace matching is provided automatically with Multi-Edit's template expansion support. Consult your Multi-Edit reference for more information about templates.

Multi-Edit language support does not include any TEX key bindings by default. However, the macros are provided, and you can install them with the "Other/Install/Key mapping..." menu. The following macros are available:

- `tex^texquote` inserts the appropriate quotation marks. This macro can be bound to `"` to provide smart quoting.

- `tex^texnquote` inserts the literal double quote. It can be bound to `Alt-"`, for example.

- `tex^texreformat` is a replacement for the reformat macro. If the filename extension is *.tex*, this macro reformats the paragraph with sensitivity to TEX macros. Otherwise it calls the default reformatting macro.

## Running TEX

Running TEX within Multi-Edit is accomplished by specifying a compiler for TEX or LATEX documents. In Figure 2-2, a batch file called *TEXIT* is being used as the compiler for documents with the extension *.tex*.

Automatic compilation and location of errors is provided by Multi-Edit language support when you have selected TEX as the language-type for *.tex* files.

# Brief

*Brief* is a powerful programmer's editor recently acquired by Borland International. It is available for both DOS and OS/2 systems. Like the other editors discussed in this section, *Brief* offers a strong set of programming features, including the ability to run compilers automatically, and a flexible, C-like macro programming language that allows you to customize the editor.

There is a LATEX editing environment for *Brief* in the CTAN archives. It includes multiple-language support (currently supporting Norwegian) and control-key shortcuts for many common LATEX commands.

The installation and setup program includes instructions for defining program compilers. TEX can be defined to process files with particular extensions. Once again, it is a good idea to have the editor run a batch file so that the batch file can determine what format file to use when processing the document.

# MicroEMACS

*MicroEMACS* is a powerful emacs-like editor for MS-DOS and Microsoft Windows.[*] Figure 2-3 shows an example of *MicroEMACS* editing a LATEX document. In this case, the LATEX extensions to *MicroEMACS* have been loaded, and "Help" is selected.

The online help for LATEX is shown in Figure 2-4. This is a Microsoft Windows help file, available independently of *MicroEMACS* (although it is nicely integrated here).

The *MicroEMACS* environment also has the ability to run other programs (including TEX to process documents) and process the error output to aid in locating errors.

# epm: OS/2's Enhanced Editor

*epm*, the enhanced editor for OS/2, can be used to edit TEX documents. The *epmtex* package adds a TEX item to the menu bar as shown in Figure 2-5.

---

[*]There are two versions of the program; the one discussed here is the version for Windows.

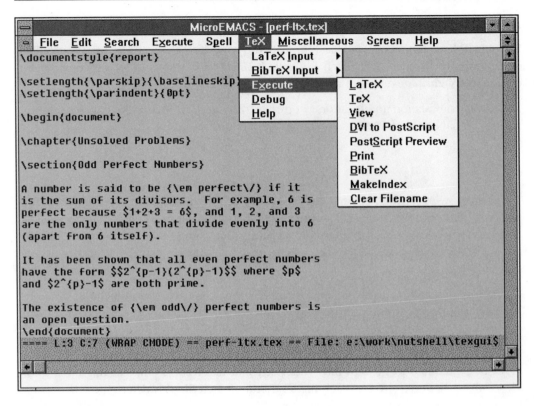

*Figure 2-3: Editing a file with MicroEMACS*

## Other Tools

There are many other editors that can be effective tools for editing TEX documents. Some of the editors that you might want to consider are idx*Jove*, an emacs-like editor; *Xnot*, a Windows port of emacs; *LSedit*, the VMS language-sensitive editor; and *Alpha* and *BBedit*, two Macintosh editors described in Chapter 15, *TEX on the Macintosh*.

There are also a number of tools designed specifically for editing TEX documents. *Scientific Word*, a commercial environment, is described in Chapter 14, *Commercial Environments*. Several free tools (*MathPad*, *Doc*, and *XTEXShell*, for example) also exist, although none were available* in time for review in this edition of *Making TEX Work*.

Another helpful tool is *LaCheck*, a LATEX syntax checker. *LaCheck* attempts to find and identify problems with your document that will cause it to format incorrectly. It runs much more quickly than TEX over a long document and may identify some things (like

---

*Or known to me, anyway.

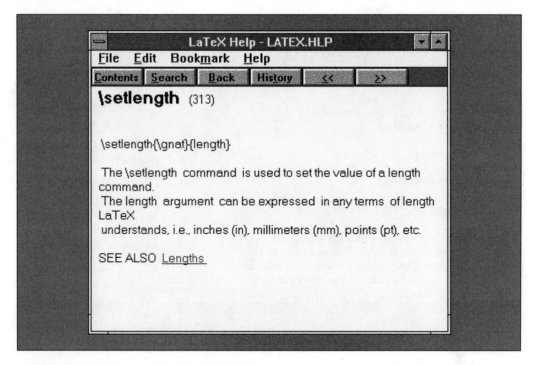

*Figure 2-4: Microsoft Windows online help for LaTeX*

missing italic correction) that are potentially incorrect, even though they are not errors that will prevent the document from formatting.

## TEX as a Compiler

This section discusses how to use TEX like a compiler from within your editor, and it is rather technical. You should read this section before you attempt to program your own editor to run TEX (if it doesn't already include support for TEX). You may not be interested in this material if you aren't planning to do that programming yourself. More details on the types of TEX output used in this section can be found in Chapter 3, *Running TEX*.

Many editors can run a compiler, capture the error messages that the compiler produces, and walk through the source file highlighting each error. Most editors with this functionality can run TEX as a "compiler" for documents.

The discussion that follows is at a very abstract level. The details vary so much from one editor to the next that presenting more detail only confuses the issue further. To implement this feature, you'll need to read your editor reference carefully, and probably experiment on your own a little bit.

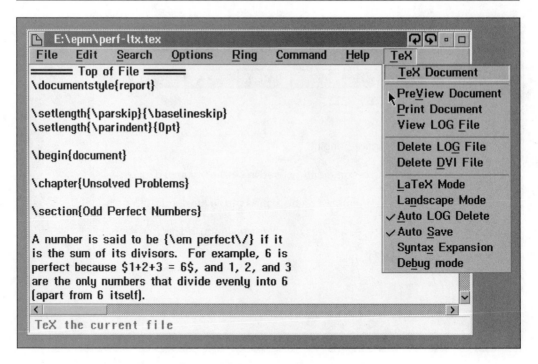

*Figure 2-5: Editing a TEX document with epm under OS/2*

## Processing a Document

Establish the TEX program as a compiler using whatever features your editor provides to set up a compiler. Experiment with your editor until you can process an error-free document.

After you have everything working, it may be desirable to modify the compiler to run a batch file or shell script instead of invoking the TEX program directly. This will allow you to program the shell script so that it can determine which format file to use.

Running TEX is only the first step. Next, you have to interpret the error messages that TEX produces. As a concrete example, Example 2-3 shows some contrived output which demonstrates an "undefined control sequence" error on line 6 of the file *wilma.tex*.

*Example 2-3: A Contrived Error*

```
This is TeX version 3.141...
** (flintstone.tex)
some
messages [1]
(fred.tex [2]
some more
```

*Example 2-3: A Contrived Error (continued)*

```
messages
[3] ) (wilma.tex [4]
! Undefined control sequence.
the dog \dino
               tipped over the car.
1.6 the dog \dino\ tipped over the car.
```

Here are some suggestions for attacking the problem of programming your favorite editor to process TeX error messages:

## Using the log file

Don't worry about capturing the error messages that TeX produces. It is much easier to get the information from the log file. Log files are described in the section called "Log Files" in Chapter 3, *Running TeX*.

## Finding error messages

Any line in the log file that begins with an exclamation point is an error message. In Example 2-3, the line that begins

```
! Undefined control sequence.
```

is an example of an error message.

## Finding the source line

Following the error message, TeX shows the context in which the error occurred. After that, the line that begins with 1.*nnn* (where *nnn* is some decimal number) identifies the line of the input file that TeX was processing when the error occurred (in Example 2-3, TeX was on line 6 when the error occurred).

## Finding the source file

When processing a document that uses the \input command to include other files, there is no guaranteed method of finding out the name of the file TeX was processing when the error occurred. Whenever TeX starts processing a file, it prints an open parenthesis followed by the name of the file. When it finishes processing the document, it prints a close parenthesis.* So the following algorithm *usually* identifies what file the error occurred in:

Beginning at the line in the log file that announces the error message (the line beginning with "!"), search backwards for the first unmatched open parenthesis. The word following that open parenthesis is probably the name of the file TeX was processing when the error occurred.

---

*Unfortunately, parentheses can occur in the log file for other reasons.

## Ignoring errors

When you run TEX "by hand," you want TEX to stop and report errors to you as they occur in your document. But if your editor is going to handle any errors that occur, it is inconvenient to have TEX stop and ask questions. In fact, it may not be possible to run TEX from your editor in a way that makes it even *feasible* for TEX to stop and ask questions. You can use several built-in control sequences to control the way TEX responds to errors. They are summarized in Table 2-3.

*Table 2-3: TEX Modes of Interaction*

| Mode | TEX's Behavior |
|------|----------------|
| \errorstopmode | Stop on errors (the default behavior) |
| \scrollmode | Scroll errors, stop on missing files |
| \nonstopmode | Scroll errors and missing files |
| \batchmode | Scroll both and don't summarize on screen |

One common way of invoking TEX from an editor to process a document is to use the command:

```
tex \nonstopmode \input flintstone
```

This uses the features discussed in the section "The Command Line" in Chapter 3 to pass a command to TEX on the command line. In this case, the command tells TEX not to stop on any kind of error.

## Handling other errors

When searching for errors in the log file, you may find it helpful to search for lines that begin with the words "Overfull box" or "Underfull box" as well as lines that begin with an exclamation point. Because TEX does not print the 1.nnn form of line-number message in this case, you will have to look for the line numbers in the warning message.

Overfull box messages have the form:

```
Overfull box (99.9pt too wide) in paragraph at lines n--m
```

The *box* will be either hbox, indicating that something is too wide, or vbox indicating that something is too tall or too deep. The distance, 99.9pt, indicates how badly the box is overfull, and $n$ is the first line of the paragraph in which the error occurs. Underfull box messages are the same, except that they begin with the word "Underfull."

There are several control sequences that you can use to control how sensitive TEX is to "bad" boxes. Any good TEX reference will discuss these parameters in detail.

# Spellchecking

Checking for spelling mistakes is an important part of any document creation process. Checking TEX documents is difficult because these documents contain control sequences that aren't words in the traditional sense.

Some editors offer ways of customizing the spellchecker. Multi-Edit, for example, allows you to indicate that any word beginning with a backslash should be ignored for the purpose of spellchecking. Figure 2-6 shows the "Other/Install/Edit Settings..." dialog where word delimiters are controlled. This simple customization goes a long way towards making spellchecking tolerable.

External spellcheckers, such as the ones described here, can also frequently be customized to ignore TEX control sequences.

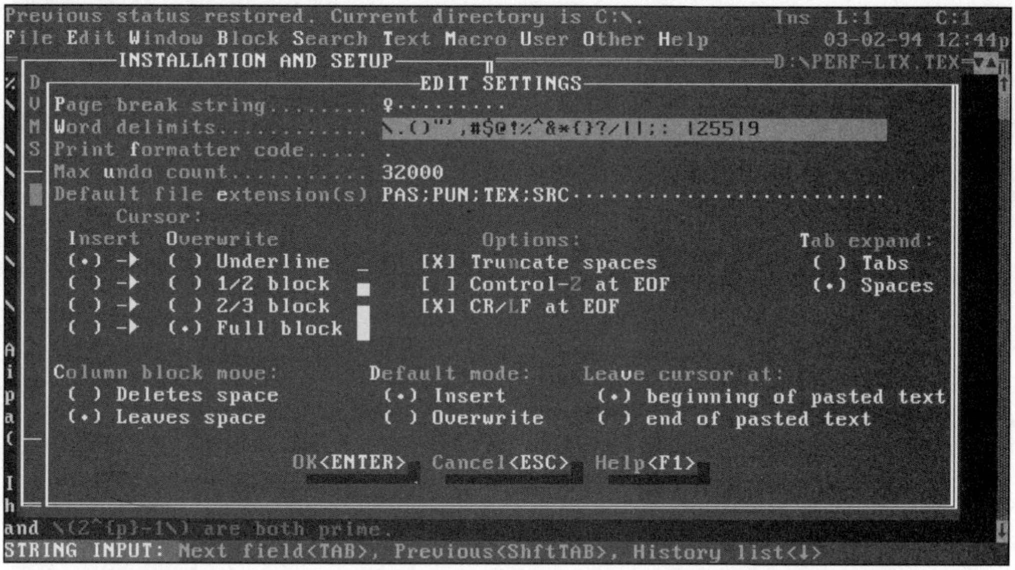

*Figure 2-6: Edit settings control word delimiters*

## ispell

*ispell* is a common UNIX spellchecker. In addition to being available from the shell prompt, GNU emacs includes an *ispell-mode* that handles TEX documents intelligently.

## amSpell

*amSpell* is an MS-DOS spellchecker that includes special support for TEX documents. When spellchecking a TEX document, *amSpell* ignores all TEX control sequences, as well as mathematics and the arguments to reference and citation commands. The standard accent primitives are also recognized, and *amSpell* can identify and correct misspellings in words that use them.

An example of *amSpell* checking a document is shown in Figure 2-7.

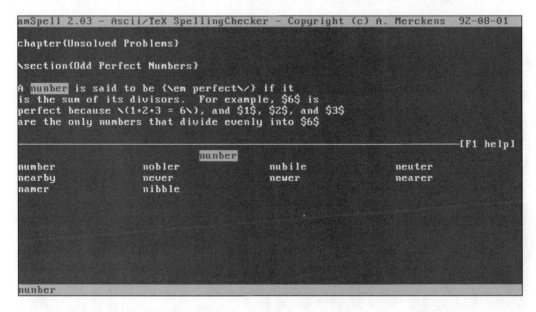

*Figure 2-7: Spellchecking a document with amSpell*

# Revision Control

Revision control allows you to track modifications to a file. It is frequently associated with programming where the ability to find and correct bugs relies on being able to recreate a problem exactly. It can be just as useful for writers wishing to keep track of changes to an evolving document. For example, I use revision control to keep track of which versions of each chapter my editor has seen.

One of the most common revision control systems is RCS, which was derived from SCCS, a commercial package. RCS is freely available under the GNU license. It is possible to use RCS under UNIX, MS-DOS, and OS/2.

The TEX macros shown in Example 2-4 can be used to include RCS information as marginal notes in a document. The marginal notes in this example are printed only when a draft is being produced.

These macros are my own, you will find others in the CTAN archives in the directory *macros/latex/contrib/misc.*

*Example 2-4: Revision Control Macros for TEX Documents Using RCS*

```
%%%%%%%%%%%%%%%%%%%%%%%%%%%%%%%%%%%%%%%%%%%%%
% RCS definitions...
%
\newif\ifdraft
\def\RCSID$#1${%
  \ifdraft{\tolerance=100000%
           \hbadness=100000%
           \raggedright%
           \marginpar{\tiny Draft #1}}%
           \typeout{Draft #1}%
  \else\typeout{Production run #1}\fi%
}

\def\RCSmargid$#1: #2 #3 #4 #5 #6 #7${%
% #1 = ``Id´´
% #2 = filename
% #3 = vers
% #4 = date
% #5 = time
% #6 = author
% #7 = state [locker]
  \ifdraft
    \setbox0=\hbox to 0pt{%
        \tolerance=100000%
        \hbadness=100000%
        \parbox{4in}{%
           \rm\tiny #2\\ #3\\ #4}%
        \hss}%
    \marginpar{\box0}%
    \typeout{Draft Id: #2 #3 #4 #5 #6 #7}%
  \fi
}
```

# TEX Shells

The iterative nature of TEX (edit, TEX, BIBTEX, make indexes, preview, repeat) can be tedious to perform by hand. As a result, several TEX "shells" have been developed which provide a more automatic interface to many aspects of the TEX process. Several of these packages are described below. In everyday use, they make TEX much more user friendly.

## TEXShell

TEXShell was designed as an add-on for emTEX (it installs directly into the emTEX directory hierarchy). This character-based interface is available for both MS-DOS and OS/2. TEXShell provides an editor, a complete help system, and fully customizable push-button access to TEX. An example of the TEXShell interface is shown in Figure 2-8. The default TEX menu and help windows are shown.

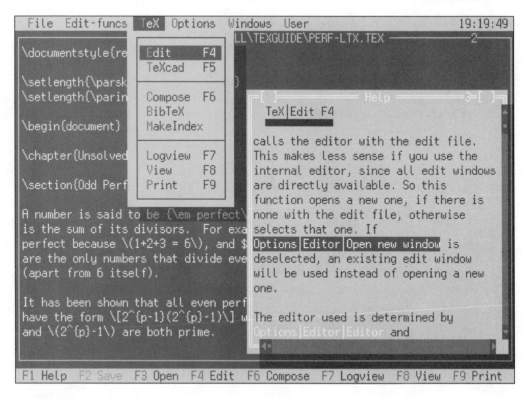

*Figure 2-8: TEXShell*

## TEXPert

TEXPert is a character-based shell for TEX. MS-DOS and OS/2 versions of TEXPert are available in either German or English. The default configuration files for TEXPert are designed to work with emTEX, but TEXPert does not install directly into the emTEX directory heirarchy. The TEXPert interface is shown in Figure 2-9.

TEXPert provides an editor, an archive tool for speedy access to commonly used files, and an interface to *grep* for quickly scanning files. The exact look and feel of TEXPert can be customized.

## 4TEX

The 4TEX system uses the *4DOS* extended batch language and a number of utilities to integrate emTEX with a wide variety of free, shareware, and commercial tools. The system is well documented in a manual that describes installation, setup, use, and customization. The 4TEX interface is shown in Figure 2-10.

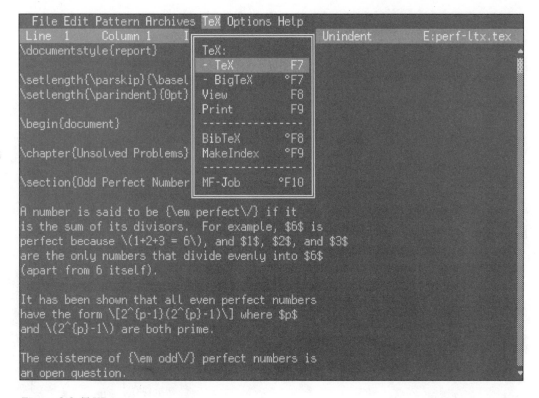

*Figure 2-9: TEXPert*

## PMTEX

PMTEX is an OS/2 presentation manager program. Although it does not provide a built-in editor, it can control four independent DOS and OS/2 sessions, one each for editing, TEX processing, previewing, and printing. The options passed to each program can be controlled from the PMTEX Options menu.

PMTEX was designed to work with emTEX, but can be configured to use any TEX system. PMTEX was also designed to support two preprocessors for phonetic transcription: the TeuTEX-P and ALDTEX-P scanners. These scanners are useful in dialectology and are available separately from PMTEX's author.

A example of the PMTEX interface is shown in Figure 2-11. Note that the menu bar is very wide and does not fit in a standard 640x480 VGA window.

## TEXit

The TEXit shell (which I wrote) is much less ambitious in many ways. Written entirely in Perl, TEXit does not offer a full screen interface or an editor at all. Instead, it provides a

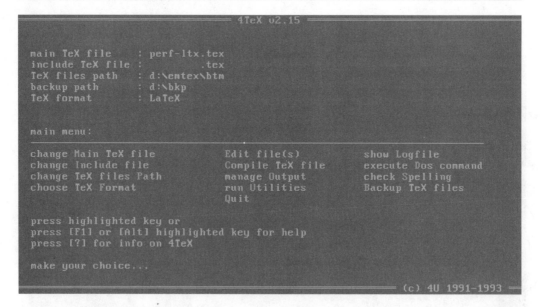

*Figure 2-10: 4TEX*

*Figure 2-11: PMTEX*

simple menu of choices as shown in Figure 2-12 (all of the menu choices are completely customizable).

```
Processing: ./driver.tex
Again? [?]status, [T]eX & View, [b]ibtex, [c]leanup,
       [e]dit a file, [p]rint, [q]uery printer, [t]ex,
       [v]iew, e[x]it:
```

*Figure 2-12: TEXit*

One of TEXit's strengths is its ability to parse the log file created by TEX and to determine when additional actions are required. For example, TEXit will recognize when a document contains unresolved references and citations and can automatically run BIBTEX and repeatedly run TEX to resolve the references. With the addition of a few "user specified" rules in the document, TEXit can easily handle index construction and other more sophisticated relationships.

# 3

# *Running TEX*

The heart of processing a document with TEX is running the TEX program. In this chapter, you'll learn what happens between the time you first start the TEX program and the time it finishes. You'll also learn what files TEX really needs (in addition to your document) and what to do when TEX finds things in your document that it doesn't understand.

## *What Do You Run?*

The first thing you have to know is what program to run. Unfortunately, the actual file you have to execute varies between platforms and implementations. If you have built and/or installed TEX yourself, you probably already know what program to run. You'll have to ask your system administrator for help if you can't figure out what the name of the TEX executable is on your computer. The rest of this chapter assumes that the command *tex* runs TEX. You should substitute the name of the executable program on your own system for *tex* in the examples that follow.

Most implementations of TEX have some hard-coded memory limits. These limitations may cause problems if you are trying to run a very complex document through TEX. To combat this problem, some distributions include two versions of the TEX executable. One version is a "small" TEX that generally runs faster but has less memory available to process your documents. The other version, a "big" TEX, can process more complex documents but may run more slowly. If you get a "TEX capacity exceeded" error, and you have a big TEX available on your system, try processing your document with the big TEX.

If you still get an error, you have a document that is simply too complex for your implementation of TEX to handle, or you have an error in one of the macros in your document. By examining the error log, described later in this chapter in the section "Log Files," you can determine what macro TEX is interpreting when the error occurs. If the error occurs in a macro that you wrote, check to make sure the macro functions the way you intended by using it in a small test document.

# What Files Does TEX Need?

Naturally, TEX needs your input file in order to process it. However, TEX must be able to find several other files as well. The files that TEX needs are normally created during the installation process. Here is a common directory layout for TEX on a UNIX system:

| | |
|---|---|
| */usr/local/lib/tex/pool* | Pool files |
| */usr/local/lib/tex/formats* | Format files |
| */usr/local/lib/tex/inputs* | "System" input files |
| */usr/local/lib/tex/macros* | (styles, macros, and miscellaneous |
| */usr/local/lib/tex/lib* | files distributed with TEX) |
| */usr/local/lib/tex/ps* | PostScript support files |
| */usr/local/lib/tex/fonts/pk* | PK fonts |
| */usr/local/lib/tex/fonts/vf* | Virtual fonts |
| */usr/local/lib/tex/fonts/tfm* | TFM metrics |

A similar layout is frequently used on other operating systems, except that the TEX files are often stored in a top-level directory (for example, *C:\TEX* under MS-DOS). Because TEX is very flexible and has many different implementations, the exact directory structure varies. Pool files are sometimes placed in the format file directory (which is sometimes called *fmt* or *fmts*, rather than *formats*). Input files may occur in one or more of the standard places listed above (*inputs*, *macros*, and *lib*) as well as a number of other places (*texinputs* is another common name).

The files under the TEX tree usually come from outside distributions, so you don't have to change them often. (You definitely *shouldn't* put your personal macro files in that tree, even if you do have access to it.)

The following sections describe, in more detail, each of the files that TEX needs.

## Pool Files

Pool files contain string constants used by TEX at runtime. Each time TEX is compiled, it creates a pool file unique to the version being compiled. The pool file from one version of TEX will not work with a different version.

In contrast to format files (discussed in the next section), if you don't have a pool file, there's nothing you can do about it. If you obtained precompiled programs (from the Internet, from a friend, or commercially) and you don't have a pool file, you received an incomplete distribution.

If you did not install TEX yourself, but find that the pool file is missing, contact the system administrator who performed the installation. He or she did something wrong.

## Format Files

As mentioned in the section "Control Sequences" in Chapter 1, *The Big Picture*, all of the control sequences and macros that your document uses must be defined somewhere. One way to do this is to use the \input command to load all of the definitions at the beginning of each document. However, with large macro packages like LATEX, this process can be very time consuming. Format files are a way of predefining control sequences and macros so they don't have to be interpreted by TEX every time they're used. If TEX didn't use format files, you'd have to wait for TEX to interpret all of LATEX every time you processed a document that used LATEX.

Format files are created by a special version of TEX, usually called iniTEX. Some implementations combine TEX and iniTEX into one program. In this case, you must select iniTEX with a special option when you run TEX. IniTEX interprets all the control sequences in a macro package and builds the in-memory data structures that the TEX program needs. After loading the whole macro package, iniTEX writes the memory image it has constructed to a format file. When TEX later loads the format file, it simply copies it into memory; no interpretation is necessary. This is why loading a format file is such a fast way to define control sequences. This is also why format files are not usually portable from one system to another,* or even between different versions of TEX on the same system. Different versions of TEX are stored differently in memory, and this difference in loading makes the format files incompatible. For this reason, you need a "big" iniTEX to make format files for a big TEX and a "small" iniTEX for a small TEX.

You will find a complete discussion of macro packages and instructions for building format files for many of the common macro packages in Chapter 4, *Macro Packages*.

## User Files

When you run TEX, you have to tell it what file to process. If you specify a complete pathname, TEX will load the specific file that you request. For example, I could process the document *myreport.tex* in the directory */home/norm/tex/* by running:

```
$ tex /home/norm/tex/myreport
```

This example applies to both UNIX and PC implementations of TEX. Even though MS-DOS and OS/2 typically use the backslash to separate directory names, *always* use a forward slash when entering filenames for TEX.

---

*The exception occurs in some UNIX versions of TEX where provisions are made for different architectures to share the same format files. The exact same version of TEX must be running on both architectures for this to work.

If you specify a simple filename without a path, TEX looks for the file in several user-defined and, possibly, system-defined locations. In the following example, TEX will attempt to locate the file *myreport.tex* in order to process it:

```
$ tex myreport
```

If the file *myreport.tex* exists in several directories, TEX will process the first file it finds without looking for any others. TEX always prints the complete name of the file it processes both on the display and in the log file, so you can always tell what file was really processed.

The most common way to specify user-defined locations is by setting the `TEXINPUTS` environment variable* to a list of subdirectories where TEX documents are kept. Setting `TEXINPUTS` specifies where TEX should look for *documents* (files that you input with `\input` or some other construct, style files, and macros). To change where TEX looks for other kinds of files (fonts, formats, pool files, etc.), setting different environment variables or performing some other customization is required. The format of the environment variable differs according to the platform you use. On UNIX systems, it is a list of directory names separated by colons. Here is a typical example:

```
.:/usr/local/lib/tex/inputs:/home/norm/tex/inputs
```

On MS-DOS and OS/2 systems, it is a list of directory names separated by semicolons. A typical example looks like this:†

```
.;\tex\inputs;\tex\styles;\tex\macros
```

Consult the documentation for your particular implementation of TEX for more information about system-defined locations where TEX looks for input files. Unfortunately, this is not always well documented. For example, an undocumented feature of version 1.4s of emTEX always searches in the directory *\emtex\texinputs* even if it does not occur in the `TEXINPUTS` path. In fact, there is no way to tell it *not* to look there, short of renaming the directory (which is what I did).

If TEX cannot find a file you specify, for example *rpt-data.tex*, it displays a prompt like this one:

```
! I can't find file `rpt-data.tex'.
<*> \input rpt-data

Please type another input filename:
```

The general form of TEX error messages is discussed in the section called "What About Errors?" later in this chapter. TEX announces an error by printing the error message on a

---

\*The exact name of the environment variable differs between implementations.

†You will notice that I've used backslashes to separate directory components in the path. Environment variables are handled by the system-dependent portions of TEX, so it's okay to use backslashes here. You can also use forward slashes, but I use backslashes because that is more typical of MS-DOS and OS/2 environments.

line that begins with an exclamation mark. Below the error, TEX provides the context in which the error occurred. In the example above, TEX encountered the command \input rpt-data and tried to find the file *rpt-data.tex* which it could not locate.

Notice that TEX automatically added the extension *.tex* to the name of the file it was looking for. In any context where you specify a filename, TEX will append *.tex* unless you specify an alternate extension.

TEX responds to a "can't find file" error by asking you to type the name of a different file. Some implementations of TEX allow you to abort by typing Ctrl-C or Ctrl-D at this point,[*] but other implementations insist that you enter a filename. In this case, you'll find it convenient to create an empty file called *nul.tex* in a directory in your TEXINPUTS path so you can get around this requirement by supplying a dummy answer to the prompt. *nul.tex* is part of many standard distributions.

# *The Command Line*

Except for the name of a document, TEX has very few command-line options. The only option that is regularly used is the name of a format file, but the use of this option is frequently buried inside a batch file or shell script.

It is helpful to think of TEX, LATEX, SLITEX, etc. as different text processors (they aren't really; they're all TEX with different format files). This illusion is easy to provide with shell scripts or batch files. For example, on an MS-DOS system, you could easily have three batch files called *tex.bat*, *latex.bat*, and *slitex.bat*:

- The *tex.bat* file runs the TEX executable with the *plain* format file specified as an option.
- The *latex.bat* file runs TEX with the *lplain* format file.
- The *slitex.bat* file runs TEX with the *splain* format file.

Now typing **tex** *filename* processes Plain TEX documents; typing **latex** *filename* processes LATEX documents; and typing **slitex** *filename* processes SLITEX documents.[†] The role of format files and macro packages is described fully in Chapter 4, *Macro Packages*.

## *Command-line Options*

A formal specification of the TEX command line looks like this:

```
$ tex <switches> <&format> <|document> <tex-commands>
```

---

[*]MS-DOS and OS/2 implementations of TEX may use Ctrl-Z (possibly followed by a carriage return) instead of Ctrl-C or Ctrl-D.

[†]On UNIX systems, the same effect is often achieved with symbolic links. Most UNIX implementations look for different standard format files based upon the name of the executable that starts them.

If this looks confusing, have no fear. I'll explain what it means in English.

After the name of the TEX program (or batch file), the first things that can go on the command line are implementation-dependent switches and options. For example, implementations of TEX that combine iniTEX and TEX into a single program may use /I as the switch to specify that iniTEX processing is desired (iniTEX, you may remember, was described in the section "Format Files," earlier in this chapter). There are no system-independent switches for TEX. Consult the documentation that comes with your implementation for more information about system-dependent switches.

After any system-dependent switches, the first thing that you can put on the TEX command line is the name of the format file to use. If you specify this option, you must include it before any other options, and you must put an ampersand (&) in front of the format file name. If you do not specify a format file, TEX will use a default format, usually Plain TEX.

After the format, TEX looks for the name of a document to process. If TEX finds a filename on the command line, it will process the document contained in that file before looking at any other options that may follow.

Finally, you can insert arbitrary TEX commands on the command line by typing them just as you would in a document. The section "TEX as a Compiler" in Chapter 2, *Editing*, describes one particular instance where this is very useful, but it isn't something that you are likely to do very often.

## Command-line Cautions

There are some special restrictions on file names used on the command line and on the way TEX interprets the command line. These restrictions are summarized here.

### Misinterpretation of the command line

Command lines that are typed at the operating system prompt are actually seen by your operating system's "command processor" before they are seen by TEX. You must be aware of special processing that might be performed by the command processor. Under UNIX, for example, the backslash is frequently interpreted as a *shell escape* character, and the ampersand has another special meaning related to job control. The ampersand is also special under some MS-DOS and OS/2 command processors where it is the default command separation character and will not be passed to TEX as you would expect.

To insert these troublesome characters literally, you must enclose the relevant sections of the command line in quotation marks or use some form of shell escape mechanism. Under UNIX, place the name of the format file, including the ampersand, in double or single quotes and use two backslashes in a row if you include TEX control sequences on the command line. For example, type:

```
$ tex ´&lplain´ \\nonstopmode \\input doc1
```

instead of

```
$ tex &lplain \nonstopmode \input doc1
```

When using OS/2, place a ^ in front of an ampersand to prevent it from being interpreted as a command separator.

### Filenames and TEX

It is easy for TEX to recognize the presence of a format file on the command line; it must be the first option and it must begin with an ampersand.* After the format file, TEX determines whether the next option is a file name by looking at the first character of the option. If the first character is not a backslash, it is a filename; otherwise it is a TEX command, and TEX assumes that no filename is present.

On some systems, notably MS-DOS and OS/2, the backslash is used to delimit the subdirectory components of a file name. On other systems, a forward slash is used. Regardless of the system you use, filenames passed to TEX *must* use forward slashes to delimit filenames.

For example, TEX will not process the file *letter.tex* in the *\tex\docs* directory of the current drive if you execute the following command line on an MS-DOS system:

```
$ tex \tex\docs\letter
```

Instead, you must type the following, regardless of the operating system you're using:

```
$ tex /tex/docs/letter
```

If you don't, TEX will complain that the control sequence \tex is undefined. Even more confusing errors may result if the first subdirectory happens to be a valid control sequence.

Unfortunately, filenames containing forward slashes are not always recognized by operating systems that use backslashes to delimit filenames. For example, under MS-DOS, IF EXIST C:/CONFIG.SYS returns false, even when a file called *config.sys* exists in the root directory of drive C:. Therefore, it is most convenient to use filenames with backslashes when other commands will be used (for example in a batch file). Filenames in batch files must have any backslashes translated into forward slashes before being passed to TEX. MS-DOS's command processor isn't really powerful enough, but the task

---

*In the unlikely event that you have a TEX document stored in a file with a name beginning with an ampersand, use the following trick to process that file: instead of running *tex &file*, run *tex \input &file* (or even *tex &format \input &file*).

is quite doable with JP Software's *4DOS* command processor. *4DOS* is a replacement for MS-DOS's normal command processor; it offers many advantages over the normal processor. You can get a shareware version of *4DOS* from many large MS-DOS archive sites on the Internet* as well as most large bulletin board systems. The following lines, written in *4DOS*'s extended batch language, will translate all backslashes in the environment variable TEXFN to forward slashes:

```
:FixBacks
  Set Count=%@Index[%TexFn,\]
  If "%Count" eq "-1" Goto FixDone
  Set Place=%@Eval[%Count+1]
  Set TexFn=%@SubStr[%TexFn,0,%Count]/%@SubStr[%TexFn,%Place]
  Goto FixBacks
:FixDone
```

These lines also work under OS/2 with JP Software's *4OS2* command processor (akin to *4DOS*; shareware versions of *4OS2* are also available). The same task can be completed in a single line with *REXX* under OS/2:

```
TEXFN = TRANSLATE(TEXFN, '\', '/')
```

*REXX* is an interpreted systems-programming language distributed with OS/2. *REXX* runs under many other IBM operating systems in addition to OS/2. Several versions of *REXX* are available for MS-DOS and UNIX systems, too.

### Multiple documents

Keep in mind that TEX interprets only the first option after the format file name as a document name. If you type the command line:

```
$ tex doc1 doc2
```

TEX will process only *doc1.tex* as a document. The result of the above command line will be exactly as if you had typed the literal word "doc2" at the very end of the file *doc1.tex*.

To get TEX to process both *doc1* and *doc2* as documents, type a command like the following:

```
$ tex doc1 \input doc2
```

or, for complete clarity,

```
$ tex \input doc1 \input doc2
```

In either case, the structure of your document files must allow them to be concatenated together. TEX does not process *doc1* and then process *doc2* separately. Instead, it processes all of *doc1* and appends the text in the file *doc2* directly onto the end of *doc1*.

---

*For example, oak.oakland.edu in the directory */pub/msdos/4DOS*.

# TEX Without Options

If you run TEX without specifying any options at all, it prints out some introductory information, then produces a ** prompt and stops. Here's what emTEX's *tex386* produces:

```
This is emTeX (tex386), Version 3.141 [3c-beta8]
**
```

This is the only situation where the ** prompt occurs. TEX now expects you to enter text. TEX will interpret anything you type after the ** prompt *exactly* as if you had typed it on the command line. All of the rules regarding slashes (described in "Misinterpretation of the command line" earlier) apply to commands that you type at the ** prompt. Remember, however, that input entered at the ** prompt is not seen by the operating system, so don't use quotation marks or doubled backslashes.

The last line of a document is usually a command telling TEX that the document is finished. TEX responds by writing the last page of the document and ending (returning control to the operating system). If a document doesn't end with such a command, TEX will wait for more input. When TEX runs out of input, it displays the * prompt (single asterisk). Anything you type at the * prompt is interpreted exactly as if it occurred in the document that TEX was processing. You cannot specify an alternate format or name a document at the * prompt. You can, however, use \input to insert another file.

If emTEX processes a document called *unended.tex*:

```
% This is UNENDED.TEX
Now is the time for all good men
to come to the aid of their country.
% Note: there's no \bye command to end
% TeX's processing...
```

the following output appears on the terminal:

```
This is emTeX (tex386), Version 3.141 [3c-beta8]
**unended
(unended.tex)
*
```

You can exit from the TEX program at the * prompt by telling TEX that it should stop processing the current document. Exactly how you get out depends on the format file you use. The following table shows the stop commands for some TEX macro packages.

| Package | Command |
|---|---|
| Plain TEX | \bye |
| LATEX | \end{document} |
| SLITEX | \end{document} |
| Lollipop | \Stop |
| TEXinfo | @bye |

If you do not know which format is in use, you can almost always get out with the following steps:*

1.  Type a control sequence that TEX will not recognize (control sequences \undefined and \gobbledygook will work). TEX will respond with the question mark prompt.

2.  Enter **x** at the prompt. The question mark prompt is discussed fully in the section "The Question Mark Prompt," later in this chapter.

To continue the above example, if I type \undefined at the * prompt, TEX will respond:

```
This is emTeX (tex386), Version 3.141 [3c-beta8]
**unended
(unended.tex)
*\undefined
! Undefined control sequence.
<*> \undefined

?
```

If I enter **x** at the question mark prompt, TEX will print several informative messages and then end, returning control to the operating system.

```
This is emTeX (tex386), Version 3.141 [3c-beta8]
**unended
(unended.tex)
*\undefined
! Undefined control sequence.
<*> \undefined

? x
No pages of output.
Transcript written on unended.log.
```

One word of caution: some macro packages redefine the meaning of the backslash (\) character so that it doesn't function as the beginning of a control sequence (for example, the TEXinfo format uses the at-sign, "@"). In this case, you must precede the undefined control sequence by the escape character, even if it isn't the backslash.

## *What About Errors?*

When you write TEX documents, you will occasionally make mistakes and as a result, TEX won't be able to process your document. There are six broad classes of mistakes you're likely to make:

1.  Naming documents or files that TEX cannot find.

---

*Typing the break character ( Ctrl-C or Ctrl-Break , for example) sometimes works as well, but some implementations of TEX don't respond to the break character at every prompt. On UNIX systems, use Ctrl-D . EmTEX responds to Ctrl-Z followed by Return .

2. Misspelling the name of a TₑX control sequence.

3. Failing to close an environment or forgetting to insert a closing brace after an opening brace.

4. Using math operators outside of math mode or forgetting to close an opened math environment.

5. Requesting a font that TₑX cannot find.

6. Everything else.

TₑX is legitimately criticized for having error messages that are very difficult to understand. TₑX frequently provides far more information than you really need or want, and the excess information often obscures the actual cause of the error.

Nevertheless, understanding what TₑX does when it encounters an error will help make error messages easier to understand. Let's begin with an example. Example 3-1 shows a simple LaTeX document using the New Font Selection Scheme (NFSS), which contains an error.* The error is that the control sequence \Large, which has been redefined to request a 17pt font, contains a typo: \fontsiz should be \fontsize.†

*Example 3-1: The Document BADFONT.TEX*

```
\documentstyle{article}
% The following definition changes the font that LaTeX
% uses for the 'Large' font.  I have introduced a typo
% into the definition, ``\fontsiz'' should be ``\fontsize''.
%
% The  first time a \Large font is requested, an error will occur.
%
\renewcommand{\Large}{\fontsiz{17}{20pt}\selectfont}
\begin{document}

This text precedes the first section header.

% Note: LaTeX uses the \Large font in section
% headers...this will fail in a confusing way
% because the error is deep within the definition
% of \section where \Large is used...
%
\section{First Section}

This is the first and only sentence of the first section.

\end{document}
```

---

*The details of LaTeX and the NFSS are discussed in Chapter 4, *Macro Packages*. It is simply convenient to use a concrete example in this case. Do not be concerned if you do not use LaTeX or the NFSS.

†In practice, redefining a control sequence like \Large in a document is a bad idea. I've done it here only to provide an example of an error that occurs inside another macro.

When TEX processes this file, using LATEX with the New Font Selection Scheme, it produces these error messages:

```
This is TeX, Version 3.1415 (C version 6.1)
LaTeX Version 2.09 <25 March 1992> with NFSS2
(badfont.tex (/work/nutshell/texguide/styles/latex/article.sty
Standard Document Style `article' <14 Jan 92>.
(/work/nutshell/texguide/styles/latex/art10.sty)) (badfont.aux)
(/usr/local/lib/tex/inputs/nfss2/T1cmr.fd)
! Undefined control sequence.
\Large ->\fontsiz
                  {17}{20pt}\selectfont
<argument> \reset@font \Large
                              \bf
\@sect ...x \ifdim \@tempskipa >\z@ \begingroup #6
                                      \relax \@hangfrom {\hskip ...
1.21 \section{First Section}

?
```

These messages exemplify the kind of confusing error messages that TEX produces. Remember the following rule: Always look at the first and last line of the TEX error message when trying to figure out what went wrong and where it went wrong. In this case, the first line is:

```
! Undefined control sequence.
```

and the last line is:

```
1.21 \section{First Section}
```

The error is that the control sequence \fontsiz is not defined and TEX was processing line 21 of the file when it occurred.

## *Log Files*

You don't have to remember or write down the error messages that TEX produces. When TEX processes a document, it produces a transcript of everything that occurs; you can refer to this transcript later if you need to recall what errors occurred when you processed your document. TEX stores this transcript in a file which has the same name as the document and the extension *.log*. For example, if you process *main.tex*, TEX produces a transcript in *main.log*.

### NOTE

Log files go in the current directory. TEX always places the log file in the current directory, even if you specify a path when you format your document. For example, if you process *lectures/main.tex*, TEX produces a transcript in *main.log*, not in *lectures/main.log* as you might expect.

## Interpreting TEX Error Messages

The first line of a TEX error message begins with an exclamation point followed by the text of the message. The lines that follow it show the context in which the error occurred.* In the previous example, the error message indicates an Undefined control sequence. This means that TEX encountered a control sequence which was not previously defined.

The final line, which says 1.21 \section{First Section}, occurs right above the question mark prompt. It identifies the line in your document that TEX was processing when it encountered the error. The error occurred when TEX was at line 21 of the file, and that line began with \section{First Section}.

Between the first and last lines, TEX prints a detailed description of how the error occurred. This is necessary because the error may have occurred inside the replacement text of a macro that you used. When TEX encounters a control sequence, like \section, it has to look up the definition to figure out how to typeset your document. The definition of a control sequence may contain other control sequences which also have to be interpreted. It is possible for TEX to be several levels deep, as it was in this case, when an error occurs. To give the person who wrote the definition of the control sequence an opportunity to figure out what went wrong, TEX prints out a *trace back* of what happened before the error. As you gain experience with a particular macro package, you'll find the intervening lines more meaningful.

Correcting an error depends entirely on the nature of the error. In this case, all you need to do is correct the typo.

As stated above, there are six general classes of errors you might encounter when you run TEX. The following sections briefly describe each class.

## Naming a File TEX Cannot Find

Missing documents are discussed in the section called "User Files," earlier in this chapter.

If you request a format file that cannot be found, TEX issues the following warning message:

```
Sorry, I can't find that format; will try the default
```

TEX then attempts to typeset your document with Plain TEX.† To correct this problem, run TEX with the correct format file name. If the format file isn't available, you will have to build it. Chapter 4, *Macro Packages*, describes how to build format files for several common macro packages.

---

*The number of lines of context shown in the error message is determined by the value of the built-in parameter \errorcontextlines.
†It is possible to make other formats the default, but in practice I've never seen it done.

## Misspelling a Control Sequence Name

Misspelling a control sequence name is one of the most common errors. For example, you might type `\ipnut{chap1}` in your document instead of `\input{chap1}`. The solution is straightforward and usually easy to identify. In many cases, you can simply proceed after encountering this error. Although TEX may not typeset your document correctly, you can continue to look for other errors. The section called "The Question Mark Prompt," later in this chapter, describes how to continue after an error.

In some cases, TEX may become badly confused by a misspelled control sequence name, in which case you should give up and fix the spelling error before trying to process your document further. This may happen if you misspell a LATEX environment name (`\begin{itemze}` instead of `\begin{itemize}`, for example),* which will make LATEX misinterpret many of the control sequences which follow.

Sometimes TEX will complain that a control sequence is undefined when you *know* that the control sequence is spelled correctly. When this occurs, make sure that you are using the correct format file (see the section "The Command Line" earlier in this chapter), loading the correct macro files, and using the correct style options.

## Failure to Close an Environment

Failure to close an environment is another very common error. There are several distinct errors in this category:

- Failure to insert a closing brace (`}`) for each opening brace may cause a "TEX capacity exceeded" error when TEX processes your document. This happens because sometimes TEX tries to read everything between braces into memory. If the closing brace is absent, TEX may run out of memory.

  If the braces are supposed to enclose the argument to a macro, you may also get this error:

  `! Paragraph ended before macro was complete.`

  In order to help detect errors of this type, TEX doesn't ordinarily allow the argument of a macro to consist of more than one paragraph, so the first blank line after the place where you failed to type the closing brace may produce this error.

- Failure to close a begin/end environment pair causes LATEX to complain about a mismatch when it encounters the next `\end{environment}` command.

- If your document ends with an open environment, TEX will warn you that:

  `! (\end occurs inside a group at level n)`

  where *n* is the number of open groups, usually 1.

---

*Technically, LATEX environment names are not a control sequence names, but they behave in very much the same way in LATEX.

- Failure to close a mathematics environment will result in the error:

  ```
  ! Missing $ inserted
  ```

  when TEX reaches a macro that does not make sense in mathematics mode (like
  \section) or when a surrounding group ends.

## Math Outside of Math Mode

TEX has a lot of operators for special treatment of mathematical formulas. These operators
must occur inside *mathematics mode*, which is usually delimited by dollar signs in your
document.

If you attempt to use math operators, superscripts, subscripts, or other math-mode control
sequences outside of mathematics mode, the following error will occur:

```
! Missing $ inserted
```

This is your clue that a mathematics environment has not been closed properly or that
you failed to open one before using a math-mode operator.

For example, the underscore character is usually defined to be a math-mode operator
which starts a subscript, in other words H$\{\}_2$O produces "$H_2O$" in your document.*
If you use the underscore outside of mathematics mode, such as in regular text:

```
The file ``test_one'' contains the ...
```

TEX will respond:

```
! Missing $ inserted
<inserted text>
                $
<to be read again>
                _
The file ``test_
                one'' contains the ...
?
```

In LATEX, the easiest way around this problem is to enclose the offending text in a
"verbatim" macro, like this:

```
The file ``\verb+test_one+'' contains the ...
```

Note that the argument to the \verb macro is delimited by any two identical characters
(in this case, two "+" signs).

---

*The empty curly braces are necessary in this example because otherwise there wouldn't be anything in front
of the subscript command for TEX to subscript below. Typically, another digit or symbol would come in front
of the subscript command. In this case, I didn't want the "H" and "O" in the math environment because letters
are printed in math-italics in math mode.

In Plain TEX or another format, the problem can be circumvented in similar ways; consult the reference for the format you are using. Also consult Table 1-2 in Chapter 1, *The Big Picture*, for a list of special characters and how to type them in your documents.

## Missing Fonts

The first time that you use each font, TEX loads font metric information about the font. The font metric information, stored in a TFM file, includes information about the sizes of each character as well as kerning and ligature information. These topics are discussed fully in Chapter 5, *Fonts*.

If you request a font that does not exist, for example *crm10* (a misspelling of *cmr10*), TEX cannot find a TFM file for the font and therefore displays:

```
Font \myfont=crm10 not loadable: Metric (TFM) file not found
```

This means that TEX attempted to associate the font described by the TFM file *crm10.tfm* with the control sequence \myfont, but the TFM file didn't exist. You must have a TFM file for every font that you use.

A second kind of error—actually, a warning—occurs when you are using the New Font Selection Scheme (NFSS). The NFSS performs font substitution, if possible, when an unknown font is requested. The NFSS is described in Chapter 4, *Macro Packages*, in the "LATEX" section.

## Everything Else

There are, unfortunately, lots of other errors that can occur. Some of the errors are directly related to TEX while others are warning and error messages associated with particular macro packages. There is no way to catalog every one of them or suggest what can be done in every case.

The best advice I can offer is to isolate the problem in as small a document as possible, consult the references you have available very carefully, and, if all else fails, forward your problem to one of the electronic forums that deal with TEX (the Info-TeX mailing list and the comp.text.tex newsgroup, for example).

# The Question Mark Prompt

When TEX encounters an error, it displays an error message and a summary of the error, as described in the section called "What About Errors?" earlier in this chapter. Following the error, TEX normally stops and displays the question mark prompt.

If you type a question mark of your own at the prompt, TeX displays the actions available
to you:

```
? ?
Type <return> to proceed,
S to scroll future error messages,
R to run without stopping, Q to run quietly,
I to insert something, E to edit your file,
1 or ... or 9 to ignore the next 1 to 9 tokens
of input, H for help, X to quit.
?
```

You can type any of the following responses at the question mark prompt:

- Type ⌈Return⌉ to proceed.

  Simply typing Return will cause TeX to ignore the error and proceed. Depending on
  the nature of the error, this may cause more errors immediately or later on.

- Type ⌈S⌉ to scroll future error messages.

  Typing ⌈S⌉ tells TeX to continue and not to stop for most future errors. TeX will
  continue to print the error messages, both to the terminal and to the log file, but it
  will not display the question mark prompt again.

  TeX will still stop and ask about missing files.

- Type ⌈R⌉ to run without stopping.

  The ⌈R⌉ option is just like ⌈S⌉ except that it tells TeX to ignore missing files as well.
  TeX will proceed blindly forward as best as it can. You will still see all of the error
  messages scroll by as TeX proceeds.

- Type ⌈Q⌉ to run quietly.

  This option is just like ⌈R⌉ except that error messages are not displayed on the screen.
  The messages are saved in the log file, however, even though they are not displayed.

- Type ⌈I⌉ to insert something.

  If you notice a simple typo, you can correct it with the ⌈I⌉ command. For example,
  suppose that TeX complains of an undefined control sequence: \cte{kn:art1}.
  You recognize that this should have been \cite{kn:art1}. You can insert the
  correct control sequence by responding i\cite to the question mark prompt. TeX
  will ignore the misspelled control sequence and insert the (correct) sequence \cite
  in its place.

  Inserting words or commands at the question mark prompt *does not* change your
  input file. It simply instructs TeX to *pretend* that your file contained a different
  sequence of words and commands. You must change the input file with an editor,
  or the same error will occur the next time you format the document.

- Type ⒠ to edit your file.

  This option terminates TEX. If your system is configured appropriately, an editor will be loaded automatically, and the cursor will be placed at the offending line in your input file. This is not possible in all environments.

- Type ⒩, where *n* is a number between 1 and 9.

  This option tells TEX to ignore some of the input. After skipping over the number of *tokens* you request, TEX returns to the question mark prompt so that you can delete more tokens.

  What's a token? When TEX reads an input file, it breaks each line down into the smallest, indivisible chunks that have meaning. These are called tokens. For the most part, tokens are individual characters. The exceptions are control sequences, which are single tokens, and white spaces which are also single tokens. There *are* other exceptions (and more technical definitions of "token"), but that's the gist of it.

- Type ⒣ for help.

  Typing ⒣ displays a slightly more verbose description of the error that occurred and, usually, suggests the nature of the corrective action that you might take.

- Type ⓧ to quit.

  Typing ⓧ tells TEX to stop immediately and ends the TEX program. If there are any completed pages (pages processed before the error, in other words), they are written to the DVI file before TEX ends.

4

# *Macro Packages*

Everyone who uses TEX uses a macro package (also called a "format"). A macro package extends TEX to provide functionality that is suited to a particular task or set of tasks.

This chapter provides a summary of TEX macro packages. General-purpose packages designed to typeset a wide range of documents—articles, books, letters, and reports—are examined first. The general-purpose packages described are Plain TEX, Extended Plain TEX, LATEX 2$_\varepsilon$, LATEX, $\mathcal{AMS}$-TEX, $\mathcal{AMS}$-LATEX, Lollipop, and TEXinfo. After surveying the general-purpose packages, several special-purpose packages designed to handle specific tasks—typesetting transparencies, music, chemistry or physics diagrams, etc.—are described. The special-purpose packages surveyed are SLiTEX, FoilTEX, Seminar, MusicTEX, ChemStruct, and ChemTEX.

There are a lot of overlapping features and similar commands in the general-purpose packages. To understand why this is the case, consider how a new macro package comes into existence. An ambitious person, who is very familiar with TEX, decides that there are some things she would like to express in her documents that are difficult to express with existing formats. Perhaps, for example, no existing format produces documents that match the precise specifications required for publishing in her field, or perhaps she has in mind a whole new document structuring paradigm. A more mundane possibility is simply that she has been customizing an existing format for some time and now feels it has enough unique features to be useful to others.

In any event, a new format is born. Now, if this format is designed for a very specific task, writing multiple-choice mathematics exams, for example, it might not have very many general-purpose writing features. On the other hand, if it is designed for writing longer, more general documents (e.g., history textbooks or papers to appear in a particular journal) then there are a number of features that it is likely to include; provisions for numbered lists, cross references, tables of contents, indexes, and quotations are all examples of features common to many documents.

To support these common features, many macro packages have similar control sequences. This stems from the fact that they are all built on top of a common set of primitives and that macro package authors tend to copy some features of other packages into their own.

You may find that you'd like to use the features of several different packages in the same document. Unfortunately, there is no provision for using multiple formats to process a single document. The features required to process most documents are shared by all of the general-purpose formats, however. You are more likely to need multiple macro packages if you want to use a special format to construct a diagram or figure and incorporate it into a document. Chapter 6, *Pictures and Figures*, describes several ways to take "electronic snippets" of one document and insert them into another, which is one possible solution to this problem.

If you're beginning to feel a little lost, have no fear. Most general-purpose formats are sufficient for most documents. And there's no reason why every document you write has to be done with the same format. Many people find LATEX and Plain TEX sufficient, but if you're writing an article for a particular journal and someone has written a format specifically for that journal's documents, by all means use it. It is more likely, however, that someone has written a style file which tailors LATEX to the requirements of the journal.

In addition to describing some common macro packages in this chapter, I'll describe how to build format files for them. If the packages that you want to use have already been installed at your site, you can ignore the installation sections.

The packages that you find most convenient will depend on the tasks you perform and how well each package suits your work style. The list of packages in this chapter is not meant to be all-inclusive, nor is it my intention to suggest which packages are best. Use the ones *you* like, for whatever reasons.

I can hear some of you already, "I don't really need a macro package," you say, "I can roll my own with just TEX."

And you are absolutely correct.

I don't recommend it, however. It's akin to using your compiler without any of the built-in functions. Most TEX primitives offer little support by themselves for writing documents.

---

### A New Perspective

LaTeX $2_\varepsilon$ (and its successor, which will be LaTeX3) seek to address many of the problems mentioned above by defining a core LaTeX format with extension packages to provide custom features.

The LaTeX $2_\varepsilon$ system provides a single format file that supports LaTeX, $\mathcal{A}\mathcal{M}\mathcal{S}$-TeX, and SLiTeX. For the time being, LaTeX $2_\varepsilon$ is described separately in this chapter along with the other formats. Be aware, however, that LaTeX $2_\varepsilon$ is now the standard LaTeX[*]and you should migrate to it as soon as possible.

---

# Installation: Making Format Files

A format file, as described in Chapter 3, *Running TeX*, is a special "compiled" version of a macro package. The iniTeX program interprets all of the control sequences in a macro package and writes the corresponding memory image into a file. Loading a format file is much faster than loading individual macro packages in your document because TeX does not have to interpret any of the control sequences while it is also processing text.

In general, all format files should be stored in the same directory.[†] If you install TeX in a directory called *tex*, then formats typically go in a directory called *formats* in the *tex* directory. This is not universally the case because you need separate format directories for big and small TeXs.[‡]

Usually, an environment variable indicates where the format files are located. Environment variables are a common way of customizing your interaction with programs. They are usually set in your *AUTOEXEC.BAT* file for MS-DOS, *CONFIG.SYS* for OS/2, or the *rc*-file for a shell (i.e., *.cshrc*, *.kshrc*) on UNIX systems. Any good reference book for your operating system or shell will describe how to use environment variables.

A common name for the environment variable that indicates where TeX formats are located is TEXFORMATS. Implementations that provide big and small TeXs need another variable to indicate the directory that contains formats for big TeX.

IniTeX is not always a separate program. Some implementations of TeX combine the functionality of TeX and iniTeX into a single program and use a special switch at runtime to determine which function to perform. In this chapter, all of the examples use the

---

[*]At the time of this writing, it's actually still in test-release, but it may be available as a standard release by the time you read this.

[†]On Macintosh systems and other environments that don't have directories, format files are typically stored in their own folders (or other metaphorically appropriate place ;-).

[‡]The distinction between big and small TeX is described in the section called "What Do You Run?" in Chapter 3.

program name *initex* to identify iniTEX. If you use an implementation that doesn't provide a separate iniTEX program, you should use the TEX program with the iniTEX switch instead. For example, for emTEX, use *tex /i* instead of *initex* when you build a format.

Like TEX, iniTEX needs to be able to find input files. Usually, this is accomplished by searching the directories listed in the TEXINPUTS environment variable. Place the input files that iniTEX needs in a directory on the TEXINPUTS path before running iniTEX unless otherwise directed. The TEXINPUTS environment variable is discussed in the "User Files" section of Chapter 3.

## Hyphenation Patterns

In order for TEX to correctly hyphenate words, every format file must contain a set of hyphenation patterns. The patterns are part of an algorithmic solution to the problem of breaking a word into syllables for hyphenation.

The details of the hyphenation algorithm (given in Appendix H of *The TEXbook* [30]) are too complex to describe here, but two aspects of this solution deserve particular emphasis. First, using patterns means that a dictionary of hyphenated words is not necessary.* This saves a lot of space and time. Second, by loading different sets of patterns, TEX can achieve equal success at hyphenating any language—even English ;-). There are actually at least two sets of hyphenation patterns for English, one for British English and one for American English. Chapter 7, *International Considerations*, describes how to load multiple sets of hyphenation patterns for typesetting multilingual documents.

# General-purpose Formats

This section describes several macro packages that are designed for formatting standard documents like articles or books. In order to provide some form of comparative measure, each macro package is used to create the same document, a one-page report that looks like Figure 4-1. I constructed this example to demonstrate a few common elements in a document: several sizes of headings, a paragraph of text, inline and displayed mathematics, and a few fonts. There are lots of other things that aren't shown (tables, figures, footnotes, etc.), and these elements vary as much as any other in the different macro packages.

Observant readers will notice that the examples are shown in the Computer Modern fonts while the rest of this book uses different fonts.† There are a number of reasons why the example is shown in Computer Modern. For one thing, all of the formats discussed here

---

*A small set of exceptions is maintained because the algorithm isn't perfect.
†Really observant readers may have noticed that it's a version of Garamond ;-)

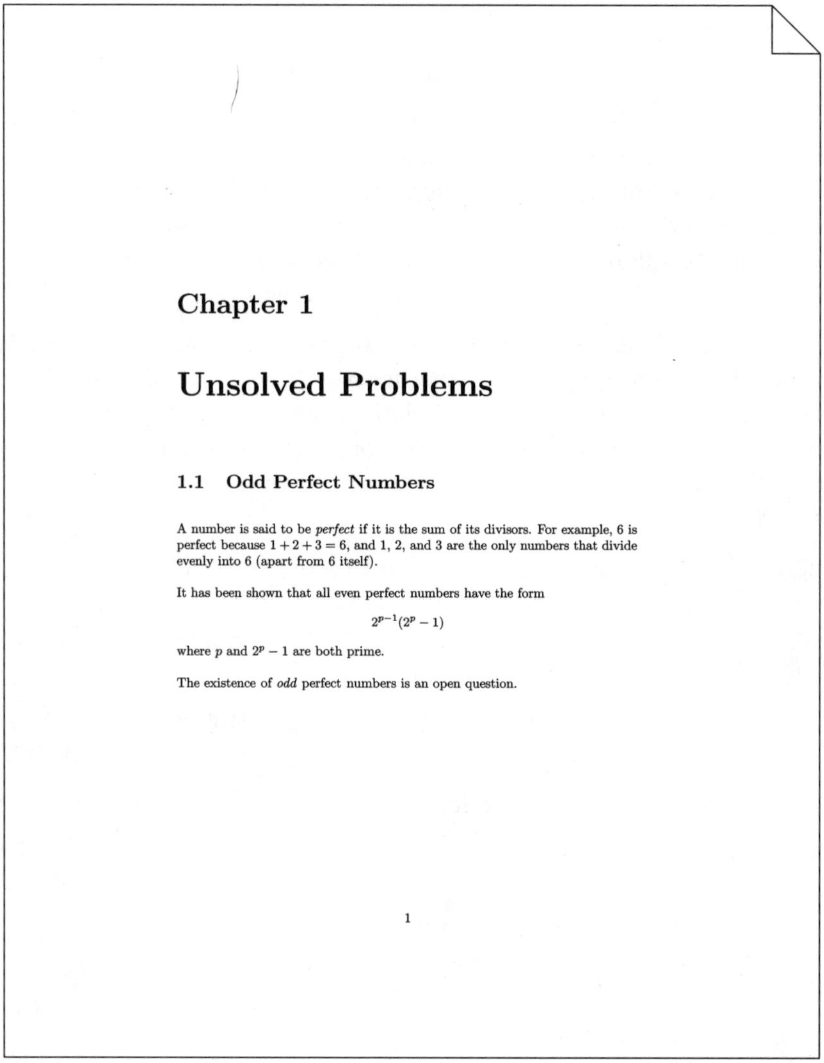

## Chapter 1

## Unsolved Problems

### 1.1 Odd Perfect Numbers

A number is said to be *perfect* if it is the sum of its divisors. For example, 6 is perfect because $1 + 2 + 3 = 6$, and 1, 2, and 3 are the only numbers that divide evenly into 6 (apart from 6 itself).

It has been shown that all even perfect numbers have the form

$$2^{p-1}(2^p - 1)$$

where $p$ and $2^p - 1$ are both prime.

The existence of *odd* perfect numbers is an open question.

1

*Figure 4-1: Sample page*

use the Computer Modern fonts by default. Using a different set of fonts would only add more complexity to each example. A more subtle problem is that I do not have appropriate mathematics fonts for Garamond. There are a number of complex issues involving the use of fonts in TEX. They are discussed in Chapter 5, *Fonts*.

## Plain TEX

Plain TEX is the format written by Donald Knuth during the development of TEX. It is described fully in *The TEXbook* [30].

Plain TEX ties together the TEX primitives in a way that makes it practical to work in TEX. If you do not have a computer programming background, you may find Plain TEX a little bit intimidating. It is definitely a "roll your own" environment. Although it demonstrably contains all of the functionality required to write everything from letters to books, there is very little "user-friendly" packaging around the internals of TEX.

Aside from user interface considerations, which are highly subjective, Plain TEX lacks some functionality when compared to other formats. There is no provision in Plain TEX for automatically numbered sections, labelled figures, tables of contents, indexes, or bibliographies. Any of these functions can be constructed in Plain TEX if you are willing to invest the time and energy required to write your own macros, but they are not built into Plain TEX.

If you enjoy writing your own macros or plan to produce novel types of documents, a firm grasp of Plain TEX will allow you to write anything in TEX. A firm grasp of Plain TEX also makes it easier to understand and modify other formats (like LATEX) that are built on top of Plain TEX.

In addition, Plain TEX is the only format that is always distributed with TEX. The other formats discussed in this chapter are freely available but do not come with TEX.

The Plain TEX input that produces the report in Figure 4-1 is shown in Example 4-1.

*Example 4-1: Plain TEX Input*

```
% Format: Plain
\font\chapfont=cmbx12 scaled 1728
\font\titlefont=cmbx12 scaled 2073
\font\secfont=cmbx12 scaled 1200

\parskip=\baselineskip
\parindent=0pt
\hsize=5in
\hoffset=.75in

\leftline{\chapfont Chapter 1}
\vskip36pt

\leftline{\titlefont Unsolved Problems}
\vskip36pt

\leftline{\secfont 1.1\ \ Odd Perfect Numbers}
\vskip12pt
```

*Example 4-1: Plain TEX Input (continued)*

```
A number is said to be {\it perfect\/} if it
is the sum of its divisors.  For example, $6$ is
perfect because $1+2+3 = 6$, and $1$, $2$, and $3$
are the only numbers that divide evenly into $6$
(apart from $6$ itself).

It has been shown that all even perfect numbers
have the form $$2^{p-1}(2^{p}-1)$$ where $p$
and $2^{p}-1$ are both prime.

The existence of {\it odd\/} perfect numbers is
an open question.
\bye
```

### Building the Plain TEX format

To build Plain TEX, you need only two files: *plain.tex* and *hyphen.tex*. These files are distributed with TEX so they should be available as soon as you have installed TEX. The *hyphen.tex* file is language-dependent. Readers who frequently work with non-English text should read Chapter 7 for more information about obtaining non-English hyphenation patterns.

The command:

```
$ initex plain \dump
```

will create the Plain TEX format. Move the resulting files, *plain.fmt* and *plain.log*, into your TEX formats directory.

## Extended Plain TEX

Extended Plain TEX extends Plain TEX in a number of useful ways without forcing you to use any particular "style" of output. The argument is this: although Plain TEX really doesn't provide all of the features that you need (tables of contents, cross references, citations, enumerated lists, convenient access to verbatim input, etc), many of these features don't have any direct impact on the appearance of your document. Unfortunately, other general-purpose macro packages like LATEX, which do provide these features, tend to force you to accept their notion of what the typeset page should look like.*

Extended Plain TEX is an attempt to solve that problem. It provides many behind-the-scenes features without providing any general page layout commands (like \chapter or \section), which means that these features can be used inside Plain TEX without much difficulty and without changing the layout of typeset pages.

---

*Of course, that's not strictly true. You can change the page layout of LATEX (and most other packages) to be almost anything, but it does require learning a lot about the macro package. If you are already familiar with Plain TEX (or some other Plain TEX-derived package), you probably have a set of macros that produce documents in the style you like. Why reinvent the wheel?

### Building the Extended Plain TEX format

To build the Extended Plain TEX format, you need the *plain.tex* and *hyphen.tex* files required to build the Plain format as well as the *eplain.tex* file distributed with Extended Plain TEX.* Make and install the Plain TEX format first, then change to the directory that contains the Extended Plain TEX distribution.

The command:

```
$ initex &plain eplain \dump
```

will create the Extended Plain TEX format. Move the resulting files, *eplain.fmt* and *eplain.log*, into your TEX formats directory.

## LATEX 2ε *Versus* LATEX

The tremendous popularity of LATEX in the TEX community has had an unfortunate side effect: because it is a very familiar and flexible format, many people have used it as the basis for extensions of one sort or another. This has resulted in a wide range of (slightly) incompatible formats and a lot of frustration.

This situation is being rectified by a new release of LATEX, currently called LATEX 2ε. The new release replaces the existing dialects of LATEX (LATEX with and without NFSS, SLITEX, AMS-LATEX, etc.) with a single core system and a set of extension packages. LATEX 2ε includes a compatibility mode which will allow it to continue to format existing documents without change (provided that they do not rely on local modifications to the LATEX format, of course). Local modifications can also be incorporated into the LATEX 2ε system as extension packages, making LATEX 2ε a complete replacement for all existing versions of LATEX and packages closely derived from LATEX.

The most significant and least compatible difference between LATEX and LATEX 2ε is the font selection scheme. There are many control sequences for selecting fonts in LATEX. Some control the typeface (`\rm`, `\tt`, `\sc`, etc.); some the size (`\small`, `\normalsize`, `\large`, etc.); and some the appearance (`\it`, `\bf`, `\em`, etc.).

Under the Old Font Selection Scheme (OFSS), the control sequences for selecting a font completely override any font selection already in place. Consider, for example, the control sequences `\it` and `\bf`, which switch to italic and boldface. Using `\bf\it` produces italic text, and `\it\bf` produces boldface text, and *neither* produces boldfaced-italic text (which is probably what you wanted).

Under the New Font Selection Scheme, typeface (called *family* in NFSS parlance), appearance (called *series* and *shape*), and size are viewed as orthogonal components in font selection. Because these parameters are independent, selecting an italic appearance with the `\it` control sequence switches to italic in the current typeface and size. Under

---

*Extended Plain TEX is available in the *macros/eplain* directory in the CTAN archives.

the NFSS, \bf\it *does* select boldface-italic in both the current typeface and size (if it is available).

LaTeX $2_\varepsilon$ supports only the NFSS, version 2 (called NFSS2). For more than a year, the NFSS (initially version 1, and more recently version 2) has been available as an extension for LaTeX 2.09. However, in light of stable test releases of LaTeX $2_\varepsilon$, the NFSS2 package for LaTeX 2.09 has been withdrawn. The discussion of NFSS in this book applies equally well to LaTeX 2.09 with NFSS2, but it is described in terms of LaTeX $2_\varepsilon$ in an effort to be more applicable in the future. The NFSS is discussed in more detail in Chapter 5.

## LaTeX $2_\varepsilon$

Leslie Lamport's LaTeX format is probably the most commonly used TeX format. It is described in *LaTeX: A Document Preparation System* [32] and many other TeX books. LaTeX $2_\varepsilon$ is the new standard LaTeX. It is described in *The LaTeX Companion* [17]. The next edition of *LaTeX: A Document Preparation System* [32] will also describe LaTeX $2_\varepsilon$.

> At the time of this writing, LaTeX $2_\varepsilon$ is available only in a test release, but by the time you read this, it is likely to be available as the new standard LaTeX. It is described first in this chapter to emphasize that you should begin using LaTeX $2_\varepsilon$ as soon as possible. Once LaTeX $2_\varepsilon$ is out of testing, it will become LaTeX, and support for older versions will not be provided (at least not by the LaTeX developers). LaTeX $2_\varepsilon$ includes a compatibility mode for old LaTeX documents so the transition should be relatively painless.

The central theme of LaTeX is "structured document preparation." An ideal LaTeX document is described entirely in terms of its structure: chapters, sections, paragraphs, numbered lists, bulleted items, tables, figures, and all the other elements of a document are identified descriptively. For example, you enclose figures in a figure *environment* identified by the control sequences \begin{figure} and \end{figure}.

When you are ready to print your document, select an appropriate document class, and LaTeX formats your document according to the rules of the selected style. In the case of the ideal document, it might first be printed in a magazine or newsletter using the article class. Later, when it is incorporated into a book, selecting the book class is *all* that is required to produce appropriate output; the document itself is unchanged.

LaTeX is written on top of Plain TeX. This means that almost any control sequence or macro that you learn about in Plain TeX can also be used in LaTeX. Of course, LaTeX insulates you from many Plain TeX commands by wrapping a much more user-friendly interface around them.

The LATEX$2_\varepsilon$ input that produces the sample page in Figure 4-1 is shown in Example 4-2. The only difference between this document and an old LATEX document is the use of the \documentclass declaration instead of the \documentstyle declaration.* For more complex documents, other minor changes may also be necessary.

*Example 4-2: LATEX$2_\varepsilon$ Input*

```
% Format: LaTeX2e
\documentclass{report}

\setlength{\parskip}{\baselineskip}
\setlength{\parindent}{0pt}

\begin{document}

\chapter{Unsolved Problems}

\section{Odd Perfect Numbers}

A number is said to be \emph{perfect} if it
is the sum of its divisors.  For example, $6$ is
perfect because \(1+2+3 = 6\), and $1$, $2$, and $3$
are the only numbers that divide evenly into $6$
(apart from 6 itself).

It has been shown that all even perfect numbers
have the form \[2^{p-1}(2^{p}-1)\] where $p$
and \(2^{p}-1\) are both prime.

The existence of \emph{odd} perfect numbers is
an open question.
\end{document}
```

### Building the LATEX$2_\varepsilon$ format

The LATEX$2_\varepsilon$ distribution is available from the directory *macros/latex2e/core* in the CTAN archives.

The following steps will build the LATEX$2_\varepsilon$ format. For more complete installation instructions, read the file *install.l2e* in the LATEX$2_\varepsilon$ distribution.

1. Place the LATEX$2_\varepsilon$ distribution in a temporary directory and make that directory the current directory. After the installation is complete, you will need to move only selected files into the standard places.

2. Restrict to only the current directory the directories that TEX searches for input files

   This can usually be accomplished by setting the environment variable TEXINPUTS[†] to a single period or the absolute path name of the current directory.

---

*LATEX$2_\varepsilon$ will process documents that use \documentstyle in LATEX 2.09 compatibility mode.
[†]Under emTEX, this variable is called TEXINPUT. On the Macintosh, file searching is frequently controlled by a configuration file or dialog box.

3. Copy the *hyphen.tex* file from the Plain TEX distribution into the current directory.

4. Issue the command:

   ```
   $ initex unpack2e.ins
   ```

   This will unpack all of the distribution files.

5. Build the format file by issuing the command:

   ```
   $ initex latex2e.ltx
   ```

   Move the resulting files *latex2e.fmt* and *latex2e.log* into the TEX formats directory.

6. In addition to the files needed to build the format, unpacking the LATEX 2$_\varepsilon$ distribution creates many files that are needed for formatting documents. These files must be placed in a location where TEX will find them. However, in order to maintain a functioning LATEX 2.09 system, you must not place the new files in the same input directory as the existing files.*

   Create a new directory (or folder) for the new files. On the UNIX system that I use, where existing input files are stored in a directory called */usr/local/lib/tex/inputs*, I created */usr/local/lib/tex/latex2e* to store the new files. You will have to add the new directory to the *front* of the list of directories that TEX searches for input files whenever you format a document with LATEX 2$_\varepsilon$.

   Move the files that the installation script produces into the new directory. Move the files *docstrip.tex*, *latexbug.tex*, *sfontdef.ltx*, *slides.ltx*, *testpage.tex*, and all of the files that end in *.cfg*, *.cls*, *.clo*, *.def*, *.fd*, and *.sty*. You should also move the files *gglo.ist* and *gind.ist* someplace where *MakeIndex* can find them. (*MakeIndex* is described in Chapter 12, *Bibliographies, Indexes, and Glossaries.*)

   One of the aspects of the test releases that continues to change is the exact list of files that must be moved. Consult the *install.l2e* file in the distribution for the exact list. The list above is from the test version of January 28, 1994.

## LATEX

This section briefly covers LATEX version 2.09. This version of LATEX is still very widely used but it is being phased out.

The LATEX input to produce the sample page in Figure 4-1 is shown in Example 4-3.

---

*Strictly speaking, this is only true for files that have the extension *.sty* because the old version of LATEX will not attempt to use the other files.

*Example 4-3: LATEX Input File*

```
% Format: LaTeX
\documentstyle{report}

\setlength{\parskip}{\baselineskip}
\setlength{\parindent}{0pt}

\begin{document}

\chapter{Unsolved Problems}

\section{Odd Perfect Numbers}

A number is said to be {\em perfect\/} if it
is the sum of its divisors.  For example, $6$ is
perfect because \(1+2+3 = 6\), and $1$, $2$, and $3$
are the only numbers that divide evenly into $6$
(apart from 6 itself).

It has been shown that all even perfect numbers
have the form \[2^{p-1}(2^{p}-1)\] where $p$
and \(2^{p}-1\) are both prime.

The existence of {\em odd\/} perfect numbers is
an open question.
\end{document}
```

Support for the NFSS in LATEX 2.09 has been withdrawn. If you need to build a format with support for NFSS, consult the "LATEX $2_\varepsilon$" section of this chapter.

### Building the LATEX format with the OFSS

The LATEX distribution* includes three subdirectories, *sty*, *doc*, and *general*. All of the LATEX files required to build the format file are in the *general* subdirectory. You will also need the *hyphen.tex* file required to build the Plain format.

In the *general* subdirectory, the command:

```
$ initex lplain
```

will create the LATEX format. Move the resulting files, *lplain.fmt* and *lplain.log*, to the TEX formats directory. In order to complete the installation, copy the files from the *sty* directory in the LATEX distribution into a directory where TEX searches for input files.

# $\mathcal{A}_\mathcal{M}\mathcal{S}$-TEX

When the American Mathematical Society selected TEX as a document preparation system, they decided to extend it in a number of ways to make the creation of papers and journals easier. They had two goals: to make it easier for authors to write mathematical papers in

---

*LATEX is available in the *macros/latex/distribs/latex* directory in the CTAN archives.

TEX and to make the resulting papers conform to a particular set of style specifications. $\mathcal{A}_{\mathcal{M}}\mathcal{S}$-TEX is described completely in *The Joy of TEX* [52].

$\mathcal{A}_{\mathcal{M}}\mathcal{S}$-TEX provides many commands that resemble LATEX environments. These have the form \\*environment* ... \end*environment*. In addition, $\mathcal{A}_{\mathcal{M}}\mathcal{S}$-TEX provides the notion of a document style to control style-related formatting issues.

Another important contribution made by the American Mathematical Society when creating $\mathcal{A}_{\mathcal{M}}\mathcal{S}$-TEX was the construction of a large number of new fonts. The American Mathematical Society provides fonts with many more mathematical symbols than the fonts that come with TEX. These fonts are available as a separate package and can be used with any TEX macro package, not just $\mathcal{A}_{\mathcal{M}}\mathcal{S}$-TEX.

The $\mathcal{A}_{\mathcal{M}}\mathcal{S}$-TEX input required to produce the document in Figure 4-2 is shown in Example 4-4. The result of formatting this document does not appear exactly like Figure 4-1 because $\mathcal{A}_{\mathcal{M}}\mathcal{S}$-TEX uses the style conventions of the American Mathematical Society.

*Example 4-4: $\mathcal{A}_{\mathcal{M}}\mathcal{S}$-TEX Input File*

```
% Format: AMSTeX
\documentstyle{amsppt}

\parindent=0pt
\parskip=\baselineskip
\hoffset=.75in

\topmatter
\title \chapter{1} Unsolved Problems\endtitle
\endtopmatter

\document
\head{1.1} Odd Perfect Numbers\endhead

A number is said to be {\it perfect\/} if it
is the sum of its divisors.  For example, $6$ is
perfect because $1+2+3 = 6$, and $1$, $2$, and $3$
are the only numbers that divide evenly into $6$
(apart from $6$ itself).

It has been shown that all even perfect numbers
have the form $$2^{p-1}(2^{p}-1)$$ where $p$
and $2^{p}-1$ are both prime.

The existence of {\it odd\/} perfect numbers is
an open question.
\enddocument
```

### Building the $\mathcal{A}_{\mathcal{M}}\mathcal{S}$-TEX format

In order to build the $\mathcal{A}_{\mathcal{M}}\mathcal{S}$-TEX format, you need the *plain.tex* and *hyphen.tex* files from Plain TEX and the *amstex.ini* and *amstex.tex* files from the $\mathcal{A}_{\mathcal{M}}\mathcal{S}$-TEX distribution.

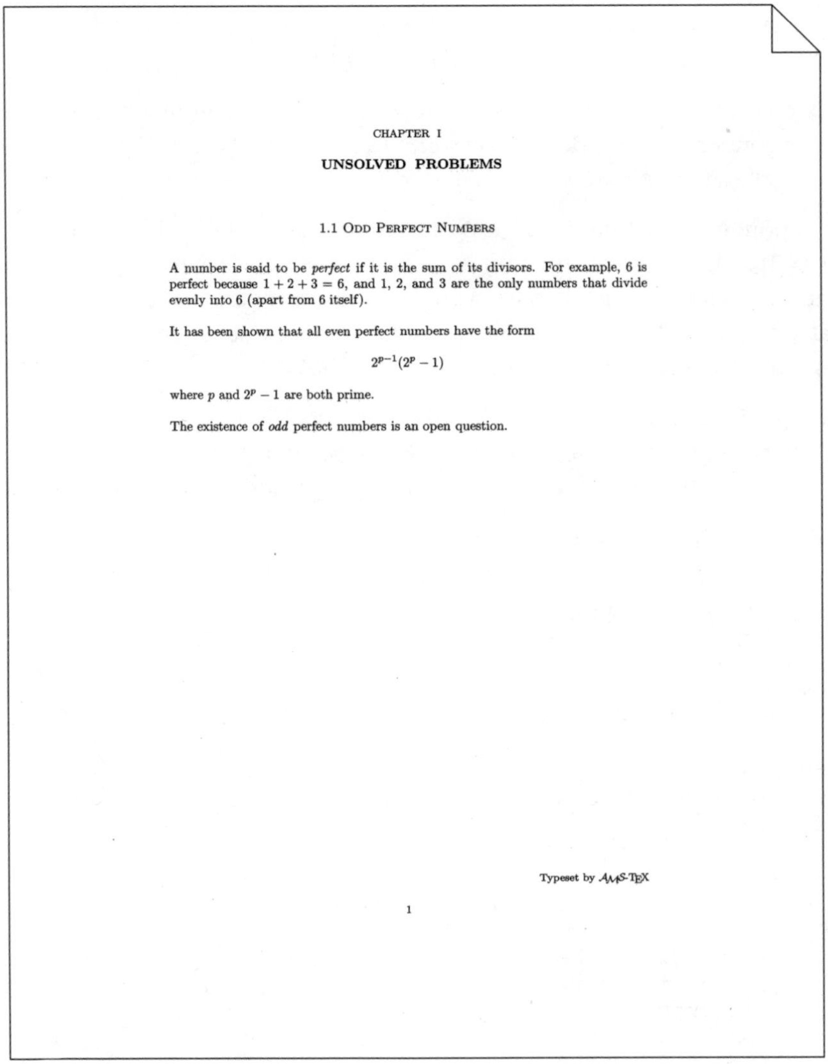

CHAPTER I

**UNSOLVED PROBLEMS**

1.1 ODD PERFECT NUMBERS

A number is said to be *perfect* if it is the sum of its divisors. For example, 6 is perfect because $1 + 2 + 3 = 6$, and 1, 2, and 3 are the only numbers that divide evenly into 6 (apart from 6 itself).

It has been shown that all even perfect numbers have the form

$$2^{p-1}(2^p - 1)$$

where $p$ and $2^p - 1$ are both prime.

The existence of *odd* perfect numbers is an open question.

Typeset by $\mathcal{A}_{\mathcal{M}}\mathcal{S}$-TEX

1

*Figure 4-2: AMS sample page*

The command:

```
$ initex amstex.ini
```

will create the $\mathcal{A}_{\mathcal{M}}\mathcal{S}$-TEX format. Move the resulting files, *amstex.fmt* and *amstex.log*, into your TEX formats directory.

# $\mathcal{A}_{\mathcal{M}}$S-LaTeX

$\mathcal{A}_{\mathcal{M}}$S-LaTeX, like $\mathcal{A}_{\mathcal{M}}$S-TeX, provides many features to make typesetting mathematics convenient while meeting the standards of the American Mathematical Society for publication. However, $\mathcal{A}_{\mathcal{M}}$S-TeX lacks many of the features that are present in LaTeX, like automatically numbered sections and tools for creating tables of contents and indexes.

When LaTeX gained popularity, many authors requested permission to submit articles to the American Mathematical Society in LaTeX. In 1987, the American Mathematical Society began a project to combine the features of $\mathcal{A}_{\mathcal{M}}$S-TeX with the features of LaTeX. The result is $\mathcal{A}_{\mathcal{M}}$S-LaTeX.

$\mathcal{A}_{\mathcal{M}}$S-LaTeX provides all of the functionality of LaTeX because it is an extension of LaTeX. It also provides the functionality of $\mathcal{A}_{\mathcal{M}}$S-TeX in LaTeX syntax and access to additional mathematical constructs and math symbols not present in LaTeX. .

The input required to produce Figure 4-1 is not shown because they do not differ significantly from the LaTeX sample. Because the sample document doesn't use any of $\mathcal{A}_{\mathcal{M}}$S-LaTeX's additional features, it is exactly the same as the LaTeX document.

### Building the $\mathcal{A}_{\mathcal{M}}$S-LaTeX format

The $\mathcal{A}_{\mathcal{M}}$S-LaTeX macros are embodied entirely in style files for LaTeX. It is not necessary to build a special format file. However, the $\mathcal{A}_{\mathcal{M}}$S-LaTeX macros require the New Font Selection Scheme (NFSS). Consult the section on LaTeX, above, for instructions on building the LaTeX format with NFSS.

# Lollipop

It can be argued that LaTeX has the following deficiency: although there are many different style options available, it is not easy for a novice user to change a style option. Changing the internals of most LaTeX style options requires a deep understanding of TeX.

The Lollipop format is very different from the other formats. The central thrust of Lollipop is that it should be easy to change and customize document styles. All Lollipop documents are built from five different generic constructs: headings, lists, text blocks, page grids, and external items.

The Lollipop input required to produce a document like the sample page in Figure 4-1 is shown in Example 4-5.

*Example 4-5: Lollipop Input File*

```
% Format: Lollipop
\DefineHeading:Chapter
   breakbefore:yes whiteafter:12pt
   line:start PointSize:20 Style:bold
      literal:Chapter Spaces:1  ChapterCounter
```

*Example 4-5: Lollipop Input File (continued)*

```
      line:stop
   vwhite:36pt
   line:start PointSize:24 Style:bold title
      line:stop
   vwhite:24pt
   Stop
\DefineHeading:Section
   whitebefore:{20pt plus 2pt} whiteafter:14pt
   line:start PointSize:14 Style:bold
      ChapterCounter . SectionCounter
      Spaces:1 title line:stop
   label:start ChapterCounter . SectionCounter
      label:stop
   Stop
\GoverningCounter:Section=Chapter
\AlwaysIndent:no
\Distance:parskip=12pt
\Distance:hoffset=.75in
\Distance:voffset=.5in
\Start
\Chapter Unsolved Problems

\Section Odd Perfect Numbers

A number is said to be {\it perfect\/} if it
is the sum of its divisors.  For example, $6$ is
perfect because $1+2+3 = 6$, and $1$, $2$, and $3$
are the only numbers that divide evenly into $6$
(apart from $6$ itself).

It has been shown that all even perfect numbers
have the form $$2^{p-1}(2^{p}-1)$$ where $p$
and $2^{p}-1$ are both prime.

The existence of {\it odd\/} perfect numbers is
an open question.
\Stop
```

### Building the Lollipop format

To make the Lollipop format, you need the Lollipop distribution and the file *hyphen.tex* from the Plain TEX distribution.

This command will create the Lollipop format:

```
$ initex lollipop \dump
```

It should be performed in the directory where you installed the Lollipop distribution so that all of the Lollipop files can be located. Move the resulting files *lollipop.fmt* and *lollipop.log* into your TEX formats directory.

# TEXinfo

The TEXinfo format is a general-purpose format, but it was designed to support a particular application: to produce both online documentation and professional quality typeset documentation from the same source file. It is discussed in more detail in Chapter 10, *Online Documentation.*

The input file shown in Example 4-6 produces the typeset output shown in Figure 4-3. The input file for this example is complicated by the fact that it contains mathematics. None of TEX's sophisticated mechanisms for handling mathematics are applicable to plain ASCII online documentation. The online documentation produced by the example in Example 4-6 is shown in Figure 4-4.

The TEXinfo format is the official documentation format of the Free Software Foundation (FSF). Although less commonly used, a LATEX variant called LATEXinfo is also available.

*Example 4-6: TEXinfo Input*

```
\input texinfo  @c -*- TeXinfo -*-
@setfilename perf-inf.inf
@ifinfo
   @paragraphindent 0
@end ifinfo
@iftex
   @defaultparindent=0pt @parindent=0pt
@end iftex

@node     Top, , (dir), (dir)
@chapter Unsolved Problems
@section Odd Perfect Numbers

A number is said to be @i{perfect} if it is
the sum of its divisors.  For example, 6 is
perfect because
@tex $1+2+3 = 6$,
@end tex
@ifinfo
1+2+3 = 6,
@end ifinfo
and 1, 2, and 3 are the only numbers that divide
evenly into 6 (apart from 6 itself).

It has been shown that all even perfect numbers
have the form
@tex $$2^{p-1}(2^{p}-1)$$ where $p$ and $2^{p}-1$
@end tex
@ifinfo
@center 2^(p-1) (2^p - 1)

where p and 2^p - 1
```

*Example 4-6: TEXinfo Input (continued)*

```
@end ifinfo
are both prime.

The existence of @i{odd} perfect numbers is an
open question.
@bye
```

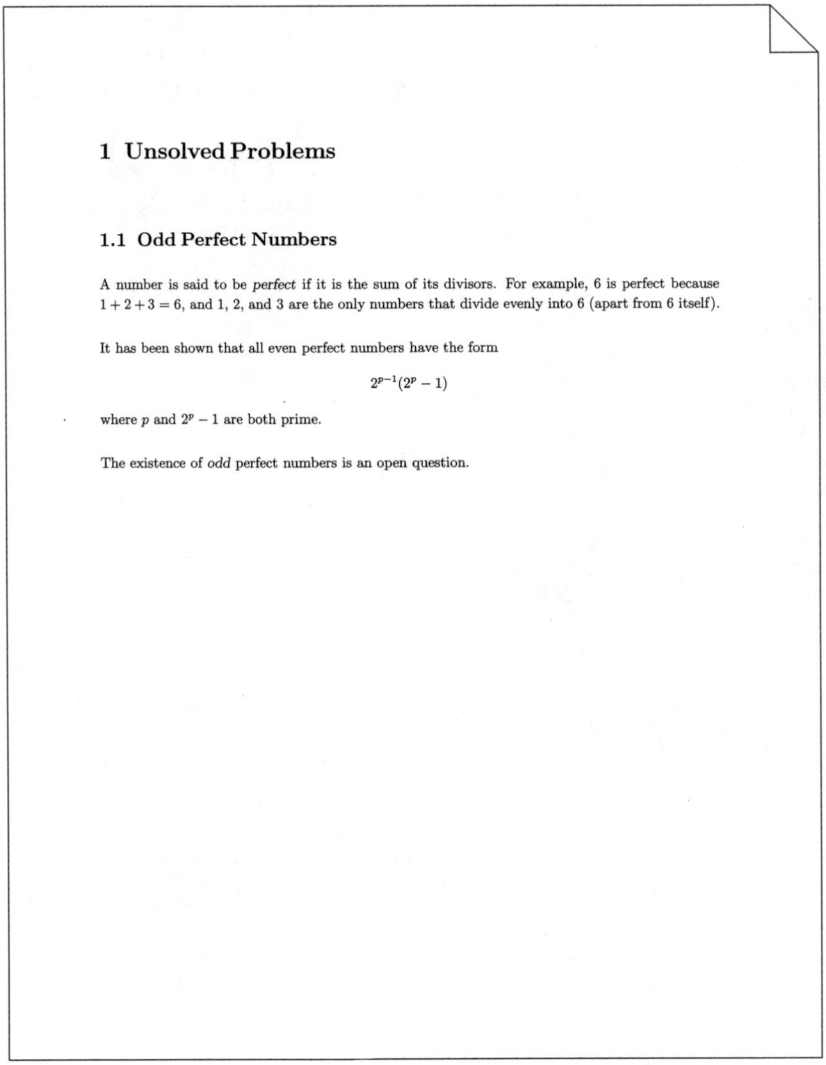

## 1  Unsolved Problems

### 1.1  Odd Perfect Numbers

A number is said to be *perfect* if it is the sum of its divisors. For example, 6 is perfect because $1 + 2 + 3 = 6$, and 1, 2, and 3 are the only numbers that divide evenly into 6 (apart from 6 itself).

It has been shown that all even perfect numbers have the form

$$2^{p-1}(2^p - 1)$$

where $p$ and $2^p - 1$ are both prime.

The existence of *odd* perfect numbers is an open question.

*Figure 4-3: TEXinfo sample page*

```
Unsolved Problems
*****************

Odd Perfect Numbers
===================

A number is said to be perfect if it is the sum
of its divisors.  For example, 6 is perfect
because 1+2+3 = 6, and 1, 2, and 3 are the only
numbers that divide evenly into 6 (apart from 6
itself).

It has been shown that all even perfect numbers
have the form

                2^(p-1) (2^p - 1)

where p and 2^p - 1 are both prime.

The existence of odd perfect numbers is an open
question.
```

*Figure 4-4: Online documentation produced by MakeInfo*

## Other Formats

There are a number of other macro packages available for TeX. Some of them are summarized below. The fact that they are not discussed more fully here (or listed below, for that matter) is not intended to reflect on the quality of the format. The formats discussed above are examples of the ways in which TeX can be extended. All of the formats below extend TeX in a way similar to one of the formats already mentioned. For any particular application, one of these macro packages might be a better choice than the formats discussed above.

**EDMAC**

Provides support for typesetting critical editions of texts in a format similar to the Oxford Classical Texts with marginal line numbers and multiple series of footnotes and endnotes keyed by line number. EDMAC is available from the CTAN archives in the directory *macros/plain/contrib/edmac*.

**INRSTeX**

Provides support for multilingual documents in French and English. INRSTeX is available from the CTAN archives in the directory *macros/inrstex*.

**LᴀᴍS-TEX**

Extends $\mathcal{A}_{\mathcal{M}}$S-TEX with LATEX-like features and improved support for commutative diagrams. LᴀᴍS-TEX is available from the CTAN archives in *macros/lamstex*.

**REVTEX**

Extends LATEX to provide support for typesetting articles for journals of the American Physical Society, the Optical Society of America, and the American Institute for Physics. REVTEX is available in the directory *macros/latex/contrib/revtex* of the CTAN archives.

**TEXsis**

Provides facilities for typesetting articles, papers, and theses. It is particularly tuned for physics papers. TEXsis also provides support for other kinds of documents, such as letters and memos. It is based upon Plain TEX. TEXsis is available from the CTAN archives in the directory *macros/texsis*.

In addition to REVTEX and TEXsis, there are several other packages in the *macros* directory on CTAN that were designed for typesetting documents about physics: PHYSE, PHYZZX, and PSIZZLE.

**TEX/Mathematica**

Supports interactive use of Mathematica on UNIX workstations running GNU emacs. Mathematica explorations can be annotated with TEX/LATEX, and Mathematica graphics can be incorporated into documents. TEX/Mathematica is available from the CTAN archives in the directory *macros/mathematica*.

**ScriptTEX**

Supports typesetting screenplays in TEX. ScriptTEX is available from the CTAN archives in the directory *macros/scripttex*.

**VerTEX**

Supports typesetting articles for economic journals. VerTEX is available from the CTAN archives in the directory *macros/plain/contrib/vertex*.

# *Special-purpose Formats*

In addition to the general-purpose packages discussed above, there are dozens, if not hundreds, of extensions to TEX that are designed for very specific tasks. Many of the extensions are LATEX style files; they provide styles for many academic journals, university theses, resumés, diagrams of various sorts, PostScript interfaces, linguistics, multinational language support, UNIX "man" pages, program listings, and countless other tasks.

To give you a feel for the range of tasks that TEX can perform, I've selected a few packages to highlight the latitude of customization that is possible. Figure 4-5 shows the chemical structure of caffeine (a molecule dear to my heart) rendered with the ChemTEX package. The source is shown in Example 4-7. Another chemistry package, ChemStruct, was used to draw Figure 4-6. Its source is shown in Example 4-8. Taking TEX in another direction, the MusicTEX package was used to typeset the first two bars of Mozart's K545 sonata in C-major in Figure 4-7. The MusicTEX input is shown in Example 4-9. Several more examples are presented in Chapter 7 where formats for typesetting non-English languages are described.

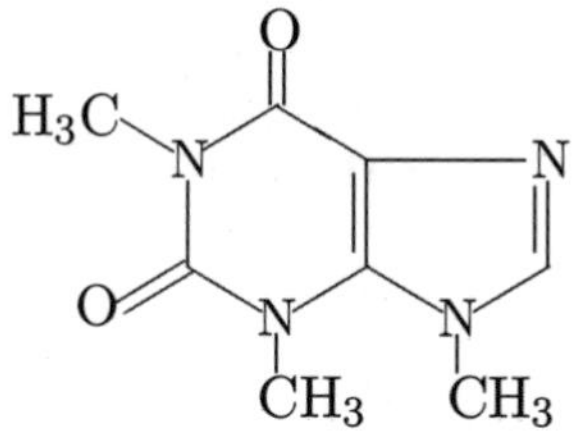

*Figure 4-5: Caffeine by ChemTEX*

*Example 4-7: The ChemTEX Source for Caffeine*

```
\initial
\len=4
\def\H{\hbox{\rm H}}
\def\C{\hbox{\rm C}}
\def\O{\hbox{\rm O}}

\[ \purine{$\H_3\C$}{$\O$}{$\C\H_3$}{Q}{$\O$}{Q}{Q}{D}{$\C\H_3$}  \]
```

*Example 4-8: The ChemStruct Source for the Lithium Cation*

```
\structure{\atom{~~Li$^+$}
\side{\nwbelow\atom{O}
\side{\nsingle\atom{H}\nnwbelow\atom{O}\side{\wsingle\atom{H}}
\nsingle\atom{H}}\swsingle\atom{H}\wnwbelow\atom{O}
\side{\wsingle\atom{H}}\nsingle\atom{H}}
\side{\nebelow\atom{O}
\side{\nsingle\atom{H}\nnebelow\atom{O}\side{\esingle\atom{H}}
\nsingle\atom{H}}\sesingle\atom{H}\enebelow\atom{O}
\side{\esingle\atom{H}}\nsingle\atom{H}}
\side{\swbelow\atom{O}
\side{\ssingle\atom{H}\sswbelow\atom{O}\side{\wsingle\atom{H}}
\ssingle\atom{H}}\nwsingle\atom{H}\wswbelow\atom{O}
\side{\wsingle\atom{H}}\ssingle\atom{H}}
\side{\sebelow\atom{O}
\side{\ssingle\atom{H}\ssebelow\atom{O}\side{\esingle\atom{H}}
\ssingle\atom{H}}\nesingle\atom{H}\esebelow\atom{O}
\side{\esingle\atom{H}}\ssingle\atom{H}}}
```

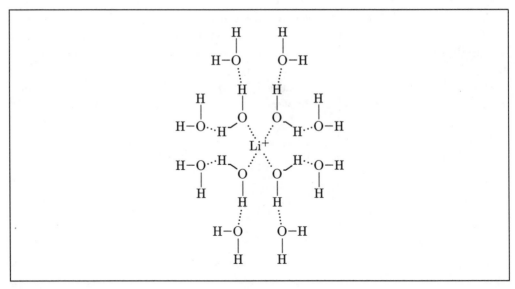

*Figure 4-6: A lithium cation rendered by ChemStruct*

*Figure 4-7: A little Mozart...*

*Example 4-9: The MusicTEX Source for Figure 4-7*

```
\begin{music}
\parindent 1cm
\def\nbinstruments{1}\relax
\def\instrumenti{Piano}%
\nbporteesi=2\relax
\generalmeter{\meterfrac{4}{4}}\relax
\debutextrait
\normal
\temps\Notes\ibu0f0\qh0{cge}\tbu0\qh0g|\hl j\enotes
\temps\Notes\ibu0f0\qh0{cge}\tbu0\qh0g|\ql l\sk\ql n\enotes
\barre
\Notes\ibu0f0\qh0{dgf}|\qlp i\enotes
```

*Example 4-9: The MusicTEX Source for Figure 4-7 (continued)*

```
\notes\tbu0\qh0g|\ibbl1j3\qb1j\tbl1\qb1k\enotes
\temps\Notes\ibu0f0\qh0{cge}\tbu0\qh0g|\hl j\enotes
\finextrait
\end{music}
```

Another popular special-purpose application of TEX is the production of transparencies, also called foils or slides. There are a few different options for this application.

## SLITEX

SLITEX is part of the standard LATEX distribution. Input to SLITEX consists of a main file and a slides file. Individual slides are composed in a `slide` environment.

SLITEX has provisions for black-and-white slides, color slides, and overlays. Unlike the other slide-making formats, which rely on `\special` printer commands* to incorporate color, SLITEX produces separate output pages for each color. For example, if you use red to highlight words on an otherwise black-and-white slide, SLITEX will produce two output pages for the slide: one with all the black text (excluding the words in red) and one with just the red words. Both of these pages will be printed in black. You must construct the colored slide by copying the pages onto colored transparencies and overlaying them. Producing slides with overlays in the same color is accomplished with a special "invisible" color. This method of producing colored transparencies has been made obsolete by modern color printers. Of course, nothing prevents you from using the `\special` extensions of your DVI driver in SLITEX to produce colored transparencies directly on a color printer.

SLITEX has always been a separate macro package, distinct from and not 100% compatible with LATEX. With the introduction of LATEX $2_\varepsilon$, SLITEX is simply an extension package to the LATEX $2_\varepsilon$ core format. Support for a separate SLITEX format is being phased out.

## FoilTEX

FoilTEX is an extension of LATEX for producing slides. The primary advantage of FoilTEX over SLITEX is that it is completely compatible with LATEX.[†] Note, however, that the defaults in many cases are not precisely the same as LATEX because of the radically different goal of FoilTEX.

FoilTEX provides support for running headers and footers, modified theorem environments for better mathematics in slides, support for AMS and PostScript fonts, and colors.

---

*The `\special` mechanism is a way of passing arbitrary information through TEX to the DVI driver that will ultimately print the document.
[†]With the caveat that it still uses the Old Font Selection Scheme.

Color slides in FoilTEX are handled by DVI driver \special commands (most commonly *dvips* \specials). However, FoilTEX includes a number of new and extended features for better handling of color. See the section "TEX in Color" later in this chapter for a detailed discussion of using color in TEX.

## Seminar

The Seminar style is another alternative for producing slides and notes. Like FoilTEX, the Seminar style is designed to work on top of LATEX. (Seminar also works with $\mathcal{A}_{\mathcal{M}}$S-LATEX.) The Seminar style is designed to produce output for a PostScript printer. It isn't strictly necessary to produce PostScript output, but if you do not, many of Seminar's features will be unavailable to you.

Seminar provides for a mixture of portrait and landscape styles and can support color using either a color-separation technique (similar to SLITEX's method) or direct use of PostScript color. In either case, the PSTricks macro package is required. (Consult the section "PSTricks" in Chapter 6, *Pictures and Figures*, for more information.)

The Seminar style has support for a number of interesting options (including two-up printing of slides), automatic resizing by changing a magnification parameter, instructions for converting your SLITEX slides, and several extensive demonstration files. Also included are explicit instructions for placing Encapsulated PostScript drawings in your slides.

# TEX in Color

With color printers and copiers becoming more common, the application of color, especially in transparencies, is more important than ever. Unfortunately, TEX knows *nothing* about color.

A little reflection about the design of TEX will make it clear why this is the case. TEX produces device-independent output. Even when color printers are as common as "regular" printers, if that ever becomes the case, it will always be true that color is an inherently device-dependent attribute. It does not make sense for TEX to understand color. However, this does not prevent TEX from using color.

At the lowest level, all that is required to use color in TEX is some way of telling the printer "start printing in *<color>* here." This is easily accomplished with a \special command. In the discussion that follows, the *dvips* \special commands are used as concrete examples, but conceptually, any color printer can be used in this way.

## Setting Up Color

Color support at the DVI driver level is provided by \special commands, but these are not typically convenient to enter directly into your document. Frequently, these commands are specified in terms of percentages of red, green, and blue (RGB color) or cyan, magenta, yellow, and black (CMYK color).

Higher-level support is provided by a collection of color control sequences. These sequences are loaded either by inputting the file *colordvi.tex* (in Plain TEX, for example) or using the *colordvi* style file (in LATEX).

*dvips* defines the colors in terms of "crayon names." If you need very precise control of the colors, you can adjust the precise mix of CMYK values in the file *colordvi.tex* after comparing the output of your printer with a standard scale (typically, the PANTONE scale). The following color names are standard in *dvips*.

| | | | |
|---|---|---|---|
| Apricot | Emerald | OliveGreen | RubineRed |
| Aquamarine | ForestGreen | Orange | Salmon |
| Bittersweet | Fuchsia | OrangeRed | SeaGreen |
| Black | Goldenrod | Orchid | Sepia |
| Blue | Gray | Peach | SkyBlue |
| BlueGreen | Green | Periwinkle | SpringGreen |
| BlueViolet | GreenYellow | PineGreen | Tan |
| BrickRed | JungleGreen | Plum | TealBlue |
| Brown | Lavender | ProcessBlue | Thistle |
| BurntOrange | LimeGreen | Purple | Turquoise |
| CadetBlue | Magenta | RawSienna | Violet |
| CarnationPink | Mahogany | Red | VioletRed |
| Cerulean | Maroon | RedOrange | White |
| CornflowerBlue | Melon | RedViolet | WildStrawberry |
| Cyan | MidnightBlue | Rhodamine | Yellow |
| Dandelion | Mulberry | RoyalBlue | YellowGreen |
| DarkOrchid | NavyBlue | RoyalPurple | YellowOrange |

## Using Color

After *dvips* has loaded *colordvi*, typesetting text in color is simply a matter of using the appropriate color control sequence. For example, to typeset something in red, use the `\Red` control sequence in your document, like this:

```
\Red{something in red}
```

Alternatively, you can change the default text color with the `\text`*color* control sequences. To make default color for all text blue, enter:

```
\textBlue
```

To change the background color, use the `\background` macro. For example, to make the current and all future pages yellow, enter:

```
\background{Yellow}
```

You can enter a precise color by specifying it in terms of its CMYK components. The `\Color` and `\textColor` macros exist for this purpose. To typeset some text in a color that is 25% cyan, 35% magenta, 40% yellow, and 10% black,* enter:

```
\Color{.25 .35 .4 .1}{some text}
```

## *Now I've Got Color, but I Need Black and White!*

If you have reason to print a colored TEX document on a black and white printer, you don't have to tear out all of the color commands. *dvips* includes a *blackdvi* file (analogous to *colordvi*—an input file or style file depending on your macro package), which translates all color commands into black and white.

Alternatively, "good" implementations of PostScript in a black and white printer should translate all colors into shades of grey. This can be an inexpensive way to preview a color document. Most screen previewers simply ignore color commands so they print in black and white even if the document is colored.

## *Color Under LATEX 2ε*

At the time of this writing, the LATEX 2ε team has not officially adopted a standard for using color. However, it is likely to follow a slightly different model than the one described above. The final design should provide color selection commands that are device-independent at the DVI driver level (in other words, the color commands will not insert device-specific commands, like snippets of PostScript, into the DVI files).

## *Color Is Subtle*

Color commands implemented as `\special` commands may introduce occasional problems. For example, if TEX introduces a page break in a paragraph that you have typeset in yellow (`\Yellow{This is a long paragraph...}`), the resulting output may print the page footer (and even the header) in yellow, although that was not intended.

Circumventing these problems may require careful use of color commands in front of text that you want to appear black. For example, in Plain TEX the difficulty described above can be avoided by specifying that the page number should be printed this way:

```
\footline{\Black{\hss\tenrm\folio\hss}}
```

---

*I made these numbers up. I take no responsibility for the artistic merits (or lack thereof) of the resulting color.

This definition guarantees that the page number will be set in black, and because it is a local color change, colored text can flow across the page around it.

You may want to make sure that other typographic elements are printed in the current global color (which may vary). *dvips* provides a local color macro called `\globalColor` for that purpose. Every time the text color is changed globally (with a `\text`*Color* command), `\globalColor` is redefined to print text in that color.

## *Further Reading*

Read the documentation for your DVI driver carefully with respect to color. Because it is device-dependent, there is a lot of room for interpretation, and it may not always be obvious why some things appear the way they do. And DVI drivers are free to implement color in any way they choose.

# II

# *Elements of a Complex Document*

Part II, *Elements of a Complex Document*, describes the major components of TEX involved in producing a non-trivial document. It discusses how to use different font technologies, how to incorporate pictures and figures into the document, how to typeset non-English languages, and how to maintain complex structures like indexes and bibliographies. This section also explains the preview and printing processes in detail.

# 5

# *Fonts*

All of the common TₑX macro packages use the Computer Modern fonts by default. In fact, the Computer Modern fonts are so frequently used in TₑX documents that some people believe they are *the* TₑX fonts and that no other options are available.

This is not the case. In fact, using different fonts in TₑX is quite easy. However, many interrelated font issues can be quite complicated, and it is possible to do things that make your documents print incorrectly (or make them unprintable).

This chapter explores all of the issues related to fonts and how these issues are resolved by a combination of font files, TₑX macros, DVI drivers, and careful planning. At a high level, it works like this:

1. TₑX macros select a font (by assigning `\font\fontid=fonttfm`). The macros may be very simple or quite complex (as is the case in LATₑX's New Font Selection Scheme).

2. TₑX loads the metric information from *fonttfm.tfm*. Many implementations of TₑX look for this file in the directories on the TEXFONTS path. TₑX cannot process your document if it cannot find the TFM file.*

3. TₑX writes a DVI file. The DVI file contains the name of each font (the name of the TFM file) and the magnification used (magnification is discussed in the section "The Issue of Size" later in this chapter).

---

*Some fonts may be preloaded in the format file. TₑX does not need TFM files for those fonts since the metric information is already available.

4.  The DVI driver attempts to locate font files for each font used at each magnification. Depending on the DVI driver, fonts can come from many places. Many drivers consult a list of built-in fonts to see if the desired font resides in the printer. Some also consult a list of font substitutions. (This can be used to substitute existing fonts for fonts that you do not have, like Computer Modern Roman in place of Times Roman if you don't have Times Roman.)

    Assuming that the font is not built-in or replaced by substitution of a built-in font, the DVI driver looks for a font file. Most modern DVI drivers look for PK fonts, although some also look for GF and PXL fonts as well.

    The exact location of these files varies. Some implementations look in the directories on the TEXFONTS path, others look in the TEXPKS or PKFONTS paths.

    A typical font directory on a UNIX system is */usr/local/lib/tex/fonts/pk*. The files in this directory typically have names of the form *tfmname.999pk*; where *tfmname* is the name of the font and *999* is the resolution.

    On file systems which have short filenames (for example, MS-DOS) a typical font directory is *\tex\fonts\999dpi* (or *\tex\fonts\dpi999*).* The files are then simply *tfmname.pk*.

    Some DVI drivers employ automatic font generation to attempt to create the font if it cannot be found.

5.  The DVI driver produces output suitable for a particular device. This may include one or more forms of downloaded fonts as well as requests for built-in fonts that are assumed to exist.

NOTE

TEX output isn't printable directly. TEX typesets a document in a device-independent fashion; it's the DVI driver that actually *prints* the document. This is important because many of the font issues are really DVI driver issues more than TEX issues, and because the distinction between TEXing a document and printing a document is another layer of complexity that can be a source of difficulty.

## *What TEX Needs To Know*

TEX needs remarkably little information about a font. Recall from Chapter 1, *The Big Picture*, that TEX typesets each page using "boxes and glue." In order to perform this function, TEX needs to know only the size of each character (its width, height, and depth). In practice, TEX fonts contain a little bit more information than simply the size of each character. Generally, they contain ligature and kerning information as well.

---

*Older DVI drivers may still use PXL files. They are frequently stored in directories with names like *pxl999*.

*Ligatures* are a typographic convention for replacing some letter combinations with single symbols. In English, this is done solely to improve the appearance of the letter combinations. Figure 5-1 shows a common ligature in English, "fi." Other common ligatures in English are "ff", "fl", and the combinations "ffi" and "ffl." Other languages have different ligatures.

*Figure 5-1: "fi" as two characters and as a ligature*

*Kerning* is the process of adding or removing small amounts of space between characters to improve the appearance of particular letter combinations. Although every character has a natural width, some combinations of characters give the illusion of too much or too little space. Figure 5-2 shows a common example in the word "We."

*Figure 5-2: "We" unkerned and kerned*

This is all the information that TEX needs, and it is all that is contained in the TFM files that TEX uses.*

## Selecting a Font in TEX

TEX's macro language includes a \font primitive for loading a font. This primitive operation associates a control sequence with the metrics in a particular TFM file. For example, the following line associates the control sequence \tinyfont with the metrics in *cmr5.tfm* (the Computer Modern Roman 5pt font):

```
\font\tinyfont=cmr5
```

---

*Actually, TFM files contain a little bit more information. The width of a space, the amount of stretch and shrink allowed between words, the amount of extra space allowed after a punctuation mark, and some specialized information used only in fonts for mathematics also appear in the TFM files. In principle, TFM files can contain even more information, although they rarely do. For a complete, detailed description of the information stored in a TFM file, consult Appendix F of *The TEXbook* [30] and *The TF To PL Processor* [26].

NOTE

Remember, only letters can appear in a TEX control sequence. You cannot say
\font\cmr5=cmr5 because \cmr5 is not a valid control sequence.

The control sequence defined with \font can subsequently be used to change the current font. After the above command, \tinyfont in your document selects the Computer
Modern Roman 5pt font as the current font.

In practice, using the primitive operations to select fonts has a number of disadvantages.
Later in this chapter, the worst of these disadvantages is described and a better alternative
is offered. For simplicity, the primitive operations are used in most of the examples in
this chapter.

## Which Character Is Which?

How does TEX know which character to use when it reads a symbol from an input file?
The answer is simple: TEX considers each font to be an array of characters. It uses the
numeric ASCII code of each character to determine what element in the array to use.*
This is a reasonable and efficient scheme as long as the ASCII values of the characters
in your input file are the same as the metric information that TEX is using.

The section called "Encoding Vectors" in this chapter describes how the ordering of
characters in a font is determined. It also discusses some of the problems that can
arise when TEX and your printer have conflicting information about the arrangement
of characters in the font. The "Virtual Fonts" section describes the TEX mechanism for
constructing fonts with different arrangements of characters.

# The Issue of Size

In the purest sense, selecting a font determines only what shape each character will have;
it does not determine the size of the font. Unfortunately in practice, the issue of shape
and size cannot be separated. The same shapes *appear* to be different at different sizes.
*Optical scaling* uses different designs to make letters at different sizes appear to have the
same shape. Conversely, linear scaling produces characters with exactly the same shape
at different sizes, although they appear slightly different.

Because the size of an object affects the way that the human eye and the brain perceive its
shape, a simple linear scaling of each character does not produce the most aesthetically
pleasing results. To overcome this problem, TEX uses two different quantities to express
the notion of size: design size and magnification.

---

*This is true even if your computer's natural character set is not ASCII. It is the responsibility of the implementor
to map the computer's natural character set into ASCII.

*Design size* addresses the issue of perception: a font looks most like the way it was designed to appear when printed at or close to its design size. Furthermore, two fonts with different design sizes (say 8pt and 12pt) that are the same typeface should *appear* identical when printed at 8pt and 12pt, respectively, even though the actual shapes may be slightly different. The design size of a font is intrinsic to the font itself and cannot be changed or influenced by TEX. It is important because it has a direct impact on the aesthetics of the typeset page.

*Magnification* addresses the notion of linear scaling. Changing magnifications changes the size of each character without altering its actual shape. Although, as noted above, changing its size may change its *apparent* shape. In general, you should print fonts as close to their design size as possible—in other words, with a magnifcation as close to 1.0 as possible. Figure 5-3 demonstrates how different characters may look when printed at very large magnifications.

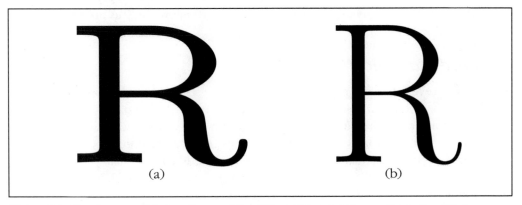

*Figure 5-3: The Computer Modern Roman letter "R" at 150pt: (a) from a 5pt design; (b) from a 17pt design*

## Expressing Design Size in TEX

The design size of a font is an integral part of the TFM file (because it is intrinsic to the font that the TFM file describes). In order to select a different design size, you must select a different TFM file. For example, the Computer Modern Roman font is usually distributed at eight design sizes: 5, 6, 7, 8, 9, 10, 12, and 17 points. Metrics for these sizes are stored in the TFM files *cmr5.tfm, cmr6.tfm, cmr7.tfm, . . .,* and *cmr17.tfm*.

Every font that you select has a specific design size, even though you may elect to use the font at another size.

## Expressing Magnification in TEX

Magnification can be expressed either implicitly or explicitly in TEX. Implicitly, magnification can be expressed by selecting a particular font at a particular size. For example, the following line defines the control sequence \big to be the Computer Modern Roman 10pt font at a size of 12pt (an implicit magnification of 120%):

```
\font\big=cmr10 at 12pt
```

Explicit magnification is selected by requesting a font scaled to a particular extent. For example, the following line defines the control sequence \bigger to be the Computer Modern Roman 10pt font at a magnification of 144% (in other words, at 14.4pt):

```
\font\bigger=cmr10 scaled 1440
```

As you can see, TEX expects the scaled magnification to be ten times the percentage of magnification. The magnification that you request must be an integer (you can't say scaled 1440.4). Multiplying the magnification by 10 allows TEX to accept fractional percentages like 104.5%.

## Standard Magnifications

TEX provides seven standard magnifications. There are several good reasons to use these magnifications whenever possible. The most important is that most TEX systems can easily print fonts at these sizes. As described later in the section "Printing Fonts," TEX's ability to select any font at any magnification does not guarantee that it can be printed at that size. By using standard sizes, you increase the likelihood that your document will be printable on your system and on other TEX systems (if portability is an issue). Using standard sizes will also give consistency to your documents. If you write many documents separately that may eventually be collected together (as a collection of short stories or a series of technical reports, for example), the internal consistency of sizes will make them appear more uniform. Finally, the standard sizes have aesthetic characteristics as well. Each size is 1.2 times the preceding size. The geometric relationship between the sizes is designed to make them appear pleasing when mixed together.

The standard sizes can be selected with the \magstep control sequence. The standard sizes (or steps) are called *magsteps* in TEX jargon. The natural size of a font is its \magstep0 size. The \magstep1 size is 20% larger. And \magstep2 is 20% larger than that (44% larger than the original design), etc. To select the Computer Modern Roman 10pt font at its next largest standard size, use:

```
\font\larger=cmr10 scaled\magstep1
```

For those occasions when you want a font that is only a little bit larger, TEX includes the control sequence \magstephalf which is halfway between \magstep0 and \magstep1.

Most TEX formats that are based upon Plain TEX define seven magsteps: `\magstep0`, `\magstephalf`, and `\magstep1` through `\magstep5`.

By using different design sizes and different standard magnifications, you gain access to a very wide range of sizes. For example, given the seven standard design sizes and seven standard magsteps, it is possible to print Computer Modern Roman at any of the following sizes (all sizes are in points):

| | | | | | | | |
|------|------|-------|-------|-------|-------|-------|-------|
| 5    | 7.67 | 9.6   | 10.95 | 13.15 | 16.59 | 19.91 | 29.38 |
| 5.48 | 8    | 9.86  | 11.52 | 13.82 | 17    | 20.4  | 29.86 |
| 6    | 8.4  | 10    | 12    | 14.4  | 17.28 | 20.74 | 35.25 |
| 6.57 | 8.64 | 10.08 | 12.1  | 14.52 | 17.42 | 22.39 | 42.3  |
| 7    | 8.76 | 10.37 | 12.44 | 14.93 | 18.62 | 24.48 |       |
| 7.2  | 9    | 10.8  | 12.96 | 15.55 | 18.66 | 24.88 |       |

## Where Do TFM Files Come From?

In order to use *any* font in TEX, you must have a TFM file for it. How you can acquire TFM files for the fonts you use depends on the kinds of fonts and where they were developed. The following list offers suggestions for the most commonly used fonts:

**PostScript fonts**

Every vendor that supplies PostScript fonts (either as font files or built-in to a printer or cartridge) should also supply Adobe Font Metric (AFM) files. AFM files provide complete metric information about the fonts.* The AFM files can be converted into TFM files with the *afm2tfm* utility distributed with *dvips*.

**LaserJet built-in fonts**

The complete metric information for LaserJet built-in fonts is supplied by Hewlett-Packard in "Tagged Font Metric" files. These are available directly from Hewlett-Packard (unfortunately, they are not distributed with the printers). The Tagged Font Metrics can be converted into TEX TFM files with *hptfm2pl*, a free utility written by, well, me, actually.

A collection of TFM files for the standard built-in fonts on the LaserJet III and IV printers is available in the CTAN archives in */tex-archive/fonts/ljmetrics*.

**LaserJet softfonts**

Bitmapped LaserJet softfonts can be converted into TEX fonts with the *SFPtoPK* utility. The resulting font includes both TEX PK and TFM files.

Scalable LaserJet softfonts should be distributed with Hewlett-Packard Tagged Font Metric files. These can be converted into TEX TFM files with the free utility *hptfm2pl*.

---

*Actually, for math fonts, TEX requires several metrics that are not usually provided. *afm2tfm* has options which allow you to specify these extra metrics when you convert the AFM file.

### TEX fonts (**METAFONT**)

The METAFONT program renders TEX MF files and produces a TFM file. Usually it produces a GF file as well, but the special mode *tfmonly* can be used to create just the TFM file.* METAFONT modes and other aspects of font creation with METAFONT are described in Chapter 11, *Introducing METAFONT*.

### TrueType fonts

Incomplete metrics are frequently distributed in the form of Windows' PFM files. Some commercial previewers for Windows can extract metric information and build a TFM file. However, at present, I do not know of any free utilities which can build TEX metrics from TrueType fonts.

# *The New Font Selection Scheme*

The New Font Selection Scheme is a method for selecting fonts in Plain TEX and LATEX. It was introduced briefly in the section "LATEX $2_\varepsilon$ Versus LATEX" of Chapter 4, *Macro Packages*. This section describes release two of the New Font Selection Scheme (known as the NFSS2) as it exists in the LATEX $2_\varepsilon$ format. Because version one is now obsolete, it is not described.

The NFSS defines a method of font selection used in place of TEX's primitive \font command. The problem with font selection using \font is that it ties a control sequence to a particular font at a particular size, which has unpleasant consequences when more than one font is used in a document. Consider the definition \font\it=cmti10. This associates the control sequence \it with the italic Computer Modern font (at 10pt). After this definition, a sentence like:

```
This requires {\it emphasis}.
```

has the desired result, if Computer Modern Roman at 10pt is the font in use when \it is encountered:

This requires *emphasis*.

If you are using some other font, perhaps in a chapter heading, you get:

## This requires *emphasis*.

This is almost certainly not what you wanted. The NFSS overcomes this difficulty by describing each font with five independent parameters: encoding, family, series, shape, and size.

---

*If your METAFONT distribution does not include a *tfmonly* mode, you can find one in the *modes.mf* file on CTAN. Consult Chapter 11, *Introducing METAFONT*, for more information.

## Font encoding

The encoding parameter identifies the encoding vector of the font. Encoding vectors play an important role in the selection of characters in a font. Encoding vectors are described more thoroughly later in this chapter. TEX Text, TEX Math Italic, and Adobe Standard are all *encoding vectors*.

## Font family

The family parameter describes the typeface of the font. Computer Modern, Times Roman, Helvetica, Galliard, and Gill Sans are all *families*.

## Font series

Font series describes the joint notions of weight and width. Weight is a measure of how darkly each character is printed, and width is a measure of how wide or narrow the font is. Standard abbreviations for weight and width are shown in Table 5-1. Normal, bold-compressed, extrabold-ultraexpanded, and light-medium are all examples of font *series*.

*Table 5-1: Standard Weight and Width Designations*

| Abbr | Weight | Abbr | Width |
|------|--------|------|-------|
| ul | Ultra-light | uc | Ultra-condensed |
| el | Extra-light | ec | Extra-condensed |
| l | Light | c | Condensed |
| sl | Semi-light | sc | Semi-condensed |
| m | Medium (normal) | m | Medium |
| sb | Semi-bold | sx | Semi-expanded |
| b | Bold | x | Expanded |
| eb | Extra-bold | ex | Extra-expanded |
| ub | Ultra-bold | ux | Ultra-expanded |

The general rule for combining weight and width to form a series abbreviation is to use the abbreviation for weight followed by the abbreviation for width, unless one is "medium," in which case it is left out. Table 5-2 shows how several weight/width combinations are used to form the series. The series designation for a light-medium font demonstrates that a single medium attribute is omitted. If both the width and weight are medium, use a single "m" for the series.

*Table 5-2: Weight and Width Are Combined to Form Series*

| Weight and Width | Series |
|------------------|--------|
| Bold extended | bx |
| Light medium | l |
| Medium extra-expanded | ex |
| Light extra-expanded | lex |
| Normal (medium, medium) | m |

## Font shape

The shape, in conjunction with series, defines the appearance of the font. Shape generally refers to the style of the face. Bold, italic, slanted, and outline are all examples of font shape.

The standard designations of font shape are shown in Table 5-3.

*Table 5-3: Standard Abbreviations of Font Shape*

| Abbr. | Shape |
|-------|-------|
| n | Normal |
| it | Italic |
| sl | Slanted |
| sc | Small caps |
| u | Upright italics |

## Font size

Font size defines both the size of the characters and the spacing between lines of text in that size. The distinction between design size and magnification, discussed at length in the first part of this chapter, is hidden within the NFSS; you need only select the size you want.[*]

The spacing between lines of text is described as the (vertical) distance between the baselines of two consecutive lines of type. It is usually about 20% larger than the size of the font. For example, a 10pt font is usually printed with 12pts between the baselines of consecutive lines. The inter-line distance that looks best depends on the font and other design elements of the document. There really isn't a good rule for the value that looks best, which is why you have to specify it.

## *Selecting Fonts with the New Font Selection Scheme*

One of the most visible differences in the NFSS2 is that you are encouraged to change the way you select fonts. The NFSS2 defines nine control sequences for user-level font selection. They are shown in Table 5-4.

*Table 5-4: User-level Font Selection Control Sequences in NFSS2*

| Control Sequence | Resulting Change |
|------------------|------------------|
| `\textrm{}` | Switch to roman family |
| `\textsf{}` | Switch to sans-serif family |
| `\texttt{}` | Switch to typewriter family |
| `\textbf{}` | Switch to bold face weight/width |

---

[*]This doesn't mean that every size you want is available. See the section "Defining Fonts with NFSS2" for information about defining font sizes in the NFSS.

*Table 5-4: User-level Font Selection Control Sequences in NFSS2 (continued)*

| Control Sequence | Resulting Change |
|---|---|
| `\textmedium{}` | Switch to medium weight/width |
| `\textit{}` | Switch to italic shape |
| `\textsl{}` | Switch to slanted shape |
| `\textsc{}` | Switch to small-caps shape |
| `\emph{}` | Switch to emphasized text |

Instead of using `\it`, for example, to change to an italic font within a group, you should use the `\textit` command with the text as an argument. For example, instead of using:

```
This is some {\it italic\/} text.
```

you should use:

```
This is some \textit{italic} text.
```

The advantage of the new scheme is that these macros are much more intelligent than the old ones. Notice that I did not specify italic correction (`\/`) in the second case. This is because the `\textit` macro is able to determine if the correction is necessary, and if so, inserts it automatically.* The macros can also be nested.

The NFSS2 allows you to use the old font selection macros, so existing documents will not be affected. If you want to set several paragraphs in a different font, you should continue to use the old selection macros because you cannot pass more than one paragraph of text to a macro.[†]

### Low-level interface to NFSS

The user-level font selection commands are implemented in terms of six low-level commands. At this level, you must specify the encoding, family, series, shape, and size of the font in order to select it. There are six control sequences for selecting a font: one each for specifying the font parameters and one for actually switching to the new font. This strategy allows the parameters to be independent; any parameters that you do not explicitly change remain the same as the current font.

These six control sequences are:

`\fontencoding{`*enc*`}`

> Selects the encoding scheme *enc*. The encoding schemes officially supported by the NFSS2 are shown in Table 5-5.

---

*If you wish to suppress italic correction, use `\nocorr` at the end (or beginning) of the text.
[†]It is possible to write macros that accept multiple paragraphs of text, but the NFSS2 font selection macros do not do so.

*Table 5-5: Encoding Schemes Supported by NFSS2*

| Encoding Scheme | Encoding Name |
|---|---|
| T1 | TEX text Cork encoding |
| OT1 | Old TEX text encoding (the CMR encoding) |
| OT2 | University of Washington Cyrillic encoding |
| OT3 | University of Washington IPA encoding |
| OML | TEX math (italic) letters |
| OMS | TEX math symbols |
| OMX | TEX math extended |
| U | Unknown encoding |

`\fontfamily{`*fam*`}`

Selects the family *fam*.

`\fontseries{`*ser*`}`

Selects the series *ser*.

`\fontshape{`*shp*`}`

Selects the shape *shp*.

`\fontsize{`*ptsize*`}{`*bskip*`}`

Selects the font size *ptsize* with a distance of *bskip* between lines. Note that *ptsize* is a simple number, whereas *bskip* is a TEX distance and you must specify units after the number. Under the NFSS2, *ptsize* specifies the *actual* size of the font,* but the NFSS2 will attempt to find a closest match if there is no exact match for the requested size. A warning message is issued if the size does not exist and a closest match has to be selected. You can control the sensitivity of the warning with the `\fontsubfuzz` parameter. It is initially set to 0.4pt, meaning that any font within 0.4pt of the requested size will be used without issuing a warning.

`\selectfont`

Switches to the font described by the current values of encoding, family, series, shape, and size.

From this description, can you figure out how the control sequence `\it` could be defined under the NFSS? The answer is on the bottom of page 128.

## *Defining Fonts with NFSS2*

The standard Computer Modern fonts and most PostScript fonts can be selected by using the appropriate style files or inputting the appropriate macros. However, if you have nonstandard fonts or fonts for some other device, you can easily add them to the NFSS.

---

*Under the NFSS1, the *ptsize* was simply a label; the actual font loaded was the nearest magstep.

The internal interface to the NFSS has been entirely redesigned. The new interface is much cleaner than the interface to the NFSS1, but similar in design.

If you are not very familiar with TEX, what follows may be a bit confusing; treat this example as a sort of "cookbook recipe" and substitute the font you wish to define for the `logo` font (the `logo` font is the typeface used for the METAFONT logo).

### Declaring a family

In order to add a new typeface, you must declare a new font family with the control sequence `\DeclareFontFamily`. If you are only adding new sizes or shapes to an existing family, do not redeclare the family.

The parameters to `\DeclareFontFamily` are the encoding, name, and loading options for the family. Loading options are any commands that should be executed every time this family is selected. For most fonts, there are no loading options.*

The following declaration creates the *logo* family with the old TEX encoding and no loading options:

```
\DeclareFontFamily{OT1}{logo}{}
```

### Declaring shapes

After a family has been created, you must specify what font shapes are available with `\DeclareFontShape`. To make the font usable, you must declare at least one font shape for each family.

The general form of a call to `\DeclareFontShape` is:

```
\DeclareFontShape{enc}%
    {fam}%
    {series}%
    {shape}%
    {sizes}%
    {loading options}
```

The family *fam* (with the appropriate encoding *enc*) must already have been created with `\DeclareFontFamily`. The *series* and *shape* parameters identify the name of the series and shape. Table 5-2 and Table 5-3 list some common series and shapes. The *sizes* parameter is a list of *font-shape declarations*, described below, and the *loading options*, if specified, override the loading options for the font family.

Each font-shape declaration indicates how the request for a font should be handled. The complete syntax for font-shape declarations is described in *Interface Description of NFSS2* [37]. Here we look at three simple cases: substituting another font for the one requested, generating the name of the TFM file for the requested font, and identifying a

---

*One possible use of loading options is to inhibit hyphenation in fixed-width fonts intended for use in verbatim material. The loading options `\hyphenchar\font=-1` have this effect.

particular TFM file for a size or range of sizes. Each of these techniques is used in the declaration of the medium, normal logo font in Example 5-1. There should be no extra spaces in the font size parameter. If you spread it over multiple lines in your input file, make sure that a comment character (%) appears at the end of each line.

*Example 5-1: Font-shape Declaration with NFSS2*

```
\DeclareFontShape{OT1}{logo}{m}{n}{%
  <-8>sub * cmr/m/n%
  <8><9><10>gen * logo%
  <10.95>logo10 at 10.95pt%
  <12->logo10}{}
```

Each font-shape declaration begins with one or more size specifications in angle brackets. This indicates either a specific size (<10> for a 10pt font) or a range of sizes (<8-9> for any size larger than or equal to 8pt and less than 9pt, <-8> for all sizes less than 8pt, or <10-> for all sizes larger than or equal to 10pt).

In Example 5-1, the first font-shape declaration indicates that font substitution should be performed for any request at a size smaller than 8pt. The string cmr/m/n indicates that medium, normal, Computer Modern Roman should be substituted in its place. In general, the substitution specifies the *family/shape/series* to be substituted.

The second declaration indicates that the name of the external font for 8pt, 9pt and 10pt fonts should be generated from the string logo and the size (at 8pt, logo8 will be used; at 9pt, logo9; and at 10pt, logo10).

The third declaration demonstrates that the font specified (logo10 at 10.95pt) can be any valid TEX font selection command. After special declarations have been processed (substitution, generation, etc.), the remaining declaration text is passed to the TEX \font primitive.

The last declaration specifies that *any* size larger than 12pt is valid. Any size larger than 12pt will use the font logo10, scaled appropriately. Automatic font generation, if it is being used, can take care of actually generating the font. Example 5-1 was constructed to demonstrate several features of the font-shape declaration syntax. A simpler, more likely declaration for the medium normal logo font is shown in Example 5-2.

*Example 5-2: Font-shape declaration with NFSS2 (simplified)*

```
\DeclareFontShape{OT1}{logo}{m}{n}{%
  <-8>sub * cmr/m/n%
  <8-9>logo8%
  <9-10>logo9%
  <10->logo10}{}
```

The 8pt design could have been scaled down for sizes less than 8pt, but you should try to avoid large deviations from the design size. Because the design for my book does not require the logo font at sizes less than 8pt, substitution was the best choice.*

## Storing Font Definitions

The NFSS will load your font definitions automatically if you store them in FD files in a directory where TeX looks for input files. Whenever an unknown encoding/family is requested, NFSS attempts to load the file *encfamily.fd*. For example, if the font declarations described in the preceding sections are stored in a file called *OT1logo.fd*, nothing special has do be done to use the logo family. The first time the logo family is selected, the definitions will be read from *OT1logo.fd*.

If you are using LaTeX 2ε (or LaTeX with the NFSS), there must already be a large number of FD files on your system. For more information about building the LaTeX 2ε format (which includes the NFSS2), consult the section "Building the LaTeX 2ε format" in Chapter 4, *Macro Packages*.

## Changing the Defaults

Sometimes you want the fonts that you define to replace the standard Computer Modern fonts. This is easily accomplished. The NFSS defines control sequences which identify the default fonts. These control sequences are listed in Table 5-6.

*Table 5-6: Default Fonts*

| Control Sequence | Font |
|---|---|
| \rmdefault | The default normal (roman) font |
| \bfdefault | The default boldface font |
| \sfdefault | The default sans-serif font |
| \itdefault | The default italic font |
| \scdefault | The default caps and small-caps font. |
| \defaultshape | The default shape (n) |
| \defaultseries | The default series (m) |

If you have defined a new font, perhaps `garamond` as I did for this book, you can make it the default normal font by changing `\rmdefault`. In LaTeX, the following command makes `garamond` the default normal font:

```
\renewcommand{\rmdefault}{garamond}
```

---

*The only reason that sizes less than 8pt need to be declared at all is that marginal notes (used for editorial comments while the book was in revision) were set in 5pt, and the logo font occasionally turned up in a marginal note.

In Plain TEX, it's written like this:

```
\def\rmdefault{garamond}
```

## NFSS Pitfalls

Defining your own fonts with the NFSS is straightforward, but it is not without its subtleties. There are several things going on behind the scenes that you must be aware of if you are going to define your own fonts.

The first consideration is font substitution. When NFSS cannot find a font, it tries to substitute a different one. First, it tries to find the font you requested in the default shape, then in the default series, and finally, in the default family. You can change the defaults used by NFSS2 with the `\DeclareFontSubstitution` command:

```
\DeclareFontSubstitution{encoding}{family}{series}{shape}
```

You must specify the defaults for each encoding you use because the encoding is never substituted.

The next consideration is the use of mathematics, which is typeset using an entirely different set of fonts. Even if you don't use any math in your document, the NFSS is prepared to function in math-mode at a moment's notice. In order to be prepared, it has to know what fonts to use. Ordinarily, mathematics is typeset using fonts at the same size as the current text font. This means that every time you change font sizes for text, NFSS changes font sizes for mathematics as well.

By default, the NFSS defines math fonts only at the following sizes: 5, 6, 7, 8, 9, 10, 11, 12, 14, 17, 20, and 25pt. If you define a new font at a different size, 24pt for example, the first time you try to use that font, you will get several warning messages indicating that `cmr/m/n/24` (Computer Modern Roman), `cmm/m/it/24` (Computer Modern Math Italic), `cmsy/m/n/24` (Computer Modern Math Symbols), and `lasy/m/n/24` (LATEX Symbols, if using LATEX), are not available. This is very confusing because it won't appear that you have selected 24pt Computer Modern *anywhere* in your document.

There are two ways to solve this problem:*

- Redefine the required fonts at the sizes requested. This involves copying the definition of each of the fonts from NFSS FD files and adding new sizes.

- Tell NFSS to use existing math sizes for the new text sizes that you define. This option is reasonable only if you won't be using any math at the new sizes (or the sizes are so close that the mathematics doesn't appear disproportional). NFSS includes a macro called `\DeclareMathSizes` for this purpose. Insert it directly after

---

*Under earlier versions of the NFSS, this problem actually resulted in an error rather than a warning. If you wish, you can simply ignore the warning; you no longer have to fix the problem.

the `\DeclareFontShape` command that declares the new font sizes. You must call `\DeclareMathSizes` once for each new size. For example, to use the 25pt math sizes with 24pt text, insert the following control sequence after you define the 24pt font:

```
\DeclareMathSizes{25}{24}{20}{17}
```

The general form of a call to `\DeclareMathSizes` is:

```
\DeclareMathSizes{text-size}%
    {math-size}%
    {script-size}%
    {script-script-size}
```

Where *math-size*, *script-size*, and *script-script-size* are the normal (123), script ($x^{123}$), and script-script ($x^{y^{123}}$) math sizes for the specified *text-size*.

LaTeX sometimes resets the current font to the `\rmdefault` font. For example, it does this when a `\ref` is going to be printed. This means that the font you define as the `\rmdefault` font should be available in every size that you use. This may require redefining the Computer Modern Roman font, as described above, if you add a new size but leave Computer Modern as the default font.

# PostScript Fonts Under NFSS

PostScript fonts and other scalable font technologies like TrueType differ from the way the "standard" TeX fonts work. They do not separate the notions of design size and magnification. Instead, PostScript fonts can be rendered at *any* size from a single design. In daily use, the PostScript fonts under NFSS are indistinguishable from non-PostScript fonts. The NFSS distribution includes style files for accessing the 35 standard PostScript fonts.

## Adjustments to Scale

Some combinations of PostScript fonts, particularly PostScript fonts with Computer Modern mathematics, look bad because there is a large discrepancy between the apparent sizes of the fonts. For example, as a consequence of design, 10pt Helvetica looks bigger than 10pt Computer Modern Math Italic. In order to correct this problem, you can specify a scaling factor when declaring PostScript fonts.* The scaling factor is specified in square brackets at the beginning of the font-shape declaration in the `\DeclareFontShape` command.

---

*Actually, you can declare a scaling factor in any font declaration, although it seems to make less sense for non-PostScript fonts.

The easiest way to find an approximation of the correct scaling factor is to look at the *x-height* of each font.* The x-height is the height of a lowercase "x" in the font. The following macro will print the x-height of a font:

```
\def\showxheight#1{%
  \font\fontfoo=#1 at 10pt%
  \message{The x-height of #1 at 10pt is \the\fontdimen5\fontfoo}}
```

The following TEX input will print the x-heights of Helvetica and Computer Modern Roman (assuming that your Helvetica font is called *phvr*):

```
\input showxheight
\showxheight{phvr}
\showxheight{cmr10}
\bye
```

On my system, the x-height of Helvetica is 5.23pt and the x-height of Computer Modern Roman is 4.30554pt. The following font declaration makes Helvetica have the same apparent size as Computer Modern Roman:

```
\DeclareFontShape{OT1}{phv}{m}{n}{%
  <-> [0.8232] phvr}{}
```

Compare scaled Helvetica to unscaled Helvetica:

**Unscaled Helvetica,** Computer Modern Roman, Scaled Helvetica.

Unscaled Helvetica looks much larger than Computer Modern, but the scaled Helvetica appears a little too small. Experimentation is the only way to find the scale that looks best.

# *When Things Go Wrong*

A number of font-related problems can arise which either prevent you from formatting and printing your document or cause the output to differ from what you anticipated. The following sections describe many common problems and their solutions.

## *When TEX Complains*

The first time an error can occur is when TEX is processing your document. Some of these errors prevent TEX from continuing while others are simply warnings.

**! Font \myfont=xxxxx not loadable: Metric (TFM) file not found.**

This error indicates that TEX tried to process a \font control sequence which assigned the font **xxxxx** to the control sequence \myfont, but TEX could not find

---

*Usually, scaling fonts to the same x-height makes them look acceptable together, but depending on the particular fonts involved, a little more or a little less scaling may be required to achieve a pleasant balance.

a TFM file for the font **xxxxx**. All the characters from the missing font will be blank in the resulting DVI file.

You cannot process your document until this error is corrected, which is a matter of fixing the offending \font command if you are using the old font selection scheme.

Under the NFSS2, this error occurs if you specify an invalid font in the command \DeclareFontShape. Examine the font that you were attempting to select and make sure that it exists.

**Warning Font/shape `x/y/z´ undefined on input line** *n*

This is a warning message from the NFSS. It indicates that you requested the font family x, series y, and shape z, but the requested font does not exist. This message is followed by another indicating which font NFSS chose to substitute in place of the one you requested. NFSS substitutes the closest possible font to the one you requested. It is usually an acceptable replacement.

For example, if you are currently using Computer Modern Bold Extended and you select Computer Modern Typewriter, the NFSS will report that there is no bold-extended-typewriter font and that normal typewriter is being substituted in its place.

**! Font x/y/z/999 not found.**

This is a fatal error from the NFSS. It indicates that you selected font family x, series y, shape z at a size of 999pts and that no such font exists. This error occurs when the size 999 is not defined in the \DeclareFontShape command for x/y/z.

**Missing character: There is no X in font foo!**

This is a warning message from TeX. Usually it occurs only in the log file. This error occurs when you attempt to access a character that does not exist in the current font. This can happen if you select the wrong font or if the selected font has a different encoding vector than anticipated. See the section "Encoding Vectors" in this chapter for more information.

## When the DVI Driver Complains

Getting TeX to successfully produce a DVI file is only half the battle. The next hurdle is getting a DVI driver to print it. Here are some of the things that can go wrong:

### Can't find PK file

When a DVI driver complains that it cannot find the appropriate PK file, there are several things that could be wrong.

- The font is built into the printer.

  If the DVI driver complains that it cannot find the PK file for a built-in font, you need to adjust the DVI driver's configuration to indicate that the font is built-in. Exactly how this is done depends on the DVI driver that you are using. For example, if you are using *dvips*, add an entry to the *psfonts.map* file. If you are using emTEX, add an entry to the font substitution file specified in the configuration file. Consult the references for your particular DVI driver for more information about using built-in fonts.

- The font does not exist on the printer you are using.

  This is the same problem as the error above except that it cannot be fixed. For example, I have TFM files for many PostScript fonts at home because it helps me format bits of documentation that I bring home from work without error. However, if I try to print one of these documents without first changing the fonts, the DVI driver complains that it cannot find several fonts. There is no way that I can correct this because the missing fonts are built-in fonts for a printer that I do not have at home. In this case, font substitution by the DVI driver may allow you to preview (and even print) the document, but it won't look very good unless the font metrics of the substituted font are very close to the metrics for the original.

- Uncommon size or font (no PK file).

  The Computer Modern family contains a number of fonts that are very rarely used. If you don't keep PK files for these fonts around all the time and attempt to use one of them (or attempt to use a common font at a very unusual size), the DVI driver will not be able to find the necessary PK file. You have to build the PK file first. Consult Chapter 11 for more information about building PK files with METAFONT. Also consult the section called "Automatic Font Generation by DVI Drivers" later in this chapter.

### Accents don't work or the wrong characters are printed

This problem is usually caused by a bad encoding vector. See the section "Encoding Vectors" in this chapter for more information.

### Printer prints the right characters but the wrong font

This is usually an indication that you are trying to use a font that does not exist on the printer. PostScript printers, for example, substitute Courier for any font that does not exist.

Another possibility is that you have configured your DVI driver incorrectly. I once told *dvips* to download Galliard when I used Garamond. It took me quite a while to find that error. Make sure that the printer contains the fonts that you think it does and make sure that you are mapping the TEX font names to the correct printer fonts.

# *Encoding Vectors*

An encoding vector describes the order and position of characters within a font. The purpose of this section is to help you understand the role that encoding vectors play in the translation of text from your input file to printed output.

Encoding vectors cause a lot of confusion. Whenever the characters that you type in your input file are printed incorrectly ("`flight`" in your input file prints out as "ight"; "`\oe{}vres`" prints out as "úvres"; or "`---`" prints out as "---" instead of "—"), you've probably encountered some sort of encoding problem.

The root of this problem is that the characters in your input file are really just numbers between 0 and 255.* The number 65 is usually a capital A, but there is nothing intrinsic to the value 65 to signify this. In order to display these byte values, they have to be translated into symbols.

These problems arise because there are at least four different translations occurring between what you type and what appears on the printed (or previewed) page:

1.  You type some symbols on the keyboard, and they are displayed by your editor. The configuration of your system determines how these characters appear. Sometimes they are from the ISO Latin-1 symbol set, sometimes US ASCII, sometimes something else, and sometimes it is user configurable. If you confine yourself to pure ASCII, you're pretty safe, but that's not convenient for languages other than English. When you are typing documents in Spanish, it's very convenient to be able to type "ñ" directly in your document.

2.  TEX reads your input file and translates it into an internal encoding (basically ASCII). (The reverse translation is performed before TEX prints any output to the terminal or the log file.) The translation tables used in this step are generally determined when the TEX program is compiled, but several modern TEXs allow you to modify these tables at runtime.

    TEX assumes that fonts use TEX's internal encoding. For example, on an IBM mainframe, which uses the EBCDIC character set, TEX translates a capital A (EBCDIC 193) into ASCII 65 and assumes that position 65 of the metric information for the current font contains the information (including ligature and kerning information) for a capital A.

3.  If you use control sequences to represent special characters (`\oe` for "œ", for example), the macro package you use is responsible for defining those control sequences so they produce the correct characters. If the macro package assumes that the "œ"

---

*In some special versions of TEX, notably those for handling languages like Japanese, this may be extended to a much larger number, but the problem is the same.

character appears at position 247 of the current font, the output will not be correct in a font with a different encoding.

4. The DVI driver reads TEX's DVI file and assumes that the encoding vector of each font used in the DVI file is the same as the encoding vector of the actual fonts in the output device. For PK fonts, this is probably true (since the DVI driver sends the font to the printer), but for fonts built into the printer, it is less likely to be true.

You may think of a font as a collection of 1 to 256 different symbols in a particular order. This is really a font plus a particular encoding vector. It is more accurate to think of a font as simply a collection of symbols (with no particular number or ordering). An encoding vector selects which symbols are used and in what order they appear. Typically, an encoding vector can contain only 256 different symbols. It is important to note that changing an encoding vector of a font does not simply permute the order of the characters in the font, it can change which symbols are actually present as well.

Encoding vectors are either implicit or explicit. Most fonts have an implicit encoding, but some (for example, Adobe Type 1 fonts) contain an explicit, configurable encoding. TEX fonts have an implicit encoding. TEX actually uses several different encoding vectors (it uses more than one because it has both text or body fonts and several kinds of math and symbol fonts). The character set tables in Appendix B, *Font Samples*, show the encoding of several different fonts.

Most macro packages assume that the TEX TEXT encoding is being used. For example, Plain TEX defines the control sequence \AE as an abbreviation for character number 29 in the current font. Even when control sequences aren't involved, problems can arise if the output font does not have the anticipated encoding. The byte-value 34 in your input file is almost always the literal double quote character (") and usually prints as a double quote (which is probably what your editor displays and probably what you expect). If the font encoding is something different, the result will not be what you expect. For example, if the current font has the TEX MATH ITALIC encoding, the result is "$\varepsilon$".

## *Virtual Fonts*

Virtual fonts (stored in VF files*) are a relatively new addition to the TEX family. When TEX was originally defined in 1970, Knuth chose a character encoding that suited his purposes, and very little effort was made to parameterize the encoding. (In fact, any TEX macro writer can use *any* encoding she wants, but no general mechanism for identifying the encoding exists.[†]) Virtual fonts combat this problem by allowing the creator to define a virtual font in terms of (multiple) characters from one or more fonts.

---

*For a complete description, consult *The VP To VF Processor* [28] and *The VF to VP Processor* [27].
[†]Version 2 of NFSS includes "encoding" as a parameter in font selection. In the long run, this will allow macro writers to hide many of these difficulties, dramatically reducing the burden currently placed on the user.

Virtual fonts are used most commonly to change the encoding vector of a font. This provides a convenient way of mapping different fonts into the required encoding so that they are easy to use in TEX. A virtual font consists of a VF file and a TFM file. TEX uses the TFM file as it would any other.

Figure 5-4 shows how a virtual font is used by the TEX system. In this case, a virtual font `ctmr` has been created combining characters from the fonts `trr0n`, `trr6m`, `trr6j`, and `trr10j`.

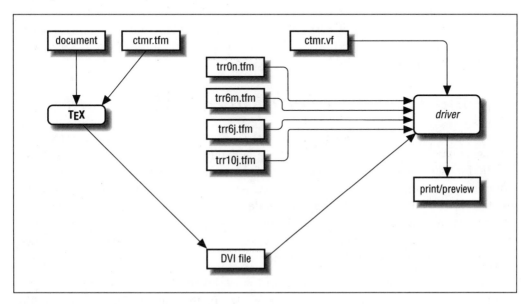

*Figure 5-4: How TEX uses a virtual font*

The document uses the font `ctmr`. TEX uses the font metric information in *ctmr.tfm* to compose the DVI file. The DVI driver, however, discovers a VF file named `ctmr`, so it uses the instructions in the virtual font to select characters from the four built-in fonts. This is a practical example. It shows how the HP LaserJet built-in fonts may be accessed with the standard TEX text encoding.

In practice, virtual fonts suffer from one limitation: A virtual font can only permute the encoding vector; it cannot access characters that do not appear in the encoding vector of the "real" font. For example, an Adobe Type 1 font might contain all of the characters that appear in the TEX text encoding, but many of them do not appear in the standard Adobe encoding vector. A virtual font alone cannot remap the characters into the TEX text encoding. The encoding vector of the font must also be changed. Several PostScript DVI drivers have this ability.

Virtual fonts are binary files and are very difficult to edit. To make it possible to construct virtual fonts by hand, TEX includes standard utilities (*VFtoVP* and *VPtoVF*) for converting the binary VF format into a human-readable VPL format. The VPL files are text files that can be edited with a text editor.

A complete description of how to create virtual fonts is beyond the scope of this book. If you are interested in experimenting with virtual fonts, I strongly recommend that you examine the *fontinst* package.* *fontinst* allows you to construct VPL files with TEX documents. This isn't as strange as it first sounds. Virtual font files have to include the metric information from TFM files for each font that they include. Because TEX can easily read this information, and the output is a plain text document anyway, TEX is a very capable, if somewhat slow, tool.

## *Automatic Font Generation by DVI Drivers*

Recent releases of many popular DVI drivers (*dvips*, *xdvi*, SeeTEX, and emTEX's DVI drivers, to name a few) include the ability to generate missing fonts automatically. Automatic font generation overcomes two problems simultaneously: it reduces disk space requirements, and it makes font generation easier. Most implementations of TEX are distributed with a complete set of Computer Modern fonts at seven or more magnifications. This can easily amount to several megabytes of disk space (even more if you are using other fonts, like the $\mathcal{AMS}$ fonts from the American Mathematical Society). In practice, you probably use only a small subset of these fonts.

One way to combat the disk-space problem is to delete all of the TEX fonts on your system and build just the ones you actually use. In the days before automatic font generation, this would have been quite unpleasant. The first time you discovered that you needed a font that you did not have, you would have to stop your DVI driver, figure out what size was missing, figure out how to get METAFONT to build the font that was missing at the appropriate resolution, run METAFONT, store the font in the right place, and return to your DVI driver. Moments later, you might discover that you had to do the whole process again for some other font.

Using a driver that provides automatic font generation makes it nearly painless to delete fonts and let them be built automatically.† The DVI driver determines the resolution required, runs METAFONT with the appropriate parameters, stores the font in the correct place, and continues processing the document uninterrupted.

The down side of automatic font generation is that you must keep the METAFONT program around and make available the source files for the Computer Modern fonts

---

*You can retrieve the *fontinst* package from the CTAN archives in the directory *fonts/utilities/fontinst*.
†It's still a bit tedious, at least on slow machines, but now you can walk away and get a cup of coffee ;-). All the fonts will be built automatically.

(and any other METAFONT fonts that you use). If you do not already have these files on your hard disk, the potential disk space savings are somewhat reduced. (METAFONT is discussed fully in Chapter 11.) Moreover, automatic font generation can only build PK files; if TFM files are also missing, you will have to build those by hand before TEX can process your document.*

Another benefit of automatic font generation is that it can be used to provide previewers, even non-PostScript previewers, with the ability to preview documents that use PostScript fonts, provided that you have the Printer Font ASCII (PFA) or Printer Font Binary (PFB) font sources and Adobe Font Metric (AFM) for your PostScript fonts.

The following lines, added to the *MakeTeXPK* script distributed with *dvips*, provide automatic font generation for PostScript fonts with *ps2pk*. This is useful even on systems where PostScript printers are used for output, because previewers like *xdvi* also use *MakeTeXPK* to build missing fonts.

```
# Look for a PostScript outline font...
if [ -r /usr/local/lib/tex/ps/outlines/$NAME.pfa ]
then
  echo Building TeX font from PostScript outline
  # Hack.  If $6 is null, $DESTDIR => $6 ...
  PStoTeXfont $1 $2 $3 $4 $5 $6 $DESTDIR
  exit 0
else
  echo Building TeX font from MetaFont outline
fi
```

In this example, PostScript fonts are stored in the */usr/local/lib/tex/ps/outlines* directory. You should change this directory to something appropriate for your system. On a UNIX system, the *PStoTeXfont* script shown in Example 5-3 is appropriate.† A *Perl* version of *MakeTeXPK* that handles both METAFONT and PostScript fonts is shown in Example D-1 in Appendix D, *Long Examples*.

*Example 5-3: The PStoTeXfont script*

```
#!/usr/local/bin/bash
#
#     This script file makes a new TeX font from a PS outline.
#
#     Parameters are:
#
#     name dpi bdpi [mag mode destdir]
#
#     `name´ is the name of the font, such as `ptmr´.  `dpi´
#     is the resolution the font is needed at.  `bdpi´ is
```

---

*Recent versions of TEX derived from the WEB2C package can build TFM files automatically as well.
†OK, so not *every* example in this book is in *Perl*.

*Example 5-3: The PStoTeXfont script (continued)*

```
#     the base resolution.
#
#     This script ignores the remaining parameters.  They are
#     left here to document the fact that the caller may provide
#     them.  They may be provided because the caller thinks
#     MetaFont is going to do the work...
#
#     Of course, this needs to be set up for your site.
#
# TEMPDIR needs to be unique for each process because of the
# possibility of simultaneous processes running this script.

TEMPDIR=/tmp/temp-tex-PS.$$
NAME=$1
DPI=$2
BDPI=$3

LOCALDIR=/usr/local/lib/mf/fonts
DESTDIR=$LOCALDIR/pk

BASENAME=$NAME.$DPI
PFADIR=/usr/local/lib/tex/ps/outlines

# Clean up on normal or abnormal exit
trap "cd /; rm -rf $TEMPDIR" 0 1 2 15

mkdir $TEMPDIR
cd $TEMPDIR

# We proceed by making a 10pt font at the resolution
# requested...
echo Making ${DPI}dpi version of $NAME.
ps2pk -X$DPI -P10 -a$PFADIR/$NAME.afm \
    $PFADIR/$NAME.pfa ${BASENAME}pk

mv ${BASENAME}pk $DESTDIR

exit 0
```

A similar script for using automatic font generation under emTEX with *4DOS* is shown in Examples D-3 and D-4 in Appendix D. Several other options are available for performing automatic font generation on a number of platforms, including a *REXX* version for OS/2 and a compiled program called *MKTeXPK*.

# *Math Fonts in TEX*

Changing math fonts is more difficult than changing text fonts. In addition to the large number of special symbols that must be available, TEX needs a lot more information to use the fonts because the characters are combined more frequently and in more complex ways. For example, the open brace character ({) in math mode is "extensible;" this means that it can be as large as required. In order for TEX to construct a brace of arbitrary size, one of the math fonts (the math extensions font) contains four different characters that TEX combines to form the brace:

$$\left\{ \phantom{x} \middle| \phantom{x} \right\}, \text{ and } \Big\{$$

Extensible recipes for characters like "{", "}", "(", and ")" are examples of additional metric information that must be available in math fonts for TEX.

In addition to the Computer Modern math fonts, there are really only three other choices at present: the $\mathcal{AMS}$ fonts (METAFONT fonts freely distributed by the American Mathematical Society which extend but do not replace the Computer Modern math fonts), the Lucida Bright+New Math fonts, and the MathTime fonts. Lucida Bright and MathTime are both sets of commercial PostScript Type 1 fonts.

# Concrete Examples

The following sections describe by example how you can use several different kinds of fonts in TEX. The tools described are generally free and generally available for multiple platforms. Where specific commercial tools are used, free alternatives are discussed.

The specific tools I mention here are not the only tools available nor are they necessarily the best, although I hope I've found the best ones. If you have found a different and better solution, don't abandon it in favor of what I use here. But please do tell me about the method that you have found. With every passing day, more free software becomes available.

## METAFONT Fonts

Chapter 11 describes how to use METAFONT to create fonts for TEX. If you have META-FONT installed, you can easily create fonts that are usable in TEX.

METAFONT reads MF files, which are plain text files that describe a font analogous to the way TEX reads TEX files that describe a document.

Appendix B, *Font Samples*, contains examples of many METAFONT fonts. Consult the "Definitive List of All Fonts Available for METAFONT" [47] for an up-to-date list with availability information.

## PostScript Type 1 Fonts

PostScript printers have many PostScript Type 1 fonts built in. If you want to use built-in fonts, you only need the metric information for them and a PostScript DVI driver. The *dvips* driver is the most popular free DVI driver. Several commercial drivers are also available.

The metric information should be available in the form of Adobe Font Metric (AFM) files from the printer vendor or directly from Adobe Systems, Inc. You need a program that will convert AFM files into TFM files. There are several free programs that will do this conversion (one is included with *dvips*), and your DVI driver may have included one. In general, if one came with your DVI driver, that is the one you should use.

If you want to use PostScript Type 1 fonts on non-PostScript devices, like most screen previewers, you need the "sources" for the fonts that you want to use. Many font vendors sell fonts in Adobe Type 1 format. In addition, there are many Type 1 fonts available on the Internet and on bulletin board systems.*

Several companies have made complete, high-quality fonts available. They are:

| | |
|---|---|
| IBM Courier | URW Antiqua |
| Bitstream Courier | URW Grotesk Bold |
| Bitstream Charter | Nimbus Roman No9 |
| Adobe Utopia | Nimbus Sans |

Check the license that accompanies these fonts to make sure that you can use them legally.

PostScript Type 1 font sources are available in Printer Font ASCII (PFA) and Printer Font Binary (PFB) formats.† The PFB format is more compact, but less portable. UNIX systems usually use PFA files, while MS-DOS and OS/2 systems use PFB files. Several existing programs can convert PFB files into PFA files and vice-versa. For the remainder of this section, I will consistently refer to PostScript Type 1 source files as PFA files, although you can use PFB files instead if they are supported on your platform.

In addition to the PFA files, you will also need metric information for the fonts. The metric information *should* be available in AFM format. If you purchased fonts from a vendor and did not receive AFM files, you should complain. Fonts from free sources, like Internet archive sites and bulletin board systems sometimes include only Printer Font Metric (PFM) files. These are Microsoft Windows printer metric files, and they do not contain enough information to make a TFM file.

It is possible to create a TFM file from the PFM file, but the metrics are not particularly good. To do this:

1.  Convert the PFM file into an incomplete AFM file with the *PFM2AFM* utility.

---

*Before you use these "free" fonts, be aware that many are of questionable legality.

†PostScript fonts for the Macintosh are stored in PFB format (essentially) in the resource fork of the printer font file. The metric information is stored in the screen font, which also contains bitmaps for on-screen display.

2. Use the *PS2PK* program to make a PK file.

3. Use *PKBBOX* to create a more complete AFM file from the incomplete AFM file and the PK file.

The AFM file manufactured in this way can be used to create a TFM file. The PK file can be used by any DVI driver that understands TEX PK fonts (almost all drivers have this ability).

Creating PK files does require more disk space, but it has the advantage that you can print TEX documents which use PostScript Type 1 fonts on non-PostScript devices. This includes fast, PK-based screen previewers like *xdvi* and emTEX's *dviscr* that do not understand PostScript.

Programs like *dvipsone* and *dviwindo* which run under the Microsoft Windows environment can use PostScript fonts directly if Adobe Type Manager (ATM) is installed on the system. However, it is still necessary to construct the TFM files for TEX.

### Using a new PostScript font in TEX (for PostScript printers)

This section presents a step-by-step description of how to use a new PostScript font in TEX with a PostScript printer or previewer. In this situation, you have a PostScript printer, and you use *dvips* to print your documents. This method also allows you to preview your documents with *Ghostscript*.

For either method, you must first obtain the PostScript sources for the font that you want to use. You *must* have a PFA or PFB file and an AFM file. As a concrete example, I'll use the "Nimbus Roman 9L Regular" font. For this font, I obtain *unmr.pfa* and *unmr.afm*. These fonts are available from the CTAN archives in the directory *fonts/urw.** In order to use the font in TEX, you must create TEX font metrics for it using *afm2tfm* (in particular, the version of *afm2tfm* that comes with *dvips*).

First, however, we must decide what encoding vector to use. Frequently, the fonts you obtain use Adobe Standard Encoding. The problem with this encoding is that it isn't very complete; it leaves out a lot of standard TEX characters (like the ligatures "fi" and "fl" as well as many accented and international letters). Instead of using Adobe Standard Encoding, I recommend using the Cork Encoding. The Cork Encoding has several advantages; it is a superset of the original TEX text encoding; it is becoming a new standard for TEX; and it is supported by the NFSS2. Of course, the Cork Encoding is not suitable for all fonts; there's no reason to try to re-encode a symbol font into the Cork Encoding—that doesn't even make any sense.

Luckily, using the Cork Encoding is no more difficult than using whatever encoding the distributed font contains. *afm2tfm* will do all the work. You only need to obtain the

---

*The Nimbus fonts actually come with TFM and VF files which makes some of the following steps redundant. But because most fonts *don't* come with TEX metrics, the example is important.

appropriate encoding file. In this case, the file is *ec.enc*, and it is distributed with both *dvips* and NFSS2. Use *afm2tfm* to generate the metrics:

```
$  afm2tfm unmr.afm -v unmr.vpl -T ec.enc unmr0.tfm
```

This command reads *unmr.afm*, the original AFM file with an arbitrary encoding, and the encoding vector *ec.enc*. It creates the virtual font *unmr.vpl* and the TFM file *unmr0.tfm*.

The relationship between these files is subtle. The AFM file contains metric information for all the possible glyphs in the font. The encoding file establishes the encoding vector— which particular characters occur in exactly what order. These two files are combined to produce character metric information for the specific encoding vector. This information is saved in the TFM file. This is a "raw" TFM file.* It does not have any ligature or kerning information and *may* have a different encoding from the virtual font (although, in this case it has the same encoding).

The next step is to produce a virtual font from the VPL file:

```
$  vptovf unmr.vpl unmr.vf unmr.tfm
```

This produces a virtual font file, *unmr.vf*, and an appropriate TFM file. This TFM file has ligature and kerning information for the characters in the font as well as the metrics for the individual glyphs.

The names of the virtual font files and the related TFM files are entirely arbitrary. You can give them any names you wish. In the long run, you will benefit if you choose a naming scheme that allows you to determine which files are which simply by examining the names. If you have a lot of fonts, take a look at *Filenames for Fonts* [10]. It is also available electronically from CTAN in the directory *info/filename*.

Now you should install the VF and TFM files in the appropriate directories and proceed to use the unmr font. TEX will do the right thing because the TFM file contains the appropriate metric information, and the DVI driver will do the right thing because it has a virtual font which specifies how the characters should be mapped into the printer.

Now that TEX is happy, we have the additional problem of making the PostScript printer happy. The easiest way to do this is to tell *dvips* to do it for us. The *psfonts.map* file used by *dvips* identifies which fonts are built into the printer and which fonts need to be downloaded.

Each line in the *psfonts.map* file describes how a particular TEX font should be interpreted. The simplest lines identify the PostScript name of fonts built into the printer. For

---

*Raw TFM files used to be identified with an "r" prefix, but recently the trend has turned towards a "0" suffix. For a more complete discussion of font names, consult *Filenames for Fonts* [10].

example, the following line indicates that *dvips* should use the PostScript font Times-Roman (which is assumed to be resident in the printer) everywhere that the DVI file uses the font `rptmr`:

```
rptmr Times-Roman
```

To automatically download a PostScript font, add `<`*`fontfile`* to the corresponding line in the *psfonts.map* file. The following entry indicates that the PostScript font CharterBT-Roman should be used where `rbchr` is used in the document. In addition, *dvips* should download the font from the file */usr/local/lib/fonts/psfonts/bchr.pfa* if it is used in the document.

```
rbchr CharterBT-Roman </usr/local/lib/fonts/psfonts/bchr.pfa
```

Additional PostScript commands can be added to the entry to perform special effects. Some of these are described in the documentation for *dvips*. They require a knowledge of PostScript that is beyond the scope of this book.

Adding the following line to *psfonts.map* will download and use the Nimbus URW font we installed above. (It is shown on two lines only because of the constraints of the page; you should enter it on one line):

```
unmr0 NimbusRomanNo9L-Regular <unmr.pfa
      "ECEncoding ReEncodeFont" <ec.enc
```

This line identifies the font `unmr0` as the NimbusRomanNo9L-Regular PostScript font, re-encoded with the ECEncoding described in the file *ec.enc*. Because this font is not resident in the printer, you must also tell *dvips* to download the font from *unmr.pfa*. If you keep encoding files or PostScript fonts (PFB or PFA files) in nonstandard locations, you will have to specify the full path of *ec.enc* and/or *unmr.pfa*.

Notice that you specify the *raw* font in the *psfonts.map* file. TEX and *dvips* will use the virtual font to determine which character(s) from which raw font(s) should *actually* be used to print your document. *afm2tfm* prints the line that should be added to the font map file when it is finished converting the font, so you don't always have to remember which is which.

The *psfonts.map* file (and the encoding and font files) are typically stored in a system-default location. On UNIX systems, this is frequently */usr/local/lib/tex/ps*. If you can't (or don't want) to change files in this directory, you can use your own font map file.

When you run *dvips*, it loads a initialization file (typically *~/.dvipsrc*). If you put the following line in that file:

```
p +/home/jdoe/myfonts.map
```

it extends the system-wide font map using the file */home/jdoe/myfonts.map*, which has the same format as the *psfonts.map* file.

If you use the `<font.pfa` syntax in your font map file to download PostScript fonts, you may discover that *dvips* is producing very large output files (or takes a long time to print, if output is going directly to a printer). The reason is that *dvips* is downloading the font at the beginning of every document that uses it. If you have a few fonts that you use all the time, it may be faster and more convenient to download the fonts manually at the beginning of the day and then remove the `<font.pfa` portion of the font mapping line (leave the encoding file, however). This will produce smaller output files because *dvips* will assume that the fonts are already downloaded. Of course, the trade-off is that your documents will not print correctly (because the appropriate fonts are not attached to the PostScript file) if you mail them to a colleague who doesn't download the same fonts you do, or if you forget to download the fonts again after someone power-cycles the printer.*

### Using a new PostScript font in TEX (for non-PostScript devices)

Using PostScript fonts for screen previewing or printing on non-PostScript printers is a very different process from printing on PostScript devices. You still need the AFM and PFA files.

This time you're going to create PK files with *ps2pk*, so virtual fonts are less useful. In fact, you have to give the AFM file the correct encoding in order to get the right PK file, so we'll avoid virtual fonts altogether. Of course, if you need several different encodings (perhaps TEX Text, Cork, and Adobe Standard) for different documents, you'll be better off with one or two raw font files and several virtual fonts, but for the moment let's imagine that that is not the case.

Example D-5 in Appendix D, *Long Examples*, is a Perl script that changes the encoding vector in an AFM file to reflect the encoding specified in an encoding file (like the ones used in the preceding section). This is an important step because *ps2pk* uses the encoding in the AFM file to determine which glyphs to render.†

To install this script, save it in a file called *enc-afm.pl* and change the top of the script (the `#!` line) to reflect where Perl is installed on your system. Users of Perl on non-UNIX systems may have to work a little harder, or simply use the syntax *perl enc-afm.pl* to run the script. UNIX users can create a symbolic link to *enc-afm.pl* called *enc-afm*, and mark it as executable.

Using this script, transform *unmr.afm* into *unmrX.afm*:

```
$ enc-afm unmr.afm ec.enc > unmrX.afm
```

---

*Some spooling software will transparently handle these problems (by downloading fonts that you forget) if the fonts are available.
†This step isn't necessary when using a PostScript printers because the PostScript font always contains all the glyphs. The font created by *ps2pk* will only contain the characters in a single encoding.

Now the *unmrX.afm* file has the Cork encoding. We can use this file to create a TFM file for TEX:

```
$ afm2tfm unmrX.afm unmr.tfm
```

This TFM file should be moved to the directory where you store TFM files for TEX.

Unlike PostScript fonts on PostScript devices, different PK files must be created for each size required. As a concrete example, let's assume we want a 14pt font. The easiest way to create a 14pt font with *ps2pk* is to use the *-P* parameter to specify the size. Unfortunately, this will cause some DVI drivers to complain because *-P* sets the design size of the PK file, and it won't match the design size in the TFM file. A better solution is to determine the resolution you need with the following formula:

$$\text{resolution} = \frac{\text{base resolution} * \text{point size}}{10}$$

The factor 10 is used because it is the nominal design size of PostScript fonts (at least, that's what *afm2tfm* uses). For example, if we are creating a 14pt font for a 300dpi laser printer, the desired resolution is $300 * 14/10 = 420$. Now we can create the font:

```
$ ps2pk -X420 -aunmrX.afm unmr.pfa unmr.420pk
```

This command creates a 420dpi PK file using the AFM file *unmrX.afm*. The font source comes from *unmr.pfa*, and the resulting PK file is called *unmr.pk*. On MS-DOS systems, name the output PK file *unmr.pk* because *unmr.420pk* is not a valid filename. Move the resulting PK file to the appropriate directory. On UNIX systems, it is probably */usr/local/lib/tex/fonts/pk*; while on MS-DOS and other systems, it is probably something like */texfonts/420dpi*.

## HP LaserJet Softfonts

Bitmapped HP LaserJet Softfonts can easily be converted into TEX PK files with the *SFPtoPK* utility. Then they can be used with almost any DVI driver.

Scalable LaserJet Softfonts can be used by TEX if two conditions are met: metric information is available, and the DVI driver that you are using can access built-in printer fonts. Metric information for Scalable LaserJet Softfonts distributed by Hewlett-Packard come in the form of Tagged Font Metric files. Tagged Font Metric files have the extension TFM, but they should not be confused with TEX TFM files. The utility *hptfm2pl* converts Tagged Font Metric files into TEX PL files (PL is a human-readable text format of TFM files). PL files are transformed into TFM files by the standard TEX utility *PLtoTF*.

To use Scalable LaserJet Softfonts, you must convert the metric information into TEX TFM files so that TEX can use the font, and then you must inform your DVI driver that the fonts are built into the printer. Before printing your document, download the Scalable LaserJet

Softfont to your printer. The *sfload* utility that is part of Sfware can download Scalable LaserJet Fonts. Many other free and shareware font downloading programs exist, too.

## TrueType Fonts

At present, TrueType fonts can be used only on systems that have built-in TrueType support (the Macintosh and MS-DOS computers running Microsoft Windows 3.1 fall into this category). You must use DVI drivers that communicate with the printer through the system's printer interface.

---

This is the answer to the question posed on page 106: "`\fontshape{it}\selectfont`"

6

# Pictures and Figures

Pictures and figures are an important component of many documents. This chapter explores how they can be incorporated into your TEX documents. There are many ways to include pictures and figures in TEX. The most important considerations are the type of image, the type of printer you will be using, what platform you are using, and how portable the document must be.

## Different Kinds of Images

Images come from many, many different sources, but they can be divided into two broad classes: bitmapped and scalable (or vector). Bitmapped images are produced whenever an image is scanned from a drawing, photograph, or other printed work. They are also produced by most simple paint programs. Scalable images are produced by some more sophisticated drawing programs, many commercial sources, and some other applications. Both classes have advantages and disadvantages.

Files that contain graphic images usually end with an extension that identifies the format of the image. The extension is a common and convenient nickname for the image format. In this chapter, I refer to graphic image formats by their extension (for example, GIF images or XBM images) without explanation. I do this partly because it is easy, but also because it is the most common way of referring to them, and you don't really need to know anything about the image formats to use them. If your DVI driver understands PCX images, you just need a PCX image; you don't have to have a detailed understanding of the format (thank goodness). If you want to know more, refer to the filename extension glossary in Appendix A, which will help you identify each of the formats discussed in this chapter.

## Bitmapped Images

Photographs and images with a lot of subtle detail are almost always stored as bitmaps. Scanners always produce bitmapped images. Some bitmap images can be converted into scalable formats. High-end graphic packages like *CorelDRAW* and *Adobe Illustrator* can do this, but most cannot. The exceptions are line drawings and other very high contrast images. Bitmaps are also "cheap" to print. Neither the computer nor the printer must do very much work to print a black-and-white bitmap image. (Color bitmap images must be dithered before they can be printed, but that's a separate consideration because it need be done only once, not every time the image is printed.) Bitmapped images are also easy to convert from one format to another.

Unfortunately, bitmap images are very device-dependent. They are stored as a two-dimensional array of dots, which gives them a fixed resolution. A $3 \times 5$-inch bitmap image that prints correctly on your 300dpi laser printer will only be a $\frac{3}{4} \times 1\frac{1}{4}$-inch picture if you make your final copy on a 1200dpi photo-typesetter.

Bitmap images also require considerable memory and disk space to store. The $3 \times 5$ image described above requires more than 150Kb of memory (if it is uncompressed).

A final consideration is that bitmap images do not scale very well. Enlarging or reducing the image requires either removing some dots (causing a loss of detail) or inserting extra dots (frequently giving slanted lines a very jagged appearance). Rescaling images by exact integer amounts (doubling or tripling its size, for example, but not making it $2\frac{1}{2}$ times as large) works reasonably well (except for jagged edges). Shaded regions, which are composed of a regular pattern of black and white dots, are frequently disrupted by irregular "blotching" if non-integral scaling is used.

## Scalable Images

Many graphic images can be represented more compactly as a collection of lines, curves, and other discrete elements. Images of this type are called *scalable* or *vector* images. Instead of storing every pixel in a rectangular array, vector images store the encoded instructions for "drawing" the image. This provides a compact representation. A circle, no matter how large, can be represented with just a few data points: the position of the center, the radius, the width and color of the line that forms the circle, and the pattern that fills the circle. It is also easy to change the size of the image; if you halve every measurement, the image is drawn at one half the size with minimal loss of detail.

One drawback of scalable images is that they require considerable computational power to render. Every printer ultimately prints the page as a large bitmap; the print engine has to translate the lines, curves, and fills of a scalable image into a bitmap before this is possible.* Previewing scalable images requires translating them into bitmaps to display them. This can be a noticeably slow process unless you have a very fast computer.

The other significant drawback of scalable images is that they are difficult to translate from one format to another. For example, to translate a PostScript image into something that can be printed on a non-PostScript printer, you have to have a program that understands all of the commands in the PostScript file. A bitmap conversion, on the other hand, doesn't require any understanding of graphics commands; it simply has to know how to rearrange the bits in the array. What it boils down to is this: it's a lot easier to write a translation program to "reverse the order of all the bits in each byte in each row" than it is to write one that can "draw the bezier curve with these three control points using a dashed, light-blue line $\frac{1}{8}$ of an inch wide."

## Device Independence Revisited

Pictures and figures are a foreign concept to TeX. Remember, TeX cares only about building pages out of boxes and glue. TeX's notion of a picture is frequently nothing more than "something special goes here (I don't know what) and it's 5 inches wide, 2 inches high, and 1 inch deep." This is device independence, of a sort, but many of the easiest ways to include pictures and figures in TeX do rely on features of a specific DVI driver or a specific kind of printer. If document portability is an issue, consider carefully before you select a particular way of including pictures and figures.

On the bright side, most DVI drivers provide some mechanism for incorporating pictures and figures. As long as it is possible to convert the images from the format originally used to a format that another DVI driver understands, document portability can be achieved. For example, it is possible to print PostScript figures on a non-PostScript device if they are first converted into another format with *Ghostscript* or some other PostScript interpreter. Unfortunately, it is usually inconvenient to convert pictures from one format to another, and some conversions may distort the images a little bit (or a lot).

## Using Only TeX

This section describes picture and figure environments that don't use any external programs. Graphics created in this way are entirely device-independent and can be printed with any DVI driver.

---

*Some devices, most notably plotters, don't work this way. They really draw lines and curves with physical pens.

## Plain TEX

Plain TEX has no built-in provision for creating pictures or figures. It is possible to do simple diagrams and graphs by writing macros that place individual points on the page. Figure 6-1 shows several data points plotted in Plain TEX. The input was derived from macros presented in Appendix D of *The TEXbook* [30]; it is shown in Example 6-1.

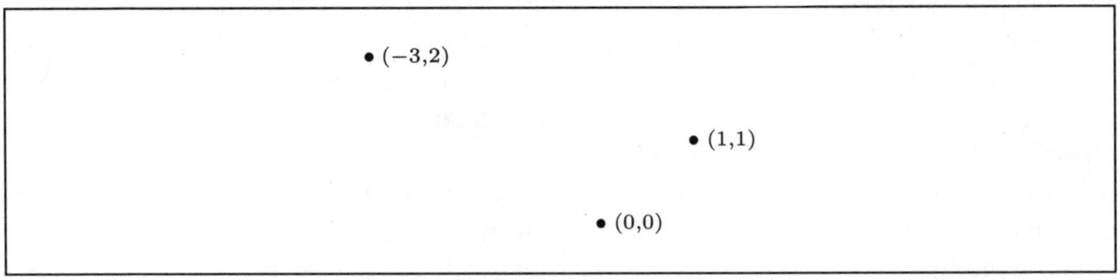

*Figure 6-1: An example diagram in Plain TEX*

*Example 6-1: The Input for the Plain TEX Diagram*

```
\newdimen\unitlength
\unitlength=1cm

\def\plot(#1,#2){%
   \rlap{\kern#1\unitlength\raise#2\unitlength%
         \hbox{$\scriptstyle\bullet\;(#1,#2)$}}}

\centerline{%
   \hbox{\plot(0,0)
         \plot(1,1)
         \plot(-3,2)}%
}
```

With special-purpose fonts, it is possible to make more complex figures in Plain TEX. However, LATEX provides a `picture` environment which greatly simplifies the process.

## LATEX

The `picture` environment in LATEX is implemented on top of the kinds of primitive operations shown in Example 6-1. Working in the `picture` environment is a lot like working on graph paper: you begin by specifing how big the graph paper is and the distance between lines on the paper (the lines aren't really there; they're just used for reference), and then inside the `picture` environment, you put *picture elements* down on the page at the intersections of the lines on the grid.

LATEX provides picture elements for text, boxes, solid and empty circles, lines, and arrows. Lines and arrows can be drawn at angles, but they are formed by taking characters from a special set of fonts so there is a limited number of angles available. The advantage of using special fonts to draw the lines is that it is relatively efficient.

Figure 6-2 is a simple figure drawn with LATEX's `picture` environment. The LATEX input for this environment is shown in Example 6-2.

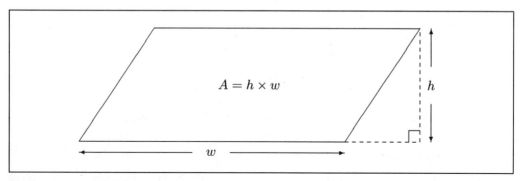

*Figure 6-2: A parallelogram in LATEX*

*Example 6-2: The LATEX Input for Figure 6-2*

```
\unitlength=1.00mm
\special{em:linewidth 0.4pt}
\linethickness{0.4pt}
\begin{picture}(93.00,40.00)
\put(0.00,10.00){\line(1,0){70.00}}
\put(70.00,10.00){\line(2,3){20.00}}
\put(90.00,40.00){\line(-1,0){70.00}}
\put(20.00,40.00){\line(-2,-3){20.00}}
\put(70.00,10.00){\line(1,0){1.00}}
\put(72.00,10.00){\line(1,0){1.00}}
\put(74.00,10.00){\line(1,0){1.00}}
\put(76.00,10.00){\line(1,0){1.00}}
\put(78.00,10.00){\line(1,0){1.00}}
\put(80.00,10.00){\line(1,0){1.00}}
\put(82.00,10.00){\line(1,0){1.00}}
\put(84.00,10.00){\line(1,0){1.00}}
\put(86.00,10.00){\line(1,0){1.00}}
\put(88.00,10.00){\line(1,0){1.00}}
\put(90.00,10.00){\line(0,1){1.00}}
\put(90.00,12.00){\line(0,1){1.00}}
\put(90.00,14.00){\line(0,1){1.00}}
\put(90.00,16.00){\line(0,1){1.00}}
\put(90.00,18.00){\line(0,1){1.00}}
\put(90.00,20.00){\line(0,1){1.00}}
\put(90.00,22.00){\line(0,1){1.00}}
\put(90.00,24.00){\line(0,1){1.00}}
\put(90.00,26.00){\line(0,1){1.00}}
\put(90.00,28.00){\line(0,1){1.00}}
\put(90.00,30.00){\line(0,1){1.00}}
\put(90.00,32.00){\line(0,1){1.00}}
\put(90.00,34.00){\line(0,1){1.00}}
\put(90.00,36.00){\line(0,1){1.00}}
```

*Example 6-2: The LATEX Input for Figure 6-2 (continued)*

```
\put(90.00,38.00){\line(0,1){1.00}}
\put(87.00,10.00){\line(0,1){3.00}}
\put(87.00,13.00){\line(1,0){3.00}}
\put(93.00,20.00){\vector(0,-1){10.00}}
\put(93.00,30.00){\vector(0,1){10.00}}
\put(93.00,25.00){\makebox(0,0)[cc]{$h$}}
\put(30.00,7.00){\vector(-1,0){30.00}}
\put(40.00,7.00){\vector(1,0){30.00}}
\put(35.00,7.00){\makebox(0,0)[cc]{$w$}}
\put(45.00,25.00){\makebox(0,0)[cc]{$A=h\times w$}}
\end{picture}
```

### The epic and eepic styles

Constructing diagrams using `picture` primitives is very tedious because each element of the picture has to be placed individually. The *epic* style extends LATEX's picture environment by adding several higher-level commands for picture construction. These commands allow you to draw solid, dotted, and dashed lines with arbitrary slopes, create matrices and grids with a single command, join several independently placed elements together, and read a list of points from an external file.

The diagrams produced by *epic.sty* are still limited by the fonts available to LATEX. The *eepic.sty* extends *epic.sty* by using \special commands to construct the more complex figure elements. The \special commands are the same as those used by *tpic* (see the "tpic" section in this chapter) and are supported by many DVI drivers.

Figure 6-3 shows a figure constructed with the *epic* macros. Figure 6-3 (a) uses *epic.sty*, and (b) uses *eepic.sty*. Notice that *eepic.sty* provides circles of arbitrary size and smooth lines at any angle. The end points of the radial lines in this figure were calculated by another program and read from a data file by *epic*. The source for these figures is shown in Example 6-3 (both diagrams were created with the same source).

*Example 6-3: The epic Input for Figure 6-3*

```
\unitlength = 1mm
\begin{picture}(50,100)(0,0)
\put(0,0){\tiny \grid(50,50)(5,5)[0,0]}
\put(25,25){\circle{50}}
\drawline(15,0)(20,5)(30,10)(50,35)
\drawline[-50](10,5)(15,10)(25,15)(45,40)
\thicklines
\dottedline{1.4}(5,10)(10,15)(15,25)(40,45)
\dashline{2}(0,15)(5,20)(10,30)(35,50)
\thinlines
\begin{drawjoin}
\jputfile{epicdata}{\picsquare}
\end{drawjoin}
\end{picture}
```

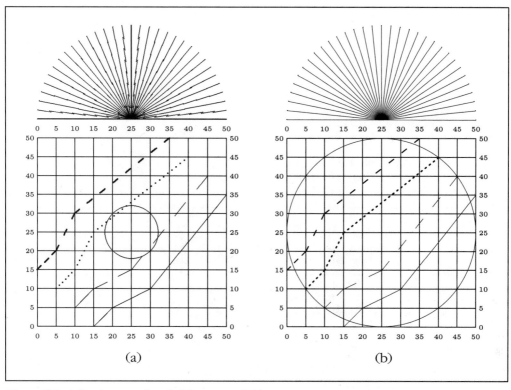

Figure 6-3: A figure created with (a) epic, and (b) eepic

### The bezier style

The *bezier* style allows you to construct curved lines in the LATEX picture environment. An example is shown in Figure 6-4. Its source is shown in Example 6-4. The grid in this example was created with *epic* for convenience.

*Example 6-4: The Input for Figure 6-4*

```
\unitlength = 1mm
\begin{picture}(100,50)(0,0)
\put(0,0){\tiny \grid(100,50)(10,10)[0,0]}
\bezier{500}(0,0)(0,0)(100,50)
\bezier{500}(0,0)(10,0)(100,50)
\bezier{500}(0,0)(20,0)(100,50)
\bezier{500}(0,0)(30,0)(100,50)
\bezier{500}(0,0)(40,0)(100,50)
\bezier{500}(0,0)(50,0)(100,50)
\bezier{500}(0,0)(60,0)(100,50)
\bezier{500}(0,0)(70,0)(100,50)
\bezier{500}(0,0)(80,0)(100,50)
\bezier{500}(0,0)(90,0)(100,50)
```

*Example 6-4: The Input for Figure 6-4 (continued)*

```
\bezier{500}(0,0)(100,0)(100,50)

\bezier{500}(0,0)(0,50)(100,50)
\bezier{500}(0,0)(0,40)(100,50)
\bezier{500}(0,0)(0,30)(100,50)
\bezier{500}(0,0)(0,20)(100,50)
\bezier{500}(0,0)(0,10)(100,50)
\bezier{500}(0,0)(0,0)(100,50)

\multiput(0,0)(10,0){11}{\circle*{1}}
\multiput(0,0)(0,10){6}{\circle*{1}}
\end{picture}
```

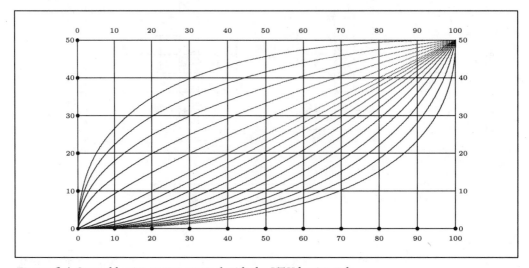

*Figure 6-4: Several bezier curves created with the LATEX bezier style*

### Other styles

In addition to these styles, there are several other style files for doing particular types of drawing. Styles exist for drawing logical circuit diagrams, bar charts, trees, and more.

### Other approaches

Because constructing LATEX drawing by hand is tedious, several programs have been written that allow you to construct diagrams visually and then produce the appropriate picture environments automatically. The *texcad* program distributed with emTEX is one such program. A similar program called *xtexcad* runs under X11 on some platforms, and there is a Fig translator for the LATEX picture environment. (For more information about Fig, see the "Fig2MF" section later in this chapter.)

# PₜCTₑX

PₜCTₑX is a macro package that you can load on top of Plain TₑX or LᴬTₑX.* It does an amazing job of plotting mathematical functions and two-dimensional graphs directly in TₑX. An example of PₜCTₑX (taken from *The PₜCTₑX Manual* [62]) is shown in Figure 6-5. The source for this figure is shown in Example 6-5.

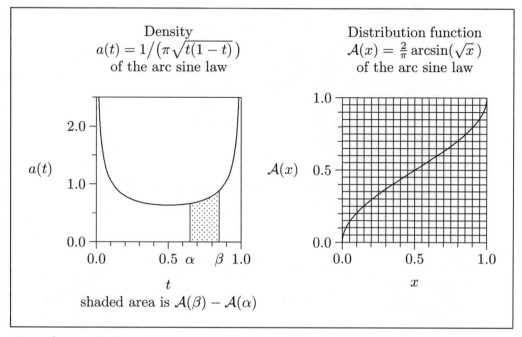

*Figure 6-5: Sample diagrams using PₜCTₑX*

*Example 6-5: PₜCTₑX Input for Figure 6-5*

```
\newdimen\unit    \unit=1.375in
\newdimen\shadeunit
\newif \ifFirstPass
\FirstPasstrue
%\FirstPassfalse  % uncomment this after you have the size you want
%
\def\DF{{\cal A}}%
%
%The following figure appears in the preface to the \PiCTeX\ manual
%
$$
\beginpicture
  \ifFirstPass
```

---

*And probably any other format derived from Plain TₑX.

*Example 6-5: PₗCTEX Input for Figure 6-5 (continued)*

```
        \savelinesandcurves on "pictex-Arcsine.tex"
    \else
      \replot "pictex-Arcsine.tex"
    \fi
%  \ninepoint  %    (See Appendix E of the TeXbook.)
    \normalgraphs
    % Density plot
    \setcoordinatesystem  units  <\unit,.4\unit>  point at 0 0
    \setplotarea x from 0 to 1, y from 0 to 2.5
    \axis bottom invisible label {\lines {$t$\cr
      shaded area is $\DF(\beta) - \DF(\alpha)$\cr}} ticks
        numbered from 0.0 to 1.0 by 0.5
        unlabeled short quantity 11
        length <0pt> withvalues $\alpha$ $\beta$ / at .65 .85 /  /
    \axis left invisible label {{$a(t)$}} ticks
      numbered from 0.0 to 2.0 by 1.0
      unlabeled short from 0.5 to 2.5 by 1.0  /
    \plotheading{\lineskiplimit=1pt \lines{%
      Density\cr
      $a(t) = 1\big/\bigl(\pi \sqrt{t(1-t)}\,\bigr)$\cr
      of the arc sine law\cr}}
    \grid 1 1
    \putrule from  .65 0.0  to  .65 .66736
    \putrule from  .85 0.0  to  .85 .89145
    \shadeunit=.2\unit  \divide\shadeunit by 12
    \setshadegrid  span <\shadeunit>  point at .75 0
    \setquadratic
    \vshade .65 0 .66736   <,,,1pt> .75 0 .73511   .85 0 .89145  /
    % Move origin to (.5,0)
    % Left half}
    \ifFirstPass
      \setcoordinatesystem  point at -.5 0
      \inboundscheckon
      \plot  -.48429 2.55990  -.47553 2.06015  -.46489 1.72936  /
      \inboundscheckoff
      \plot  -.46489 1.72936  -.43815 1.32146  -.40451 1.08308
             -.36448  .92999  -.31871  .82623  -.26791  .75400
             -.21289  .70358  -.12434  .65727   .0       .63662  /
      % Right half
      \inboundscheckon
      \plot   .48429 2.55990   .47553 2.06015   .46489 1.72936  /
      \inboundscheckoff
      \plot   .46489 1.72936   .43815 1.32146   .40451 1.08308
              .36448  .92999   .31871  .82623   .26791  .75400
              .21289  .70358   .12434  .65727   .0      .63662  /
    \fi
    % Distribution function
    % Set origin of new coordinate system 1.7*1.375in=2.34in
    %   to the right of the original origin.
    \setcoordinatesystem  units <\unit,\unit>  point at -1.7 0
```

*Example 6-5: P~CT~X Input for Figure 6-5 (continued)*

```
\setplotarea x from 0 to 1, y from 0 to 1
\axis bottom label {$x\vphantom{t}$} ticks
   numbered from 0.0 to 1.0 by 0.5  unlabeled short quantity 11 /
\axis left label {$\DF(x)$} ticks
   numbered from 0.0 to 1.0 by 0.5  unlabeled short quantity 11 /
\plotheading{\lines{%
  Distribution function\cr
  $\DF(x) = {2\over \raise1pt\hbox{\seveni ^^Y}}
     \arcsin(\sqrt{x}\,)$\cr
  of the arc sine law\cr}}
\linethickness=.25pt  \grid {20} {20}
\linethickness=.4pt   \grid 2 2
% Left half
% Now move origin of coordinate system up to (.5,.5)
\ifFirstPass
  \setcoordinatesystem  point at -2.2 -.5
  \plot           -.50000 -.50    -.49901 -.48    -.49606 -.46
     -.49104 -.44  -.48439 -.42    -.47553 -.40    -.46489 -.38
     -.43815 -.34  -.40451 -.30    -.36448 -.26    -.31871 -.22
     -.26791 -.18  -.21289 -.14    -.12434 -.08    .0      .0   /
  % Right half
  \plot            .50000  .50     .49901  .48     .49606  .46
      .49104  .44   .48439  .42     .47553  .40     .46489  .38
      .43815  .34   .40451  .30     .36448  .26     .31871  .22
      .26791  .18   .21289  .14     .12434  .08     .0      .0   /
\fi
\endpicture
$$
```

The primary drawback of P~CT~X is that it requires a considerable amount of memory to use. Even relatively simple looking graphs require a big T~X to plot with P~CT~X. P~CT~X also produces very, very large DVI files (the graphs are drawn by interpreting and plotting each pixel individually). This usually results in very large output files from the DVI driver, and some printers may have difficulty printing your documents.

The P~CT~X macros are freely available, but the manual is not. You can purchase the manual directly from the author of P~CT~X or from the T~X User's Group.

## X~y~-pic

*X~y~-pic* is another add-on macro package for T~X, L~T~X, and other formats. It provides considerably more flexibility than the L~T~X picture environment without resorting to the resource-expensive strategy of P~CT~X.

*X~y~-pic* provides many more arrows than L~T~X (including curved and self-pointing forms), a wider variety of dashed and dotted lines, provision for lines that bend and go around other picture elements, and annotations for lines and arrows. It seems especially well suited to typesetting commutative diagrams, simple state-transition diagrams, and complex annotated matrices.

The syntax used in *Xy-pic* diagrams is not as straightforward as LaTeX's picture environment. An example of a complex *Xy-pic* diagram is shown in Figure 6-6. The corresponding source is shown in Example 6-6.

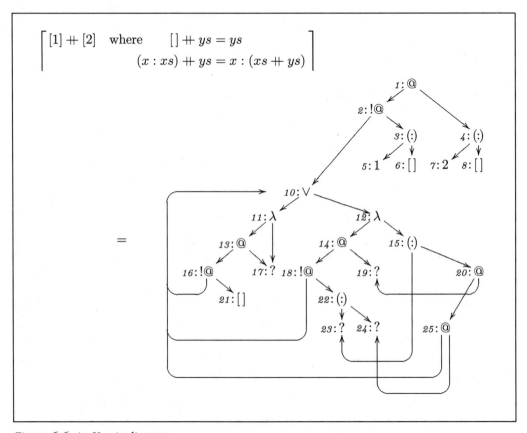

*Figure 6-6: An Xy-pic diagram*

*Example 6-6: The Xy-pic Input for Figure 6-6*

```
% Graph representing BAWL term [1]++[2].          [XY-pic & -*-tex-*-]
% by Kristoffer H. Rose <kris@diku.dk>
%
\def\n#1{\llap{{\sevenit#1\/}:\,}}
\def\op#1{(\mskip-.5\thinmuskip{#1}\mskip-.5\thinmuskip)}
\def\concat{\mathbin{\text{\rm+\kern-.5em+}}}
%
```

*Example 6-6: The Xy-pic Input for Figure 6-6 (continued)*

```
\def\du#1#2{%
  % #1: slidesign, #2: #rows to go down.
  \save\aftergo{\go="p",[0,0]!<#1\jot,0pt>%
    \xto`d[#2,0]+<-2.5pc,-.8pc>`"p" "p"\restore}}
%
\def\dul#1#2#3{%
  % #1: slidesign, #2: #rows to go down; #3: #columns to go left.
  \save\aftergo{\go="p",[0,0]!<#1\jot,0pt>%
  \xto`d[#2,0]+<-2.5pc,-.8pc>`[#2,-#3]+<-2.5pc,0pc> `"p" "p"\restore}}
%
\spreaddiagramrows{-1.4pc}
\spreaddiagramcolumns{-1pc}
%
$$
\displaylines{\quad
  \left\lceil\openup-\jot\eqalign{
  [1]\concat[2] \quad\text{where}\qquad
    [\,] \concat ys     &= ys \cr
    (x:xs) \concat ys   &= x:(xs \concat ys)}\right\rceil
\hfill\cr\hfill
 =\qquad
 {\diagram&&        &       &       &&\n1\@\dlto\xto[2,2]\\
   &        &       &       &       &\n2{!\@}\xto[3,-2]\drto\\
   &        &       &       &       &&\n3\op:\dlto\dto&&\n4\op:\dlto\dto\\
   &        &       &       &       &\n51&\n6[\,] &\n72&\n8[\,]\\
   &        &       &\n{10}\lor\dlto\drrto \go+<-3em,0em>="10"\\
   &        &\n{11}\lambda \dlto\ddto&&&\n{12}\lambda \dlto\drto\\
   &\n{13}\@\dlto\drto&&    &\n{14}\@\dlto\drto
                                   &&\n{15}\op:\du04[3,-2]\drrto\\
\n{16}{!\@}\dul000"10"\drto&&\n{17}{?}&\n{18}{!\@} \dul023"10" \drto
                                   &&\n{19}{?}&&&\n{20}\@\ddlto\du00[0,-3]\\
   &\n{21}[\,]&      &       &\n{22}\op:\dto\drto&&  &       &\\
   &        &       &       &\n{23}{?}&\n{24}{?}
                            &&\n{25}\@ \dul-27"10"\du+3[0,-2]\\
   &        &       &       &       &       &\\
   &        &       &       &       &       &\\
   &        &       &       &       &       &\enddiagram}
\quad\cr}
$$
```

## DraTEX

DraTEX is a macro package that can be loaded on top of Plain TEX or LATEX and provides many sophisticated drawing features. An example is shown in Figure 6-7. The source is in Example 6-7.

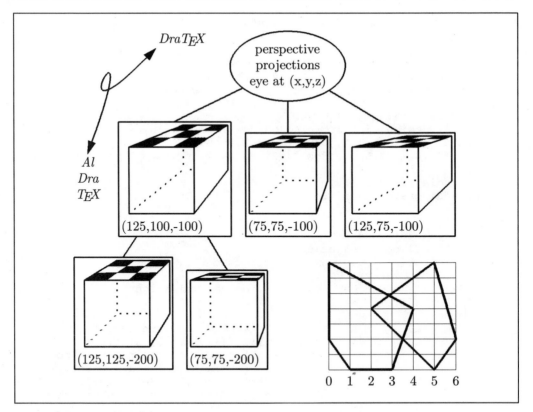

*Figure 6-7: An DraTEX diagram*

*Example 6-7: The DraTEX Input for Figure 6-7*

```
\Draw     \Ragged(4)      %%%%%%%%%% tree %%%%%%%%%%%%%

\Define\DotsToLoc(1){    \MarkLoc(x)
    \CSeg\DoLine(x,#1)(5){
          \MoveF(-3)\LineF(1)} }
\PictNode(3){       \IF \EqText(,#2) \THEN \Text(--#1--) \ELSE
    \ThreeDim(#1,#2,#3)
       \MarkPLoc(1)    \Line(50,0,0)    \MarkPLoc(2) \Line(0,50,0)
       \MarkPLoc(3)    \Line(-50,0,0)   \MarkPLoc(4) \Line(0,-50,0)
       \Move(0,0,50)   \MarkPLoc(1´)
       \Move(50,0,0)   \MarkPLoc(2´)    {\Line(0,0,-50)}
       \Line(0,50,0)   \MarkPLoc(3´)    {\Line(0,0,-50)}
       \Line(-50,0,0) \MarkPLoc(4´)    {\Line(0,0,-50)}
       \Do(1,4){    \Do(1,4){
          \MarkPLoc(p\Val\I) \I+1; \Move(0,0,-16.66666)
          } \Move(16.66666,0,66.66666)   }
       \TwoDim
```

*Example 6-7: The DraTEX Input for Figure 6-7 (continued)*

```
            \MoveToLL(3,4)(4´,1´) \DotsToLoc(1´) \DotsToLoc(1)
            \MoveToLL(2,3)(1´,2´) \DotsToLoc(1´)
            \PaintQuad(p0,p1,p5,p4)        \PaintQuad(p2,p3,p7,p6)
            \PaintQuad(p5,p6,p10,p9)       \PaintQuad(p8,p9,p13,p12)
            \PaintQuad(p10,p11,p15,p14)
            \MoveToLoc(1)  \CSeg[0.5]\Move(1,2) \Move(0,-5)
            \EntryExit(0,1,0,0)  \Text(--(#1,#2,#3)--)
        \EndTwoDim
    \EndThreeDim        \FI    }

\Define\MyEdge(2){\EdgeTo(#1,#2,0,1)} \TreeAlign(V,0,-1)(0,0,0)
\TreeSpec(o,\OvalNode&r,\RectNode)()(\MyEdge)
\TreeSpace(C,10,15)        \AdjTree(A,0..0,0,-201,201,0 )
\Tree()(
  3,o,perspective~~projections~~eye~at~{(x,y,z)},, //
  2,r,125,100,-100 & 0,r,75,75,-100 & 0,r,125,75,-100 //
  0,r,125,125,-200 & 0,r,75,75,-200 //)

%%%%%%%%% graph %%%%%%%%%%%%

\MoveToNode(2..1,2.5,-1)    \MarkLoc(1)
\MoveToNode(1..2,1,-1.5)    \MarkLoc(2)
\CSeg\Scale(1,2)    \Scale(0.16666,0.14286)

\Axis(1,2)(E3,&&&&&&)
\Axis(1,2)(S3,0&1&2&3&4&5&6)
    \MoveToLoc(1)
\Table\x{ -1,2 & 0,5 & 4,-3 & -1,-4 & -2,0 }
    \PenSize(1.5pt)  \Move(1,0)  \x(0,99){\Line}
\Table\x{ 3,3 & 1,-5 & -1,-2 & -3,4 }
                  \Move(1,4)  \x(0,99){\Line}

%%%%%%%%% DraTeX+AlDraTeX logos %%%%%%%%%%%%

\it \TextNode(1){\Text(--#1--)}
\MoveToNode(0..0,0,1) \Units(1pt,1pt) \Move(-60,0)
\EntryExit(1,1,0,0)  \Node(d)(--Dra\TeX--)
\MoveToNode(2..0,-1,1)  \Move(0,40) \EntryExit(-1,-1,0,0)
\Node(a)(--Al~~Dra~~\TeX--)        \PenSize(0.75pt)
\ArrowHeads(2) \CurvedEdgeAt(d,-1,-1,a,0,1)(225,1.1,70,1.3)

\EndDraw
```

DraTEX offers a wide variety of low-level drawing commands: straight lines at arbitrary angles, circles of any size, bezier curves, rectangular or polar coordinate systems, perspective for three-dimensional figures, user-definable shading patterns, clipping, repetition, and user-definable drawing objects and commands. A supporting package, AlDraTEX, provides high-level drawing commands for pie charts, XY charts, bar charts, spread diagrams, grid diagrams, trees, and diagram annotations (arrows, edges, labels).

Although it is a flexible and portable solution, beware that complex figures may require considerable time to compute and will almost certainly require a big TEX. The resulting DVI files tend to be large as well.

DraTEX and AlDraTEX are described in *TEX & LATEX: Drawing and Literate Programming* [18].

# Using a Little Help

On most platforms, if you have TEX, METAFONT is available. Because METAFONT was designed for drawing, it has much better support for pictures and figures than TEX. There are three utilities that allow you to combine TEX and METAFONT to create pictures: *MFPic* and *Fig2MF*.

## MFPic

*MFPic*'s `picture` environment and LATEX's `picture` environment are implemented very differently. The commands in *MFPic* don't attempt to typeset your diagram with special fonts; instead, they write METAFONT commands to another file. This file must be processed with METAFONT before your document can be viewed.

Because METAFONT is used to draw the actual diagram, the *MFPic* macros are much more flexible than the LATEX picture creation commands. *MFPic* macros provide lines (at any angle), rectangles, polygons, circles (of any size), ellipses, cyclic and acyclic curves, arcs, and wedges (all empty, shaded, or filled).

Unlike *Fig2MF*, described below, *MFPic* can plot user-specified functions (parametrically or directly, using polygonal or bezier interpolation).

Finally, because *MFPic* works so directly with TEX, it can include labels and captions in the figure as well as allowing "METAFONT hackers" to insert METAFONT code directly.

## Fig2MF

The "Fig" in *Fig2MF* stands for the Fig graphics code (in this case, Fig version 2.1). Fig is a device-independent way of representing figures. Like TEX DVI files, Fig graphics are always translated into a device-dependent form before they are printed. *Fig2MF* translates Fig graphics into METAFONT code, which can be rendered into a font that is usable by TEX on any platform.

At present, there are a few limitations on *Fig2MF*: text objects are ignored, and arrowed and non-solid line styles are not supported. The advantage of *Fig2MF* is that very good interactive drawing programs, like *xfig*, can be used to create figures.

## METAFONT

If the idea of programming directly in METAFONT is appealing to you, start by reading "Simple Drawings in METAFONT" [58]. This is a short document (freely available) that describes how simple drawings can easily be rendered directly in METAFONT.

In order to use METAFONT creatively, *The METAFONTbook* [29] is really a necessity, but you can get a feel for the picture creation process in METAFONT without it.

# Using a Little More Help

A couple of TeX macro packages combine the convenience of using only TeX commands to produce pictures and figures with the power of PostScript. Using these macros makes your documents less portable because they rely on a PostScript printer or PostScript interpreter to be printed.

## PSTricks

The *PSTricks* macro package is a TeX-PostScript hybrid. The advantage of this approach is that *PSTricks* is able to provide much wider functionality than the preceding packages without leaving TeX. The disadvantage is that it makes your documents dependent on a PostScript printer.

One of the neatest features of *PSTricks* is the ability to interact with other TeX objects. You can add PostScript annotations (curved lines, labels, etc.) to the entries in a table, for example, or point to other elements on the page, like this:

In addition to allowing you to insert essentially arbitrary PostScript commands directly into your document, *PSTricks* provides TeX macros for most common picture elements including: commands for curved and straight lines (at arbitrary angles), a wide variety of arrow heads and tails, pattern-filled regions, regular and irregular polygonal shapes, text scaling and rotation, and grids.

## TeXdraw

TeXdraw, like *PSTricks*, provides support for pictures and figures by relying on a PostScript back end.

TeXdraw is organized into a toolbox of simple routines from which more complex commands can be constructed. The TeXdraw manual [23] includes several examples of how complex commands can be built from toolbox routines.

## tpic

The "pic" drawing language was designed for *troff* documents. The *tpic* program interprets pic drawings and produces TeX output to render them. The output relies on a set of \special commands, which must be implemented by the DVI driver to actually produce the output. The *tpic* \specials are implemented by many DVI drivers.

# Using a Lot of Help

Although many nice effects can be achieved directly in TEX or with METAFONT, you will probably want to include some other form of image (e.g., an encapsulated PostScript figure or a scanned photograph) in a TEX document eventually.

There are a myriad of choices when this occurs. To a large extent, the options available depend on the kind of printer you have, which DVI drivers you use, and to what extent you are willing to sacrifice device independence.

## Electronic Cut-and-paste

Documents that require complex graphics may be difficult to produce as a single TEX document. You may exceed the memory limitations of your version of TEX if you try to put too many figures on a given page, or you may wish to include graphics from incompatible macro packages (suppose you are using the Lollipop format for example, and you want to include a LATEX picture).

You can always leave blank space in your document, print the graphic on a separate page, and then combine the two pages with scissors, glue, and a photocopy machine. However, there are many times when this is inappropriate (not to mention the aesthetic sensibilities it may disturb).

Another solution is to use a program that can perform cut-and-paste operations on the output files before they are printed. If you use Plain TEX or LA$_M$S-TEX, one option is *DVIpaste*. *DVIpaste* can insert parts of one DVI file into another. It is part of the LA$_M$S-TEX distribution. The documentation for *DVIpaste* contains a good example of its use. Unfortunately, *DVIpaste* relies on macros that are incompatible with most other macro packages.

Some DVI drivers like *dvimsp*,* which comes with emTEX, can translate DVI files into bitmapped images that can then be incorporated into your document directly. Figures 4-5, 4-6, and 4-7 in Chapter 4, *Macro Packages*, were inserted into this book using *dvidot*.

## Scalable Image Formats

Several of the most commonly encountered scalable image formats are PostScript (usually encapsulated), HPGL (Hewlett-Packard's Plotter language), DXF (Autocad's vector format), and the Fig graphics language. PostScript and HPGL are used by specific printers

---

* *dvimsp* has been replaced by *dvidot* in the beta test distributions.

and plotters, DXF files are created by many computer-aided design programs, and Fig is a graphic language understood by several free editing tools—it is always converted into something else before it is printed. Many programs that can edit scalable images have their own vendor-specific formats. Luckily, these programs can usually produce PostScript or HPGL output as well.

PostScript images are the most commonly encountered scalable images. Drawing packages that output PostScript generally produce *encapsulated PostScript* (EPS). Similarly, most PostScript clip-art is distributed in EPS format. Encapsulated PostScript is a subset of the PostScript language. One of the most important features of EPS images is a *bounding box*. The bounding box identifies the size of the EPS image. This information is used to determine the scaling factor required to get an image of the correct size.

Generic PostScript can sometimes be converted into encapsulated PostScript. For example, the *ps2epsi* program that comes with *Ghostscript* attempts to convert generic PostScript into encapsulated PostScript.

Some software produces reasonable PostScript figures, but fails to include the bounding box. For those situations, the *bbfig* program that comes with *dvips* may help. *bbfig* uses the printer to calculate a bounding box that you can insert into the figure. After you have printed the figure, you can construct a bounding box by hand, if necessary (sometimes *bbfig* gets confused). Simply measure the height and width of the figure and its position on the page (measured from the bottom-left corner). The bounding box is a rectangle measured from the lower-left corner of the figure to the upper-right corner. An example is shown in Figure 6-8.

The bounding box is measured in PostScript points. There are 72 PostScript points to the inch, so the image in Figure 6-8 has the following bounding box:

```
%%BoundingBox: 115.2 180 468 626.4
```

If you are printing your document on a PostScript printer, you will find that PostScript images are easy to handle; every PostScript DVI driver that I have seen allows you to incorporate encapsulated PostScript with one or more `\special` commands. The section "Inserting PostScript Images into TEX" later in this chapter describes two ways of incorporating encapsulated PostScript images into Plain TEX or LATEX documents for printing on a PostScript printer.

PostScript output on non-PostScript devices is much more difficult, although it can be achieved with a PostScript interpreter like *Ghostscript*.* For a detailed description of how PostScript images can be converted into another format with *Ghostscript*, see the "Ghostscript" section later in this chapter.

---

*In fairness, the degree of difficulty depends on the platform you work on. Some systems, like the Amiga, have very good support for PostScript output, even on non-PostScript devices. Alternatively, if you have a fast computer, the extra translation through *Ghostscript* may be quite painless.

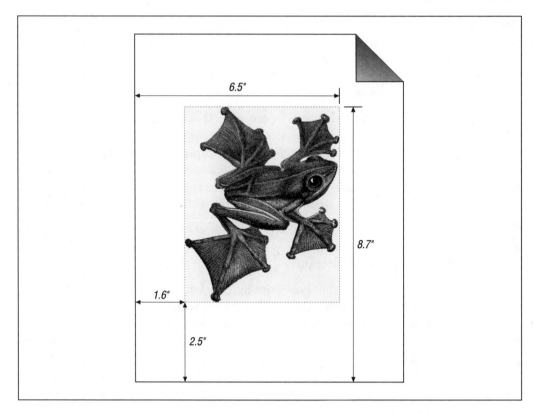

*Figure 6-8: A PostScript bounding box example*

Hewlett-Packard HPGL is the plotter language developed by HP for its line of pen-based plotting devices. Many computer-aided design and drafting programs can produce HPGL. In addition to plotters, the HP LaserJet III and more recent HP LaserJet printers also understand HPGL. On an HP LaserJet III or later model printer, you can print HPGL directly if your DVI driver allows you to include printer-specific data. This ability was introduced in version 1.4t of the emTEX *dvihplj* driver.

If your DVI driver does not support printer-specific files or your printer does not understand HPGL, there are at least two conversion programs (*hp2xx* and *hp2ps*) that may be able to convert your HPGL drawings into another form you can use.

The Fig graphics language was designed to represent pictures and figures in an easy to interpret and portable manner. The *Fig* and *xfig* drawing programs work with Fig graphics. Several other programs, like *gnuplot*, can also produce Fig graphics. See the "Fig2MF" section for more information.

# Bitmapped Image Formats

Including bitmapped images is easier than including scalable images because no real interpretation of commands is necessary. Over the years, lots of different ways have been developed for including bitmapped images in TEX documents. Since the development of the *bm2font* program, most of these methods have become obsolete. As a result, this section examines only a few methods.

### DVI driver \special

The first method is DVI driver-specific: if your DVI driver includes a `\special` command for including bitmapped graphic images, you can simply use that command. The disadvantage of using a DVI driver `\special` is that it makes the document less portable. Instead of being printable with any DVI driver, it now requires a DVI driver that recognizes a particular `\special` command. Note also that some DVI drivers do not handle color images very well; you may need to convert the image to black and white first. (Many programs described in the "Manipulating Images" section later in this chapter can perform this operation.)

### bm2font

On most platforms, *bm2font* provides an ideal solution for including bitmapped images. This program translates bitmapped images into PK fonts and produces a snippet of TEX code that can be used to print the image in your document. Because most DVI drivers can use PK fonts, a high degree of portability is maintained. Some portability is still lost since the bitmapped image has a fixed resolution, but that is a consequence of using the bitmapped image, not *bm2font*. All of the bitmap images in this book were included with the *bm2font* program.

This book is a good example of an instance where portability is required. I could easily have included the graphics with the `\special` command of the DVI driver that I use most frequently (*dvihplj*), but then I couldn't have produced pages suitable for final publication.

*bm2font* can read a number of common graphic image formats including GIF, Windows BMP, and PCX. It can translate color images into black and white using a number of dithering methods, and it can scale the image to a specific size (although scaling bitmap images is not usually very effective).

### pbmtopk

The *pbmtopk* program provides a solution similar to *bm2font*. Because *pbmtopk* is a smaller program, it may be easier to port to other systems. The *pbmtopk* distribution includes *pktopbm*, which can translate PK files back into PBM bitmaps.

# Inserting PostScript Images into TEX

If you are using Plain TEX or LATEX and printing your documents on a PostScript printer, there are several (essentially equivalent) style files that you can use to include your figures.

One is *epsfig.sty*, which can be used as a LATEX style option or be inserted directly into Plain TEX documents with \input.* The *epsfig* style option is supported by LATEX $2_\varepsilon$ as well.

After the style file is loaded, you can use the macro \epsfig to include your figure. The complete syntax for \epsfig is:

```
\epsfig{figure=, height=, width=, rheight=, rwidth=,
        bbllx=, bblly=, bburx=, bbury=,
        clip=, angle=, silent=}
```

In practice, only a few of these options are commonly used. Here is a description of each:

figure=

Identifies the name of the file containing the PostScript figure. This option is required.

height=, width=

Specify the height and width of the figure. If only one is specified, the other will be scaled automatically to keep the proportions of the original figure. If both are given, the figure will be scaled (anamorphically) to the requested size.

rheight=, rwidth=

Provide the "reserved" height and width of the figure. This is how big the TEX box that encloses the figure will be. By default, the box is as big as the figure.

bbllx=, bblly=, bburx=, bbury=

Specify the bounding box of the figure. If not specified (it usually isn't), the bounding box is read from the PostScript figure.

clip=

Indicates whether or not the figure should be "clipped" at its bounding box. Clipping prevents lines in the figure from extending beyond the bounding box.

angle=

Allows you to specify that the figure should be rotated. Always specify the angle of rotation in degrees. The figure is always rotated counter-clockwise.

silent=

Turns off informative messages printed by the macros as the figure is processed.

---

*The *epsfig.sty* style relies on *epsf.tex* to provide low-level support for including EPS images. The *epsf.tex* file is part of the *dvips* distribution.

The parameters to the \epsfig macro have to obey TEX's strict parsing rules. In particular, you must not put spaces around the equal sign in any option. The clip= and silent= options have no values, but you must include the equal sign anyway.

For example, Figure 6-9 was inserted by \epsfig using the following commands:

```
\begin{figure}
  \epsfig{figure=figs/sample.eps}
  \caption{An example of an encapsulated figure.}
  \label{fig:psfigure}
\end{figure}
```

*Figure 6-9: An example of an encapsulated figure*

Figure 6-10 demonstrates a few of other *epsfig* options:

```
\begin{figure}
  \epsfig{figure=figs/sample.eps,width=6cm,angle=45}
  \caption{An example of an encapsulated figure}
  \label{fig:psfigurerot}
\end{figure}
```

## *Manipulating Images*

There are literally dozens of software packages available for manipulating graphic images. The discussion that follows focuses on a small handful of these programs. The programs selected are representative of the kinds of tools available, but this is by no means an

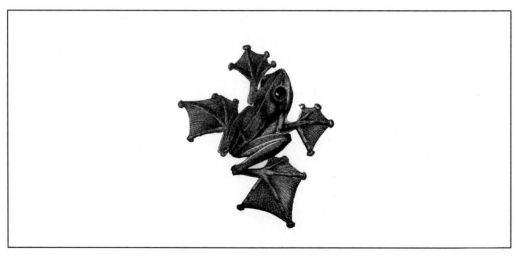

*Figure 6-10: Another example of an encapsulated figure (resized and rotated)*

endorsement that these are the best tools. Table 6-1 summarizes the programs described in this section.

If you cannot find any way of converting a particular image, remember that you may be able to display the image and capture it with another program that can save the image in a more tractable format.

*Table 6-1: Graphics Manipulation Packages*

| Program | Platforms | Cost | Purpose |
|---------|-----------|------|---------|
| *Image Magick* | UNIX | Free | Display, manipulate, convert and capture images |
| *PBMplus* | All | Free | Convert and manipulate images |
| *xv* | UNIX | SW[1] | Display, manipulate, convert and capture images |
| *xloadimage* | UNIX | Free | Display images |
| *Image Alchemy* | MS-DOS[2] | SW | Convert images |
| *CView* | MS-DOS | SW | Convert images |
| *Jpeg4* | MS-DOS | SW | Convert images |
| *PMView* | OS/2 | SW | Display and convert images |
| *txt2pcx* | MS-DOS | SW | Translate text into graphic image format |
| *Ghostscript* | All | Free | Convert PostScript to other formats |
| *hp2xx* | UNIX | Free | Convert HPGL to other formats |

[1]Shareware: "Try before you buy," but not free.

[2]Also available for Sun workstations; see documentation.

# Image Magick

*Image Magick* is a collection of eight programs for manipulating images. These programs work with MIFF files by default. MIFF is the "machine-independent file format" developed by the package's author. If you are going to manipulate images with these tools, the author recommends converting them to MIFF format first. The *convert* program reads and writes a large number of image formats, so conversion to and from MIFF format is straightforward.

*Image Magick* requires the Independent JPEG Group's JPEG library in order to manipulate JPEG images. Similarly, Sam Leffler's TIFF software library is required to manipulate TIFF images. Both of these are compile-time options. If you did not build *Image Magick*, you may not be able to manipulate JPEG or TIFF images. To manipulate PostScript images, *Ghostscript* must be available.

The programs described below are the *Image Magick* tools that allow you to manipulate images in ways that may be necessary or useful for creating printable images. Other tools, like *animate*, included in the *Image Magick* distribution, aren't described here because they have no bearing on printability.

### display

This program allows you to preview images on an X11 display. The number of colors in the image is reduced to match the number of colors of your display, if necessary. Program options allow you to specify a variety of image-processing operations on the image (noise reduction, scaling, manipulation of the color map, etc.).

Conversion to MIFF format, as recommended above, isn't necessary for simply displaying the image.

### import

This program allows you to capture visible portions of an X11 display. You can capture any visible window, the entire display, or any rectangular portion of the display. *import* can save the image in any format recognized by *convert*.

### convert

As the name implies, this utility converts images between graphics formats. The following standard formats are recognized:

| MIFF | BMP | CMYK | EPS | FAX | GIF | IRIS | JPEG | PICT | PNM |
|------|-----|------|-----|-----|------|------|------|------|-----|
| PS | RGB | RLE | SUN | TGA | TEXT | TIFF | XBM | XWD | |

Additionally, a few less-standard formats are recognized. A complete list is available in the manual page for *convert*.

### combine

This program combines two images by blending them together. The result varies tremendously, depending on the kind of blending used. Simple overlaps, various kinds of cutouts, and more complex color blendings are possible.

*montage*

> Unlike *combine*, *montage* combines multiple images by *tiling*. (The images are laid next to each other rather than on top of each other.) Optionally, the image name can appear below each tile.

*mogrify*

> *mogrify* is used to transform an image (or series of images). You can specify alternate color maps in a variety of ways, as well as dithering and error correcting transformations. The images can also be rolled, rotated, rescaled, and sheared. (Shearing transforms a rectangle into a parallelogram by shifting the X or Y axis.)

## *PBMplus*

The *PBMplus* package is a large collection of image translation programs. This package was written originally for UNIX, but has since been ported to MS-DOS and OS/2.

*PBMplus* defines three file formats:

- PBM—The Portable Bitmap format for black and white images
- PGM—The Portable Graymap format for grayscaled images
- PPM—The Portable Pixmap format for color images

Translation from one format to another is accomplished by translating into the appropriate portable format first, and then translating the portable bitmap into the destination format.

The following image formats are supported by the PBMPlus tools:

| | |
|---|---|
| Abekas YUV bytes | MGR bitmaps |
| Andrew Toolkit raster objects | MTV or PRT ray traced images |
| Atari Degas .pi1 images | MacPaint files |
| Atari Degas .pi3 files | Macintosh PICT files |
| Atari Spectrum files | PCX files |
| AutoCAD slides | PostScript "images" |
| Bennet Yee "faces" | QRT ray tracer files |
| CMU window manager bitmaps | Raw grayscale bytes |
| Doodle brush files | Raw RGB bytes |
| FITS files | Sun icons |
| GIF files | Sun rasterfiles |
| Gould scanner files | TIFF images |
| Group 3 faxes | TrueVision Targa files |
| HIPS files | Usenix FaceSaver(tm) images |
| HP PaintJet files | X10/X11 window dumps |
| IFF ILBM files | X11 pixmaps |
| IMG (GEM) images | XBM files |
| Img-whatnot files | Xim file |
| Lisp Machine bitmaps | |

The *PBMplus* tools translate the image into the appropriate portable format (PBM, PGM, or PPM) depending on the nature of the image. Similarly, the tools can all work with "lower" formats. (PPM tools can work with PGM and PBM files, and PGM tools can work with PBM files.) For example, there is no "*pbmtopcx*," however the *ppmtopcx* tool will create a black and white PCX file if you use a PBM file as the input. Once converted into a portable format, the image can be translated back into (almost) any of the supported formats.

In addition to image conversion, the PBMPlus tools include programs to perform a wide variety of image manipulations.

| | |
|---|---|
| Apply Conway's rules of life | Create a blank image |
| Create a mask bitmap | Reduce/enlarge an image |
| Convert text into a bitmap | Create a UPC bitmap |
| Bentleyize a greymap | Apply edge-detection |
| Apply edge-enhancement | Generate a histogram |
| Normalize contrast | Apply an "oil-painting" filter |
| Create a "ramp" | Generate textural features |
| Perform bitwise arithmetic | Perform MxN convolution |
| Crop an image | Cut/Paste rectangles |
| Color-reduce | Flip/rotate |
| Apply gamma-correction | Build a visual index |
| Invert an image | Add a border to an image |
| Scale an image | Shear an image |
| Smooth an image | Build a tiled image |
| Colorize a graymap | Dither color images |
| Create fractal terrain | Apply Laplacian-relief filter |

## *xv*

*xv* is an interactive image viewing/converting tool that runs on X11 servers (including MS-DOS implementations of X11 such as Desqview/X).

You can view GIF, PBM, XBM, Sun rasterfile, JPEG, and TIFF images. You can save any image in one of those formats or in encapsulated PostScript. In addition, you can capture any visible portion of the X11 server window interactively with *xv*.

Like most of the tools described here, *xv* includes a number of image manipulation tools (cropping, scaling, editing the color map, etc.). If you try to view an image that is larger than your display, *xv* automatically scales it to fit. I find that *xv*'s interactive nature makes it easier to use for image manipulation than the command-driven tools.

# *xloadimage*

The *xloadimage* program is another X11 picture display tool. Like *xv* and *Image Magick's display*, it has a number of picture manipulation options (although they are not interactive).

One advantage of *xloadimage* is that it does not rescale images that are too large to fit within the display. Instead, it places them in a scrollable window. I find this behavior superior to *xv's* solution of rescaling a very large image even though you are interested only in a small section of it.

# *Image Alchemy*

*Image Alchemy* is a shareware tool for converting graphic images between various formats. Although the manual mentions a version for Sun workstations, I have only seen the MS-DOS version.

Note that the unregistered shareware version of this program will only convert images which are 640×480 pixels or smaller.

The following is a list of the graphic formats recognized by version 1.5 of *Image Alchemy*:

| | |
|---|---|
| ADEX | PCPAINT/Pictor Page Format |
| Autologic | PCX |
| Binary Information Files (BIF) | Portable BitMap (PBM) |
| Encapsulated PostScript (EPS) | Q0 |
| Erdas LAN/GIS | QDV |
| Freedom of the Press | QRT |
| GEM VDI Image File | Scodl |
| GIF | Silicon Graphics Image |
| HP Printer Command Language (PCL) | Stork |
| HP Raster Transfer Language (RTL) | Sun Raster |
| HSI JPEG | TIFF |
| HSI Palette | Targa |
| HSI Raw | Utah Raster Toolkit (RLE) |
| IFF/ILBM | Vivid |
| JPEG/JFIF | Windows Bitmap (BMP) |
| Jovian VI | WordPerfect Graphic File |
| Macintosh PICT/PICT2 | XBM |
| MTV Ray Tracer | XWD |

*Image Alchemy* can also perform a number of image manipulations like rescaling, cropping, and color map changes.

# ColorView

*ColorView* is a shareware MS-DOS program for displaying and converting graphic images. Although designed to work with VESA SuperVGA adapters, *ColorView* can also work with plain VGA adapters. It does require a 80286 or a more powerful processor.

*ColorView* can read JPEG, GIF (87 and 89), BMP, and RLE images. It can write GIF (87), 8-bit BMP, 24-bit BMP, JPEG, and RLE images. It can perform image translation without displaying the images, so a VGA or SuperVGA adapter is not required for translation.

# Jpeg4

This is the Independent JPEG Group's JPEG Software. The compression tool can convert GIF, PPM, and Targa (TGA) images into JPEG format. The decompression tool converts JPEG images into GIF, PPM (or PGM), or Targa formats.

# pmjpeg

The *pmjpeg* program is an OS/2 2.x program that can read and display JPEG, TIFF, Targa, GIF, PCX, and Windows or OS/2 BMP images. In addition, *pmjpeg* can write images in any of these formats except Windows BMP. *pmjpeg* can also capture all or part of the desktop.

Some of the other features of *pmjpeg* are color map editing, contrast enhancement, image cropping, scaling, rotation, batch translation of images into JPEG format, cyclic slideshow presentations, and the ability to reduce an image to the system palette colors.

# txt2pcx

*txt2pcx* is a memory-resident MS-DOS utility that captures text-mode screens as PCX graphic images. See the discussion of screen capturing in the "Screen Dumps" section of this chapter for more information about why this is sometimes desirable.

# Ghostscript

*Ghostscript* is distributed by the Free Software Foundation (FSF). It is one of the few freely available programs that can convert PostScript images into other formats.

*Ghostscript* is a (mostly) complete PostScript interpreter. Converting an entire page of PostScript into another format is straightforward with *Ghostscript*. The following example converts the PostScript file *file.ps* into a monochrome GIF image called *image1.gif*:

```
$ gs -r300 -sDEVICE=gifmono -sOutputFile=image1.gif file.ps
```

The parameter *-r300* indicates that *Ghostscript* should generate output at a resolution of 300dpi. This controls the size of the bitmap. If you plan to print the resulting bitmap, you should specify the same resolution as your printer.

If *file.ps* contains more than one page, you can use a `%d` in the output file's name to identify how multiple pages should be handled. For example, if *file.ps* contains three pages, the following command will extract the first page into *image1.gif*, the second page into *image2.gif*, and the third page into *image3.gif*:*

```
$ gs -r300 -sDEVICE=gifmono -sOutputFile=image%d.gif file.ps
```

For incorporating images into TEX, it is more common to convert an encapsulated PostScript (EPS) image into a bitmapped format than it is to convert entire pages. Encapsulated PostScript is described earlier in this chapter in the section "Scalable Image Formats." It is slightly more difficult to convert encapsulated PostScript because of the bounding box. To convert this into a bitmap of exactly the right size, you have to tell *Ghostscript* to move the image to the upper-left corner of the page (where *Ghostscript* always begins its conversion) and tell it how big the image is in pixels.

The following steps are necessary to produce exactly the right size bitmap of the encapsulated PostScript figure:

1.  Find the size of the bounding box. Examine the PostScript file using a text editor. Find the line that begins with `%% BoundingBox:` followed by four numbers. Those numbers are the lower-left x-coordinate (llx), the lower-left y-coordinate (lly), the upper-right x-coordinate (urx), and the upper-right y-coordinate (ury), respectively.

2.  Create another file called *trans.ps* that contains the single line:

    `llx neg lly neg translate`

3.  Calculate the width of the bounding box: $width_{bb} = urx - llx$.

4.  The width you have just calculated is the width at 72dpi. To convert this to the resolution that you will be using, multiply by the resolution and divide by 72. For example, if you will be printing at 300dpi and the width of the bounding box $width_{bb}$ is 216, the width at 300dpi, *width*, is $(216 \times 300) \div 72 = 900$.

5.  Calculate the corrected height in an analogous manner using $height_{bb} = ury - lly$ as a starting point. For example, if $height_{bb} = 360$, the height you get at 300dpi is 1500.

---

*Under MS-DOS and OS/2, remember that the command processor performs variable substitution with the percent sign. Use two consecutive percent signs.

6. Finally, run *Ghostscript* using the *-g* parameter to select the image size (*width* × *height*). For example, to translate the EPS file *card.ps* into the GIF file *card.gif* at 300dpi assuming the height and width calculated above, run:

```
$ gs -r300 -g900x1500 -sDEVICE=gifmono \
      -sOutputFile=card.gif trans.ps card.ps
```

The *Perl* script shown in Example 6-8 automates this process.

*Example 6-8: Converting Encapsulated PostScript to a Bitmap with Ghostscript*

```perl
#! perl
#
# Usage: gs-eps epsfile <outputfile> <resolution> <device>
#
# Where: epsfile is the encapsulated postscript file
#        outputfile is the output file (the default name
#           is <basename epsfile>.<device>)
#        resolution is the output resolution (default=300)
#        device is the GS driver to use (default=pbm)

($epsfile,$outputfile,$res,$device) = @ARGV;

if (! $epsfile) {
  printf "Usage: gs-eps epsfile <outputfile> <resolution>";
  printf " <gsdriver>\n";
  printf "Note: parameters are positional.  To specify a";
  printf " driver, you\n";
  printf "must also specify an outputfile and resolution.\n";
  exit 1;
  }

$epsfile =~ tr/\\/\//; # translate \foo\bar -> /foo/bar

if (! -r $epsfile) {
  printf "Cannot read file: $epsfile\n";
  exit 1;
  }

if (! $res)      { $res = 300 }
if (! $device)   { $device = "pbm" }

if (! $outputfile ) {
  @pathname = split(/\//,$epsfile);
  $outputfile = $pathname[$#pathname];
  $outputfile =~ s/.eps$//;
  $outputfile = join(".", $outputfile, $device);
  }

printf "Converting $epsfile to $outputfile at ${res}dpi...\n";
```

*Example 6-8: Converting Encapsulated PostScript to a Bitmap with Ghostscript (continued)*

```
open (EPSFILE,$epsfile);

undef $bbox;
undef $showpg;
while (<EPSFILE>) {
    $bbox = $_ if /\%\%\s*BoundingBox:\s*\d+\s+\d+\s+\d+\s+\d+/;
    $showpage = $_ if /showpage/;
    last if ($bbox && $showpage);
    }

if (! $bbox) {
    printf "Cannot find a bounding box in $epsfile";
    exit 1;
    }

$bbox =~ s/\D*//;    # remove everything preceding the digits

($llx,$lly,$urx,$ury) = split(/\s/,$bbox);

$xsize = sprintf("%d", (($urx - $llx) * $res / 72) + 0.5);
$ysize = sprintf("%d", (($ury - $lly) * $res / 72) + 0.5);

printf "$llx neg $lly neg translate > gs-eps-a.$$\n";
printf "quit > gs-eps-b.$$\n";

if (! $showpg) {
    printf "showpage > gs-eps-b.$$\n";
    printf "quit >> gs-eps-b.$$\n";
    }

# join sillyness to keep the length of lines in the
# script small enough to print in the book.
$gscmd = join(" ", "gs -sDEVICE=$device",
                    "-q -sOutputFile=$outputfile",
                    "-g${xsize}x${ysize} -r$res",
    "gs-eps-a.$$ $epsfile -",
    "< gs-eps-b.$$");

printf "$gscmd\n";

printf "rm -f gs-eps-a.$$ gs-eps-b.$$\n";
```

The primary disadvantage of *Ghostscript* is that the selection of free PostScript fonts
is quite limited. The only freely available fonts are: IBM Courier, Bitstream Courier,
Bitstream Charter, Adobe Utopia, URW Antiqua, URW Grotesk Bold, Nimbus Roman
No9, and Nimbus Sans. Unless you have the PostScript sources for other fonts used in
your figures (PFA or PFB and AFM files), *Ghostscript* will use crude approximations of
the desired font.

# GoScript

*GoScript* is a commercial PostScript interpreter sold by LaserGo, Inc. *GoScript* is available for MS-DOS systems only. A special version is available for Microsoft Windows.

The primary advantage of a commercial interpreter is that it comes with more high-quality fonts. The *GoScript* program comes with "clones" of the 13 standard PostScript fonts:

| | |
|---|---|
| Times Roman | Times Italic |
| Times Bold | Times Bold Italic |
| Helvetica | Helvetica Oblique |
| Helvetica Bold | Helvetica Bold Oblique |
| Courier | Courier Oblique |
| Courier Bold | Courier Bold Oblique |
| Symbol | |

The *GoScript Plus* program includes clones of all 35 standard fonts (the standard 13 plus AvantGarde, Bookman, Helvetica-Narrow, New Century Schoolbook, Palatino in four styles, Zapf Chancery Italic, and Zapf Dingbats). For MS-DOS users, this program has the additional advantage of being quite a bit faster than *Ghostscript*.

Although *GoScript* can use any PostScript Type 1 or Type 3 font, the fonts supplied with *GoScript* are not in a standard PostScript format, so they cannot be used with other applications.

On a 300dpi LaserJet printer, *GoScript* did not seem to align the baseline of bitmapped PostScript fonts with great accuracy. This is unfortunate, because the Computer Modern fonts created with METAFONT for TEX are bitmapped.

# hp2xx

*hp2xx* converts scalable images in HPGL into other formats. HPGL is Hewlett-Packard's command language for controlling pen-based plotters. (HP's LaserJet series of printers, starting with the LaserJet III, also understand HPGL.)

Many computer-aided drafting packages can save diagrams in HPGL format. Other software that works with scalable images is likely to be able to save in HPGL format as well. Because HPGL support is uncommon in printers, you will probably have to convert HPGL diagrams into another format to include them in your TEX documents.

*hp2xx* output comes in three flavors: scalable graphics, TEX commands, and bitmapped graphics.

### Scalable graphics

The supported scalable graphics formats are encapsulated PostScript and METAFONT source code.

### TEX commands

HPGL drawings composed of mostly straight lines can be rendered in TEX. *hp2xx*'s TEX output is designed for either the emTEX DVI drivers (it relies on \special commands to draw lines at arbitrary angles) or the *epic* macros (which also use \special commands that must be supported by your DVI driver).

### Bitmapped graphics

Bitmaps can be produced in PBM, PCX, or PCL (HP LaserJet bitmap) formats. You can select image size and resolution to produce a bitmap that will print at the correct size for your printer.

# *Image Editors*

Although many images are available on the Net and commercially, it is very likely that you will want to create your own pictures and diagrams for some of the documents that you write. A few common drawing tools are described below. Table 6-6 summarizes the packages discussed here. There are many more commercial packages for image editing—so many, in fact, that I'm not going to make any effort to describe them here.

*Table 6-6: Graphics Editing Packages*

| Program | Platforms | Cost | Purpose |
|---------|-----------|------|---------|
| *xfig* | UNIX | free | Edit scalable Fig drawings |
| *idraw* | UNIX | free | Edit encapsulated PostScript images |
| *tgif* | UNIX | free | Edit scalable drawings |
| *pixmap* | UNIX | free | Edit X11 XBM and XPM files |
| *texcad* | MS-DOS | free | Edit LATEX picture environments |
| *xtexcad* | UNIX | free | An X11 implementation of *texcad* |

## *xfig*

*xfig* is an editing tool for scalable images stored in the Fig format, described in the "Fig2MF" section of this chapter. An example of a drawing being constructed with *xfig* is shown in Figure 6-11.

The objects in Fig are arcs, circles, open and closed splines, ellipses, regular and irregular polygons, polylines, boxes, arc-boxes (boxes with rounded corners), text, and encapsulated PostScript. Compound objects can be constructed by binding these objects together.

As a consequence of Fig's device independence, it can be translated into a number of different output formats. A completed Fig drawing can be rendered in PostScript, PICTEX,

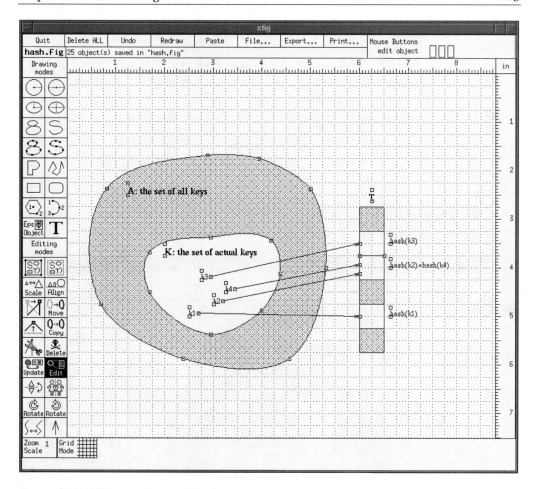

*Figure 6-11: Editing an image with xfig*

LATEX's `picture` environment, **METAFONT**, or any of the pic, epic, eepic, box, eepicemu and `\special` environments. Figures can also be saved as X11 bitmaps. Not all of the output formats support all of the features of Fig. For example, arbitrarily sloped lines are not supported by the LATEX `picture` environment, and encapsulated PostScript makes sense only for PostScript output.

*xfig* supports rotation, flipping, scaling, and duplication of objects. However, it imposes some limitations on the figures that you create. Objects that contain boxes, arc-boxes, circles, or ellipses can be rotated only in 90 degree increments. Text objects cannot be flipped over.

When objects are placed on the "canvas," you can elect to have *xfig* restrict their placement to $\frac{1}{16}$, $\frac{1}{4}$, or $\frac{1}{2}$-inch intervals. Restricted placement makes alignment of a large number of objects easier. Unrestricted placement is also allowed, and there is an alignment operator that can center (vertically and horizontally) any number of objects. A nonprinting grid is available in several sizes, independent of the restriction on object placement. In a similar way, *xfig* can be instructed to draw sloped lines within specific limits (for example, only allowing lines at slopes supported by LATEX's `picture` environment). Precise numeric-coordinate placement of individual objects is also supported.

*xfig* provides access to the standard 35 PostScript fonts as well as the standard LATEX fonts. Eight-bit input, allowing access to international symbols, is also provided.

## *idraw*

*idraw*, the InterViews drawing editor, is an X Windows application for editing encapsulated PostScript figures. Figure 6-12 shows a drawing constructed with *idraw*.

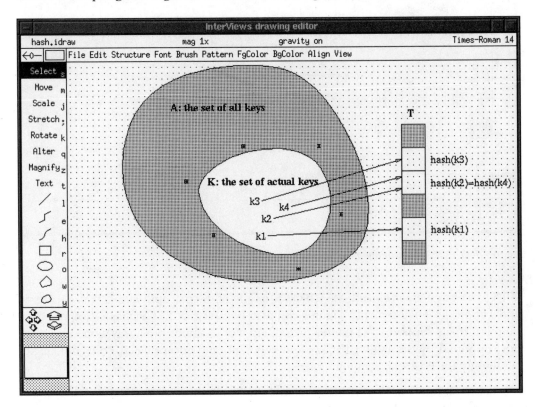

*Figure 6-12: Editing an image with idraw*

The objects in *idraw* are lines, ellipses, open and closed splines, irregular polygons, polylines, rectangles, and text. Compound objects can be constructed by gluing these objects together. Fonts, brushes, and patterns can be customized and extended with X-defaults. *idraw* supports the full complement of rotation, flip, scale, and duplicate operations with or without grid lines and optional gravity.

Unfortunately, the "gravity" option, which allows you to create horizontally and vertically aligned objects, is not preserved when a file is saved. It is very difficult to recover the alignment of a file when it has been saved and reloaded.

Graphics in TIFF, encapsulated PostScript, X11 bitmap format, and Unidraw format can be imported into *idraw* figures.

## *tgif*

*tgif*, like *xfig* and *idraw*, is an editor for scalable drawings. The "gif" in *tgif* has nothing to do with the bitmap GIF format. The captured screen in Figure 6-13 shows a drawing being constructed with *tgif*.

*tgif* stores objects as a set of Prolog "facts." Several programs are provided for interpretation of *tgif* objects outside of *tgif*. Only four output types are built into *tgif*: PostScript, encapsulated PostScript (EPS), X11 bitmaps, and X11 pixmaps.

*tgif* has a number of interesting features including the ability to design hierarchical drawings in either a "top down" or "bottom up" manner, and the separation of an object's *representation* from its *instantiation*. In addition, arbitrary text-based attributes can be attached to each object. *tgif* uses these attributes in a number of ways, such as the execution of system commands based upon object attributes.

The objects supported by *tgif* are arcs, ellipses, rectangles, rounded-corner rectangles, polylines, polygons, open and closed splines, text, X11 bitmaps, some forms of X11 pixmaps, and encapsulated PostScript. These objects can be grouped together.

*tgif* supports only five fonts (Times, Courier, Helvetica, New Century Schoolbook, and Symbol) at a few fixed sizes. The fill patterns, line styles, text-styles, and other attributes are similarly fixed (although more generous in number).

## *bitmap/pixmap*

*bitmap* and *pixmap* are standard tools distributed with the X11 Window System. The *pixmap* tool provides a superset of the functions in *bitmap*, including support for color images. An example of the *bitmap* program editing a small X icon is shown in Figure 6-14.

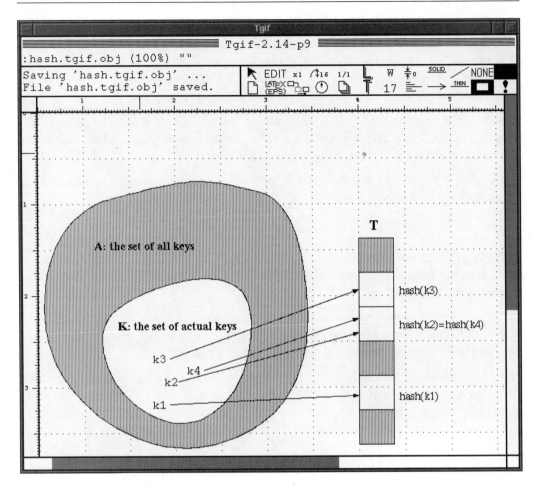

*Figure 6-13: Editing an image with tgif*

## Other Bitmap Editors

Free or inexpensive bitmap editors are available for almost every computer system. The selection of a particular package depends in large part on what kinds of diagrams you need to create.

The primary disadvantage of bitmap editing is that it is difficult to create bitmaps large enough to be used at printer resolution. Even a "full screen" image on a high-resolution monitor is only a couple of inches across (at best) on a laser printer.

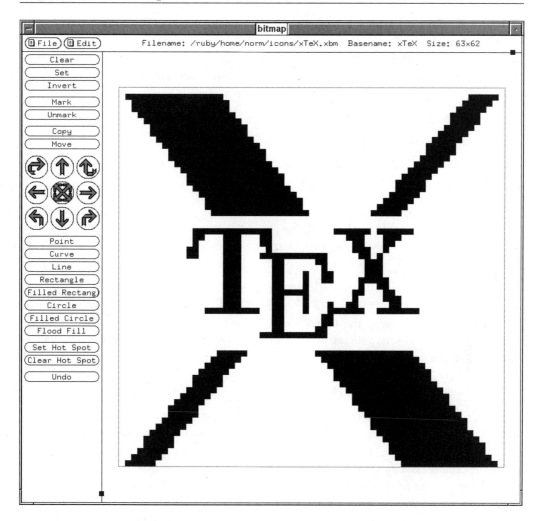

*Figure 6-14: An example of bitmap editing an icon*

## texcad/xtexcad

*texcad* is an MS-DOS program (distributed with emTeX) for editing LaTeX `picture` environments. *xtexcad* is a similar program that runs under the X11 Window system.

The LaTeX `picture` environment suffers from two limitations: it can only draw relatively simple diagrams, and it is very difficult to use. *texcad* and *xtexcad* remove the second limitation. With one of these programs, the LaTeX `picture` environment becomes a viable option for many diagrams.

# Screen Dumps

If you are writing a document that describes a computer program, it is frequently desirable to include an image of the running program (a captured screen or screen dump) in the document. There are several ways that this can be accomplished:

- *Screen Thief* for MS-DOS
- *GrabIt* for Microsoft Windows
- *xv*, *Image Magick*, or *xwd* for X11 workstations
- *PM-Cam*, *Nikon II*, or *pmjpeg* for OS/2

The captured screen may be in a graphics format that is directly usable by your DVI driver or by *bm2font*. If not, one or more of the conversion programs described in "Manipulating Images" earlier in this chapter will help you convert it into a usable format.

The most common output devices for TEX are laser printers with a resolution of 300dpi or higher. By contrast, the resolution of a typical display is around 80dpi. This discrepancy may require you to enlarge the bitmap image to make it legible in your document. For example, a 640x480 bitmap image is only about two inches wide when printed at 300dpi. In color images, *dithering*, which increases the number of dots used to represent each pixel in the original image, has a natural enlarging effect on the image, and this reduces the magnitude of the problem. However, some scaling may still be necessary.

If the screen you want to include is only text (this includes IBM's line-drawing characters and other symbols), you can include it as a special "verbatim" environment if you have an appropriate font. The advantages of this method are that the actual screen text can be incorporated directly into your document (making the document more portable and easier to distribute, if that is a concern), and that the resulting document is small and easy to print. The disadvantage of this approach is that information about color is lost. If parts of the on-screen text appear in different colors for highlighting, using a pure-text approach may not produce acceptable results. For example, compare Figure 6-15 with the results in Figure 2-2 in Chapter 2, *Editing*.

To insert pure-text screen captures, you have to have a font with exactly the same encoding as the text on the screen (for more information about font encodings, see the section "Encoding Vectors" in Chapter 5, *Fonts*). On MS-DOS and OS/2 PCs, this is sometimes a problem because the IBM line drawing characters do not appear in most fonts. Several commercial fonts provide the appropriate character set, but so do the freely available IBM Courier fonts (distributed by IBM for the X11 Consortium). The IBM Courier fonts are PostScript Type 1 fonts. If you need TEX PK fonts, use the *ps2pk* program as described in the section called "PostScript Type 1 Fonts" in Chapter 5.

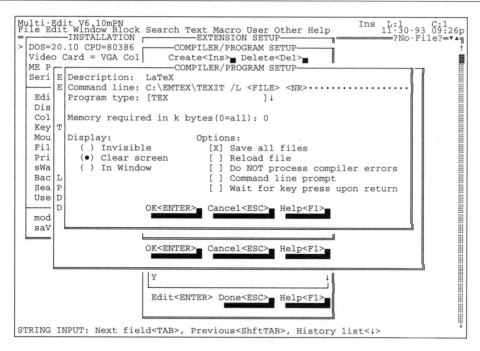

```
Multi-Edit V6.10mPN                                    Ins  L:1    C:1
File Edit Window Block Search Text Macro User Other Help      11-30-93 09:26p
=─────INSTALLATION ┌──────EXTENSION SETUP─────┐ ═══════════?No-File?=▼▲┓
> DOS=20.10 CPU=80386 ┌──────COMPILER/PROGRAM SETUP──────┐              ↑
  Video Card = VGA Col│   Create<Ins>▪ Delete<Del>▪      │              ▓
  ME P┌──────────────────COMPILER/PROGRAM SETUP──────────────┐
  Seri│E│Description:  LaTeX                                  │
  ────│E│Command line: C:\EMTEX\TEXIT /L <FILE> <NR>·········│·
  Edi │ │Program type: [TEX                 ]↓              │
  Dis │ │                                                    │
  Col │ │Memory required in k bytes(0=all): 0                │
  Key │T│                                                    │
  Mou │ │Display:                Options:                    │
  Fil │ │  ( ) Invisible         [X] Save all files          │
  Pri │ │  (●) Clear screen      [ ] Reload file             │
  sWa │ │  ( ) In Window         [ ] Do NOT process compiler errors │
  Bac │L│                        [ ] Command line prompt     │
  Sea │P│                        [ ] Wait for key press upon return │
  Use │D│                                                    │
  ────│D│        OK<ENTER>▪  Cancel<ESC>▪  Help<F1>▪         │
  mod │ │        ████████    █████████      ███████          │
  saV └─┴────────────────────────────────────────────────┘
      └──────────────────────────────────────────────────┐
              OK<ENTER>▪  Cancel<ESC>▪  Help<F1>▪         │
              ████████    █████████      ███████          │
          └──┬───────────────────────────────────────────┘
             │Y                                     ↓
             │    Edit<ENTER> Done<ESC>▪  Help<F1>▪ │
             │    ████████    █████████   ███████   │
             └─────────────────────────────────────┘
STRING INPUT: Next field<TAB>, Previous<ShftTAB>, History list<↕>
```

*Figure 6-15: A text mode screen dump.*

To use the IBM Courier fonts to print captured screens, you will need AFM files that have the correct encoding vector. AFM files with the IBM OEM character set encoding are available from the CTAN archives in the directory *fonts/courier*.

After the appropriate font is available, you are almost ready to reproduce a captured screen. One problem remains: TEX cannot \input binary files. Because screen dumps frequently contain characters from outside the normal ASCII range, they must be considered binary in this context. To overcome this difficulty, it is necessary to process the screen dump and convert it into a text file. The *Perl* script in Example D-8 in Appendix D, *Long Examples*, will perform this conversion.

After conversion, the TEX code shown in Example 6-9 will insert the screen. This code will work in both Plain TEX and LATEX. Similar code can be written for other formats. Figure 6-15 was produced with this code.

*Example 6-9: Script for Inserting a Captured Text Screen*

```
% use any IBM OEM encoded fixed width font!
\font\screenfont=ncrr-ibm at 7pt
%%%%%%%%%%%%%%%%%%%%%%%%%%%%%%%%%%%%%%%%%%%%%%%%%%%%%%%%%%%%%%%%%%%%%%%
% These macros are derived from The TeXbook pg 380-381
\def\uncatcodespecials{\def\do##1{\catcode`##1=12 }\dospecials}
```

*Example 6-9: Script for Inserting a Captured Text Screen (continued)*

```
\def\setupverbatim{\screenfont%
  \def\par{\leavevmode\endgraf\relax}%
  \obeylines\uncatcodespecials%
  \catcode`\\=0\catcode`\{=1\catcode`\}=2\obeyspaces}
{\obeyspaces\global\let =\ } % let active space be a control space
\def\screenlisting#1{\par\begingroup%
  \def\c##1{\char##1}\setupverbatim\input{#1}%
  \endgroup}
%%%%%%%%%%%%%%%%%%%%%%%%%%%%%%%%%%%%%%%%%%%%%%%%%%%%%%%%%%%%%%%%%%%%%%%%
\def\screenbox#1{%
  \vbox{\offinterlineskip%
    \parskip=0pt\parindent=0pt%
    \screenlisting{#1}}}
%%%%%%%%%%%%%%%%%%%%%%%%%%%%%%%%%%%%%%%%%%%%%%%%%%%%%%%%%%%%%%%%%%%%%%%%
% Input converted file `#1' and set it inside a box with `#2' padding
% space around the image.
\def\screendump#1#2{%
  \hbox{\vrule%
    \vbox{\hrule%
      \hbox{\hskip#2%
        \vbox{\vskip#2%
          \def\twentyxs{xxxxxxxxxxxxxxxxxxxx}%
    \setbox0=\hbox{\screenfont\twentyxs\twentyxs\twentyxs\twentyxs}%
          \hbox to \wd0{\screenbox{#1}\hss}%
        \vskip#2}%
      \hskip#2}%
    \hrule}%
  \vrule\hss}}
```

7

# *International Considerations*

Although the standard TEX macro packages and the Computer Modern fonts were designed to typeset documents written primarily in English, TEX enjoys widespread international use.

From a technical standpoint, languages can be divided into two categories: those that are "like English" (meaning that they use a relatively small number of characters and are typeset horizontally, left to right) and those that are not. German, French, and Russian are all "like English" in this sense. Hebrew, Chinese, and Japanese are not (Hebrew is typeset right to left, and Chinese and Japanese use thousands of characters).*

This chapter explores some of the issues that arise when TEX is used to typeset languages other than English. For simplicity, we'll look at languages like English first, and then describe some environments for typesetting much more complex languages.

## *Typesetting in Any Language*

In order to typeset any language with TEX, three things have to happen:

1.  TEX has to read the input file and perform the correct mapping from the input file's character set to its internal representation of each character. The character set used in the input file will vary depending upon the language. For instance, if you're writing a document in French, it is as natural to use "é" in your input file as it is to use any other letter.

---

*Chinese and Japanese are also typeset vertically. At present, TEX does not support vertical typesetting, although there is at least one effort underway to provide that feature. See the section called "ASCII Nihongo TEX" for more information on vertical typesetting.

2. TEX has to typeset the document according to the rules of the language being used. Naturally, this means that there must be some way of declaring what language is being used, and appropriate macros have to exist to embody the rules of that language. Users familiar only with English may not recognize the importance of language-specific rules because English has so few rules. Other languages have many. In German, for example, if the consonants "ck" in a word are broken by a hyphen, the "c" becomes a "k" ("k-k"). In French, small amounts of extra space are placed around various punctuation marks.

   A good reference manual for internationalization is *Software Internationalization and Localization: An Introduction* [56].

3. The DVI file that results from typesetting the document must be printed correctly. In other words, all of the accented characters and symbols used by the language must be available (or constructed) for previewing and printing.

Early attempts to write documents in languages other than English were hampered by several limitations in the TEX program. In particular, fonts were limited to 128 characters, and only a single set of hyphenation patterns could be loaded (effectively preventing multilingual documents from being hyphenated correctly). These technical problems were corrected in TEX version 3.x (first released in 1990). The remaining difficulties—mostly a lack of standardization and the need to develop relevant language-specific macros—are being addressed by the TUG Technical Working Group on Multiple Language Coordination (TWGMLC).

## Reading Input Files

The first point to consider when typesetting is that every input file is written in some character set. For example, because this book is written in English and I work in the United States, the source code for this book is written in 7-bit ASCII. If this book were written in another language, a different character set, perhaps ISO Latin1, would be more appropriate.

When TEX reads your input file, characters like "é" and "«" have to be translated into a form that TEX can use. For example, "é" should be translated into \´e and, if the DC fonts are in use, "«" should be translated into character 19; otherwise, if the DC fonts are not in use, "«" should be translated into $<<$ which will give the approximate result. The DC fonts are discussed in the section called "Printing the Result," later in this chapter.

It is always possible to access characters from another symbol set by using a control sequence. Table 7-1 shows the standard TEX control sequences for accessing accented characters and characters from other alphabets.*

---

*The accent macros are shown with a lower case e; naturally, any letter that needs to be accented can be used in place of the e.

*Table 7-1: Standard Control Sequences for Symbols from Other Character Sets*

| Control Sequence | Symbol | Control Sequence | Symbol |
|---|---|---|---|
| \`e | è | \oe | œ |
| \'e | é | \ae | æ |
| \"e | ë | \o | ø |
| \u{e} | ĕ | \aa | å |
| \.e | e̥ | \l | ł |
| \t{ee} | e͡e | \OE | Œ |
| \d{e} | ẹ | \AE | Æ |
| \H{e} | e̋ | \O | Ø |
| \^e | ê | \AA | Å |
| \v{e} | ě | \L | Ł |
| \=e | ē | ?` | ¿ |
| \~e | ẽ | !` | ¡ |
| \c{e} | ȩ | \ss | ß |
| \b{e} | e̠ | | |

Table 7-2 shows new control sequences proposed by the TWGMLC for characters not available in standard TEX and LATEX distributions.[*]

*Table 7-2: New Control Sequences Proposed by TWGMLC*

| Control Sequences | | Symbols | | Description |
|---|---|---|---|---|
| ,, | `` | „ | " | German quotations („Gänsefüßchen") |
| << | >> | « | » | French quotations (guillemets) |
| \dh | \DH | ð | Ð | Icelandic eth |
| \dj | \DJ | đ | Ð | Serbocroation dj |
| \ng | \NG | ŋ | Ŋ | Sami ng |
| \th | \TH | þ | Þ | Icelandic thorn |
| \k e | | ę | | Polish ogonek subscript |
| \r u | | ů | | Czech circle accent |
| \v{d} | \V{D} | ď | Ď | Czech d and D with haček |
| \v{l} | \V{l} | ľ | Ľ | Slovakian l and L with haček |
| \v{t} | \V{T} | ť | Ť | Czech t and T with haček |

The only technical problem associated with using language-specific character sets in your input files is that you must have some way of telling TEX to perform the appropriate substitutions. One method is to use a special style file like *isolatin1*.[†] This style uses

---

[*]These characters are available in the DC fonts and were not previously available in standard TEX.
[†] *isolatin1.sty* is available from the CTAN archives in *macros/latex/contrib/misc/*.

"active characters" to map the ISO Latin1 input character set to TEX's representation. It could be adapted to other character sets as well. Another possibility is to rely on system-dependent extensions to TEX. For example, emTEX provides extensive support for "code pages," which address this problem.

The only other problem created by using different input character sets is one of compatibility. If you write files using the ISO Latin1 character set and send them to someone who uses a different character set, the file will appear to be incorrect.[*]

### Appearances can be deceiving

A document stored on disk is really just a file containing a series of characters, each represented by a unique numerical value. For an editor to display a document, each numerical value must be translated into a visual representation of the character. Frequently this translation is performed by the operating system or computer hardware. In an analogous way, each numeric value must be translated into a printable character when the document is typeset.

Figure 7-1 shows how this translation is performed for display by the operating system and for printing by TEX (using the *isolatin1* style, for example). This figure shows the disparity that occurs if the two translation tables are not the same.

How can this arise? Well, suppose, for example, that a colleague is writing a document in French. He has a TEXnical problem that he would like me to investigate. I agree to take a look, and he sends the file to me. My colleague is using the ISO Latin1 character set in his input file because it contains many symbols that are convenient for writing French (including the guillemets). I receive the file and edit it on my PC. The file that I see displayed looks like gibberish. That's because I'm using the IBM OEM encoding on my PC, which is sufficient for English. All of the special characters in the ISO Latin1 character set appear incorrect. Bewildered, I TEX and preview the document to see what it's supposed to look like. To my surprise, the previewed document looks fine.

In this case, I can correct the problem by changing the "code page" used on my PC or by translating the input file with a program like GNU *recode*.[†]

## Changing the Rules

In order to select languages, the TWGMLC has proposed a set of language switching macros. These are shown in Table 7-3.[‡]

---

[*] If you use electronic mail to send files that use any characters other than the printable subset of 7-bit ASCII (space through tilde), you are bound to run into problems. You can combat this problem by using a wrapper (like uuencoding or MIME messages) when you send the mail, but those tools are outside the scope of this book. Ask your system administrator for more assistance with sending binary mail.

[†] *recode* is available from `prep.ai.mit.edu` and other places where GNU software is archived.

[‡] These are "low-level" macros. A higher-level interface will be provided for each language. See the section called "The Babel Styles" later in this chapter for more information.

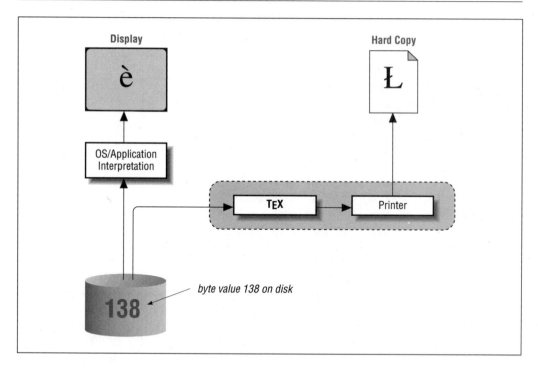

*Figure 7-1: Character mapping example*

Selecting a language has three effects:

- It establishes the correct hyphenation environment.

    Language-specific hyphenation patterns are loaded, if necessary, and correct values for the minimum length of a hyphenated word fragment are set.

    At the time of this writing, hyphenation patterns are already available, or under development, for Armenian, Bulgarian, Cambodian, Catalan, Croation, Czech, Danish, Dutch, English (U.K. and U.S.), Esperanto, Estonian, Finnish, French, German, Greek (both modern and ancient), Hungarian, Icelandic, Italian, Kirundi, Latin, Lithuanian, Norwegian, Polish, Portuguese, Russian, Slovak, Swahili, Swedish, Yiddish, and Yoruba.

- It loads the correct fonts and special characters.

    Even languages which use the same alphabet may have different fonts in order to provide specific features of the language. For example, the "fi" ligature makes sense only when typesetting English, and the \th and \TH macros make sense only when typesetting languages that need "þ" and "Þ."

*Table 7-3: Language Switch Macros Proposed by TUG*

| Macro Switch | Language | Macro Switch | Language | Macro Switch | Language | Macro Switch | Language |
|---|---|---|---|---|---|---|---|
| \AB | Abkhazian | \FY | Frisian | \MG | Malagasy | \SB | Sorbian |
| \OM | Afan Oromo | \GL | Galician | \ML | Malayalam | \ES | Spanish |
| \FF | Afar | \KA | Georgian | \MS | Malay | \SU | Sudanese |
| \AF | Afrikaans | \DE | German | \MT | Maltese | \SW | Swahili |
| \SQ | Albanian | \EL | Greek | \MI | Maori | \SV | Swedish |
| \AM | Amharic | \KL | Greenlandic | \MR | Marathi | \TL | Tagalog |
| \AR | Arabic | \GN | Guarani | \MO | Moldavian | \TG | Tajik |
| \HY | Armenian | \GU | Gujarati | \NA | Nauru | \TA | Tamil |
| \AS | Assamese | \HA | Hausa | \NE | Nepali | \TT | Tatar |
| \AY | Aymara | \HE | Hebrew | \NO | Norwegian | \TE | Telugu |
| \AZ | Azerbaijani | \HI | Hindi | \OC | Occitan | \TY | Thai |
| \BA | Bashkir | \HU | Hungarian | \OR | Oriya | \BO | Tibetan |
| \EU | Basque | \IS | Icelandic | \PS | Pashto | \TI | Tigrinya |
| \BN | Bengali | \ID | Indonesian | \FA | Persian | \TO | Tonda |
| \DZ | Bhutani | \IA | Interlingua | \PL | Polish | \TS | Tsonga |
| \BH | Bihari | \IE | Interlingue | \PT | Portuguese | \TR | Turkish |
| \BI | Bislama | \IU | Inuktitut | \PA | Punjabi | \TK | Turkmen |
| \BR | Breton | \IK | Inupiak | \QU | Quechua | \TW | Twi |
| \BG | Bulgarian | \GA | Irish | \RM | Rhaeto-Roman | \GB | U.K. English |
| \MY | Burmese | \IT | Italian | \RO | Romanian | \US | U.S. English |
| \BE | Byelorussian | \JA | Japanese | \RU | Russian | \UG | Uigur |
| \KM | Cambodian | \JW | Javanese | \SE | Sami | \UK | Ukrainian |
| \CA | Catalan | \KN | Kannada | \SM | Samoan | \UR | Urdu |
| \ZH | Chinese | \KS | Kashmiri | \SG | Sangho | \UZ | Uzbek |
| \CO | Corsican | \KK | Kazakh | \GD | Scots Gaelic | \VI | Vietnamese |
| \HR | Croatian | \RW | Kinyarwanda | \SR | Serbian | \VO | Volapuk |
| \CS | Czech | \KY | Kirghiz | \ST | Sesotho | \CY | Welsh |
| \DA | Danish | \RN | Kirundi | \TN | Setswana | \WO | Wolof |
| \NL | Dutch | \KO | Korean | \SN | Shona | \XH | Xhosa |
| \EO | Esperanto | \KU | Kurdish | \SD | Sindhi | \YI | Yiddish |
| \ET | Estonian | \LO | Laothian | \SI | Singhalese | \YO | Yoruba |
| \FO | Faroese | \LV | Latvian | \SS | Siswati | \ZA | Zhuang |
| \FJ | Fiji | \LN | Lingala | \SK | Slovak | \ZU | Zulu |
| \FI | Finnish | \LT | Lithuanian | \SL | Slovenian | | |
| \FR | French | \MK | Macedonian | \SO | Somali | | |

- It defines special primitive operations, if appropriate.

  For example, right-to-left typesetting primitives are necessary only for languages like Hebrew which are typeset right-to-left.

## *Printing the Result*

The Computer Modern Fonts are insufficient for typesetting languages other than English. In order to overcome this difficulty, the TEX User's Group has extended the Computer Modern encoding vector and established a new standard.

The new standard fonts are known variously as the Cork fonts, the DC fonts, and the EC fonts. These are all synonymous. The new standard was created following discussions at the TEX User's Group meeting in Cork, Ireland in 1990, hence the name Cork. The METAFONT fonts, which embody this encoding, will eventually become the EC fonts. The current versions, available now, are still being refined (in the sense that some of the letter forms are being refined; the encoding will not change). These are called the DC fonts.

There is a distinction between the standard encoding vector and the METAFONT fonts that replace Computer Modern. Therefore, I will refer to the standard encoding as the "Cork Encoding" and to the METAFONT fonts as the "DC fonts".*

At the time of this writing, the DC fonts are not a complete superset of Computer Modern because the DC Math fonts have not yet been released. (The DC fonts will contain the upper-case Greek alphabet, which is currently missing from the DC fonts.) When the DC Math fonts are released, the DC fonts will be a complete superset of Computer Modern. The only apparent difference will be that the accents on the DC fonts are not at exactly the same height as the accented characters constructed with the \accent primitive using Computer Modern.[†]

The Cork Encoding is shown in Table B-3 in Appendix B, *Font Samples*. There are 255 symbols in this vector with one blank for special purposes. Unlike the Computer Modern fonts, which have different encoding vectors in some typefaces (Computer Modern Roman is not the same as Computer Modern Typewriter, for example), all of the DC fonts have the same encoding vector.

Several people have commented that the Cork Encoding suffers from a "design error" because it places characters in positions 0-31, which are frequently inaccessible in other applications, and because it places a nonstandard character at position 32, where a space usually occurs. This is not a design error. Bear in mind that the DC fonts are designed to be TEX output fonts. Font creators, working in other environments (for example,

---

[*]Because the "EC fonts" don't exist yet, I won't mention them again.

[†]Actually, the issue of accents is a difficult one. Different languages which have the same letters do not always place accents at the same height. This is yet another problem that will have to be resolved.

TrueType or PostScript) are free to divide the Cork Encoding into two separate font files and provide a virtual font for TEX that establishes the correct encoding. The motivation for putting as many symbols as possible in a single font is that TEX cannot kern across fonts.

This is not meant to imply that the DC fonts should always be virtual. In fact, the DC fonts should be the "real" fonts upon which virtual fonts are based. A virtual Computer Modern font based upon the real DC fonts is infinitely preferable to a virtual DC font built on Computer Modern because:

- You need a "real" font to make virtual fonts, and the Computer Modern fonts don't contain enough *real* characters.

- Expressing accented characters in METAFONT is much better than building accents inside a virtual font. The virtual font has less information to work with (it has only boxes).

- Different languages use accents at different heights. A simple "patch" to the METAFONT code for a real font with accents is far superior to introducing another set of virtual fonts for every language.

From a purely practical point of view, the correct way to deal with these and related problems is to use the babel style files.

## *The Babel Styles*

The babel styles are a collection of style files for LATEX that provide features for typesetting in many languages. The babel styles are compatible with Plain TEX and all versions of LATEX. (In particular, they are being adopted as the standard multilingual styles in LATEX $2_\varepsilon$ and will be the standard in LATEX3 when it is released.)

To date, babel styles exist for Catalan, Croatian, Cyrillic, Czech, Danish, Dutch, English, Esperanto, Finnish, French, Galician, German, Italian, Hungarian, Norwegian, Polish, Portuguese, Romanian, Russian, Slovak, Slovenian, Spanish, Swedish, and Turkish, as well as several dialects (American as a dialect of English, for example).

Example 7-1 shows the skeletal structure of a document using the English and French styles. Within the document, the \selectlanguage control sequence is used to switch between languages.* The language that is in effect by default is determined when the format file is created.

---

*Another control sequence, \iflanguage, is provided so that you can write macros which are sensitive to the language in use when they are expanded.

*Example 7-1: A Sample Multilingual Document Using English and French*

```
\documentstyle[english,francais]{article}
\begin{document}
This is a document which uses both English and
French. \selectlanguage{french} Mais, je ne parle plus
fran\c{c}ais. \selectlanguage{english}  So I won't try
to make this example very long.
\end{document}
```

Selecting a language automatically has the following effects:

- It selects hyphenation patterns for the language. This means that paragraphs of text will be hyphenated according to the conventions of the language in use.* Switching hyphenation patterns is possible only if the format file being used by TEX contains hyphenation rules for language.

- It automatically translates the names of all the document elements into the selected language. For example, if you insert the \tableofcontents when French is the selected language, the table of contents will be called the "Table des matières" instead of "Table of Contents."

- It alters the format of the date produced by the \today macro to fit the conventions of the selected language. In American, \today is "January 30, 1994"; in English it is "30th January 1994"; and in French it is "30 janvier 1994."

- It defines particular typing shortcuts to make writing the selected language more convenient for the typist. For example, the French style makes several punctuation characters into macros so that extra space is automatically inserted before them according to French typographic conventions.

## Building Multilingual Babel Formats

Building a multilingual format file is very much like building a format for a single language. The only difference is that instead of loading a single set of hyphenation patterns (generally from a file called *hyphen.tex*), you will need hyphenation patterns for each language that you want to use. These can be obtained from the CTAN archives in the directory *tex-archive/language/hyphenation*.

If you have a file called *hyphen.tex* on your system, rename it. This file is distributed as part of the standard TEX distribution and contains American English hyphenation patterns, so *ushyphen.tex* is an appropriate name.

Next, create a file called *language.dat* that contains one line for each language you want to use. Each line should list the language name and the file containing hyphenation

---

*Paragraphs that contain multiple languages will be hyphenated according to the rules of the language in effect when the paragraph ends.

patterns for that language. For example, an appropriate *language.dat* file for the format used to typeset Example 7-1 might contain these lines:

```
english ehyphen.tex
francais fr8hyph.tex
```

Now, proceed to construct the format file using iniTEX according to the instructions distributed with the format or by following the suggestions in Chapter 4, *Macro Packages*. When iniTEX complains that it cannot find *hyphen.tex*, provide the alternate name *babel.hyphen*. This will use *language.dat* to load the appropriate hyphenation patterns and associate them with the languages you specified.

NOTE

The first language that you list in *language.dat* will be the default language for the format file that you create.

## *TEX Pitfalls*

TEX 3.x, the Cork Encoding, and language-specific macro files are not "magic bullets" that can solve all of the problems that arise in typesetting multilingual documents or writing macros that are useful in all language contexts. Some of the deficiencies are really insoluble without changing the TEX program in ways that are not allowed by Knuth. Two such problems are mentioned here:

- The \uppercase and \lowercase primitives are problematic.

  There is a strict one-to-one mapping between lowercase and uppercase letters in TEX. Unfortunately, accented letters may require different mappings. Consider these examples:

  | | | |
  |---|---|---|
  | \"I with two dots | Ï with two dots | What you typed |
  | \"i with two dots | ï with two dots | Result of \lowercase |
  | \"\i\ with two dots | ï with two dots | Correct lowercase |

  Because no information about the accent is known, the result of passing your text to the \lowercase primitive is not correct.

  This problem can be minimized by using an input character set which contains the accented letters that you need. This allows you to establish the appropriate one-to-one relationships.

  Some of the characters chosen for the Cork encoding were driven by this weakness as well. The only reason that "SS" is a glyph is so that it can be the \uppercase character for "ß."

- TEX doesn't distinguish between a dash used in a compound word (for example, "wish-fulfillment") and a dash used for hyphenation.

This distinction isn't necessary in English because English doesn't have any end-of-word ligatures. Imagine a language where "sh" should become "x" at the end of a word.* A compound word like "push-ready" should be typeset "pux-ready" whereas a word like "pushover" should remain "push-over" if it is hyphenated across a line break.

# *Very Complex Languages*

The following sections describe TEX packages (collections of macros, fonts, and other files) that allow you to typeset languages very different from English.

## *Japanese*

Typesetting Japanese involves solving several problems. The first is the task of entering Japanese text with an editor. There are many editors on many platforms that can handle Japanese input. Although there are also established ways to romanize Japanese text so that it can be displayed on terminals that do not provide support for Japanese input, these are bound to be inconvenient for anyone seriously writing in Japanese. If you are in a position to edit Japanese text, you are probably already aware of several good editors.

The second problem is that typesetting Japanese with TEX requires many, many fonts. The fact that a single font can hold no more than 256 symbols means that dozens (perhaps hundreds) of fonts are required to represent all of the myriad symbols used in everyday Japanese writing. There are some hard-coded limits on the number of fonts that a single TEX document can use, and it is possible to bump into them pretty quickly when typesetting a language like Japanese.

Another problem is printing the output. Assembling a collection of fonts that contain high-quality glyphs for all of the necessary characters is a time consuming and potentially expensive task. At present, the freely-available fonts are of relatively low quality.

A complete discussion of these issues, and many others can be found in *Understanding Japanese Information Processing* [35].

### *ASCII Nihongo TEX*

ASCII Nihongo TEX (also known as JTEX) is a complete, Japanized version of TEX. Instead of trying to shoehorn Japanese into traditional TEX programs, all of the programs have been modified to accept files containing standard Japanese text (two bytes per character). This section describes the ASCII Corporation's version of JTEX. See the section called "NTT JTEX" for information about NTT's version of JTEX. You can get the ASCII version of JTEX from `ftp.ascii.co.jp` (133.152.1.1).

---

*This is a concocted example; to my knowledge, it doesn't actually appear in any language.

ASCII Nihongo TEX is based on TEX 2.9 and can read input files coded with JIS, Shift-JIS, EUC, and KUTEN. The DVI files produced by ASCII JTEX are not standard DVI files. In order to support the large character set for Japanese writing, the DVI files use commands that are not output by standard TEX, so many drivers do not support them. You cannot process DVI files produced by ASCII JTEX with most standard DVI drivers.

Release notes with version 1.7 of JTEX indicate that it will be the last public release of JTEX. Another product, called pTEX (for Publishing TEX) may be released at some time in the future. One advantage of pTEX will be the ability to typeset vertically.

The primary disadvantage of the JTEX system is that there are no freely-available fonts for it. The authors assume that you will be using fonts resident in your printer. You may be able to purchase Japanese fonts from some font vendors, although I've seen no detailed instructions for using them with JTEX. Other, albeit more minor, disadvantages are the need to build and maintain an entire parallel TEX distribution and the fact that standard DVI drivers cannot process JTEX DVI files.

### NTT JTEX

JTEX is a complete, Japanized version of TEX. Instead of trying to shoehorn Japanese into traditional TEX programs, all of the programs have been modified to accept files containing standard Japanese text (two bytes per character). This section describes NTT's version of JTEX. See the section called "ASCII Nihongo TEX" for information about ASCII Corporation's version of JTEX. You can get the NTT version of JTEX from `ftp.math.metro-u.ac.jp` (133.86.76.25)

NTT JTEX is based on TEX 3.14 and can read input files coded with JIS, Shift-JIS, and EUC. In addition to support for commercial Japanese fonts, NTT JTEX includes a set of fonts generated from 24x24 dot bitmaps (JIS C-6234). Unlike ASCII JTEX, NTT produces standard DVI files.

### Poor Man's Japanese TEX

Poor Man's Japanese TEX (pmJ日本語) is a freely-available Japanese typesetting system that sits on top of standard TEX. The Japanese sections of the input file must use the Shift-JIS encoding; a conversion program is supplied to convert JIS encoded input files into Shift-JIS. If you use another encoding, such as EUC, you will have to find some way to convert it into Shift-JIS before you can use pmJ日本語.

pmJ日本語 solves the font problem in a clever way: METAFONT outlines for Japanese characters are mechanically produced from freely-available bitmaps. This results in relatively low quality characters, but at least they're free!

The Paulownia Court, the opening passage from the 800-year-old novel *The Tale of the Genji*, is shown in Figure 7-2. This sample was typeset by pmJ日本語.

## The Paulownia Court

づれの御時にか、女御更衣あまたさぶら ひたまひける
中に、いとやむごとなき際に はあらぬが、すぐれて時めき
たまふありけ り。はじめより我はと思ひあがりたまへる御
方々、めざまし きものにおとしめそねみたまふ。同じほど
、それより下臈の 更衣たちは、ましてやすからず。朝夕の
宮仕につけても、人 の心をのみ動かし、恨みを負ふつもり
にやありけん、いとあ つしくなりゆき、もの心細げに里が
ちなるを、いよいよあか ずあはれなるものに思ほして、人
のそしりをもえ憚らせたま はず、世の例にもなりぬべき御
もてなしなり。上達部上人な ども、あいなく目を側めつつ
、いとまばゆき人の御おぼえな り。唐土にも、かかる事の
起りにこそ、世も乱れあしかりけ

*Figure 7-2: Poor Man's Japanese*

The pmj日本語 documentation lists the following advantages and disadvantages:

pmj日本語 Advantages

- It is available now.

- It is free.

- It works with standard TeX.

- It is device independent, but has relatively poor quality fonts. The relative lack of quality is magnified by higher resolution output devices, unfortunately.

- It uses a set of free fonts mechanically produced from bitmaps.

pmj日本語 Disadvantages

- It is somewhat crude and unlikely to be improved upon to any great extent.

- It uses low quality fonts.

- It requires a large number of fonts and as a result, lots of disk space.

- It provides no access to slanted, bold, or other Japanese type-styles.

- It cannot typeset vertically.

- It may take days to build the required fonts.

## JemTEX

JemTEX is a lot like pmJ日本語; it uses fonts constructed from a collection of 24x24 dot bitmaps. The JemTEX font maker includes a number of options for tailoring the appearance of the characters.

A sample of Japanese typeset with JemTEX is shown in Figure 7-3.

The Paulownia Court

いづれの御時にか、女御更衣あまたさぶら ひたまひける中に、いとやむごとなき際に はあらぬが、すぐれて時めきたまふありけり。はじめより我はと思ひあがりたまへる御方々、めざまし きものにおとしめそねみたまふ。同じほど、それより下臈の 更衣たちは、ましてやすからず。朝夕の宮仕につけても、人 の心をのみ動かし、恨みを負ふつもりにやありけん、いとあ つしくなりゆき、もの心細げに里がちなるを、いよいよあか ずあはれなるものに思ほして、人のそしりをもえ憚らせたま はず、世の例にもなりぬべき御もてなしなり。上達部上人など も、あいなく目を側めつつ、いとまばゆき人の御おぼえなり。唐土にも、かかる事の起りにこそ、世も乱れあしかりけ

*Figure 7-3: JemTEX sample*

JemTEX takes a very different approach to processing Japanese text. Instead of providing TEX macros to interpret two-byte Japanese symbols in the input file, JemTEX provides a preprocessor which translates the Japanese input into equivalent TEX input. The preprocessor understands EUC and Shift-JIS input files.

Using a preprocessor has several advantages:

- TEX can process the files very quickly. Because the input files are not edited by hand, they are designed to be processed quickly by TEX rather than by human eyes.

- Only the fonts that are actually used must be loaded. A system like pmJ日本語 must load all of the Japanese fonts because it does not know which ones will actually be used. JemTEX knows exactly which fonts are required for each document.

- The preprocessor can handle subtle spacing issues automatically.

- The preprocessor can provide discretionary hyphens for TEX, thereby allowing TEX to hyphenate Japanese correctly.

# *Chinese*

The general problems that apply to Japanese typesetting also apply to Chinese.

### *Poor Man's Chinese TEX*

Poor Man's Chinese TEX (pmC) is closely related to pmJ日本語. The Chinese input files should be encoded with 8-bit GB encoding (GB 2312-80). If you use another encoding, you will have to convert it into the 8-bit GB encoding before you can use pmC.

The pmC package uses the same technique as pmJ日本語 to construct Chinese fonts. The relative advantages and disadvantages of pmJ日本語 apply equally to pmC.

Two sets of Chinese characters are available: traditional and simplified. A sample of Chinese created with pmC using the traditional Chinese characters is shown in Figure 7-4. A similar example, using the simplified characters, is shown in Figure 7-5.

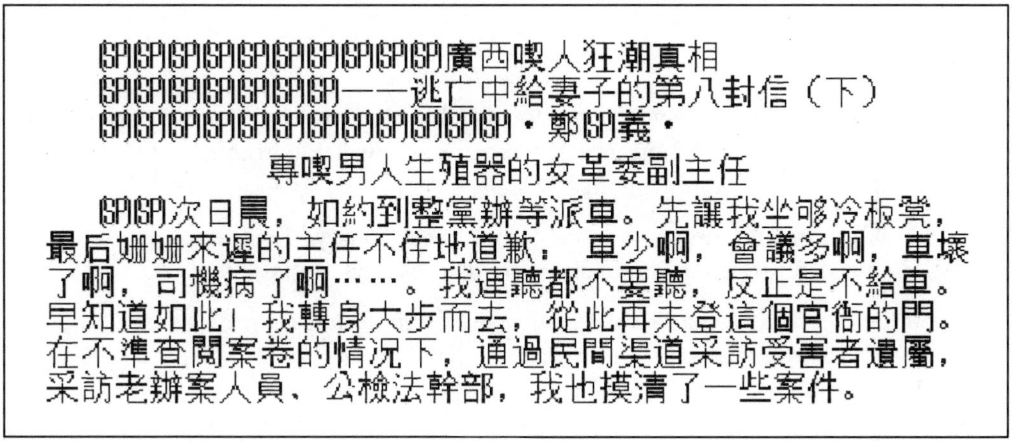

(SP)(SP)(SP)(SP)(SP)(SP)(SP)(SP)(SP)(SP)廣西喫人狂潮真相
(SP)(SP)(SP)(SP)(SP)(SP)(SP)——逃亡中給妻子的第八封信（下）
(SP)(SP)(SP)(SP)(SP)(SP)(SP)(SP)(SP)(SP)(SP)(SP)・鄭(SP)義・
專喫男人生殖器的女革委副主任
(SP)(SP)次日晨，如約到整黨辦等派車。先讓我坐够冷板凳，最后姍姍來遲的主任不住地道歉：車少啊，會議多啊，車壞了啊，司機病了啊……。我連聽都不要聽，反正是不給車。早知道如此！我轉身大步而去，從此再未登這個官衙的門。在不準查閱案卷的情況下，通過民間渠道采訪受害者遺屬，采訪老辦案人員、公檢法幹部，我也摸清了一些案件。

*Figure 7-4: Poor Man's Chinese with traditional characters*

# *Arabic*

Typesetting in Arabic can be accomplished with the ArabTEX package. ArabTEX includes a complete set of fonts and macros for producing documents in Persian, Arabic, and related scripts. An example of Arabic is shown in Figure 7-6 on page 187.

广西吃人狂潮真相
－－逃亡中给妻子的第八封信（下）
·郑　义·
专吃男人生殖器的女革委副主任
次日晨，如约到整党办等派车。先让我坐够冷板凳，
最后姗姗来迟的主任不住地道歉：车少啊，会议多啊，车坏
了啊，司机病了啊……。我连听都不要听，反正是不给车。
早知道如此！我转身大步而去，从此再未登这个官衙的门。
在不准查阅案卷的情况下，通过民间渠道采访受害者遗属，
采访老办案人员、公检法干部，我也摸清了一些案件。

*Figure 7-5: Poor Man's Chinese with simplified characters*

## Hebrew

Typesetting left-to-right Hebrew (or occasional Hebrew words in an English document) is relatively easy. The required fonts and TEX macros are available from `noa.huji.ac.il` and on the CTAN archives in *language/hebrew*.*

Typesetting right-to-left Hebrew is more complicated. First, you will need an editor that handles right-to-left text entry, preferably one that displays Hebrew text.

After you have constructed a document that uses right-to-left Hebrew, you will need a special version of TEX, called XET, to process it. XET is a version of TEX that understands right-to-left typesetting.

Early versions of XET, called TEX-XET, produced nonstandard DVI files called IVD files. If you use TEX-XET, a special program called *ivd2dvi* must be used to translate the IVD files into DVI files before they can be printed. More recently, XET has been reimplemented to produce standard DVI files. The new version is called TEX--XET.† They are functionally identical. You can get UNIX and PC versions of XET from `noa.huji.ac.il`. An example of Hebrew is shown in Figure 7-7 on page 188.

---

*At the time of this writing, the material at `noa.huji.ac.il` is more up-to-date than the material in the CTAN archives.

†Yes, the only difference between the names really is the number of hyphens!

جُحَا وَحِمَارُهُ *ğuḥā wa-ḥimāruhu*

*ʾatā ṣadīqun ʾilā ğuḥā yaṭlubu minhu ḥimārahu li-yarkabahu fī safratin qaṣīratin wa-qāla lahu:*

أَتَى صَدِيقٌ إِلَى جُحَا يَطْلُبُ مِنْهُ حِمَارَهُ لِيَرْكَبَهُ فِي سَفْرَةٍ قَصِيرَةٍ وَقَالَ لَهُ :

*sawfa ʾuʿīduhu ʾilayka fī 'l-masāʾi , wa-ʾadfaʿu laka ʾuğratan.*

سَوفَ أُعِيدُهُ إِلَيْكَ فِي المَسَاءِ ، وَأَدْفَعُ لَكَ أُجرَةً .

*fa-qāla ğuḥā:*

فَقَالَ جُحَا :

*ʾanā ʾāsifun ğiddan ʾannī lā ʾastaṭīʿu ʾan ʾuḥaqqiqa laka rağbataka, fa-'lḥimāru laysa hunā 'l-yawma.*

أَنَا آسِفٌ جِدًّا أَنِّي لَا أَسْتَطِيعُ أَن أُحَقِّقَ لَكَ رَغْبَتَكَ ، فَالحِمَارُ لَيسَ هُنَا اليَومَ .

*wa-qabla ʾan yutimmu ğuḥā kalāmahu badaʾa 'l-ḥimāru yanhaqu fī 'ṣṭablihi.*

وَقَبَلَ أَن يُتِمَّ جُحَا كَلَامَهُ بَدَأَ الحِمَارُ يَنْهَقُ فِي اصطَبلِهِ .

*fa-qāla lahu ṣadīquhu:*

فَقَالَ لَهُ صَدِيقُهُ :

*ʾinnī ʾasmaʿu ḥimāraka yā ğuḥā yanhaqu.*

إِنِّي أَسْمَعُ حِمَارَكَ يَا جُحَا يَنْهَقُ .

*fa-qāla lahu ğuḥā:*

فَقَالَ لَهُ جُحَا :

*ğarībun ʾamruka yā ṣadīqī! ʾa-tuṣaddiqu 'l-ḥimāra wa-tukaddibunī?*

غَرِيبٌ أَمرُكَ يَا صَدِيقِي ! أَتُصَدِّقُ الحِمَارَ وَتُكَذِّبُنِي ؟

*Figure 7-6: Arabic text typeset with ArabTEX*

## 1    גם שוקולד הורג

הכרתי פעם בעל "חנות טבע" שהיה סמל לבריאות. "אני לא מעשן, לא שותה, לא נוגע
בבשר, בחמאה ובמטוגנים", אמר וגרם ללקוחותיו רגשי נחיתנות. בוקר אחד, במקום
לפגוש את פני שופעי הבריאות, ראיתי מודעת אבל על דלת חנותו הנעולה. בן 38 היה
במותו. מת בבריאות טובה. לעומתו צ'רצ'יל, שתה כמו חזיר, עישן סיגרים, מקטרות
וסיגריות, אכל כל דבר שאפשר להעלות על הדעת ומת בן 90. קצת סנילי, אך בריא
למדי.

## 2    באותו נושא

קחו תצלום של מנהיגי המדינה ואלופיה מימי תש"ח והשוו עם תצלום של מקביליהם
היום. מה ההבדל? הכרס, כמובן. קחו תצלום מלפני שנה וחצי ושימו לב מה קרה לכמה
משרינו, פקידינו וקציninו הבכירים. פניהם התעגלו, כרסיהם בין שיניהם, אחדים מהם
נראים ככדורים מתגלגלים.

חומר למחשבה: אם להשתעבד לתאוות בשרים, האם לא עדיפה השיטה הבריטית
הבלתי משמינה - אשה מהצד?

חלק ממאמר של יואל מרקוס: "6 הערות על המצב", **הארץ** 18.2.94

*Figure 7-7: Hebrew*

8

# *Printing*

The emphasis in this book so far has been on getting TEX to process a document that contains all the desired typographic elements without error. The result of this effort is a DVI file.

The next step is translating the DVI file into a printed document. That is the focus of this chapter. Usually, you want to preview a document before you print it, but in many ways previewers are just a special kind of printer. The two do differ significantly, however, so we will discuss them separately. (Chapter 9, *Previewing*, describes previewers.)

This chapter explores the issues related to printing a DVI file. There are sections concerning the printing of fonts, the printing of pictures and figures, and descriptions of several kinds of drivers you can use to print TEX documents.

## *Printing Fonts*

If you have a TFM file for a font, you can use that font in TEX. In fact, you can use that font at an arbitrary magnification in TEX, which means that you can use Courier at 13.4pt as easily as Computer Modern Roman at 10pt. Unfortunately, this ease of use does not imply that the resulting DVI file will be easy to print. It doesn't even imply that it will be possible to print the document. For example, if you request Courier at 13.4pt, but it is available in your printer only at 10pt and 12pt (and you have no other source for Courier), there is no way to print your document without distortion.

This section discusses the issues involved in getting the desired fonts to print from your DVI file. Both bitmapped and scalable fonts are considered, as well as fonts built into the printer. You will also gain a better understanding of why some documents do not print, and learn alternatives that may enable you to print your documents.

Every font can be classified in two broad, independent ways: internal versus external, and scalable versus bitmapped. Each class of fonts has some advantages and some unique problems. In general, there are more restrictions on built-in fonts than on external fonts, and more restrictions on bitmapped fonts than on scalable fonts.

## Built-in Fonts

Built-in fonts, whether scalable or bitmapped, pose two problems. First, you must obtain the appropriate TFM files. Usually, the metric information has to be supplied by the vendor and then translated into TEX TFM format using a conversion tool. No vendor that I am aware of distributes TEX metric information directly. The section called "Where Do TFM Files Come From?" in Chapter 5, *Fonts*, describes several options for obtaining metric information for built-in fonts.

The second problem is that the DVI driver you are using must "know" somehow that the TFM file corresponds to one of the printer's internal fonts. When the DVI driver examines the DVI file, the only information available about each font is the name of the TFM file that describes its metrics. The most common way DVI drivers handle this problem is with a font translation file or a font substitution file.

### Font substitution in emTEX

emTEX's DVI driver reads a user-specified font substitution file before processing the DVI file. A line like the following in the font substitution file informs the *dvihplj* driver that *lpr1610u* is an internal font and describes the LaserJet control sequence required to select it:

```
lpr1610u 300 => pcl: 10U s0P s16.66H s8.5V s0S s0B s0T
```

Other substitutions are also possible. For example, if you work with documents that come from other systems that allow long filenames, you can substitute the long names for shorter filenames that are legal under MS-DOS. The following line in a font substitution file tells emTEX that the font "tmsrmn" should be used anywhere that a DVI file uses the font "Times-Roman":

```
Times-Roman -> tmsrmn
```

You can use even more sophisticated substitutions, including pattern matching, for example. Consult *The emTEX DVI Driver Manual* [36] for more information.

### Font substitution in dvips

The *dvips* program, which translates DVI files into PostScript, also reads a font substitution file before processing a DVI file. In addition to identifying which fonts are built into the printer, the substitution file can also instruct *dvips* to download PostScript fonts that are not resident in your printer if they are used in a document.

*dvips* has a system-wide font substitution file called *psfonts.map*. This file is distributed with *dvips* and can be customized by your system administrator. You can tell *dvips* to load a personal font substitution file by using the *p* command in *dvips*'s initialization file (called *.dvipsrc* in your home directory on UNIX systems). Consult the *dvips* documentation for more information about setting up an initialization file.

The following lines in a font substitution file indicate that the font *grbk* (which is the name of the TFM file) corresponds to the built-in printer font Garamond-Book. The TFM file *hlvcd* corresponds to the printer font Helvetica-Condensed. Helvetica-Condensed is not built into the printer but is stored in the file */home/walsh/fonts/helvcd.pfb*. If *hlvcd* is used in a document, *dvips* will download *helvcd.pfb* automatically when it converts the document.

```
grbk   Garamond-Book
hlvcd  Helvetica-Condensed </home/walsh/fonts/helvcd.pfb
```

### Font substitution in other drivers

Other DVI drivers, particularly those written for operating environments like Microsoft Windows that provide a standard interface to printers, may leave the distinction between built-in and external fonts up to the operating environment. If this is the case, you must use the tools provided by the operating system to support the printers and fonts that you require.

If your DVI driver does use a font substitution file, make sure that the translations specified actually exist. The DVI driver cannot practically determine if the font you have specified as built into the printer really exists or not. If it doesn't, you won't get the output you expect, and the DVI driver will not be able to diagnose the problem.

The most significant disadvantage of using built-in fonts is that they are not usually available for on-screen previewing of your document. Some form of font substitution has to be employed to preview a document. Sometimes this reduces the utility of on-screen previewing. Chapter 9, *Previewing,* discusses this issue in more detail.

## External Fonts

External fonts, those that aren't built into the printer, pose a different set of problems. First, they have to be available to the DVI driver, and they have to be represented in a manner that the DVI driver understands. For the vast majority of DVI drivers, this means that the fonts must be stored in files on your hard disk in PK format. The PK files contain a compressed, bitmapped rendering of the font at a particular resolution. For more information about PK files and other bitmapped-font issues, see "Bitmapped Fonts" later in this chapter.

Most DVI drivers locate fonts by searching in the directories contained in an environment variable or in some system-dependent locations.

Once the fonts are available, the DVI driver has two options for using them: it can download them to the printer, or it can send them as bitmapped graphic images. Most laser printers can accept downloadable fonts, although they may require additional memory to accept large numbers of fonts. In either case, the printable files are generally larger and print more slowly than documents that use the printer's built-in fonts. Of course, using external fonts does give you far more flexibility than using only built-in fonts.

Unlike a missing internal font, if you attempt to use an external font that is not available, your DVI driver will be able to detect the problem and may be able to substitute another font or compensate in some other way.

---

## Increasing Printing Speed

How can you increase printing speed if you frequently print, on a laser printer, documents that use a small number of external fonts (for example, several sizes of Computer Modern)? A handy trick is to download the fonts manually and then tell the DVI driver that the fonts are built-in.

Suppose you use the 7pt, 10pt, and 12pt sizes of Computer Modern Roman, and the 12pt and 14pt sizes of Computer Modern Bold Extended in most of your documents. If you are printing on an HP LaserJet printer with emTEX's *dvihplj*, you could convert the relevant PK files into HP LaserJet softfonts with *PKtoSFP* (see the discussion of bitmapped fonts in the next section to determine which PK files are relevant). Then download them to the printer every morning with a utility like *Sfload*. *Sfload* is part of the *Sfware* package. (Disclaimer: I wrote *Sfware* so I'm partial to it. There are many other programs that can download softfonts.) In the font-substitution file for *dvihplj*, simply indicate that those fonts are built-in, and *dvihplj* will no longer download them for each document. This can significantly decrease the amount of data that must be sent to the printer for each document.

Beware, however, that if you fail to download the fonts, you will get very badly garbled output when you print a document.

---

## Bitmapped Fonts

Each character in a bitmapped font is represented by a rectangular array of dots. Some of the dots in this array are "on," and some are "off." When the dots are printed very close together, they provide the illusion of a solid character. Bitmapped fonts are common in the TEX community because all of the fonts created by METAFONT are printed in bitmapped form.

The notion of magnification discussed in the section called "The Issue of Size" in Chapter 5 is interpreted as an issue of resolution when dealing with bitmapped fonts.

Resolution is used in a slightly counter-intuitive way by DVI drivers. Generally, resolution is described as a feature of a device that affects the *appearance* of images printed on that device and not their *size*. For example, in comparing two drawings in which one was printed on 150dpi dot-matrix printer and the other was printed on a 300dpi laser printer, I might say, "the laser printed page looks better because it was printed at a higher resolution."

That's true, but what isn't usually stated explicitly is that the comparison is between a 150dpi drawing rendered at 150dpi and a 300dpi drawing rendered at 300dpi. This is the situation shown in Figure 8-1 where a 4dpi image is printed at 4dpi next to an 8dpi image printed at 8dpi.

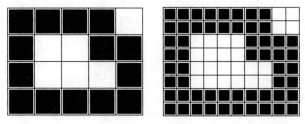

*Figure 8-1: Resolution of the bitmap and the device changed simultaneously*

What if the resolution of the printer were held constant? That's the situation shown in Figure 8-2. The 4dpi image printed at 4dpi is shown next to the 8dpi image printed at 4dpi. The result is that the size of the image is doubled.

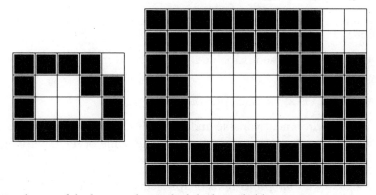

*Figure 8-2: Resolution of the bitmap changed while device held constant*

This is the technique that DVI drivers use to print a larger magnification of the same font; they print a version of the font designed for a correspondingly higher-resolution device. The same technique is used to print at smaller magnifications.

Most DVI drivers use bitmapped fonts stored in PK files. The PK format is a highly compressed binary format.* Two other bitmapped font formats (sometimes accepted by DVI drivers) are associated with TEX: GF and PXL files. The GF format is a very flat, uncompressed bitmap format produced by several utility programs, including METAFONT. The *GFtoPK* program converts GF files into PK files. The PXL format is an uncompressed bitmap format; it has been superseded by the PK format (which achieves better compression) and is completely obsolete. If you still have PXL files, you should convert them to PK format with the *PXtoPK* utility. If you are using a DVI driver that still requires PXL files, you should find out about an upgrade; the program is obsolete.

The fact that DVI drivers use different resolutions of the same font file to obtain different magnifications introduces a naming problem. How can the DVI driver distinguish between *cmr12.pk* at 300dpi and *cmr12.pk* at 360dpi (or any other resolution)?

On UNIX systems, this problem is usually resolved by putting the resolution in the filename in front of the extension *pk*. For example, *cmr12.300pk* is *cmr12* at 300dpi while *cmr12.360pk* is *cmr12* at 360dpi.

On many other systems, where the operating system imposes limits on the length of filenames, a solution is achieved by storing the fonts in different subdirectories. On MS-DOS, for example, the 300dpi version of *cmr12* might be stored in *\texfonts\300dpi\cmr12.pk* while the 360dpi version is stored in *\texfonts\360dpi\cmr12.pk.*

In either case, you should obey the conventions specified by your DVI driver to assure that the DVI driver can find the fonts. One common solution to the problem of finding fonts is to use an environment variable to list the directories where PK files occur. For example, on a UNIX system, the environment variable TEXPKS might hold a list of directories separated by colons:†

```
TEXPKS=/usr/local/lib/tex/fonts:/usr/local/lib/tex/fonts/pk:\
/usr/local/lib/mf/fonts:/usr/local/lib/mf/fonts/pk
```

Under MS-DOS, the environment variable DVIDRVFONTS might hold a list of directories separated by semicolons:

```
DVIDRVFONTS=C:\TEXFONTS;C:\MYFONTS
```

The format of the environment variable and how it is created or modified is determined by the operating environment that you are using. The name of the environment variable differs according to the DVI driver.

To recap, TEX works with *magnifications* of abstract, scalable measurements; DVI drivers work with *resolutions* of fixed, bitmapped images.

---

*For a complete, detailed description of the PK and GF formats, consult *The GF to PK Processor* [24].
†A backslash is used here to escape the end of the first line. This is a standard way to continue a line in most UNIX shells. Naturally, you can simply enter it as one line in your editor, if you prefer.

To convert a magnification into a resolution, multiply the resolution of your output device by the magnification. A font at a magnification of 120% on a 300dpi laser printer has a resolution of 360dpi.

To convert a resolution into a magnification, divide the font resolution by the resolution of the printer. A 420dpi font on a 300dpi laser printer has a magnification of 140%.

## Scalable Fonts

Although scalable fonts used to be very uncommon, the proliferation of PostScript printers and products like Adobe Type Manager (not to mention built-in support for TrueType fonts in Apple System 7.0 and Microsoft Windows 3.1) have made these fonts very common. It is important to remember that scalable fonts are ultimately converted into bitmapped fonts. All printers eventually treat the page as a very large bitmap and either do or do not deposit a small amount of ink in each position in the bitmap.

Most DVI drivers leave the work of performing this rasterization to someone else. If you are not using a PostScript printer, you probably rely on some other piece of software to do the work. Adobe Type Manager and built-in support for TrueType are the most common software solutions. Some printers, like the LaserJet III, have built-in scalable fonts as well, even though they are not PostScript printers.

## Font Printing Pitfalls

Sometimes you need a font at a size that is not available. Because scalable fonts are available at any size, this is a problem only with bitmapped fonts. Remember that META-FONT creates bitmapped fonts, but they can be scaled because the MF source for the font is not a bitmap. You can't scale the PK file, but you can generate a new PK file at the size you need. In order to do this, you must have METAFONT installed, and you must have the MF source for the font. Chapter 11, *Introducing METAFONT*, describes how to create a METAFONT font at any size.

If the font isn't a METAFONT font, or you don't have the MF source, you may still be able to scale the font. However, you should be aware before you try that the result may be unacceptable. Scaling bitmapped fonts causes ugly, jagged edges if the font is scaled larger, and loss of detail if it is scaled smaller. Small changes in size are sometimes manageable.

The *dvips* driver will scale bitmapped fonts if it cannot find or build the requested font. Alternatively, the *sffx* program can scale HP LaserJet softfonts. I don't know of any other scaling options.

Non-scalable fonts that are built into the printer cannot be scaled at all. If you need to have a built-in font at an unavailable size, you will have to substitute another font in place of the built-in one.

# *Printing Pictures and Figures*

Pictures and figures are frequently the least portable elements of a document. Chapter 6, *Pictures and Figures*, describes many of the options that are available for including pictures and figures in a document.

If the method used is supported by the DVI driver and printer that you use, pictures and figures are transparently printed. They are even less difficult to print than fonts. On the other hand, if you are attempting to print a document which incorporates pictures and figures using a method not supported by your DVI driver or printer, it may be exceptionally difficult to print the document.

## *Unsolvable Problems*

DVI files are not always "complete" with respect to pictures and figures. Many documents use \special commands to access DVI driver or printer-specific features in order to include pictures and figures. These \specials may have just the name of an external file that contains the graphic image to be included. For example, using the emTEX drivers, I can include a bitmapped graphic image with the command \special{em:graph spslogo}. When emTEX's DVI drivers process this command, the graphic image in the file *spslogo.pcx* is included in the output. If I transmit this DVI file to another computer but forget to transmit the file *spslogo.pcx*, there is no way to print the DVI file with the SPS logo.

At first, it may seem that a good solution to the problem described above would be to include the actual data for the image in the \special command. But to do that, TEX would have to process the image data, defeating the purpose of the \special mechanism. The \special mechanism is better because it is open ended—it can handle new types of graphics, for example, without changing TEX.

The second, essentially unsolvable, problem involves DVI files containing \special commands that have embedded data. For example, one set of picture drawing \special commands are the tpic \specials. If your DVI driver does not understand these commands, there is no practical way to extract them from the DVI file in order to convert them into a format your DVI driver understands. There may not even be a practical way of extracting them from the TEX document to construct a printable image. You simply can't print that document with the tpic figures intact.

## *Solvable Problems*

If you have a document that includes an external picture or figure using a method that your DVI driver or printer does not understand, and you have the file that contains the graphic image and the TEX source for the document, you may be able to print it.

The section called "Manipulating Images" in Chapter 6, lists a wide variety of picture conversion tools that may allow you to convert the image into a printable form. For example, if the document in question uses a \special command to include a PCX graphic image, but your DVI driver only understands the Macintosh PICT format, you could use the *PBMplus* utilities to convert the PCX image into PICT format.

A conversion that might frequently be necessary if you work on both PostScript and non-PostScript printers is conversion from encapsulated PostScript to a bitmap format. This is a translation that *Ghostscript* or some other PostScript interpreter can perform.

## Pictures Using Only TEX

Device-independent pictures created using only TEX pose no particular printing problems. These include the LATEX picture environment, as well as the PICTEX and *Xy-pic* macro packages.

## METAFONT Figures

Pictures created with METAFONT (using *MFPic*, *Fig2MF*, or METAFONT directly) are really METAFONT fonts. As a result, they can be created for almost any raster output device.* As long as METAFONT is available and the figures aren't too large, they pose no problems. Very large images may break some DVI drivers or may not be printable on some output devices.

## Scalable Images

Scalable formats, primarily PostScript and HPGL, are difficult to convert to other printing technologies. However, the *Ghostscript* program is one option for PostScript figures, and *hp2xx* can convert a subset of HPGL commands into other formats.

## Bitmap Images

Bitmap images are generally the easiest to convert from one format to another, but there is another issue that is more difficult to deal with—resolution. Printing a bitmap image at 1200dpi if the original is only 300dpi is not easy.

# Selected Drivers

Table 8-1 lists a number of common DVI drivers used to print TEX documents (as opposed to previewing them). These drivers are discussed in more detail in this section. The list of drivers described here is nowhere near complete. The presence or absence

---

*Because figures are frequently much larger than individual characters, METAFONT may have difficulty with large figures at very high resolutions.

of a particular driver from this list is not intended as a reflection on the quality of the driver. I tried to select a representative set of free and commercial drivers. Drivers for other printers usually offer similar features.

*Table 8-1: Common DVI Drivers*

| DVI driver | Supplier | System | Printers |
|---|---|---|---|
| *dvihplj* | Free (emTEX) | | HP LaserJet compatible |
| *dvidot* | Free (emTEX) | MS-DOS+OS/2 | Most dot matrix |
| *dvipcx* | Free (emTEX) | | PCX graphic images |
| *dvilj2* | Free (*dvi2xx*) | Most | HP LaserJet compatible |
| *dvips* | Free (*dvips*) | Most | PostScript |
| *DVILASER/HP* | ArborText | MS-DOS, Unix | HP LaserJet compatible |
| *DVILASER/PS* | ArborText | MS-DOS, Unix | PostScript |
| *PTI Laser/HP* | Personal TEX | MS-DOS | HP LaserJet compatible |
| *PTI Laser/PS* | Personal TEX | MS-DOS | PostScript |
| *PTI Jet* | Personal TEX | MS-DOS | HP DeskJet compatible |
| *dvipsone* | Y&Y | MS-DOS | PostScript |

## emTEX Drivers

The emTEX distribution includes three DVI drivers: *dvihplj* for printing on HP LaserJet, DeskJet, PaintJet, QuietJet printers (as well as the Kyocera laser printer), *dvidot* for printing on a wide variety of dot-matrix printers, and *dvipcx* for translating DVI files into PCX graphics images (for faxing, for example). The printers that *dvidot* supports are listed below. If your dot-matrix printer isn't listed, detailed instructions in the emTEX documentation will probably allow you to construct an appropriate parameter file.

| | |
|---|---|
| Apple Imagewriter | IBM Proprinter 4202 |
| C.ITOH 8510A | IBM Proprinter 4207 |
| Canon Bubble Jet BJ-10e | IBM Proprinter 4208 |
| EPSON FX and RX series | NEC P6, Panasonic KX-P1124 |
| EPSON LQ series | NEC P7 |
| IBM Proprinter 4201 | Tandy DMP-130 |

All of the emTEX drivers support several \special commands for including bitmapped graphics and lines at any angle.

The Computer Modern fonts in PK format occupy several directories and considerable space on disk. To minimize the impact of keeping several magnifications of fonts around, the emTEX drivers introduced the concept of *font libraries*. Font libraries are single files that contain many, many PK fonts. The fonts distributed with emTEX are distributed in font library format. The *fontlib* program, distributed with emTEX, allows you to create and maintain font libraries of your own.

The emTEX drivers support automatic font generation starting with version 1.4S. This is accomplished by a second program, *dvidrv*, that runs the DVI driver and then *MFjob*, if required, to build the fonts. The relationship between these components is shown in Figure 8-3.

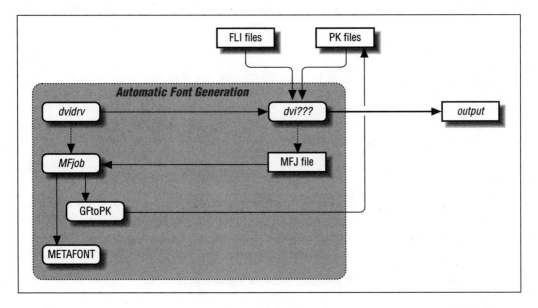

*Figure 8-3: Previewing and printing with emTEX*

Starting with version 1.4t,* emTEX's *dvihplj* supports 600dpi fonts (for the LaserJet 4 series) and built-in printer fonts.

The following list of features highlights some of the capabilities of the emTEX drivers:

- Printing of a range of pages
- Printing of multiple copies (with or without collating)
- Reverse ordering of pages
- Selection of duplex printing
- Ability to scale PK files to the requested size if an appropriate PK file is unavailable. This may result in poorer output quality due to distortion, but that's not emTEX's fault.
- Extremely flexible support for printing booklets and "n-up" arrangements of pages

---

*In alpha-testing at the time of this writing.

- Selection of paper size and dimensions (margins, etc.)

- Transformations (rotation by a multiple of 90 degrees)

- Changes in magnification and resolution of output

- Support for font libraries

- Support for font compression in printers with that feature

- Ability to download each page as a large bitmap (to overcome font limitations in some printers)

- Support for automatic font generation

## *dvilj2*

*dvilj2* is a free driver for the HP LaserJet Series II printer. It is part of the *dvi2xx* distribution, which also includes drivers for the HP LaserJet Series IIP and III printers, as well as a driver for the IBM 3812 page printer.

## *dvips*

*dvips* is one of the most popular PostScript DVI drivers. It is available for UNIX, MS-DOS, and OS/2 platforms. It may also be available on other platforms because the source code is freely available. *dvips* supports a wide range of \special commands for controlling the PostScript output, including pictures and figures and raw PostScript code.

The following list of features highlights some of *dvips*'s capabilities:

- Inclusion of printer-specific prologue files

- Support for compressed PostScript pictures and figures

- Automatic creation of pseudo-bold and pseudo-italic fonts

- Ability to run as a filter

- Automatic splitting of documents into sections to prevent out-of-memory errors on the printer

- Printing of crop marks

- Printing of a range of pages (by physical sheet or TEX page number)

- Selection of manual-feed on the printer

- Limit on number of output pages

- Reverse order of pages

- Selection of paper type

- Changes in magnification of the output

- Printing of odd/even pages only

- Printing of multiple copies (with or without collating)
- Stripping of comments (to avoid printer/spooler bugs)
- Moving of printed image left/right or up/down page
- Compression of fonts before downloading

An option to the *dvips* driver can be used to indicate which printer the output is destined for. This allows many printer-specific options (resolution, paper sizes, etc.) to be specified in a configuration file, removing from the user the burden of remembering them.

Automatic font generation is supported by *dvips*, as described above. *dvipsk*, a modified version of *dvips*, also supports a font-searching mechanism that greatly simplifies the task of specifying which directories contain font files. If any directory specification in the font path ends with two slashes, *dvips* searches that directory and all of its subdirectories for the font files. This allows you to create a font directory structure like the one shown here:

```
/usr/local/lib/tex/fonts/supplier
/usr/local/lib/tex/fonts/supplier/typeface
/usr/local/lib/tex/fonts/supplier/typeface/src
/usr/local/lib/tex/fonts/supplier/typeface/tfm
/usr/local/lib/tex/fonts/supplier/typeface/vf
/usr/local/lib/tex/fonts/supplier/typeface/vpl
/usr/local/lib/tex/fonts/supplier/typeface/glyphs
/usr/local/lib/tex/fonts/supplier/typeface/glyphs/pk
```

This arrangement is advantageous because it organizes your fonts and simplifies maintenance of the directories that contain them. If */usr/local/lib/tex/fonts//* is in the font search path, *dvips* will search through all of the font directories for the files that it needs. For example, it might find the TFM file for cmr10 in */usr/local/lib/tex/fonts/free/cm/tfm*. The directory */usr/local/lib/tex/fonts/adobe/garamond/glyphs/type1* is the location for the PostScript source of the Garamond-Italic font.

The *dvips* distribution includes the *afm2tfm* program for creating TEX font metrics from Adobe AFM files. This version of *afm2tfm* can perform several useful tasks such as automatically creating appropriate virtual fonts (for mapping TEX font encodings to PostScript encodings) or changing the encoding of the PostScript font.

## *DVILASER/HP*

ArborText's *DVILASER/HP* DVI driver translates TEX DVI files into a format that can be printed on HP LaserJet printers. These drivers are available for both MS-DOS and supported UNIX workstations. The following discussion is based on experiences with *DVILASER/HP* version 5.3.3, the MS-DOS implementation of ArborText's HP LaserJet driver.

*DVILASER/HP* functions in the way you would expect, generating LaserJet printable documents from TEX DVI files. It also has many special features. Some of the more interesting features are summarized below. *DVILASER/HP* can print documents using PK files, HP LaserJet softfonts, and built-in fonts (including fonts from cartridges).

ArborText supplies a complete set of Computer Modern fonts in PK format. Recent releases of *DVILASER/HP* can use the virtual fonts introduced in TEX version 3.0.

ArborText's *DVILASER/HP* DVI driver provides the following features:

- Selectable number of copies

- Optional reverse ordering of pages

- Selectable manual-feed

- Portrait or landscape orientation

- Selectable page size

- Ability to scale PK files to the requested size if an appropriate PK file is unavailable. This may result in poorer output quality due to distortion, but that's not *DVILASER/HP*'s fault.*

- Page movement and reordering options (for printing multiple pages on a single sheet of paper, for example)

- Configurable font substitution

- Support for LaserJet "overlays." *DVILASER/HP* recognizes \special commands for inserting raw HP LaserJet format documents and inserting HP LaserJet overlays[†]

- An interactive mode (useful for printing only selected pages from a document without re-running *DVILASER/HP* many times or when many options are going to be used)

- Selectable paper tray

Many other utilities come with *DVILASER/HP*; they are summarized in Table 8-3.

*Table 8-3: Other DVILASER/HP Utilities*

| Utility | Description |
|---------|-------------|
| *aftovp* | Converts VPL from AFM file |
| *gftopk*[1] | Converts GF files into PK files |
| *hpformat* | A print formatter for ASCII files |
| *packpxl* | Creates packed (byte-aligned) PXL file |
| *painthp* | Converts MacPaint files into HP LaserJet format |
| *pcltopk*[1] | Converts HP LaserJet softfonts into PK/TFM file |
| *pktopx*[1] | Converts PK files into PXL files |

---

*The scaling uses the next larger-sized PK file, and ArborText claims that this results in good quality over a large range of point sizes without providing PK files for every exact size.

[†]Consult your HP LaserJet reference manual for more information about overlays.

*Table 8-3: Other DVILASER/HP Utilities (continued)*

| Utility | Description |
|---|---|
| *pxtopk*[1] | Converts PXL files into PK files |
| *spr* | A serial-line print spooler |
| *tftovp* | Converts VPL from TFM file |
| *unpkpxl* | Creates standard, word-aligned PXL file |
| *vftovp*[1] | Converts VF files into VPL files |
| *vptovf*[1] | Converts VPL files into VF files |

[1]A standard, or otherwise freely available, utility.

ArborText recently released *DVILASER/HP3 drivers* for the HP LaserJet III and IV printers. In addition to the features described above, *DVILASER/HP3* supports more complex documents, compressed font downloading, 600dpi and duplex printing, paper tray and output bin selection, and the ability to include TIFF images via a \special command.

## *DVILASER/PS*

ArborText's *DVILASER/PS* DVI driver translates TEX DVI files into PostScript. These drivers are available for both MS-DOS and supported UNIX workstations. The following discussion is based on experiences with *DVILASER/PS* version 6.3.5, the MS-DOS implementation of ArborText's PostScript driver.

PostScript DVI drivers are more flexible than many other DVI drivers because PostScript is a very powerful page description language. Some of *DVILASER/PS*'s more interesting features are summarized below. *DVILASER/PS* can print documents using PK files, downloadable PostScript fonts, and built-in fonts. ArborText supplies TFM files for many built-in PostScript fonts. Recent releases of *DVILASER/PS* can use the virtual fonts introduced in TEX version 3.0.

ArborText's *DVILASER/PS* DVI driver provides the following features:

- Options for loading custom PostScript prologue code
- Ability to be used as a filter (sends PostScript code to standard output)
- Selectable number of copies
- Optional reverse ordering of pages
- Portrait or landscape orientation
- Selectable page size
- Ability to scale PK files to the requested size if an appropriate PK file is unavailable. This may result in poorer output quality due to distortion, but that's not *DVILASER/PS*'s fault.
- Page movement and reordering options (for printing multiple pages on a single sheet of paper, for example)

- Selectable paper tray

- Configurable font substitution

- Support for LaserJet "overlays"

- An interactive mode (useful for printing only selected pages from a document without re-running *DVILASER/PS* many times or when many options are going to be used)

- Ability to download PK files permanently, speeding printing of future documents

- Document, page, or encapsulated PostScript document structuring options

- Optional clipping of characters that fall outside the normally printable page area

Many other utilities come with *DVILASER/PS*. They are summarized in Table 8-4.

*Table 8-4: Other DVILASER/PS Utilities*

| Utility | Description |
|---------|-------------|
| *afmtopl* | Converts AFM files into unmapped PL files |
| *afmtoplm* | Converts AFM files into mapped PL files[2] |
| *aftovp* | Converts VPL from AFM file |
| *gftopk*[1] | Converts GF files into PK files |
| *packpxl* | Creates packed (byte-aligned) PXL file |
| *pktopx*[1] | Converts PK files into PXL files |
| *pltotf*[1] | Converts PL files into TFM files |
| *psformat* | A print formatter for ASCII files |
| *pxtopk*[1] | Converts PXL files into PK files |
| *spr* | A serial-line print spooler |
| *tftopl*[1] | Converts TFM files into PL files |
| *tftovp* | Converts VPL from TFM file |
| *unpkpxl* | Creates standard, word-aligned PXL file |
| *vftovp*[1] | Converts VF files into VPL files |
| *vptovf*[1] | Converts VPL files into VF files |

[1] A standard, or otherwise freely available, utility.

[2] Mapping changes the encoding vector of the font.

*DVILASER/PS* recognizes `\special` commands for inserting raw PostScript files and commands, encapsulated PostScript files, and automatic page overlays (which can be selectively enabled and disabled). Other `\special` commands allow you to set most of the *DVILASER/PS* command-line options directly in the document, rotate any TEX "box" to any angle, and print change bars. For LaTeX users, ArborText includes a plug-in replacement for LaTeX's picture environments that uses PostScript instead of special fonts to draw each figure.

## PTI Laser/HP and PTI Jet

*PTI Laser/HP* and *PTI Jet* are distributed together by Personal TEX, Inc. *PTI Laser/HP* is an HP LaserJet driver. *PTI Jet* is a DeskJet driver. The *PTI Jet* driver works with a standard DeskJet printer; no additional options or memory are required. The *PTI Laser/HP* driver is for HP LaserJet II and III series printers. A separate program, *PTI Laser/HP4*, is sold for LaserJet 4 series printers (to support 600dpi fonts, for example).

The following features are available in these drivers:

- Support for font substitution
- Support for built-in fonts
- Printing multiple copies of each page
- Setting page size
- Printing in landscape mode
- Selecting magnification
- Ability to print a range of pages (by physical sheet or TEX page number)
- Reversing order of pages
- Ability to move the page image left/right or up/down the page
- Support for 256 character fonts

*PTI Laser/HP* offers the following additional features, which are not supported by *PTI Jet*:

- Ability to reserve printer font ID numbers
- A utility program, *sftopk*, for converting HP LaserJet softfonts into TEX PK fonts
- Support for directly including HP LaserJet printer commands via the \special mechanism in TEX

## PTI Laser/PS

*PTI Laser/PS* is Personal TEX's PostScript DVI driver. In addition to the DVI driver, the *PTI Laser/PS* package includes utilities for spooling output to a serially-connected printer and converting AFM files into TFM files.

Some of *PTI Laser/PS*'s more interesting options are summarized below.

- Ability to select different printer resolutions
- Selectable number of copies
- Configurable font substitution
- Selectable page size

- An interactive mode for selecting options and reacting to errors (characters that fall off the page, missing fonts, etc.)

- Portrait or landscape orientation

- Selectable TEX magnification

- Option files for storing frequently used options.

- Selectable output filename

- Options to select individual pages or ranges of pages by TEX page number or physical sheet number

- Optional reverse ordering of pages

- Adjustable page offset (adjusts the position of the printed page on the physical page)

- Support for 256-character fonts

- Special support for the eccentricities of the Apple LaserWriter printer

*PTI Laser/PS* recognizes a \special command for inserting raw PostScript files into the printed document. The horizontal and vertical size of the inserted image can be changed.

## *dvipsone*

*dvipsone* is a commercial PostScript driver for MS-DOS distributed by Y&Y Inc. It produces PostScript output from a TEX DVI file. *dvipsone* is designed for a "bitmap-free" environment. This makes *dvipsone* almost unique among DVI drivers because it *cannot* use standard PK fonts. To use *dvipsone*, you must have PostScript fonts for every font that you use (or the font must be built into the printer).* Y&Y sells a complete set of Computer Modern fonts in Adobe Type 1 format.

*dvipsone* has a rich set of features:

- Printing multiple DVI files with a single command

- Printing pages in reverse order

- Printing only odd or even pages

- Ability to force output to conform to EPS standards

- Assumption that all requested fonts are printer-resident

- Insertion of verbatim PostScript

- Printing a range of pages

- Resizing of the output

- Rotation of output by arbitrary angle

---

*The *dvipsone* distribution includes a utility which can convert PK fonts into bitmapped PostScript fonts. This program translates a PK file into an Adobe Type 3 font. Once in Type 3 format, *dvipsone* can use the font. Using Type 3 fonts created in this way adds resolution-dependence to your PostScript file.

- Shifting output left/right or up/down

- Printing arbitrary number of copies

- Selection of paper type (letter, landscape, legal, etc.)

- Insertion of user-specified PostScript prologue

- Conservation of memory by downloading partial fonts

- Remapping of the font encoding on-the-fly

- Support for ten different styles of \special commands for including encapsulated PostScript images

Perhaps the most interesting feature of the *dvipsone* driver is its ability to download partial PostScript fonts. Y&Y claim that partial font downloading is a feature unique to *dvipsone*. A moderately complex TEX document may use twenty or more fonts and each font is typically between 20K and 30K. This means that the DVI driver downloads roughly 500K of font data for the document. In addition to requiring considerable printer memory, all that font data increases the amount of time that it takes to send your document to the printer. The partial font downloading feature of *dvipsone* means that only the characters that are actually used in your document are sent to the printer. The ability to download partial fonts can result in a substantially smaller PostScript file.

Several other utilities are distributed with *dvipsone*. They are summarized in Table 8-5.

*Table 8-5: Other dvipsone Utilities*

| Utility | Description |
|---------|-------------|
| *download* | Robust font-downloading program for PostScript fonts |
| *afmtotfm*[1] | Converts AFM files into TFM files |
| *tfmtoafm* | Converts TFM files into AFM files |
| *pfatopfb*[1] | Convert PFA files into PFB files |
| *pfbtopfa*[1] | Convert PFB files into PFA files |
| *twoup* | Reorders pages in a PostScript file |
| *pktops* | Provides access to PK fonts for *dvipsone* |

[1] A standard, or otherwise freely available, utility.

# 9

# *Previewing*

Because TEX is not interactive, most TEX documents are developed iteratively. After adding a significant amount of text or changing the format of a document, you'll want to see what the document looks like. Then you can add more text or try different formats. Then, it's helpful to see it again . . .

You could print the document, but that's wasteful and slow (not to mention environmentally unfriendly). This is where screen previewers enter the picture. They allow you to look at your document on a video display.

Accurate previewing is more difficult than printing your document for several reasons. Screen displays are much more diverse than printers (previewing on a PC is very different from previewing on a workstation running X11 even though printing to a LaserJet printer is essentially the same from both places). Also, it's very difficult to preview documents that use printer-specific features. For example, if you use a PostScript figure in your document, it will be very easy to print on a PostScript printer, but on most platforms it is much more difficult to preview that document on the screen (two exceptions are the Amiga and NeXT which have integrated support for displaying PostScript images).

In the following sections I'll explore options for previewing on several platforms. The X Window System is usually associated with UNIX workstations, but several PC implementations (running under both MS-DOS and OS/2) are now available. The X11 previewers described here may be available for those systems, but I haven't seen them. *Ghostscript* is another previewing option that is available on several platforms so it is described in its own section.

Table 9-1 summarizes the previewers described here.

*Table 9-1: Common Previewers*

| Previewer | Supplier | OS | Comments |
|---|---|---|---|
| xdvi | Free (xdvi) | Unix/DesqView | X11 |
| XTEX | Free (XTEX) | Unix | X11 |
| Ghostscript | Free (gs) | most | PostScript |
| Ghostview | Free (Ghostview) | Unix, Windows | PostScript |
| dviscr | Free (emTEX) | MS-DOS, OS/2 | |
| dvipm | Free (emTEX) | OS/2 | Presentation Manager |
| dvivga | Free (dvivga) | MS-DOS | EGA/VGA |
| TEX Preview | ArborText | MS-DOS, Unix | |
| dvideo | Kinch Software | MS-DOS | EGA |
| PTI View | Personal TEX | MS-DOS | |
| dvimswin | Free (dvimswin) | MS-DOS | Windows |
| dviwin | Free (dviwin) | MS-DOS | Windows |
| wdviwin | Kinch Software | MS-DOS | Windows |
| DVIWindo | Y&Y | MS-DOS | Windows |
| dvi2tty | Free (dvi2tty) | Most | ASCII |
| dvigt/dvitovdu | Free | Most | |
| crudetype | Free | VMS | ASCII |

# Previewing Under X11

The three most common X11 previewers are *xdvi*, XTEX, and *Ghostview* (really a PostScript previewer). *Ghostview* runs on top of *Ghostscript* and is described in the "Previewing with Ghostscript" section of this chapter.

## Previewing with xdvi

You can retrieve *xdvi* from the CTAN archives in the directory *dviware/xdvi*.

Figure 9-1 shows the preview process under *xdvi*. *xdvi* reads the DVI file and loads the PK files for any fonts that are required. If *xdvi* cannot find a requested font, it will run *MakeTeXPK* to create the font. *MakeTeXPK* is a shell script (or a batch file called *maketexp* under MS-DOS) that tries to use METAFONT or *ps2pk* to build the font.

After forming each page, *xdvi* passes it off to the X11 Window Manager to be displayed. Previewing under *xdvi* is shown in Figure 9-2.

Screen resolution is typically much lower than printer resolution. Because *xdvi* uses the PK files at printer resolution, it must scale them before using them for display purposes. The scaling process allows *xdvi* to use *anti-aliasing* to improve image quality on color displays. Anti-aliasing is a technique used to improve the appearance of scaled images by using colored pixels around the edges of the image to provide the illusion of partial

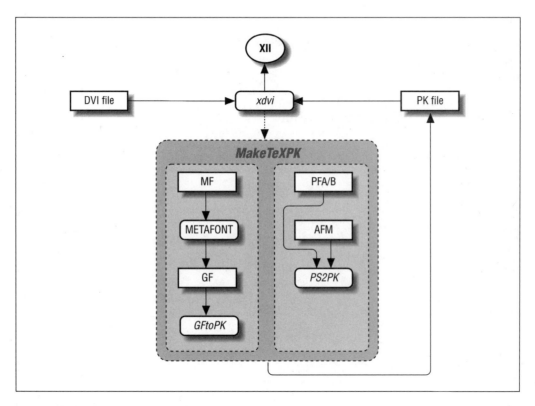

*Figure 9-1: How Previewing with xdvi Works*

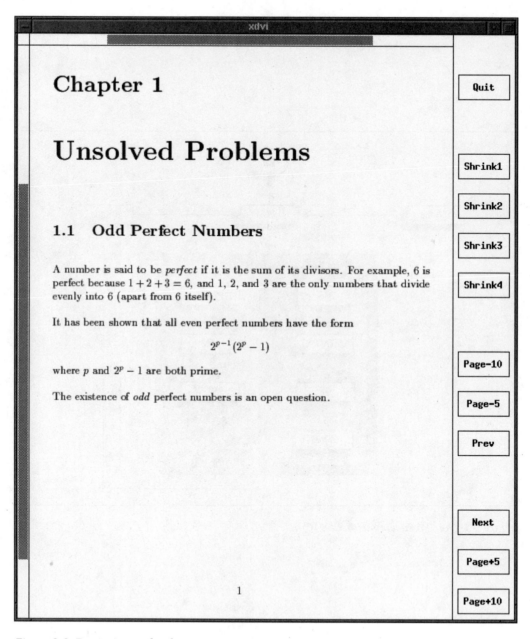

*Figure 9-2: Previewing with xdvi*

pixels. This can dramatically improve the readability of the displayed text. If the PostScript font files are available, *xdvi* can display documents that use PostScript fonts; otherwise, it performs font substitution.

A recent addition to *xdvi* is the ability to preview documents that include PostScript figures. The figures are rendered behind the scenes by *Ghostscript* and displayed by *xdvi*. In my opinion, this addition really makes *xdvi* one of the finest X11 previewers available. It is fast, uses printer fonts, has anti-aliasing for superb readability on color displays, and can include PostScript figures.

## Previewing with XTEX

The XTEX previewer is very similar to *xdvi*. The primary difference is that XTEX uses X11 fonts for display. This means that XTEX must build fonts at the appropriate resolution. After the fonts have been built, XTEX is typically a very fast previewer.

You can retrieve XTEX from the CTAN archives in the directory *dviware/xtex*.

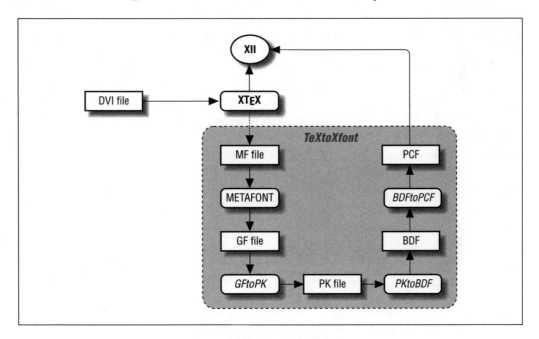

*Figure 9-3: How Previewing with XTEX Works*

Figure 9-3 shows the preview process under XTEX. Like *xdvi*, XTEX uses the *MakeTeXPK* program to build PK files for fonts that are unavailable. Additionally, XTEX uses the *TeXtoXfont* shell script, or batch file, to convert PK fonts into X11 display fonts.

The XTEX previewer relies on the X11 Window Manager to build the display. However, if PostScript figures are present in your document, XTEX will attempt to display them. When XTEX is built, you can specify that *Ghostscript* or another PostScript interpreter be used to handle PostScript figures.

An example of XTEX's display is shown in Figure 9-4.

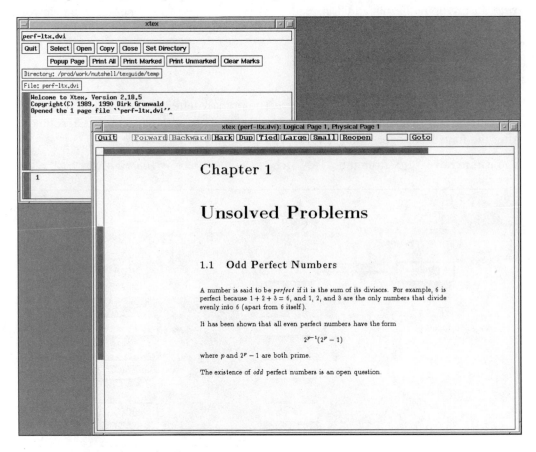

*Figure 9-4: Previewing with XTEX*

## *Previewing with Ghostscript*

Previewing with *Ghostscript* is quite different from previewing with *xdvi* and XTEX. Most previewers process the DVI file to build the display. *Ghostscript* is a general-purpose program for displaying PostScript files. Under X11, an additional program called *Ghostview* provides more sophisticated control of previewing.

*Ghostscript* and *Ghostview* are products of the Free Software Foundation (FSF). You can retrieve them from the GNU archives on `prep.ai.mit.edu` in the directory */pub/gnu* or from any mirror of those archives.

*Ghostscript* reads and interprets the PostScript file created by a program such as *dvips*. It provides its own means of handling font substitution if the appropriate fonts are unavailable. Because *dvips* converts the TEX DVI file into PostScript, *Ghostscript* can display all of the elements of the document including PostScript figures and other PostScript printer-specific commands.

An example of *Ghostview*'s display is shown in Figure 9-5.

# *Previewing with emTEX*

Figure 8-3 in Chapter 8, *Printing*, shows the relationship between the various components involved when processing a DVI file with emTEX. Previewing and printing are very similar operations with emTEX. To preview, you use the *dviscr* driver, and the result is displayed on the screen. To print, use one of the other DVI drivers, and the result is a file that can be sent directly to your printer. Chapter 13, *Non-commercial Environments*, discusses emTEX in more detail.

*dvidrv* runs the appropriate DVI driver: *dviscr* for previewing, *dvihplj* for printing to an HP LaserJet printer, or *dvidot* for printing to other dot matrix printers.

The DVI driver reads the DVI file and loads fonts from PK files or FLI font libraries. If your document uses graphics, they are loaded from PCX or MSP files.

If your document uses a font that is not available, the DVI driver writes the commands necessary to build the font to the MFJ file.* Before performing font substitution, the driver will ask if you wish to build the missing fonts. If you elect to build them, the DVI driver stops and returns control to the *dvidrv* program.

*dvidrv* notices that the DVI driver stopped because of missing fonts and runs *MFjob* to build them. After building the fonts, the previewer is run again to display the document.

The *dvidrv* program is quite simple. With some care, it can be replaced by a batch file that does more work.† For example, I have replaced *dvidrv* with a *4DOS* batch file called *dvidxx* that can automatically build PostScript fonts by calling *ps2pk* in addition to building **METAFONT** fonts with *MFjob*. The *dvidxx* batch file is printed in Example D-3 in Appendix D, *Long Examples*.

---

*Some setup is required to obtain this functionality. By default, the driver asks for the name of a font to substitute in place of the missing font.

†Particularly in networked environments where *dvidrv* assures that temporary filenames won't collide between users.

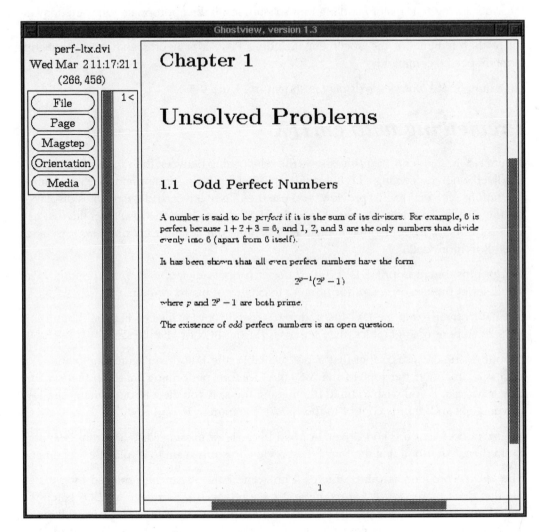

*Figure 9-5: Previewing with Ghostview*

A full-screen preview with *dviscr* is shown in Figure 9-6.

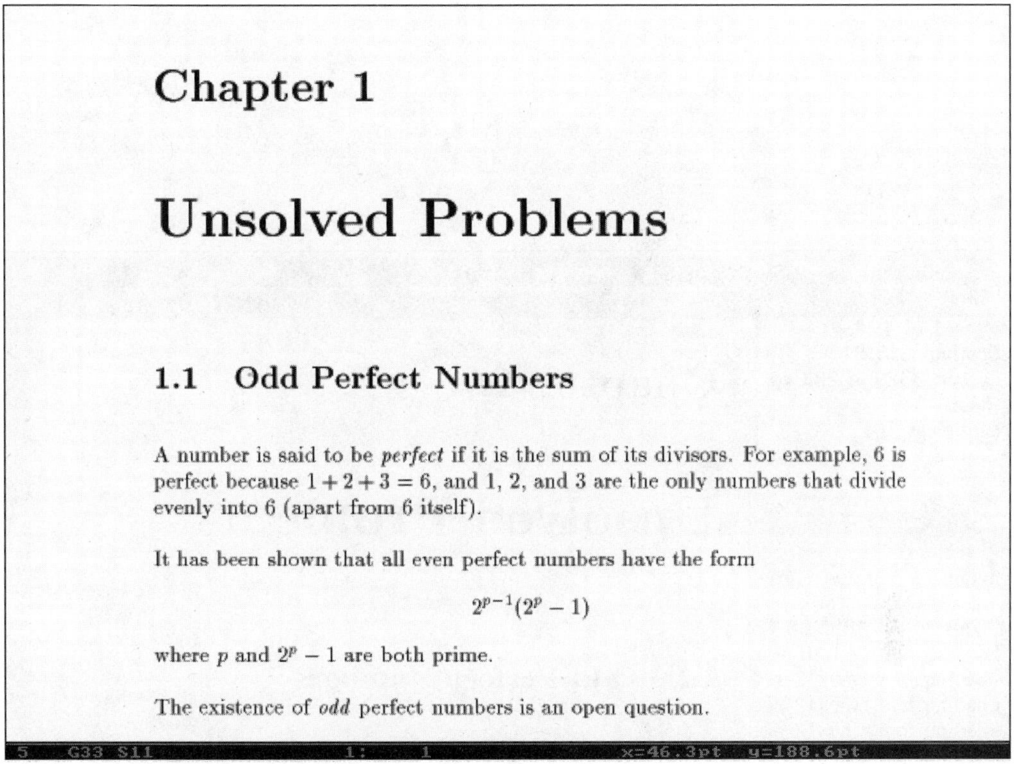

---

# Chapter 1

# Unsolved Problems

## 1.1   Odd Perfect Numbers

A number is said to be *perfect* if it is the sum of its divisors. For example, 6 is perfect because $1 + 2 + 3 = 6$, and 1, 2, and 3 are the only numbers that divide evenly into 6 (apart from 6 itself).

It has been shown that all even perfect numbers have the form

$$2^{p-1}(2^p - 1)$$

where $p$ and $2^p - 1$ are both prime.

The existence of *odd* perfect numbers is an open question.

`5    G33 S11                        1:     1            x=46.3pt   y=188.6pt`

---

*Figure 9-6: Previewing with emTEX's dviscr*

Under OS/2, the *dvipm* previewer offers more power. A sample *dvipm* display is shown in Figure 9-7 later in this chapter.

The *dviscr* and *dvipm* previewers use *anti-aliasing* to obtain better image quality on a color display. However, this translates into a poorer quality image when captured for display in a black-and-white book.

## *Previewing with dvivga*

*dvivga* is an MS-DOS previewer for EGA and VGA displays. You can retrieve *dvivga* (and a complete set of the Computer Modern fonts in PK format) from the CTAN archives in the directory *dviware/dvivga*. *dvivga* requires PK fonts at screen-resolutions (around 100dpi); that is why a special set of fonts is provided. If you are using a dot-matrix printer with a similar resolution, the special fonts may already be installed on your system.

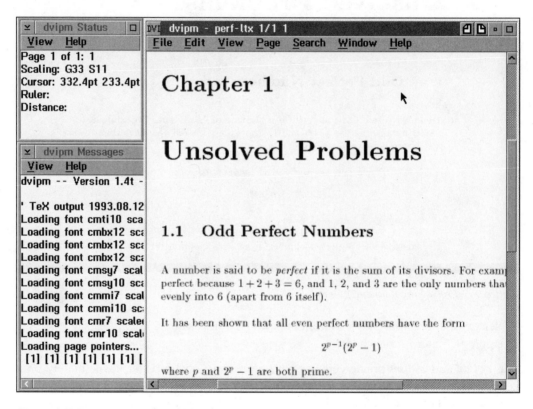

*Figure 9-7: Previewing with emTEX's dvipm*

*dvivga* does not support any \special commands for including pictures or figures, but it does support configurable font-substitution for fonts that are unavailable.

Figure 9-8 shows a preview of the sample document from Chapter 4. This image is from a VGA display.

# Chapter 1

# Unsolved Problems

## 1.1 Odd Perfect Numbers

A number is said to be *perfect* if it is the sum of its divisors. For example, 6 is perfect because $1 + 2 + 3 = 6$, and 1, 2, and 3 are the only numbers that divide evenly into 6 (apart from 6 itself).

It has been shown that all even perfect numbers have the form

$$2^{p-1}(2^p - 1)$$

where $p$ and $2^p - 1$ are both prime.

The existence of *odd* perfect numbers is an open question

*Figure 9-8: Previewing with dvivga*

# TEX Preview

*TEX Preview* is the ArborText DVI previewer for MS-DOS. A similar previewer is available for UNIX workstations running the X Window System (versions for Motif and Open Look environments are also available). The following discussion is based on experiences with *TEX Preview* version 6.1.2, the MS-DOS implementation of ArborText's TEX previewer.

*TEX Preview* supports a wide range of graphics adapters, including EGA, VGA, and Hercules adapters as well as the Olivetti Monochrome Graphics adapter, the Tecmar Graphics Master, the Genius VHR Full Page Display Monitor, the ETAP Neftis Monitor, the Toshiba 3100, and the AT&T PC6300 display.

Figure 9-9 shows a preview of the sample document from Chapter 4, *Macro Packages*. This image is from a VGA display. Three additional features of the driver, not exercised in this example, are the ability to scale fonts to any size, display rulers and bitmapped graphics, and a "two-up" mode for viewing two pages at a time.

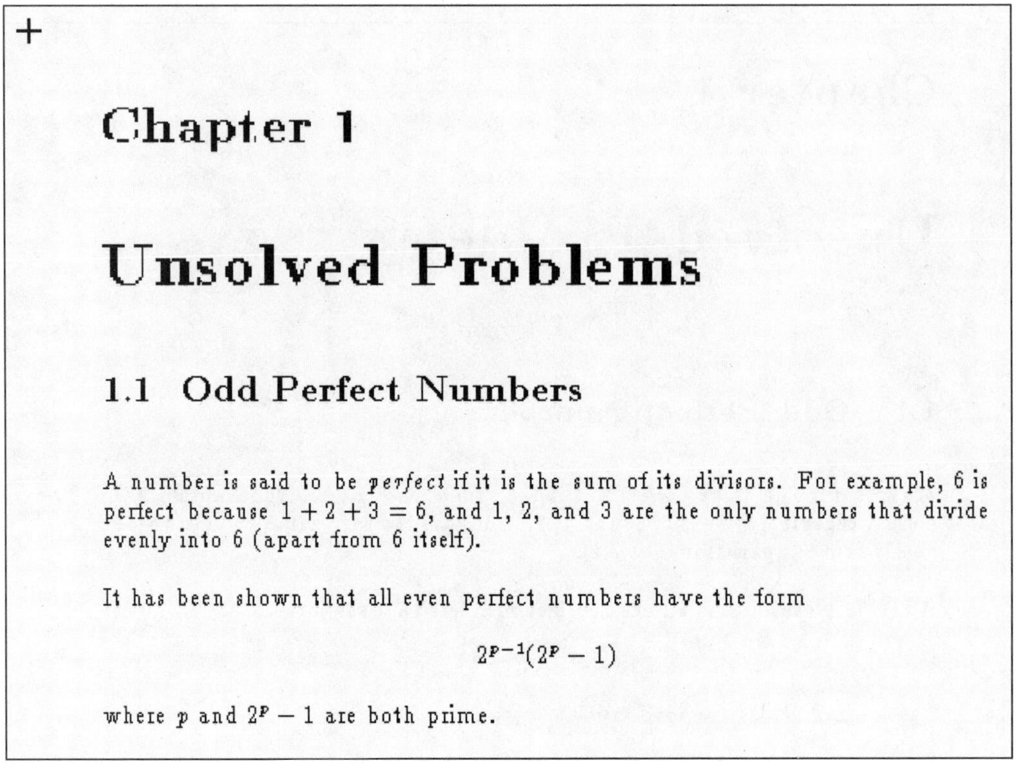

+

# Chapter 1

# Unsolved Problems

## 1.1  Odd Perfect Numbers

A number is said to be *perfect* if it is the sum of its divisors. For example, 6 is perfect because $1 + 2 + 3 = 6$, and 1, 2, and 3 are the only numbers that divide evenly into 6 (apart from 6 itself).

It has been shown that all even perfect numbers have the form

$$2^{p-1}(2^p - 1)$$

where $p$ and $2^p - 1$ are both prime.

*Figure 9-9: Previewing with ArborText's Previewer*

When *TEX Preview* is displaying a DVI file, you can move around the page and between pages; you can change the magnification, search for text in the DVI file, show the attributes of the character under the cursor (font, dimensions, magnification, etc.), and switch to another file. A configuration file allows you to specify a wide range of options to control how *TEX Preview* appears when it starts up.

ArborText supplies a full set of Computer Modern Roman PK files at screen resolutions as well as a complete set of Times Roman and Helvetica fonts at screen resolutions. The additional PostScript fonts are derived from official Adobe sources and allow you to preview documents that will be printed on PostScript printers (provided that they use only Times, Helvetica, and Computer Modern fonts). They are designed specifically to work with TFM files provided with *DVILASER/PS*, ArborText's PostScript DVI driver.

If you want to use additional fonts, for example the $\mathcal{A}\mathcal{M}\mathcal{S}$-fonts or Computer Modern fonts at unusual sizes, you may wish to generate PK files at the appropriate resolutions. *TEX Preview* will perform font substitution for missing fonts (you can control what substitutions are made) and can use the DVI driver metric information, so generating additional fonts is not necessary.

*TEX Preview* understands the virtual font mechanisms introduced in TEX version 3.0. Several additional utilities provided with *TEX Preview* allow you to construct virtual fonts. These utilities are summarized in Table 9-2.

*Table 9-2: TEX Preview Utilities*

| Utility | Description |
|---------|-------------|
| *aftovp* | Converts VPL from AFM file |
| *gftopk*[1] | Converts GF files into PK files |
| *packpxl* | Creates packed (byte-aligned) PXL file |
| *pktopx*[1] | Converts PK files into PXL files |
| *pxtopk*[1] | Converts PXL files into PK files |
| *tftovp* | Converts VPL from TFM file |
| *unpkpxl* | Creates standard, word-aligned PXL file |
| *vftovp*[1] | Converts VF files into VPL files |
| *vptovf*[1] | Converts VPL files into VF files |

[1] A standard, or otherwise freely available, utility.

ArborText's *TEX Preview* program recognizes \special commands for drawing change bars and for rotating *any* TEX "box" through a multiple of 90 degrees. These are the same \special commands recognized by other ArborText DVI drivers.

# *dvideo*

The MS-DOS based EGA previewer *dvideo* is distributed as part of the TurboTEX distribution by the Kinch Computer Company. TurboTEX is described more completely in the section called "TurboTEX" in Chapter 14, *Commercial Environments*. TurboTEX also includes a Microsoft Windows previewer.

Figure 9-10 shows a *dvideo* preview of the sample document from Chapter 4.

The preview displayed here uses the default set of fonts distributed with TurboTEX. This does not include several of the large sizes used by this example. In practice, you will have to purchase or build many fonts before you can use TurboTEX.

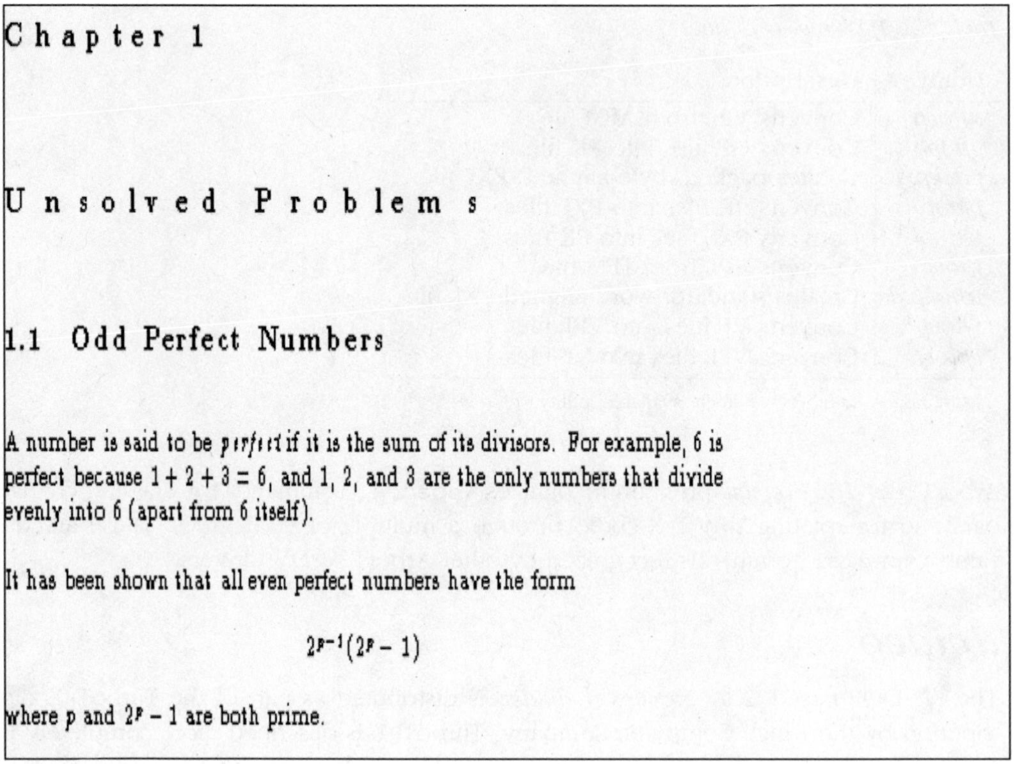

# Chapter 1

# Unsolved Problem s

## 1.1 Odd Perfect Numbers

A number is said to be *perfect* if it is the sum of its divisors. For example, 6 is perfect because $1 + 2 + 3 = 6$, and 1, 2, and 3 are the only numbers that divide evenly into 6 (apart from 6 itself).

It has been shown that all even perfect numbers have the form

$$2^{p-1}(2^p - 1)$$

where $p$ and $2^p - 1$ are both prime.

*Figure 9-10: Previewing with TurboTEX dvideo (using limited selection of fonts)*

# PTI View

*PTI View* is the MS-DOS previewer that comes with PCTEX, distributed by Personal TEX, Inc. PCTEX is described in the section called "PCTEX" in Chapter 14, *Commercial Environments*.

Figure 9-11 shows a *PTI View* preview of the sample document from Chapter 4.

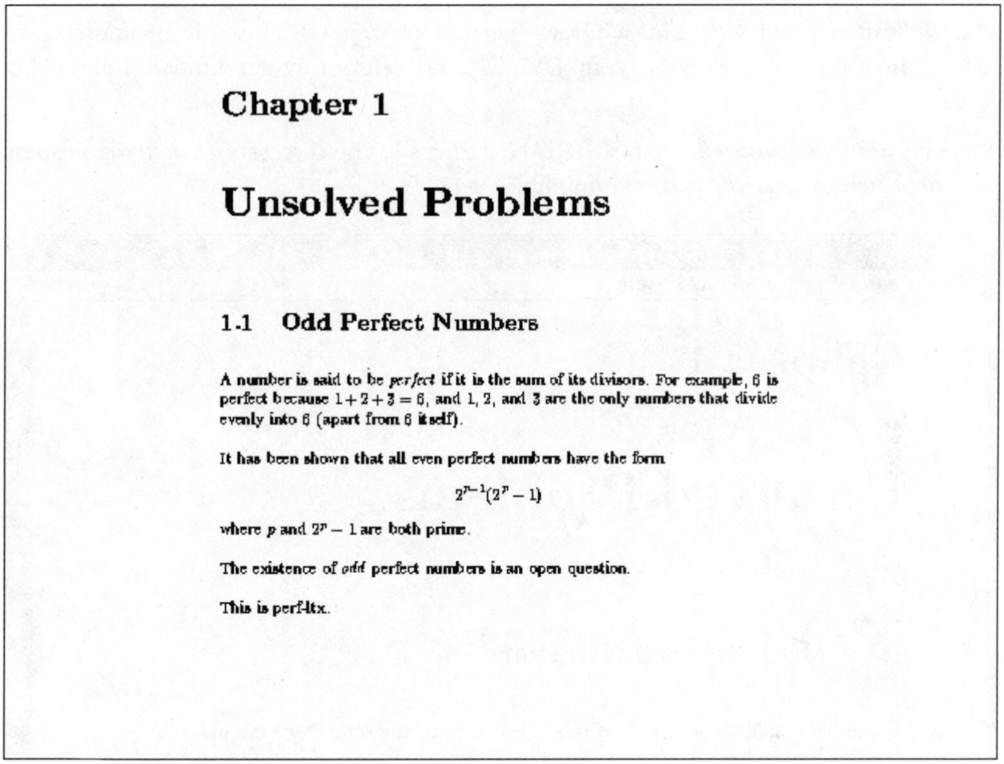

**Chapter 1**

**Unsolved Problems**

**1.1  Odd Perfect Numbers**

A number is said to be *perfect* if it is the sum of its divisors. For example, 6 is perfect because $1 + 2 + 3 = 6$, and 1, 2, and 3 are the only numbers that divide evenly into 6 (apart from 6 itself).

It has been shown that all even perfect numbers have the form

$$2^{p-1}(2^p - 1)$$

where $p$ and $2^p - 1$ are both prime.

The existence of *odd* perfect numbers is an open question.

This is perf-ltx.

*Figure 9-11: Previewing with Personal TEX's Previewer*

*PTI View* is distributed with a complete set of the Computer Modern fonts in PK format (*PTI View* can use the same PK fonts as your printer, regardless of the printer's resolution). It can display the preview in many video modes, including several high-resolution super VGA modes.

# *Previewing Under Windows*

Most MS-DOS previewers are inappropriate for previewing in Windows because they assume that they can control the entire display. Recently, several commercial and free previewers for Windows have become available. They are described in this section.

## *dvimswin*

The *dvimswin* previewer is a Windows version of *dvivga*. It uses the same screen-resolution fonts for displaying your DVI file and offers font-substitution for missing fonts.

You can retrieve *dvimswin* from the CTAN archives in the directory *dviware/dvimswin*. The *dvimswin* previewer is shown in Figure 9-12.

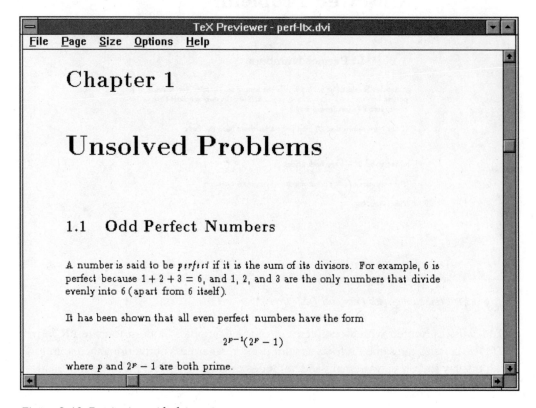

*Figure 9-12: Previewing with dvimswin*

## dviwin

The *dviwin* previewer is another free Microsoft Windows previewer. *dviwin* can use either screen or printer resolution fonts to display your DVI file. You can retrieve *dviwin* from the CTAN archives in the directory *dviware/dviwin*.

What makes *dviwin* unique is its support for \special commands. *dviwin* understands \special commands for including pictures and figures, as well as the emTeX and *tpic* drawing primitives.

*dviwin* has built-in support for PCX, BMP, and MSP graphic formats. Additionally, it can use any graphics filter installed in your Windows environment. Many commercial programs include additional filters to handle the images that they construct. *dviwin* also supports emTeX font libraries and customizable automatic font generation. By using *dviwin*, you can print your DVI files on any Microsoft Windows-supported printer. The *dviwin* previewer is shown in Figure 9-13.

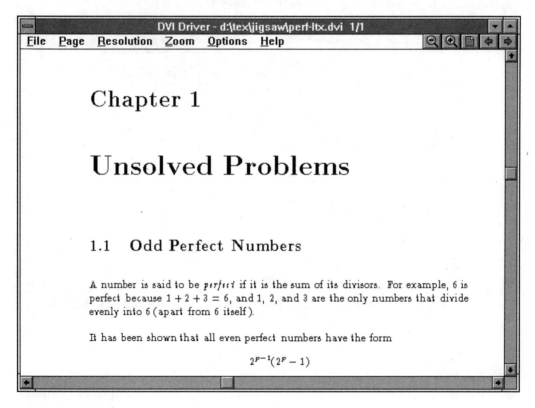

*Figure 9-13: Previewing with dviwin*

The *dviwin* distribution includes two additional utilities: *clipmeta* for creating MSP graphic files from any image captured in the Windows clipboard, and *wbr*, a text-file browser.

## wdviwin

As mentioned above, the TurboTEX package includes a Windows DVI driver, *wdviwin*, distributed by the Kinch Computer Company. Sample output from this previewer is shown in Figure 9-14. This sample shows the status window, the preview window, and a few of the available tools.

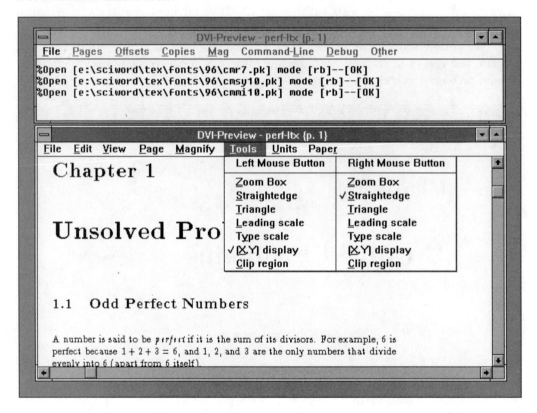

*Figure 9-14: Previewing with TurboTEX's wdviwin*

## DVIWindo

The *DVIWindo* previewer by Y&Y is unique among the previewers used here. *DVIWindo* has no support for PK fonts; it relies entirely on scalable fonts provided by Microsoft Windows. (This means either PostScript Type 1 fonts rendered by *Adobe Type Manager* or built-in TrueType font support.) As a result, to use the *DVIWindo* previewer, you must purchase the Computer Modern fonts in TrueType or Adobe Type 1 format (or not use them at all).

The *DVIWindo* previewer is shown in Figure 9-15. The pull-down menu shown in this image is the "TEX Menu," a new feature of *DVIWindo* 1.1. This menu, which can be customized to include any programs you wish, allows *DVIWindo* to function as a TEX shell. Once *DVIWindo* is running, you can edit files and format documents with TEX directly from this menu.

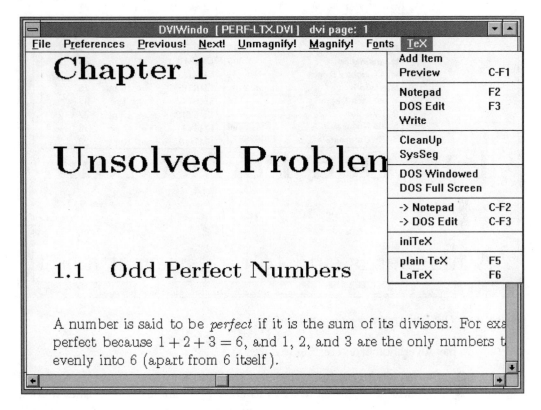

*Figure 9-15: Previewing with Y&Y's DVIWindo*

The real advantage of using scalable fonts is that you can resize the image in arbitrary ways.* For example, Figure 9-16 shows a much-enlarged version of the same page. Similar enlargement with non-scalable fonts would require that the PK fonts exist at very high-resolutions (occupying considerable disk space) or produce very jagged output. The jaggedness of the image shown here is the result of magnifying the captured screen

---

*Most previewers support resizing, but they are generally limited to the resolutions for which PK fonts are available.

image, not the previewer. Several useful information boxes are also shown in these images.

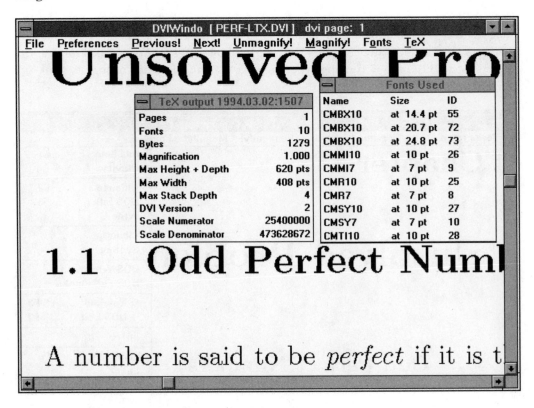

*Figure 9-16: DVIWindo preview much enlarged*

*DVIWindo* has several other interesting features:

- Portions of a document may be copied into the Windows clipboard and then pasted into other applications. This allows you to construct complex mathematics in TEX, for example, and paste them into another Windows application. The pasted material will appear as a single graphical object that can be moved, resized, and cropped. The material is not rendered as a bitmap, so it can be resized without loss of quality!

- TIFF images are displayed in the document. If you use *dvipsone* (Y&Y's PostScript printer driver) and create both TIFF and EPS (encapsulated PostScript) versions of an image, *DVIWindo* will automatically display the TIFF image, and *dvipsone* will automatically print the EPS image.

- Colored text and rules can be incorporated into a document with \special commands.

- You can create "hypertext" buttons in your document. Selecting a button (an area of text or a rule) automatically moves you to a destination marker in the document. These buttons are only meaningful to *DVIWindo*, but they do allow you to move around quickly in a document while you are writing it. Of course, they could also be very handy if you use DVI files for online documentation.

In addition to the *DVIWindo* executable, several programs are provided to help you work with PostScript fonts under Windows. They are summarized in Table 9-3.

*Table 9-3: DVIWindo Utilities*

| Utility | Description |
|---|---|
| *pfatopfb*[1] | Convert PFA files into PFB files |
| *pfbtopfa*[1] | Convert PFB files into PFA files |
| *tifftags* | Show the tags used in a TIFF image |
| *reencode* | Change the encoding of a PostScript font |
| *afmtotfm*[1] | Convert AFM files into TFM files |
| *tfmtoafm* | Convert TFM files into AFM files |
| *afmtopfm* | Convert AFM files into PFM files |
| *pfmtoafm* | Convert PFM files into AFM files |
| *safeseac* | Circumvents problem with accented letters in PS fonts under Windows |
| *cleanup* | Removes inactive Windows from the desktop |
| *sysseg* | Displays information about Windows system memory |

[1]A standard, or otherwise freely available, utility.

# *Previewing on a TTY*

Graphical workstations and personal computers with graphics capabilities are a natural environment for previewing TEX output. Unfortunately, they aren't always available. This section describes several previewers that work in less sophisticated environments.

## *dvi2tty*

The *dvi2tty* program attempts to convert TEX output into ASCII text. This program is designed to provide an approximation of *troff*'s *nroff* processor. To get the best results, you will have to reformat your document using a limited subset of TEX's capabilities. A LATEX style file is included for this purpose. You can retrieve *dvi2tty* from the CTAN archives in the directory *dviware/dvi2tty*.

The output from *dvi2tty* is imperfect in many ways, but it can provide a workable ASCII document. I used it to produce plain ASCII documentation in my *Sfware* package, for example. *dvi2tty* also provides a quick-and-dirty method of applying some standard text processing tools, like *grep*, to TEX output.

## *dvgt/dvitovdu*

These programs share a common history. As a result, they offer an overlapping set of features. The most recent work has been done on the *dvgt* processor. You can retrieve *dvgt* from the CTAN archives in the directory *dviware/dvgt*.

Unlike *dvi2tty*, which is a conversion program, *dvgt* is an interactive previewer. One very neat feature of *dvgt* is its ability to preview TEX output on a number of graphics terminals, including Tektronix 4010, VT240, VT640, Gigi, Regis, VIS500, VIS550, VIS603, and VIS630 terminals. The importance of this feature is that many versions of *Kermit* and *NCSA Telnet* (and possibly other communications programs) support one of these terminal types. This means that you can preview documents even when you are away from your workstation, by using dial-up access with either a graphics terminal or plain ASCII.

Even when output is limited to plain ASCII, *dvgt* attempts to make its output resemble the printed page. To do this, it frequently drops characters out of the middle of words and performs other space-saving abbreviations. The result is a crude, but workable preview, on a plain ASCII terminal.

Figure 9-17 shows an example of *dvgt* display in tek4010 emulation. This is a somewhat contrived example since the emulation is being performed by an xterm.

*dvitovdu* is an older version of the program. It is available in source code form in both C and Pascal. You can retrieve *dvitovdu* from the CTAN archives in the directory *dviware/dvitovdu*.

## *crudetype*

*crudetype* is another plain-ASCII previewer. It provides features similar to *dvgt* and *dvitovdu*. It is written in WEB, but it cannot be translated to C with the *web2c* conversion tool (so you will have to have a Pascal compiler).

The *crudetype* program was written with VMS in mind, although it may be portable to other systems. You can retrieve *crudetype* from the CTAN archives in the directory *dviware/crudetype*.

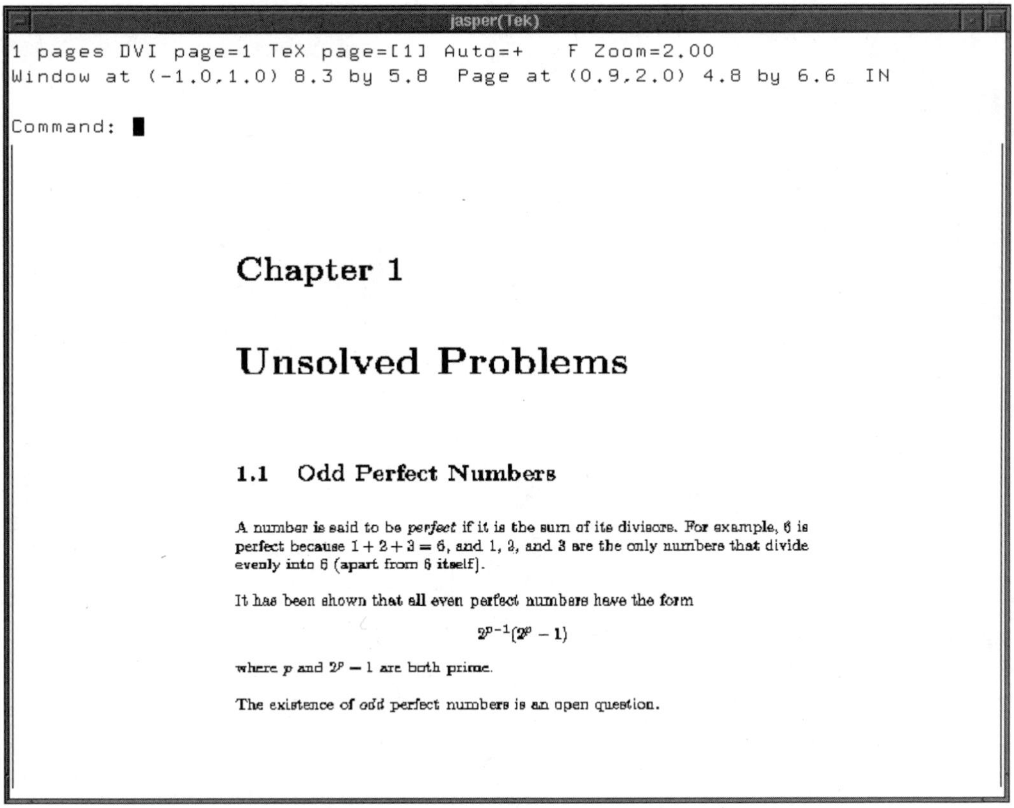

```
jasper(Tek)
1 pages DVI page=1 TeX page=[1] Auto=+    F Zoom=2.00
Window at (-1.0,1.0) 8.3 by 5.8   Page at (0.9,2.0) 4.8 by 6.6   IN

Command: █
```

# Chapter 1

# Unsolved Problems

### 1.1   Odd Perfect Numbers

A number is said to be *perfect* if it is the sum of its divisors. For example, 6 is perfect because $1 + 2 + 3 = 6$, and 1, 2, and 3 are the only numbers that divide evenly into 6 (apart from 6 itself).

It has been shown that all even perfect numbers have the form

$$2^{p-1}(2^p - 1)$$

where $p$ and $2^p - 1$ are both prime.

The existence of odd perfect numbers is an open question.

*Figure 9-17: Previewing with dvgt under Tektronix 4010 emulation*

# 10

# *Online Documentation*

Some common kinds of documentation—for example, manuals for computer programs—present a unique challenge to the author. In many cases, it would be nice to be able to provide online documentation in addition to a typeset manual.

One option is to maintain two different documents: one for publication and one for online access. This is difficult to maintain and is prone to error. As the documentation evolves, it is almost inevitable that some changes to one document will not be implemented in the other.

Another option is to include only very limited formatting information in the document designed for publication so that it is easy to "strip out" the formatting commands and produce an online manual. The unfortunate side effect of this approach is that the resulting typeset documentation doesn't have a very professional appearance.

With care, TEX can be the basis for a middle-ground approach to this problem.* If you are starting a new documentation project, TEXinfo and LameTEX provide two alternatives for the production of typeset and online documentation from the same source. LATEX2HTML and LATEX2hy provide alternatives that may be suitable for existing documentation.

You'll find that the best results occur when you plan ahead: if you know that you need both typeset and ASCII documentation, try to use tools that will make the task easier. But, even if you try to plan ahead, it's not uncommon to find out after the fact that you need or want ASCII documentation. If you don't have the TEX sources, you'll just have to take the best results you can get with one of the tools described later in this chapter and do whatever hand-editing is required.

---

*Structured markup languages like SGML also address this problem, but they introduce their own set of difficulties. Regardless of whatever advantages they may hold, I'm not going to discuss them here.

If you have the TEX sources for a document, here are some guidelines that can help improve the quality of the conversion to plain ASCII:

- Redefine all font commands to use \tt. This makes TEX work with a fixed-width font. You will probably get many, many overfull and underfull box messages. This can't be helped. Setting \tolerance and \hbadness to large values (10000 with TEX 2.x or 100000 with TEX 3.x, for example) will reduce the number of warnings.

  Similarly, redefine all the commands that change font size to select the same size (probably 10pt or 12pt will work best, but larger values may be better if you have wide margins).

- Don't use any special fonts—no picture environments in LaTeX, for example. Take out rules, too.

- Use \raggedright. There's no point in trying to line up the right margin.

- Remove or redefine all mathematics to avoid the use of math-mode. It won't work; don't ask TEX to try.

- Remove all tables (\halign in Plain TEX, tabular environments in LaTeX).

- Remove floating environments; this may help.

- Depending on your level of expertise and the number of documents that you have to convert, redefine footnotes and other environments to give you more marginal improvements.

The *ascii.sty* style for LaTeX encapsulates many of these rules for you.

# *Something Is Lost*

Many things that can easily be represented on paper cannot be represented in plain ASCII. One reason for this is that plain ASCII output is not proportionally spaced. Also, in ASCII you can move up or down only by rows, and left or right only by columns; you can't move down "3 points" on a terminal to typeset a subscript, for example.

These differences combine to make many things impossible. For all of its marvelous sophistication, TEX cannot help you typeset mathematics in plain ASCII. It just can't be done. Most tables can't be done in plain ASCII either (at least not if you want lines that are only 80 characters or so long).

The following sections describe tools that may help you achieve the goal of online and typeset documentation from the same sources. Each tool has its own advantages and disadvantages. The ones that work best for you will depend on the type of documentation you are producing and the amount of work you are willing to do.

# TEXinfo

TEXinfo is the document formatting system adopted by the Free Software Foundation (FSF) and the GNU Project. It is a special TEX format that is very different from standard TEX.* The goal of TEXinfo is to devise an input format that can be processed by TEX to produce typeset output and then be processed by another program to produce *hypertext* output. (The other program in this case is *MakeInfo*.)

TEXinfo supports ordinary text, sectioning commands, itemize and enumeration environments, footnotes, cross-references, tables of contents, lists of figures and tables, and multiple indexes.

The TEXinfo example from Chapter 4, *Macro Packages*, is reproduced in Example 10-1 (the TEXinfo input), Figure 10-1 (the typeset page), and Figure 10-2 (the resulting online documentation).

*Example 10-1: TEXinfo Commands*

```
\input texinfo  @c -*- TeXinfo -*-
@setfilename perf-inf.inf
@ifinfo
   @paragraphindent 0
@end ifinfo
@iftex
   @defaultparindent=0pt @parindent=0pt
@end iftex

@node    Top, , (dir), (dir)
@chapter Unsolved Problems
@section Odd Perfect Numbers

A number is said to be @i{perfect} if it is
the sum of its divisors.  For example, 6 is
perfect because
@tex $1+2+3 = 6$,
@end tex
@ifinfo
1+2+3 = 6,
@end ifinfo
and 1, 2, and 3 are the only numbers that divide
evenly into 6 (apart from 6 itself).

It has been shown that all even perfect numbers
have the form
@tex $$2^{p-1}(2^{p}-1)$$ where $p$ and $2^{p}-1$
@end tex
@ifinfo
```

---

*A L^ATEX implementation, called L^ATEXinfo, is also available.

*Example 10-1: TEXinfo Commands (continued)*

```
@center 2^(p-1)  (2^p - 1)

where p and 2^p - 1
@end ifinfo
are both prime.

The existence of @i{odd} perfect numbers is an
open question.
@bye
```

The output from *MakeInfo* is very nearly pure ASCII. The motivation for hypertext output is to make cross references dynamic when the "info" version of the document is used for online reference.* The result is close enough to pure ASCII that converting it to pure ASCII is not (usually) too difficult. For example, the *comp.fonts* newsgroup's Frequently Asked Questions list is maintained as a TEXinfo document. It is posted as an info version that has been processed by a Perl script to "flatten" the hypertext.

The TEXinfo format is well documented, so a brief description here will suffice. First, the backslash, which is ordinarily used to introduce control sequences in TEX, is not special. Instead the "@"-sign is used. Second, a TEXinfo document is divided into "nodes." A node corresponds roughly to a chapter or a large section of a chapter. In the online documentation, it is easy to jump between related nodes.

Because the info version of the document is ASCII text, many of the special typesetting features of TEX aren't applicable. To support them in the typeset document, TEXinfo allows you to specify that some portions of the input should be seen only by TEX and some should be seen only by *MakeInfo*. Example 10-1 uses this feature to typeset mathematics using the best features of both TEX and *MakeInfo*.

# LATEX2HTML

LATEX2HTML attempts to convert LATEX documents into HTML, the document structuring language used by the World Wide Web (WWW) project. HTML stands for HyperText Markup Language; it is a way of describing documents in terms of their structure (headings, paragraphs, lists, etc.). SGML, the Standard Generalized Markup Language, provides a framework for developing structured documentation; HTML is one specific SGML document type. HTML documents are displayed by special programs called browsers that interpret the markup and present the information in a consistent manner. Because an HTML document is described in terms of its structure and not its appearance, HTML documents can be effectively displayed by browsers in non-graphical environments.

---

*"Info" is the name of both the output format and a program for displaying the text in a hypertext fashion. Another common way to access info files is with the GNU emacs online help system.

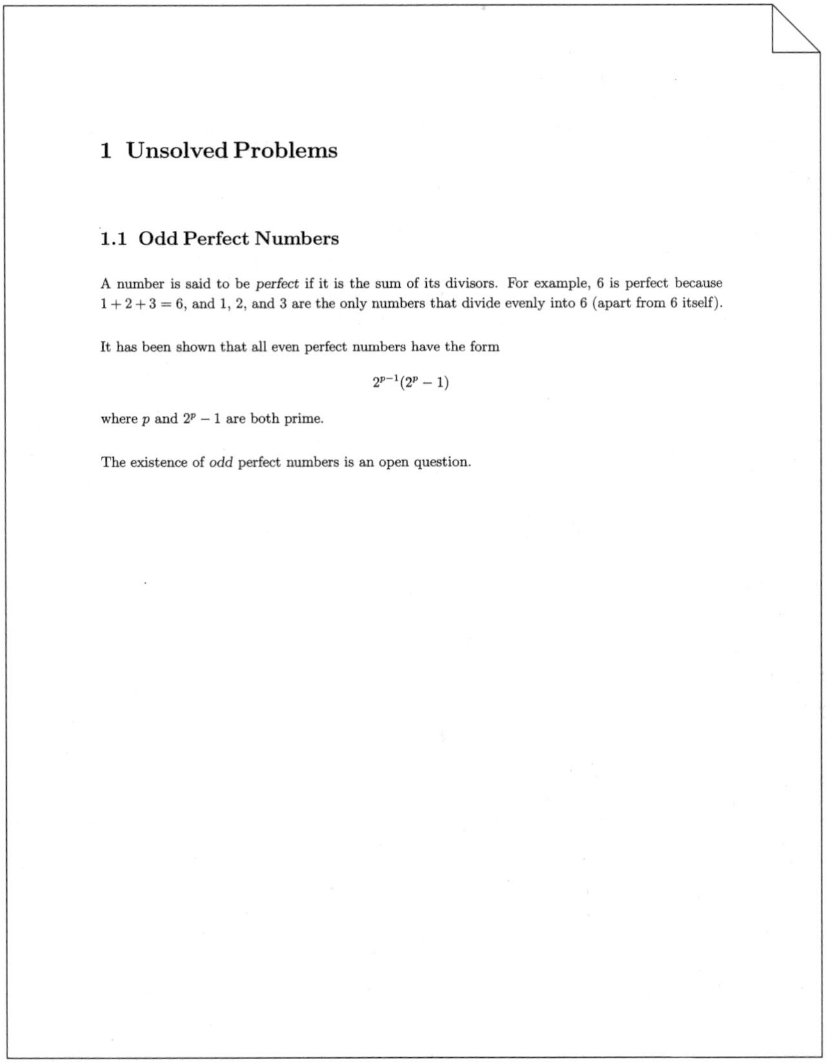

## 1 Unsolved Problems

### 1.1 Odd Perfect Numbers

A number is said to be *perfect* if it is the sum of its divisors. For example, 6 is perfect because $1 + 2 + 3 = 6$, and 1, 2, and 3 are the only numbers that divide evenly into 6 (apart from 6 itself).

It has been shown that all even perfect numbers have the form

$$2^{p-1}(2^p - 1)$$

where $p$ and $2^p - 1$ are both prime.

The existence of *odd* perfect numbers is an open question.

*Figure 10-1: TEXinfo sample page*

One of the most important features of HTML documents is the ability to form hypertext links between documents. Hypertext links allow you to build dynamic relationships between documents. For example, selecting a marked word or phrase in the current document displays more information about the topic, or a list of related topics.

LATEX2HTML preserves many of the features of a LATEX document in HTML. Elements that are too complex to represent in HTML, such as mathematical equations and logos like "TEX," are converted into graphic images that can be displayed online by graphical

```
Unsolved Problems
*****************

Odd Perfect Numbers
===================

A number is said to be perfect if it is the sum
of its divisors.  For example, 6 is perfect
because 1+2+3 = 6, and 1, 2, and 3 are the only
numbers that divide evenly into 6 (apart from 6
itself).

It has been shown that all even perfect numbers
have the form

            2^(p-1) (2^p - 1)

where p and 2^p - 1 are both prime.

The existence of odd perfect numbers is an open
question.
```

*Figure 10-2: Online documentation produced by MakeInfo*

browsers. All types of cross referencing elements (including footnotes) are preserved as hypertext links.

When installed, LaTeX2HTML understands many basic LaTeX commands, but it can be customized to handle other styles. LaTeX2HTML is written in *Perl*.

All in all, LaTeX2HTML is one of the easiest and most effective tools for translating typeset documentation into a format suitable for online presentation. In a graphical environment like X11, Microsoft Windows, or the Macintosh, HTML documents offer very good support for online documentation.

# LameTₑX

LameTₑX is a PostScript translator for a (very limited) subset of LaTeX. One of its original design goals, the inclusion of sophisticated PostScript commands directly in a LaTeX document, has been superseded by the PSTricks package. However, one of the side effects of a special-purpose translator for LaTeX is the ability of that translator to produce different kinds of output, including plain ASCII.

The primary advantage of this method is that it does not require learning an entirely foreign macro package like TEXinfo. The disadvantage is that it understands only a very small subset of LATEX. This subset includes *only* the following commands:

| | | |
|---|---|---|
| \# | \footnotesize | \ref |
| \$ | \hspace | \rm |
| \% | \hspace* | \sc |
| \& | \huge | \scriptsize |
| \Huge | \include | \section |
| \LARGE | \input | \section* |
| \Large | \it | \setlength |
| \_ | \item | \sf |
| \addtolength | \itemize | \sl |
| \backslash | \label | \small\smallskip |
| \begin | \large | \subparagraph |
| \bf | \ldots | \subparagraph* |
| \bigskip | \medskip | \subsection |
| \center | \newlength | \subsection* |
| \chapter | \newline | \subsubsection |
| \chapter* | \normalsize | \subsubsection* |
| \clearpage | \par | \tiny |
| \description | \paragraph | \today |
| \document | \paragraph* | \tt |
| \documentstyle | \part | \verbatim |
| \em | \part* | \verbatim* |
| \end | \quotation | \verse |
| \enumerate | \quote | \vspace |
| \flushleft | \raggedleft | \vspace* |
| \flushright | \raggedright | |

In addition, unlike LATEX, LameTEX doesn't understand any Plain TEX commands (other than the ones listed).

# *latex2hy*

*latex2hy* is a LATEX-to-ASCII converter. It has several options for controlling the input and output character sets. In addition, *latex2hy* has a number of options for improving the quality of both ASCII and printed documentation. For example, input documents can contain both TEX and ASCII representations for complex objects (like mathematical formulae). The printed documentation uses the TEX version while *latex2hy* uses the ASCII version. Provision is also made for "fixups," which allow character sequences from the input text to be translated into different sequences on output. For example, "$9.81^m/_{s^2}$" can be automatically translated into 9.81m/s^2. By adding specific fixups to each document that you translate, you can obtain successively better approximations automatically.

*latex2hy* gives particular attention to cross references. Cross references are translated into "links" between topics in *hypertext* output formats. Currently, only the *TurboVision* hypertext format is supported, although several other formats are being considered.

# *detex*

*detex* is a simple program that does little more than strip control sequences and other TEXish character sequences from your document. Doing this makes the document more amenable to other kinds of processing (like spellchecking) but does a poor job of producing "online documentation." Still, it's an option.

# *dvispell*

The *dvispell* program produces plain text output from a DVI file. It is not a spellchecker, but it was designed to extract the words from a TEX document which were then fed to a spellchecking program that was unable to ignore TEX control sequences.

The *dvispell* program is part of the emTEX package, and it is remarkably sophisticated. There are many ways in which *dvispell* can be programmed to perform complex manipulations. One special strength of *dvispell* is its ability to handle conversion of accented characters and Greek symbols.

*dvispell* differs from the other programs described here because it works with TEX output, the DVI file. On the one hand, this provides *dvispell* with more information (character positions, line breaks, floating bodies, etc). On the other hand, all of the formatting commands are missing, so it isn't easy to determine what the user had in mind. (It's a bit like reverse-engineering a piece of software—without the source code, it's not always easy to tell why things look the way they do.) But *dvispell* gives you access to most of the information that is present in the DVI file.

# 11

# *Introducing* METAFONT

TEX builds pages out of boxes and glue. The smallest boxes are usually individual characters. METAFONT is a tool that creates the actual characters.

In the last few years, a real explosion has taken place in the number of readily available fonts. Today, many people have access to a large number of high quality typefaces. Not too long ago (before Adobe Type Manager (ATM) was available for the Macintosh and Microsoft Windows), fonts were too expensive to be generally available. In those days, a font building tool like METAFONT was essential if TEX was going to have a number of typefaces and a large number of mathematical symbols. Today, the role of METAFONT is diminishing. Many people choose to use PostScript fonts almost entirely. In fact, with PostScript alternatives to the Computer Modern Math fonts now available, it's possible to use TEX without using METAFONT fonts at all.

On the other hand, lots of people do still use the Computer Modern fonts, and there are many other METAFONT fonts (for non-English languages like Arabic and Japanese, for example), so METAFONT is still a useful tool. Also, it can be used to make nice portable diagrams.

This chapter cannot teach you how to harness all of METAFONT's power. The only practical way to learn how to design your own images with METAFONT is to read *The METAFONTbook* [29] (even if your images are nowhere near as complex as an entire font).

What you will learn from this chapter is how to run **METAFONT** to create TEX PK fonts and TFM files from existing **METAFONT** programs. The Computer Modern fonts, the $\mathcal{AMS}$ fonts, and the DC Fonts are all created with **METAFONT**. It is not unreasonable to imagine that you might someday want to create one of these fonts at a non-standard size or unusual magnification.

Knowing how to run **METAFONT** will also help you set up a system for performing automatic font generation. This can save a lot of disk space. See the section called "Automatic Font Generation by DVI Drivers" in Chapter 5, *Fonts*, for more information about setting up automatic font generation.

From many perspectives, TEX and **METAFONT** behave in analogous ways. Where TEX reads a plain text TEX document, processes it, and produces a DVI file, **METAFONT** reads a plain text MF program, processes it, and produces a generic bitmap font file as output.

Because you probably aren't going to be writing your own font programs for **METAFONT**, you have to get them from somewhere. Many distributions of TEX include **METAFONT** and the font files for the Computer Modern fonts. This chapter will concentrate on just the Computer Modern font programs because those are the most likely to be available.

Many **METAFONT** fonts can be retrieved from the CTAN archives. Table 11-1 lists some common fonts and their location in the CTAN archives. A collection of font samples is shown in Appendix B, *Font Samples*.

*Table 11-1: Some Popular METAFONT Fonts on the CTAN Archives*

| Fonts | Location |
|---|---|
| Standard Computer Modern | *fonts/cm* |
| Standard LATEX | *macros/latex/distribs/base/fonts* |
| $\mathcal{AMS}$ Fonts | *fonts/ams* |
| DC Fonts | *fonts/dc* |
| Concrete | *fonts/concrete* |
| Pandora | *fonts/pandora* |
| Ralph Smith's Script Font | *fonts/rsfs* |
| St. Mary's Road | *fonts/stmary* |

# *What to Run?*

Like TEX itself, the actual **METAFONT** file you have to execute varies between platforms and implementations. If you have built and/or installed TEX, you probably already know what program to run. You'll have to ask your system administrator for help if you cannot figure out what the name of the **METAFONT** executable is on your computer. In the rest of this chapter, I'll assume that the command *mf* runs METAFONT. You should substitute the name of the executable program on your system for *mf* in the examples that follow.

METAFONT comes in big and small versions just like TEX. You will need the big META-FONT if you are building fonts for very high-resolution devices or at very large sizes. Most fonts can be built with a small METAFONT.

# What Files Does METAFONT Need?

In addition to the METAFONT programs, METAFONT must be able to find several other files. The files that are needed are normally created during the installation process. The sections that follow describe each of the files that METAFONT needs.

## Pool Files

The pool file for each version of METAFONT has the same purpose as the pool file created for TEX. It is created when METAFONT is compiled. If you don't have a pool file, there's nothing you can do about it. If you obtained precompiled programs (from the Internet, from a friend, or commercially) and you don't have the pool file needed by METAFONT, you received an incomplete distribution.

If you did not install METAFONT, and the pool file is missing, contact the system administrator who performed the installation. Something was done incorrectly.

## Base Files

Base files for METAFONT are analogous to format files for TEX. Unlike TEX, which has many different format files, there are relatively few base files for METAFONT.

Base files are created by a special version of METAFONT, usually called *iniMF*. However, some implementations combine METAFONT and *iniMF* into one program, in which case you must select *iniMF* with a special option when you run the program.

Like iniTEX, *iniMF* interprets all the control sequences in a set of base macros and builds the in-memory data structures that the METAFONT program needs. After loading all the files, *iniMF* writes the memory image into a base file. When METAFONT loads the base file, it simply copies it into memory; no interpretation is necessary.

Because METAFONT loads the base files without interpretation, they are not generally portable from one system to another, or even between different versions of METAFONT on the same system. Different versions of METAFONT load differently in memory, and this makes the base files incompatible. For example, you need a big *iniMF* to make base files for big METAFONT and small *iniMF* for a small METAFONT.

The "Building a Base File" section later in this chapter describes how to build a base file, if you do not already have one.

## METAFONT *Programs*

When you run METAFONT, you have to tell it what file (METAFONT program) to process. METAFONT programs are stored in files with the extension *.mf*. If you specify a complete pathname, METAFONT will load the specific file that you request. If you specify a simple filename without a path, METAFONT looks for the file in several user-defined and, possibly, system-defined locations. The most common way to specify user-defined locations is by setting the `MFINPUTS` environment variable to a list of subdirectories where METAFONT programs are kept. The format of the environment variable differs according to the platform you use. On UNIX systems, it is a list of directory names separated by colons. On MS-DOS and OS/2 systems, it is a list of directory names separated by semicolons. Consult the documentation for the particular implementation of METAFONT you use for more information about system-defined locations where METAFONT looks for input files.

# *Command-line Options*

In addition to the name of the METAFONT program, METAFONT has very few command-line options. The name of a base file is the only option regularly used. In this section, I'll explain what can go on the METAFONT command line.

A formal specification of the METAFONT command line looks like this:

```
$ mf switches &base mf-program mf-commands
```

After the name of the METAFONT program, the first things that you can specify on the command line are implementation-dependent switches and options. For example, implementations of METAFONT that combine *iniMF* and METAFONT into a single program may use the switch */I* to specify that *iniMF* processing is desired. There are no system-independent switches for METAFONT. Consult the documentation that comes with your implementation for more information about system-dependent switches.

After any system-dependent switches, you can specify the name of the base file to use. This option, if present, must come before any other options, and you must put an ampersand (&) in front of the base file name. If you do not specify a base file, METAFONT will use a default base.

After the base, METAFONT looks for the name of a METAFONT program file. If META-FONT finds a filename on the command line, it will process the program contained in that file before looking at any other options that may follow.

Finally, you can insert arbitrary METAFONT commands on the command line by typing them just as you would in a program. In fact, this is frequently done to change the size or magnification of the font being created. Exactly how this is accomplished is described in the section called "Making a GF Font" later in this chapter.

Please read the section called "Command-line Cautions" in Chapter 3, *Running TEX*, for a detailed description of some common problems with **METAFONT** commands on the command line. They are exactly the same problems that can occur on the TEX command line.

Also, the behavior of **METAFONT** when run without any options at all is the same as the behavior of TEX as described in the section called "TEX Without Options" in Chapter 3.

# Building a Base File

Building a base file for **METAFONT** is exactly analogous to building a format file for TEX. Fortunately, there are far fewer base files. The two most common base files are the *plain* base and the *cmbase* (the base used for the Computer Modern fonts). Use the *iniMF* program to build a base file. For example, to build the plain base, use:

```
$ inimf plain
```

Move the resulting files, *plain.base* and *plain.log*, into the directory where **METAFONT** looks for base files (typically in a *bases* or *formats* subdirectory under the standard TEX directory).

The *cmbase* is actually an extension of the plain base. To build it, use the command:

```
$ inimf &plain cmbase
```

Remember to use appropriate quotation or shell escape characters to prevent the ampersand from being misinterpreted.

# Running METAFONT

The sections that follow describe how to use **METAFONT** to make a font from an existing MF file. You should reread the sections "The Issue of Size" from Chapter 5, *Fonts*, and "Bitmapped Fonts" from Chapter 8, *Printing*, if you are unfamiliar with the notions of bitmap and device resolution and magnification and design size in TEX fonts.

## Picking a Mode

The input to **METAFONT** is an "outline" description of a font. The output is a set of bitmaps that realize the outline on a particular device at a particular size.

Output from **METAFONT** is naturally device-dependent because different printers have different resolutions. But even two printers with the same resolution sometimes produce different looking results from the same bit patterns. For example, some laser printers are "write white" printers, and some are "write black" printers—depending on whether the printer fills in the black (text) areas or the white (non-text) areas of the page. A small, intricate bitmap (like a character from a font) designed for a write-black printer may not look as good on a write-white printer and vice versa.

There are several internal parameters that can be modified to produce optimal output on any given device. These parameters are grouped together in a *mode*. Whenever you run METAFONT to create a new set of bitmaps, you must select a mode.

There are no rules for determining what parameters produce the best mode for a particular printer; it's just done by trial and error (set some values, print a font, see if it looks good, adjust some values, print another font, etc.).

Luckily, a large collection of predefined METAFONT modes is available in the CTAN archives. The file *fonts/modes/modes.mf* contains appropriate METAFONT modes for many printers.

Each mode has a name. For example, `laserwriter` and `LNOthree` are two modes from *modes.mf*. See "Making a GF Font," later in this chapter for how to select a mode when you run METAFONT.

Internally, METAFONT has a variable called `mode` that it uses to keep track of the current mode. The examples in this chapter use the `laserwriter` mode because that is appropriate for my printer.

### Proofing mode

Proofing mode is the mode that METAFONT uses if you do not select another mode. In proofing mode, METAFONT displays each character on the screen. This mode does not usually produce a useful font because it sets the device resolution to 2601.72 dots per inch (dpi). That resolution is chosen so that there are exactly 36 pixels per point (one point is 1/72.27 inches in TeX).

Because font designers are going to want to look at a font on the screen far more often than they will want to print it, METAFONT uses proofing mode as the default.

If you find that METAFONT is producing fonts with huge resolutions (thousands of dots per inch) or fonts without TFM files, you're probably running in proofing mode. Remember to use the mode-setting commands on the command line when you run METAFONT. These commands are described in "Making a GF Font," later in this chapter.

## Selecting a Size

The design size of the font you are creating is determined by the MF file you use. For example, the design size of *cmr10.mf* is 10pt. The design size of *cmr12.mf* is 12pt, etc. To select how large you want the bitmaps to be, you must set the magnification. There is no other way to select the size when you are running METAFONT.

If you know the design size of a font and the size of the bitmaps that you actually want to produce, it is easy to calculate the magnification required. The magnification is simply the ratio of the size you want to the design size.

For example, suppose you need a 16pt version of Computer Modern Roman. First, pick the font that has a design size closest to the size you want—in this case, Computer Modern Roman 17pt (*cmr17.mf*). To calculate the magnification, simply divide 16 by 17; in other words, the desired magnification is 0.9412. To make a 13pt version of *cmr12*, use a magnification of 1.0833. Remember, in order to use these fonts in TEX, you will have to use the `at` or `scaled` operators (for example, `\font\cmrxvi=cmr17 at 16pt`).

## *Making a GF Font*

After you have selected a mode and a magnification, running METAFONT is easy. In general, you use a command line like the following:

```
$ mf \mode=selected-mode; mag=desired-magnification; \input mf-file
```

For example, on a UNIX system, the following command line would make a GF file for the Computer Modern Roman 12pt font at a size of 13pt:

```
$ mf '\mode=laserwriter; mag=1.0833; \input cmr12'
```

Note the use of quotation marks to avoid shell-expansion of the backslash characters.

On an MS-DOS or OS/2 system, where the backslash is not a special character, the 13pt version of *cmr12* is made with the following command:

```
$ mf \mode=laserwriter; mag=1.0833; \input cmr12
```

As you can see, the semicolons are *required* in both cases.

Magnification can be expressed with the `magstep()` function if the font is being built at a standard magstep size. For example, the following command builds a 14.44pt version of *cmr12*:

```
$ mf \mode=hplaser; mag=magstep(1); \input cmr12
```

This corresponds to `\magstep1`. This example also illustrates how a different mode can be selected. In this case, the font is being built for an HP LaserJet printer. The command is shown without quotations, but they are still necessary on UNIX systems.

## *Making a PK Font*

Running METAFONT, as shown above, produces a TFM file and a GF file. TEX only needs the TFM file, which can simply be copied to the appropriate directory. For the Computer Modern fonts, you probably already have copies of the TFM files, so the duplicates produced by METAFONT can be deleted. The TFM file does not change at different magnifications, so you do not need to save different TFM files for different sizes.

The GF file contains a font in the "generic bitmap" format. Most DVI drivers use PK files. The *GFtoPK* program converts GF fonts into PK fonts. If METAFONT creates the file *cmr12.gf*, you can convert it into a PK file by issuing the command:

```
$ gftopk cmr12.gf cmr12.pk
```

After conversion, you should move the PK file to the appropriate directory for your DVI driver and delete the GF file. PK files are generally stored in one of two directory structures. On operating systems that support long filenames, it is most common to store all the PK files for a given font in the same directory, using the extension to identify the resolution. In this case, a 360dpi version of *cmr10* would be stored as *cmr10.360pk*. Under operating systems like MS-DOS, which do not support long filenames, different resolutions are stored in their own directories. In this case the 360dpi font just described would be stored as *cmr10.pk* in a directory called *360dpi* or *dpi360*.

## *What About Errors?*

Because I'm operating under the assumption that you are not writing your own META-FONT programs, errors are far less likely. Nevertheless, there are a few things that can go wrong.

Figure 11-1 shows a simple figure eight created with METAFONT. The code which creates this symbol is shown in Example 11-1.

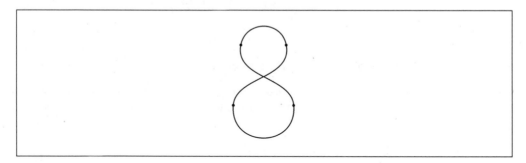

*Figure 11-1: A figure eight created with METAFONT*

*Example 11-1: The Code for the Figure Eight*

```
mode_setup;
u# := 2mm#;
define_pixels(u);

beginchar("A", 8u#, 9u#, 5u#);
  z1 = ( 0u,  0u);
  z2 = ( 8u,  0u);
```

*Example 11-1: The Code for the Figure Eight (continued)*

```
      z3 = ( 1u,  8u);
      z4 = ( 7u,  8u);
      pickup pencircle scaled 1u#;
      draw z4 .. z1 .. z2 ..  z3 .. cycle;
      pickup pencircle scaled 3u#;
      drawdot z1;
      drawdot z2;
      drawdot z3;
      drawdot z4;
   endchar;

   \end
```

Let's look at some of the things that can go wrong. In the following examples, a UNIX implementation of METAFONT is being used. Quotation marks are used to prevent misinterpretation of the backslashes.

## ! I can´t find file `mode=laserwriter.mf´.

If you forget to put a backslash in front of the mode parameter, METAFONT thinks that mode specification is the name of the MF file. For example, mode=laserwriter is misinterpreted as the filename:

```
$ mf ´mode=laserwriter; \input eight´
This is METAFONT, Version 2.71 (C version 6.1)
! I can´t find file `mode=laserwriter.mf´.
<*> mode=laserwriter
                     ; \input eight
Please type another input file name:
```

## ! Value is too large (xxxx).

This error occurs if some element of the image goes outside of the bounds allowed by METAFONT. Frequently, this occurs in proofing mode when the image is so large that it can't be rendered.* In this example, METAFONT is in proofing mode because I forgot the \mode=laserwriter parameter on the command line:

```
$ mf ´\input eight´
This is METAFONT, Version 2.71 (C version 6.1)
(eight.mf
! Value is too large (4097).
<recently read> ;

beginchar->...rdp:=(EXPR3);w:=hround(charwd*hppp);
                                  h:=vround(charht*hppp);
1.5 beginchar("A", 8u#, 9u#, 5u#)
                                   ;

?
```

---

*Obtaining this error from *eight.mf* required changing unit size from 2mm to 5mm.

This doesn't mean that METAFONT can't render very large images; it just means that my design isn't robust enough to handle an extremely high resolution.

## ! Curve out of range.

This error is also caused by an image that is too large to be rendered.* Again, META-FONT is trying to create the image at an extremely high resolution; it is in proofing mode because I forgot the \mode=laserwriter parameter on the command line:

```
$ mf '\input eight'
This is METAFONT, Version 2.71 (C version 6.1)
(eight.mf
! Curve out of range.
<to be read again>
                       ;
l.11    draw z4 ..  z1 .. z2 ..  z3 .. cycle;

?
```

## unknown string

This is what happens if you forget the semicolon after the \mode parameter. In this example, METAFONT thinks that "laserwriter \input eight" is the mode, which doesn't make sense:

```
$ mf '\mode=laserwriter \input eight'
This is METAFONT, Version 2.71 (C version 6.1)
(eight.mf
>> unknown string mode_name0
! Not a string.
<to be read again>
                   ;
mode_setup->...nput  "&mode)else:mode_name[mode]fi;
                                            if.unknown.mag:...
l.1 mode_setup
              ;
?
```

## ! Extra tokens will be flushed.

Oops, another missing semicolon:

```
$ mf '\mode=laserwriter; mag=magstep(1) \input eight'
This is METAFONT, Version 2.71 (C version 6.1)
(eight.mf
! Extra tokens will be flushed.
<to be read again>        ,
                    warningcheck
mode_setup->warningcheck
                    :=0;if.unknown.mode:mode=proof;fi...
l.1 mode_setup
?
```

---

*Obtaining this error from *eight.mf* required changing unit size from 2mm to 4mm.

**Nothing happens...**

METAFONT is sitting at the asterisk prompt waiting for you to do something. You forgot to \input the font:

```
$ mf '\mode=laserwriter; eight'
This is METAFONT, Version 2.71 (C version 6.1)

*
```

**Output written on eight.nnngf...**

Success! A 300dpi version of *eight.mf* has been created and stored in the file *eight.300gf*:

```
$ mf '\mode=laserwriter; \input eight'
This is METAFONT, Version 2.71 (C version 6.1)
(eight.mf [65] )
Font metrics written on eight.tfm.
Output written on eight.300gf (1 character, 1964 bytes).
Transcript written on eight.log.
```

On systems that place restrictions on the length of a filename extension, it is abbreviated to *eight.300*. The next step is to run *gftopk eight.300gf*. This will produce *eight.300pk*, which our DVI driver can use.

## Other Errors

The list of errors in the preceding sections is hardly exhaustive. For example, the gothic fonts (see Appendix B, *Font Samples*) produce two more errors when rendered at low resolutions: *! inconsistent equation*, caused by apparently contradictory statements (probably due to rounding errors) and *! strange path*, caused by a path that does not appear to run counter-clockwise (again probably caused by rounding errors, these are very complex fonts).*

Most of the other errors that are encountered can be ignored (the preceding examples from the gothic fonts can certainly be ignored—at least at 300dpi). Entering ⒣ at META-FONT's question mark prompt will describe the cause of the error in more detail.

# Output at Very High Resolutions

Producing METAFONT output for very high resolution devices like phototypesetters is sometimes difficult. This will frequently require a big METAFONT for the same reasons that processing a large document requires a big TEX.

---

*There are very specific rules about which way paths must be drawn so that METAFONT's algorithms for filling in the character's outline can succeed.

It is possible to construct examples that cannot be rendered at very high resolutions because they are simply too large and complex.

## Output at Very Low Resolutions

The intricate detail of many characters is difficult to render at very low resolutions. Yet, it is sometimes desirable to produce output at low resolutions for on-screen previewers and dot matrix printers.

Usually, errors like "`strange turning path`" that result from attempting to produce output at low resolutions can be ignored, but sometimes the resulting characters will be distorted.

# 12

# *Bibliographies, Indexes, and Glossaries*

Bibliographies and indexes are typically difficult to incorporate into a document. Bibliographies have stringent, but varying, presentation requirements (the MLA wants bibliographies to look one way, the Association of Computing Machinery wants them another, etc.). Indexes don't vary that much, but they are tedious to put together.

BIBTEX provides a powerful mechanism for handling bibliographies and citations. *Tib* is another bibliography package for TEX. The *MakeIndex* program helps manage the construction of one or more indexes for a document. Glossaries are also constructed with the *MakeIndex* program.

## *BIBTEX*

What's wrong with doing bibliographies by hand? Two things. First, it is tedious to typeset each bibliography entry according to the strict requirements of the publisher. Chances are, you'll have to look up the requirements each time, and you're bound to make mistakes. Second, no matter what field you work in, it's likely that you'll cite some of the same articles and books in more than one publication. Computers are supposed to reduce effort, not replicate it.

BIBTEX provides a powerful mechanism for dealing with bibliographies in a mechanical way, considerably reducing effort on your part. Rather than formatting each bibliography entry, you build a database of bibliography information. Each time you want to make a citation, you simply use BIBTEX to build the bibliography from your database into your document. That's easy to do, as you'll see in a few minutes.

The idea of a bibliography database is introduced in Appendix B of *LATEX: A Document Preparation System* [32] and is described in more detail in *BIBTEXing* [44] and *Designing*

*BIBTEX Styles* [43]. The purpose of this chapter is to familiarize you with the concepts of a bibliography database and to describe many of the freely available tools for manipulating databases. It is not intended to replace any of the preceding documents.

## How BIBTEX Works

The LATEX command \cite inserts citations into your document.* You use a short *key* to identify the publication you cite. For example, in this book, when I want to cite *The TEXbook* [30], I use the command \cite{kn:texbook}. The string kn:texbook is the key. When you build your bibliography database, you assign a key to each document in the database.

When LATEX processes your document, it stores information about the documents that you cite (including the key for each document) in the AUX file. The following commands identify how the bibliography should be formatted and what bibliography databases contain the publications you cite. LATEX also writes this information to the AUX file:

```
\bibliographystyle{abbrv}
\bibliography{texpubs}
```

BIBTEX examines the AUX file and extracts the appropriate entries from the bibliography database. It then formats those entries according to the *bibliography style* that you specify. The bibliography style (stored in a plain text file with the extension BST) tells BIBTEX exactly how each entry should be formatted. After formatting the entries, BIBTEX writes a BBL file that LATEX incorporates into your document (at the place where the \bibliography command occurs) the next time you process it.

Sometimes it seems confusing to use LATEX to create a bibliography. If LATEX keeps warning you about "unknown citations" for documents that you *know* are in the database, try the following: run LATEX, then BIBTEX, then LATEX, and then LATEX again.

The first time you run LATEX, it writes the citation keys to the AUX file (but it doesn't know what publications they refer to). BIBTEX writes the BBL file, which includes the printable, formatted bibliography and information about what publication corresponds to each citation. The second time you run LATEX, it still doesn't know what publication each citation refers to because it hasn't seen the BBL file yet (bibliographies are usually at the end of a document). During the second pass, LATEX writes the citation referents to the AUX file. Finally, on the third LATEX pass, it knows what each citation refers to, so it can typeset the citations as well as the bibliography!

---

*For Plain TEX and other formats derived from Plain, the *btxmac.tex* macros provide these commands.

# Building a Bibliography Database

A bibliography database is a plain text file that contains information about a collection of publications. Bibliography databases generally have the extension *.bib*. Example 12-1 is an example of a single database entry. This entry is from a database of TEX-related publications that I put together while writing this book.

*Example 12-1: A Sample BIBTEX entry*

```
@book{kn:texbook,
  author =   "Donald E. Knuth",
  title =    "The {\TeX}book",
  publisher =    "Addison-Wesley",
  year =   1989,
  edition =    "Fifteenth",
}
```

The entry in Example 12-1 describes *The TEXbook* by Donald Knuth. The key for this entry is `kn:texbook`.

## NOTE

All of the keys in a BIBTEX database must be unique. If you use multiple databases for a single document, all of the keys in all of the databases must be unique.

In database jargon, the bibliography database contains a collection of records describing publications. There may be several types of records in the same database. Each record contains several fields, some of which are required and some optional. The required fields vary according to the type of record.

In English, this means that each entry in the database describes a specific type of publication (book, article, technical report, etc.). Every publication is described by its characteristics. For example, books have a title, an author or editor, a publisher, and a year of publication. Some books also have a publisher's address, a volume or number, a series, edition, or month of publication (or some combination of these elements). These characteristics are called *fields*, and they are identified by their name.

## Database entries

This is the general structure of an entry in a bibliography database:

```
@type{key,
    field1 = "value1",
    field2 = "value2",
    . . .
    fieldn = "valuen"
}
```

Always enter complete bibliography information in mixed case. Never abbreviate or set field values in all upper or all lowercase, even if the bibliography style that you most frequently use specifies, for example, that book titles appear in uppercase or that only the author's first initial should appear. BIBTₑX will take care of formatting the entry according to the style. If you store incomplete information in the database, BIBTₑX can't work correctly if you change styles.

### Entry types

Table 12-1 shows the required and optional fields for article and book entries. Similar lists exist for the other standard entry types: booklet, conference, inbook, incollection, inproceedings, manual, mastersthesis, phdthesis, proceedings, techreport, unpublished, and a catch-all miscellaneous type.

*Table 12-1: Types of Entries with Required and Optional Fields*

| Type | Required Fields | Optional Fields |
|------|-----------------|-----------------|
| article | author<br>journal<br>title<br>year | month<br>number<br>pages<br>volume<br>note |
| book | author or editor<br>publisher<br>title<br>year | address<br>edition<br>month<br>volume or number<br>series<br>note |

Fields that are neither required nor optional are ignored. Therefore, you can and should associate arbitrary information about a publication in its entry. Abstracts and keywords, for example, are two additional pieces of information that you might keep for some publications. They can be stored in `abstract` and `keyword` fields in each entry, even though it is unlikely that they will ever occur in a bibliography.

## NOTE

The types of records that are valid, and the required and optional fields they contain are determined solely by the bibliography style. There is nothing in the BIBTₑX program that makes *book* and *article* entries more legitimate than *reptile* or *cartoon* entries.

### Abbreviations

The database entry structure that I've shown isn't entirely accurate. In my example, every field has a quoted string value. The truth is, every value is either a quoted string or an abbreviation or a number. An abbreviation is created with the `@string` command. Typically, `@string` commands are placed at the top of the bibliography database. For example, the following command defines `ora` to be an abbreviation for O'Reilly & Associates.

```
@string{ora = "O´Reilly & Associates, Inc."}
```

The months of the year should always be specified with abbreviations so that bibliography styles can redefine how they appear in the bibliography (for this reason, three-letter abbreviations for the months are defined in the standard styles—you don't have to define them yourself). The names of journals that you cite frequently are also obvious candidates for abbreviation.

### Preamble

Sometimes it is helpful to define TEX control sequences in a bibliography database. BIBTEX provides a `@preamble` entry for this purpose.

Consider the following example, paraphrased from *BIBTEXing* [44]: You have a database which contains entries for each volume of a two-volume set by the same author. It happens that Volume One has been reprinted, so it has a more recent date than Volume Two. The standard styles sort by author and then date, so as it stands, the bibliography would list Volume Two before Volume One.

To correct this problem, you could specify the dates for Volume One as:

```
year = "{\noopsort{1990a}}1992"
```

and for Volume Two:

```
year = "{\noopsort{1990b}}1990"
```

BIBTEX will sort "1990a" before "1990b," so they will appear in the correct order, and the following definition for `\noopsort` will simply discard its argument, so nothing extra will appear in the bibliography:*

```
\def\noopsort#1{}
```

The best place to put this definition is in the database that uses it (so that it will always be present when that database is used). The `@preamble` command simply copies its argument to the top of the BBL file, so this definition at the top of the database will do exactly what we want:

```
@preamble{"\def\noopsort#1{}"}
```

---

*This example uses Plain TEX syntax rather than a LATEX `\newcommand`, because BIBTEX databases can be used from Plain TEX as well as LATEX.

### Comments

Anything that does not appear inside a @*type*{ } command is a comment. However, many programs that manipulate bibliography databases will misplace comments appearing before or after an entry if the entries are reordered.

BIBTEX includes a @comment entry for backwards compatibility with older systems. Unlike TEX, the percent sign (%) is *not* a comment character in BIBTEX.

### Special characters

Inserting TEX control sequences (to form accented characters, for example) into a bibliography entry requires special care. Some styles specify that entries should be shifted to upper or lowercase, and shifting the case control sequence names would make them different.

BIBTEX is aware of the case sensitivity of TEX control sequence names and will not change them. To specify accents or other special characters, always enclose them in { and } braces. The same treatment should be given to portions of an author's name that should remain in lowercase even if the rest of the name is shifted to uppercase.

## Bibliography Styles

BIBTEX styles are really programs written in a simple but powerful stack-based language and interpreted by BIBTEX.* Don't confuse bibliography styles (BST files) with LATEX styles (STY files); they are unrelated. Although a complete description of the BIBTEX language is not presented here, a short example will help give you a sense of the language.

Each BST file defines a number of functions. The highest level functions determine how each entry is formatted: when BIBTEX needs to format a "book" entry, it executes the book function, which must be defined by the BST file in use or an error will result.

Let's consider part of the task of formatting a book entry. These code fragments are from the standard bibliography style *plain.bst*. When the book function is ready to output the book title, it calls the format.btitle function, shown here:

```
FUNCTION {format.btitle}
{ title emphasize
}
```

This function places the *title* field on top of the stack and calls emphasize:

```
FUNCTION {emphasize}
{ duplicate$ empty$
    { pop$ "" }
    { "{\em " swap$ * "}" * }
  if$
}
```

---

*A complete description of BIBTEX's programming language can be found in *Designing BIBTEX Styles* [43].

This is what `emphasize` will do when the *title* is not an empty field:

1.  Duplicate what is on the top of the stack.

2.  Test the value on the top of the stack. The `empty$` function removes the top value from the stack and places a boolean "true" value there if what it removed was an empty field, and a "false" value otherwise.

3.  Push { `pop$` `""` } onto the stack.

4.  Push { `"{\em "` `swap$` `*` `"}"` `*` } onto the stack.

5.  Test the condition. The `if$` function takes three values from the stack: a boolean value, something to do if that value is true, and something to do if that value is false. In this case, the title is not an empty field, so the value is false. The { `pop$` `""` } value is discarded, and { `"{\em "` `swap$` `*` `"}"` `*` } is evaluated.

6.  Push {\em␣ onto the top of the stack.

7.  Swap the top two items on the stack. Now \em␣ is below the book title on the stack.

8.  Concatenate the top two items on the stack. Now the top of the stack holds the value \em␣*book title*.

9.  Push } onto the top of the stack.

10. Concatenate the top two items on the stack. Now the top of the stack holds the value {\em␣*book title*}.

The resulting value left on top of the stack when `emphasize` is finished is the TeX code required to print the book title with emphasis.

### Special-purpose styles

A number of styles have been written to allow you to develop special-purpose bibliographies. A few of them are listed here:

*   *bibunits* supports multiple bibliographies in different sections of a single document.

*   *chapterbib* supports separate bibliographies in each chapter of a single document.

*   *makebst* asks a number of questions about the bibliography style you need and constructs an appropriate BIBTEX style.

## Bibliography Database Tools

There are a lot of programs designed to help you extract information from bibliography databases, sort the entries, build subset-bibliographies that contain only some of the entries from a larger bibliography, and enter or edit information in an existing or new database. A lot of these programs are written in UNIX shell script languages and rely on existing text-processing tools like *awk*, *sed*, *sort*, and *grep*. Of course, many of these text-processing tools have been ported to other operating systems. Most of the utilities written in shell script languages can be modified to work in other environments by an ambitious individual.

### bibsort

The *bibsort* shell script reorders the entries in a bibliography database into alphabetical order by entry key name. `@string` commands are reordered by macro name. This program cannot deal correctly with comments that appear outside of an entry. These comments are always associated with the preceding entry, which is frequently incorrect.

Consider carefully before you reorder the entries in a database. BIBTEX places some restrictions on the available orderings. Cross references, for example, must appear before the entry to which they refer.

### biblook

*biblook* is an interactive program that searches rapidly through a bibliography database for key words in specified fields. Compound conditions (using "and" and "or") can be specified. The entries located by a search can be saved into a separate file.

To use *biblook*, you must preprocess the database with *bibindex*, which builds a binary index of the entries. Differences in case are removed, TEX control sequences are stripped out, and non-alphanumeric characters are removed. This increases the likelihood of correct matches.

### bibclean

*bibclean* is a syntax checker for bibliography databases. Running *bibclean* before using *bibsort*, *biblook*, or any other programs described here can eliminate a lot of the problems these programs may encounter. Although bibliography databases are plain text files with a very loose structure, some tools are more easily confused than others.

*bibclean* identifies possible problems in the database and pretty-prints it in a standard way. The following formatting changes are made by *bibclean*:

- The structure of each database entry is made consistent with respect to the following criteria: the "@" sign that begins the entry type is moved into column 1; each line in the entry is changed to contain exactly one "field = value" pair; and the closing right brace is placed in column 1 on a line of its own. Additionally, outer parentheses are converted into braces; tabs are expanded into blanks; hyphens in a sequence of pages are converted into en-dashes; and month names are converted into standard abbreviations.

- Long string values are split at a blank and continued on the following line. The continuation lines are indented.

- Individual names in the author and editor fields are normalized. A single space is placed after periods that separate initials, and all entries are converted into "first-name middle-name last-name" form (instead of "last-name, first-name" form, for example).

- The checksums of ISBN and ISSN numbers are verified.

- Uppercase letters that appear outside of braces are enclosed in braces to prevent them from being erroneously shifted to lowercase by some bibliography styles.

- Text outside of entries is not changed. Entries are separated by a single blank line.

### citetags

When documents must be transmitted in "source" form (meaning that the actual TEX files will be shipped around), it's generally unnecessary to include entire bibliography databases. In these cases, it would be more convenient to send only the bibliography entries that are actually used.

The *citetags* program extracts the citations from an AUX file. This list of citations can be passed to the *citefind* program to build a small bibliography database of just the required entries.

### citefind

*citefind* processes a list of citations and a list of bibliography databases and writes out a new database containing just the entries required to match the citations present. This provides a minimal database that can be shipped with the document if the TEX files must be processed on another computer.

### bibextract

Given a list of fields and values (specified as regular expressions), *bibextract* creates a new database containing only the entries that match one or more of the specified values in one or more of the specified fields. The necessary `@string` and `@preamble` commands are also included in the new database.

### lookbibtex

*lookbibtex* offers the same features as *bibextract*. However, *lookbibtex* is written in *Perl* rather than a shell script language.

### bibdestringify

As the name implies, *bibdestringify* replaces all `@string` macros in a database by their textual expansions.

### edb

*edb*, or the "Emacs Database" is a powerful database programming system built on top of GNU Emacs Lisp. *edb* has been used to write a database-editing mode for BIBTEX databases. It can be extended to handle new entry types.

### Emacs BIBTEX mode

BIBTEX mode is a mode for editing BIBTEX databases in emacs. It provides some template expansion and alignment features, but is essentially a text-editing mode (as opposed to *edb*, which is specifically a database-entry editor).

## bibview

*bibview* is an X Window-based program for editing bibliography databases. Figure 12-1 shows an example of *bibview* editing a database entry.

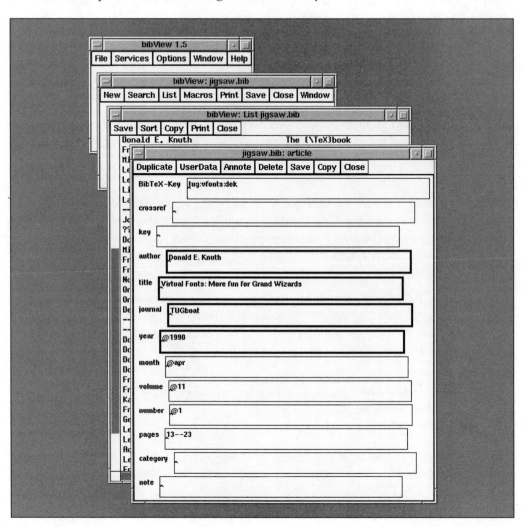

*Figure 12-1: Editing an article entry with bibview*

Unlike the *xbibtex* program, *bibview* can handle optional and ignored fields in bibliography entries. It does not handle new entry types.

## xbibtex

*xbibtex* is an X Window-based program for creating bibliography databases. Figure 12-2 shows an example of *xbibtex* creating a bibliography entry.

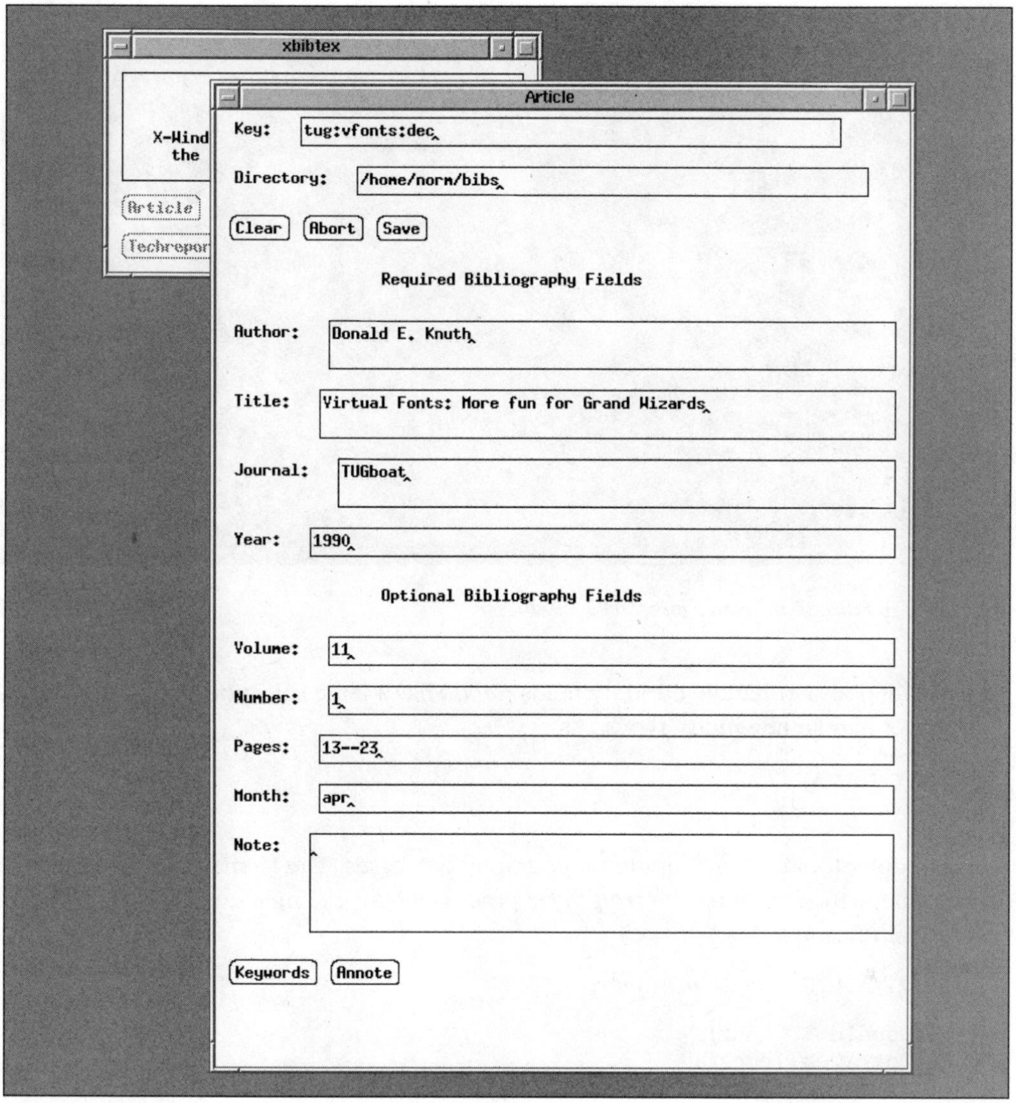

*Figure 12-2: Editing an article entry with xbibtex*

It does not appear that *xbibtex* can edit existing entries. It also does not handle unexpected fields or new entry types.

### bibdb

The *bibdb* program is an MS-DOS-based bibliography database editor. The screen capture in Figure 12-3 shows an example of *bibdb* editing a bibliography entry. *bibdb* displays only fields that have values.

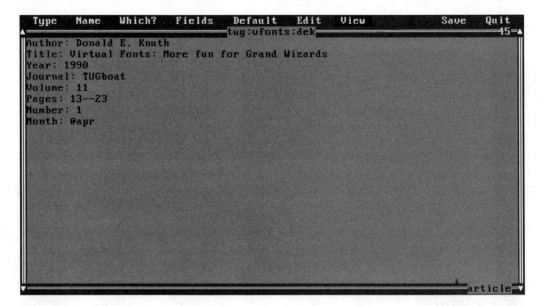

Figure 12-3: Editing an article entry with bibdb

Although it does not handle arbitrary fields, *bibdb* has a large selection of optional fields. It does not handle new entry types.

# Tib

*Tib* is another tool for maintaining bibliography databases. The format of a *Tib* database is the same as the format for the *troff refer* processor.* An example entry for *The TEXbook* is shown in Example 12-2.

*Example 12-2: A Tib style database entry*

```
%A  Donald E. Knuth
%T  The \TeX{}book
%I  Addison-Wesley
%D  1989
```

Unlike BIBTEX, which relies on the citation macros to format citations correctly, *Tib* actually replaces the citations with the appropriate information. In other words, *Tib*-style citations are not control sequences; they are just text strings. The *Tib* processor creates an entirely new document file that should be passed to TEX.

The general format of a *Tib* citation is [.*citation key(s)*.]. *Tib* databases do not contain a key field; instead, the citation keys can come from any fields in the database

---

* *refer* databases can reportedly be converted to and from BIBTEX format.

entry (you can exclude some fields if you wish). The punctuation around citations in square brackets is adjusted by *Tib*. An alternate form of citation using angle brackets inserts a citation without adjusting any of the surrounding punctuation.

The bibliography is inserted into your document wherever the string "`. [ ]`" occurs at the beginning of a line. Analogous to BIBTEX, the format of the reference list is controlled by a *Tib* style. Styles for roughly fifteen technical journals are provided.

# Making Indexes

Constructing an index for a TEX document is relatively straightforward. First, you must identify each occurrence of each word or concept that you want indexed. To do this, you must insert `\index` entries into your document.\* When you format your document containing the index entries, an IDX file is created that contains all of the entries along with the page number where each entry occurred.

The *MakeIndex* program[†] reads the IDX file, sorts and collates the entries, and writes an IND file. The *MakeIndex* program can also load an index style file, discussed in the next section.

When LATEX processes your document, it inserts the contents of the IND file into your document at the point where you use the `\printindex` control sequence.

## Index Entries

Index entries use special characters to identify different types of entries (simple entries, multiple-level entries, see-also's, etc.). The exact characters used are controlled by the index style file, and it may be convenient to select an alternate style. For example, *MakeIndex* uses the double-quote character by default to identify literal characters in the index entry, but the German Babel style makes the literal double quote character a shortcut for the umlaut accent; this use makes it unavailable as the quotation character in index entries.

Another point to consider when coding index entries is that the arguments to the index macros are expanded by TEX. This makes it difficult to insert some control sequences in an index entry (for example `\index{TeX@\TeX}`). In LATEX, you can combat this problem by using the `\protect` control sequence: `\index{TeX@\protect\TeX}`.

A complete list of the different kinds of index entries that can be created is included in *MakeIndex: An Index Processor for LATEX* [33].

---

\*The format you use must also provide support for indexing. In LATEX, most of the support is built in, but you must use the makeidx style option. In Plain TEX and other Plain-derived formats, input the *idxmac.tex* macros at the top of your document. The rest of this section assumes that you use LATEX, although the principles hold for any macro package that supports indexing.
[†]Frequently called *makeidx* on MS-DOS systems.

## *Index Format*

The format of the index is controlled by both the index style (which specifies whether or not headings should be present, what the delimiters should be, etc.) and the definition of several control sequences:*

`\theindex`

> Controls what happens just before the index is printed. This sequence should establish a new page, set up running headers and footers, select multiple columns, and do whatever other global setup is desired.

`\item`

> Executed just before a first-level entry.

`\subitem`

> Executed just before a second-level entry.

`\subsubitem`

> Executed just before a third-level entry.

`\indexspace`

> Executed between alphabetical sections.

`\endtheindex`

> Controls what happens just after the index is printed. This sequence should undo anything that was started by `\theindex`.

## *Special-purpose styles*

A number of styles have been written to allow you to develop special-purpose indexes. *multind* and *index* are described here.

*multind* supports multiple indexes in a single document.

*index* is a reimplementation of the LATEX indexing commands. It stores index entries in the AUX files so that portions of a document can be reformatted without losing the entire index. It also provides support for multiple indexes and replaces the *makeidx* style option.

# *Making Glossaries*

The LATEX command `\glossary` can be used to accumulate words and concepts for a document glossary. The output, stored in a GLO file, is very similar to an IDX file. Like an index, the glossary file can be processed by *MakeIndex* to produce a sorted list of

---

*In LATEX, these control sequences have default definitions that you may not need to change.

terms. To produce a glossary, you must create an index style for the glossary. Here is a minimal *glossary.ist*:

```
keyword "\\glossaryentry"
preamble "\n\\begin{theglossary}\n"
postamble "\n\\end{theglossary}\n"
```

The output file that *MakeIndex* creates will have to be edited by hand, naturally, in order to incorporate the definitions of the entries. You will also have to define an appropriate glossary environment by defining the control sequences used to make the glossary:

`\theglossary`

Controls what happens just before the glossary is printed. This sequence should establish a new page, set up running headers and footers, and do whatever other global setup is desired.

`\item`

Executed just before a glossary item.

`\endtheglossary`

Controls what happens just after the glossary is printed. This sequence should undo anything that was started by `\theglossary`.

Finally, you will have to `\input` or `\include` the glossary in your document.

# III

## A Tools Overview

Part III, *A Tools Overview*, summarizes the tools you can use in processing TeX documents. It describes the major free and commercial implementations of TeX, and then briefly summarizes the many TeXnical tools available.

In this Chapter:
- Web2C
- emTEX
- texas
- sbTEX
- gTEX

# 13

# *Non-commercial Environments*

This chapter offers an overview of several common free and shareware TEX systems. If you notice any conflicts between the information in this chapter and the documentation that comes with the software, please consider the documentation to be more accurate and up-to-date. I've attempted to provide hints and practical suggestions, but software installation is largely dependent on your system configuration and the way you want to use TEX.

## *Web2C*

The official sources for all of the standard TEX programs are distributed in a format known as WEB.* WEB is an implementation of a programming style known as "literate programming." One central tenet of literate programming is that source code and documentation should be written in parallel. Literate programming enforces this tenet by combining the two in a single file. WEB source files contain a mixture of source code and documentation.

In WEB files, the documentation is written in TEX, and the source code is written in Pascal. (Other literate programming environments use different documentation and programming languages.) To print the documentation, a special preprocessor called *weave* transforms the WEB source into a TEX document that can be formatted and printed. Another preprocessor, called *tangle*, transforms the WEB source into a Pascal program that can be compiled and executed.

In practice, it is far more likely that you have access to a C compiler than to a Pascal compiler. This is where *Web2C* comes in. *Web2C* is a special-purpose Pascal-to-C translator

---

*Hence the spider on the cover, by the way.

that makes it possible to compile and build the TEX sources in most UNIX environments (and probably many other environments as well).

Karl Berry maintains the *Web2C* distribution. You can retrieve it from the CTAN archives in the directory *systems/unix/web2c.*

Preparing to build TEX with the *Web2C* distribution is very straightforward. Unpack the archive files, read the file named *README*, and follow the instructions in the file named *INSTALL*. Many people have built TEX using these sources. If you have difficulty, readers of the `Info-TeX` mailing list or the `comp.text.tex` newsgroup will almost certainly be able to help.

In my experience, there are only two parts of the installation that are likely to cause any difficulty: compiling *tangleboot.c* and building the X Windows support in METAFONT.

Because *tangle* is written in WEB, there is an obvious bootstrapping problem (how do you *tangle tangle.web* in order to compile *tangle?*). The *Web2C* distribution includes a small C program called *tangleboot.c,* which overcomes this hurdle. It's possible that getting *tangleboot.c* to compile on your machine may require some tinkering. I had this problem on one machine with one release of *Web2C.* Subsequent releases of *Web2C* seem to have corrected this problem (in my case, at least).

Compiling X Window support for METAFONT has regularly been a thornier problem. If you are not comfortable programming in C, I cannot suggest a simple way to correct these difficulties in the general case. (However, asking for help in the appropriate newsgroups is very likely to produce a solution for any particular problem.)

The most common errors that I've encountered in building the X Windows support for METAFONT are conflicting prototypes and type definitions. My solution to these problems, inelegant though it may be, has generally been to "correct" or remove the offending declarations from the METAFONT sources. (Note: the X Window support is written directly in C, not WEB, so it is considerably easier to edit.) In my experience, this has always been successful, but your mileage may vary.

# *emTEX*

The emTEX distribution is a very complete, free distribution of TEX for MS-DOS and OS/2 systems. emTEX will run on any 80x86 processor, although some of the larger, faster executables require at least a 386. There is no single right way to install TEX, so what follows is only one possible installation. This installation uses the default directories and assumes a single-user environment. Installing emTEX in a network environment is mentioned briefly in "*Installing emTEX on a Network,*" later in this chapter. Incorporating the more recent, beta test versions of emTEX is described in the section called

"Installing the Beta Test Versions of emTEX." emTEX is available on CTAN in the directory *systems/msdos/emtex*.

On the whole, the installation instructions for emTEX are provided in the distribution. Begin by reading the English or German versions of the documentation provided. Additionally, you should read the DVI driver documentation at least once. (It's quite long, and you may not remember all of it after a single reading, but at least you'll have a feel for what can be done.)

Table 13-1 summarizes the files in the distribution. The standard emTEX distribution occupies six high-density floppy disks. A complete installation requires more than 12 megabytes of storage without fonts. You must also get a set of fonts (available in font library format for emTEX) or set up automatic font generation.

*Table 13-1: Summary of the emTEX Distribution*

| File | Abbreviated Contents | Size | Expanded Size |
|---|---|---|---|
| *\*.eng* | English documentation | 125Kb | 125Kb |
| *\*.ger* | German documentation | 140Kb | 140Kb |
| *\*.exe* | Delete, remove, pkunzip | 227Kb | 227Kb |
| *tex1.zip* | TEX executables, TFMs, inputs | 368Kb | 645Kb |
| *tex2.zip* | Plain formats, more TFMs | 262Kb | 403Kb |
| *blatex.zip* | Big TEX LATEX format | 227Kb | 494Kb |
| *latex1.zip* | Documentation and formats | 243Kb | 393Kb |
| *latex2.zip* | LATEX styles and TFMs | 233Kb | 705Kb |
| *latexdoc.zip* | LATEX style documentation | 110Kb | 315Kb |
| *makeindx.zip* | *MakeIndex* | 52Kb | 152Kb |
| *pictex.zip* | PICTEX macros | 43Kb | 144Kb |
| *texware.zip* | *texchk, texconv, maketcp,* TEXware | 265Kb | 433Kb |
| *dvidrv1.zip* | Driver configuration, batch, and setup files | 119Kb | 370Kb |
| *dvidrv2.zip* | Driver executables | 345Kb | 551Kb |
| *dvidrv3.zip* | Preview executables | 293Kb | 506Kb |
| *texcad.zip* | TEXCad | 118Kb | 236Kb |
| *bmf1.zip* | Big METAFONT | 261Kb | 472Kb |
| *mf1.zip* | METAFONT executables | 245Kb | 398Kb |
| *mf2.zip* | METAFONT sources, OS/2 executable | 337Kb | 613Kb |
| *mf3.zip* | METAFONT sources | 273Kb | 768Kb |
| *mfware1.zip* | GF tools, PK tools | 320Kb | 504Kb |
| *bibtex.zip* | BIBTEX | 117Kb | 319Kb |
| *bmf2.zip* | OS/2 executable, Big METAFONT bases | 266Kb | 564Kb |
| *btex1.zip* | Big TEX executables | 259Kb | 447Kb |
| *btex2.zip* | Big TEX Plain format | 269Kb | 533Kb |
| *emsy.zip* | Special fonts from emTEX | 8Kb | 11Kb |

*Table 13-1: Summary of the emTEX (continued)*

| File | Abbreviated Contents | Size | Expanded Size |
|------|----------------------|------|---------------|
| *mfware2.zip* | *MFjob*, some more inputs | 138Kb | 230Kb |
| *misc_mf.zip* | Miscellaneous inputs | 36Kb | 130Kb |
| *pkedit.zip* | *PKEdit* | 51Kb | 97Kb |
| *dvidrvma.zip* | DVI driver manual | 178Kb | 494Kb |
| *web.zip* | WEB tools | 128Kb | 252Kb |
| *g*.zip* | German versions of TEX | 800Kb | 1614Kb |

For simplicity, the discussion that follows assumes that you have enough disk space to install the entire 12Mb distribution. If you can't get that much space (even temporarily), you can perform the steps discussed in the section "Making emTEX Smaller" as you install.

## Where to Start

Begin by reading the English (*\*.eng*) or German (*\*.ger*) documentation files on the first disk. Where there is disagreement between this book and those files, believe the files—especially if a new version of emTEX has been released.

## Unpacking the Archives

The emTEX distribution is a collection of ZIP files spread over six disks. You must install these files into your hard drive. If you have more than one hard disk, you may install emTEX on any drive you choose. Select one with more than 12Mb of free space, at first. You can copy the files onto another drive after you've deleted things that you don't need.

All of the emTEX files are installed in a subdirectory tree rooted at *emtex*. If you absolutely must use a different subdirectory tree, unpack each archive file into a temporary directory and then copy the files into the subtree you want to use. You will have to do much more extensive customization of the batch files and configuration files before emTEX will work. That sort of customization isn't described here in detail.

Make the root directory of the hard disk that you wish to install onto the current directory, and then use the *pkunzip* program distributed on the first disk, or any later version of *pkunzip*, to unpack each of the archive files. You can also use the *Info-Zip* version of *unzip* (version 5.0 or later) to unpack the archives. If you do not want the German versions of the TEX macro files, do not bother to unpack the *lkurz.zip* or *g\*.zip* files on disk six.

After you have unpacked the files, you will have a directory tree rooted at *\EMTEX* containing about 12Mb of files and the following additional directories: *bibinput, bmfbases, btexfmts, doc, mfbases, mfinput, MFjob, remove, texfmts, texinput,* and *tfm*.

## Setting Up the Environment

A lot of information about where and how things are installed for emTEX is stored in the environment. If you are unfamiliar with the DOS or OS/2 environment, consult your operating system reference for more details. In brief, the environment is a collection of named strings. For example, your PATH is in the environment.

The emTEX distribution includes a batch file called *set-tex*, which sets all of the environment variables that emTEX uses. Edit this file and change all references to C: to the drive where you installed emTEX. If you installed emTEX on drive C:, you needn't change anything. The section "Basic Customization" later in this chapter describes the variables used by emTEX in greater detail.

If you are using MS-DOS and haven't already made the environment larger than its default size, you may need to do so in order to use emTEX. Insert the following command, or something like it, in your *CONFIG.SYS* file:

```
SHELL=C:\COMMAND.COM /P /E:1024
```

This is very system-dependent. You will have to use different settings if you keep *COMMAND.COM* in a subdirectory or if you use a different command processor.

## Testing the Installation

After you have set up the environment, make the *emtex* directory the current directory and test TEX by typing:

```
C:\EMTEX> tex
This is emTeX, Version 3.0 [3a] (no format preloaded)
** \relax

* This is a test

* \bye
[1]
Output written on texput.dvi (1 page, 224 bytes).
Transcript written on texput.log.
```

This will produce a small DVI file called *texput.dvi*. Keep this file; you can use it in a few minutes to test the previewer.

To test LATEX, enter the command:

```
$ tex &lplain testpage
```

See the section "Command-line Cautions" in Chapter 3, *Running TEX*, for an explanation of some potential problems with using the ampersand (&) character on the command line.

## Installing Fonts

There are several sets of fonts available for emTEX. You should select the set that is appropriate for your printer. They are summarized in Table 13-2. The CTAN directory *systems/msdos/emtex* contains the libraries or disks of libraries.

*Table 13-2: Fonts Libraries Available for emTEX on CTAN*

| CTAN Directory | Resolution | Description |
| --- | --- | --- |
| *fx_fonts* | 240x216 | Epson FX series printers, Tandy DMP-130 printer |
| *fx_med_fonts* | 240x144 | Epson FX series (for Windows drivers) |
| *ito_fonts* | 160x144 | C. ITOH 8510A printers |
| *lj_fonts* | 300x300 | 300dpi Laser printers |
| *p6h_fonts* | 360x360 | Epson LQ series, NEC P6 & P7, IBM Proprinter, and Panasonic KX-P1124 printers |
| *p6m_fonts* | 360x180 | Epson LQ series, NEC P6 & P7, IBM Proprinter, and Panasonic KX-P1124 printers |
| *p6l_fonts* | 180x180 | Epson LQ series, NEC P6 & P7, IBM Proprinter and Panasonic KX-P1124 printers |
| *psfonts* | 300x300 | Standard 35 PostScript fonts |

Not every font set is appropriate for every model of the series mentioned. If your printer isn't mentioned, use the *dvidot* program included with emTEX to generate an appropriate configuration file. Select the font set with the same resolution as your printer.

The PostScript fonts included in the *psfonts* libraries are suited primarily for previewing. The quality of many of the fonts is substandard. (They were generated from unhinted outlines with *Ghostscript*.) A font substitution file is provided for 300dpi, 180dpi, and 360dpi printers.

Once you have retrieved the font libraries that you need, unpack them (if they are in ZIP archives) and place the FLI files in the \\*TEXFONTS* directory of the drive where you installed emTEX. The amount of disk space required depends on the font set that you install. It can be more than 5.5 megabytes. The section called "Automatic Font Generation with emTEX," later in this chapter, provides an overview of automatic font generation under emTEX. This can save a considerable amount of disk space.

### Testing font installation

After you have installed a font set, you should be able to preview and print TEX documents. If you followed the instructions in "Testing the Installation," earlier in this chapter, you have two DVI files in your \\*EMTEX* directory.

First, figure out which configuration file is appropriate for your installation. The table near the top of *dvidrv.doc* in the emTEX documentation directory should help you determine which one is appropriate.

The default configuration file for previewing is the LaserJet configuration. If you installed the LaserJet fonts (*lj_*.fli*), you do not have to change the previewer. Otherwise, edit the preview batch file (*v.bat* for MS-DOS systems and *v.cmd* for OS/2 systems) and change the configuration file. The preview batch file looks like this:

```
@echo off
dviscr @lj.cnf /ocr=1 /fl=-1 %1 %2 %3 %4 %5 %6 %7 %8 %9
```

The configuration file name is *lj.cnf*. If, for example, you are using the Epson FX series printer fonts, you would change this to *fx.cnf*:

```
@echo off
dviscr @fx.cnf /ocr=1 /fl=-1 %1 %2 %3 %4 %5 %6 %7 %8 %9
```

Now type **v texput** to preview the test file. Under OS/2, you should do this from a full-screen session, not a windowed session. You can type **v testpage** to preview the LaTeX test page, if you created it.

## *Making emTeX Smaller*

The complete distribution of emTeX is much larger than the practical requirements. This section discusses the pros and cons of deleting (or at least archiving) parts of the emTeX distribution.

### *Deleting extra documentation*

The \\*emtex\\doc* directory contains two complete sets of documentation, one in English and the other in German. Delete the set that you do not need. This will save about 500Kb.

### *Deleting extra executables*

There are six versions of the TeX and **METAFONT** executables in the emTeX distribution. You can probably delete at least four from each. Follow these guidelines:

- If you have a 80286 or larger processor, delete the non-286 versions: *btex.exe, tex.exe, bmf.exe,* and *mf.exe.*

- If you do not have OS/2, delete the OS/2 versions: *btexp.exe, texp.exe, bmfp.exe,* and *mfp.exe.* Conversely, if you have OS/2 and you are satisfied that you will never want to run TeX or **METAFONT** under DOS or Windows, delete the non-OS/2 versions: *btex286.exe, tex286.exe, bmf286.exe, mf286.exe,* and the non-286 versions listed above. If you need both, you'll have to keep both around, of course.

- Finally, if disk space is at a premium and/or you have a fast computer, you may choose to delete the small versions of TeX and **METAFONT**. The small versions are faster than the big versions, but large or complex documents and fonts may require the big versions, so don't delete them. If you want to delete the small versions, delete *tex.exe, tex286.exe, mf.exe, mf286.exe, texp.exe,* and *mfp.exe.* In this case you must keep at least one of *btex.exe*, *btex286.exe*, and *btexp.exe* depending on your environment. Similarly, you must keep at least one of the big METAFONTs. If you've decided to delete the small versions, you can also delete two directories: *emtex\mfbases* and *emtex\texfmts*. These contain the format files and base files for the small versions of TEX and METAFONT.

Suppose that you have a 80386 computer running MS-DOS (not OS/2) and you are willing to sacrifice the speed of the small versions of TEX and METAFONT. You would keep the *btex286.exe* and *bmf286.exe* executables and delete the rest plus the formats and bases that you don't need, saving 2704Kb. You can save an equivalent amount of space by deleting the big 80286 versions and keeping the big non-286 versions, or by deleting all of the non-OS/2 versions, depending on your environment.

Table 13-3 summarizes the other executables in the emTEX distribution. This will help you decide which programs you need to keep. Programs that you don't feel you need should probably be stored in archive files, possibly on diskettes, in case you change your mind.

*Table 13-3: Other emTEX Executables*

| Program | Size | Description |
|---------|------|-------------|
| *ask.exe* | 6Kb | Prompts user in batch file, only used by gh.bat |
| *bibtex.exe* | 94Kb | BIBTEX |
| *chtopx.exe* | 39Kb | Obsolete: converts CHR files to PXL format |
| *pxtoch.exe* | 40Kb | Obsolete: converts PXL files to CHR format |
| *pxtopk.exe* | 49Kb | Obsolete: converts PXL files to PK format |
| *dvidot.exe* | 129Kb | Dot matrix printer driver |
| *dvihplj.exe* | 134Kb | HP LaserJet printer driver |
| *makedot.exe* | 54Kb | Updates dot matrix printer parameters |
| *dvimsp.exe* | 128Kb | Converts DVI files into graphic images |
| *fontlib.exe* | 67Kb | Font library management |
| *maketcp.exe* | 28Kb | Change the TEX code page |
| *MFjob.exe* | 51Kb | METAFONT driver |
| *pcltomsp.exe* | 56Kb | Converts HP LaserJet graphics into MSP or PCX format |
| *pkedit.exe* | 94Kb | Edits PK files |
| *pktopx.exe* | 55Kb | Converts PK files to PXL format |
| *texcad.exe* | 79Kb | Interactive LATEX drawing tool |
| *texchk.exe* | 49Kb | Syntax checker for LATEX |
| *texconv.exe* | 27Kb | Converts input files (see "code pages") |
| *dviscr.exe* | 215Kb | Previewer |
| *dviscrs.exe* | 164Kb | Previewer for small-memory configurations |
| *dvivik.exe* | 142Kb | Previewer for Viking I displays |
| *dvitype.exe* | 72Kb | Texware: shows DVI file |
| *pltotf.exe* | 74Kb | Texware: converts PL files to TFM format |
| *tftopl.exe* | 48Kb | Texware: converts TFM files to PL format |
| *gftodvi.exe* | 69Kb | Mfware: makes proof sheets for a font |
| *gftopk.exe* | 53Kb | Mfware: converts GF files to PK format |

*Table 13-3: Other emTEX Executables (continued)*

| Program | Size | Description |
|---|---|---|
| *gftopxl.exe* | 59Kb | Mfware: converts GF files to PXL format |
| *gftype.exe* | 61Kb | Mfware: shows GF file |
| *mft.exe* | 55Kb | Mfware: pretty-prints MF files |
| *pktogf.exe* | 47Kb | Mfware: converts PK files to GF format |
| *pktype.exe* | 45Kb | Mfware: shows PK file |
| *makeindx.exe* | 102Kb | Builds indices for documents |
| *pooltype.exe* | 31Kb | Web: shows contents of pool files |
| *tangle.exe* | 52Kb | Web: creates compilable file |
| *weave.exe* | 72Kb | Web: creates documentation file |
| *vftovp.exe* | 69Kb | Virtual fonts: converts VF files to VPL format |
| *vptovf.exe* | 73Kb | Virtual fonts: converts VPL files to VF format |

Deciding which programs to remove from the emTEX directory depends, to a large extent, on how you use TEX. If you haven't been using TEX for very long, try to keep as many things as you can until you get a better feel for what you'll be using. Save copies of all the programs you delete on floppy disks so that they are easy to get back. Here are some suggestions:

- Delete the previewer and printer drivers that you don't need.

- Delete obsolete programs unless you know you need them.

- Delete WEB programs if you'll never be compiling TEX yourself or reading TEX program source code.

- Delete *Mfware* programs if you won't be doing a lot of work with fonts. Note: keep *gftopk.exe* if you want to use automatic font generation.

- Delete *Texware* and *Virtual* font programs if you won't be working with virtual fonts. (You can probably delete *dvitype.exe*, in any case).

- Delete *bibtex.exe* if you won't be working with bibliographic databases.

- Delete *makeindx.exe* if you won't be working with indexes.

- Delete *ask.exe* if you won't be using *gh.bat*.

Next, figure out what batch files you'll be using and delete (or archive) all the others. If you aren't using OS/2, this includes all of the *\*.cmd* files.

### Deleting extra printer drivers

Read about the *dvidot* program for printing to a dot matrix printer, if you have one. When you figure out which of the DOT parameter files you need, delete (or archive) the rest. Follow these guidelines:

- If you don't have a Viking I display, delete *dvivik.exe*.

- If you don't have a laser printer, delete *dvihplj.exe*.

- Delete *dviscrs.exe* if you have enough memory to use *dviscr* instead. If you are always going to use a Windows or OS/2 previewer, you can delete *dviscr.exe* as well.

## Basic Customization

There are two ways to customize emTEX. One way is to customize the environment variables that emTEX uses; the other is to customize the configuration files that emTEX uses for previewing and printing (configuration files have no effect on TEX itself).

### Environment variables

There are thirteen environment variables that emTEX uses. For simplicity in the following discussion, assume that emTEX is installed on drive C:. If it is not, change *every* reference to C: to the drive actually in use.

EMTEXDRV (Not set by default)

Special note: this variable will become obsolete with the next release of emTEX.

This variable tells emTEX what drive to use when searching for default paths. Although I don't recommend it, if you use entirely standard paths for your files, you can rely on the compiled-in defaults in the emTEX executables.* The EMTEXDRV environment variable should be set to the single letter of the drive on which these paths reside. For example, if you installed emTEX on drive C: (in completely standard directories), you could set EMTEXDRV=C.

EMTEXDIR (Not set by default)

Special note: this is a new variable; it will become available with the next release of emTEX. EMTEXDIR replaces EMTEXDRV.

This variable tells emTEX what path to use when searching for default paths. The EMTEXDIR environment variable should be set to the root path where emTEX is installed (for example, C:\EMTEX).

TEXINPUT

Defines the directories that emTEX uses when searching for TEX input files. You would typically leave *C:\EMTEX\TEXINPUT* in this path and extend it with directories of your own in place of *C:\MYTEX*.

TEXFMT

Specifies where small versions of TEX look for format files. Typically you would leave this set as it is and add new format files to that directory. You do not have to set this variable if you are not using the small versions of TEX.

---

*One of the reasons I don't recommend it is that it isn't easy to determine precisely what the compiled-in defaults are, and they may change without notice.

BTEXFMT

Specifies where large versions of TeX look for format files. You will typically leave this set as it is and add new format files to the directory specified. If you do not use large versions of TeX, you need not set this variable.

TEXTFM

TeX uses the directories stored in this variable when searching for TFM files for fonts used in your documents. If you install new fonts, you should put the TFM files for these fonts in their own directory and add the name of that directory to the TEXTFM path.

MFINPUT

The METAFONT program looks for input files in this path. It is analogous to the TEXINPUT variable. If you add new METAFONT fonts to your system, for example, the $\mathcal{AMS}$ fonts, place them in a different directory and add that directory to this path. If you do not use METAFONT, you do not need this variable.

MFBAS

Analogous to TEXFMT. Specifies where small versions of METAFONT look for base files. If you do not use METAFONT, you do not need this variable.

BMFBAS

Analogous to BTEXFMT. Specifies where large versions of METAFONT look for base files. If you do not use METAFONT, you do not need this variable.

MFJOB

Specifies where *MFjob* looks for input files. If you are not using METAFONT or *MFjob* for font generation, you do not need this variable.

BIBINPUT

Specifies where *bibtex* searches for bibliography database files (BIB files). Clearly, if you're not using BibTeX, you don't need BIBINPUT.

DVIDRVINPUT

This tells the emTeX DVI drivers where to search for DVI files. In practice, I simply set this to "." so that only the current directory is used. If you find it convenient to search for DVI files, by all means set it to an appropriate path. The default path includes *C:\EMTEX\DOC* so that it is easy to preview or print the local guide.

DVIDRVFONTS

This tells the emTeX DVI drivers where to search for fonts. The *C:\TEXFONTS* directory is the default location for font libraries. If other fonts are installed, it's natural to include them in this path. For example, preview versions of the PostScript fonts are now available from CTAN in font library format. If you install those libraries in

*C:\PSFONTS*, you should change the DVIDRVFONTS environment variable to include both paths.

DVIDRVGRAPH

The emTEX DVI drivers can incorporate PCX and MSP graphics with a \special command. The DVIDRVGRAPH environment variable tells the drivers where to look for the graphic files. The $r portion of the path is replaced by the resolution of the image required. For example, I set this to *C:\TEXGRAPH\GR$r* and put 300dpi graphic images in *C:\TEXGRAPH\GR300*, 420dpi images in *C:\TEXGRAPH\GR420*, etc. The default value of this variable is set so that the local guide will print properly.

### *Setting up configuration files*

Configuration file options are described completely in the DVI driver documentation that accompanies emTEX. Read the English or German versions of *dvidrv.doc* carefully. The "out of the box" configuration is sufficient for most uses, but specifying a new configuration file is a convenient way to alter the default size of the page in preview mode or set up emTEX to print pages in "two-up" or "four-up" variations (for printing booklets, for example).

## *Installing the Beta Test Versions of emTEX*

It has been several years since the standard distribution of emTEX was assembled. In that time, several other releases have been made. These are beta test releases, but they are as rock-solid as the standard distribution. Personally, I encourage you to install the beta test versions, especially because they offer features not found in the standard release.

The beta test versions are stored in a series of ZIP files at CTAN in the directory *systems/msdos/emtex/betatest*. Table 13-4 summarizes the files in the beta test distribution.[*]

*Table 13-4: The Beta Test Files for emTEX*

| File | Contents |
|---|---|
| *btexb8.zip* | Big TEX executables |
| *dvidrv_1.zip* | New drivers and support files |
| *dvispell.zip* | *dvispell* |
| *maketcp.zip* | *maketcp* |
| *mfb1.zip* | METAFONT executables |
| *MFjob11l.zip* | *MFjob* |
| *mfpm.zip* | OS/2 support for METAFONT preview |
| *pkeditpm.zip* | OS/2 PM version of *PKEdit* |
| *tex386b8.zip* | 386 version of TEX |
| *texb5.zip* | Small TEX executables |

---

[*]As this chapter is being written, Eberhard Mattes is working on a new version of emTEX. This new version will, at some point, replace the existing beta test files, making this section somewhat out of date. Use the *READ.ME* files in the actual distribution as the definitive source of information.

To install the beta test versions, simply unpack the archives into your \emtex directory, replacing any existing files with the new versions. After you have installed the beta test versions, you can repeat the space-saving steps suggested earlier in this chapter.

What are the advantages of the beta test versions?

- Automatic font generation is supported. This means that you do not need large font library files.

- The beta test versions are TEX version 3.141; the standard distribution is the slightly older version 3.0.

- The beta test distribution includes a 386-specific version of TEX, which is much faster than other versions.

- For OS/2 users, a Presentation Manager DVI previewer is provided.

## *Running emTEX 386 in Windows*

The 386-specific version of TEX provided by the beta test distributions of emTEX has some compelling advantages over the other TEX executables: it's a big TEX and it's fast. Unfortunately, it does not run in Windows (or some other MS-DOS environments).

The problem is memory management. In order to be large and fast, the *tex386* executable relies on some advanced features of the 386 (and higher) processors. These features are provided under MS-DOS by a "DOS extender." The DOS extender allows MS-DOS applications to use "protected mode," where they can address more than 640Kb of memory. There are several competing standards for protected mode memory management. *emx*, the extender implemented in emTEX, is not compatible with the DPMI standard used by Microsoft Windows and some other MS-DOS extenders (for example, MS-DOS sessions under OS/2).

Luckily, there is a freely available MS-DOS extender, which is compatible with both DPMI and emTEX, the RSX extender. Starting with version beta-11 of emTEX, the is very easy to use.*

There are two versions of the extender: *rsx*, for use in MS-DOS with DPMI extenders, and *rsxwin*, for use in Windows. Both versions are available on the CTAN archives in the directory *support/msdos/dpmi/rsx*.

To use the RSX extender in MS-DOS with *tex386* version beta-11 or later, simply put *rsx.exe* somewhere on your PATH. When emTEX discovers a DPMI extender, it will use *rsx* instead of *emx*.

---

*Earlier versions of *tex386.exe* had the *emx* extender "bound" into the executable, which made the process more complicated. The *emx* extender had to be unbound before the new one could be used.

To use the RSX extender in Windows, you must modify the command line that is executed to run *tex386*. Where you currently use:

```
d:\path1\tex.exe options
```

you must now use:

```
d:\path2\rsxwin.exe -e d:\ path1\tex386.exe options
```

The *rsxwin* extender will set up an extender for emTEX and then run TEX.

## *Automatic Font Generation with emTEX*

### NOTE

Automatic font generation is not supported by the standard distribution of emTEX. You must install the beta test versions to use automatic font generation.

The new versions of the emTEX DVI drivers include a program called *dvidrv*, which handles automatic font generation. The *dvidrv* program runs the driver and if the driver indicates that fonts are missing, gives you the opportunity to use font substitution or build new fonts. The *MFjob* program is used to build the fonts. *MFjob* runs the **METAFONT** and *GFtoPK* to produce and install the necessary fonts. *MFjob* installs the PK files into the first directory on the font path.

The *dvidrv* program can be replaced by a batch file that can select an appropriate font-rendering program (something other than **METAFONT**, for example) to build the necessary fonts. This feature is only available in the OS/2 versions of emTEX releases 1.4t and later. The batch file in Example D-3 in Appendix D, *Long Examples*, is a replacement for *dvidrv*. It uses *ps2pk* to make PK versions of PostScript Type 1 fonts if an appropriate PFB file can be found. Otherwise, it calls *MFjob* in the same way that *dvidrv* does.

## *Installing emTEX on a Network*

Ordinarily, emTEX does not require write access to any of its data files, so installation on a network is not a problem. The location of temporary files that must be writable is controlled with environment variables. If automatic font generation is being used, there are two applicable cautions.

First, if you use the batch file approach to automatic font generation in order to support different rendering software, be aware that your batch file must handle the fact that multiple files may be written to the same directory from different users. Don't let filenames collide.

Second, it is ideal if you can provide a single world-writable location for automatically generated fonts. If multiple users are working with similar documents, each will not need private copies of the fonts they require. If your networking software tracks the time of last file access, you can determine which files to delete from this global font area on a regular basis.

# *texas*

*texas* is a 32-bit MS-DOS version of TeX. It is a big TeX. Unlike *tex386*, which comes with emTeX, the *texas* executable uses a royalty-free, commercial DOS extender. The advantage of this extender is that it can run under Windows and other protected-mode environments such as DESQview.

Before you install *texas*, you should get a complete TeX system from some other location (emTeX or gTeX, for example). The *texas* distribution does not include anything other than the TeX executable and the MS-DOS extender—no format files, no input files, nothing.

The *-i* switch runs *texas* in iniTeX mode. Using the instructions from Chapter 4, *Macro Packages*, you should be able to build new format files for use with *texas* if you have another TeX distribution to work from.

*texas* uses the following environment variables:

TEXINPUTS

> Defines the directories that *texas* uses when searching for TeX input files. You would typically leave the defaults in this path and extend it with directories of your own in place of *C:\MYTEX*.

TEXFORMATS

> Specifies where *texas* looks for format files. Typically you would leave this set as is and add new format files to that directory.

TEXFONTS

> TeX uses the directories stored in this variable when searching for TFM files for fonts used in your documents. If you install new fonts, you should put the TFM files in their own directory and add the name of that directory to the TEXFONTS path.

TEXPOOL

> Specifies where *texas* looks for its pool file. Unless you have installed *texas* in an unusual way, you will not have to change this setting.

DOS4GVM

> *texas* uses a DOS extender to overcome memory limitations under MS-DOS. If the extender runs out of memory, it writes parts of the memory-image that it is maintaining out to disk. This environment variable specifies where that information should be written. You do not usually need to change this setting.

# *sbTEX*

sbTEX is another MS-DOS implementation of TEX. The *sb38tex* distribution includes TEX and iniTEX executables, TFM files for the Computer Modern Roman fonts, and TEX sources for the Plain TEX format. This is TEX version 3.141. You will have to get DVI drivers and other TEX tools from a different package.

The *sb32xet* distribution is XET version 3.1.* The source files for the XET *nailp* format are included, as well as the supporting files for Hebrew.

The *sbmf13* distribution is **METAFONT** version 2.71. Only the sources for the Plain **METAFONT** base file are provided. Like the sbTEX distribution, this is a very minimal set of files. Only the *GFtoPK* utility is included; all of the other **METAFONT** programs you need will have to be obtained from another package.

The default directories for sbTEX are \\*TEX*\\*INPUTS* for input files, \\*TEX*\\*FORMATS* for format files, and \\*TEX*\\*FONTTFMS* for TFM files. The default drive is C:, but that can be changed with the *sb38set* program.

You can also modify these paths by setting the `TEXINPUTS` environment variable for input files, the `FMTSB` environment variable for format files, and the `FONTTFMS` environment variable for TFM files. Additionally, sbTEX uses the `SBFTMP` environment variable to determine where temporary files should be located if font caching is performed. Here is a more complete description of sbTEX's environment variables:

`TEXINPUTS`

> Defines the directories that sbTEX uses when searching for TEX input files. You would typically leave the defaults in this path and extend it with directories of your own in place of *C:\\MYTEX*.

`FMTSB`

> Specifies where sbTEX looks for format files. Typically you would leave this set as it is and add new format files to that directory.

`FONTTFMS`

> TEX uses the directories stored in this variable when searching for TFM files for fonts used in your documents. If you install new fonts, you should put the TFM files for these fonts in their own directory and add the name of that directory to the `FONTTFMS` path.

`SBFTMP`

> When font-caching is enabled, sbTEX writes cached information to disk when it runs out of memory. This environment variable specifies where that information should be written. You do not usually need to change this setting.

---

*XET is a variant of TEX that can typeset in both left-to-right and right-to-left modes.

# gTEX

The gTEX package is distributed in two ways. One way is intended to supplement (actually, replace part of) the emTEX distribution. The advantage of gTEX executables over emTEX is that they will run under Windows. The 386 versions of emTEX executables will not run under Windows. On the other hand, although gTEX will run in an MS-DOS session under OS/2, only the emTEX executables will actually run in a native OS/2 session. The other distribution is a complete set of TFM files, source, and input files for Plain TEX, LATEX, and *AMS*-TEX. In either distribution, you must get DVI drivers and some ancillary programs from another complete package (like emTEX).

The following programs are included in the gTEX distribution:

| | | |
|---|---|---|
| BIBTEX | *GFtoPK* | *VFtoVP* |
| *DVItype* | *MFT* | *VPtoVF* |
| *DVIcopy* | *PKtoGF* | *MakeIndx* |
| *GFtoDVI* | *PKtype* | METAFONT |

*amSpell* (a third party spell-checker, not traditionally part of TEX)

*MEwin* (an Emacs-like editor for Windows, also not traditionally part of TEX)

The gTEX executables use the same environment variables as emTEX.

# 14

# *Commercial Environments*

There are several commercial versions of TEX on the market. The advantage of commercial programs over free ones is that they provide an automated installation procedure and some level of technical support. There's no reason to believe that a commercial implementation of TEX is necessarily better than a free one (or vice versa, for that matter) because the source code for TEX is in the public domain.

The following sections highlight several commercial implementations of TEX.

## *µTEX by ArborText*

ArborText sells µTEX for MS-DOS systems as well as an implementation of TEX for UNIX workstations. The ArborText previewer and DVI driver software are also available for both UNIX and MS-DOS systems. The following discussion is based on experiences with µTEX version 3.14B, the MS-DOS implementation of ArborText's TEX package.

The µTEX package is a complete TEX implementation for MS-DOS. The additional utilities, *PLtoTF*, *TFtoPL*, and BIBTEX, are also included. Neither METAFONT nor *MakeIndex* is provided.

The default installation of µTEX creates format files for Plain TEX and LATEX. To be as fast as possible, µTEX creates executable versions of TEX for each of these formats; these versions have the appropriate macro packages preloaded into the executable. You can use the standard notation to load alternate macro packages if you wish to save disk space.

ArborText includes a lot of support for using TEX for non-English documents. Several files of international hyphenation patterns (English, French, German, Dutch, and Portuguese) are provided, as well as reprints of the TUGboat articles describing new features of TEX version 3.0 and virtual fonts.

Designed for an MS-DOS environment having only limited memory, $\mu$TEX uses a swap file (potentially located in EMS or XMS memory) to process large files. Several environment variables can be used to alter the size of internal TEX data structures when a new format is being produced. In terms of big and small versions, $\mu$TEX can be configured either way. These choices are made when you create the format file however, so you will need to use iniTEX (included with $\mu$TEX) to make a "bigger" TEX.

One of the most interesting features of $\mu$TEX is a quick-and-dirty preview mode provided by the TEX executable. After at least one page of your document has been processed, you can switch to a preview mode and see what the page looks like while TEX continues processing your document. This previewer is not particularly attractive, but it's quick and easy to use. No other previewer is provided. ArborText sells a fully functional previewer as a separate package.

To print your documents, you must purchase or obtain a DVI driver separately. ArborText sells two drivers, one for HP LaserJet printers and another for PostScript printers. The $\mu$TEX distribution includes a complete set of TFM files, but it does not include any PK files.

The ArborText previewer is summarized in the section called "TEX Preview" in Chapter 9, *Previewing*. The ArborText printer drivers, *DVILASER/HP* and *DVILASER/PS*, are described in Chapter 8, *Printing*.

# Y&YTEX

Y&YTEX is an MS-DOS implementation of TEX by Y&Y Inc. (a 386 or higher processor is required). Y&YTEX is sold as a bundled package with *DVIWindo*, *dvipsone*,[*] and a set of PostScript fonts (either the Computer Modern fonts, the Lucida Bright and Lucida New Math fonts, or the MathTime fonts). The installation provides format files for Plain TEX and LATEX.

Y&YTEX stands out among TEX systems because of its memory management. Unlike other TEX systems, which exist in big and small versions, all of Y&YTEX's memory management is dynamic. All of the buffers that TEX uses (main memory, font memory, string memory, etc.) will expand to meet the needs of the most complex documents you create. The memory required for hyphenation patterns is dynamically allocated as well, which means that you can construct multilingual formats with as many sets of hyphenation patterns as you need (multilingual formats are discussed in more detail in Chapter 7, *International Considerations*). The advantage of dynamic memory management over a fast and big

---

[*] *DVIWindo* is described in Chapter 9, and *dvipsone* is described in Chapter 8.

TEX is that Y&YTEX starts out small (big TEXs reserve a large fixed amount of memory even when processing simple jobs that don't require very much). In a multitasking environment where several programs are competing for memory, one large program can slow the progress of the entire system. Y&YTEX's memory manager supports XMS, VCPI, and DPMI. This means that it can run under MS-DOS with any of the common memory managers and under Windows, Windows NT, and DOS sessions in OS/2.

Y&YTEX has a couple of additional strengths for multilingual use: it supports customizable input character translation and more than 255 internal font numbers. Most versions of TEX only support a maximum of 255 fonts in any single document.

# Textures

*Textures* is a commercial implementation of TEX for the Macintosh distributed by Blue Sky Research. It is described fully in Chapter 15, *TEX on the Macintosh*.

# TurboTEX

TurboTEX is a complete TEX system for MS-DOS with full support for Microsoft Windows. It is distributed by the Kinch Computer Company. The programs included in TurboTEX version 3.0 are shown in Table 14-1. The *dvideo* and *wdviwin* previewers are described in Chapter 9.

*Table 14-1: TurboTEX Programs*

| Program | Description |
|---------|-------------|
| *dvialw*[1] | A PostScript DVI driver |
| *dvideo* | An EGA (non-Windows) previewer |
| *wdviwin* | A Windows previewer |
| *dvielq*[1] | An Epson LQ driver |
| *dvieps*[1] | An Epson/IBM graphics printer driver |
| *dvijep*[1] | An HP LaserJet PLus/Series II driver |
| *dvijet*[1] | An HP LaserJet/DeskJet driver |
| *dvilj4*[1] | An HP LaserJet 4 driver |
| *initex*[1] | iniTEX for building new format files |
| *latex*[1] | TEX with the LATEX format preloaded |
| *tex*[1] | TEX with the Plain format preloaded |
| *texidx* | The GNU TEX indexing program |
| *tif2hp* | Converts TIFF bitmapped graphics to HP LaserJet bitmaps |
| *virtex*[1] | TEX with no format preloaded |

[1] Windows version included.

The Microsoft Windows version of TurboTEX is a superset of the DOS version (you must install both, but you can delete the non-Windows executable programs that have Windows versions, if you wish).

TurboTEX includes a complete **METAFONT** distribution. In addition to the programs shown in Table 14-2, the complete sources for the Computer Modern, LaTeX, and *AMS*-fonts are also provided.

*Table 14-2: TurboTEX METAFONT Programs*

| Program | Description |
|---------|-------------|
| *gftodvi*[1] | Creates proof sheets of **METAFONT** characters |
| *inimf* | **METAFONT** with no base file preloaded |
| *mfscript* | A script generator (for building multiple fonts) |
| *mfcga* | **METAFONT** for CGA displays |
| *mfhga* | **METAFONT** for Hercules displays |
| *gftopk*[1] | Converts GF files to PK files |

[1] A standard, or otherwise freely available, utility.

At the time of this writing, a new version of TurboTEX is actively being developed. Unfortunately, it was not available for review in time for this edition of *Making TEX Work*. The Kinch Computer Company claims that the next release will include a big TEX running under Windows 3.1/Win32s and Windows NT as a native, protected-mode 32-bit application. A new Windows previewer will also be available, and it takes advantage of Windows "multiple document interface" to preview multiple documents in the same session. Kinch will also provide a set of the standard Computer Modern Fonts in TrueType and Type 1 formats.

# *PCTEX*

PCTEX is a complete TEX system for MS-DOS distributed by Personal TEX, Inc. It is one of two offerings from PTI. The version for Windows is described later in this chapter.

PCTEX is sold in two configurations. The PCTEX Starter System includes the latest releases of PCTEX and PCTEX/386, *PTI View* (for previewing), one printer driver with the appropriate Computer Modern fonts in PK format, *LaTeX For Everyone* [20], and the sources for Plain TEX, LaTeX, and *AMS*-TEX. The PCTEX Laser System includes Big PCTEX/386, LaserJet, LaserJet 4, PostScript and DeskJet printer drivers (along with a complete set of Computer Modern fonts in PK format at 300dpi and 600dpi), and the *PC TEX Manual*, in addition to everything contained in the Starter System.

The discussion that follows is based on experiences with the PCTEX Starter System with PCTEX version 3.14 and the *PTI Laser/HP* DVI driver.

In addition to the TEX executables and macro packages mentioned above, PCTEX includes these standard TEX utilities: BIBTEX, *PLtoTF*, *TFtoPL*, *PXtoPK*, and *PKtoPX*. It does not include any of the other standard utilities or the *MakeIndex* processor. METAFONT is available as a separate package (although it is being discontinued, so it may not be available for long).

Several additional features make PCTEX an attractive commercial alternative:

- It uses a text-based "menu system" for processing documents. This program makes the edit/format/preview cycle a simple matter of selecting the appropriate menu item. Figure 14-1 shows this system in use.

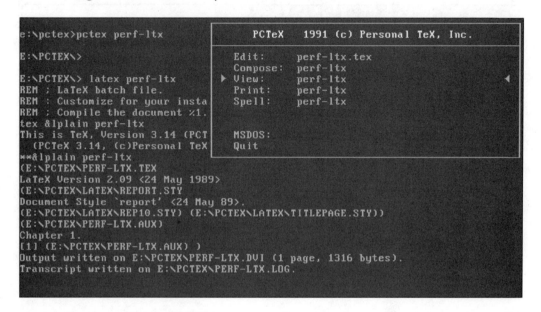

```
e:\pctex>pctex perf-ltx                   PCTeX   1991 (c) Personal TeX, Inc.

E:\PCTEX\>                           Edit:     perf-ltx.tex
                                     Compose:  perf-ltx
E:\PCTEX\> latex perf-ltx          ▶ View:     perf-ltx                        ◀
REM ; LaTeX batch file.              Print:    perf-ltx
REM : Customize for your insta       Spell:    perf-ltx
REM ; Compile the document %1.
tex &lplain perf-ltx
This is TeX, Version 3.14 (PCT       MSDOS:
  (PCTeX 3.14, (c)Personal TeX       Quit
**&lplain perf-ltx
(E:\PCTEX\PERF-LTX.TEX
LaTeX Version 2.09 <24 May 1989>
(E:\PCTEX\LATEX\REPORT.STY)
Document Style `report' <24 May 89>.
(E:\PCTEX\LATEX\REP10.STY) (E:\PCTEX\LATEX\TITLEPAGE.STY))
(E:\PCTEX\PERF-LTX.AUX)
Chapter 1.
[1] (E:\PCTEX\PERF-LTX.AUX) )
Output written on E:\PCTEX\PERF-LTX.DVI (1 page, 1316 bytes).
Transcript written on E:\PCTEX\PERF-LTX.LOG.
```

*Figure 14-1: The PCTEX menu system*

- Support is provided for Bitstream fonts. Bitstream is a vendor of high-quality scalable typefaces. The utilities included with PCTEX allow you to create TFM and PK files from Bitstream compressed outline fonts.

- If you prepare multilingual documents, you'll appreciate the attention they receive in the PCTEX documentation. Although the ability to compose multilingual documents is really a feature of TEX version 3, not PCTEX in particular, PTI provides step-by-step instructions for building a multilingual format file. Support files for English, French, and Spanish are included.

PTI's previewer, *PTI View*, is described in Chapter 9, *Previewing*. The *PTI Laser/HP* and *PTI Laser/PS* printer drivers are discussed in Chapter 8, *Printing*. Drivers for DeskJet and Epson printers are also available.

# *PCTEX For Windows*

PCTEX For Windows is a new offering from Personal TEX, Inc. PCTEX For Windows is a superset of Personal TEX's MS-DOS version of PCTEX.

This version of PCTEX is an integrated system with a built-in editor (with complete on-line help), previewer, and push-button access to PCTEX for composing your documents. Figure 14-2 shows PCTEX For Windows in action.

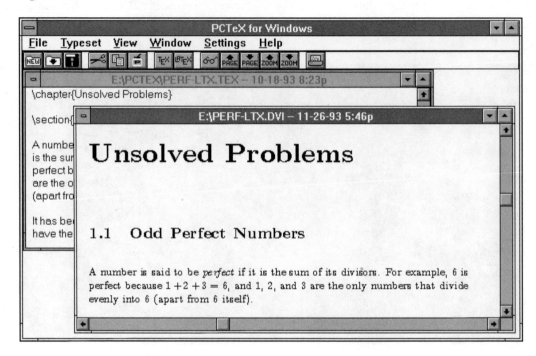

*Figure 14-2: PCTEX For Windows editing and previewing a LATEX document*

*PCTEX For Windows* includes a complete set of Computer Modern and $\mathcal{AMS}$ fonts in scalable TrueType format. This allows PCTEX to print directly to any printer (or other device) supported by Microsoft Windows. To provide better access to other TrueType fonts that you may have installed, PCTEX includes a TFM generator for TrueType fonts. This generator is shown in Figure 14-3.

Except for the *PXtoPK* and *PKtoPX* utilities, *PCTEX For Windows* has all of the features of the MS-DOS version of PCTEX.

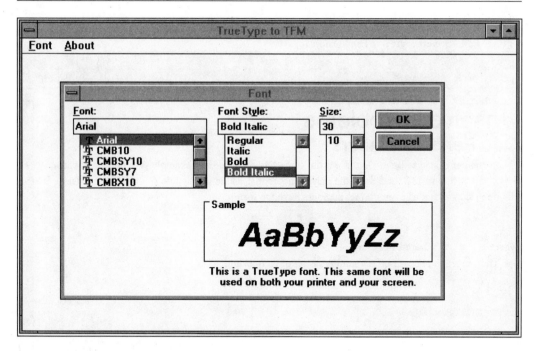

*Figure 14-3: PCTEX For Windows TrueType font metric builder*

## Scientific Word

*Scientific Word*, a commercial package from TCI Software Research, bridges the gap between TEX and word processing by providing a more or less WYSIWYG interface on top of TEX. *Scientific Word* requires Microsoft Windows. Figure 14-4 shows a sample document being edited by *Scientific Word*.

*Scientific Word* is a powerful program that might prove to be invaluable in some circumstances. An ideal candidate for *Scientific Word* is someone with little or no desire to learn TEX, but who wants professional quality output for documents containing a lot of mathematics. *Scientific Word* is not simply a fast, interactive previewer; it really is a visual editor that produces TEX code behind the scenes. You enter document elements (even complex elements like mathematics) in an interactive push-button fashion, and *Scientific Word* translates it into the appropriate LATEX input. This is very different from Blue Sky Research's *Textures* where the user types in TEX but has nearly instantaneous feedback.

Unfortunately, the complexity of TEX vastly exceeds *Scientific Word's* ability to act as a visual editor, and this leads to a number of potentially confusing discrepancies. For example, in a TEX document, the \parindent and \parskip control sequences control the indentation of the first line of a paragraph and the distance between paragraphs. In

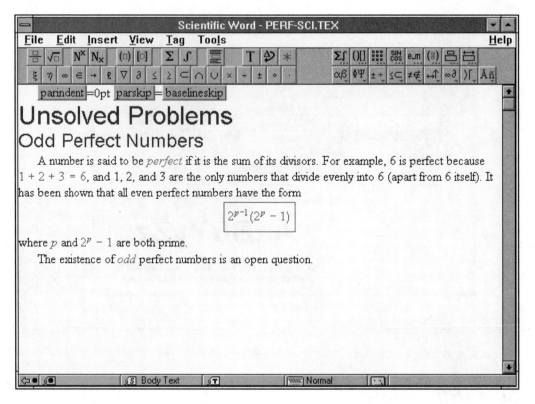

*Figure 14-4: Editing a document with Scientific Word*

*Scientific Word*, the on-screen appearance of the document is controlled separately. This difference is apparent in Figure 14-4, where the paragraphs appear to be indented with no additional space between them, and Figure 14-5 (the same document shown in the previewer) where the paragraphs are not indented but have additional space between them.

These discrepancies arise because *Scientific Word* was designed with the same philosophy as LATEX: separation of content and form. The purpose of the *Scientific Word* editor is to allow you to organize your thoughts and perfect the content of your document. It is the job of LATEX, in conjunction with the document style options that you select, to perfect the appearance of your document. The display shown in Figure 14-4 is not incorrect in any way, it just isn't WYSIWYG. TCI Research claims that "by going beyond WYSIWYG, *Scientific Word* allows you to focus on the creative process . . . and not the layout commands necessary to typeset [your document]."

When *Scientific Word* encounters TEX code that it does not understand, it leaves a labelled grey box in the display (you can see two such boxes above the chapter title

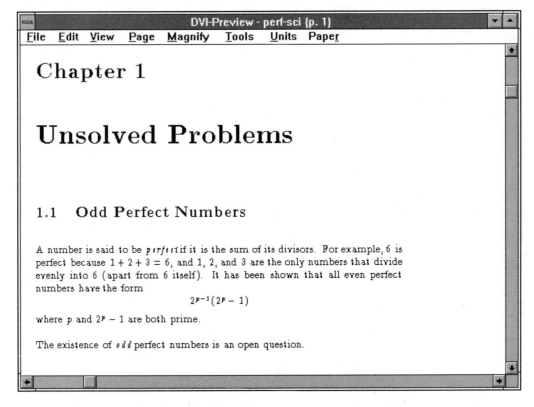

*Figure 14-5: Preview of the Scientific Word document shown in Figure 14-4*

"Unsolved Problems" in Figure 14-4).* This means that you can edit all of the TeX code in your document from within *Scientific Word*, and small amounts of customization do not require abandoning the program. The *Scientific Word* technical reference, included online with the program, describes how you can tailor *Scientific Word* to recognize many of your customizations.

Behind the scenes, *Scientific Word* documents are processed by a full-fledged TeX processor (TurboTeX by the Kinch Computer Company). This includes integrated document formatting and previewing under Windows. Starting with version 1.1 of *Scientific Word*, instructions are included to switch to a different version of TeX, or different previewers and DVI drivers, if you prefer.

---

*I forced the issue of unrecognized control sequences by inserting \parskip and \parindent control sequences into the body of the document. They really belong in a document style option.

# 15

# TEX on the Macintosh

For the most part, using TEX on the Macintosh is like using TEX on any other system. Certainly, the TEX documents that you edit are the same, and the output (on paper) is the same as the output from any other version of TEX.

However, because they are immersed in a consistent graphical environment, Macintosh tools have a substantially different appearance from their non-graphical counterparts.*

There are four implementations of TEX available for the Macintosh. Of these four, one is commercial, two are shareware, and one is (mostly) free. The following sections present an overview of each implementation, in alphabetical order.

## CMacTEX

The CMacTEX package includes the most recent versions of TEX and METAFONT and all of the standard tools. A port of *dvips* is also included, as well as a DVI previewer and a *PrintPS* tool for printing PostScript files directly to a LaserWriter printer over AppleTalk.

Each utility is a straightforward port of its UNIX counterpart. Command-line options have been replaced by standard Mac dialog boxes and menus where appropriate. TEX has been extended to include a built-in editor, although it is not necessary to use that editor if you have another favorite.

By design, CMacTEX is a very modular package. This makes it easy to substitute different tools, or different ports of the same tools, where it is advantageous to do so. For example, you can use *MacGS* (a Macintosh version of *Ghostscript*) as a previewer if you like.

---

*I'm not going to argue about the relative merits of graphical and non-graphical environments or particular implementations of graphical environments. When all is said and done, the Mac *is* different. At least today.

Small versions of TEX, iniTEX, METAFONT, and *iniMF* are provided in the free distribution of CMacTEX. Big versions are available only in a commercial distribution purchased directly from the author. At the time of this writing, the commercial distribution is available on diskettes and via email. The commercial version also provides fully automated font generation (see "Automatic Font Generation by DVI Drivers" in Chapter 5, *Fonts*) and faster versions of TEX and METAFONT.

The configuration files used by CMacTEX resemble the environment variables used by implementations of TEX on other systems. You can set up multiple search folders for input files and fonts, for example, by providing a list of folder names separated by colons.

Table 15-1 summarizes the CMacTEX version 2.1 distribution available on the CTAN archives (in *systems/mac/cmactex*) as of July, 1993. The top-level folders and their contents are presented, not a list of the archive files that form the distribution.

*Table 15-1: Summary of the CMacTEX Distribution at CTAN*

| Folder | Description |
|--------|-------------|
| *TeX* | Small versions of TEX |
| *Metafont* | Small versions of METAFONT |
| *view&print* | DVI previewer and *PrintPS* |
| *dvips5516* | Complete distribution of *dvips*, version 5.516. |
| *Utilities* | All of the standard TEXware and *MFware* utilities |
| *ams* | Versions of $\mathcal{A}_{\mathcal{M}}\mathcal{S}$-TEX and $\mathcal{A}_{\mathcal{M}}\mathcal{S}$-LATEX |
| *ams-pk* | $\mathcal{A}_{\mathcal{M}}\mathcal{S}$-fonts in PK format |
| *ams-tfm* | TFM files for the $\mathcal{A}_{\mathcal{M}}\mathcal{S}$-fonts |
| *amsfonts* | METAFONT sources for version 2.0 of the $\mathcal{A}_{\mathcal{M}}\mathcal{S}$-fonts |
| *tfms* | TFM files for the CMR and LATEX fonts |
| *cmpk300* | The CMR fonts in PK format |
| *lpk300* | The LATEX extensions to CMR in PK format |

The installation instructions for CMacTEX are easy to understand, but you will have to configure CMacTEX before you try to use it. Unfortunately, the default configuration files do not reflect the layout of folders that results directly from unpacking the archive files.

CMacTEX includes a prebuilt format file for Plain TEX, but if you want to use LATEX, you will have to build the format file with iniTEX first.

# *DirectTEX*

DirectTEX is a Macintosh Programmer's Workshop (MPW) based TEX package. It is distributed in archive files containing eight disk images. You will have to copy each disk image onto a diskette (using a tool provided) before you can install DirectTEX.

Because I don't have access to a Mac with MPW installed, there is very little that I can say about DirectT<sub>E</sub>X at this point.

# OzT<sub>E</sub>X

OzT<sub>E</sub>X is a complete T<sub>E</sub>X package that includes an integrated DVI previewer. OzT<sub>E</sub>X can print T<sub>E</sub>X DVI files directly to any printer selected by the *Chooser*. Because OzT<sub>E</sub>X does not include METAFONT, you may need to get from some other source PK files at a resolution appropiate for your printer. The standard OzT<sub>E</sub>X distribution includes a complete set of PK files for 300dpi and 360dpi printers.

A default configuration file and a selection of specialized configuration files for different printers and environments are provided with OzT<sub>E</sub>X. The distinction between big and small implementations of T<sub>E</sub>X has been replaced by configurable memory limits. With enough RAM and appropriate configuration, you should be able to get OzT<sub>E</sub>X to process any T<sub>E</sub>X file you give it.

OzT<sub>E</sub>X includes a simple text editor called Σ*Edit*, but you can replace it with any editor you choose. Table 15-2 summarizes the OzT<sub>E</sub>X version 1.5 distribution available on the CTAN archives (in *systems/mac/oztex*) as of July, 1993. The top-level folders and their contents are given, not a list of the archive files that form the distribution.

*Table 15-2: Summary of the OzT<sub>E</sub>X Distribution at CTAN*

| Folder | Contents |
|---|---|
| *Configs* | Configuration files |
| *TeX-formats* | Format files for Plain T<sub>E</sub>X and L<sup>A</sup>T<sub>E</sub>X |
| *TeX-fonts* | TFM files for CMR, L<sup>A</sup>T<sub>E</sub>X, and PostScript fonts |
| *Help-files* | Online help files |
| *PS-files* | PostScript sources for OzT<sub>E</sub>X's PostScript built-in driver |
| *TeX-docs* | Example T<sub>E</sub>X files |
| *LaTeX-docs* | L<sup>A</sup>T<sub>E</sub>X sources for a 26 page User's Guide to OzT<sub>E</sub>X |
| Σ*Edit* | A simple text editor desk accessory |
| *TeX-inputs* | Input files for Plain T<sub>E</sub>X and L<sup>A</sup>T<sub>E</sub>X |
| *PK-files* | A set of PK files for 300dpi and 360dpi printers |

The OzT<sub>E</sub>X DVI printer recognizes \special commands for inserting PICT, PNTG (*Mac-Paint*), and EPSF images into your documents. Provision is also made for including raw PostScript code if the selected printer is a PostScript printer.

OzT<sub>E</sub>X is a shareware program. If you continue to use it after a reasonable trial period, you are expected to purchase it.

# *Textures*

*Textures* is a commercial implementation of TEX from Blue Sky Research. It has a number of features that make it unique in the TEX market. It is supported by a complete user's guide and access to telephone and email product support.

*Textures* supports an interactive preview mode called *Lightning Textures*. It is this feature that really sets *Textures* apart from other implementations. In this mode, changes to your document are reflected immediately in the preview window. In an environment with sufficient resources (memory and processing speed), the result is striking. Constructing complex items like tables and mathematical formulae is much easier, especially for the TEX novice, than using the conventional edit, TEX, preview, debug cycle. Because the log file is also visible, it's easy to see when you've written erroneous TEX code.

Note that *Lightning Textures* is not really a WYSIWYG environment (like *Scientific Word*, for example) because you still enter regular TEX commands in a purely textual fashion. You get immediate feedback in a different window.

*Textures* is fast. Extensive instrumentation and hand-tuning of the program has produced an executable that is several (maybe many) times faster than other TEX executables on similar hardware.

A complete set of Computer Modern Roman fonts is provided in Adobe Type 1 format. This means that any font can be rendered at any size without loss of quality. PostScript versions of the $\mathcal{A}\mathcal{M}\mathcal{S}$-fonts are also available. The fonts can be purchased separately in either Macintosh or Adobe PFB formats.

*Textures* is a very integrated environment. This can hardly be labelled a disadvantage considering how well it works, but it does mean that some extra effort is required if you want access to your document in a less integrated fashion. Using another editor to compose your document is possible, but it prevents you from using *Lighting Textures*. Starting with version 1.6, the *Textures* editor includes a macro programming language, so you can customize it with features that you find useful. Blue Sky Research provides the tools you need to incorporate other fonts into TEX or extract TEX files (like DVI files) that are normally hidden from view by *Textures*.

Figure 15-1 shows an example of a *Textures* session. The preview quality in this image is less than optimal because the Macintosh that *Textures* is running on does not have Adobe Type Manager.

Because the Computer Modern Roman fonts are included in Adobe Type 1 format, METAFONT is not provided in the *Textures* package. Recently, BSR made their version of METAFONT freely available. BSR's METAFONT was designed to work with *Textures*, and creates output files that are suitable for *Textures*, but not necessarily the standard GF and TFM files you might expect. Those files can be obtained elsewhere, of course.

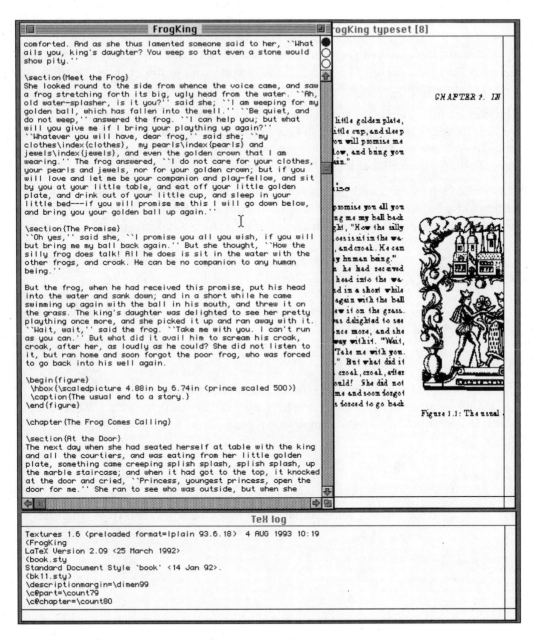

*Figure 15-1: Editing, previewing, and typesetting in Textures*

The *Textures* package includes implementations of many auxiliary TEX programs including BIBTEX, *MakeIndex*, the *Excalibur* spellchecker (see the "Excalibur" section later in this chapter), a *DVITool* for importing and exporting DVI files, and font tools for importing and exporting fonts. (Because *Textures* doesn't use PK files directly, the standard *MFware* tools are not provided.) The *Textures* font tools are freely available from Blue Sky Research; see the "BSR Font Tools" section later in this chapter. *Textures* also supports virtual fonts.

*Textures* includes the Eplain and Midnight macro packages in addition to Plain TEX and LATEX. iniTEX is built into *Textures*, so you can make additional format files as described in Chapter 4, *Macro Packages*. Making format files with *Textures* requires a Macintosh Plus or other system with at least 1Mb of memory.

The *Textures* previewer and printing operations understand bitmap or scalable (EPSF) pictures inserted into your document with `\special` commands. Although not visible on the previewer, raw PostScript can also be inserted for documents printed on PostScript devices.

# *Other Tools*

The following sections describe Macintosh versions of other common tools. Some of these programs are unique to the Mac, while others are ports of tools from other systems.

## *Alpha*

*Alpha* is a sophisticated shareware editor for text files. *Alpha* uses *Tcl*, an interpreted C-like language, as a macro programming language for extending the editor. LATEX support, which is written in *Tcl*, is very complete. An example of the *Alpha* editor is shown in Figure 15-2.

## *BBEdit*

*BBEdit* is another shareware editor. Like *Alpha*, it has a wide range of features including a LATEX-aware editing mode. An example of the *BBEdit* editor is shown in Figure 15-3.

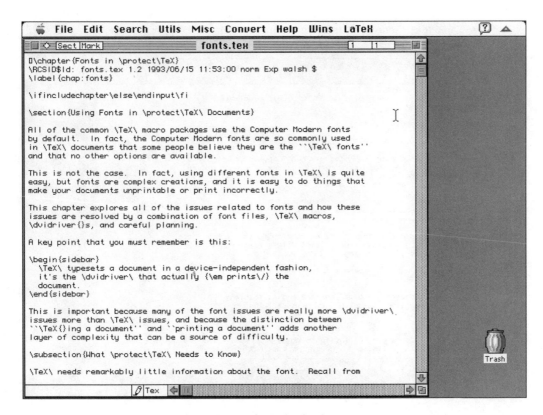

*Figure 15-2: Alpha editing the fonts chapter from this book*

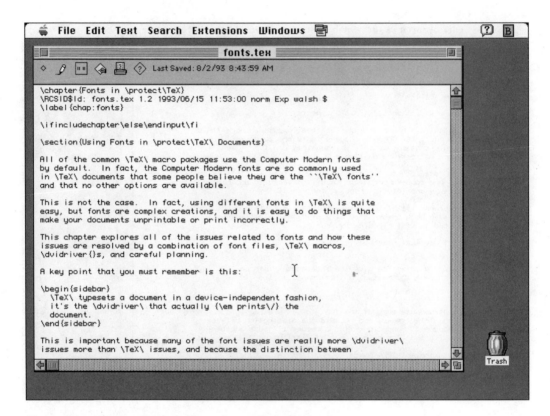

*Figure 15-3: BBEdit editing the fonts chapter from this book*

## BSR Font Tools

The Macintosh Programmer's Workshop (MPW) is required to use the Blue Sky Research Font Tools. These tools were written for *Textures* users so that they could make other fonts, like those created with METAFONT, for example, usable in *Textures*. In practice however, they create standard Macintosh font resources, so the resulting fonts can be used by any Mac application. Table 15-3 describes the tools included in the *BSR Font Tools* package.

*Table 15-3: Font Tools in the BSR package*

| Tool | Description |
|------|-------------|
| *GFtoPK* | Converts METAFONT GF files into standard PK format |
| *PKtoFOND* | Creates Mac FOND resource from PK and TFM files |
| *TFMtoSuit* | Creates a font metrics suitcase |
| *NFNTcon* | Finds NFNT resource numbering conflicts |
| *TFtoPL* | Converts TFM files into PL files |
| *PLtoTF* | Translates PL files (back) into TFM files |

## Excalibur

*Excalibur* is a spellchecker designed to work with LATEX documents. An example of *Excalibur* is shown in Figure 15-4.

## HyperBɪʙTₑX

This is a hypercard stack for maintaining bibliographic databases suitable for use with BɪʙTₑX. BɪʙTₑX is described in Chapter 12, *Bibliographies, Indexes, and Glossaries*. An example of HyperBɪʙTₑX is shown in Figure 15-5.

## MacGS

*MacGS* is a Macintosh port of GNU *Ghostscript*, described in Chapter 9, *Previewing*.

## dvidvi

*dvidvi* is a Macintosh port of the *dvidvi* utility for rearranging pages in a DVI file.

## MacDVIcopy

*MacDVIcopy* is a port of the *DVICOPY* utility, which transforms virtual font references in a DVI file into the appropriate non-virtual fonts or commands. This allows DVI drivers and previewers that lack support for virtual fonts to preview documents that use them.

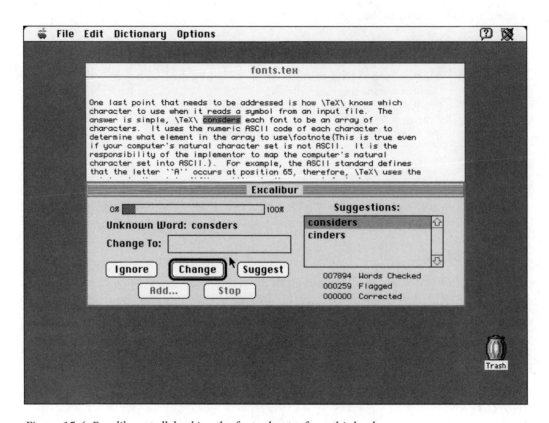

*Figure 15-4: Excalibur spellchecking the fonts chapter from this book*

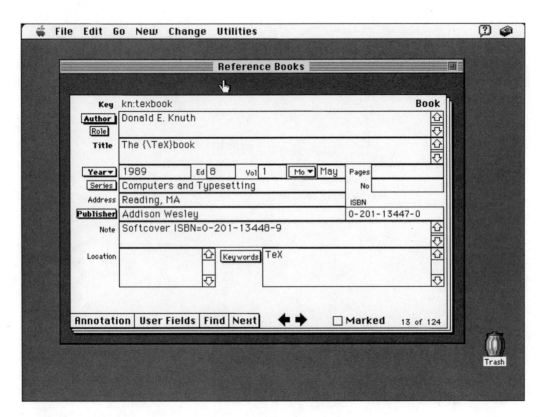

*Figure 15-5: The HyperBiBTEX view of a bibliographic database*

## *MacBIBTEX*

MacBIBTEX is a port of the standard BIBTEX utility for accessing bibliographic databases in a document. BIBTEX is described in Chapter 12.

## *MacMakeIndex*

*MacMakeIndex* is a port of the standard *MakeIndex* for creating sorted, multilevel indexes in a document. *MakeIndex* is described in Chapter 12.

# 16

# *T<small>E</small>X Utilities*

This chapter offers a brief summary of a large number of T<small>E</small>X utilities (some more commonly used than others). Some of these programs are mentioned elsewhere in this book in connection with the particular tasks that they perform.

Although many programs are described in this chapter, there is no way that it can be entirely complete. There are just too many programs on CTAN for me to be familiar with *all* of them. This list is representative of the collection of programs present in the archives during the winter of 1993. Regrettably, programs not documented in English are not included at this time. Take the time to explore the CTAN archives yourself; you won't be disappointed.

> Use the Web, Luke! One of the most convenient online tools for search-
> ing the archives is the World Wide Web (WWW) interface available at
> *http://jasper.ora.com/ctan.html*. The WWW interface is constructed automatically
> from the most recent list of files in the CTAN archives with annotations taken from
> this chapter from the *TeX-index*, and from the *ctan.dat* descriptions maintained
> by the CTAN archivists.

This chapter attempts to describe only part of the archives. Here are some of the things that are *not* described in this chapter:

* The thirty or more packages in the *archive-tools* directory. This directory contains sources and executables for almost every archiving tool imaginable. If you retrieve a file from an FTP site and you don't have the tool necessary to unpack it, you'll

probably find it in here. You'll also find other archive-related programs like an FTP server and the *Gopher* sources.

- Files from the *digests*, *documentation*, and *help* directories. These are collections of electronic digests, documents, and articles that discuss aspects of TEX. They are recommended reading.

- Files from the *fonts* directory. These are summarized in Chapter 5, *Fonts*.

- Files from the *languages* directory. These are summarized in Chapter 7, *International Considerations*.

- The many special macro files in the *macros* subtree. Many macro formats are described in Chapter 4, *Macro Packages*.

- Architecture-specific applications from the *systems* subtree. These include applications for Amiga, Atari, Macintosh, MS-DOS, OS/2, UNIX, VMS, and Xenix systems. The Common-TEX distribution is also available under this directory, as well as the standard TEX distributions by Knuth.

# *List of Tools*

These tools are available in the CTAN archives in the directories specified. This list is sorted by CTAN path name so that related utilities appear near each other.

### *bib2dvi*
Directory: *biblio/bibtex/utils/bib2dvi*
*bib2dvi* is a shell script that creates a printable listing of an entire BIBTEX database.

### *bibcard*
Directory: *biblio/bibtex/utils/bibcard*
*bibcard* is an X11 based database editor for BIBTEX databases. This is an OpenWindows application requiring the *xview* and *olgx* libraries.

### *bibclean*
Directory: *biblio/bibtex/utils/bibclean*
*bibclean* syntax-checks and pretty-prints a BIBTEX database.

### *bibextract*
Directory: *biblio/bibtex/utils/bibextract*
*bibextract* extracts bibliographic entries from a list of BIBTEX databases based upon a user-supplied regular expression.

### *citefind*
Directory: *biblio/bibtex/utils/bibextract*
*citefind* extracts bibliographic entries from a list of BIBTEX databases based upon a user-supplied list of keys.

## citetags

Directory: *biblio/bibtex/utils/bibextract*

*citetags* extracts citation tags from a list of LATEX source files. These tags can be fed to *citefind* to produce a bibliography database customized for a particular document.

## bibindex

Directory: *biblio/bibtex/utils/bibindex*

*bibindex* creates a bibliographic index for the *biblook* program.

## biblook

Directory: *biblio/bibtex/utils/bibindex*

*biblook* uses a binary index constructed by *bibindex* to perform very fast lookups into BIBTEX databases.

## bibsort

Directory: *biblio/bibtex/utils/bibsort*

*bibsort* sorts a BIBTEX database.

## bibtool

Directory: *biblio/bibtex/utils/bibtool*

*bibtool* performs a number of operations on BIBTEX databases. It can pretty-print and syntax-check a database, automatically build new keys, extract particular entries, sort a database, and perform a number of other operations. The operation of *bibtool* can be customized with one or more resource files.

## aux2bib

Directory: *biblio/bibtex/utils/bibtools*

*aux2bib* extracts citations from a LATEX AUX file and constructs a bibliography that contains only the entries required by the document.

## bibify

Directory: *biblio/bibtex/utils/bibtools*

*bibify* attempts to generate an AUX file that contains appropriate references for citations. This eliminates one LATEX pass over the document and may be much faster for large documents. *bibify* cannot handle documents that use multiple AUX files.

## bibkey

Directory: *biblio/bibtex/utils/bibtools*

Lists all entries in a BIBTEX database that contain a particular keyword in the keyword field.

## cleantex

Directory: *biblio/bibtex/utils/bibtools*

Deletes temporary files (AUX, LOF, etc.) created by LATEX.

### looktex

Directory: *biblio/bibtex/utils/bibtools*

Lists all BIBTEX database entries that match a specified regular expression.

### makebib

Directory: *biblio/bibtex/utils/bibtools*

*makebib* creates a "portable" BIBTEX database by performing string substitutions, removing comments, and optionally discarding all entries that do not match a given list of keys.

### printbib

Directory: *biblio/bibtex/utils/bibtools*

*printbib* creates a printable listing of an entire BIBTEX database. *printbib* is also available in the *biblio/bibtex/utils/printbib* directory.

### bibview

Directory: *biblio/bibtex/utils/bibview*

*bibview* is an interactive Perl script that allows you to view and search through a BIBTEX database.

### HyperBibTeX

Directory: *biblio/bibtex/utils/hyperbibtex*

*HyperBibTeX* is a Macintosh tool for manipulating BIBTEX databases.

### bibdestringify

Directory: *biblio/bibtex/utils/lookbibtex*

*bibdestringify* performs BIBTEX string substitution on a BIBTEX database.

### lookbibtex

Directory: *biblio/bibtex/utils/lookbibtex*

Lists all BIBTEX database entries that match a specified regular expression.

### r2bib

Directory: *biblio/bibtex/utils/r2bib*

*r2bib* converts *refer* databases into BIBTEX databases.

### ref2bib

Directory: *biblio/bibtex/utils/ref2bib*

*ref2bib* converts *refer* databases into BIBTEX databases.

### xbibtex

Directory: *biblio/bibtex/utils/xbibtex*

*xbibtex* is an X11 program for manipulating BIBTEX databases.

### Public Doman DVI Driver Family

Directory: *dviware/beebe*

A collection of DVI drivers. This code has been used as the basis for many other DVI-aware programs. Table 16-1 summarizes the drivers included in this package.

*Table 16-1: The Public Doman DVI Driver Family*

| Driver | Description |
|--------|-------------|
| *dvialw* | PostScript (Apple LaserWriter laser printer) |
| *dvibit* | Version 3.10 BBN BitGraph terminal |
| *dvica2* | Canon LBP-8 A2 laser printer |
| *dvican* | Canon LBP-8 A2 laser printer |
| *dvidjp* | Hewlett-Packard Desk Jet plus (from LaserJet) |
| *dvie72* | Epson 9-pin family 240/216-dpi dot matrix printer |
| *dvie72* | Epson 9-pin family 60/72-dpi dot matrix printer |
| *dvieps* | Epson 9-pin family 240/216-dpi dot matrix printer |
| *dvieps* | Epson 9-pin family 60/72-dpi dot matrix printer |
| *dvigd* | Golden Dawn Golden Laser 100 laser printer |
| *dviimp* | imPRESS (Imagen laser printer family) |
| *dvijep* | Hewlett-Packard LaserJet Plus laser printer |
| *dvijet* | Hewlett-Packard 2686A Laser Jet laser printer |
| *dvil3p* | Digital LN03-PLUS 300 dpi laser printer |
| *dvil3p* | Digital LN03-PLUS 150 dpi laser printer |
| *dvil75* | DEC LA75 144h x 144v dot matrix printer |
| *dvil75* | DEC LA75 72h x 72v dot matrix printer |
| *dvim72* | Apple ImageWriter 144 dpi dot matrix printer |
| *dvim72* | Apple ImageWriter 72 dpi dot matrix printer |
| *dvimac* | Apple ImageWriter 144 dpi dot matrix printer |
| *dvimac* | Apple ImageWriter 72 dpi dot matrix printer |
| *dvimpi* | MPI Sprinter 144h x 144v dot matrix printer |
| *dvimpi* | MPI Sprinter 72h x 72v dot matrix printer |
| *dvio72* | OKIDATA Pacemark 2410 144 dpi dot matrix printer |
| *dvio72* | OKIDATA Pacemark 2410 72 dpi dot matrix printer |
| *dvioki* | OKIDATA Pacemark 2410 144 dpi dot matrix printer |
| *dvioki* | OKIDATA Pacemark 2410 72 dpi dot matrix printer |
| *dviprx* | Printronix 300/600 60h x 72v dpi dot matrix printer |
| *dvitos* | Toshiba P-1351 180h x 180v dpi dot matrix printer |

### bitpxl

Directory: *dviware/bitpxl*

Converts HP LaserJet bitmaps into PXL files.

### cdvi

Directory: *dviware/cdvi*

MS-DOS DVI file previewer. Does not support external fonts, but has 16 Computer Modern fonts built in.

### *Crudetype*

Directory: *dviware/crudetype/version3*

A DVI-to-text translator. *Crudetype* attempts to make a readable DVI file. An interactive mode is available on some platforms. A 132-column display is expected for most output.

### *DVItoVDU*

Directory: *dviware/dvgt*

*DVItoVDU* is a terminal previewer for DVI files. The *dvgt* version supports graphics preview using various graphics terminals and limited typeset preview on other terminals such as the VT100 and VT220. Tektronix emulation allows remote previewing of DVI files through Telnet or using Kermit from a PC, for example.

### *DVI2PCL*

Directory: *dviware/dvi2pcl*

Translates DVI files into HP LaserJet format.

### *dvi2ps*

Directory: *dviware/dvi2ps*

There are a number of translators called *dvi2ps*. Some appear to be older DVI to PostScript translators supporting the MIT *printcap* entries and Apple LaserWriter printers, while others offer support for Asian fonts compatible with the tools used by the Japanese TEX User's Group and the *chfont* program, better support for built-in printer features, and faster execution.

### *psdvi*

Directory: *dviware/dvi2ps/psdvi*

This program translates DVI files into resolution-independent PostScript files. This allows the PostScript output to be printed on high-resolution phototypesetting equipment. Many other DVI-to-PostScript converters assume that the output resolution is 300dpi, which makes the PostScript more difficult, or impossible, to print on high-resolution devices.

Because bitmapped fonts are inherently resolution-dependent, documents that use them cannot be translated with this driver. This means that none of the Computer Modern or $\mathcal{AMS}$ fonts can be used unless you have them in PostScript Type 1 format.

### *DVI2QMS*

Directory: *dviware/dvi2qms*

Translates DVI files into output suitable for QMS 800/1200/2400 printers.

### *DVI2TTY*

Directory: *dviware/dvi2tty*

Translates DVI files into plain ASCII text.

## dvi2xx

Directory: *dviware/dvi2xx*

Translates DVI files into output suitable for the HP LaserJet family of printers and compatible printers. It also supports output to the IBM 3812 printer. MS-DOS and OS/2 executables are provided.

## dviapollo

Directory: *dviware/dviapollo*

A screen previewer for Apollo workstations.

## dvibit

Directory: *dviware/dvibit*

A screen previewer for BBN BitGraph terminals.

## dvibook

Directory: *dviware/dvibook*

Rearranges DVI file pages into a sequence suitable for printing and folding into a book. Actually, it produces signatures, which are small groups of pages that can be folded together. A signature is composed of several folded pages; a book is composed of many signatures bound together.

## DVIChk

Directory: *dviware/dvichk*

*DVIChk* examines a DVI file and prints out the page numbers that occur in the document in the order in which they occur. Pages in a DVI file do not have to occur in any particular order.

## DVICOPY

Directory: *dviware/dvicopy*

This program copies a DVI file that contains references to virtual fonts and creates an equivalent DVI file with all references to virtual fonts translated into references to the appropriate non-virtual fonts.

## DVIDIS

Directory: *dviware/dvidis*

A DVI file previewer for VaxStations running VMS.

## dvidoc

Directory: *dviware/dvidoc*

Translates DVI files into plain ASCII. Although it does not attempt to form the same page breaks, it does claim to get the interword spacing correct.

### DVIDVI

Directory: *dviware/dvidvi*

Rearranges pages in a DVI file. The resulting file is a new DVI file containing only the selected pages. A Macintosh executable is available in *dviware/dvidvi/mac*.

### DVIEW

Directory: *dviware/dview*

A very old previewer for MS-DOS. This program relies on PXL files and requires the antique Almost Modern fonts to print the user manual.

### DVIIMP

Directory: *dviware/dviimp*

Translates DVI files into a format suitable for printing on an Imagen printer. This program reads GF files rather than PK files.

### dvimerge

Directory: *dviware/dvimerge*

*dvimerge* is a shell script (written in *sb*) that uses *dvidvi* and *dviconcat* to merge two DVI files together.

### DVIMSWin

Directory: *dviware/dvimswin*

A DVI previewer for MS-DOS running Windows 3.1. This program uses PK fonts at screen resolution. These can be generated by METAFONT or obtained from the *dvivga* distribution.

### dvipage

Directory: *dviware/dvipage*

A DVI previewer for workstations running SunView version 3.0 or later.

### dvipj

Directory: *dviware/dvipj*

This program is a modification of the *dvijet* driver that supports color printing on the HP PaintJet printer. To build this program, you need source from the Public Doman DVI Driver Family.

### dvips

Directory: *dviware/dvips*

The *dvips* program is the de facto standard DVI to PostScript translator. Several versions are available, although the most recent release seems to offer a superset of the features provided by all the other versions.

### *dvipsk*

Directory: *dviware/dvipsk*

*dvipsk* is a modification of *dvips* version 5.516 that supports an extended path searching algorithm for PK fonts.

### *DVISUN*

Directory: *dviware/dvisun*

A DVI previewer for Sun II terminals.

### *dvitodvi*

Directory: *dviware/dvitodvi*

Rearranges pages in a DVI file, producing a new DVI file.

### *dvitool*

Directory: *dviware/dvitool*

A DVI previewer for workstations running SunView.

### *dvitops*

Directory: *dviware/dvitops/dvitops*

*dvitops* is a DVI-to-PostScript translator. *psfont* can be used to download PostScript fonts. *pfbtops* decodes printer font binary files into printer font ASCII files. *aftopl* builds a PL file from a PostScript AFM file. PL files can be further translated into TFM files with the standard *PLtoTF* utility.

### *dvitovdu*

Directory: *dviware/dvitovdu*

A DVI previewer for terminals. *dvitovdu* handles plain ASCII terminals as well as some graphics terminals. Includes VMS and UNIX ports.

### *dvitovdu*

Directory: *dviware/dvitovdu32*

Another version of the *dvitovdu* DVI previewer for terminals. *dvitovdu* handles plain ASCII terminals as well as some graphics terminals. This version seems to read only PXL files.

### *dvitty*

Directory: *dviware/dvitty*

A simple previewer for ASCII display of DVI files.

### *DVIVGA*

Directory: *dviware/dvivga*

The *DVIVGA* distribution includes a program for previewing DVI files on PCs with EGA, VGA, or MCGA displays. *DVIVGA* is derived from the Public Doman DVI Driver Family. The *DVIVGA* distribution also includes a full set of PK fonts at many resolutions: 70, 76,

84, 92, 100, 110, 121, 132, 145, 174, 208, 250, and 300dpi. Other previewers that require PK fonts at screen resolution (typically near 100dpi) can also use these fonts.

### DVIWIN
Directory: *dviware/dviwin*
A screen previewer for MS-DOS running Windows 3.1. This program includes the ability to use emTEX FLI font libraries.

### eps
Directory: *dviware/epson/eps-0.2*
Prints a DVI file on an Epson dot-matrix printer. Some PK fonts at the appropriate resolutions are included in *dviware/epson/epson*.

### ivd2dvi
Directory: *dviware/ivd2dvi*
The TEX-XET driver produces IVD files, which are like DVI files except that they use some special commands to perform reflection, which allows them to print *right-to-left*.

This program translates an IVD file into a standard DVI file by replacing all of the special commands with standard DVI file commands.

### dvijep
Directory: *dviware/kane*
Another DVI-to-HP LaserJet+ driver.

### dvijep_p
Directory: *dviware/kane*
A modified version of *dvijep* with Centronics PP8 workarounds *removed* where they might confuse a real LaserJet+ printer.

### dvi2kyo
Directory: *dviware/kyocera*
A DVI translator that produces Kyocera's native Prescribe command language rather than relying on Kyocera's somewhat limited HP LaserJet compatibility mode.

### kyodev
Directory: *dviware/kyocera*
This DVI driver produces output in Kyocera's native Prescribe format.

### dviplus
Directory: *dviware/laserjet*
An old DVI-to-HP LaserJet Plus translator that uses PXL files.

### LN03 Driver
Directory: *dviware/ln03*
Translates DVI files into a format suitable for printing on a Digital LN03 printer.

## PSPrint

Directory: *dviware/psprint*

A PostScript printing program that can handle DVI files, raw PostScript files, or text files. This program is a combined DVI-to-PostScript translator and file-printing utility.

UNIX and VMS sources are provided, but a Pascal compiler is required.

## QMS

Directory: *dviware/qms*

An old VMS DVI driver for QMS printers.

## QuicSpool

Directory: *dviware/quicspool*

This is a collection of programs for printing files to QMS and Talaris laser printers. Support for DVI files is included.

## SCREENVIEW

Directory: *dviware/screenview*

A VMS tool based on *Crudetype* for previewing DVI files at an ASCII terminal.

## SeeTEX

Directory: *dviware/seetex*

The *SeeTEX* package contains a number of tools for working with DVI files. The most substantial of these tools are the *xtex* and *texsun* previewers for workstations running the X Window system and the SunView window system, respectively.

*xtex* is unique among X11 previewers because it uses X Window fonts. This makes *xtex* quite fast. It also means that *xtex* has to build a lot of new X Window fonts the first few times that you use it. The *mftops* program converts TEX PK fonts into X Window fonts. *xtex* uses the *MakeTeXPK* program to build new PK fonts at the necessary resolutions. *xtex* also uses *Ghostscript* to display the PostScript figures in your document. This is typically much faster than using *GhostView* to preview the entire document. The *texx* previewer is a much simpler X Window previewer. It cannot interpret PostScript, but it does recognize most of the *tpic* specials. *SeeTEX* also includes *iptex*, an Imagen printer driver.

## TEXtool

Directory: *dviware/textool*

This is a TEX previewer for the SunView window system.

## umddvi

Directory: *dviware/umddvi*

*dvidmd* is a DVI previewer for DMD 5620 displays. *dvipr* is a DVI driver for Versatec printers. *iptex* is a DVI driver for Imagen printers. Finally, *dviselect* extracts pages from a DVI file and produces a new DVI file containing the selected pages.

## VUTEX

Directory: *dviware/vutex*

Another VMS DVI previewer for ASCII terminals.

## xdvi

Directory: *dviware/xdvi*

A screen previewer for workstations running the X11 Window System. MS-DOS executables, useful only if you have an X11 Window system running on your PC, are available in the *dviware/xdvi-dos* directory.

## xdvik

Directory: *dviware/xdvik*

*xdvik* is a modification of *xdvi* that supports an extended path searching algorithm for PK fonts.

## bit2spr

Directory: *graphics/bit2spr*

*bit2spr* converts X11 XBM bitmaps into a "sprite" format that can be included directly in TEX documents. The resulting sprites are fully portable, although they require a lot of memory, which may make large bitmaps impractical.

## bm2font

Directory: *graphics/bm2font*

The *bm2font* program converts bitmapped images into TEX, TFM, and PK files. *bm2font* also generates the Plain TEX or LATEX statements necessary to insert the figure into your document. Color images can be dithered in a number of different ways. This is one of the most portable ways to insert pictures into a document; almost every available DVI driver can print TEX PK fonts.

## fig2MF

Directory: *graphics/fig2mf*

Translates Fig code into METAFONT source. This allows you to use interactive drawing tools like *xfig* to construct diagrams that can be included into your document in a portable manner with *fig2MF*.

## gnuplot

Directory: *graphics/gnuplot*

*gnuplot* is an interactive function plotting program. Several different types of output are supported and can be included directly into your document.

## hpgl2ps

Directory: *graphics/hpgl2ps*

This program translates HPGL Plotter language commands into encapsulated PostScript.

## mactotex

Directory: *graphics/mactotex*

This program cleans up Macintosh PostScript so it can be included into your documents with *psfig*. (Some printers have difficulty printing PostScript output generated on a Macintosh because the PostScript is tailored towards the Apple LaserWriter series of printers.)

## MFPic

Directory: *graphics/mfpic*

*MFPic* is a flexible replacement for the LATEX `picture` environment. Instead of relying on special fonts to generate pictures, *MFPic* writes METAFONT code, which generates a font containing the picture specified. This makes *MFPic* more flexible than the standard `picture` environment without losing portability.

## pbmtopk

Directory: *graphics/pbmtopk*

Translates PBM files into TEX PK fonts.

## PiCTeX

Directory: *graphics/pictex*

A sophisticated macro package that works on top of Plain TEX and LATEX. It provides a device-independent way of producing many kinds of figures. The PICTEX implementation frequently generates documents that are too complex for "small" versions of TEX to render. The PICTEX manual is not freely available and must be purchased before PICTEX can be used.

## Glo+Index

Directory: *indexing/glo+index*

These are tools for automatic construction of indexes and glossaries. The glossary building tool uses `\glossary` entries from your document in conjunction with a database of word definitions to automatically construct a glossary. The *idxtex* program provides many of the same features as the *MakeIndex* program.

## MakeIndex

Directory: *indexing/makeindex*

This is the standard tool for processing `\index` entries from LATEX documents. *MakeIndex* reads the entries, sorts them, handles a number of useful features (multilevel indexes, special sorting criteria, etc.) and produces LATEX source code, which produces a typeset index.

### RTF Translator

Directory: *support/RTF-1_06a1*

The *RTF Translator* package includes several programs for converting RTF (Rich Text Format) files. RTF files contain information about the structure as well as the content of a document. Microsoft Word and several NeXT tools can produce RTF files.

Table 16-2 summarizes the translators provided. Note that there is no TEX or LATEX translator in this package at present.

*Table 16-2: RTF Translators*

| Program | Translation |
|---------|-------------|
| *rtf2null* | Removes RTF codes |
| *rtf2text* | Translates to ASCII text |
| *rtf2troff* | Translates to *ms* macros in *troff* |
| *rtfwc* | Counts actual words in an RTF document |
| *rtfdiag* | Verifies the RTF parser (or the RTF document) |
| *rtfskel* | A skeleton for producing new translators |

### accents

Directory: *support/accents*

*accents* generates a virtual font containing accented letters arranged according to the KOI8-CS character set. This program constructs the accented letters from characters and accent marks, if necessary. If the input font is in Adobe Standard Encoding, *accents* can rearrange it into TEX Text encoding.

### addindex

Directory: *support/addindex*

*addindex* inserts LATEX \index commands into your document. Presented with a list of words and index entries, *addindex* reads your LATEX files and indexes every word from the list that occurs in your document.

### amSpell

Directory: *support/amspell*

The *amSpell* program is an interactive MS-DOS spellchecker for plain ASCII and TEX documents.

### atops

Directory: *support/atops*

A simple program to convert ASCII text files into PostScript.

### AUC-TEX

Directory: *support/auctex*

A comprehensive TEX editing environment for GNU emacs.

## basix

Directory: *support/basix*

*basix* is a BASIC interpreter written entirely in TEX. Honest. ;-)

## BibDB

Directory: *support/bibdb*

An MS-DOS program for editing BIBTEX bibliographic databases.

## brief_t

Directory: *support/brief_t*

The *brief_t* package is a LATEX editing environment for Borland International's *Brief* editor.

## c++2latex

Directory: *support/c++2LaTeX-1_1*

This program parses your C or C++ programs and creates LATEX source code for pretty-printing them. The syntactic elements of the source (keywords, identifiers, comments, etc.) can be set in different fonts. Compiling this program requires *flex*.

## C2LATEX

Directory: *support/c2latex*

*C2LATEX* is a filter designed to provide simple literate programming support for C programming. This filter massages LATEX-coded C comments and source code into a LATEX document.

## chi2tex

Directory: *support/chi2tex*

*chi2tex* is an MS-DOS program for converting *ChiWriter* documents into TEX.

## detex

Directory: *support/detex*

*detex* removes TEX control sequences from a document. The *texspell* script pipes the resulting output through a spell checker.

## bibtex-mode, web-mode

Directory: *support/emacs-modes*

GNU emacs macros that provide an enhanced editing environment for BIBTEX databases and *Web* source files. Another substantial set of modes for editing LATEX documents is provided by AUC-TEX, listed separately.

## flow

Directory: *support/flow*

*flow* reads a plain text description of a flow chart and produces the appropriate LATEX `picture` environment for printing the flow chart.

### byte2tex

Directory: *support/foreign/byte2tex*

A translator for multilingual documents that use the upper range of the ASCII character set as a second alphabet. The translation performed is controlled by a plain text description of the alphabet. See also *EDI* and *cyrlatex*.

### cyrlatex

Directory: *support/foreign/cyrlatex*

A LATEX style for using the $\mathcal{A}_{\mathcal{M}}\mathcal{S}$ Cyrillic fonts as a second alphabet under LATEX. See also *EDI* and *byte2tex*.

### EDI

Directory: *support/foreign/edi*

An MS-DOS editor for multilingual (particularly Cyrillic) documents. *EDI* uses the upper range of the ASCII character set as a programmable second alphabet. See also *byte2tex* and *cyrlatex*. MS-DOS and Atari executables are available.

### genfam

Directory: *support/genfam*

The *genfam* script reads a configuration file that describes a set of fonts and then runs the appropriate METAFONT commands to produce them. A sample configuration file, *modern*, is provided for the Computer Modern Roman family.

### Ghostview

Directory: *support/ghostview*

*Ghostview* provides an interactive interface to *Ghostscript*, the GNU PostScript interpreter. *Ghostview* requires X11, but there are ports to Microsoft Windows and OS/2.

### Stanford GraphBase

Directory: *support/graphbase*

This is a collection of *CWeb* programs for studying combinatorial algorithms. It is related to TEX only because *CWeb* files are part TEX.

### HPTFM2PL

Directory: *support/hp2pl*

This program reads Hewlett-Packard Tagged Font Metric files and creates TEX PL files. The PL files can be further translated into TEX TFM files with the standard utility *PLtoTF*.

Hewlett-Packard distributes metric information about LaserJet built-in fonts and font cartridges in Tagged Font Metric format, so this program gives you a way of getting TEX metrics for those fonts. To actually use them, you must have both the metrics and a DVI driver that can use built-in fonts.

## HP2TeX

Directory: *support/hp2tex*

*HP2TeX* translates HPGL files into TeX documents that use the \special commands found in emTeX for drawing lines at arbitrary angles. This makes diagrams in HPGL format that use only straight lines printable directly with TeX. See also *HP2XX*.

## HP2XX

Directory: *support/hp2xx*

*HP2XX* converts HPGL diagrams into PostScript or one of several bitmapped formats. It can also translate some diagrams directly into TeX if \special commands are available for drawing lines at any angle.

MS-DOS, Sparc, Convex 210, and HP9000 executables are available. A Windows front-end is also available for MS-DOS.

## HPtoMF

Directory: *support/hptomf*

*HPtoMF* converts HPGL (Hewlett-Packard's plotter language) into a variety of other vector and raster formats.

## HTMLtoLaTeX

Directory: *support/html2latex*

This program converts HTML documents into LaTeX source for printing.

## Icons

Directory: *support/icons*

This is a collection of icons for TeX and METAFONT. They were designed by Donald Knuth for OpenWindows and have subsequently been translated into Microsoft Windows, OS/2, and X11 XBM format.

## Imake-TeX

Directory: *support/imaketex*

*Imake-TeX* helps you create an Imakefile for TeX documents. Imakefiles are used to generate custom makefiles for an application, in this case a LaTeX document.

## ispell

Directory: *support/ispell*

An interactive spellchecker. *ispell* is intelligent about TeX documents and can handle languages other than English.

## jspell

Directory: *support/jspell*

*jspell* is an MS-DOS spellchecker. It includes special support for TeX documents.

## TEXTools

Directory: *support/kamal*

The *TEXTools* package includes several tools for manipulating TEX documents. *detex* strips TEX commands from a file. *texeqn* extracts displayed equations from a document. *texexpand* merges documents loaded with \input or \include into a single file. *texmatch* checks for matching delimiters. *texspell* uses *detex* to spellcheck the filtered version of a document.

## LaCheck

Directory: *support/lacheck*

*LaCheck* reads a LATEX document and reports any syntax errors it finds. This is faster than running the document through TEX if you are only interested in finding TEXnical mistakes.

## LATEX2HTML

Directory: *support/latex2html*

Converts LATEX documents into HTML documents, suitable for browsing with a WWW browser. Many complex document elements are handled automatically.

## LATEXMk

Directory: *support/latexmk*

LATEXMk is a *Perl* script that attempts to determine what operations need to be performed on a document to produce a complete DVI file. LATEXMk runs LATEX, BIBTEX, etc. until a complete document has been built.

## lgrind

Directory: *support/lgrind*

*lgrind* formats program sources using LATEX. Syntactic elements are identified by typographic changes in the printed sources.

## LSEdit

Directory: *support/lsedit*

This is an add-on package for the VAX/VMS Language Sensitive Editor (*LSEDI*). It provides an editing environment for LATEX documents.

## make_latex

Directory: *support/make_latex*

Provides a set of *make* rules for LATEX documents.

## MakeProg

Directory: *support/makeprog*

*MakeProg* is a system for doing Literate Programming in TEX. It provides a mechanism for combining documentation with TEX macros. Donald Knuth's original articles on Literate Programming are included with the documentation.

## *MathPad*

Directory: *support/mathpad*

MathPad is an X11 editor for TeX sources. It was not available (or known to me) in time for review in this edition of *Making TeX Work*.

## *MCTeX*

Directory: *support/mctex*

A TeX macro package for pretty-printing *Lisp* code.

## *MEWLaTeX*

Directory: *support/mewltx*

An extension to *microEMACS* for Windows. It provides a LaTeX editing environment that allows you to write, spellcheck, process, and view your document from within *microEMACS*.

## *MNU*

Directory: *support/mnu*

*MNU* is an MS-DOS menu system written with batch files. It was designed for running TeX but can be extended to other applications.

## *pbm2TeX*

Directory: *support/pbm2tex*

*pbm2TeX* converts PBM files into LaTeX `picture` environments. This provides a portable way to include bitmap images in documents. The documents take a long time to typeset, however, and may require a big TeX.

## *PCWriTeX*

Directory: *support/pcwritex*

Adds TeX to *PC-Write* as a special kind of printer. Documents "printed" to the TeX printer can be processed with TeX to get typeset output.

## *PMTeX*

Directory: *support/pmtex*

An OS/2 Presentation Manager application that provides a shell around common TeX-related activities (editing, TeXing, previewing, printing, etc.).

## *PP*

Directory: *support/pp*

A Pascal or Modula-2 pretty-printer. It translates code into a Plain TeX or LaTeX document. An MS-DOS executable is provided.

## *PS2EPS*

Directory: *support/ps2eps*

Attempts to convert PostScript output from other programs into encapsulated PostScript output suitable for including in TeX documents with *dvips*, for example. Support is included for converting output from *GEM* 3.0, *DrawPerfect* 1.1, *PSpice* 4.05, *OrCAD* 3.11, *PrintGL* 1.18, *Mathcad* 3.0, and *GNUPlot* 3.0.

### PS Utils

Directory: *support/psutils*

A collection of utilities for transforming PostScript output files in various ways. *psbook* rearranges pages into signatures. *psselect* selects ranges of pages. *pstops* performs arbitrary rearrangement and selection of pages. *psnup* prints multiple pages on a single sheet of paper. *epsffit* rescales an encapsulated PostScript figure to fit within a specified bounding box. These programs can be used to rearrange the output from PostScript DVI drivers like *dvips*.

*PS Utils* also includes scripts for displaying character information and "fixing" PostScript output from other sources. (Some PostScript output is nonstandard and must be fixed-up before it can be used with the *PS Utils*.) These scripts are summarized in Table 16-3.

*Table 16-3: Additional Scripts in PS Utils*

| Script | Purpose |
|---|---|
| *getafm* | Retrieves font metrics from the printer |
| *showchar* | Prints a character and its metrics |
| *fixfmps* | Fixes output from *FrameMaker* |
| *fixwpps* | Fixes output from *WordPerfect* |
| *fixwfwps* | Fixes output from *Word* for Windows |
| *fixmacps* | Fixes Macintosh PostScript |
| *fixpsditps* | Fixes *Transcript psdit* files |
| *fixpspps* | Fixes output from *PSPrint* |

### rtf2LaTeX

Directory: *support/rtf2LaTeX*

A conversion program to translate RTF sources into LaTeX.

### rtf2TeX

Directory: *support/rtf2TeX*

A conversion program to translate RTF sources into TeX.

### RTF-to-LaTeX

Directory: *support/rtflatex*

Another conversion program to translate RTF sources into LaTeX.

### S2LaTeX

Directory: *support/s2latex*

A *Scribe*-to-LaTeX converter. Requires *lex* and *yacc* to compile.

## SchemeTEX

Directory: *support/schemetex*

*SchemeTEX* provides support for Literate Programming in *Scheme*. *Lex* is required to build *SchemeTEX*.

## TEXOrTho

Directory: *support/spelchek*

*TEXOrTho* is a spellchecking filter for text files. It was designed for spellchecking TEX and LATEX documents, but it is parameter-file driven so it may be possible to extend it to other formats.

## Tek2EEPIC

Directory: *support/tek2eepic*

A filter for Tektronix 4015 escape sequences that allows graphics output designed for a Tektronix 4015 display to be included in a TEX document. The resulting DVI file must be processed by a DVI driver that recognizes the *tpic* \special commands.

## TEXcalc

Directory: *support/texcalc*

*TEXcalc* is an *InstaCalc* spreadsheet for calculating TEX typeface design sizes based upon magnification and scaling factors.

## TEXinfo2HTML

Directory: *support/texi2html*

Translates GNU TEXinfo sources into HTML.

## TEXi2roff

Directory: *support/texi2roff*

This is a TEXinfo-to-*nroff* converter (although it should be possible to process most documents with *troff* as well).

## TEXit

Directory: *support/texit*

A *Perl* script for processing TEX documents intelligently.

## texproc

Directory: *support/texproc*

*texproc* is a filter that inserts the output from a command into your document. This can be used, for example, to automatically insert the output from *GNUPlot* directly into your TEX document (assuming that you use one of the TEX-compatible output terminals in *GNUPlot*).

### tgrind

Directory: *support/tgrind*

*tgrind* is a source code pretty-printer modelled after the standard BSD UNIX *vgrind* utility. It produces a TEX or LATEX document that typesets an attractive program listing from your source code.

### tr2LATEX

Directory: *support/tr2latex*

Translates *troff* sources into LATEX.

### tr2TEX

Directory: *support/tr2tex*

Translates *troff* sources into Plain TEX.

### TRANSLIT

Directory: *support/translit*

*TRANSLIT* transliterates ASCII character codes. Single characters can be translated into multiple characters and vice versa, in addition to simple permutations. This program allows files written in one national character set to be translated into another character set without losing characters or meaning.

### TSpell

Directory: *support/tspell*

A spellchecking filter for TEX documents. It strips TEX and LATEX macros out of a document, runs the document through a spellchecker, and restores the TEX and LATEX macros. It looks like it was designed for VAX machines.

### umlaute

Directory: *support/umlaute*

A collection of style files for processing TEX documents with accented characters using machine-native character encodings. Support for the ISO standard character set (ISO Latin1) and the MS-DOS code page 437 character set is provided.

### undump

Directory: *support/undump*

*undump* combines a core dump and an executable program to build a new executable using the core dump to provide initial values for all of the program's static variables. One use of this program is to construct TEX executables with macro packages preloaded. This is unnecessary on most modern computers (they're fast enough to simply load the format files). *undump* is no longer a supported program.

## untex

Directory: *support/untex*

Removes all LaTeX control sequences from a document. Can optionally remove arguments to control sequences, as well as all math-mode text. Replaces many accented characters with their IBM OEM character set equivalents.

## VMSSpell

Directory: *support/vmsspell*

A VMS spellchecking tool. Distributed in a VMS-style archive package.

## VorTEX

Directory: *support/vortex*

A GNU emacs editing mode for TEX documents. Also provides support for BIBTEX databases.

## windex

Directory: *support/windex*

*windex* is an aid for building indexes in LaTeX documents. It modifies the LaTeX indexing macros to produce a different output format. The *windex* program can then sort the terms and construct an index for you.

## WP2LATEX

Directory: *support/wp2latex-5_1*

This program attempts to translate WordPerfect v5.1 documents into LaTeX.

## xet

Directory: *support/xet*

The *xet* program removes all commands and mathematical formulae from Plain TEX and LaTeX documents. *xet* has a number of options for handling different aspects of a document (such as accents and LaTeX environments) and claims to be useful as a simple syntax checker for TEX files.

## xetal

Directory: *support/xetal*

This is a more recent version of *xet*, described above.

## xlatex

Directory: *support/xlatex*

An X11 Windows application that ties together several aspects of TEXing a document. It provides a "push button" interface to editing, processing, previewing, and printing your document.

# Filename Extension Summary

This chapter summarizes many common filename extensions. The extensions are listed in alphabetical order. All extensions can be shortened to three letters for consistency with operating systems that do not allow longer file extensions. On other file systems, they may be slightly different. For example, EPS files are sometimes called EPSF files on UNIX systems, which allow longer filenames.

## *ABF*

An Adobe binary screen font file contains a binary encoding of a BDF (bitmap distribution format) file. Binary encoding makes the files smaller, but it also makes them less portable and unintelligible to humans. The binary format is described in Adobe's ABF Format Specification [2]. BDF files are described below.

## *AFM*

Adobe font metrics files are ASCII files distributed with PostScript Type 1 fonts. Type 1 fonts are the linearly scalable fonts that PostScript printer users are most familiar with. Bounding boxes, an encoding vector (what characters go where), kerning, and ligature information are among the things described in this file. The AFM file format is described completely in Adobe's AFM Format Specification [4].

PostScript fonts (available through commercial vendors or from the Internet) are supplied with AFM files. Generally, the only occasion that you would have to modify an AFM file would be to change the encoding vector.

## *AUX*

Auxiliary files are built by LaTeX each time it formats a document. LaTeX writes information about cross references, citations, etc., to the auxiliary file for post-processing by other tools, or for TeX processing the next time this document is formatted.

### BBL

Bibliography files are created by BIBTEX from the citations in your document, the bibliography databases (BIB) that you specify, and the bibliography style (BST) you use. BIBTEX writes the resulting bibliography to the BBL file, which is automatically included in your LATEX document at the place where you define the bibliography.

### BDF

Bitmap distribution format files are ASCII files that describe a bitmap font. They are frequently used to distribute bitmap versions of scalable fonts in screen resolution at common sizes. They are resolution specific, but they are portable from one architecture to another. The BDF file format is described completely in Adobe's BDF Format Specification [3].

Some fonts packages are distributed with BDF files. Other BDF files are created as part of the conversion process from native format to X11 format. It is unlikely that you would ever create one purely by hand.

### BIB

Bibliography databases contain bibliographic information. These are generally hand-written and may contain bibliographic information for all of the sources that you are (ever) likely to cite. The BIBTEX program reads information about each work that you \cite{} from the BIB file. Consult the documentation for BIBTEX for more information about the format of BIB files.

### BLG

BIBTEX log files record the status of the last run of BIBTEX.

### BST

Bibliography style files are used by BIBTEX to define the layout of the citations. BIBTEX produces LATEX commands in the BBL file that define the citations in the format specified by the BST file.

You may eventually write or modify a bibliography style file, but it is less common than modifying LATEX style files because bibliographies have a more rigidly defined format. Consult the documentation for BIBTEX for more information about the format of BST files.

### BZR

The GNU fontutils define the BZR format to hold generic scalable font data. The file actually contains the specification for a series of bezier curves. The BZR file format is defined in the TEXinfo pages that accompany the GNU fontutils. The GNU fontutils create BZR files.

## DVI

TEX produces device-independent output in the DVI file. This file describes the TEXed document in a simple stack language that can be rendered on any device. The format of DVI files is described in the WEB documentation for *DVItype*, or in *The DVI Drivers Standard* [53].

TEX (and some *MFware* utilities) produces DVI files.

## EPSF

Encapsulated PostScript files contain scalable PostScript images and extra information (such as the size of the image's bounding box) that is necessary to scale the image appropriately for printing, unlike generic PostScript. Using encapsulated PostScript images in your TEX document requires a DVI driver that understands PostScript \specials. How to include pictures and figures via encapsulated PostScript is described in detail in Chapter 6, *Pictures and Figures*.

You are unlikely to create encapsulated PostScript files by hand, but many drawing and drafting programs can create them for you.

## FIG

FIG files are created by the *XFig* program (and possibly other programs). The scalable representation of a collection of graphics objects is stored in ASCII form in FIG files. The *transfig* program can translate FIG files into a number of other formats including EPSF, HPGL, and a variety of LATEX environments.

## FLI

Font libraries are distributed with emTEX. They contain a collection of PK files. Font libraries have several advantages over a directory full of PK files: they are easier to maintain (because you don't have to deal with hundreds of files); they are faster to search (because they are indexed more efficiently than a directory); they are smaller (because *each* PK file wastes an average of half a cluster of disk space); and the name of each font is not limited to eight characters as it is under MS-DOS file naming conventions.

Note: *dvips* can also use emTEX FLI files.

## GF

Generic font files contain bitmap data for the characters of a font. The GF format is very simple, and many TEX related programs that create fonts produce GF files. The disadvantage of GF files is that they are very large (because no compression is performed). The format of GF files is described in the WEB documentation for *GFtoPK* (or any of the GF-related *MFware* programs).

METAFONT is the primary source for GF files. Some other programs (some of the GNU fontutils, for example) also produce GF files.

### GIF

Graphics interchange format is a CompuServe bitmap graphics standard. GIF files are very popular, and a number of converters (e.g., *BM2FONT*) can translate GIF files into a format usable by TEX.

### GLO

Glossary files are produced by the LATEX \glossary command. They are analogous to the IDX files produced by the \index commands. The glossary is inserted in your document wherever the \makeglossary command occurs.

### GSF

Ghostscript fonts are scalable fonts very similar to PostScript Type 1 fonts. Theoretically, *Ghostscript* can use PostScript Type 1 fonts directly, although I have never tried. Several GSF fonts are distributed with *Ghostscript*.

### HPGL

Hewlett-Packard GL is a plotter language. Many programs can produce vector graphics in HPGL format.

### HPTFM

Hewlett-Packard tagged font metric files are a lot like TEX TFM files. It is unfortunate that both files have the extension TFM because they are completely incompatible. You can generate TEX TFM files from HPTFMs with the *HPTFM2PL* program.

### IDX

Index files are produced automatically when you use the \index commands in LATEX. The IDX file contains raw indexing data that will be used by the *MakeIndex* program to build an index for your document. You must include the *makeidx* style in your documentstyle command, and you must turn on indexing with \makeindex in the preamble of your document if you wish to (re)build the index. See the entry for IND files below for more information.

### ILG

*MakeIndex* log files record the status of the last run of *MakeIndex*.

### IMG

The IMG format is a particular bitmapped image format used by the GEM Window System (a PC-based windowed desktop interface product). The GNU fontutils read IMG files as their default format. The *PBMplus* utilities* can convert between many graphics file formats, including IMG.

---

*The *PBMplus* utilities are a collection of programs that allow conversion between different graphic formats by using the PBM format as a transition step.

Some scanning software produces IMG files directly. Other IMG files are distributed by the Free Software Foundation as part of an ongoing project to produce high-quality, free typefaces.

## IND

Index files are produced by the *MakeIndex* and automatically get included into your LaTeX document wherever you put the `\printindex` command. The `\index` commands in your LaTeX document write raw indexing data to the IDX file. *MakeIndex* reads the IDX file, sorts and formats the index according to the IST file, and produces an IND file for your document.

## IST

Index specification files are used by *MakeIndex* to format the index file. Consult the documentation for *MakeIndex* for more information.

## JPEG

JPEG files are compressed bitmap images. Because JPEG files use a "lossy" compression algorithm, they are frequently much smaller than other formats.

## LOF

List of figures files are produced by the `\listoffigures` command in LaTeX. After seeing `\listoffigures`, LaTeX writes figure captions to the LOF file. The next time the document is formatted, LaTeX will insert the LOF file at the point where you issue the `\listoffigures` command.

## LOG

Log files are always produced by TeX and METAFONT. The LOG file is generally uninteresting. Status and warning messages deemed too trivial (or too detailed) for the display are written to the log file (all messages written to the display are also written to the log).

## LOT

List of tables files are exactly analogous to LOF files.

## MF

Just as TeX reads TEX files, which are plain ASCII descriptions of a typeset document, METAFONT reads MF files, which are plain ASCII descriptions of a typeface. META-FONT and MF files are the topic of Knuth's *METAFONTbook* [29]. Unlike PostScript fonts, METAFONT fonts are not linearly scaled.*

The standard TeX distribution contains the MF files for the Computer Modern fonts. Knuth has produced several more MF files to demonstrate METAFONT. The American

---

*Linear versus non-linear scaling is a typographic issue better discussed elsewhere. I mention it here just for completeness.

Mathematical Society has extended Computer Modern with several more. The *MFpic* macro package produces MF files from a picture-like environment in TEX. *The METR-FONTbook* describes how to create your own fonts with METAFONT.

The *List of MetaFonts* [47] is posted occasionally to the newsgroups `comp.text.tex` and `comp.fonts`.

Chapter 11, *Introducing METAFONT*, describes METAFONT in more detail. The TEX fonts available in METAFONT format are listed in Chapter 5, *Fonts*.

## *MFJ*

MFjob files are plain ASCII files that contain instructions for *MFjob*, an emTEX program that builds groups of METAFONT fonts. MFJ files can be created by hand to automate the process of building a set of fonts. They are also created by the emTEX DVI drivers if automatic font generation is being used.

## *MSP*

Microsoft Paint files contain bitmapped graphic images. They can be included in a TEX document with \special commands recognized by the emTEX DVI drivers.

## *PBM*

The portable bitmap format is a flexible bitmap representation introduced by the *PBMplus* package. The *PBMplus* utilities allow for the conversion of PBM format files to and from almost anything else. The PBM format (and all the utilities) are described in the manpages that accompany the *PBMplus* toolkit distribution.

The PBM toolkit and many other X11 graphics utilities can read and write PBM files (e.g. XV).

## *PCF*

The PCF format is one of several X11 bitmap font formats. Architecture-specific versions of X11 use PCF files. Other architectures use one of a number of other architecture-specific formats (e.g., SNF). PCF files are used by at least the DEC versions of the X11 server. The X11 distribution for your architecture includes a program that will convert BDF files to the standard adopted for your architecture.

PCF files are almost invariably created from some other source. It is unlikely that you will ever create one by hand.

## *PCL*

PCL files contain printer commands for HP LaserJet printers. DVI drivers for HP LaserJet printers create PCL files. It is possible to get information out of some PCL files with *pcltomsp*.

## *PCX*

PCX files contain bitmapped graphic images. They can be included in a TEX document with \special commands recognized by the emTEX DVI drivers.

## *PFA*

Printer font ASCII files contain scalable outline data that describes each character in a Type 1 font. A large portion of this file is encrypted, so it is an ASCII file only in the sense that the binary portion is represented as a string of hexadecimal ASCII digits. This is traditional PostScript because it is pure ASCII. See PFB below.

Type 1 outline fonts are created by special font editing programs or conversion tools (e.g. the GNU fontutils).

## *PFB*

Printer font binary files, like PFA files, contain the outline data for PostScript Type 1 fonts. The binary format was adopted to save space (they are generally about half the size of their PFA counterparts).* Because they are binary files, it is more difficult to transfer them from one architecture to another (endian-ness, binary transmission, etc.). PostScript purists are apt to disparage them.

## *PFM*

Printer font metric files are a Microsoft Windows standard. They are encountered frequently in archives that contain Type 1 fonts. Unfortunately, these archives occasionally fail to include AFM files, which are more standard outside of the Windows community. Even more unfortunately, PFM files do not contain all of the information that is in an AFM file. However, the *PFM2AFM* program can construct a partial AFM file. I believe that the PFM file format is described in a Microsoft technical note; however, I have never seen it.

Unless you use Microsoft Windows, PFM files are likely to be useless. If you need PFM files, the MS-DOS program *Refont* can create them from AFM files.

## *PK*

Most TEX DVI conversion programs read packed bitmap font files. The PK font format defines a clever scheme that allows bitmap fonts to be compressed significantly. The format of PK files is described in the WEB documentation for *PKtype* (or any of the PK-related *MFware* programs).

You are unlikely to create PK files by hand, per se, but there are a number of utility programs that ultimately create PK files (e.g., *GFtoPK*, METAFONT, *MFpic*, *PS2PK*).

## *PL*

A property list file contains an ASCII representation of a binary file. The property list format was created during TEX development to allow binary files (specifically TFM files) to be hand-coded. Most users have no reason to create PL files; however, some programs create PL files that must be converted into TFM files with the TEXware program *PLtoTF*. The PL format is described in the WEB documentation for *PLtoTF*.

---

*The proof is left as an exercise to the reader (I always wanted to say that).

If you need to edit TEX font metric information for a particular font, you will almost certainly do so by editing the PL file. You can create a PL file from a TFM file with the *TFtoPL* utility.

## PS

PostScript is a page description language. The PostScript language is described in a series of volumes from Adobe Systems. PS is a common extension for PostScript files.

Unless you are inclined to enter the Obfuscated PostScript Contest, you are unlikely to create PostScript files by hand. PostScript files are created by many common tools.

## PXL

This format is obsolete. It has been completely superseded by the PK format. If you still have PXL files, you can convert them to PK format with the *PXtoPK* program. If you are still using a DVI driver that needs PXL files, you need an upgrade.

## SFL

These files contain HP LaserJet softfonts in landscape orientation. LaserJet softfonts are device specific bitmap representations of a typeface. The bitmap versions are described thoroughly in the *LaserJet Technical Reference Manual* [21] for each of the HP LaserJet printers. Newer laser printers can perform automatic rotation of fonts (in 90 degree increments, at least), so the distinction between landscape and portrait font files is disappearing.

## SFP

These files contain HP LaserJet softfonts in portrait orientation. See the entry for SFL files, above.

## SFS

Scalable softfonts are HP LaserJet softfonts for the new (HPLJ III and higher) LaserJet printers. These are really in AGFA IntelliFont Scalable format [7].

## SNF

Server native format fonts are another version of X11 bitmap font. See the entry for PCF files, above, for more information.

## STY

Style files are used by LaTeX to define the layout of a LaTeX document (by redefining the meaning of commands like \section{}, for example). They are also used commonly to extend LaTeX. See the LaTeX manual [32] for more information.

Style files are really just TEX files that perform specific tasks. You will eventually write or modify a style file, but it isn't something you are likely to do every day.

## TEX

TEX files describe the layout of a typeset document in the TEX programming language,* as defined by *The TEXbook* [30]. Most people use some form of macro package on top of TEX to make the language easier to swallow. If a TEX file begins with \documentstyle{} or has \begin{document} somewhere near the top, it is probably a LATEX document. Otherwise, look for the \input commands to see what macro packages are being included.

Documents that do not appear to be LATEX documents and do not appear to \input special macro packages may be using a special *format*. Formats are fast-loading precompiled macro packages. If you know the name of the format file, you can tell TEX to use it by typing &*format-name* as a parameter to TEX.

## TIFF

TIFF files contain bitmapped or vector graphic images in a very flexible form. The "T" in TIFF stands for "tagged." All of the different kinds of information (regarding number of colors, compression, etc.) that might appear in a TIFF file are given unique tags that allow a TIFF file reader to skip over information that it does not understand.

## TFM

TEX font metric files contain information about fonts. TEX doesn't know anything about the intrinsic shape of the characters that it lays down on the page. TEX deals entirely with boxes. Every character is described by the rectangular box that (usually) surrounds it. The TFM file for a font describes the size of each character's box, as well as ligature and kerning information for the font. A human-readable version of a TFM file can be produced with the *TFtoPL* program. The format of TFM files is described thoroughly in the WEB documentation for *TFtoPL*.

If you have reason to modify a TFM file, you will almost certainly do so by converting it to PL format first. You can convert it back into a TFM file with the *PLtoTF* utility.

See also HPTFM files.

## TOC

Table of contents files are produced by the \tableofcontents command in LATEX. After seeing \tableofcontents, LATEX writes chapter, section, subsection, etc., names to the TOC file. The next time the document is formatted, LATEX will insert the TOC file at the point where you issue the \tableofcontents command.

## TXT

Generic ASCII text.

---

*You already knew this, didn't you?

**VF**

Virtual font files. They are described in more detail in Chapter 5, *Fonts*. In short, a virtual font maps a character to an arbitrary sequence of DVI file commands. This may be another character in a different font, a different character in the same font, or something else entirely.

**VPL**

The virtual property list is a property list file for virtual fonts (as opposed to being some sort of property list file that was itself virtual ;-). VPL files serve the same purpose for VF files that PL files serve for TFM files. The VPL format is defined in the WEB documentation for *VPtoVF*.

**XBM**

X11 bitmap files contain a bitmapped image. X11 icons are frequently stored in XBM files. They also occur in `.icon` files and files without extensions (e.g., in */usr/include/X11/bitmaps*). I mention them here only because I like to use icons on my X11 desktop, and I have used *PKtoBM* to create several nice ones from TEX PK files.

X11 bitmap files are used for all bitmap displays in the X11 server (not just icons). Because they are ASCII and not binary, they are architecture independent, which makes them very portable.

# B

# *Font Samples*

This appendix showcases a number of METAFONT fonts. First, several examples of encoding vectors are presented and then samples of many fonts from the CTAN archives are provided.

## *Font Encodings*

Font encoding vectors are described in Chapter 5, *Fonts*. Table B-1 shows the Computer Modern Text encoding, Table B-2 shows the Computer Modern Math Italic encoding, Table B-3 shows the Cork encoding, and Table B-4 shows the Adobe Standard encoding.

*Table B-1: The Computer Modern Roman Font Encoding*

|   | 0 | 1 | 2 | 3 | 4 | 5 | 6 | 7 |
|---|---|---|---|---|---|---|---|---|
| **0** | Γ<br>0 | Δ<br>1 | Θ<br>2 | Λ<br>3 | Ξ<br>4 | Π<br>5 | Σ<br>6 | Υ<br>7 |
|  | Φ<br>8 | Ψ<br>9 | Ω<br>10 | ff<br>11 | fi<br>12 | fl<br>13 | ffi<br>14 | ffl<br>15 |
| **1** | ı<br>16 | J<br>17 | `<br>18 | ´<br>19 | ˇ<br>20 | ˘<br>21 | ¯<br>22 | ˚<br>23 |
|  | ˛<br>24 | ß<br>25 | æ<br>26 | œ<br>27 | ø<br>28 | Æ<br>29 | Œ<br>30 | Ø<br>31 |
| **2** | ˝<br>32 | !<br>33 | ”<br>34 | #<br>35 | $<br>36 | %<br>37 | &<br>38 | ’<br>39 |
|  | (<br>40 | )<br>41 | *<br>42 | +<br>43 | ,<br>44 | -<br>45 | .<br>46 | /<br>47 |
| **3** | 0<br>48 | 1<br>49 | 2<br>50 | 3<br>51 | 4<br>52 | 5<br>53 | 6<br>54 | 7<br>55 |
|  | 8<br>56 | 9<br>57 | :<br>58 | ;<br>59 | ¡<br>60 | =<br>61 | ¿<br>62 | ?<br>63 |
| **4** | @<br>64 | A<br>65 | B<br>66 | C<br>67 | D<br>68 | E<br>69 | F<br>70 | G<br>71 |
|  | H<br>72 | I<br>73 | J<br>74 | K<br>75 | L<br>76 | M<br>77 | N<br>78 | O<br>79 |
| **5** | P<br>80 | Q<br>81 | R<br>82 | S<br>83 | T<br>84 | U<br>85 | V<br>86 | W<br>87 |
|  | X<br>88 | Y<br>89 | Z<br>90 | [<br>91 | “<br>92 | ]<br>93 | ^<br>94 | ˙<br>95 |
| **6** | ‘<br>96 | a<br>97 | b<br>98 | c<br>99 | d<br>100 | e<br>101 | f<br>102 | g<br>103 |
|  | h<br>104 | i<br>105 | j<br>106 | k<br>107 | l<br>108 | m<br>109 | n<br>110 | o<br>111 |
| **7** | p<br>112 | q<br>113 | r<br>114 | s<br>115 | t<br>116 | u<br>117 | v<br>118 | w<br>119 |
|  | x<br>120 | y<br>121 | z<br>122 | –<br>123 | —<br>124 | ˝<br>125 | ~<br>126 | ¨<br>127 |
|  | **8** | **9** | **A** | **B** | **C** | **D** | **E** | **F** |

*Table B-2: The Computer Modern Math Italic Font Encoding*

|   | 0 | 1 | 2 | 3 | 4 | 5 | 6 | 7 |
|---|---|---|---|---|---|---|---|---|
| **0** | $\Gamma$ 0 | $\Delta$ 1 | $\Theta$ 2 | $\Lambda$ 3 | $\Xi$ 4 | $\Pi$ 5 | $\Sigma$ 6 | $\Upsilon$ 7 |
|   | $\Phi$ 8 | $\Psi$ 9 | $\Omega$ 10 | $\alpha$ 11 | $\beta$ 12 | $\gamma$ 13 | $\delta$ 14 | $\epsilon$ 15 |
| **1** | $\zeta$ 16 | $\eta$ 17 | $\theta$ 18 | $\iota$ 19 | $\kappa$ 20 | $\lambda$ 21 | $\mu$ 22 | $\nu$ 23 |
|   | $\xi$ 24 | $\pi$ 25 | $\rho$ 26 | $\sigma$ 27 | $\tau$ 28 | $\upsilon$ 29 | $\phi$ 30 | $\chi$ 31 |
| **2** | $\psi$ 32 | $\omega$ 33 | $\varepsilon$ 34 | $\vartheta$ 35 | $\varpi$ 36 | $\varrho$ 37 | $\varsigma$ 38 | $\varphi$ 39 |
|   | ↼ 40 | ↽ 41 | ⇀ 42 | ⇁ 43 | ˓ 44 | ˒ 45 | ▷ 46 | ◁ 47 |
| **3** | 0 48 | 1 49 | 2 50 | 3 51 | 4 52 | 5 53 | 6 54 | 7 55 |
|   | 8 56 | 9 57 | . 58 | , 59 | < 60 | / 61 | > 62 | ⋆ 63 |
| **4** | $\partial$ 64 | A 65 | B 66 | C 67 | D 68 | E 69 | F 70 | G 71 |
|   | H 72 | I 73 | J 74 | K 75 | L 76 | M 77 | N 78 | O 79 |
| **5** | P 80 | Q 81 | R 82 | S 83 | T 84 | U 85 | V 86 | W 87 |
|   | X 88 | Y 89 | Z 90 | ♭ 91 | ♮ 92 | ♯ 93 | ⌣ 94 | ⌢ 95 |
| **6** | $\ell$ 96 | a 97 | b 98 | c 99 | d 100 | e 101 | f 102 | g 103 |
|   | h 104 | i 105 | j 106 | k 107 | l 108 | m 109 | n 110 | o 111 |
| **7** | p 112 | q 113 | r 114 | s 115 | t 116 | u 117 | v 118 | w 119 |
|   | x 120 | y 121 | z 122 | ı 123 | ȷ 124 | ℘ 125 | → 126 | ⌢ 127 |
|   | **8** | **9** | **A** | **B** | **C** | **D** | **E** | **F** |

## Table B-3: The Cork Font Encoding

| | 0 | 1 | 2 | 3 | 4 | 5 | 6 | 7 |
|---|---|---|---|---|---|---|---|---|
| | ` | ´ | ^ | ~ | ¨ | ″ | ° | ˇ |
| | 0 | 1 | 2 | 3 | 4 | 5 | 6 | 7 |
| **0** | ˘ | — | ˙ | ᷄ | ˓ | ˒ | ‹ | › |
| | 8 | 9 | 10 | 11 | 12 | 13 | 14 | 15 |
| | " | " | „ | « | » | – | — | |
| | 16 | 17 | 18 | 19 | 20 | 21 | 22 | 23 |
| **1** | 0 | 1 | J | ff | fi | fl | ffi | ffl |
| | 24 | 25 | 26 | 27 | 28 | 29 | 30 | 31 |
| | ␣ | ! | " | # | \$ | % | & | ' |
| | 32 | 33 | 34 | 35 | 36 | 37 | 38 | 39 |
| **2** | ( | ) | * | + | , | - | . | / |
| | 40 | 41 | 42 | 43 | 44 | 45 | 46 | 47 |
| | 0 | 1 | 2 | 3 | 4 | 5 | 6 | 7 |
| | 48 | 49 | 50 | 51 | 52 | 53 | 54 | 55 |
| **3** | 8 | 9 | : | ; | < | = | > | ? |
| | 56 | 57 | 58 | 59 | 60 | 61 | 62 | 63 |
| | @ | A | B | C | D | E | F | G |
| | 64 | 65 | 66 | 67 | 68 | 69 | 70 | 71 |
| **4** | H | I | J | K | L | M | N | O |
| | 72 | 73 | 74 | 75 | 76 | 77 | 78 | 79 |
| | P | Q | R | S | T | U | V | W |
| | 80 | 81 | 82 | 83 | 84 | 85 | 86 | 87 |
| **5** | X | Y | Z | [ | \ | ] | ^ | — |
| | 88 | 89 | 90 | 91 | 92 | 93 | 94 | 95 |
| | ' | a | b | c | d | e | f | g |
| | 96 | 97 | 98 | 99 | 100 | 101 | 102 | 103 |
| **6** | h | i | j | k | l | m | n | o |
| | 104 | 105 | 106 | 107 | 108 | 109 | 110 | 111 |
| | p | q | r | s | t | u | v | w |
| | 112 | 113 | 114 | 115 | 116 | 117 | 118 | 119 |
| **7** | x | y | z | { | \| | } | ~ | - |
| | 120 | 121 | 122 | 123 | 124 | 125 | 126 | 127 |
| | **8** | **9** | **A** | **B** | **C** | **D** | **E** | **F** |

*Table B-3: The Cork Font Encoding (continued)*

| | 0 | 1 | 2 | 3 | 4 | 5 | 6 | 7 |
|---|---|---|---|---|---|---|---|---|
| **8** | Ă 128 | Ą 129 | Ć 130 | Č 131 | Ď 132 | Ĕ 133 | Ę 134 | Ğ 135 |
| | Ĺ 136 | Ľ 137 | Ł 138 | Ń 139 | Ň 140 | Ŋ 141 | Ő 142 | Ŕ 143 |
| **9** | Ř 144 | Ś 145 | Š 146 | Ş 147 | Ť 148 | Ţ 149 | Ű 150 | Ů 151 |
| | Ÿ 152 | Ź 153 | Ž 154 | Ż 155 | IJ 156 | İ 157 | đ 158 | § 159 |
| **A** | ă 160 | ą 161 | ć 162 | č 163 | ď 164 | ĕ 165 | ę 166 | ğ 167 |
| | í 168 | ľ 169 | ł 170 | ń 171 | ň 172 | ŋ 173 | ő 174 | ŕ 175 |
| **B** | ř 176 | ś 177 | š 178 | ş 179 | ť 180 | ţ 181 | ű 182 | ů 183 |
| | ÿ 184 | ź 185 | ž 186 | ż 187 | ij 188 | ı 189 | ¿ 190 | £ 191 |
| **C** | À 192 | Á 193 | Â 194 | Ã 195 | Ä 196 | Å 197 | Æ 198 | Ç 199 |
| | È 200 | É 201 | Ê 202 | Ë 203 | Ì 204 | Í 205 | Î 206 | Ï 207 |
| **D** | Đ 208 | Ñ 209 | Ò 210 | Ó 211 | Ô 212 | Õ 213 | Ö 214 | Œ 215 |
| | Ø 216 | Ù 217 | Ú 218 | Û 219 | Ü 220 | Ý 221 | Þ 222 | SS 223 |
| **E** | à 224 | á 225 | â 226 | ã 227 | ä 228 | å 229 | æ 230 | ç 231 |
| | è 232 | é 233 | ê 234 | ë 235 | ì 236 | í 237 | î 238 | ï 239 |
| **F** | ð 240 | ñ 241 | ò 242 | ó 243 | ô 244 | õ 245 | ö 246 | œ 247 |
| | ø 248 | ù 249 | ú 250 | û 251 | ü 252 | ý 253 | þ 254 | ß 255 |
| | **8** | **9** | **A** | **B** | **C** | **D** | **E** | **F** |

*Table B-4: The Adobe Standard Font Encoding*

|   | 0 | 1 | 2 | 3 | 4 | 5 | 6 | 7 |
|---|---|---|---|---|---|---|---|---|
| **0** | (0) | (1) | (2) | (3) | (4) | (5) | (6) | (7) |
|  | (8) | (9) | (10) | (11) | (12) | ' (13) | ¡ (14) | ¿ (15) |
| **1** | 1 (16) | (17) | ` (18) | ´ (19) | ˇ (20) | ˘ (21) | ¯ (22) | ° (23) |
|  | ˛ (24) | ß (25) | æ (26) | œ (27) | ø (28) | Æ (29) | Œ (30) | Ø (31) |
| **2** | (32) | ! (33) | " (34) | # (35) | $ (36) | % (37) | & (38) | ' (39) |
|  | ( (40) | ) (41) | * (42) | + (43) | , (44) | - (45) | . (46) | / (47) |
| **3** | 0 (48) | 1 (49) | 2 (50) | 3 (51) | 4 (52) | 5 (53) | 6 (54) | 7 (55) |
|  | 8 (56) | 9 (57) | : (58) | ; (59) | < (60) | = (61) | > (62) | ? (63) |
| **4** | @ (64) | A (65) | B (66) | C (67) | D (68) | E (69) | F (70) | G (71) |
|  | H (72) | I (73) | J (74) | K (75) | L (76) | M (77) | N (78) | O (79) |
| **5** | P (80) | Q (81) | R (82) | S (83) | T (84) | U (85) | V (86) | W (87) |
|  | X (88) | Y (89) | Z (90) | [ (91) | \ (92) | ] (93) | ^ (94) | _ (95) |
| **6** | ` (96) | a (97) | b (98) | c (99) | d (100) | e (101) | f (102) | g (103) |
|  | h (104) | i (105) | j (106) | k (107) | l (108) | m (109) | n (110) | o (111) |
| **7** | p (112) | q (113) | r (114) | s (115) | t (116) | u (117) | v (118) | w (119) |
|  | x (120) | y (121) | z (122) | { (123) | \| (124) | } (125) | ~ (126) | ¨ (127) |
|   | 8 | 9 | A | B | C | D | E | F |

*Table B-4: The Adobe Standard Font Encoding (continued)*

| | 0 | 1 | 2 | 3 | 4 | 5 | 6 | 7 |
|---|---|---|---|---|---|---|---|---|
| **8** | Λ 128 | ~ 129 | ê 130 | ë 131 | á 132 | î 133 | ü 134 | ò 135 |
| | ú 136 | û 137 | Á 138 | ì 139 | Î 140 | ä 141 | Ê 142 | š 143 |
| **9** | è 144 | ž 145 | ã 146 | å 147 | ô 148 | Ë 149 | ÿ 150 | ý 151 |
| | í 152 | Â 153 | Ú 154 | é 155 | Ò 156 | à 157 | Ü 158 | â 159 |
| **A** | Ì 160 | Ù 161 | ¢ 162 | £ 163 | / 164 | ¥ 165 | ƒ 166 | § 167 |
| | ¤ 168 | Û 169 | " 170 | « 171 | ‹ 172 | › 173 | fi 174 | fl 175 |
| **B** | Š 176 | – 177 | † 178 | ‡ 179 | · 180 | Ï 181 | ¶ 182 | • 183 |
| | , 184 | „ 185 | " 186 | » 187 | ... 188 | ‰ 189 | ï 190 | È 191 |
| **C** | Ó 192 | Ã 193 | Å 194 | Ö 195 | Ä 196 | Ñ 197 | Ž 198 | · 199 |
| | Í 200 | É 201 | Ÿ 202 | ù 203 | ñ 204 | " 205 | ¸ 206 | Õ 207 |
| **D** | — 208 | õ 209 | À 210 | Ý 211 | Ô 212 | ó 213 | ö 214 | 215 |
| | 216 | 217 | 218 | 219 | 220 | 221 | 222 | 223 |
| **E** | 224 | 225 | 226 | ª 227 | 228 | 229 | 230 | 231 |
| | Ł 232 | 233 | 234 | º 235 | 236 | 237 | 238 | 239 |
| **F** | 240 | 241 | 242 | 243 | 244 | 245 | 246 | 247 |
| | ł 248 | 249 | 250 | 251 | 252 | 253 | 254 | 255 |
| | **8** | **9** | **A** | **B** | **C** | **D** | **E** | **F** |

# Font Samples

METAFONT, like TEX, has been widely ported and many people have developed fonts using it. The remainder of this appendix shows examples of many of the fonts available in the CTAN archives in February, 1994.

## *fonts/ams/amsfonts/cyrillic*

### *wncyb10*

˘АБЦДЕФГХИЈКЛМНОПЧРСТУВЩШЫЗ
абцдефгхијклмнопчрстувщшыз
!"Ђ˘%´'()*Ђ,-./0123456789:;«ı»?
ЉЦЭІЄЋЊ нъљцэієђ ЮЖЙЁV ФSЯ южйёv ф sяъ

### *wncyi10*

˘АБЦДЕФГХИЈКЛМНОПЧРСТУВЩШЫЗ
*абцдефгхијклмнопчрстувщшыз*
*!"Ђ˘%´'()*њ,-./0123456789:;«ı»?*
*ЉЦЭІЄЋ Ћ нъљцэієђ ЮЖЙЁV ФSЯ южйёv ф sяв*

### *wncyr10*

˘АБЦДЕФГХИЈКЛМНОПЧРСТУВЩШЫЗ
абцдефгхијклмнопчрстувщшыз
!"Ђ˘%´'()*Ђ,-./0123456789:;«ı»?
ЉЦЭІЄЋ Ћњ љцэіеђ ЮЖЙЁV ФSЯ южйёv ф sяъ

### *wncysc10*

˘АБЦДЕФГХИЈКЛМНОПЧРСТУВЩШЫЗ
АБЦДЕФГХИЈКЛМНОПЧРСТУВЩШЫЗ
!"Ђ˘%´'()*ъ,-./0123456789:;«й»?
ЉЦЭІЄЋ Ћњ љцэієъ Ћ ЮЖЙЁV ФSЯ южйёv ф sяъ

### *wncyss10*

˘АБЦДЕФГХИЈКЛМНОПЧРСТУВЩШЫЗ
абцдефгхијклмнопчрстувщшыз
!"Ђ˘%´'()*Ђ,-./0123456789:;«ı»?
ЉЦЭІЄЋ Ћњ љцэіеђ Ћ ЮЖЙЁV ФSЯ южйёv ф sяъ

## fonts/ams/amsfonts/euler

### euex10

### eufb10

$\mathfrak{ABCDEFGHIJKLMNOPQRSTUVWXYZ}$
$\mathfrak{abcdefghijklmnopqrstuvwxyz}$
!&'()*+,−./0123456789:;=?
ðffgﬅﬆ Y3"1

### eufm10

$\mathfrak{ABCDEFGHIJKLMNOPQRSTUVWXYZ}$
$\mathfrak{abcdefghijklmnopqrstuvwxyz}$
!&'()*+,−./0123456789:;=?
ðffgﬅtu"1

### eurb10

∂ABCDEFGHIJKLMNOPQRSTUVWXYZ
abcdefghijklmnopqrstuvwxyz
ωεϑϖφ0123456789.,</>
ΔΘΛΞΠΣΥΦΨΩαβγδεζηθικλμνξπρστυφχ

### eurm10

∂ABCDEFGHIJKLMNOPQRSTUVWXYZ
abcdefghijklmnopqrstuvwxyz
ωεϑϖφ0123456789.,</>
ΔΘΛΞΠΣΥΦΨΩαβγδεζηθικλμνξπρστυφχ

### eusb10

$\mathscr{XABCDEFGHIJKLMNOPQRSTUVWXYZ}$
{}|\§
¬ℜℑ
∼

*eusm10*

ℵ*ABCDEFGHIJKLMNOPQRSTUVWXYZ*
{}|\§
¬ℜℑ
~

# *fonts/ams/amsfonts/extracm*

*cmbsy9*

ℵ*ABCDEFGHIJKLMNOPQRSTUVWXYZ*
⊣⊔⊓{}⟨⟩|||‡⋔\≀ ⊔∇⨿⊓⊏⊒≡§†‡
→↑↓↔↖↗↘≃⇐⇒⇑⇓⇔↙↗∝∫∞∈∋△▽⊭∄∃⊬∅ℝℜℑ⊤⊥
·×∗÷⋄±∓⊕⊖⊗⊘⊙⊚∘•≍≡⊑⊒≤≥⪯⪰∼≈⊏⊐≪≫⋖⋗♠

*cmcsc9*

@ABCDEFGHIJKLMNOPQRSTUVWXYZ
ABCDEFGHIJKLMNOPQRSTUVWXYZ
!"#$%&'()*+,-./0123456789:;<=>?
ΔΘΛΞΠΣΥΦΨΩ↑↓'';¡¿ıȷ`´˘¯˚¸ßæœøÆŒØ¨

*cmex9*

*cmmib9*

∂*ABCDEFGHIJKLMNOPQRSTUVWXYZ*
*abcdefghijklmnopqrstuvwxyz*
ω*εϑϖϱςφ←⇐→⇀↼↽*0123456789.,<*/*>⋆
ΔΘΛΞΠΣΥΦΨΩαβγδεζηθικλμνξπρστυφχ^

# *fonts/ams/amsfonts/symbols*

### *msam10*

⊏⊐▷⊲▷⊲★◊▼▶◀→←△▲▽⊨≦≧≡≶≷≳≂¥⇛⇚✓⋎⋏
⌢∈⋑⋓⋒⋏⋎⋏⋌⊆⊇⋍⊜⩵≖⋘⋙⌐⌐Ⓡ⑤⋔†⋍⌐⌐✠
⟿↝↾⇁≐≑≒≓≈≋·∴∵÷≜≏≎≺≻⋠⋡⋨⋩≼≽≀≐≓≒≻≽≳≷
⊞⊠∎∎.◊◆○○⇌⊸⊟||⊩⊦⊣→←⇐⇛⫫⫼||||↦↤⊂⊐⊤⊤⊖

### *msbm10*

♯ABCDEFGHIJKLMNOPQRSTUVWXYZ
℧℧ℸ≈⊐⊐⌐⊲⊳⋉⋊⋉⋌⋌⋉⋈∼≈≋≂⋍⋍⌢⌢*F*
≨≩≨⊊⊋⊊⊋⊋⊊⊋⊊⊋⋬⋭⫅⫆⫋⫌⫋⫌⊄⊅←↛↠↞↣↢⇸⇷⇹⇸*⊛⊘
⪇⪈⋨⋩⪉⪊⋨⋩⪇⪈⋦⋧⋬⋭⋨⋩⪇⪈⪇⪈⪌⪍≨≩≨≩∼≉⌿⟍⌐

# *fonts/apl*

### *cmapl10*

ABCDEFGHIJKLMNOPQRSTUVWXYZ
abcdefghijklmnopqrstuvwxyz
!А×$÷∧'()∗+,-./0123456789:;<=>?
□∇Δαωε¨∨◊≥ρⲓ₀∘∪∩⊂⊃_¯~≠τ⊥⊦⊩⌊⌈⌐→↓

# *fonts/astro*

### *astrosym*

# *fonts/bard*

### *bard*

ᚹᚺ᚜᚛ᚾᚼᚷᚺᛁᛁ᚜ᚲᚹᚾᚮᚱᚣᛗᚣᛏᚡᛖᚷᛏᚣᚣ
ᚹᚺ᚜᚛ᚾᚼᚷᚺᛁᛁ᚜ᚲᚹᚾᚮᚱᚣᛗᚣᛏᚡᛖᚷᛏᚣᚣ
'᚛ᛁᚭᚹᚹᛏᚱᚲ᚜:
ᛂᚾᚲᚹᛏᚣᚦᚡᚦᛈᚲᚤᚺᚾᚡ

## *fonts/bashkirian*

### *jkbash10*

˘АБЦДЕФГХИЈКЛМНОПЧРСТУВШШЫЗ
абцдефгхијклмнопчрстувшшыз
!"Ђ˘%´'()*Ђ,-./0123456789:;«ı»?
ЉЦЗІЄЂЋњљцзієђћЮЖЙЁVӨSЯюжйёvӨsяъ
FҐКНӨҮЂӘFκнҩγhə

### *jkcyr10*

˘АБЦДЕФГХИЈКЛМНОПЧРСТУВШШЫЗ
абцдефгхијклмнопчрстувшшыз
!"Ђ˘%´'()*Ђ,-./0123456789:;«ı»?
ЉЦЗІЄЂЋњљцзієђћЮЖЙЁVӨSЯюжйёvӨsяъ
FҐКНӨҮЂӘFκнҩγhə

## *fonts/bbding*

### *bbding10*

## *fonts/bbold*

### *bbold10*

ΘABCDEFGHIJKLMNOPQRSTUVWXYZ
abcdefghijklmnopqrstuvwxyz
!"#$%&'()*+,-./0123456789:;<=>?
ΔΘΛΞΠΣϒΦΨΩαβγδεζηθικλμνξπρστυφχω

### *cspex10*

# fonts/blackletter

## blackletter

ABCDEFGHIJKLMNOPQRSTUVWXYZ
abcdefghijklmnopqrstuvwxyz
!$&'()*+,-./0123456789:;=?

# fonts/calligra

## callig15

ABCDEFGHIJKLMNOPQRSTUVWXYZ
abcdefghijklmnopqrstuvwxyz
!$&'()*,.0123456789:;?
'~¨""—fifl ¥ÿ¡£ÀÁÂÃÄÅÆÇÈ
ÉÊËÌÍÎÏÑÒÓÔÕÖŒ ÙÚÛÜàáâãäåæçèéêë
ìíîïñòóôõöœùúûüß

# fonts/chess

## chess10

## chessf10

# fonts/cirth

## cirbf

## cirsl

## cirss

## cirth

## *fonts/cm*

### *cmb10*

**@ABCDEFGHIJKLMNOPQRSTUVWXYZ**
**abcdefghijklmnopqrstuvwxyz**
**!”#$%&’()*+,-./0123456789:;¡=¿?**
**ΔΘΛΞΠΣΥΦΨΩﬀﬁﬂﬃﬄıȷ` ´ˇ˘¯˚¸ßæœøÆŒØ¨**

### *cmbsy10*

ℵ$\mathcal{ABCDEFGHIJKLMNOPQRSTUVWXYZ}$
⊣⌊⌋⌈⌉{}⟨⟩|‖↕⇕\≀√∐∇∫⊔⊓⊑⊒§†‡
→↑↓↔↗↘≃⇐⇒⇑⇓⇔↖↙∝′∞∈∋△▽/∀∃¬∅ℜℑ⊤⊥
·×∗÷⋄±∓⊕⊖⊗⊘⊙◯∘•≍≡⊆⊇≤≥⪯⪰∼≈⊂⊃≪≫≺≻♠

### *cmbx10*

**@ABCDEFGHIJKLMNOPQRSTUVWXYZ**
**abcdefghijklmnopqrstuvwxyz**
**!”#$%&’()*+,-./0123456789:;¡=¿?**
**ΔΘΛΞΠΣΥΦΨΩﬀﬁﬂﬃﬄıȷ` ´ˇ˘¯˚¸ßæœøÆŒØ¨**

### *cmbxsl10*

***@ABCDEFGHIJKLMNOPQRSTUVWXYZ***
***abcdefghijklmnopqrstuvwxyz***
***!”#$%&’()*+,-./0123456789:;¡=¿?***
***ΔΘΛΞΠΣΥΦΨΩﬀﬁﬂﬃﬄıȷ` ´ˇ˘¯˚¸ßæœøÆŒØ¨***

### *cmbxti10*

***@ABCDEFGHIJKLMNOPQRSTUVWXYZ***
***abcdefghijklmnopqrstuvwxyz***
***!”#£%&’()*+,-./0123456789:;¡=¿?***
***ΔΘΛΞΠΣΥΦΨΩﬀﬁﬂﬃﬄıȷ` ´ˇ˘¯˚¸ßæœøÆŒØ¨***

### *cmcsc10*

@ABCDEFGHIJKLMNOPQRSTUVWXYZ
ABCDEFGHIJKLMNOPQRSTUVWXYZ
!”#$%&’()*+,-./0123456789:;<=>?
ΔΘΛΞΠΣΥΦΨΩ↑↓'¡¿ıȷ` ´ˇ˘¯˚¸SSÆŒØÆŒØ¨

**cmdunh10**

@ABCDEFGHIJKLMNOPQRSTUVWXYZ
abcdefghijklmnopqrstuvwxyz
!"#$%&'()*+,-./0123456789:;¡=¿?
ΔΘΛΞΠΣΥΦΨΩ ﬀﬁﬂﬃﬄ ıȷ ` ´ ˇ ˘ ¯ ° ¸ ß æ œ ø Æ Œ Ø ¨

**cmex10**

**cmff10**

@ABCDEFGHIJKLMNOPQRSTUVWXYZ
abcdefghijklmnopqrstuvwxyz
!"#$%&'()*+,-./0123456789:;¡=¿?
ΔΘΛΞΠΣΥΦΨΩ ﬀﬁﬂﬃﬄ ıȷ ` ´ ˇ ˘ ¯ ° ¸ ß æ œ ø Æ Œ Ø

**cmfi10**

@ABCDEFGHIJKLMNOPQRSTUVWXYZ
abcdefghijklmnopqrstuvwxyz
!"#£%&'()*+,-./0123456789:;¡=¿?
ΔΘΛΞΠΣΥΦΨΩ ﬀﬁﬂﬃﬄ ıȷ ` ´ ˇ ˘ ¯ ° ¸ ß æ œ ø Æ Œ Ø ¨

**cmfib8**

@ABCDEFGHIJKLMNOPQRSTUVWXYZ
abcdefghijklmnopqrstuvwxyz
!"#$%&'()*+,-./0123456789:;¡=¿?
ΔΘΛΞΠΣΥΦΨΩ ﬀﬁﬂﬃﬄ ıȷ ` ´ ˇ ˘ ¯ ° ¸ ß æ œ ø Æ Œ Ø ¨

**cmitt10**

@ABCDEFGHIJKLMNOPQRSTUVWXYZ
abcdefghijklmnopqrstuvwxyz
!"#£%&'()*+,-./0123456789:;<=>?
ΔΘΛΞΠΣΥΦΨΩ↑↓'¡¿ıȷ ` ´ ˇ ˘ ¯ ° ¸ ß æ œ ø Æ Œ Ø ¨

**cmmi10**

∂*ABCDEFGHIJKLMNOPQRSTUVWXYZ*
*abcdefghijklmnopqrstuvwxyz*
ωεϑϖϱϕ←⟵⟶→⟶⟶‹›▷◁0123456789.,</>⋆
ΔΘΛΞΠΣΥΦΨΩαβγδεζηθικλμνξπρστυφχ ˆ

**cmmib10**

∂***ABCDEFGHIJKLMNOPQRSTUVWXYZ***
***abcdefghijklmnopqrstuvwxyz***
***ωεϑϖϱϕ←⟵⟶→⟶⟶‹›▷◁0123456789.,</>⋆***
***ΔΘΛΞΠΣΥΦΨΩαβγδεζηθικλμνξπρστυφχ*** ˆ

**cmr10**

@ABCDEFGHIJKLMNOPQRSTUVWXYZ
abcdefghijklmnopqrstuvwxyz
!"#$%&'()*+,-./0123456789:;¡=¿?
ΔΘΛΞΠΣΥΦΨΩ ff fi fl ffi ffl ı ȷ ` ´ ˇ ˘ ¯ ˚ ¸ ß æ œ ø Æ Œ Ø ¨

**cmsl10**

@*ABCDEFGHIJKLMNOPQRSTUVWXYZ*
*abcdefghijklmnopqrstuvwxyz*
*!"#$%&'()*+,-./0123456789:;¡=¿?*
*ΔΘΛΞΠΣΥΦΨΩ ff fi fl ffi ffl ı ȷ ` ´ ˇ ˘ ¯ ˚ ¸ ß æ œ ø Æ Œ Ø ¨*

**cmsltt10**

@*ABCDEFGHIJKLMNOPQRSTUVWXYZ*
*abcdefghijklmnopqrstuvwxyz*
*!"#$%&'()*+,-./0123456789:;<=>?*
*ΔΘΛΞΠΣΤΦΨΩ↑↓'¡¿ıȷ` ´ ˇ ˘ ¯ ˚ ¸ ß æ œ ø Æ Œ Ø ¨*

**cmss10**

@ABCDEFGHIJKLMNOPQRSTUVWXYZ
abcdefghijklmnopqrstuvwxyz
!"#$%&'()*+,-./0123456789:;¡=¿?
ΔΘΛΞΠΣΥΦΨΩ ff fi fl ffi ffl ı ȷ ` ´ ˇ ˘ ¯ ˚ ¸ ß æ œ ø Æ Œ Ø ¨

**cmssbx10**

**@ABCDEFGHIJKLMNOPQRSTUVWXYZ**
**abcdefghijklmnopqrstuvwxyz**
**!"#$%&'()*+,-./0123456789:;¡=¿?**
**ΔΘΛΞΠΣΥΦΨΩ ff fi fl ffi ffl ı ȷ ` ´ ˇ ˘ ¯ ˚ ¸ ß æ œ ø Æ Œ Ø ¨**

*cmssdc10*

@ABCDEFGHIJKLMNOPQRSTUVWXYZ
abcdefghijklmnopqrstuvwxyz
!"#$%&'()*+,-./0123456789:;¡=¿?
ΔΘΛΞΠΣΥΦΨΩﬀﬁﬂﬃﬄﬆıȷ` ´˜¯˘˙¸ ßæœøÆŒØ¨

*cmssi10*

@*ABCDEFGHIJKLMNOPQRSTUVWXYZ*
*abcdefghijklmnopqrstuvwxyz*
*!"#$%&'()*+,-./0123456789:;¡=¿?*
*ΔΘΛΞΠΣΥΦΨΩﬀﬁﬂﬃﬄﬆıȷ` ´˜¯˘˙¸ ßæœøÆŒØ¨*

*cmssq8*

@ABCDEFGHIJKLMNOPQRSTUVWXYZ
abcdefghijklmnopqrstuvwxyz
!"#$%&'()*+,-./0123456789:;¡=¿?
ΔΘΛΞΠΣΥΦΨΩﬀﬁﬂﬃﬄﬆıȷ` ´˜¯˘˙¸ ßæœøÆŒØ¨

*cmssqi8*

@*ABCDEFGHIJKLMNOPQRSTUVWXYZ*
*abcdefghijklmnopqrstuvwxyz*
*!"#$%&'()*+,-./0123456789:;¡=¿?*
*ΔΘΛΞΠΣΥΦΨΩﬀﬁﬂﬃﬄﬆıȷ` ´˜¯˘˙¸ ßæœøÆŒØ¨*

*cmsy10*

ℵ*ABCDEFGHIJKLMNOPQRSTUVWXYZ*
⊣⊔⊓{}⟨⟩∥↕⇕\≀ √ ⨿∇∫⊔⊓⊑⊒§†‡
→↑↓↔↦↗↘≃⇐⇒⇑⇓⇔↖↙∝∞∈∋△▽⊬⊣¬∅ℜℑ℘℘⊤⊥
·×∗÷⋄±∓⊕⊖⊗⊘⊙○∘•≍≡⊆⊇≤≥⪯⪰∼≈⊏⊐≪≫⊰⊱♠

*cmtcsc10*

@ABCDEFGHIJKLMNOPQRSTUVWXYZ
ABCDEFGHIJKLMNOPQRSTUVWXYZ
!"#$%&'()*+,-./0123456789:;<=>?
ΔΘΛΞΠΣΥΦΨΩ↑↓' '¡¿IJ` ´˜¯˘˙¸ ßssæœøÆŒØ¨

*cmtex10*

@ABCDEFGHIJKLMNOPQRSTUVWXYZ
abcdefghijklmnopqrstuvwxyz
!"#$%&'()*+,-./0123456789:;<=>?
↓αβ∧¬∈πλγδ↑±⊕ω∂⊂⊃∪∩∀∃⊗↰↔→≠◇≲≥≡∨∫

**cmti10**

> @*ABCDEFGHIJKLMNOPQRSTUVWXYZ*
> *abcdefghijklmnopqrstuvwxyz*
> *!"#£%&'()*+,-./0123456789:;¡=¿?*
> *ΔΘΛΞΠΣΥΦΨΩ ﬀ ﬁ ﬂ ﬃ ﬄ ıȷ ` ´ ˇ ˘ ¯ ˚ ¸ ß æ œ ø Æ Œ Ø ¨*

**cmtt10**

> @ABCDEFGHIJKLMNOPQRSTUVWXYZ
> abcdefghijklmnopqrstuvwxyz
> !"#$%&'()*+,-./0123456789:;<=>?
> ΔΘΛΞΠΣΥΦΨΩ↑↓'¡¿ıȷ ` ´ ˇ ˜ ¯ ˚ ¸ ß æ œ ø Æ Œ Ø ¨

**cmu10**

> @ABCDEFGHIJKLMNOPQRSTUVWXYZ
> abcdefghijklmnopqrstuvwxyz
> !"#£%&'()*+,-./0123456789:;¡=¿?
> ΔΘΛΞΠΣΥΦΨΩ ﬀ ﬁ ﬂ ﬃ ﬄ ıȷ ` ´ ˇ ˘ ¯ ˚ ¸ ß æ œ ø Æ Œ Ø ¨

**cmvtt10**

> @ABCDEFGHIJKLMNOPQRSTUVWXYZ
> abcdefghijklmnopqrstuvwxyz
> !"#$%&'()*+,-./0123456789:;¡=¿?
> ΔΘΛΞΠΣΥΦΨΩ ﬀ ﬁ ﬂ ﬃ ﬄ ıȷ ` ´ ˇ ˜ ¯ ˚ ¸ ß æ œ ø Æ Œ Ø ¨

## *fonts/cm/utility*

**grdov5**

**logo10**

> AEFMNOPST

**logo10**

> AEFMNOPST

**logobf10**

> **AEFMNOPST**

**logobf10**

> **AEFMNOPST**

*logosl10*

AEFMNOPST

*logosl10*

AEFMNOPST

*slaps4*

*sldov6*

## *fonts/cmastro*

*cmastro10*

℧♈☊☉♈♀♁☌♃☽♅♆○

## *fonts/cmcyr*

*cmcbx10*

@АБЦДЕФГХИКЛМНОПЧРСТУВЩШЫЗ
абцдефгхиклмнопчрстувщшыз
!"#$%&'()*+,-./0123456789:;=?
ЭэЮЖЙЯюжйяъ

*cmcbxsl10*

@АБЦДЕФГХИКЛМНОПЧРСТУВЩШЫЗ
абцдефгхиклмнопчрстувщшыз
!"#$%&'()*+,-./0123456789:;=?
ЭэЮЖЙЯюжйяъ

*cmcbxti10*

@АБЦДЕФГХИКЛМНОПЧРСТУВЩШЫЗ
абцдефгхиклмнопчрстувщшыз
!"#£%&'()*+,-./0123456789:;=?
ЭэЮЖЙЯюжйяъ

*cmcitt10*

@АБЦДЕФГХИКЛМНОПЧРСТУВЩШЫЗ
абцдефгхиклмнопчрстувщшыз
!"#£%&'()*+,-./0123456789:;=?
ЭэЮЖЙЯюжйяъ

### cmcsl10

@АБЦДЕФГХИКЛМНОПЧРСТУВЩШЫЗ
абцдефгхиклмнопчрстувщшыз
!"#$%&'()*+,-./0123456789:;=?
ЭэЮЖЙЯюжйяъ

### cmcss10

@АБЦДЕФГХИКЛМНОПЧРСТУВЩШЫЗ
абцдефгхиклмнопчрстувщшыз
!"#$%&'()*+,-./0123456789:;=?
ЭэЮЖЙЯюжйяъ

### cmcssdc10

@АБЦДЕФГХИКЛМНОПЧРСТУВЩШЫЗ
абцдефгхиклмнопчрстувщшыз
!"#$%&'()*+,-./0123456789:;=?
ЭэЮЖЙЯюжйяъ

### cmcti10

@АБЦДЕФГХИКЛМНОПЧРСТУВЩШЫЗ
абцдефгхиклмнопчрстувщшыз
!"#£%&'()*+,-./0123456789:;=?
ЭэЮЖЙЯюжйяъ

### cmctt10

@АБЦДЕФГХИКЛМНОПЧРСТУВЩШЫЗ
абцдефгхиклмнопчрстувщшыз
!"#$%&'()*+,-./0123456789:;=?
ЭэЮЖЙЯюжйяъ

### cmcyr10

@АБЦДЕФГХИКЛМНОПЧРСТУВЩШЫЗ
абцдефгхиклмнопчрстувщшыз
!"#$%&'()*+,-./0123456789:;=?
ЭэЮЖЙЯюжйяъ

## fonts/cmoefont

### cmoebx10

ĐƷÞðӡ ‚þþ

### cmoer10

ĐƷÞðӡ ‚þþ

### cmoesc10

Ð3Ðꝺ3 ‚Þ

### cmoesl10

Ð3Ðẟ3 ‚þþ

### cmoeti10

*Ð3Ðẟ3 ‚þ*

### cmoett10

Ð3Ðẟ3 ‚þþ

## *fonts/cmpica*

### cmpicab

@ABCDEFGHIJKLMNOPQRSTUVWXYZ
abcdefghijklmnopqrstuvwxyz
!"#$%&'()*+,-./0123456789:;<=>?
ΔΘΛΞΠΣΤΦΨΩ↑↓'¡¿ıJ` ´˘¯˝ ¸ßæœøÆŒØ¨

### cmpicati

*@ABCDEFGHIJKLMNOPQRSTUVWXYZ*
*abcdefghijklmnopqrstuvwxyz*
*!"#$%&'()*+,-./0123456789:;<=>?*
*ΔΘΛΞΠΣΤΦΨΩ↑↓'¡¿ıJ` ´˘¯˝ ¸ßæœøÆŒØ¨*

### cmpica

@ABCDEFGHIJKLMNOPQRSTUVWXYZ
abcdefghijklmnopqrstuvwxyz
!"#$%&'()*+,-./0123456789:;<=>?
ΔΘΛΞΠΣΤΦΨΩ↑↓'¡¿ıJ` ´˘¯˝ ¸ßæœøÆŒØ¨

## *fonts/concrete*

### cccsc10

@ABCDEFGHIJKLMNOPQRSTUVWXYZ
ABCDEFGHIJKLMNOPQRSTUVWXYZ
!"#$%&'()*+,-./0123456789:;<=>?
ΔΘΛΞΠΣΥΦΨΩ↑↓'¡¿IJ` ´˘¯˝ ¸ssæœøÆŒØ¨

**ccmi10**

∂ABCDEFGHIJKLMNOPQRSTUVWXYZ
abcdefghijklmnopqrstuvwxyz
ωεϑϖϱςφ↼↽⇀⇁↻▷◁0123456789.,</>⋆
ΔΘΛΞΠΣΥΦΨΩαβγδεζηθικλμνξπρστυφχ⌢

**ccr10**

@ABCDEFGHIJKLMNOPQRSTUVWXYZ
abcdefghijklmnopqrstuvwxyz
!"#$%&'()*+,-./0123456789:;¡=¿?
ΔΘΛΞΠΣΥΦΨΩﬀﬁﬂﬃﬄıȷ`´˜¯˘˙¸ßæœøÆŒØ¨

**ccsl10**

@ABCDEFGHIJKLMNOPQRSTUVWXYZ
abcdefghijklmnopqrstuvwxyz
!"#$%&'()*+,-./0123456789:;¡=¿?
ΔΘΛΞΠΣΥΦΨΩﬀﬁﬂﬃﬄıȷ`´˜¯˘˙¸ßæœøÆŒØ¨

**ccslc9**

@ABCDEFGHIJKLMNOPQRSTUVWXYZ
abcdefghijklmnopqrstuvwxyz
!"#$%&'()*+,-./0123456789:;¡=¿?
ΔΘΛΞΠΣΥΦΨΩﬀﬁﬂﬃﬄıȷ`´˜¯˘˙¸ßæœøÆŒØ¨

**ccti10**

@ABCDEFGHIJKLMNOPQRSTUVWXYZ
abcdefghijklmnopqrstuvwxyz
!"#£%&'()*+,-./0123456789:;¡=¿?
ΔΘΛΞΠΣΥΦΨΩﬀﬁﬂﬃﬄıȷ`´˜¯˘˙¸ßæœøÆŒØ¨

# *fonts/duerer*

**cdb10**

ABCDEFGHIJKLMNOPQRSTUVWXYZ

**cdi10**

ABCDEFGHIJKLMNOPQRSTUVWXYZ

**cdr10**

ABCDEFGHIJKLMNOPQRSTUVWXYZ

**cdsl10**

ABCDEFGHIJKLMNOPQRSTUVWXYZ

**cdss10**

ABCDEFGHIJKLMNOPQRSTUVWXYZ

**cdtt10**

ABCDEFGHIJKLMNOPQRSTUVWXYZ

# fonts/eiad

### eiad10

@ABCDEFGIÐCLMNOPFRSTUÐMTȘS
abcdefgiðclmnopfrrtuðmtȘr
!"#$%&'()*+,-./0123456789:;¡=¿?
ÞÁÉÍÓÚÞáéíóú` ´ ˜ ¯ ° ˛ ¸ ⸴ ⸍ ¨

### eiadbf10

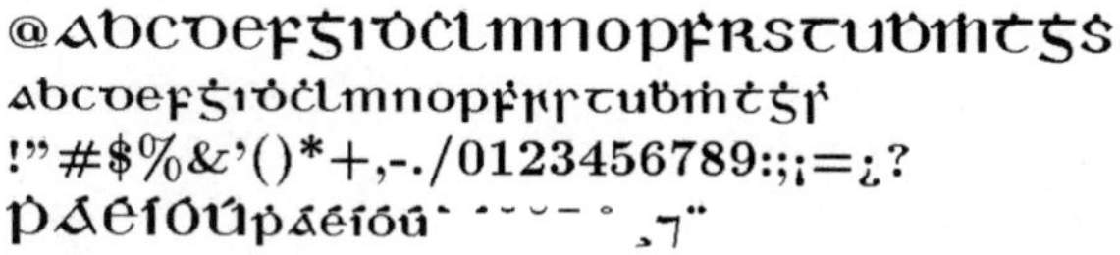

@ABCDEFGIÐCLMNOPFRSTUÐMTȘS
abcdefgiðclmnopfrrtuðmtȘr
!"#$%&'()*+,-./0123456789:;¡=¿?
ÞÁÉÍÓÚÞáéíóú` ´ ˜ ¯ ° ˛ ¸ ⸴ ⸍ ¨

# fonts/elvish

### teng10

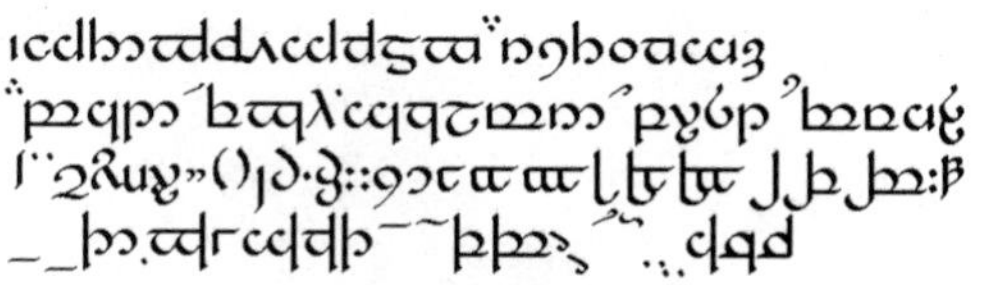

ıcdlɔⲧⲇⲇʌⲥⲇⲓⲇȝⲧⲁ̈ɳ9ɦoⲁⲥⲁȝ
̈ⲡⲁɋⲡɔ̓ɓⲧɋʎ̔ⲥɋɋⲧⲝⲉⲝⲝⲝ ́ⲡʏ6ⲣ ̓ɓ�ɔⲁɋ
l ̓ ⳋⱤⳙⲩ ⸗ ()ð·ȝ::9ɔⲧⲧⲧⱳ[ⱦⱦ ⲧ Jɓ Jɔ:ɓ
_Jɔⳋⲧɟⲥⲇⲇ‖ɓ ̄ ̃ɓɓɔȝ ̂ ⸴.. ɋɋⲇ

# fonts/engwar

### engwar

ⰑbⲥⲇⲉⱤ9ɦjjⰍⰌⲙⲛoⲡⰋⲅstuⲅⲩⲭyz
ⰑbⲥⲇⲉⱤ9ɦjjⰍⰌⲙⲛoⲡⰋⲅstuⲅⲩⲭyz
!" '().~::0123456789:≈?
ɪj` ´˅˅-..

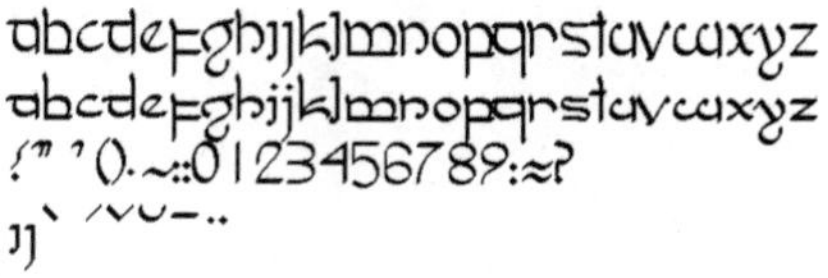

## fonts/fc

### b-fcbx10

@ABCDEFGHIJKLMNOPQRSTUVWXYZ
abcdefghijklmnopqrstuvwxyz
!"#$%&'()*+,-./0123456789:;<=>?
´^˜"˝°˘˅¯˛ ̧‹›""„«»——oıfffiflffiffl-
ƁÐƐƷFĚƳHKΚNƆŃſDUYƇPŠŇN̦Ş3ƷŤĖȨTƮƲfjđˮ
ɓɗɛəfɛχħkɲɔſɲʋɣƈƥšň̦ɳ̦ʂʒťɛ̦ʠț˝¿˙
ĿIJĊÃMÕǼÆÇÈÉÊËĘ̄ĒĔĨĐÑÒÓÔÕÖŒØǪǬŌŎŲŨ-
ıȷ̃ēāḿõæçèéêëȩ̄ēĕĩdᷩñòóôõöœøǫǭōŏŭũß

### b-fcbxi10

@ABCDEFGHIJKLMNOPQRSTUVWXYZ
abcdefghijklmnopqrstuvwxyz
!"#£%&'()*+,-./0123456789:;<=>?
´^˜"˝°˘˅¯˛ ̧‹›""„«»——oıȷ- ƁÐƐƷF
ĚƳHKΚNƆŃſDUYƇPŠŇN̦Ş3ƷŤĖȨTƮđˮɓɗɛəfɛƥ
ħkɲɔſɲʋɣƈƥšň̦ɳ̦ʂʒťɛ̦ț˝¿˙ ĿIJĊÃMÕÆ
ÇÈÉÊËĘ̄ĒĔĨĐÑÒÓÔÕÖŒØǪǬŌŎŲŨ-ıȷ̃ēāḿõæ
çèéêëȩ̄ēĕĩdᷩñòóôõöœøǫǭōŏŭũß

### b-fcbxsl10

@ABCDEFGHIJKLMNOPQRSTUVWXYZ
abcdefghijklmnopqrstuvwxyz
!"#$%&'()*+,-./0123456789:;<=>?
´^˜"˝°˘˅¯˛ ̧‹›""„«»——oıfffiflffiffl-
ƁÐƐƷFĚƳHKΚNƆŃſDUYƇPŠŇN̦Ş3ƷŤĖȨTƮƲfjđˮ
ɓɗɛəfɛχħkɲɔſɲʋɣƈƥšň̦ɳ̦ʂʒťɛ̦ț˝¿˙
ĿIJĊÃMÕÆÇÈÉÊËĘ̄ĒĔĨĐÑÒÓÔÕÖŒØǪǬŌŎŲŨ-
ıȷ̃ēāḿõæçèéêëȩ̄ēĕĩdᷩñòóôõöœøǫǭōŏŭũß

### b-fcbxu10

@ABCDEFGHIJKLMNOPQRSTUVWXYZ
abcdefghijklmnopqrstuvwxyz
!"#£%&'()*+,-./0123456789:;<=>?
´^˜"˝°˘˅¯˛ ̧‹›""„«»——oıȷ- ƁÐƐƷF
ĚƳHKΚNƆŃſDUYƇPŠŇN̦Ş3ƷŤĖȨTƮđˮɓɗɛəfɛƥ
ħkɲɔſɲʋɣƈƥšň̦ɳ̦ʂʒťɛ̦ț˝¿˙ ĿIJĊÃMÕÆ
ÇÈÉÊËĘ̄ĒĔĨĐÑÒÓÔÕÖŒØǪǬŌŎŲŨ-ıȷ̃ēāḿõæ
çèéêëȩ̄ēĕĩdᷩñòóôõöœøǫǭōŏŭũß

## b-fccsc10

@ABCDEFGHIJKLMNOPQRSTUVWXYZ
ABCDEFGHIJKLMNOPQRSTUVWXYZ
!"#$%&'()*+,-./0123456789:;<=>?
´ˆ˜¨˝°˘¯˙¸ ̦‹›""„«»–—0IJFFFIFLFFIFFL-
ƁƊƐƎƑĔƔĦKƝƆŃƒȢUYĆPŠŃŅŞƷŦĖȨŦƮTʃƒJƋ¨
ƁƊƐƎƑĔƔĦKƝƆŃƒȢUYĆPŠŃŅŞƷŦĖȨŦƮ"¡¿´
ĿĮĔĀŃÕÆÇÈÉÊËĘĒĔĮĐÑÒÓÔÕÖŒØǪǪŌŎŮŨ‾
ĿĮĔĀŃÕÆÇÈÉÊËĘĒĔĮĐÑÒÓÔÕÖŒØǪǪŌŎŮŨSS

## b-fci10

@ABCDEFGHIJKLMNOPQRSTUVWXYZ
abcdefghijklmnopqrstuvwxyz
!"#£%&'()*+,-./0123456789:;<=>?
´ˆ˜¨˝°˘¯˙¸ ̦‹›""„«»–—0ŋ-ƁƊƐƎƑ
ĔƔĦKƝƆŃƒȢUYĆPŠŃŅŞƷŦĖȨŦƮđ¨ɓɗɛəfĕɣ
ħkɲɔŋʃɲʋyćpšńŅŞʒŧėȩŧ"¡¿´ĿĮĔĀŃÕÆ
ÇÈÉÊËĘĒĔĮĐÑÒÓÔÕÖŒØǪǪŌŎŮŨ-ĮĭĕãŃõæ
çèéêëĘēĕĮđñòóôõöœøǫǫōŏůũß

## b-fcitt10

@ABCDEFGHIJKLMNOPQRSTUVWXYZ
abcdefghijklmnopqrstuvwxyz
!"#£%&'()*+,-./0123456789:;<=>?
´ˆ˜¨˝°˘¯˙¸ ̦‹›""„«»––,ɩŋ-ƁƊƐƎƑ
ĔƔĦKƝƆŃƒȢUYĆPŠŃŅŞƷŦĖȨŦƮđ¨ɓɗɛəfĕɣ
ħkɲɔŋʃɲʋycpšńŅŞʒŧėȩŧ"¡¿´ĿĮĔĀŃÕÆ
ÇÈÉÊËĘĒĔĮĐÑÒÓÔÕÖŒØǪǪŌŎŮŨ-Įĭ ĕãŃõæ
çèéêëĘēĕĮđñòóôõöœøǫǫōŏůũß

## b-fcr10

@ABCDEFGHIJKLMNOPQRSTUVWXYZ
abcdefghijklmnopqrstuvwxyz
!"#$%&'()*+,-./0123456789:;<=>?
´ˆ˜¨˝°˘¯˙¸ ̦‹›""„«»–—0ŋfffiflffiffl-
ƁƊƐƎƑĔƔĦKƝƆŃƒȢUYĆPŠŃŅŞƷŦĖȨŦƮʧffjƋ¨
ɓɗɛəfĕɣħkɲɔŋʃɲʋyćpšńŅŞʒŧėȩŧ"¡¿´
ĿĮĔĀŃÕÆÇÈÉÊËĘĒĔĮĐÑÒÓÔÕÖŒØǪǪŌŎŮŨ‾
ĮĭĕãŃõæçèéêëęēĕĮđñòóôõöœøǫǫōŏůũß

*b-fcsibx10*

@ABCDEFGHIJKLMNOPQRSTUVWXYZ
abcdefghijklmnopqrstuvwxyz
!"#$%&'()*+,-./0123456789:;<=>?
´`˜"„°˘¯¸˝ ,‚‹›""„«»——◦ıffffifflffiffl-
Ƀ'ƉƐƷFĚȣHKNƆŃʃƊɄYĆʼPŠŃŊŞƷŦÈĘŦȽɣfjȡ¨
ɓɗɛəfěɣħkɲɔ̃ʃɲʊyćʼpšŋ̣ŋ̣ṣẓṭéęŧ¨ı̨¿˙
ĿŀĮÃMÕÆÇÈÉÊËĘĒĖĪ-ĐÑÒÓÔÕÖŒØǪǪŌŎÙŪ̃
ı̨ɛ̃ãm̃õæçèéêëẹēēĩȡ̃ñòóôõöœøǫọōŏųũß

*b-fcsitt10*

@ABCDEFGHIJKLMNOPQRSTUVWXYZ
abcdefghijklmnopqrstuvwxyz
!"#$%&'()*+,-./0123456789:;<=>?
´`˜"„°˘¯¸˝ ,‚‹›""„«»——◦ıʃfffififlffiffl-
Ƀ'ƉƐƷFĚȣHKNƆŃʃƊɄYĆʼPŠŃŊŞƷŦÈĘŦȽɣfjȡ¨
ɓɗɛəfěɣħkɲɔ̃ʃɲʊyćʼpšŋ̣ŋ̣ṣẓṭéęŧ¨ı̨¿˙
ĿŀĮÃMÕÆÇÈÉÊËĘĒĖĪ-ĐÑÒÓÔÕÖŒØǪǪŌŎÙŪ̃
ı̨ɛ̃ãm̃õæçèéêëẹēēĩȡ̃ñòóôõöœøǫọōŏųũß

*b-fcsl10*

@ABCDEFGHIJKLMNOPQRSTUVWXYZ
abcdefghijklmnopqrstuvwxyz
!"#$%&'()*+,-./0123456789:;<=>?
´`˜"„°˘¯¸˝ ,‚‹›""„«»——◦ıffffifflffiffl-
Ƀ'ƉƐƷFĚȣHKNƆŃʃƊɄYĆʼPŠŃŊŞƷŦÈĘŦȽɣfjȡ¨
ɓɗɛəfěɣħkɲɔ̃ʃɲʊyćʼpšŋ̣ŋ̣ṣẓṭéęŧ¨ı̨¿˙
ĿŀĮÃMÕÆÇÈÉÊËĘĒĖĪ-ĐÑÒÓÔÕÖŒØǪǪŌŎÙŪ̃
ı̨ɛ̃ãm̃õæçèéêëẹēēĩȡ̃ñòóôõöœøǫọōŏųũß

*b-fcss10*

@ABCDEFGHIJKLMNOPQRSTUVWXYZ
abcdefghijklmnopqrstuvwxyz
!"#$%&'()*+,-./0123456789:;<=>?
´`˜"„°˘¯¸˝ ,‚‹›""„«»——◦ıffffifflffiffl-
Ƀ'ƉƐƷFĚȣHKNƆŃʃƊɄYĆʼPŠŃŊŞƷŦÈĘŦȽɣfjȡ¨
ɓɗɛəfěɣħkɲɔ̃ʃɲʊyćʼpšŋ̣ŋ̣ṣẓṭéęŧ¨ı̨¿˙
ĿŀĮÃMÕÆÇÈÉÊËĘĒĖĪ-ĐÑÒÓÔÕÖŒØǪǪŌŎÙŪ̃
ı̨ɛ̃ãm̃õæçèéêëẹēēĩȡ̃ñòóôõöœøǫọōŏųũß

*b-fcssbx10*

@ABCDEFGHIJKLMNOPQRSTUVWXYZ
abcdefghijklmnopqrstuvwxyz
!"#$%&'()*+,-./0123456789:;<=>?
´˜˝¨¸˚˛¯˘˙, ,‹›""„«»——•ıjffffifflffiffl-
ʙʪDƐꟻFɣƎHKꞁNƆꞃNꞂƲUYƇʿPŠŃ<u>N</u>Ş3ŦĖƐŦŦƴꝥȸ¨
ƃɗɛəfɛ̌ɣꞕkꞁɔꞃʃɲʊyƈꝓšń<u>n</u>ş<u>z</u>ŧėeŧ̧¨¡¿´
ĿIĔÃḾʃÆÇÈÉÊĔ<u>Ë</u>ĒĔĪÐÑÒÓÔÕÖŒØǪQÕÕ<u>Y</u>Ũ—
Ŀiĕãḿʃæçèéêĕ<u>ë</u>ēĕĩ<u>d</u>ñòóôõöœøọ<u>o</u>õõ<u>y</u>ũß

*b-fcssi10*

@*ABCDEFGHIJKLMNOPQRSTUVWXYZ*
*abcdefghijklmnopqrstuvwxyz*
*!"#$%&'()\*+,-./0123456789:;<=>?*
*´˜˝¨¸˚˛¯˘˙, ,‹› "" „«»——•ıjffffifflffiffl-*
*ʙʪDƐꟻFɣꞁHKꞁNƆꞃNꞂƲUYƇʿPŠŃ<u>N</u>Ş3ŦĖƐŦŦƴꝥȸ¨*
*ƃɗɛəfɛ̌ɣꞕkꞁɔꞃʃɲʊyƈꝓšń<u>n</u>ş<u>z</u>ŧėeŧ̧¨¡¿´*
*ĿIĔÃḾʃÆÇÈÉÊĔ<u>Ë</u>ĒĔĪÐÑÒÓÔÕÖŒØǪQÕÕ<u>Y</u>Ũ—*
*Ŀiĕãḿʃæçèéêĕ<u>ë</u>ēĕĩ<u>d</u>ñòóôõöœøọ<u>o</u>õõ<u>y</u>ũß*

*b-fcsstt10*

```
@ABCDEFGHIJKLMNOPQRSTUVWXYZ
abcdefghijklmnopqrstuvwxyz
!"#$%&'()*+,-./0123456789:;<=>?
```
´˜˝¨¸˚˛¯˘˙, ,‹›"" „«»—•ıjffffifflffiffl-
ʙʪDƐꟻFɣꞁHKꞁNƆꞃNꞂƲUYƇʿPŠŃ<u>N</u>Ş3ŦĖƐŦŦƴꝥȸ¨
ƃɗɛəfɛ̌ɣꞕkꞁɔꞃʃɲʊyƈꝓšń<u>n</u>ş<u>z</u>ŧėeŧ̧¨¡¿´
ĿIĔÃḾʃÆÇÈÉÊĔ<u>Ë</u>ĒĔĪÐÑÒÓÔÕÖŒØǪQÕÕ<u>Y</u>Ũ—
Ŀiĕãḿʃæçèéêĕ<u>ë</u>ēĕĩ<u>d</u>ñòóôõöœøọ<u>o</u>õõ<u>y</u>ũß

*b-fctt10*

```
@ABCDEFGHIJKLMNOPQRSTUVWXYZ
abcdefghijklmnopqrstuvwxyz
!"#$%&'()*+,-./0123456789:;<=>?
```
´˜˝¨¸˚˛¯˘˙, ,‹›"" „«»—•ıjffffifflffiffl-
ʙʪDƐꟻFɣꞁHKꞁNƆꞃNꞂƲUYƇʿPŠŃ<u>N</u>Ş3ŦĖƐŦŦƴꝥȸ¨
ƃɗɛəfɛ̌ɣꞕkꞁɔꞃʃɲʊyƈꝓšń<u>n</u>ş<u>z</u>ŧėeŧ̧¨¡¿´
ĿIĔÃḾʃÆÇÈÉÊĔ<u>Ë</u>ĒĔĪÐÑÒÓÔÕÖŒØǪQÕÕ<u>Y</u>Ũ—
Ŀiĕãḿʃæçèéêĕ<u>ë</u>ēĕĩ<u>d</u>ñòóôõöœøọ<u>o</u>õõ<u>y</u>ũß

### b-fcu10

@ABCDEFGHIJKLMNOPQRSTUVWXYZ
abcdefghijklmnopqrstuvwxyz
!"#£%&'()*+,-./0123456789:;<=>?
´˜¨"˝ ˚ ˘�'‚ ‛ ‹›""„«»–— oŋ-ƁƊƐꟻF
ĚƔ̵HKꞋNƆŃʃꝹUYĆP̧ŠŇŅṢ3ŦĖȨꝋꝹd ̈bɗɛəfëꝑ
ħ kꞩⱭ ꞗuy ̧ćp ̧šňn ̧ṣ3ꞑ́ eꝑꞩt"¡¿'ꞐĨÃMÕÆ
ÇÈÉÊËĒ ̱Ē̄ĪĐÑÒÓÔÕÖŒØǪꝹ̱Ō̄ŌŮŨ-ꞑ̲ĩ̲ẽ̲ãm̃̄Ꝓ̃̄æ
çèéêëē ̱ ē̄ĩđñòóôõöœøǫꝹ̱ō̄ŏůũß

## fonts/futhark

### futhol10

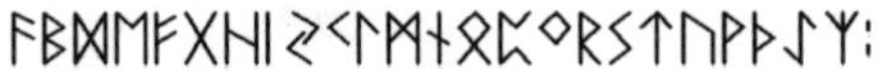

ᚠᛒᛗᛖᛘᚠᚷᚺᛁ ᛉᛍᛏᛘᛏᛉᛕ ᛟᛉᛋᛏᚾᛈᛒ ᛋᛉ:

## fonts/georgian

### georgian

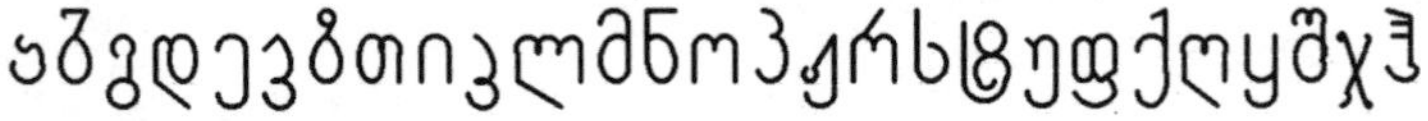

აბგდევზთიკლმნოპჟრსტუფქღყშჩ

### mxed10

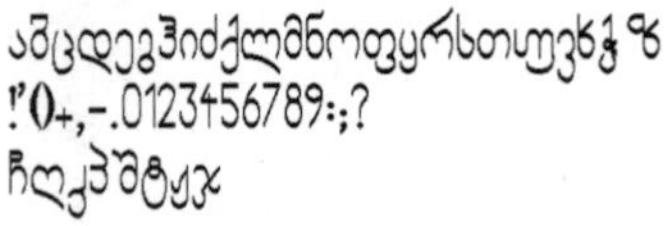

ამცdეგჳndკლღმნოთ ̂ვ ̂ yრსთ ̂ უჳ ̂ კჴꞁ ჵ
!'0+,-.0123456789:;?
ჩ ̂ cꞁꝑ̂ ̂ ꝑꝺ̂ ̂ ꝺ ̂ ꝑꝺ ̂ ꝑ ̂ y ꝺ

### mxedbf10

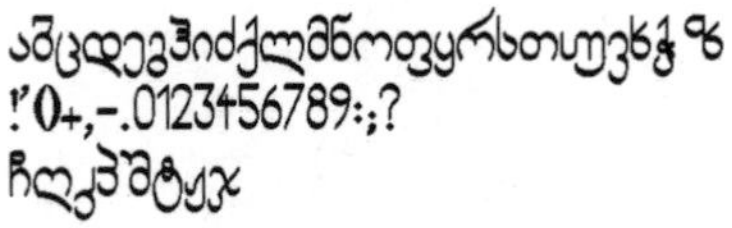

ამცdეგჳndკლღმნოთ ̂ვ ̂ yრსთ ̂ უჳ ̂ კჴꞁ ჵ
!'0+,-.0123456789:;?
ჩ ̂ cꞁꝑ̂ ̂ ꝑꝺ̂ ̂ ꝺ ̂ ꝑꝺ ̂ ꝑ ̂ y ꝺ

## fonts/go

### go10

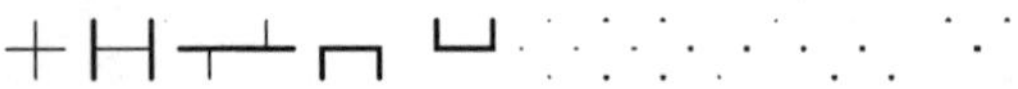

+ ┤├ ┬ ┴ ┌ ┐ ┘ └ · ·· ··· ···· ····· ······ ·

### go1bla10

64 65 66 67 68 69 70 71 72 73 74 75 76 77 78 79 80 81 82 83 84 85 86 87 88 89 90
97 98 99 100 101 102 103 104 105 106 107 108 109 110 111 112 113 114 115 116 117 118 119 120 121 122
33 34 35 36 37 38 29 40 41 42 43 44 45 46 47 48 49 50 51 52 53 54 55 56 57 58 59 60 61 62 63
1 2 3 4 5 6 7 8 9 10 11 12 13 14 15 16 17 18 19 20 21 22 23 24 25 26 27 28 29 30 31 127

## go1whi10

⑥④⑥⑤⑥⑥⑥⑦⑥⑧⑥⑨⑦⓪⑦①⑦②⑦③⑦④⑦⑤⑦⑥⑦⑦⑦⑧⑦⑨⑧⓪⑧①⑧②⑧③⑧④⑧⑤⑧⑥⑧⑦⑧⑧⑧⑨⑨⓪
⑨⑦⑨⑧⑨⑨⑩⓪⑩①⑩②⑩③⑩④⑩⑤⑩⑥⑩⑦⑩⑧⑩⑨⑪⓪⑪①⑪②⑪③⑪④⑪⑤⑪⑥⑪⑦⑪⑧⑪⑨⑫⓪⑫①⑫②
③③③④③⑤③⑥③⑦③⑧②⑨④⓪④①④②④③④④④⑤④⑥④⑦④⑧④⑨⑤⓪⑤①⑤②⑤③⑤④⑤⑤⑤⑥⑤⑦⑤⑧⑤⑨⑥⓪⑥①⑥②⑥③
①②③④⑤⑥⑦⑧⑨⑩⑪⑫⑬⑭⑮⑯⑰⑱⑲⑳㉑㉒㉓㉔㉕㉖㉗㉘㉙㉚㉛⑫⑦

## go2bla10

⑲②⑲③⑲④⑲⑤⑲⑥⑲⑦⑲⑧⑲⑨②⓪⓪②⓪①②⓪②②⓪③②⓪④②⓪⑤②⓪⑥②⓪⑦②⓪⑧②⓪⑨②①⓪②①①②①②②①③②①④②①⑤②①⑥②①⑦②①⑧
②②⑤②②⑥②②⑦②②⑧②②⑨②③⓪②③①②③②②③③②③④②③⑤②③⑥②③⑦②③⓪②③⑨②④⓪②④①②④②②④③②④④②④⑤②④⑥②④⑦②④⓪②④⑨②⑤⓪
①⑥①①⑥②①⑥③①⑥④①⑥⑤①⑥⑥①⑥⑦①⑥⑧①⑥⑨①⑦⓪①⑦①①⑦②①⑦③①⑦④①⑦⑤①⑦⑥①⑦⑦①⑦⑧①⑦⑨①⑧⓪①⑧①①⑧②①⑧③①⑧④①⑧⑤①⑧⑥①⑧⑦①⑧⑧①⑧⑨①⑨⓪①⑨①
①②⑨①③⓪①③①①③②①③③①③④①③⑤①③⑥①③⑦①③⑧①③⑨①④⓪①④①①④②①④③①④④①④⑤①④⑥①④⑦①④⑧①④⑨①⑤⓪①⑤①①⑤②①⑤③①⑤④①⑤⑤①⑤⑥①⑤⑦①⑤⑧①⑤⑨△

## go2whi10

⑲②⑲③⑲④⑲⑤⑲⑥⑲⑦⑲⑧⑲⑨②⓪⓪②⓪①②⓪②②⓪③②⓪④②⓪⑤②⓪⑥②⓪⑦②⓪⑧②⓪⑨②①⓪②①①②①②②①③②①④②①⑤②①⑥②①⑦②①⑧
②②⑤②②⑥②②⑦②②⑧②②⑨②③⓪②③①②③②②③③②③④②③⑤②③⑥②③⑦②③⑧②③⑨②④⓪②④①②④②②④③②④④②④⑤②④⑥②④⑦②④⑧②④⑨②⑤⓪
①⑥①①⑥②①⑥③①⑥④①⑥⑤①⑥⑥①⑥⑦①⑥⑧①⑥⑨①⑦⓪①⑦①①⑦②①⑦③①⑦④①⑦⑤①⑦⑥①⑦⑦①⑦⑧①⑦⑨①⑧⓪①⑧①①⑧②①⑧③①⑧④①⑧⑤①⑧⑥①⑧⑦①⑧⑧①⑧⑨①⑨⓪①⑨①
①②⑨①③⓪①③①①③②①③③①③④①③⑤①③⑥①③⑦①③⑧①③⑨①④⓪①④①①④②①④③①④④①④⑤①④⑥①④⑦①④⑧①④⑨①⑤⓪①⑤①①⑤②①⑤③①⑤④①⑤⑤①⑤⑥①⑤⑦①⑤⑧①⑤⑨△

# *fonts/gothic*

## yfrak

𝔄𝔅ℭ𝔇𝔈𝔉𝔊ℌℑ𝔍𝔎𝔏𝔐𝔑𝔒𝔓𝔔ℜ𝔖𝔗𝔘𝔙𝔚𝔛𝔜ℨ

abcdefghijklmnopqrstuvwxyz

!" #ℨ%&'()*+,-./0123456789:;§=?

ıȷ` ´ˇ˘˙° ¸ßﬁﬂﬀﬃﬄchckáâäߎëëöóúüü§œ

## ygoth

𝔄𝔅ℭ𝔇𝔈𝔉𝔊ℌℑ𝔍𝔎𝔏𝔐𝔑𝔒𝔓𝔔ℜ𝔖𝔗𝔘𝔙𝔚𝔛𝔜ℨ

abcdefghijklmnopqrstuvwxyz

!" ѡqßſ'()ßſſi,·ſſi0123456789:;ſtſtß?

kebochckckdaæwhahrßtitbtbtiſtifflyhppaxepohjgßwaßæœœllvebu

*yinit*

*yswab*

ABCDEFGHJIKLMNOPQRSTUVWXYZ
abcdefghijklmnopqrstuvwxyz
!"#%'()*+,-./0123456789:§=?
ıȷ`´˘ˇ¯˙¸ßfflfffffffchckàäâßéëôöúü§ß

## fonts/greek/kd

*kdbf10*

˜ΑΒΔΕΦΓΗΙΘΚΛΜΝΟΠΧΡΣΤΥ˝ΩΞΨΖ
αβςδεφγηιθχλμνοπχρστυωξψζ
!¨˜˝%´()*+,-./0123456789:˙˙=';
˙˜˜ῒῑῒῢῧῢῧ˝˘¯—άέήόώίύᾶὰᾱέήόὼίύῆά
έήόώίύῶᾆᾇῒᾅᾇῷ˜῁ῢῗᾶᾆᾇῒᾅᾇῷ˜῁ῢῧᾶὰᾆᾇ
ῆᾆῒῢᾶᾇῆᾆῐ˜῁ῢᾶᾀᾄῄῆ˜ῒῢᾶᾀᾄῆῄῷ˜ῒῢᾶᾀῃῆῳῷ
῁ᾶᾀᾄῆῃῳῷ῁ῲ῁ᾶᾀᾄῆῃῳῷ῁ῲῤᾶᾀᾄῆῃῳῷ῁ῲῤᾶᾀῆῆῆῲῷ῁ῲ

*kdgr10*

˜ΑΒΔΕΦΓΗΙΘΚΛΜΝΟΠΧΡΣΤΥ˝ΩΞΨΖ
αβςδεφγηιθχλμνοπχρστυωξψζ
!¨˜˝%´()*+,-./0123456789:˙˙=';
˙˜˜ῒῑῒῢῧῢῧ˝˘¯—άέήόώίύᾶὰᾱέήόὼίύῆά
έήόώίύῶᾆᾇῒ˜ῢῗᾶᾆᾇῒ˜ῢῧᾶὰᾆᾇῒῢᾶᾀᾄῄῆ
ῆᾆῒῢᾶᾇῆᾆῒ˜ῢᾶᾀᾄῄῆ˜ῒῢᾶᾀᾄῆῄῷ˜ῒῢᾶᾀῃῆῳῷ
῁ᾶᾀᾄῆῃῳῷ῁ῲ῁ᾶᾀᾄῆῃῳῷ῁ῲῤᾶᾀᾄῆῃῳῷ῁ῲῤᾶᾀῆῆῆῲῷ῁ῲ

### kdsl10

˝ΑΒΔΕΦΓΗΙΘΚΛΜΝΟΠΧΡΣΤΥ˝ΩΞΨΖ
αβςδεφγηιθκλμνοπχρστυωξψζ
!¨˚˜%´()*+,-./0123456789:·˙`=´;
˚˜ïíīĭüúūŭ'´˘¯—άέήόώίύāάέήόώίύῆά
έήόώίύῶᾱἔῆᾌῑῠῑᾱἔῆᾌῑῠῡὰὲἠὸὼὶὺᾱ̆ἔ
ῆὃῶῑῠᾱ̆ἔῆὃῶῑῠᾱ̆άῆῆῶῑῠᾱ̆άῆῆῶῑῠᾱ̆αῆηῶώ
ῶὰᾱῆηῶώῶ̆ᾱᾱῆῆῶώ̆ῶῤὰᾱῆῆῶώ̆ῶῤᾱᾱῆῆῶ̆ῶ̆

### kdti10

˝ΑΒΔΕΦΓΗΙΘΚΛΜΝΟΠΧΡΣΤΥ˝ΩΞΨΖ
αβςδεφγηιθκλμνοπχρστυωξψζ
!¨˚˜%´()*+,-./0123456789:·˙`=´;
˚˜ïíīĭüúūŭ'´˘¯—άέήόώίύāάέήόώίύῆά
έήόώίύῶᾱἔῆᾌῑῠῑᾱἔῆᾌῑῠῡὰὲἠὸὼὶὺᾱ̆ἔ
ῆὃῶῑῠᾱ̆ἔῆὃῶῑῠᾱ̆άῆῆῶῑῠᾱ̆άῆῆῶῑῠᾱ̆αῆηῶώ
ῶὰᾱῆηῶώῶ̆ᾱᾱῆῆῶώ̆ῶῤὰᾱῆῆῶώ̆ῶῤᾱᾱῆῆῶ̆ῶ̆

### kdtt10

˝ΑΒΔΕΦΓΗΙΘΚΛΜΝΟΠΧΡΣΤΥ˝ΩΞΨΖ
αβςδεφγηιθκλμνοπχρστυωξψζ
!¨˚˜%´()*+,-./0123456789:·˙`=´;
˚˜ïíīĭüúūŭ'´˘¯—άέήόώίύāάέήόώίύῆά
έήόώίύῶᾱἔῆᾌῑῠῑᾱἔῆᾌῑῠῡὰὲἠὸὼὶὺᾱ̆ἔ
ῆὃῶῑῠᾱ̆ἔῆὃῶῑῠᾱ̆άῆῆῶῑῠᾱ̆άῆῆῶῑῠᾱ̆αῆηῶώ
ῶὰᾱῆηῶώῶ̆ᾱᾱῆῆῶώ̆ῶῤὰᾱῆῆῶώ̆ῶῤᾱᾱῆῆῶ̆ῶ̆

## fonts/greek/kelly

### cmg10

@ΑΒΔΕΓΧΙΚΛΜΝΟΠΡΣΤΥΩΞΗΖ
αβδεγχικλμνοπρστυωξης
!"#$%&'()*+,-./0123456789:;=?
ψϑϑκΦΨΘϖρςφε`´˘¯˚ˌ¨

### cmgb10

@ΑΒΔΕΓΧΙΚΛΜΝΟΠΡΣΤΥΩΞΗΖ
αβδεγχικλμνοπρστυωξης
!"#$%&'()*+,-./0123456789:;=?
ψϑϑκΦΨΘϖρςφε`´˘¯˚ˌ¨

*cmgi10*

@ΑΒΔΕΓΧΙΚΛΜΝΟΠΡΣΤΥΩΞΗΖ
αβδεγχικλμνοπρστυωξης
!"#$%&'()*+,-./0123456789:;=?
ψϑθκΦΨΘϖρςφε`´˘¯˚˛¨

*cmgtt10*

ΘΑΒΔΕΓΧΙΚΛΜΝΟΠΡΣΤΤΩΞΗΖ
αβδεγχικλμνοπρστυωξης
!"#$%&'()*+,-./0123456789:;=?
ψϑθκΦΨΘϖρςφε`´˘¯˚˛¨

## *fonts/greek/moschovakis*

*gecmbx10*

@ABCDEFGHIJKLMNOPQRSTUVWXYZ
abcdefghijklmnopqrstuvwxyz
!"#$%&'()*+,-./0123456789::¡=¿?
ΔΘΛΞΠΣΥΦΨΩ fffifl ffiffl ıȷ`´˘¯˚˛ßæœøÆŒØ¨
ΑΒΓΔΕΖΗΘΙΚΛΜΝΞΟΠΡΣΤΥΦΧΨΩαβγδεζηθ
ικλμνξοπρσςτυφχψΆΈΉΊΌΎΏὰᾶάᾱᾰὲἐ
ἐἔἕἠἡἤἥἰῒῗῒ ὸὀὄὅὺῦύὑὕ ὦᾠ ὠᾧᾦ
ωάέήῒίόύϋώΰ '«»`˜ʹʺ˚ʹʺˠˠˠᾳῃῳᾁῄῴ

*gecmml10*

∂ABCDEFGHIJKLMNOPQRSTUVWXYZ
abcdefghijklmnopqrstuvwxyz
ωεϑϖρςφ⟶⟵⟶⟶⟶↺▷◁0123456789.,</>⋆
ΔΘΛΞΠΣΥΦΨΩαβγδεζηθικλμνξπρστυφχ^
ΑΒΓΔΕΖΗΘΙΚΛΜΝΞΟΠΡΣΤΥΦΧΨΩαβγδεζηθ
ικλμνξοπρσςτυφχψΆΈΉΊΌΎΏωάέήῒίόύϋ
ώΰ '«»

*gecmr10*

@ABCDEFGHIJKLMNOPQRSTUVWXYZ
abcdefghijklmnopqrstuvwxyz
!"#$%&'()*+,-./0123456789::¡=¿?
ΔΘΛΞΠΣΥΦΨΩ fffifl ffiffl ıȷ`´˘¯˚˛ßæœøÆŒØ¨
ΑΒΓΔΕΖΗΘΙΚΛΜΝΞΟΠΡΣΤΥΦΧΨΩαβγδεζηθ
ικλμνξοπρσςτυφχψΆΈΉΊΌΎΏὰᾶάᾱᾰὲἐ
ἐἔἕἠἡἤἥἰῒῗῒ ὸὀὄὅὺῦύὑὕ ὦᾠ ὠᾧᾦ
ωάέήῒίόύϋώΰ '«»`˜ʹʺ˚ʹʺˠˠˠᾳῃῳᾁῄῴ

## gecmsc10

@ABCDEFGHIJKLMNOPQRSTUVWXYZ
ABCDEFGHIJKLMNOPQRSTUVWXYZ
!"#$%&'()*+,-./0123456789:;<=>?
ΔΘΛΞΠΣΥΦΨΩ↑↓'¡¿ıɪȷ` ´˝˜¯˚ ¸ssæœøÆŒØ¨
ABΓΔEZHΘIKΛMNΞOΠPΣTYΦXΨΩABΓΔEZHΘ
IKΛMNΞOΠPΣTYΦXΨA E H I O Y Ω AAAAAAEEE
EEHHHHHHHIIIIIIIOOOOOYYYYYYΩΩΩΩΩΩΩ
AEHÏIOYŸΩÏŸ˙⁽ʰ⁾AHΩAHΩ

## gecmsl10

@ABCDEFGHIJKLMNOPQRSTUVWXYZ
abcdefghijklmnopqrstuvwxyz
!"#$%&'()*+,-./0123456789:;¡=¿?
ΔΘΛΞΠΣΥΦΨΩﬀﬁﬂﬃﬄıȷ` ´˝˜¯˚ ¸ßæœøÆŒØ¨
ABΓΔEZHΘIKΛMNΞOΠPΣTYΦXΨΩαβγδεζηθ
ιxλμνξοπρςστυφχψ´A´E´H´I´O´Y´Ω˜àãáăǎèê
êẽěɛ̃η̃η̃η̃η̃η̃ǐìíïîǐòóõǒõǔùúüǔǔǔὠὤὣὥὥ
ωάéήίïíóúüώûυ˙'«»` ˜ ˑ ˓ ˟ ˤ ˟ ˠ ˟ ˠ ˠ αηωάήώ

## gecmss10

@ABCDEFGHIJKLMNOPQRSTUVWXYZ
abcdefghijklmnopqrstuvwxyz
!"#$%&'()*+,-./0123456789:;¡=¿?
ΔΘΛΞΠΣΥΦΨΩﬀﬁﬂﬃﬄıȷ` ´˝˜¯˚ ¸ßæœøÆŒØ¨
ABΓΔEZHΘIKΛMNΞOΠPΣTYΦXΨΩαβγδεζηθ
ιxλμνξοπρςστυφχψ´A´E´H´I´O´Y´Ω˜àãáăǎèê
êẽěɛ̃ηη̃η̃η̃η̃ǐìíïîǐòóõǒõǔùúüǔǔǔὠὤὣὥὥ
ωάéήίïíóúüώυ˙'«»` ˜ ˑ ˓ ˟ ˤ ˟ ˠ ˟ ˠ ˠ αηωάήώ

## gecmti10

@ABCDEFGHIJKLMNOPQRSTUVWXYZ
abcdefghijklmnopqrstuvwxyz
!"#£%&'()*+,-./0123456789:;¡=¿?
ΔΘΛΞΠΣΥΦΨΩﬀﬁﬂﬃﬄıȷ` ´˝˜¯˚ ¸ßæœøÆŒØ¨
ABΓΔEZHΘIKΛMNΞOΠPΣTYΦXΨΩαβγδεζηθ
ιxλμνξοπρςστυφχψ´A´E´H´I´O´Y´Ω˜àãáăǎèê
êẽěɛ̃ηη̃η̃η̃η̃ǐìíïîǐòóõǒõǔùúüǔǔǔὠὤὣὥὥ
ωάéήίïíóúüώûυ˙'«»` ˜ ˑ ˓ ˟ ˤ ˟ ˠ ˟ ˠ ˠ αηωάήώ

*gecmtt10*

```
@ABCDEFGHIJKLMNOPQRSTUVWXYZ
abcdefghijklmnopqrstuvwxyz
!"#$%&'()*+,-./0123456789:;<=>?
ΔΘΛΞΠΣΤΦΨΩ↑↓'¡¿ıȷ`´˜¯˘˙¸ßæøŒŒØ¨
ΑΒΓΔΕΖΗΘΙΚΛΜΝΞΟΠΡΣΤΥΦΧΨΩαβγδεζηθ
ικλμνξοπρςτυφχψ˝ãäåàăèéêěëèḧñ̈ḧ
ḧ̄ḧ̄ı̃ı̈ı̀ı̌ı̈ı̈òóôõöùũúủüûũ̈ũ̄ũ̄ũ̄ũ̄ãáéñ̈ı̈ı̈ó
úüöı̈ü˙ `˜ʼˊˇ˘˝ʺˀʽʼʼαηωάήώ
```

# *fonts/greek/yannis*

## *mrgrbf10*

```
᾽ΑΒὀΔΕΦΓΗΙΘΚΛΜΝΟΠΧΡΣΤΥ῾ΩΞΨΖ
αβςδεφγηιθκλμνοπχρστυύωξψζ
!῀῁ἐ%ἐ᾽()*+,-./0123456789:῾=;
ααάάάηηήήήήωωωώώώιιίίίίυυύύʼύεέ
```

## *mrgrrg10*

```
᾽ΑΒὀΔΕΦΓΗΙΘΚΛΜΝΟΠΧΡΣΤΥ῾ΩΞΨΖ
αβςδεφγηιθκλμνοπχρστυύωξψζ
!῀῁ἐ%ἐ᾽()*+,-./0123456789:῾=;
ααάάάηηήήήήωωωώώώιιίίίίυυύύʼύεέ
```

## *mrgrsl10*

```
᾽ΑΒὀΔΕΦΓΗΙΘΚΛΜΝΟΠΧΡΣΤΥ῾ΩΞΨΖ
αβςδεφγηιθκλμνοπχρστυύωξψζ
!῀῁ἐ%ἐ᾽()*+,-./0123456789:῾=;
ααάάάηηήήήήωωωώώώιιίίίίυυύύʼύεέ
```

## *mrgrti10*

```
᾽ΑΒὀΔΕΦΓΗΙΘΚΛΜΝΟΠΧΡΣΤΥ῾ΩΞΨΖ
αβςδεφγηιθκλμνοπχρστυύωξψζ
!῀῁ἐ%ἐ᾽()*+,-./0123456789:῾=;
ααάάάηηήήήήωωωώώώιιίίίίυυύύʼύεέ
```

## *rgrbf10*

```
῀ΑΒὀΔΕΦΓΗΙΘΚΛΜΝΟΠΧΡΣΤΥ῀ΩΞΨΖ
αβςδεφγηιθκλμνοπχρστυύωξψζ
!῀῁ἐ%ἐ᾽()*+,-./0123456789:῾῾=᾽;
ἀἀάἄᾶᾱηἠήήῆῆῆωὠώῴῶῶιιίίίιυυύύʼύεέ
```

## rgrrg10

˘ΑΒόΔΕΦΓΗΙΘΚΛΜΝΟΠΧΡΣΤΥ˚ΩΞΨΖ
αβςδεφγηιθκλμνοπχρστυῦωξψζ
!¨˜έ%ἓ´()*+,-./0123456789:·˙˚=';
ἀἀάἆᾶᾱήἠἤἧἦὦὠὤὦὦῶἳἷἵῒἳῗῢὺύΰ'ῠέἔ

## rgrsl10

˘ΑΒόΔΕΦΓΗΙΘΚΛΜΝΟΠΧΡΣΤΥ˚ΩΞΨΖ
αβςδεφγηιθκλμνοπχρστυῦωξψζ
!¨˜έ%ἓ´()*+,-./0123456789:·˙˚=';
ἀἀάἆᾶᾱήἠἤἧἦὦὠὤὦὦῶἳἷἵῒἳῗῢὺύΰ'ῠέἔ

## rgrti10

˘ΑΒόΔΕΦΓΗΙΘΚΛΜΝΟΠΧΡΣΤΥ˚ΩΞΨΖ
αβςδεφγηιθκλμνοπχρστυῦωξψζ
!¨˜έ%ἓ´()*+,-./0123456789:·˙˚=';
ἀἀάἆᾶᾱήἠἤἧἦὦὠὤὦὦῶἳἷἵῒἳῗῢὺύΰ'ῠέἔ

# fonts/halftone

**halftone**

# fonts/hge

hge

@ABCDEFGHIJKLMNOPQRSTUVWXYZ
abcdefghijklmnopqrstuvwxyz
!"#$%&'()*+,-./0123456789:;<=>?
'o

# fonts/hieroglyph

*diacr10*

@ȝdḥśṯḫˁbdfghỉjklmnpḳrstwḥyz
!"#£%&'()*+,-./0123456789:;=?

# fonts/karta

## karta15

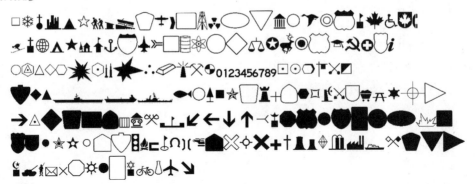

# fonts/klinz

## klinz

# fonts/knot

## knot1

## knot2

## knot3

*knot4*

*knot5*

*knot6*

*knot7*

## *fonts/levy*

*grbld10*

˜ΑΒ˚ΔΕΦΓΗΙΘΚΛΜΝΟΠΧΡΣΤΥ˝ΩΞΨΖ
αβσδεφγηιθκλμνοπχρστυωξψζ
!"˜˚%´()*+,-./0123456789:·˙=';
σασβσ'σδσεσφσγσησισθσκσλσμσνσοσπσχσρσσστσυσωσξσφσζ''˘¯—àá
àσàὰά̀ά̆σάά̆ᾰ̆ᾱ̆σά̆ᾱ̆ᾰ̆σᾱ̆ᾰ̆ὰ̆σᾱ̆ᾰ̆ὰ̀σὰ̃ηὴησηὴ̆ή̆σηὴ̆ὴ̆ή̆σηή̃ή̃
ή̆σή̆ή̃ή̆σή̆ηὴ̃ησηῃ̃ὴ̆ή̆σηῃ̃ηὴ̃σηὴ̆ὼ̀ὼ̃ὼ̀σὼ̀φ̀φ̀φ̆σφ̀ὼ̆ὼ̃σφ̀ώ̆φ̆φ̆σφ̀ῶ̃ῶ̃
ῶ̃σῶ̃ῶ̃φ̃φ̃φ̃σφ̃ὶ̀ὶ̀σὶ̀ὶ̀ὶ̀ὶ̀σὶ̀ΰ̈ΐ̈σἳΰ̈ΰ̈σὓἱ̈ἱ̈σἱ̃ὺ̃ὺ̃σὺ̃ὲ̀έ̀
ὲ̀σὲ̀ὸ̀ὸ̀ὸσὸ̀ὲ̃έ̃ἒ̃σέ̆ό̃ό̃ό̆σό̃ẗ̈ẗ̈ẗ̈ΰ̈ΰ̆ΰ̆ΰ̃ᾳηῳῥ̀ῥ̆σ`σ´σ˜

### grreg10

ˇΑΒ˚ΔΕΦΓΗΙΘΚΛΜΝΟΠΧΡΣΤΥˇΩΞΨΖ
αβσδεφγηιθκλμνοπχρστυωξψζ
!¨˚˚%´()*+,-./0123456789:˙˙=᾽;
σασβσ᾽σδσεσφσγσησισθσκσλσμσνσοσπσχσρσσστσυσωσξσψσζ᾽᾽˘¯—àá
àσàᾳᾳᾳσαᾰᾰσάᾳᾰᾳσᾳᾶᾰᾰσᾶᾳᾰᾳσᾳἡἠἠσἠἡἠἡσηἠἦ
ἦσἠἥἦἧσἠἥἦἧσἦἦἦἧσηὠὠωσὠᾠᾠωσωᾧᾧσωᾧᾧᾧσᾠῶ
ᾦσῶᾤᾥᾧσᾩἱἰισιὺὺσυἰῗῗσίῠῠῠσυῗῗσιῦῦῦσυὲέ
ἐσὲὸὸσὸέἔἒἕσέόὄὂσόῒῗῗῢὺῢῢᾳηῳρρσˋσ´σ˜

### grtt10

ˇΑΒ˚ΔΕΦΓΗΙΘΚΛΜΝΟΠΧΡΣΤΤˇΩΞΨΖ
αβσδεφτηιθκλμνοπχρστυωξψζ
!¨˚˚%´()*+,-./0123456789:˙˙=᾽;
σασβσ᾽σδσεσφστσησισθσκσλσμσνσοσπσχσρσσστσυσωσξσψσζ᾽᾽˘¯—àá
àσàᾳᾳᾳσαᾰᾰσάᾳᾰᾳσᾳᾶᾰᾰσᾶᾳᾰᾳσᾳἡἠἠσἠἡἠἡσηἠἦ
ἦσἠἥἦἧσἠἥἦἧσἦἦἦἧσηὠὠωσὠᾠᾠωσωᾧᾧσωᾧᾧᾧσᾠῶ
ᾦσῶᾤᾥᾧσᾩἱ ἱισιὺὺσυἰῗῗσίῠῠῠσυῗῗσιῦῦῦσυὲέ
ἐσὲὸὸσὸέἔἒἕσέόὄὂσόῒῗῗῢὺῢῢᾳηῳρρσˋσ´σ˜

## fonts/malvern

### fmvX10

ΑΒΓΔΕΖΗΘΙΞΚΛΜΝΟΠΦΡΣΤΥΦΧΨΩμο
῾῾ʹ~0123456789<>
→↑↓↔↕⊕0123456789

### fmvb10

@ABCDEFGHIJKLMNOPQRSTUVWXYZ
abcdefghijklmnopqrstuvwxyz
!˝#$%&'()*+,-./0123456789:;<=>?
´`^¨˝˝˙˘ˇ¯˙¸˚.,<>""„«»-—◦ıﬀﬁﬂﬃﬄ·
ÄĄĆČDĘĜĹŁŃŇĦŔŘŚŞŤŢŨŸŹŻŽĿJðŠą¢
čđěęğíΓłńňηíŕśšşł¿ûüźžżij¡¿£ÀÁÂÃÄ
ÅÆÇÈÉÊËÌÍÎÏÐÑÒÓÔÕÖŒØÙÚÛÜÝPàáâãäå
æçèéêëìíîïðñòóôõöœøùúûüýþß

### fmvi10

@ABCDEFGHIJKLMNOPQRSTUVWXYZ
abcdefghijklmnopqrstuvwxyz
!"#$%&'()*+,-./0123456789:;<=>?
´˜¨˝•˘¯˗˙„◇""„«»-—ıȷfffiflﬀﬃ-
ÄĄĆČĎĚĘĞĹĿŃŇŊĴŔŘŚŠŢŤŮŸŹŽŻĲĴđ§ăąć
čďěęğĩľłńňŋřśšşţţůüÿźžż ij¡¿£ÀÁÂÄ
ÅÆÇÈÉÊËÌÍÎÏÐÑÒÓÔÕÖŒØÙÚÛÜÝÞàáâãäå
æçèéêëìíîïðñòóôõöœøùúûüýþß

### fmvr10

@ABCDEFGHIJKLMNOPQRSTUVWXYZ
abcdefghijklmnopqrstuvwxyz
!"#$%&'()*+,-./0123456789:;<=>?
´˜¨˝•˘¯˗˙„◇""„«»-—ıȷfffiflﬀﬃ-
ÄĄĆČĎĚĘĞĹĿŃŇŊĴŔŘŚŠŢŤŮŸŹŽŻĲĴđ§ăąć
čďěęğĩľłńňŋřśšşţţůüÿźžż ij¡¿£ÀÁÂÄ
ÅÆÇÈÉÊËÌÍÎÏÐÑÒÓÔÕÖŒØÙÚÛÜÝÞàáâãäå
æçèéêëìíîïðñòóôõöœøùúûüýþß

## fonts/ocr-a

### ocr10

@ABCDEFGHIJKLMNOPQRSTUVWXYZ
abcdefghijklmnopqrstuvwxyz
!"#$%&'()*+,-./0123456789:;<=>?
.,?'-ЛЧн|ÄÄÆÑØÖÜ£¥■

## fonts/ocr-b

### ocrb10

@ABCDEFGHIJKLMNOPQRSTUVWXYZ
abcdefghijklmnopqrstuvwxyz
!"#$%&'()*+,-./0123456789:;<=>?
ΔΘΛΞΠΣΤΦΨΩ↑↓ˊˋ¡¿ıȷˋˊˇ˘¯˙˙¸ßæœøÆŒØ¨
äöüÄÖÜ§¤| "

## fonts/pandora

### pnb10

@ABCDEFGHIJKLMNOPQRSTUVWXYZ
abcdefghijklmnopqrstuvwxyz
!"#$%&'()*+,-./0123456789:;¡=¿?
ΔΘΛΞΠΣΤΦΨΩﬀﬁﬂﬃﬄıȷ˜˜˝˙ßæœøÆŒØ¨

*pnr10*

@ABCDEFGHIJKLMNOPQRSTUVWXYZ
abcdefghijklmnopqrstuvwxyz
!"#$%&'()*+,-./0123456789:;¡=¿?
ΔΘΛΞΠΣΥΦΨΩﬀﬃﬂﬁﬄﬃıȷ˜˝˜˘¯˚¸ßæœøÆŒØ¨

*pnsl10*

*@ABCDEFGHIJKLMNOPQRSTUVWXYZ*
*abcdefghijklmnopqrstuvwxyz*
*!"#$%&'()*+,-./0123456789:;¡ =¿ ?*
*ΔΘΛΞΠΣΥΦΨΩﬀﬃﬂﬁﬄﬃıȷ˜˝˜˘¯˚¸ßæœøÆŒØ¨*

*pnss10*

@ABCDEFGHIJKLMNOPQRSTUVWXYZ
abcdefghijklmnopqrstuvwxyz
!"#$%&'()*+,-./0123456789:;¡=¿?
ΔΘΛΞΠΣΥΦΨΩﬀﬃﬂﬁﬄﬃıȷ˜˝˜˘¯˚¸ßæœøÆŒØ¨

*pnssb10*

**@ABCDEFGHIJKLMNOPQRSTUVWXYZ**
**abcdefghijklmnopqrstuvwxyz**
**!"#$%&'()*+,-./0123456789:;¡=¿?**
**ΔΘΛΞΠΣΥΦΨΩﬀﬃﬂﬁﬄﬃıȷ˜˝˜˘¯˚¸ßæœøÆŒØ¨**

*pnssi10*

*@ABCDEFGHIJKLMNOPQRSTUVWXYZ*
*abcdefghijklmnopqrstuvwxyz*
*!"#$%&'()*+,-./0123456789:;¡ =¿ ?*
*ΔΘΛΞΠΣΥΦΨΩﬀﬃﬂﬁﬄﬃıȷ˜˝˜˘¯˚¸ßæœøÆŒØ¨*

*pntt9*

```
@ABCDEFGHIJKLMNOPQRSTUVWXYZ
abcdefghijklmnopqrstuvwxyz
!"#$%&'()*+,-./0123456789:;<=>?
ΔΘΛΞΠΣΥΦΨΩ↑↓'¡¿ıȷ˜˝˜˘¯˚¸ßæøÆŒØ¨
```

# fonts/phonetic

### cmph10

ɒBɔdǝfjgdKʍɲ几Ƀ'Dʌ
aɓɔðǝɹɓɦɨɟʞɯɲþɹʃɥʍʒʎˈ
ωεϑϖϱϛϕʔ
λℲɷˌυαβγδεζηθικλμνξπρστυφχ

### cmphb10

ɒBɔdǝfjgdKʍɲ几Ƀ'Dʌ
aɓɔðǝɹɓɦɨɟʞɯɲþɹʃɥʍʒʎˈ
ωεϑϖϱϛϕʔ
λℲɷˌυαβγδεζηθικλμνξπρστυφχ

### cmphi10

ɒBdʌfjdKʍɲ几Dɔðǝɾɓɦɨɟʞɯɲþɹʃʎʒɦ
ωεϑϖϱϛϕʔ
λℲɷυαβγδεζηθικλμνξπρστυφχ

# fonts/punk

### punk10

ＤABCDEFGHJJKLMNOPQRSTUVWXYZ
ABCDEFGHIJKLMNOPQRSTUVWXYZ
!'#$%&'()*+,-./0128453789:;(=)?
ΔΘΛΞΠΣΥΦΨΩↄ↓'¡¿ı`´˘ˇ˜˝¸˛˙ˌ_ ßÆŒØÅ̊ÇØ̈

### punkbx20

ＤABCDEFGHJJKLMNOPQRSTUVWXYZ
ABCDEFGHJJKLMNOPQRSTUVWXYZ
!'#$%&'()*+ - /0123456789:;⟨=⟩?
ΔΘΛΞΠΣΥΦΨΩↄ↓'¡¿ı`´˘ˇ˜
˝¸˛˙ˌ ˉ
ßÆŒØÅ̊ÇØ̈

### punksl20

ＤABCDEFGHJJKLMNOPQRSTUVWXYZ
ABCDEFGHJJKLMNOPQRSTUVWXYZ
!'#$%&'()*+ - /0123456789:;⟨=⟩?
ΔΘΛΞΠΣΥΦΨΩↄ↓'¡¿ı ˌ ßÆŒØÅ̊ÇØ̈

# fonts/redis

### redis10

תשרקץקפפֿעסננמסלבכרֿיטחזוהדגב
!#%'()*+,./:;=

### redisbx10

תשרקץקפפֿעסננמסלבכרֿיטחזוהדגב
!#%'()*+,./:;=

### rediss10

תשרקץקפפֿעסננמסלבכרֿיטחזוהדגב
!#%'()*+,./:;=

# fonts/rsfs

### rsfs10

ABCDEFGHI JKLMNOPQRSTUVWXYZ

# fonts/rune

### rune

ᛒᛚᛩᛗᛈᛦᚷᚱᛇᚠᛁᚦᛚᛋᛗᛂᛖᚲᛦᛔᛑᛗᚾᛆᚻᛁᚪᛘᛁᛦᛏᚷᚱᚲᛞᛒ
!"#$%&'()*+,-./0123456789:;(=)?

### srune

ᛒᛈᚲᛩᛗᛈᛦᚷᚻᛁᛋᛁᚱᛈᛗᛁᚲᚲᛏᚱᛞᛗᛮᛆᛈᚱᛂᛆᛦ
ᛒᛈᚲᛩᛗᛈᛦᚷᚻᛁᛋᛁᚱᛈᛗᛁᚲᚲᛏᚱᛞᛗᛮᛆᛈᚱᛂᛆᛦ
!"#$%&'()*+,-./0123456789:;(=)?
ᛏᛈᚷᚻᛁᛗᚷᚷᛉᛊᛦᛏ

# fonts/srune

### srune

ᛒᛈᚲᛩᛗᛈᛦᚷᚻᛁᛋᛁᚱᛈᛗᛁᚲᚲᛏᚱᛞᛗᛮᛆᛈᚱᛂᛆᛦ
ᛒᛈᚲᛩᛗᛈᛦᚷᚻᛁᛋᛁᚱᛈᛗᛁᚲᚲᛏᚱᛞᛗᛮᛆᛈᚱᛂᛆᛦ
!"#$%&'()*+,-./0123456789:;(=)?
ᛏᛈᚷᚻᛁᛗᚷᚷᛉᛊᛦᛏ

# fonts/stmary

### stmary10

# fonts/tengwar

### tengwar

# fonts/tsipa

### tsipa10

# fonts/twcal

### twcal14

## fonts/va

### va14

### vacal14

## fonts/wasy

### wasy10

## fonts/wasy2

### wasy10

### wasyb10

# *fonts/wsuipa*

### *wbxipa10*

ꝏɷꝓꝑꝕꝗꝗꝗꝗꝗ.ɪʀʁ§ʃʃꝋꞇʧɟθꜧꝕʊᴜꝕʋᴍ
ʒʔꙅꝑꝢ‿‚ˈ‚ꞁꞇꞇ﹣‑‧‥ ‹ˆˇ‹›˚ ˳ ˖
ʀʟʋħɦɟɥ̶ɟɥ̶ɥ̶ʇ ᴴɟ ꞁꝋλꞁƞ ᴍ ꞁꞁ ꞁꞁ ɲ ŋ ꞁ ɴ ⊙ θ ɷ ω
ɑ ɑ ꝺ ʌ ᵬ ᵬ ᵬ ᵬ ᵬ ᵬ ɟ ꜩ ꞇ ꝺ ꝺ ꝺ ꝺ ꝺ ꝺ ꝺ ꝺ ᶑ ꝺ ꝺ ꝺ ꝺ ꝺ ꝺ ꝺ ꝺ ꞇ ɣ ˎ

### *wslipa10*

ꝏɷꝓꝑꝕꝗꝗꝗꝗꝗ.ɪʀʁ§ʃʃꝋꞇʧɟθꜧꝕʊᴜꝕʋᴍ
ʒʔꙅꝑꝢ‿‚ˈ‚ꞁꞇꞇ﹣‑‧‥ ‹ˆˇ‹›˚ ˳ ˖
ʀʟʋħɦɟɥ̶ɟɥ̶ɥ̶ʇ ᴴɟ ꞁꝋλꞁƞ ᴍ ꞁꞁ ꞁꞁ ɲ ŋ ꞁ ɴ ⊙ θ ɷ ω
ɑ ɑ ꝺ ʌ ᵬ ᵬ ᵬ ᵬ ᵬ ᵬ ɟ ꜩ ꞇ ꝺ ꝺ ꝺ ꝺ ꝺ ꝺ ꝺ ꝺ ᶑ ꝺ ꝺ ꝺ ꝺ ꝺ ꝺ ꝺ ꝺ ꞇ ɣ ˎ

### *wsuipa10*

ꝏɷꝓꝑꝕꝗꝗꝗꝗꝗ.ɪʀʁ§ʃʃꝋꞇʧɟθꜧꝕʊᴜꝕʋᴍ
ʒʔꙅꝑꝢ‿‚ˈ‚ꞁꞇꞇ﹣‑‧‥ ‹ˆˇ‹›˚ ˳ ˖
ʀʟʋħɦɟɥ̶ɟɥ̶ɥ̶ʇ ᴴɟ ꞁꝋλꞁƞ ᴍ ꞁꞁ ꞁꞁ ɲ ŋ ꞁ ɴ ⊙ θ ɷ ω
ɑ ɑ ꝺ ʌ ᵬ ᵬ ᵬ ᵬ ᵬ ᵬ ɟ ꜩ ꞇ ꝺ ꝺ ꝺ ꝺ ꝺ ꝺ ꝺ ꝺ ᶑ ꝺ ꝺ ꝺ ꝺ ꝺ ꝺ ꝺ ꝺ ꞇ ɣ ˎ

# *macros/latex/distribs/latex/fonts*

### *lasy10*

⟨⟩ ˏ ˅ ℧ ⋈ □ ◇ ⤳ → ⊏ ⊐
◁ ⊴ ▷ ⊵

### *lasyb10*

⟨⟩ ˏ ˅ ℧ ⋈ □ ◇ ⤳ → ⊏ ⊐
◁ ⊴ ▷ ⊵

### *lcircle10*

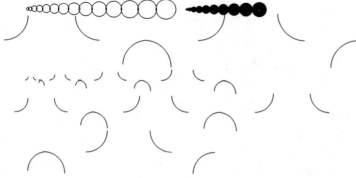

*lcirclew10*

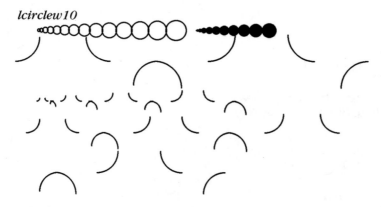

*lcmss8*

@ABCDEFGHIJKLMNOPQRSTUVWXYZ
abcdefghijklmnopqrstuvwxyz
!"#$%&'()*+,-./0123456789:;¡=¿?
ΔΘΛΞΠΣΥΦΨΩﬀﬁﬂﬃﬄıȷ`´˜¯˘˙ˌßæœøÆŒØ¨

*lcmssb8*

@ABCDEFGHIJKLMNOPQRSTUVWXYZ
abcdefghijklmnopqrstuvwxyz
!"#$%&'()*+,-./0123456789:;¡=¿?
ΔΘΛΞΠΣΥΦΨΩﬀﬁﬂﬃﬄıȷ`´˜¯˘˙ˌßæœøÆŒØ¨

*lcmssi8*

@ABCDEFGHIJKLMNOPQRSTUVWXYZ
abcdefghijklmnopqrstuvwxyz
!"#$%&'()*+,-./0123456789:;¡=¿?
ΔΘΛΞΠΣΥΦΨΩﬀﬁﬂﬃﬄıȷ`´˜¯˘˙ˌßæœøÆŒØ¨

*line10*

*linew10*

**C**

## *Resources*

This appendix lists the resources described in this book. Each of the tools (with the exception of tools mentioned only in Chapter 16, *T<sub>E</sub>X Utilities*, which are already listed in a similar format) described in the book is presented here. Each entry credits the author and provides information about where the software can be obtained.

Most of the resources in this appendix are availble from the CTAN archives. Where other sites are listed (for example, *oak.oakland.edu* for MS-DOS software), the addresses are only one possibility. Most of these archives are mirrored around the world. When possible, use an FTP site that is geographically nearby. If you are connected to the Internet, the *archie* service can help you locate nearby sites.

## *TUG: The T<sub>E</sub>X Users Group*

The T<sub>E</sub>X Users Group TUG, begun in 1980, is the international group for T<sub>E</sub>X users. Their mission is to encourage and expand the use of T<sub>E</sub>X, **METAFONT**, and related systems; to ensure the integrity and portability of these systems; and to foster innovation in high-quality electronic document preparation.

Membership includes the quarterly TUGboat, the newsletter TTN (also a quarterly), and a membership directory; as well, TUG publishes an occasional series called T<sub>E</sub>Xniques, for special topics (e.g., P<sub>I</sub>CT<sub>E</sub>X, `edmac.sty`).

TUG annual meetings are held in various locations, currently in North America and Europe, in a regular rotation; proceedings are published in TUGboat. Most of the publications now available on T<sub>E</sub>X, **METAFONT**, and related systems are available from the TUG office, which also distributes the main public domain T<sub>E</sub>X implementations.

In addition to its publications, TUG promotes active development work via the Technical Council and its Technical Working Groups. Efforts here include the CTAN archive work, multilingual TEX, TEX for the disabled, and the intersection of TEX with SGML and with Acrobat.

Information about joining TUG, receiving TUGboat, and attending the annual meetings is available from:

TEX Users Group
P.O. Box 869
Santa Barbara, California
93102 USA

## Other User Groups

There are also many other user groups, often based on language or geography: German-speaking users (DANTE), French-speaking users (GUTenberg), Dutch-speaking users (NTG), users in the Nordic countries (the Nordic group), users in the UK (UK TEX Users Group). There are active groups in existence in Japan, in Russia (CyrTUG), in Estonia, in Poland (GUST), and in the Czech Republic (CsTUG), to name but a few.

Contact TUG for details on how to get in touch with these or other TEX user groups.

# TEX Software

### CMacTEX
Author:     Thomas R. Kiffe
FTP:        *CTAN:systems/mac/cmactex*

### DirectTEX
Author:     Wilfried Ricken
FTP:        *CTAN:systems/mac/directtex*

### emTEX
Author:     Eberhard Mattes
FTP:        *CTAN:systems/msdos/emtex*

### gTEX
Author:     Young U. Ryu
FTP:        *CTAN:systems/msdos/gtex*

## PCTℰX

| | |
|---|---|
| Author: | Personal TℰX, Inc. |
| Address: | 12 Madrona Avenue |
| | Mill Valley, CA 94941 |
| | USA |
| Phone: | (415) 388–8853 / (413) 388–8865 FAX |

## sbTℰX

| | |
|---|---|
| Author: | Wayne G. Sullivan |
| FTP: | *CTAN:systems/msdos/sbtex* |

## TℰX

| | |
|---|---|
| Author: | Donald Knuth |
| FTP: | *CTAN:systems/web2c* |
| Comments: | The WEB sources and the WEB2C programs are both available here. |

## texas

| | |
|---|---|
| Author: | Shih-Ping Chan |
| FTP: | *CTAN:systems/msdos/texas* |

## Textures

| | |
|---|---|
| Author: | Blue Sky Research |
| Address: | 534 SW Third Avenue |
| | Portland, OR 97204 |
| | USA |
| Phone: | (800) 622–8398 or (503) 222–9571 / (503) 222–1643 FAX |

## TurboTℰX

| | |
|---|---|
| Author: | Kinch Computer Company |
| Address: | 501 Meadow Street |
| | Ithaca, NY 14850 |
| | USA |
| Phone: | (607) 273–0222 / (607) 273–0484 FAX |

## μTℰX

| | |
|---|---|
| Author: | ArborText |
| Address: | 1000 Victors Way |
| | Ann Arbor, MI 48108 |
| | USA |
| Phone: | (313) 996–3566 / (313) 996–3573 FAX |

**Y&YTEX**

Author:     Y&Y, Inc.
Address:    106 Indian Hill
             Carlisle, MA 01741
             USA
Phone:     (508) 371–3286 / (508) 371–2004 FAX

# TEX Shells

### 4TEX
Author:    Wietse Dol, Erik Frambach, Arjen Merckens, and Maarten van der Vlerk
FTP:        *CTAN:systems/msdos/4tex*

### PMTEX
Author:    Guillaume Schiltz
FTP:        *CTAN:systems/os2/pmtex*

### TEXPert
Author:    Johannes Martin
FTP:        *CTAN:systems/msdos/texpert*

### TEXShell
Author:    Jürgen Schlegelmilch
FTP:        *CTAN:systems/msdos/texshell*

### XTEXShell
Author:    Michael Hofmann
FTP:        *tsx-11.mit.edu:pub/linux/packages/TeX*

# Editors

### ΣEdit
See:       OzTEX, page 392.

### Alpha
Author:    Pete Keheler
FTP:        *CTAN:systems/mac*

### BBEdit

| | |
|---|---|
| Author: | Rich Siegel |
| FTP: | *mac.archive.umich.edu:/mac/util/text* |

### Brief

| | |
|---|---|
| Author: | Borland International, Inc. |
| Address: | 1800 Green Hills Road |
| | P.O. Box 660001 |
| | Scotts Valley, CA 95067–0001 |
| Phone: | (408) 438–8400 |

### demacs

| | |
|---|---|
| Author: | Manabu Higashida and Hirano Satoshi |
| FTP: | *oak.oakland.edu:/pub/msdos/demacs* |

### Doc

| | |
|---|---|
| See: | idraw, page 409. |

### emacs

| | |
|---|---|
| See: | GNU emacs, page 395. |

### epm

| | |
|---|---|
| Author: | International Business Machines |
| FTP: | *ftp.cdrom.com:/pub/os2/ibm/epm* |

### GNU emacs

| | |
|---|---|
| Author: | Free Software Foundation |
| Address: | 675 Massachusetts Avenue |
| | Cambridge, MA 02139 |
| | USA |
| FTP: | *prep.ai.mit.edu:/pub/gnu* |

### Jove

| | |
|---|---|
| Author: | Jonathan Payne |
| FTP: | *oak.oakland.edu:/pub/msdos/editor* |

### MathPad

| | |
|---|---|
| Author: | Roland Backhouse, Richard Verhoeven, and Olaf Weber |
| FTP: | *CTAN:support/mathpad* |

### MEwin

Author:      Pierre Perret
FTP:         *oak.oakland.edu:/pub/msdos/windows3*

### MicroEMACS

See:         MEwin, page 395.

### Multi-Edit

Author:      American Cybernetics
Address:     1830 West University Drive, Suite 112
             Tempe, AZ 85821
Phone:       (602) 968–1945 / (602) 966–1654 FAX

### Scientific Word

Author:      TCI Software Research
Address:     1190 Foster Road
             Las Cruces, NM 88001
             USA
Phone:       (505) 522–4600 / (505) 522–0116

### Xnot

Author:      Julie Melbin
FTP:         *oak.oakland.edu:/pub/msdos/editor*

# Macro Packages (Formats)

### $\mathcal{A}_{\mathcal{M}}\mathcal{S}$-TEX

Author:      American Mathematical Society
FTP:         *CTAN:fonts/ams/amstex*

### Eplain

See:         Extended Plain TEX, page 396.

### Extended Plain TEX

Author:      Karl Berry
FTP:         *CTAN:macros/eplain*

### LameTEX
Author:        Jonathan Monsarrat
FTP:           *CTAN:misc/lametex*

### I̴A̴MS-TEX
Author:        Michael Spivak
FTP:           *CTAN:macros/lamstex*

### LATEX
Author:        Leslie Lamport
FTP:           *CTAN:macros/latex/core*

### LATEX $2_\varepsilon$
Author:        Leslie Lamport, et. al.
FTP:           *CTAN:macros/latex2e/core*

### Lollipop
Author:        Victor Eijkhout
FTP:           *CTAN:macros/lollipop*

### MusicTEX
Author:        Daniel Taupin
FTP:           *CTAN:macros/musictex*

### Plain TEX
Author:        Donald Knuth
FTP:           *CTAN:macros/plain/base*

### SLiTEX
Author:        Leslie Lamport
FTP:           *CTAN:macros/latex/core*

# Styles and Macros

### AMS-LATEX
Author:        American Mathematical Society
FTP:           *CTAN:fonts/ams/amslatex*

### ArabTEX
Author:    Klaus Lagally
FTP:       *CTAN:language/arabtex*

### ascii.sty
Author:    R. W. D. Nickalls
FTP:       *CTAN:fonts/ascii*

### Babel
Author:    J. L. Braams
FTP:       *language/babel*

### bibunits.sty
Author:    Jose Alberto
FTP:       *CTAN:macros/latex/contrib/misc*

### chapterbib
Author:    Niel Kempson and Donald Arseneau
FTP:       *CTAN:macros/latex/contrib/misc*

### ChemTEX
Author:    Roswitha T. Haas and Kevin C. O'Kane
FTP:       *CTAN:macros/latex/contrib/chemtex*

### ChemStruct
Author:    Michael Ramek
FTP:       *CTAN:macros/latex/contrib/chemstruct*

### DraTEX
Author:    Eitan M. Gurari
FTP:       *CTAN:macros/generic/dratex*

### EDMAC
Author:    John Lavagnino
FTP:       *CTAN:macros/plain/contrib/edmac*

### eepic.sty
Author:    Conrad Kwok
FTP:       *CTAN:macros/latex/contrib/eepic*

## epic.sty

Author:      Sunil Podar

FTP:         *CTAN:macros/latex/contrib/epic*

## epsf.tex

See:         dvips, page 406.

## epsfig.sty

Author:      Sebastian Rahtz, Tom Rokicki, Trevor Darrell, et. al.

FTP:         *CTAN:macros/latex/contrib/epsfig*

## FoilTEX

Author:      James Hafner

FTP:         *CTAN:macros/foiltex*

## idxmac.tex

FTP:         *CTAN:indexing/makeindex/lib*

## INRSTEX

Author:      Michael J. Ferguson

FTP:         *CTAN:macros/inrstex*

## isolatin1.sty

FTP:         *CTAN:macros/latex/contrib/misc*

## Midnight

Author:      Marcel van der Goot

FTP:         *CTAN:macros/generic/midnight*

## multind

Author:      F. W. Long

FTP:         *CTAN:macros/latex/contrib/misc*

## PiCTEX

Author:      Michael Wichura

FTP:         *CTAN:graphics/pictex*

### REVTEX
Author:       American Physical Society, American Institute of Physics, and Optical Society
              of America
FTP:          *CTAN:macros/latex/contrib/revtex*

### ScriptTEX
Author:       Adrian McCarthy
FTP:          *CTAN:macros/scripttex*

### Seminar
Author:       Timothy Van Zandt
FTP:          *CTAN:macros/latex/contrib/seminar*

### TEX/Mathematica
Author:       Dan Dill
FTP:          *CTAN:macros/mathematica*

### TEXsis
Author:       Eric Myers and Frank E. Paige
FTP:          *CTAN:macros/texsis*

### VerTEX
Author:       Hal Varian
FTP:          *CTAN:macros/plain/contrib*

### XY-pic
Author:       Kristoffer H. Rose
FTP:          *ftp.diku.dk:/diku/users/kris*

## Styles That Produced This Book

This book was formatted with an extensively modified version of the standard LATEX
book style. In addition to the *pstricks*, *index.sty*, *epsfig.sty*, *epic.sty*, and *eepic.sty* files
described above, the following styles were used to format this book:

### pageframe.sty
Author:       Cameron Smith
FTP:          *CTAN:macros/latex/contrib/pageframe*

### footnpag.sty

Author:      Joachim Schrod

FTP:         *CTAN:macros/latex/contrib/footnpag*

### fancybox.sty

Author:      Timothy Van Zandt

FTP:         *CTAN:macros/latex/contrib/misc*

### fancyheadings.sty

Author:      Piet van Oostrum

FTP:         *CTAN:macros/latex/contrib/fancyheadings*

### array.sty

Author:      Frank Mittelbach and David Carlisle

FTP:         *CTAN:macros/latex/distribs/array*

### dcolumn.sty

Author:      David Carlisle

FTP:         *CTAN:macros/latex/distribs/array*

### tabularx.sty

Author:      David Carlisle

FTP:         *CTAN:macros/latex/distribs/array*

### longtable.sty

Author:      David Carlisle

FTP:         *CTAN:macros/latex/distribs/array*

### verbatim.sty

Author:      Rainer Schöpf

FTP:         *CTAN:macros/latex/distribs/verbatim*

### vrbinput.sty

Author:      Bernd Raichle

FTP:         *CTAN:macros/latex/distribs/verbatim*

**path.sty**

Author:        Philip Taylor
FTP:           *CTAN:macros/latex/contrib/misc*

# Utilities

**afm2tfm**

See:           dvips, page 406.

**amSpell**

Author:        Erik Frambach
Address:       Faculty of Econometrics
               University of Groningen
               Netherlands
FTP:           *CTAN:support/amspel*

**animate**

See:           Image Magick, page 409.

**AUC-TEX**

Author:        Kresten Krab Thorup and Per Abrahamsen
FTP:           *CTAN:support/auctex*

**awk**

Author:        Free Software Foundation
Address:       675 Massachusetts Avenue
               Cambridge, MA 02139
               USA
FTP:           *prep.ai.mit.edu:/pub/gnu*
Comments:      The FSF's version of *awk* is called *gawk*. Many commercial implementations
               of *awk* are also available.

**bbfig**

Author:        Ned Betchelder
FTP:           *CTAN:dviware/dvips/dvips/contrib/bbfig*

**bibclean**

Author:        Nelson H. F. Beebe
FTP:           *CTAN:bibtex/utils/bibclean*

### *bibdb*
Author:     Eyal Doron
FTP:        *CTAN:support/bibdb*

### *bibdestringify*
See:        lookbibtex, page 410.

### *bibextract*
Author:     Nelson H. F. Beebe
FTP:        *CTAN:biblio/bibtex/utils/bibextract*

### *bibindex*
Author:     Nelson H. F. Beebe
FTP:        *CTAN:biblio/bibtex/utils/bibindex*

### *biblook*
See:        bibindex, page 403.

### *bibsort*
Author:     Nelson H. F. Beebe
FTP:        *CTAN:biblio/bibtex/utils/bibsort*

### *BIBTEX*
Author:     Oren Patashnik
FTP:        *CTAN:biblio/bibtex*

### *bibview*
Author:     Holger Martin, Peter Urban, and Armin Liebl
Comments:   Available from volume 18 of the `comp.sources.x` newsgroup.

### *Bitmap*
Author:     Davor Matic
FTP:        *ftp.x.org:/contrib*

### *Bm2font*
Author:     Friedhelm Sowa
FTP:        *CTAN:graphics/bm2font*

### *citefind*
See:        bibextract, page 403.

## citetags
See:      bibextract, page 403.

## combine
See:      Image Magick, page 409.

## convert
See:      Image Magick, page 409.

## crudetype
Author:    R. M. Damerell
FTP:      *CTAN:dviware/crudetype*

## detex
Author:    Daniel Trinkle
FTP:      *CTAN:support/detex*

## display
See:      Image Magick, page 409.

## dvgt
Author:    Geoffrey Tobin
FTP:      *CTAN:dviware/dvgt*

## dvi2tty
Author:    Marcel J. E. Mol
FTP:      *CTAN:dviware/dvi2tty*

## dvi2xx
Author:    Gustaf Neumann
FTP:      *CTAN:dviware/dvi2xx*

## dvicopy
Author:    Peter Breitenlohner
FTP:      *CTAN:dviware/dvicopy*

## dvideo
See:      TurboTEX, page 393.

### dvidot
See:            emTEX, page 392.

### dvidrv
See:            emTEX, page 392.

### dvidvi
Author:      Tom Rokicki
FTP:            *CTAN:dviware/dvidvi*

### dvidxx
Comments:  See Example D-3 in Chapter D, *Long Examples*.

### dvihplj
See:            emTEX, page 392.

### DVILASER/HP
See:            μTEX, page 393.

### DVILASER/PS
See:            μTEX, page 393.

### DVILASER/HP
See:            μTEX, page 393.

### DVILASER/PS
See:            μTEX, page 393.

### dvilj2
See:            dvi2xx, page 404.

### dvimsp
See:            emTEX, page 392.

### dvimswin
Author:      J. D. McDonald
FTP:            *CTAN:dviware/dvimswin*

### dvipaste
Author:      Michael Spivak
FTP:         *CTAN:macros/lamstex/dvipaste*

### dvipcx
See:         emTEX, page 392.

### dvipm
See:         emTEX, page 392.

### dvips
Author:      Tomas Rokicki
FTP:         *CTAN:dviware/dvips*

### dvipsk
Author:      Karl Berry
FTP:         *CTAN:dviware/dvipsk*
Comments:    *dvips* enhanced to support path searching for fonts.

### dvipsone
See:         Y&YTEX, page 393.

### dviscr
See:         emTEX, page 392.

### dvispell
See:         emTEX, page 392.

### DVITool
Author:      Jeff W. McCarrell
FTP:         *CTAN:support/vortex/dvitool*
Comments:    Unrelated to the *Textures* tool of the same name.

### dvitovdu
Author:      Andrew Trevorrow
FTP:         *CTAN:dviware/dvitovdu*

### dvitype
See:         TEXware, page 417.

### dvivga

FTP:			*CTAN:dviware/dvivga*

### dviwin

Author:			Hippocrates Sendoukas
FTP:			*CTAN:dviware/dviwin*

### DVIWindo

See:			Y&YTEX, page 393.

### enc-afm.pl

Comments:	See Example D-5 in Chapter D, *Long Examples*.

### epmtex

Author:			Jon Hacker
FTP:			*CTAN:systems/os2/epmtex*

### Excalibur

Author:			Rick Zaccone
FTP:			*CTAN:systems/mac/excalibur*

### Fig

Author:			Supoj Sutanthavibul

### Fig2MF

Author:			Anthony Starks
FTP:			*CTAN:graphics/fig2mf*

### fontinst

Author:			Alan Jeffrey
FTP:			*CTAN:fonts/utilities/fontinst*

### fontlib

See:			emTEX, page 392.

### GFtoDVI

See:			*MFware*, page 412.

### GFtoPK

See:			*MFware*, page 412.

### Ghostscript

Author:     Aladdin Enterprises
Address:    P.O. box 60264
            Palo Alto, CA 94306
            USA
Phone:      (415) 322–0103 / (415) 322–1734 FAX
FTP:        *prep.ai.mit.edu:/pub/gnu*

### Ghostview

Author:     Timothy O. Theisen
FTP:        *prep.ai.mit.edu:/pub/gnu*

### gnuplot

Author:     Free Software Foundation
Address:    675 Massachusetts Avenue
            Cambridge, MA 02139
            USA
FTP:        *prep.ai.mit.edu:/pub/gnu*

### GoScript

Author:     LaserGo, Inc.
Address:    9369 Carroll Park Drive, Suite A
            San Diego, CA 92121
            USA
Phone:      (619) 450–4600 / (619) 450-9334 FAX

### GoScript Plus

See:        GoScript, page 408.

### groff

Author:     Free Software Foundation
Address:    675 Massachusetts Avenue
            Cambridge, MA 02139
            USA
FTP:        *prep.ai.mit.edu:/pub/gnu*
Comments:   The FSF's version of *troff* is called *groff*. Many commercial implementations
            of *troff* are also available.

## *hp2xx*

Author:     Heinz W. Werntges
FTP:        *CTAN:support/hp2xx*

## *HPTFM2PL*

Author:     Norman Walsh
FTP:        *CTAN:support/hp2pl*

## *HyperBIBTEX*

Author:     Evan Antwork
FTP:        *mac.archive.umich.edu:/mac/misc/tex*

## *idraw*

FTP:        *interviews.stanford.edu*

## *Image Alchemy*

Author:     Handmade Software, Inc.
Address:    15951 Los Gatos Blvd., Ste. 17
            Los Gatos, CA 95032
            USA
Phone:      (408) 358–1292 / (408) 358–2694
FTP:        *oak.oakland.edu:/pub/msdos/graphics*

## *Image Magick*

Author:     John Cristy
FTP:        *ftp.x.org:/contrib*

## *import*

See:        Image Magick, page 409.

## *Info-Zip*

Author:     Mark Adler, et. al.
FTP:        *ftp.uu.net:/pub/archiving/zip*

## *iniMF*

See:        METAFONT, page 411.

## *iniTEX*

See:        TEX, page 393.

### *ispell*

FTP:          *CTAN:support/ispell*

### *ivd2dvi*

Author:      Larry Denenberg
FTP:          *CTAN:dviware/ivd2dvi*

### *JemTEX*

Author:      François Jalbert
FTP:          *CTAN:systems/msdos/jemtex2*

### *LaCheck*

Author:      Kresten Krab Thorup and Per Abrahamsen
FTP:          *CTAN:support/lacheck*

### *lookbibtex*

Author:      John Heidemann
FTP:          *CTAN:biblio/bibtex/utils/lookbibtex*

### *MacBIBTEX*

Author:      Michael Kahn
FTP:          *CTAN:systems/mac*
Comments: This is a Mac port of BIBTEX.
See:          BIBTEX, page 403.

### *MacDVIcopy*

Author:      Yannis Haralambous
Comments: This is a Mac port of *dvicopy*.
See:          dvicopy, page 404.

### *MacGS*

Author:      Martin Fong
FTP:          *mac.archive.umich.edu:/mac/graphics/graphicsutil*
Comments: This is a Mac port of *GhostScript*.
See:          GhostScript, page 407.

### MacMakeIndex
Author:      Johnny Tolliver
FTP:         *CTAN:systems/mac*
Comments: This is a Mac port of *MakeIndex*.
See:         MakeIndex, page 411.

### makebst
Author:      Patrick W. Daly
FTP:         *CTAN:macros/latex/contrib/custom-bib*

### makeidx.sty
FTP:         *CTAN:indexing/makeindex/lib*

### MakeIndex
Author:      Pehong Chen
FTP:         *CTAN:indexing/makeindex*

### MakeIndx
See:         MakeIndex, page 411.

### MakeInfo
See:         TEXinfo, page 416.

### maketcp
See:         emTEX, page 392.

### MakeTeXPK
Comments: There are several versions of this file available. See Example D-1 in Chapter D, *Long Examples*.
See:         dvips, page 406.

### MakeTeXTFM
Comments: See Example D-2 in Chapter D, *Long Examples*.

### METAFONT
Author:      Donald Knuth
FTP:         *CTAN:systems/web2c*
Comments: The WEB sources and the WEB2C programs are both available here.

### METAFONT *for Textures*

Author:      Blue Sky Research
Address:     534 SW Third Avenue
             Portland, OR 97204
             USA
Phone:       (800) 622–8398 or (503) 222–9571 / (503) 222–1643 FAX
FTP:         *CTAN:systems/mac/metafont/bluesky*

### MFjob

See:         emTEX, page 392.

### MFpic

Author:      Thomas Leathrum
FTP:         *CTAN:graphics/mfpic*

### MFT

See:         *MFware*, page 412.

### MFware

Author:      Donald Knuth
FTP:         *CTAN:systems/web2c*
Comments:    The WEB sources and the WEB2C programs are both available here.

### mogrify

See:         Image Magick, page 409.

### montage

See:         Image Magick, page 409.

### Nikon II

Author:      Bitware, Software & Services
Address:     P.O. Box 3097
             Manuka A.C.T. 2603
             Australia
FTP:         *ftp.cdrom.com:/pub/os2/2_x/graphics*

### nroff

See:         groff, page 408.

### PBMplus
Author:      Jef Poskanzer
FTP:         *ftp.x.org:/contrib*

### pbmtopk
Author:      Angus Duggan
FTP:         *CTAN:graphics/pbmtopk*

### pfatopfb
See:         t1utils, page 417.

### pfbtopfa
See:         t1utils, page 417.

### PFM2AFM
Author:      Ken Borgendale
FTP:         *CTAN:fonts/utilities/pfm2afm*

### pixmap
Author:      Lionel Mallet
FTP:         *ftp.x.org:/contrib/pixmap*

### PKBBOX
Author:      Norman Walsh
FTP:         *CTAN:fonts/utilities/pkbbox*

### PKEdit
See:         emTEX, page 392.

### PKtoGF
See:         *MFware*, page 412.

### pktopbm
See:         pbmtopk, page 413.

### pktops
See:         Y&YTEX, page 393.

### PKtoPX
See:         *MFware*, page 412.

### PKtoSFP
Author:     Norman Walsh
FTP:        *CTAN:font/softfonts*

### PKtype
See:        *MFware*, page 412.

### PLtoTF
See:        TEXware, page 417.

### PM-Cam
Author:     J. von Kaenel
FTP:        *ftp.cdrom.com:/pub/os2/ibm/ews*

### pmC
Author:     Tom Ridgeway
FTP:        *CTAN:fonts/poorman*

### pmJ
Author:     Tom Ridgeway
FTP:        *CTAN:fonts/poorman*

### Pmjpeg
Author:     Norman Yee
FTP:        *ftp.cdrom.com:/pub/os2/2_x/graphics*

### ps2epsi
See:        ghostscript, page 407.

### PS2PK
Author:     Piet Tutelaers
FTP:        *CTAN:fonts/utilities/ps2pk*

### PSTricks
Author:     Timothy Van Zandt
FTP:        *CTAN:graphics/pstricks*

### PTI Jet
See:        PCTEX, page 392.

### PTI Laser/HP
See:              PCT<sub>E</sub>X, page 392.

### PTI Laser/HP4
See:              PCT<sub>E</sub>X, page 392.

### PTI Laser/PS
See:              PCT<sub>E</sub>X, page 392.

### PTI View
See:              PCT<sub>E</sub>X, page 392.

### PXtoPK
Author:      Peter Breitenlohner
FTP:          *systems/msdos/utilities*

### RCS
Author:      Walter F. Tichy
FTP:          *prep.ai.mit.edu:/pub/gnu*

### Recode
Author:      Francois Pinard
FTP:          *prep.ai.mit.edu:/pub/gnu*

### REXX
Author:      International Business Machines

### sbMF
See:              sbT<sub>E</sub>X, page 393.

### sed
Author:      Free Software Foundation
Address:     675 Massachusetts Avenue
             Cambridge, MA 02139
             USA
FTP:          *prep.ai.mit.edu:/pub/gnu*
Comments:  Many commercial implementations of *sed* are also available.

## SeeTEX
Author:     David Grunwald
FTP:        *CTAN:dviware/seetex*

## sffx
See:        Sfware, page 416.

## Sfload
See:        Sfware, page 416.

## SFPtoPK
Author:     Norman Walsh
FTP:        *CTAN:font/softfonts*

## Sfware
Author:     Norman Walsh
FTP:        *CTAN:font/softfonts/sfware*

## tangle
See:        WEB2c, page 420.

## tar
Author:     Free Software Foundation
Address:    675 Massachusetts Avenue
            Cambridge, MA 02139
            USA
FTP:        *prep.ai.mit.edu:/pub/gnu*
Comments:   Many commercial implementations of *tar* are also available.

## tex386
See:        emTEX, page 392.

## TEX Preview
See:        $\mu$TEX, page 393.

## texcad
See:        emTEX, page 392.

## texchk
See:        emTEX, page 392.

### *texconv*
See:          emTEX, page 392.

### *TEXinfo*
Author:      Free Software Foundation
Address:    675 Massachusetts Avenue
              Cambridge, MA 02139
              USA
FTP:           *prep.ai.mit.edu:/pbu/gnu*

### *TeXtoXfont*
Comments:  See Example D-6 in Chapter D, *Long Examples*.

### *TEXware*
Author:      Donald Knuth
FTP:           *CTAN:systems/web2c*
Comments:  The WEB sources and the WEB2C programs are both available here.

### *TFtoPL*
See:          TEXware, page 417.

### *Tgif*
Author:      William Chia-Wei Cheng
FTP:           *ftp.x.org:/contrib*

### *Tib*
Author:      James C. Alexander
FTP:           *CTAN:biblio/tib*

### *TEX Preview*
See:          $\mu$TEX, page 393.

### *troff*
See:          groff, page 408.

### *t1utils*
Author:      I. Lee Hetherington
FTP:           *CTAN:fonts/utilities/t1utils*

### txt2pcx

| | |
|---|---|
| Author: | DECISIONS Software |
| Address: | P.O. Box 31418 |
| | Phoenix, AZ 85046 |
| | USA |
| Phone: | (602) 992–0310 |

### unzip

| | |
|---|---|
| See: | Info-Zip, page 409. |

### VFtoVP

| | |
|---|---|
| See: | *MFware*, page 412. |

### VPtoVF

| | |
|---|---|
| See: | *MFware*, page 412. |

### wbr

| | |
|---|---|
| See: | dviwin, page 407. |

### wdviwin

| | |
|---|---|
| See: | TurboTEX, page 393. |

### weave

| | |
|---|---|
| See: | WEB2c, page 420. |

### xbibtex

| | |
|---|---|
| Author: | Nicholas Kelly and Christian H. Bischof |
| FTP: | *CTAN:biblio/bibtex/utils/xbibtex* |

### Xdvi

| | |
|---|---|
| Author: | Paul Vojta |
| FTP: | *CTAN:dviware/xdvi* |

### XET

| | |
|---|---|
| FTP: | *noa.huji.ac.il:/tex* |
| Comments: | Several implementations of XET--TEX are available here. |

### xfig

| | |
|---|---|
| Author: | Brian V. Smith |
| FTP: | *ftp.x.org:/contrib* |

### xloadimage
Author:    Jim Frost
FTP:      *ftp.x.org:/contrib*

### XTEX
See:      SeeTEX, page 415.

### Xtexcad
Comments: Available from volume 17 of the `comp.sources.x` newsgroup.

### xv
Author:    John Bradley
FTP:      *ftp.x.org:/contrib*

# Miscellaneous

### 4DOS
Author:    JP Software Inc.
Address:   P.O. Box 1470
          E. Arlington, MA 02174
          USA
Phone:    (617) 646–3975
FTP:      *oak.oakland.edu:/pub/msdos/4dos*

### 4OS2
Author:    JP Software Inc.
Address:   P.O. Box 1470
          E. Arlington, MA 02174
          USA
Phone:    (617) 646–3975
FTP:      *ftp.cdrom.com:/pub/os2/2_x/sysutils*

### Channel 1®
Address:   1030 Massachusetts Avenue
          Cambridge, MA 02138
Phone:    (617) 864–0100 voice / (617) 354-3230 v32.bis modem
Comments: The Channel 1 BBS carries a TEX conference with many MS-DOS tools available for downloading to registered users.

### *edb*

Author:     Michael Ernst
FTP:        *theory.lcs.mit.edu:/pub/emacs/edb*
Comments:   Database manager for GNU Emacs.

### *Linux*

Author:     Linus Torvalds
FTP:        *ftp.cdrom.com:/pub/linux*

### *mewltx*

Author:     Michael F. Reid
FTP:        *CTAN:support/mewltx*
Comments:   LATEX extensions for *MicroEMACS*.
See:        MEwin, page 395.

### *modes.mf*

Author:     Karl Berry
FTP:        *CTAN:fonts/modes*

### *Perl*

Author:     Larry Wall

### *TeX-index*

Author:     David Jones
FTP:        *CTAN:info*
Comments:   Also known as *tex-styles-and-macros.txt*.

### *tex-styles-and-macros.txt*

See:        TeX-index, page 420.

### **Web2c**

Author:     Karl Berry
FTP:        *CTAN:systems/web2c*

# D

# *Long Examples*

This appendix contains the source for several scripts that seemed too long to place in the running text. These scripts are provided as examples only, they may not run on your system without some modification.

These examples are available online, see the Preface for more information about retrieving online examples.

The *MakeTeXPK.pl* script builds PK files from **METAFONT** and PostScript fonts.

*Example D-1: MakeTeXPK.pl*

```
#!/usr/local/bin/perl
#
# MakeTeXPK.pl version 1.0, Copyright (C) 1993,94 by Norman Walsh.
# NO WARRANTY.  Distribute freely under the GNU GPL.
#
# This script attempts to make a new TeX PK font, because one wasn't
# found.  Parameters are:
#
# name dpi bdpi [[[magnification] mode] subdir]
#
# `name'   is the name of the font, such as `cmr10' (*NOT* cmr10.mf).
# `dpi'    is the resolution the font is needed at.
# `bdpi'   is the base resolution, useful for figuring out the mode to
#          make the font in.
# `magnification' is a string to pass to MF as the magnification.
# `mode'   if supplied, is the mode to use.
#
# This script was designed with two goals in mind: to support recursive
# subdirectory searching for fonts and to provide support for PK files
# built from both MF fonts and PS fonts.  It also supports the Sauter
# and DC fonts which can be built at any design size.
#
```

*Example D-1: MakeTeXPK.pl (continued)*

```
# This script was designed and tested with the following directory structure
# in mind: each typeface is stored in its own directory with appropriate
# subdirectories for font sources, metrics, and glyphs.  The script may not
# work exactly right if you use a different directory structure (the font
# installation, in particular, will probably be incorrect).  However,
# several other versions of MakeTeXPK exist which will handle simpler
# directory structures, so you need not feel compelled to use the one
# described here.
#
# For MF fonts: (... is usually something like /usr/local/lib/tex/fonts)
#
# .../typeface/src          holds the sources
#             /tfm          holds the TFM files
#             /glyphs       root for glyphs
#             /glyphs/mode  holds the PK files for "mode".
#
# For PS fonts: (... is usually something like /usr/local/lib/tex/fonts)
#
# .../typeface/afm          holds the AFM files
#             /tfm          holds the TFM files
#             /vf           holds the VF files
#             /vpl          holds the VPL files
#             /glyphs       root for glyphs
#             /glyphs/pk/999dpi  holds the PK files at 999 dpi created by ps2pk
#             /glpyhs/type1 holds the type1 PFA/PFB sources for the fonts
#

require "getopts.pl";
$rc = &Getopts ('v');            # Get options from the user...

$USE_MODE_IN_DEST = 1;            # Does the destination directory name include
                                 # the name of the mode?

$VERBOSE = $opt_v || $ENV{"DEBUG_MAKETEXPK"}; # Verbose?

chop($CWD = `pwd`);              # Where.are we?
$TEMPDIR = "/tmp/mkPK.$$";       # Where do temp files go?
$MFBASE = "&plain";              # What MF base do we use by default?

# Where are fonts stored?
$TEXFONTS = $ENV{"TEXFONTS"} || ".:/usr/local/lib/fonts//";

# Define modes that should be used for base resolutions...
$DPI_MODES{300}  = "laserwriter";
$DPI_MODES{200}  = "FAX";
$DPI_MODES{360}  = "lqhires";
$DPI_MODES{400}  = "nexthi";
$DPI_MODES{600}  = "QMSmoa";
$DPI_MODES{100}  = "nextscreen";

$DPI_MODES{100}  = "videodisplayi";
$DPI_MODES{110}  = "videodisplayii";
$DPI_MODES{118}  = "videodisplayiii";
```

*Example D-1: MakeTeXPK.pl (continued)*

```perl
$DPI_MODES{120}  = "videodisplayiv";
$DPI_MODES{124}  = "videodisplayv";
$DPI_MODES{130}  = "videodisplayvi";
$DPI_MODES{140}  = "videodisplayvii";
$DPI_MODES{150}  = "videodisplayviii";

$DPI_MODES{72}   = "MacTrueSize";
$DPI_MODES{635}  = "linolo";
$DPI_MODES{1270} = "linohi";
$DPI_MODES{2540} = "linosuper";

# Where are the DC fonts stored and what base names can be used?
$DCR_DIR = '/usr/local/lib/fonts/free/dc/src';
@DCR_GEN = ('dcb','dcbom','dcbx','dcbxsl','dcbxti','dccsc','dcdunh','dcff',
            'dcfi','dcfib','dcitt','dcr','dcsl','dcsltt','dcss','dcssbx',
            'dcssi','dctcsc','dcti','dctt','dcu','dcvtt' );

# Where are the Sauter fonts stored and what base names can be used?
$SAUTER_DIR = '/usr/local/lib/fonts/free/sauter/src';
@SAUTER_GEN = ('cmb','cmbizx','cmbozx','cmbsy','cmbszx','cmbx','cmbxsl',
               'cmbxti', 'cmbz', 'cmbzx', 'cmcsc', 'cmdszc', 'cmdunh',
               'cmex', 'cmff', 'cmfi', 'cmfib', 'cminch', 'cmitt', 'cmmi',
               'cmmib', 'cmr', 'cmrcz', 'cmrisz', 'cmritz', 'cmriz',
               'cmrotz', 'cmroz', 'cmrsz', 'cmrtz', 'cmruz', 'cmrz',
               'cmsl', 'cmsltt', 'cmss', 'cmssbx', 'cmssdc', 'cmssi',
               'cmssq', 'cmssqi', 'cmsy', 'cmtcsc', 'cmtex', 'cmti',
               'cmtt', 'cmu', 'cmvtt', 'czinch', 'czssq', 'czssqi',
               'lasy', 'lasyb');

$SAUTER_ROUNDING{11} = '10.954451';
$SAUTER_ROUNDING{14} = '14.4';
$SAUTER_ROUNDING{17} = '17.28';
$SAUTER_ROUNDING{20} = '20.736';
$SAUTER_ROUNDING{25} = '24.8832';
$SAUTER_ROUNDING{30} = '29.8685984';

# Get the command line arguments...
($NAME, $DPI, $BDPI, $MAG, $MODE, $FORCEDEST, $EXTRA) = @ARGV;

open (TTY, ">/dev/tty");            # Open the TTY (so we can print messages
select (TTY); $| = 1; select(STDOUT); # even if STDERR and STDOUT are both
                                   # redirected)

if ($VERBOSE) {
    print TTY "$0: font name: $NAME\n";
    print TTY "$0: dpi: $DPI\n";
    print TTY "$0: base dpi: $BDPI\n";
    print TTY "$0: magnification: $MAG\n" if $MAG;
    print TTY "$0: mode: $MODE\n" if $MODE;
    print TTY "$0: force destination directory: $FORCEDEST\n" if $FORCEDEST;
    print TTY "$0: extra: $EXTRA\n" if $EXTRA;
}
```

*Example D-1: MakeTeXPK.pl (continued)*

```perl
# Make sure we got enough arguments, but not too many...
die "$0: Invalid arguments.\n" if ($BDPI eq "" || $EXTRA ne "");

# Calculate the magnification from the requested resolutions if no
# magnification string was provided.
if (!$MAG) {
    $MAG = "$DPI/$BDPI";
    print TTY "$0: magnification: $MAG\n" if $VERBOSE;
}

# Calculate the mode if the mode was not given.  Die if we don't know
# what mode to use for the requested base resolution.
if ($MODE eq "") {
    $MODE = $DPI_MODES{$BDPI};
    die "$0: No mode for ${BDPI}dpi base resolution.\n" if $MODE eq "";
    print TTY "$0: mode: $MODE\n" if $VERBOSE;
}

######################################################################

# Really start the work...
print TTY "Attempting to build PK file for: $NAME at ${DPI}dpi.\n";

$mfFile = $NAME;
$mfFile =~ /^(.*[^0-9])(\d+)$/;
$mfBase = $1;
$mfSize = $2;

# Presumably, we got here because the PK file doesn't exist.  Let's look
# for the MF file or the PFA or PFB file...

#   ... it's more complicated than that...

# If the font is from a PFA/B file, it may have the name "rxxx" or
# "xxx0" because virtual fonts extract glyphs from the "raw" font.
# We need to find the PFA/B file and install the font with the right name.
# I'm not sure what the best solution would really be, but this will work.
# Luckily, it gets installed with the right name 'cause we already
# figured that out...
#
# A better solution on Unix machines might be to make "xxx0.pfa" or
# "rxxx.pfa" a symbolic link to "xxx.pfa".  But that won't work for other
# architectures...

$t1source = "";
$t1source = $1 if $mfFile =~ /^r(.*)$/;
$t1source = $1 if $mfFile =~ /^(.*)0$/ && ($t1source eq "");

if ($t1source) {
    $fontSource = &find_fonts($TEXFONTS,
                    ("$mfFile.mf", "$mfFile.pfa", "$mfFile.pfb",
                     "$t1source.pfa", "$t1source.pfb"));
} else {
```

*Example D-1: MakeTeXPK.pl (continued)*

```perl
        $fontSource = &find_fonts($TEXFONTS,
                                  ("$mfFile.mf", "$mfFile.pfa", "$mfFile.pfb"));
    }

    if ($fontSource) {
        if ($fontSource =~ /\.pfa$/ || $fontSource =~ /\.pfb$/) {
            print TTY "Building PK file from PostScript source.\n";
            &make_and_cd_tempdir();
            &make_from_ps($fontSource);
        } elsif ($fontSource =~ /\.mf$/) {
            local($fpath, $fname);
            print TTY "Building PK file from MF source.\n";
            &make_and_cd_tempdir();

            if ($fontSource =~ /^(.*)\/([^\/]*)$/) {
                $fpath = $1;
                $fname = $2;

                $fpath = $CWD if $fpath eq ".";
                $fpath = "$CWD/.." if $fpath eq "..";
            } else {
                $fpath = "";
                $fname = $fontSource;
            }

            &make_from_mf($fpath, $fname);
        } else {
            print TTY "$0: Cannot build PK font for $NAME.\n";
            print TTY " " x length($0), "  Unprepared for $fontSource.\n";
            die "\n";
        }
    } else {
        if (grep(/^$mfBase$/, @DCR_GEN)) {

            print TTY "Building PK file from DC source.\n";

            &make_and_cd_tempdir();

            $MFBASE = "&dxbase";
            open (MFFILE, ">$mfFile.mf");
            print MFFILE "gensize:=$mfSize; generate $mfBase;\n";
            close (MFFILE);

            &make_from_mf("$DCR_DIR","$mfFile.mf");

        } elsif (grep(/^$mfBase$/, @SAUTER_GEN)) {

            print TTY "Building PK file from Sauter source.\n";

            &make_and_cd_tempdir();

            if (defined($SAUTER_ROUNDING{$mfSize})) {
                $designSize = $SAUTER_ROUNDING{$mfSize};
```

*Example D-1: MakeTeXPK.pl (continued)*

```
            } else {
                $designSize = $mfSize;
            }

            open (MFFILE, ">$mfFile.mf");
            print MFFILE "design_size := $designSize;\n";
            print MFFILE "input b-$mfBase;\n";
            close (MFFILE);

            &make_from_mf("$SAUTER_DIR","$mfFile.mf");

    } else {
        print TTY "$0: Cannot build PK file.  Can't find source.\n";
        die "\n";
    }
}

&cleanup();

exit 0;

#######################################################################

sub run {
    local(@cmd) = @_;
    local($rc);

    open  (SAVEOUT, ">&STDOUT");
    open  (SAVEERR, ">&STDERR");
    close (STDOUT);
    open  (STDOUT, ">&TTY");
    close (STDERR);
    open  (STDERR, ">&TTY");

    # Chdir seems to return a funny exit code.  So do it internally...
    # (this is a hack)
    if (@cmd[0] eq "chdir") {
        $rc = chdir(@cmd[1]);
        $rc = !$rc;
    } else {
        $rc = system(@cmd);
    }

    close (STDOUT);
    open  (STDOUT, ">&SAVEOUT");
    close (SAVEOUT);

    close (STDERR);
    open  (STDERR, ">&SAVEERR");
    close (SAVEERR);

    if ($rc) {
        printf TTY "%s\n", "*" x 72;
```

*Example D-1: MakeTeXPK.pl (continued)*

```perl
            print  TTY "$0 error : system return code: $rc\n";
            print  TTY "$0 failed: @cmd\n";
            printf TTY "%s\n", "*" x 72;
        }

        $rc;
}

sub make_and_cd_tempdir {
    &run ("mkdir", "$TEMPDIR");
    &run ("chdir", "$TEMPDIR");
}

sub cleanup {
    &run ("chdir", "$CWD");
    &run ("rm", "-rf", "$TEMPDIR");
}

sub install_font {
    local($source_path, $font, $subdir, $mode) = @_;
    local($pkdirs, @paths, $ptarget);
    local($target) = "";

    if ($VERBOSE) {
        print "Install: source_path: $source_path\n";
        print "Install: font       : $font\n";
        print "Install: subdir     : $subdir\n";
        print "Install: mode       : $mode\n";
    }

    $pkdirs = $ENV{"TEXPKS"} || $ENV{"PKFONTS"} || "";
    @paths = split(/:|;/,$pkdirs);

    # Need to find an installable target for the PK files.  Try
    # ../glyphs/$subdir and ../$subdir then give up and use the best $pkdirs
    # path...

    if (!$target) {
        ($ptarget = $source_path) =~ s#/[^/]*$##;
        $target = "$ptarget/glyphs/$subdir"
            if -d "$ptarget/glyphs/$subdir"
                || (-d "$ptarget/glyphs"
                    && -w "$ptarget/glyphs"
                    && ! -f "$ptarget/glyphs/$subdir");
    }

    if (!$target) {
        ($ptarget = $source_path) =~ s#/[^/]*$##;
        $target = "$ptarget/$subdir"
            if -d "$ptarget/$subdir"
                || (-d $ptarget && -w $ptarget && ! -f "$ptarget/$subdir");

        # what a minute, suppose we just made a font in the current
```

```
            # directory...let's put the PK file there too...
            if (! -d "$target" && ($source_path eq $CWD)) {
                $target = $source_path;
                $USE_MODE_IN_DEST = 0;
            }
    }

    while (!$target && ($ptarget = shift @paths)) {
        $target = $ptarget if ($ptarget ne "." && $ptarget ne ".."
                                && -d $ptarget && -w $ptarget);
    }

    if ($target) {
        if (! -d $target) {
            &run ("mkdir", "$target");
            &run ("chmod", "777", "$target");
        }

        if ($USE_MODE_IN_DEST) {
            $target .= "/$mode";
            if (! -d $target) {
                &run ("mkdir", "$target");
                &run ("chmod", "777", "$target");
            }
        }

        print TTY "Installing $font in $target.\n";
        &run ("cp", "$font", "$target/fonttmp.$$");
        &run ("chdir", "$target");
        &run ("mv", "fonttmp.$$", "$font");
        &run ("chmod", "a+r", "$font");
        &run ("chdir", "$TEMPDIR");
        print STDOUT "$target/$font\n";
    } else {
        print TTY "$0: Install failed: no where to put $font.\n";
    }
}

sub make_from_mf {
    local ($source_path, $source_file) = @_;
    local ($mfsource, $mfinputs, $cmd);
    local ($gfname, $pkname, $realdpi, $testdpi);
    local ($cmpath);

    print "source_path: $source_path\n" if $VERBOSE;
    print "source_file: $source_file\n" if $VERBOSE;

    &run ("chdir", "$TEMPDIR");

    if (!$source_file) {
        $mfsource = $source_path;
        ($source_path = $mfsource) =~ s#/[^/]*$##;
        ($source_file = $mfsource) =~ s#^.*/([^/]*)$#$1#;
```

*Example D-1: MakeTeXPK.pl (continued)*

```perl
    }

    $mfinputs = $ENV{"MFINPUTS"};
    $mfinputs =~ s/^:*(.*):*$/$1/ if $mfinputs;
    $ENV{"MFINPUTS"} = ".:$source_path";
    $ENV{"MFINPUTS"} .= ":$mfinputs" if $mfinputs;

    print "MFINPUTS: $ENV{MFINPUTS}\n" if $VERBOSE;

    $cmpath = "/usr/local/lib/fonts/free/cm/src";
    if (-d $cmpath && $ENV{"MFINPUTS"} !~ /$cmpath/) {
        $ENV{"MFINPUTS"} .= ":$cmpath";
    }

    $cmd = "$MFBASE \\mode:=$MODE; mag:=$MAG; scrollmode; " .
           "\\input $source_file";
    print TTY "virmf $cmd\n";

    $saveTERM = $ENV{"TERM"};
    $saveDISPLAY = $ENV{"DISPLAY"};
    delete $ENV{"DISPLAY"};
    $ENV{"TERM"} = "vt100";

    $rc = &run ("virmf", "$cmd");

    $ENV{"DISPLAY"} = $saveDISPLAY;
    $ENV{"TERM"} = $saveTERM;

    $realdpi = $DPI;
    $gfname = "./$mfFile.${realdpi}gf";

    for ($testdpi = $realdpi-2; $testdpi < $realdpi+3; $testdpi++) {
        $gfname = "./$mfFile.${testdpi}gf", $realdpi = $testdpi
            if ! -f $gfname && -f "./$mfFile.${testdpi}gf";
    }

    $gfname = "./$mfFile.${realdpi}gf";
    $pkname = "./$mfFile.${realdpi}pk";

    $rc = &run ("gftopk", "$gfname", "$pkname");

    &install_font($source_path, "$mfFile.${realdpi}pk", 'pk', "$MODE");
}

sub make_from_ps {
    local ($source_path, $source_file) = @_;
    local ($pssource, @cmd);
    local ($basename, $afmFile, $afmtest, $part);

    &run ("chdir", "$TEMPDIR");

    if (!$source_file) {
        $pssource = $source_path;
```

*Example D-1: MakeTeXPK.pl (continued)*

```perl
        ($source_path = $pssource) =~ s#/[^/]*$##;
        ($source_file = $pssource) =~ s#^.*/([^/]*)$#$1#;
    }

    # Need to find the AFM file...
    $afmFile = "";
    ($basename = $source_file) =~ s/\.pf[ab]$//;
    # First, look in ../afm:
    ($afmtest = $source_path) =~ s#/[^/]*$##;
    $afmtest .= "/afm/$basename.afm";
    $afmFile = $afmtest if -r $afmtest;

    # Then, look in ../../afm:
    ($afmtest = $source_path) =~ s#/[^/]*$##;
    $afmtest =~ s#/[^/]*$##;
    $afmtest .= "/afm/$basename.afm";
    $afmFile = $afmtest if !$afmFile && -r $afmtest;

    die "$0: Cannot find AFM file for $source_file.\n" if !$afmFile;

    @cmd = ('ps2pk', "-a$afmFile", "-X$DPI",
            "$source_path/$source_file", "./$mfFile.${DPI}pk");

    foreach $part (@cmd) {
        print TTY "$part ";
    }
    print TTY "\n";

    $rc = &run (@cmd);

    &install_font($source_path, "$mfFile.${DPI}pk", 'pk', "${DPI}dpi");
}

sub find_fonts {
# This subroutine searches for font sources.  It looks in all the directories
# in the path specified.  Recursive searches are preformed on directories
# that end in //, !, or !!.  The emTeX directive "!", which should search
# only one level deep, is treated exactly like "!!".
#
    local($path, @fonts) = @_;
    local(@dirs, $dir, $font);
    local(@matches) = ();
    local(@recursive_matches);

    $path =~ s/!!/\/\//g;
    $path =~ s/!/\/\//g;
    $path =~ s/\\/\//g;

    print TTY "CWD: ", `pwd` if $VERBOSE;
    print TTY "Find: @fonts\n" if $VERBOSE;
    print TTY "Path: $path\n" if $VERBOSE;

    @dirs = split(/:|;/, $path);
```

*Example D-1: MakeTeXPK.pl (continued)*

```perl
        while (@dirs) {
            $dir = shift @dirs;
            next if !$dir;

            if ($dir =~ /\/\//) {
                @recursive_matches = &recursive_search($dir, @fonts);
                push (@matches, @recursive_matches)
                    if @recursive_matches;
            } else {
                $dir =~ s/\/*$//;                # remove trailing /, if present
                foreach $font (@fonts) {
                    push (@matches, "$dir/$font")
                        if -f "$dir/$font";
                }
            }
        }

        $font = shift @matches;

        if (@matches) {
            print TTY "$0: Found more than one match.\n";
            print TTY " " x length($0), "  Using: $font\n";
        }

        $font;
    }

    sub recursive_search {
        local($dir, @fonts) = @_;
        local(@matches) = ();
        local(@dirstack, $rootdir, $font, $fontmask);

        $dir =~ /^(.*)\/\/(.*)$/;
        $rootdir = $1;
        $fontmask = $2;

        $rootdir =~ s/\/*$//;                   # remove trailing /'s

        # Note: this perl script has to scan them all, the mask is meaningless.
        # Especially since I'm looking for the font *source* not the TFM or
        # PK file...

        $fontmask =~ s/\$MAKETEX_BASE_DPI/$BDPI/g;
        $fontmask =~ s/\$MAKETEX_MAG/$MAG/g;
        $fontmask =~ s/\$MAKETEX_MODE/$MODE/g;

        print TTY "Search root=$rootdir\n" if $VERBOSE;
        print TTY "Search mask=$fontmask (ignored by $0)\n" if $VERBOSE;

        @dirstack = ($rootdir);

        while ($rootdir = shift @dirstack) {
            opendir (SEARCHDIR, "$rootdir");
```

*Example D-1: MakeTeXPK.pl (continued)*

```
        while ($dir = scalar(readdir(SEARCHDIR))) {
            if ($dir ne "." && $dir ne ".." && -d "$rootdir/$dir") {
                push(@dirstack, "$rootdir/$dir");
                foreach $font (@fonts) {
                    if (-f "$rootdir/$dir/$font") {
                      print TTY "Matched: $rootdir/$dir/$font\n" if $VERBOSE;
                        push(@matches, "$rootdir/$dir/$font");
                    }
                }
            }
        }
        closedir (SEARCHDIR);
    }

    @matches;
}
```

The *MakeTeXTFM.pl* script builds TFM files from METAFONT and PostScript (AFM file) fonts.

*Example D-2: MakeTeXTFM.pl*

```
#!/usr/local/bin/perl
#
# MakeTeXTFM.pl version 1.0, Copyright (C) 1993,94 by Norman Walsh.
# NO WARRANTY.  Distribute freely under the GNU GPL.
#
# This script attempts to make a new TeX TFM file, because one wasn't
# found.  The only argument is the name of the TFM file, such as
# `cmr10.tfm' (*NOT* just `cmr10').
#
# This script was designed with two goals in mind: to support recursive
# subdirectory searching for fonts and to provide support for PK files
# built from both MF fonts and PS fonts.  It also supports the Sauter
# and DC fonts which can be built at any design size.
#
# This script was designed and tested with the following directory structure
# in mind: each typeface is stored in its own directory with appropriate
# subdirectories for font sources, metrics, and glyphs.  The script may not
# work exactly right if you use a different directory structure (the font
# installation, in particular, will probably be incorrect).  However,
# several other versions of MakeTeXPK exist which will handle simpler
# directory structures, so you need not feel compelled to use the one
# described here.
#
# For MF fonts: (... is usually something like /usr/local/lib/tex/fonts)
#
# .../typeface/src         holds the sources
#             /tfm         holds the TFM files
#             /glyphs      root for glyphs
#             /glyphs/mode holds the PK files for "mode".
#
# For PS fonts: (... is usually something like /usr/local/lib/tex/fonts)
#
# .../typeface/afm         holds the AFM files
#             /tfm         holds the TFM files
#             /vf          holds the VF files
#             /vpl         holds the VPL files
#             /glyphs      root for glyphs
#            /glyphs/pk/999dpi  holds the PK files at 999 dpi created by ps2pk
#             /glpyhs/type1 holds the type1 PFA/PFB sources for the fonts
#
# The TFM files constructed for PostScript fonts are mapped to the Old TeX
# encoding.
#

require "getopts.pl";
$rc = &Getopts ('v');            # Get options from the user...

$VERBOSE = $opt_v || $ENV{"DEBUG_MAKETEXPK"}; # Verbose?

chop($CWD = `pwd`);              # Where are we?
```

*Example D-2: MakeTeXTFM.pl (continued)*

```
$TEMPDIR = "/tmp/mkPK.$$";          # Where do temp files go?
$MFBASE = "&plain";                 # What MF base do we use by default?

# Where are fonts stored?
$TEXFONTS = $ENV{"TEXFONTS"} || ".:/usr/local/lib/fonts//";

# Define modes that should be used for base resolutions...
$DPI_MODES{300}  = "laserwriter";
$DPI_MODES{200}  = "FAX";
$DPI_MODES{360}  = "lqhires";
$DPI_MODES{400}  = "nexthi";
$DPI_MODES{600}  = "QMSmoa";
$DPI_MODES{100}  = "nextscreen";

$DPI_MODES{100}  = "videodisplayi";
$DPI_MODES{110}  = "videodisplayii";
$DPI_MODES{118}  = "videodisplayiii";
$DPI_MODES{120}  = "videodisplayiv";
$DPI_MODES{124}  = "videodisplayv";
$DPI_MODES{130}  = "videodisplayvi";
$DPI_MODES{140}  = "videodisplayvii";
$DPI_MODES{150}  = "videodisplayviii";

$DPI_MODES{72}   = "MacTrueSize";
$DPI_MODES{635}  = "linolo";
$DPI_MODES{1270} = "linohi";
$DPI_MODES{2540} = "linosuper";

# Where are the DC fonts stored and what base names can be used?
$DCR_DIR = '/usr/local/lib/fonts/free/dc/src';
@DCR_GEN = ('dcb','dcbom','dcbx','dcbxsl','dcbxti','dccsc','dcdunh','dcff',
            'dcfi','dcfib','dcitt','dcr','dcsl','dcsltt','dcss','dcssbx',
            'dcssi','dctcsc','dcti','dctt','dcu','dcvtt' );

# Where are the Sauter fonts stored and what base names can be used?
$SAUTER_DIR = '/usr/local/lib/fonts/free/sauter/src';
@SAUTER_GEN = ('cmb','cmbizx','cmbozx','cmbsy','cmbszx','cmbx','cmbxsl',
               'cmbxti', 'cmbz', 'cmbzx', 'cmcsc', 'cmdszc', 'cmdunh',
               'cmex', 'cmff', 'cmfi', 'cmfib', 'cminch', 'cmitt', 'cmmi',
               'cmmib', 'cmr', 'cmrcz', 'cmrisz', 'cmritz', 'cmriz',
               'cmrotz', 'cmroz', 'cmrsz', 'cmrtz', 'cmruz', 'cmrz',
               'cmsl', 'cmsltt', 'cmss', 'cmssbx', 'cmssdc', 'cmssi',
               'cmssq', 'cmssqi', 'cmsy', 'cmtcsc', 'cmtex', 'cmti',
               'cmtt', 'cmu', 'cmvtt', 'czinch', 'czssq', 'czssqi',
               'lasy', 'lasyb');

$SAUTER_ROUNDING{11} = '10.954451';
$SAUTER_ROUNDING{14} = '14.4';
$SAUTER_ROUNDING{17} = '17.28';
$SAUTER_ROUNDING{20} = '20.736';
$SAUTER_ROUNDING{25} = '24.8832';
$SAUTER_ROUNDING{30} = '29.8685984';
```

*Example D-2: MakeTeXTFM.pl (continued)*

```perl
open (TTY, ">/dev/tty");
select (TTY); $| = 1; select(STDOUT);

$tfmFile = @ARGV[0];
if (!$tfmFile) {
    print TTY "$0 error: No TFM file specified.\n";
    die "\n";
}

print TTY "\nAttempting to build TFM file: $tfmFile.\n";

# This is the *wierdest* bug I've ever seen.  When this script is called
# by virtex to build a TFM file, the argument (as interpreted by Perl)
# has (at least one) ASCII 16 attached to the end of the argument.  This
# loop removes all control characters from the $tfmFile name string...
$tfmFile =~ /(.)$/;
$char = ord ($1);
while ($char <= 32) {
    $tfmFile = $`;
    $tfmFile =~ /(.)$/;
    $char = ord ($1);
}

# Now we know the name of the TFM file.  Next, get the name of the MF file
# and the base name and size of the MF file.

($mfFile = $tfmFile) =~ s/\.tfm$//;
$mfFile =~ /^(.*[^0-9])(\d+)$/;
$mfBase = $1;
$mfSize = $2;

# Presumably, we got here because the TFM file doesn't exist.  Let's look
# for the MF file or the AFM file...

$tfmSource = &find_fonts($TEXFONTS, ("$mfFile.mf", "$mfFile.afm"));

if ($tfmSource) {
    if ($tfmSource =~ /\.afm$/) {
        print TTY "Building $tfmFile from AFM source.\n";
        &make_and_cd_tempdir();
        &make_from_afm($tfmSource);
    } elsif ($tfmSource =~ /\.mf$/) {
        local($fpath, $fname);
        print TTY "Building $tfmFile from MF source.\n";
        &make_and_cd_tempdir();

        if ($tfmSource =~ /^(.*)\/([^\/]*)$/) {
            $fpath = $1;
            $fname = $2;

            $fpath = $CWD if $fpath eq ".";
            $fpath = "$CWD/.." if $fpath eq "..";
        } else {
```

*Example D-2: MakeTeXTFM.pl (continued)*

```perl
                    $fpath = "";
                    $fname = $tfmSource;
            }

            &make_from_mf($fpath, $fname);
        } else {
            print TTY "$0: Cannot build $tfmFile.\n";
            print TTY " " x length($0), "  Unprepared for $tfmSource.\n";
            die "\n";
        }
    } else {
        if (grep(/^$mfBase$/, @DCR_GEN)) {

            print TTY "Building $tfmFile from DC source.\n";

            &make_and_cd_tempdir();

            $MFBASE = "&dxbase";
            open (MFFILE, ">$mfFile.mf");
            print MFFILE "gensize:=$mfSize; generate $mfBase;\n";
            close (MFFILE);

            &make_from_mf("$DCR_DIR","$mfFile.mf");

        } elsif (grep(/^$mfBase$/, @SAUTER_GEN)) {

            print TTY "Building $tfmFile from Sauter source.\n";

            &make_and_cd_tempdir();

            if (defined($SAUTER_ROUNDING{$mfSize})) {
                $designSize = $SAUTER_ROUNDING{$mfSize};
            } else {
                $designSize = $mfSize;
            }

            open (MFFILE, ">$mfFile.mf");
            print MFFILE "design_size := $designSize;\n";
            print MFFILE "input b-$mfBase;\n";
            close (MFFILE);

            &make_from_mf("$SAUTER_DIR","$mfFile.mf");

        } else {
            print TTY "$0: Cannot build $tfmFile.  Can't find source.\n";
            die "\n";
        }
    }

    &cleanup();

    exit 0;
```

*Example D-2: MakeTeXTFM.pl (continued)*

```perl
sub run {
    local(@cmd) = @_;
    local($rc);

    open (SAVEOUT, ">&STDOUT");
    open (SAVEERR, ">&STDERR");
    close (STDOUT);
    open (STDOUT, ">&TTY");
    close (STDERR);
    open (STDERR, ">&TTY");

    # Chdir seems to return a funny exit code.  So do it internally...
    # (this is a hack)
    if (@cmd[0] eq "chdir") {
        $rc = chdir(@cmd[1]);
        $rc = !$rc;
    } else {
        $rc = system(@cmd);
    }

    close (STDOUT);
    open (STDOUT, ">&SAVEOUT");
    close (SAVEOUT);

    close (STDERR);
    open (STDERR, ">&SAVEERR");
    close (SAVEERR);

    if ($rc) {
        printf TTY "%s\n", "*" x 72;
        print  TTY "MakeTeXTFM error : system return code: $rc\n";
        print  TTY "MakeTeXTFM failed: @cmd\n";
        printf TTY "%s\n", "*" x 72;
    }

    $rc;
}

sub make_and_cd_tempdir {
    &run ("mkdir", "$TEMPDIR");
    &run ("chdir", "$TEMPDIR");
}

sub cleanup {
    &run ("chdir", "$CWD");
    &run ("rm", "-rf", "$TEMPDIR");
}

sub install_font {
    local($source_path, $font, $subdir) = @_;
    local(@paths) = split(/:|;|,/,$ENV{"TEXFONTS"});
    local($target) = "";
    local($ptarget);
```

```perl
        if (!$target && $source_path =~ /\/src$/) {
            $ptarget = $source_path;
            $ptarget =~ s/(.*)\/src$/$1/;
            $ptarget .= "/$subdir";
            $target = $ptarget if (-d $ptarget && -w $ptarget);
        }

        if (!$target && $source_path =~ /\/afm$/) {
            $ptarget = $source_path;
            $ptarget =~ s/(.*)\/afm$/$1/;
            $ptarget .= "/$subdir";
            $target = $ptarget if (-d $ptarget && -w $ptarget);
        }

        if (!$target && ($source_path eq $CWD)) {
            $target = $source_path;
        }

        while (!$target && ($ptarget = shift @paths)) {
            $target = $ptarget if ($ptarget ne "." && $ptarget ne ".."
                                   && -d $ptarget && -w $ptarget);
        }

        if ($target) {
            print TTY "Installing $font in $target.\n";
            &run ("cp", "$font", "$target/fonttmp.$$");
            &run ("chdir", "$target");
            &run ("mv", "fonttmp.$$", "$font");
            &run ("chmod", "a+r", "$font");
            &run ("chdir", "$TEMPDIR");
            print STDOUT "$target/$font\n";
        } else {
            print TTY "$0: Install failed: no where to put $font.\n";
        }
    }

sub make_from_mf {
    local ($source_path, $source_file) = @_;
    local ($mfsource, $mfinputs, $cmd);

    &run ("chdir", "$TEMPDIR");

    if (!$source_file) {
        $mfsource = $source_path;
        ($source_path = $mfsource) =~ s#/[^/]*$##;
        ($source_file = $mfsource) =~ s#^.*/([^/]*)$#$1#;
    }

    $mfinputs = $ENV{"MFINPUTS"};
    $mfinputs =~ s/^:*(.*):*$/$1/ if $mfinputs;
    $ENV{"MFINPUTS"} = ".:$source_path";
    $ENV{"MFINPUTS"} .= ":$mfinputs" if $mfinputs;
```

*Example D-2: MakeTeXTFM.pl (continued)*

```perl
        print "MFINPUTS: $ENV{MFINPUTS}\n" if $VERBOSE;

        $cmd = "$MFBASE \\mode:=laserwriter; scrollmode; \\input $source_file";
        print TTY "virmf $cmd\n";

        $saveTERM = $ENV{"TERM"};
        $saveDISPLAY = $ENV{"DISPLAY"};
        delete $ENV{"DISPLAY"};
        $ENV{"TERM"} = "vt100";

        $rc = &run ("virmf", "$cmd");

        $ENV{"DISPLAY"} = $saveDISPLAY;
        $ENV{"TERM"} = $saveTERM;

        &install_font($source_path, $tfmFile, 'tfm');
    }

sub make_from_afm {
    local ($afmFile) = @_;
    local ($source_path);

    print TTY "afm2tfm $afmFile -v $mfFile ${mfFile}0\n";
    $rc = &run ("afm2tfm", "$afmFile", "-v", "$mfFile", "${mfFile}0");

    print TTY "vptovf $mfFile.vpl $mfFile.vf $mfFile.tfm\n";
    $rc = &run ("vptovf", "$mfFile.vpl", "$mfFile.vf", "$mfFile.tfm");

    ($source_path = $afmFile) =~ s#/[^/]*$##;
    &install_font($source_path, "$mfFile.tfm", 'tfm');
    &install_font($source_path, "${mfFile}0.tfm", 'tfm');
    &install_font($source_path, "$mfFile.vpl", 'vpl');
    &install_font($source_path, "$mfFile.vf", 'vf');
}

sub find_fonts {
    local($path, @fonts) = @_;
    local(@dirs, $dir, $font);
    local(@matches) = ();
    local(@recursive_matches);

    print "Find fonts on path: $path\n" if $VERBOSE;

    @dirs = split(/:|;/, $path);
    while ($dir = shift @dirs) {
        print "Search: $dir\n" if $VERBOSE;
        if ($dir =~ /\/\//) {
            @recursive_matches = &recursive_search($dir, @fonts);
            push (@matches, @recursive_matches)
                if @recursive_matches;
        } else {
            $dir =~ s/\/*$//;               # remove trailing /, if present
```

*Example D-2: MakeTeXTFM.pl (continued)*

```
            foreach $font (@fonts) {
                push (@matches, "$dir/$font")
                    if -f "$dir/$font";
            }
        }
    }

    $font = shift @matches;

    if (@matches) {
        print TTY "$0: Found more than one match.\n";
        print TTY " " x length($0), "  Using: $font\n";
    }

    $font;
}

sub recursive_search {
    local($dir, @fonts) = @_;
    local(@matches) = ();
    local(@dirstack, $rootdir, $font, $fontmask);

    $dir =~ /^(.*)\/\/(.*)$/;
    $rootdir = $1;
    $fontmask = $2;

    $rootdir =~ s/\/*$//;                      # remove trailing /'s

    # Note: this perl script has to scan them all, the mask is meaningless.
    # Especially since I'm looking for the font *source* not the TFM or
    # PK file...

    $fontmask =~ s/\$MAKETEX_BASE_DPI/$BDPI/g;
    $fontmask =~ s/\$MAKETEX_MAG/$MAG/g;
    $fontmask =~ s/\$MAKETEX_MODE/$MODE/g;

    print "Search root=$rootdir\n" if $VERBOSE;
    print "Search mask=$fontmask (ignored by $0)\n" if $VERBOSE;

    @dirstack = ($rootdir);

    while ($rootdir = shift @dirstack) {
        opendir (SEARCHDIR, "$rootdir");
        while ($dir = scalar(readdir(SEARCHDIR))) {
            if ($dir ne "." && $dir ne ".." && -d "$rootdir/$dir") {
                push(@dirstack, "$rootdir/$dir");
                foreach $font (@fonts) {
                    if (-f "$rootdir/$dir/$font") {
                        print "Matched: $rootdir/$dir/$font\n" if $VERBOSE;
                        push(@matches, "$rootdir/$dir/$font");
                    }
                }
            }
        }
```

*Example D-2: MakeTeXTFM.pl (continued)*

```
        }
        closedir (SEARCHDIR);
    }

    @matches;
}
```

The *dvidxx.btm* script is written in *4DOS*'s extended batch language. It performs automatic font generation for **METAFONT** and PostScript fonts using emTₑX's drivers (version 1.4s).

*Example D-3: dvidxx.btm*

```
@echo off
: ---------------------------------------------------------------------
: DVIDXX Copyright (C) 1992,94 by Norman Walsh
:
: This file is free.  You can do anything you like with it with one
: exception: if you change this file, you MUST rename it!
:
: Requirements: 4DOS, emTeX drivers 1.4s or higher, MAKEPK.BTM
:
: Usage: DVIDXX emtexDriver driverOptions
:
: Note: DVIDXX requires a fair amount of free environment space in order
:       to function properly.
:
: Norman Walsh
: <norm@ora.com>
:
: 12/09/1992: - Vers 0.5
:             - This is a first attempt.  It works, but it doesn't have
:               any bells and whistles.  It would be nice, for example,
:               if it noticed that PS2PK failed for a particular font...
: ---------------------------------------------------------------------
:
: This batch file is a replacement for emTeX's dvidrv program.  It offers
: one additional feature.  In addition to using MFjob to build fonts that
: don't exist, DVIDXX can use PS2PK to build PK files for PostScript fonts.
: Note: You must have the AFM and PFA/B files for the PS fonts in question.
:
: Why did you write this as a 4DOS BTM file?  For two reasons.  First, I
: wanted it to be interpreted rather than compiled so that it would be
: easy to change, modify, and extend.  Second, I did it in 4DOS BTM language
: because DOS's batch language is too primitive.  Yes, maybe I _could_ have
: done it with a plain BAT file, but I had no desire to try.
:
: ---------------------------------------------------------------------
:
: This file relies on MAKEPK.BTM to actually build the fonts with PS2PK.
:
: Both MAKEPK and DVIDXX are somewhat dependant on the layout of your
: hard disk.  Well, on the layout of mine, actually ;-)
:
: Here's how my HD is organized:
:
: C:\PSFONTS\            Root of my PostScript fonts directory.
:                        This is stored in the %[PSFONTS] env. variable
: %[PSFONTS]\PFB         Where .PFB files are kept
: %[PSFONTS]\AFM         Where .AFM files are kept
: %[PSFONTS]\UTIL        Where MAKEPK is kept
:
```

*Example D-3: dvidxx.btm (continued)*

```
: ---------------------------------------------------------------------
: Make sure this is 4DOS...
if "%@eval[2+2]" == "4"  goto start
echo Sorry, this batch file can only be run with 4Dos.
goto end
: ---------------------------------------------------------------------
: Call the driver (maybe we won't have to do anything else)
: In a network environment, you may have to make the mfjob-file unique
: for each user in some way...
: ---------------------------------------------------------------------
:start
if not "%_dos" == "DOS" goto os2ok
iff %_env lt 128 then
  echo Sorry, this batch file requires at least 128 bytes of free environment
  echo space.  Consult your 4DOS manual for information about increasing it.
  goto end
endiff
:os2ok
setlocal
set MFJOBFN=dvidxx.mfj

%1 %2$ +mfjob-file:%MFJOBFN +batch-mode
iff not errorlevel == 8 then
  endlocal
  goto end
endiff
: ---------------------------------------------------------------------
: Ok, we have to build some fonts...
:
:   NEWJOB     = name of the MFjob file that will actually be used
:   PSJOB      = name of the batch file that will build fonts with PS2PK
:   PSCNT      = number of PS fonts to build
:   MFCNT      = number of MF fonts to build
:   MFJOBLEN   = number of lines in the original MFjob file
:   LNUM       = current line number (in original MFjob file)
:   LINE       = text of the current line
:   FONT       = name of font
:   SIZE       = ptsize of current font (assumes designsize of 10pt)
:   PSFNT      = 0/1 flag determines if the %FONT in question is PS or not
: ---------------------------------------------------------------------
echo Looking at MFJob file...
set NEWJOB=%@unique[%@path[%MFJOBFN]]
set PSJOB=%@unique[%@path[%MFJOBFN]]
ren %NEWJOB %NEWJOB.mfj /q
ren %PSJOB %PSJOB.btm   /q
set NEWJOB=%NEWJOB.mfj
set PSJOB=%PSJOB.btm
set PSCNT=0
set MFCNT=0
set MFJOBLEN=%@lines[%MFJOBFN]
set LNUM=0

: Create the batch file and the new MFjob file...
```

*Example D-3: dvidxx.btm (continued)*

```
echo %% > %NEWJOB
echo pushd %PSFONTS > %PSJOB


: -----------------------------------------------------------------
: Loop through the entire MFjob file.  Lines that begin "{font=" are
: analyzed further to determine what kind of font it is.  All other lines
: are simply copied to the new MFjob file.
: -----------------------------------------------------------------


:looptop

if %LNUM gt %MFJOBLEN goto loopover

: Deleting this percent stuff will save a small amount of time, but
: since reading from the MFjob file is pretty slow, I find it reassuring...
set PERC=%@eval[%LNUM / %MFJOBLEN * 100]
set p=%@index[%PERC,.]
if %p gt 0 set PERC=%@substr[%PERC,0,%p]
echos %@CHAR[13]Working:
echos   %[PERC]%%

set LINE=%@line[%MFJOBFN,%LNUM]
:
: We employ a convoluted compound test because %@substr["%foo",1,5] fails
: with a "no closing quote" error if the %@len["%foo"] < 5...
:
set FOUND=0
iff %@len["%LINE"] gt 5 then
  if (%@substr["%LINE",1,5]) == ({font) set FOUND=1
endiff

: If we found a font, %FOUND will be 1
iff %FOUND == 1 then
  Rem Extract the font name and the size
  set p=%@index["%LINE",;]
  set FONT=%@substr["%LINE",7,%@eval[%p - 7]]
  set p=%@index["%LINE",mag=]
  set q=%@index["%LINE",}]
  set SIZE=%@substr["%LINE",%@eval[%p+4],%@eval[%q-%p-5]]
  set SIZE=%@eval[%SIZE*10]

  Rem This is where we test to see if it is a PS font.  I've got a really
  Rem simple test below.  Basically, I keep all my PFB files for PS fonts
  Rem in a single directory.  If the font in question isn't in that directory,
  Rem I assume it is an MF font.
  set PSFNT=0
  gosub ispsfont
  iff %PSFNT == 1 then
    Echo %FONT at %[SIZE]pt will be built by PS2PK
    Rem I keep MAKEPK in C:\PSFONTS\UTIL so that's what I write to the batch
    Rem file.  If you keep it somewhere else, you'll have to change this.
    echo call %[psfonts]\util\makepk %FONT %SIZE >> %PSJOB
    set PSCNT=%@eval[%PSCNT + 1]
```

*Example D-3: dvidxx.btm (continued)*

```
   else
     Echo %FONT at %[SIZE]pt will be built by MFjob
     echo %LINE >> %NEWJOB
     set MFCNT=%@eval[%MFCNT + 1]
   endiff
else
  echo %LINE >> %NEWJOB
endiff

set LNUM=%@eval[%LNUM + 1]
goto looptop
:loopover

: ------------------------------------------------------------------------

: Finish up the PSJOB file and clean up the messages on the screen
echo popd >> %PSJOB
echos %@CHAR[13]                      %@CHAR[13]

: ------------------------------------------------------------------------

: Go for it!
iff %MFCNT gt 0 then
   echo Attempting to build %MFCNT fonts with MFjob
   mfjob %NEWJOB
endiff
del %NEWJOB /q

: Get back the environment space that we (may) need in MAKEPK...
unset MFJOBLEN LNUM LINE FONT SIZE PSFNT MFCNT NEWJOB

iff %PSCNT gt 0 then
   echo Attempting to build %PSCNT fonts with PS2PK
   call %PSJOB
endiff
del %PSJOB /q

: ------------------------------------------------------------------------
: Try to run the driver again...this time it should succeed!

del %MFJOBFN /q
%1 %2$ +mfjob-file:%MFJOBFN +batch-mode
iff errorlevel == 8 then
   echo Font building must have failed for at least one font.  Look in
   echo the %MFJOBFN file to see which font(s) failed.
endiff

endlocal
goto end

: ------------------------------------------------------------------------
: This really simple subroutine is how I look for PS fonts.  This routine
: should set PSFNT=1 iff the %FONT variable names a PostScript font.
```

*Example D-3: dvidxx.btm (continued)*

```
      :
      :ispsfont
      if exist %[psfonts]\pfb\%FONT.pfb set PSFNT=1
      return

      : -------------------------------------------------------------------
      :end
```

The *makepk.btm* script is used by *dvidxx.btm*, shown in Example D-3 in this appendix.

*Example D-4: makepk.btm*

```
@echo off
: ----------------------------------------------------------------------
: MAKEPK Copyright (C) 1992,94 by Norman Walsh
:
: This file is free.  You can do anything you like with it with one
: exception: if you change this file, you MUST rename it!
:
: Requirements: 4DOS, ps2pk, afm2tfm, pfm2afm, pkbbox
:
: Usage: MAKEPK fontfn ptsize [pkfn] [-opts]
:
: Norman Walsh
: <norm@ora.com>
:
: 12/09/1992: - Vers 0.5
:----------------------------------------------------------------------
: See usage info below
:
: This batch file relies on the following directory structure:
:
: C:\PSFONTS\                Root of the PostScript fonts directory.
:                           This is stored in the %[PSFONTS] env. variable
: %[PSFONTS]\PFB             Where .PFB files are kept
: %[PSFONTS]\AFM             Where .AFM files are kept
: %[PSFONTS]\PFM             Where .PFM files are kept (only required if the
:                           AFM file does not exist)
: %[PSFONTS]\TFM             Where _all_ TFM files are kept for PS fonts
: C:\BIN\PS2PK               Where all the PS2PK utils are kept
:----------------------------------------------------------------------
: Make sure the parameters are ok...
iff %# lt 1 then
   echo Usage: %0 fontfn ptsize [pkfn] [-opts]
   echo.
   echo MAKEPK rasterizes ´fontfn´ at ´ptsize´ and stores it in ´pkfn´.  The
   echo default ´pkfn´ is the name of the ´fontfn´.  All fonts are stored in
   echo the %[psfonts]\@Rrdpi\ directory.  If -opts are supplied, they are
   echo passed to PS2PK.
   quit 1
endiff

: Setup local environment
setlocal
pushd %[psfonts]

: Parse the command line
set pfbfn=%@name[%1]
set ptsz=%2
set pkfn=%@name[%3]
shift 2
:toshift
iff ‡%@substr[%1,0,1]‡ == ‡-‡ then
```

*Example D-4: makepk.btm (continued)*

```
    set pkopts=%pkopts %1
else
    set pkfn=%@name[%1]
endiff
shift
if %# gt 0 goto toshift
: ----------------------------------------------------------------------
: Figure out the name of the appropriate PK directory.  Create it if it
: doesn't exist.  Abort if a filename exists with that name...
:
: TeX seems to underestimate the font size by a very small amount.  We
: compensate (in the calculation of the directory) by adding the small
: amount 0.0005 to the point size before truncating to integer...
:
set pkres=%@int[(%@eval[(%@eval[%ptsz+0.0005] * 300) / 10]]
set pkdir=%[pkres]dpi
if isdir %pkdir goto okdir
iff not exist %pkdir then
    md %pkdir
    goto okdir
endiff
echo MakePK: Cannot create directory: %pkdir
quit 1
:okdir
: ----------------------------------------------------------------------
: Setup the %PKFN if it wasn't set by a parameter
if "%pkfn" == "" set pkfn=%@name[%pfbfn]

: If the font and TFM alread exist, don't bother making them
iff exist %[pkdir]\%[pkfn].pk .and. .\tfm\%@filesize[%[pkfn].tfm] gt 0 then
    popd
    quit 0
endiff

: Check to see if an AFM file exists (and has a reasonable size)...
iff %@filesize[.\afm\%[pfbfn].afm] gt 0 then
    set afmok=1
else
    set afmok=0
endiff
: ----------------------------------------------------------------------
: Make sure we have everything we need...a PFB and an AFM or PFM...
set ok=1
iff not exist .\pfb\%[pfbfn].pfb then
    echo Cannot find PFB file: .\pfb\%[pfbfn].pfb
    set ok=0
endiff
iff not exist .\pfm\%[pfbfn].pfm .and. %afmok == 0 then
    echo Cannot find PFM file (.\pfm\%[pfbfn].pfm) and
    echo cannot find AFM file (.\afm\%[pfbfn].afm)
    set ok=0
endiff
if "%ok" == "0" quit 1
```

*Example D-4: makepk.btm (continued)*

```
set ok=
: -------------------------------------------------------------------
: If we didn't find an AFM file, make one...
iff %afmok == 0 then
   echo PFMtoAFM...
   \bin\ps2pk\pfm2afm .\pfm\%[pfbfn].pfm .\afm\%[pfbfn].afm
endiff


: -------------------------------------------------------------------
: Build the font...
echo Rasterizing...
::: The lines marked *** MERGE *** should be joined onto the end of the
::: preceding line.  They were broken only to fit within the margins of
::: this book.
echo ps2pk -P10 -X%[pkres] -a.\afm\%[pfbfn].afm %pkopts
*** MERGE ***    .\pfb\%[pfbfn].pfb %[pkdir]\%[pkfn].pk
ps2pk -V -P10 -X%[pkres] -a.\afm\%[pfbfn].afm %pkopts
*** MERGE ***    .\pfb\%[pfbfn].pfb %[pkdir]\%[pkfn].pk

: If we didn't get a descent AFM then we built it with AFM2PFM.
: Unfortunately, the bounding boxes are missing if we did that.
: So add the bounding boxes with the UGLY HACKISH PKbbox program...
iff %afmok == 0 then
   echo PKbbox to make bounding boxes...
   set tempafm=%@unique[.]
   c:\tex\util\pkbbox %pkdir\%pkfn.pk .\afm\%[pfbfn].afm > %tempafm
   move %tempafm .\afm\%[pfbfn].afm
endiff

: If there's no TFM, build it...
iff not exist .\tfm\%[pkfn].tfm then
   echo AFMtoTFM...
   afm2tfm .\afm\%[pfbfn].afm .\tfm\%[pkfn].tfm
endiff

::: If we didn't build a 10pt font, scale it appropriately
::iff not "%ptsz" == "10" then
::   c:\tex\util\pkscale %[pkdir]\%[pkfn].pk .\tfm\%[pkfn].tfm /designsize:10
::   del %[pkdir]\%[pkfn].bak /q
::endiff


:
: -------------------------------------------------------------------
: We're all done...
popd
endlocal
quit 0
```

The *enc-afm.pl* script changes the encoding vector in an AFM file.

*Example D-5: enc-afm.pl*

```
#! /usr/local/bin/perl
#
# Usage: enc-afm afm-file enc-file > encoded-afm-file
#
# Where: afm-file is the original AFM file with an arbitrary
#        encoding enc-file is the encoding file (in PS
#        format, a la dvips .enc files) encoded-afm-file is
#        the new AFM file with 'enc-file' encoding.
#

# what about .notdef?

$afmfile = @ARGV[0];
$encfile = @ARGV[1];

print STDERR "Reading encoding file: $encfile\n";
&read_encfile($encfile);
print STDERR "Reading AFM file: $afmfile\n";
&read_afmfile($afmfile);

# Assign the correct encoding position to each char
$missing = 0;
for ($count = 0; $count < $vectorlen; $count++) {
    $missing_glyphs{@encoding[$count]} = 1, $missing = 1
if !defined($vectorplace{@encoding[$count]})
        && @encoding[$count] ne ".notdef";
    $vectorplace{@encoding[$count]} = $count; .
}

&print_long_list("Note: the following glyphs are missing "
  . "from the AFM file: ",
 sort (keys %missing_glyphs))
     if $missing;

# Construct the CharMetrics lines
@output_encoding = ();
foreach $name (keys %metrics) {
    push (@output_encoding,
  sprintf("C %3d ; %s",
  $vectorplace{$name}, $metrics{$name}));
}

# Sort the CharMetrics lines
@sorted_encoding = sort (@output_encoding);

# Move the unused characters to the end of the list
@output_encoding = grep(/^C\s+\d+/, @sorted_encoding);
@minusone_encoding = grep(/C\s+-1/, @sorted_encoding);
push(@output_encoding, @minusone_encoding);

# Print the new AFM file
```

*Example D-5: enc-afm.pl (continued)*

```perl
print $line, "\n" while ($line = shift @preamble);

print "Comment Encoded with enc-afm from $encfile.\n";
print "EncodingScheme $encname\n";
printf "StartCharMetrics %d\n", $#output_encoding+1;
print $line, "\n" while ($line = shift @output_encoding);
print "EndCharMetrics\n";

print $line, "\n" while ($line = shift @postamble);

exit 0;

sub read_afmfile {
    local ($afmfile) = @_;
    local ($inpreamble, $inmetrics, $inpostamble) = (1,0);
    local ($width, $name, $bbox, $prname);

    @preamble = ();
    %metrics = ();
    %vectorplace = ();
    @postamble = ();

    open (AFM, $afmfile)
|| die "Can't open afm file: $afmfile\n";

    while (<AFM>) {
chop;

push(@postamble, $_) if $inpostamble;
push(@preamble, $_)
    if $inpreamble && ! /^EncodingScheme\s/i;

if (/^EndCharMetrics/) {
    $inmetrics = 0;
    $inpostamble = 1;
}

if ($inmetrics) {
    $width = $1 if /[;\s]+WX\s+([0-9]+)[;\s]+/;
    $name = $1 if /[;\s]+N\s+(\w+)[;\s]+/;
    $bbox = $1 if /[;\s]+B\s+([^;]+)[;\s]+/;
    die "Invalid line in AFM file: $_\n"
if ($name eq "");
    $metrics{$name} = sprintf("WX %4d ; N %s ; B %s ;",
      $width, $name, $bbox);
    $vectorplace{$name} = -1;
}

if (/^StartCharMetrics/) {
    $inpreamble = 0;
    $inmetrics = 1;
}
    }
```

*Example D-5: enc-afm.pl (continued)*

```perl
    }

    sub read_encfile {
        local ($encfile) = @_;
        local ($place, $line);

        open (ENC, $encfile)
    || die "Can't open encoding file: $encfile\n";

        $encname = "";
        @encoding = ();
        $#encoding = 256; # set the array length
        $vectorlen = 0;
        $done = 0;
        while (<ENC>) {
    chop;
    next if /^\s*%/;

    $line = $_;
    if ($encname eq "") {
        die "Invalid line in encoding file: $_\n"
    if ! /\s*\/(.*)\s*\[(.*)$/;
        $encname = $1;
        $line = $2;
    }

    $place = index($line, "%");
    $line = substr($line,$[,$place-1) if $place >= $[;

    $place = index($line, "]");
    if ($place >= $[) {
        $line = substr($line,$[,$place-1);
        $done = 1;
    }

    while ($line =~ /^\s*\/(\S*)\s*(.*)$/) {
        @encoding[$vectorlen++] = $1;
        $line = $2;
    }

    last if $done;
        }
    }

    ##############################################################
    # This routine prints a message followed by a potentially
    # long list of items, seperated by spaces.  It will never
    # allow "word wrap" to occur in the middle of a word.  There
    # has to be a better way, using Perl's report generation to
    # do this, but I haven't looked yet.
    #
    sub print_long_list {
      local ($message,@thelist) = @_;
```

*Example D-5: enc-afm.pl (continued)*

```
    local ($line) = $message;
    local ($item, $displaystring) = ("", "");

    foreach $item (@thelist) {
        if (length($line . $item) < 73) {
    $line .= $item . ", ";
        } else {
    $displaystring .= $line . "\n";
    $line = $item . ", ";
        }
    }

    $line =~ s/(.*),\s*$/$1/; # remove the last ", "...
    $displaystring .= $line . "\n";

    print STDERR $displaystring;
}
```

The *TeXtoXfont* script is a UNIX shell script (written in *bash*) which builds an X11 font from a METAFONT or PostScript font.

*Example D-6: TeXtoXfont*

```
#!/usr/local/bin/bash
#
#    This script file makes a new X/TeX screen font, because one wasn't
#    found.  Parameters are:
#
#    name dpi bdpi magnification destdir
#
#    `name' is the name of the font, such as `cmr10'.  `dpi' is
#    the resolution the font is needed at.  `bdpi' is the base
#    resolution, useful for figuring out the mode to make the font
#    in.  `magnification' is a string to pass to MF as the
#    magnification.  'destdir' is the directory in which to cache the new
#    font.
#
#    Note that this file must execute Metafont, mftobdf, and then bdftosnf,
#    and place the result in the correct location for X
#    to find it subsequently.
#
#    Of course, it needs to be set up for your site.
#
# TEMPDIR needs to be unique for each process because of the possibility
# of simultaneous processes running this script.
TEMPDIR=/tmp/bdf-snf.$$
NAME=$1
DPI=$2
BDPI=$3
MAG=$4
MODE=$5
DESTDIR=$6
umask 0

#declare -i cmfound=0
#MFDIRS=`echo $MFINPUTS | gawk -F: '{ for (i=1; i<=NF; i++) print $i }'`
#for f in $MFDIRS
#do
#  if [ -r $f/$NAME.mf ]; then
#    declare -i cmfound=1
#  fi
#done

if [ -r /usr/local/lib/tex/fonts/ps-outlines/$NAME.pfa ]
then
  echo Building X-font from PostScript outline
  PStoXfont $1 $2 $3 $4 $5 $6
  exit 0
else
  echo Building X-font from MetaFont outline
fi

#   Something like the following is useful at some sites.
```

*Example D-6: TeXtoXfont (continued)*

```
GFNAME=$NAME.$DPI'gf'
BDFNAME=$NAME.$DPI.'bdf'
SNFNAME=$NAME.$DPI.pcf

COMPRESS=1

# check if we're not running with MIT server after all
if xdpyinfo|grep -s 'vendor string: *.*MIT.*'; then
#        DESTDIR=/usr/lib/X11/fonts/xtex
#        SNFNAME=$NAME.$DPI.'snf'
         COMPRESS=0
         MITSERVER=1
fi

if test "$COMPRESS" = "1"
then
  SNFZNAME=${SNFNAME}'.Z'
else
  SNFZNAME=${SNFNAME}
fi

# Clean up on normal or abnormal exit
trap "cd /; rm -rf $TEMPDIR $DESTDIR/bdftmp.$$ $DESTDIR/snftmp.$$" 0 1 2 15

mkdir $TEMPDIR
cd $TEMPDIR

if test -r $DESTDIR/$BDFNAME
then
   echo "$DESTDIR/$BDFNAME already exists!"
    exit 0
fi

if test -r $DESTDIR/$SNFNAME
then
    echo "$DESTDIR/$SNFNAME already exists!"
    exit 0
fi

if test -r $DESTDIR/$SNFZNAME
then
    echo "$DESTDIR/$SNZFNAME already exists!"
    exit 0
fi


##
# First try mftobdf, maybe it exists...
##

echo "1st mftobdf -dpi" $DPI $NAME
mftobdf -dpi $DPI $NAME
if test ! -r $BDFNAME
```

*Example D-6: TeXtoXfont (continued)*

```
then
  pwd
  echo mf "\mode:=$MODE; mag:=$MAG/1000; scrollmode; input $NAME </dev/null"
  mf "\mode:=$MODE; mag:=$MAG/1000; scrollmode; input $NAME" </dev/null
  if test ! -r $GFNAME
  then
#
# My local metafont gives bogus names occasionally. Don't know why.
#
      echo "Unable to find $GFNAME in directory "`pwd`
      OLDDPI=$DPI
      NEWDPI=`expr $DPI - 1`
      if [ -r $NAME.$NEWDPI'gf' ] ; then
        DPI=$NEWDPI
      fi
      NEWDPI=`expr $DPI + 1`
      if [ -r $NAME.$NEWDPI'gf' ] ; then
        DPI=$NEWDPI
      fi
      if [ -r $NAME.$DPI'gf' ] ; then
        GFNAME=$NAME.$DPI'gf'
        BDFNAME=$NAME.$DPI.'bdf'
        SNFNAME=$NAME.$DPI.pcf
        echo "Metafont built $GFNAME instead of $NAME.${OLDDPI}gf, \
but that's ok..."
        gftopk $GFNAME
      else
        echo "Metafont failed for some reason on $GFNAME, \
but continuing anyway"
      fi
  else
    gftopk $GFNAME
  fi

  echo "mftobdf -dpi" $DPI $NAME
  mftobdf -dpi $DPI $NAME
  if test ! -r $BDFNAME
  then
      echo "Mftobdf failed for some reason on $BDFNAME"
      exit 1
  fi
fi

echo "$FONTCOMPILER"
if [ $MITSERVER ]; then
        bdftopcf $BDFNAME > $SNFNAME
else
        /usr/bin/dxfc $BDFNAME > $SNFNAME
fi
if test ! -r $SNFNAME
then
    echo "Font compiler failed for some reason on $SNFNAME"
    exit 1
```

*Example D-6: TeXtoXfont (continued)*

```
fi

# Install the BDF and SNF files carefully, since others may be doing
# the same as us simultaneously.

#cp $BDFNAME $DESTDIR/bdftmp.$$
cp $SNFNAME $DESTDIR/snftmp.$$
cd $DESTDIR
#mv bdftmp.$$ $BDFNAME
mv snftmp.$$ $SNFNAME

if test "$COMPRESS" = "1"
then
  compress -f $SNFNAME
fi

if [ $MITSERVER ]; then
        mkfontdir $DESTDIR
else
        /usr/bin/dxmkfontdir $DESTDIR
fi
xset +fp $DESTDIR
xset fp rehash

exit 0
```

The *PStoXfont* script is used by *TeXtoXfont*, shown in Example D-6 in this appendix.

*Example D-7: PStoXfont*

```
#!/usr/local/bin/bash
#
#   This script file makes a new X/TeX screen font, because one wasn't
#   found.  Parameters are:
#
#   name dpi bdpi mag mode destdir
#
#   `name' is the name of the font, such as `cmr10'.  `dpi' is
#   the resolution the font is needed at.  `bdpi' is the base
#   resolution, useful for figuring out the mode to make the font
#   in.  `magnification' is a string to pass to MF as the
#   magnification.  'destdir' is the directory in which to cache the new
#   font.
#
#   Note that this file must execute Metafont, mftobdf, and then bdftosnf,
#   and place the result in the correct location for X
#   to find it subsequently.
#
#   Of course, it needs to be set up for your site.
#
# TEMPDIR needs to be unique for each process because of the possibility
# of simultaneous processes running this script.
#
# This temp directory has to be under /users/oos/bin (or somewhere globally
# accessible) because this script runs PS2PK on ibis even if it is started
# elsewhere (e.g. on a Sparc).  To do so, it uses the "ibis [cmd]" shortcut
# and passes the temp directory.  If the TEMPDIR was /tmp/whatever then,
# it would fail because /tmp on a Sparc isn't /tmp on ibis.
TEMPDIR=/users/oos/bin/PStemp/temp-X-PS.$$

NAME=$1
DPI=$2
BDPI=$3
MAG=$4
MODE=$5
DESTDIR=$6

BASENAME=$NAME.$MAG.$BDPI
PTSIZE=`echo "2 k $MAG 100 / p q" | dc`
PFADIR=/usr/local/lib/tex/fonts/ps-outlines/

# Clean up on normal or abnormal exit
trap "cd /; rm -rf $TEMPDIR" 0 1 2 15

mkdir $TEMPDIR
cd $TEMPDIR

echo Making ${PTSIZE}pt ${BDPI}dpi version of $NAME.
ps2pk -v -X$BDPI -P$PTSIZE -a$PFADIR/$NAME.afm \
    $PFADIR/$NAME.pfa $BASENAME.pk
```

*Example D-7: PStoXfont (continued)*

```
pktobdf $BASENAME.pk | gawk -vname=$NAME.$DPI -f \
   /usr/local/lib/tex/ps/PStoXfont.awk > $BASENAME.bdf
bdftopcf $BASENAME.bdf > $BASENAME.pcf
mv $BASENAME.pcf $DESTDIR

mkfontdir $DESTDIR
xset +fp $DESTDIR
xset fp rehash

exit 0
```

The *txt2verb.pl* script translates arbitrary text lines into a format suitable for including in \verbatim material in TEX.

*Example D-8: txt2verb.pl*

```
#!/usr/local/bin/perl
#
# txt2verb  Copyright (C) 1993 by Norm Walsh <norm@ora.com>
#           Distribute freely under the terms of the GNU Copyleft.
#
# Converts a text "screen" into a form suitable for \inputing into TeX
# and printing as a screen dump.  The original form is assumed to be
# a series of 80-byte lines with any character in the range 0-255 present
# (including CR and LF in the middle of a line).
#
# The output form is a series of lines of varying length.  There is
# one output line for each input line.  TeX special characters and all
# characters in the ranges 0-31 and 127-255 are replaced by control
# sequences.
#
# Usage:
#
#   txt2verb screenfile <texfile>
#
#   If texfile is not specified, stdout is assumed.
#
# Options:
#
#   -1    File of lines.  Input file contains lines of varying length,
#         but no imbedded CR or LF chars.
#   -v    Verbose: print each input line as it's read.
#   -q    Quiet: no messages.
#   -L #  Set line length to '#' characters.
#
# To incorporate the resulting screen dump in your Plain TeX or LaTeX
# document, insert the following macro definitions before the first
# screen dump:
#
#  \font\screenfont=cr-pc8 at 8pt % use any IBM OEM encoded fixed width font!
#
#  %%%%%%%%%%%%%%%%%%%%%%%%%%%%%%%%%%%%%%%%%%%%%%%%%%%%%%%%%%%%%%%%%%%%%%%%
#  % These macros are derived from The TeXbook pg 380-381
#  \def\uncatcodespecials{\def\do##1{\catcode`##1=12 }\dospecials}
#  \def\setupverbatim{\screenfont%
#    \def\par{\leavevmode\endgraf\relax}%
#    \obeylines\uncatcodespecials%
#    \catcode`\\=0\catcode`\{=1\catcode`\}=2\obeyspaces}
#  {\obeyspaces\global\let =\ } % let active space be a control space
#  \def\screenlisting#1{\par\begingroup%
#    \def\c##1{\char##1}\setupverbatim\input{#1}%
#    \endgroup}
#  %%%%%%%%%%%%%%%%%%%%%%%%%%%%%%%%%%%%%%%%%%%%%%%%%%%%%%%%%%%%%%%%%%%%%%%%
#  \def\screenbox#1{%
#    \vbox{\offinterlineskip%
#      \parskip=0pt\parindent=0pt%
```

*Example D-8: txt2verb.pl (continued)*

```
#        \screenlisting{#1}}}
#    %%%%%%%%%%%%%%%%%%%%%%%%%%%%%%%%%%%%%%%%%%%%%%%%%%%%%%%%%%%%%%%%%%%%%%%%%%
#    % Input converted file ´#1´ and set it inside a box with ´#2´ padding
#    % space around the image.
#    \def\screendump#1#2{%
#      \hbox{\vrule%
#        \vbox{\hrule%
#          \hbox{\hskip#2%
#            \vbox{\vskip#2%
#      \def\twentyxs{xxxxxxxxxxxxxxxxxxxx}%
#      \setbox0=\hbox{\screenfont\twentyxs\twentyxs\twentyxs\twentyxs}%
#      \hbox to \wd0{\screenbox{#1}\hss}%
#    \vskip#2}%
#          \hskip#2}%
#        \hrule}%
#      \vrule\hss}}
#    %%%%%%%%%%%%%%%%%%%%%%%%%%%%%%%%%%%%%%%%%%%%%%%%%%%%%%%%%%%%%%%%%%%%%%%%%%
#
# To include the converted image ´screen.tex´ in your document with 2pt
# of padding around the image, use:
#
#    \screendump{screen}{2pt}
#
# in your document.  Note: since this is set as an ´hbox´, you may need
# to use \leavevmode\screendump{screen}{2pt}
#
###########################################################################

require ´getopts.pl´;
do Getopts(´lvqL:´);

die "$0: options make no sense: -l and -L $opt_L.\n" if $opt_l && $opt_L;

$FILEOFLINES = $opt_l;
$VERBOSE     = $opt_v;
$QUIET       = $opt_q;
$LINELENGTH  = $opt_L || 80;

$capturefile = @ARGV[0] || die "Usage: $0 capturefile <texfile>";
$texfile     = @ARGV[1] || "-";

select(STDERR); $| = 1; select(STDOUT); # no buffering of stderr

%badchars = (); # These characters are illegal on input

# anything in the control character range
for ($byte = 0; $byte < 32; $byte++) {
    $char = sprintf("%c", $byte);
    $badchars{$char} = "\\c{$byte}";
}

# and anything over 126
for ($byte = 127; $byte < 256; $byte++) {
```

*Example D-8: txt2verb.pl (continued)*

```perl
    $char = sprintf("%c", $byte);
    $badchars{$char} = "\\c{$byte}";
}

$badchars{"\%"} = '\%';
$badchars{"\$"} = '\$';
$badchars{"\&"} = '\&';
$badchars{"\#"} = '\#';
$badchars{"\{"} = '\c{123}';
$badchars{"\}"} = '\c{125}';
$badchars{"\\"} = '\c{92}';
$badchars{"\_"} = '\c{95}';
$badchars{"\^"} = '\c{94}';

open (CAPTFILE, $capturefile)
    || die "Can't open capture file: $capturefile\n";
open (TEXFILE, ">$texfile")
    || die "Can't open TeX file: $texfile\n";
while ($line = &get_line()) {
    print STDERR "." if $texfile ne "-" && !$VERBOSE && !$QUIET;
    print STDERR "$line\n" if $VERBOSE;

    $outputbuf = "";
    while (length($line) > 0) {
$char = substr($line,0,1);
$line = substr($line,1);

if (defined($badchars{$char})) {
    $outputbuf .= $badchars{$char};
} else {
    $outputbuf .= $char;
}
    }
    print TEXFILE "$outputbuf\n";
}

close(CAPTFILE);
close(TEXFILE);

exit 0;

sub get_text_line {
    local($line);

    if ($line = scalar(<CAPTFILE>)) {
chop($line);
    }

    $line;
}

sub get_data_line {
    local($datalen, $line);
```

*Example D-8: txt2verb.pl (continued)*

```perl
    if ($datalen = read(CAPTFILE, $line, $LINELENGTH)) {
# if we got a complete line, look to see if the next
# characters in the file are CR, CR/LF, or LF.  If so, remove
# them (assume the are line breaks in the file)
if ($datalen = $LINELENGTH) {
    $place = tell(CAPTFILE);
    $datalen = read(CAPTFILE, $line, 1);
    if ($line eq "\015") {
$place++;
$datalen = read(CAPTFILE, $line, 1);
if ($line ne "\012") {
    seek(CAPTFILE, $place, 0);
}
    } elsif ($line ne "\012") {
seek(CAPTFILE, $place, 0);
    }
}
    } else {
return undef;
    }

    $line;
}

sub get_line {
    local($line);
    if ($FILEOFLINES) {
$line = &get_text_line();
    } else {
$line = &get_data_line();
    }

    $line;
}
```

# *Bibliography*

[1] Adobe Systems Incorporated. *Supporting Downloadable PostScript Fonts*. Tech. Rep. 5040, Mountain View, CA, January 1988.
`CTAN:fonts/postscript/adobe/Documents/5040.Download_Fonts.ps`.

[2] Adobe Systems Incorporated. *Adobe Binary Screen Font Files*. Tech. Rep. 5006, January 1989.
`CTAN:fonts/postscript/adobe/Documents/5006.ABF_Spec.ps`.

[3] Adobe Systems Incorporated. *Character Bitmap Distribution Format*. Tech. Rep. 5005, January 1989.
`CTAN:fonts/postscript/adobe/Documents/5005.BDF_Spec.ps`.

[4] Adobe Systems Incorporated. *Adobe Font Metric Files*. Tech. Rep. 5004, March 1990.
`CTAN:fonts/postscript/adobe/Documents/5004.AFM_Spec.ps`.

[5] Adobe Systems Incorporated. *Adobe Type 1 Font Format, version 1.1*, first edition, August 1990.

[6] Adobe Systems Incorporated. *Macintosh FOND Resources*. Tech. Rep. 0091, July 1990.
`jasper.ora.com:/pub/AdobeDocs/Specifications/0091-FondResources.ps`.

[7] Agfa Compugraphic Division. *IntelliFont Scalable Typeface Format*, first edition, April 1991.

[8] Beck, Micah and A. Siegal. "Transfig: Portable Graphics for TEX". *TUGboat*, 11(3):373–380, September 1990.

[9] Berendt, Gerhard. "On the implementation of graphics into TEX". *TUGboat*, 11(2):190–194, June 1990.

[10] Berry, Karl. "Filenames for Fonts". *TUGboat*, 11(4):517–520, November 1990.

[11] Bodenheimer, Bobby. *TₑX, ᴌᴬTₑX, etc.: Frequently Asked Questions with Answers*, December 1992.
rtfm.mit.edu:/pub/usenet/comp.text.tex/*.

[12] Cameron, Debra and Bill Rosenblatt. *Learning GNU Emacs*. O'Reilly & Associates, Sebastopol, CA, 1991.

[13] Carlisle, David. *The implementation of the ᴌᴬTₑX Colour interface*, February 1994.

[14] Clark, Adrian F. "Practical halftoning in TₑX". *TUGboat*, 12(1):157–165, March 1991.

[15] Ferguson, Michael J. *INRSTₑX Manual*. INRS Communications, 1991.

[16] Fößmeier, Reinhard. "X bitmaps in TₑX". *TUGboat*, 12(2):229–232, June 1991.

[17] Goossens, Michel et al. *The ᴌᴬTₑX Companion*. Addison Wesley, 1994.

[18] Gurari, Eitan M. *TₑX & ᴌᴬTₑX: Drawing and Literate Programming*. McGraw Hill, 1993.

[19] Guy, Richard K. *Unsolved Problems in Number Theory*, volume 1 of *Unsolved Problems in Intuitive Mathematics*. Springer-Verlag, 1981.

[20] Hahn, Jane. *ᴌᴬTₑX For Everyone*. Personal TₑX, Inc., second edition, 1991.

[21] Hewlett Packard. *PCL 5 Printer Language Technical Reference Manual*, first edition, September 1990.

[22] Hobby, John D. *A User's Manual for MetaPost*.
research.att.com:/pub/research/cstr/162.Z.

[23] Kabal, Peter. *TₑXdraw: PostScript drawings from TₑX*, 1.4a edition, July 1992.
CTAN:graphics/texdraw/manual/*.

[24] Knuth, Donald E. *The GF to PK Processor.*

[25] Knuth, Donald E. *The PL to TF Processor.*

[26] Knuth, Donald E. *The TF to PL Processor.*

[27] Knuth, Donald E. *The VF to VP Processor.*

[28] Knuth, Donald E. *The VP to VF Processor.*

[29] Knuth, Donald E. *The METAFONTbook*. Addison Wesley, 1986.

[30] Knuth, Donald E. *The TₑXbook*. Addison Wesley, fifteenth edition, 1989.

[31] Knuth, Donald E. "Virtual Fonts: More fun for Grand Wizards". *TUGboat*, 11(1):13–23, April 1990.

[32] Lamport, Leslie. *ᴌᴬTₑX: A Document Preparation System*. Addison Wesley, 1986.

[33] Lamport, Leslie. *MakeIndex: An Index Processor for ᴌᴬTₑX*, February 1987.
CTAN:indexing/makeindex/doc/*.

[34] Lewis, Chris and Nils-Peter Nelson. *Frequently Asked Questions for `comp.text`*, June 1993.
`rtfm.mit.edu:/pub/usenet/comp.text.tex`.

[35] Lunde, Ken. *Understanding Japanese Information Processing.* O'Reilly & Associates, Sebastopol, CA, first edition, 1993.

[36] Mattes, Eberhard. *The emTEX DVI Driver Manual*, June 1993.

[37] Mittelbach, Frank. *Interface description of NFSS2*, 1993.

[38] Mittelbach, Frank and Chris Rowley. *The LATEX3 Project*, April 1993.
`CTAN:info/ltx3pub/l3d001.tex`.

[39] Mittelbach, Frank and Rainer Schöpf. "A new font selection scheme for TEX macro packages—the basic macros". *TUGboat*, 10(2):222–238, July 1989.

[40] Mittelbach, Frank and Rainer Schöpf. "The new font family selection—User Interface to Standard LATEX". *TUGboat*, 11(1):297–305, June 1990. Reprinted with corrections in TUGboat 11:2.

[41] Mittelbach, Frank and Rainer Schöpf. *The New Font Selection Scheme—User Interface Standard to LATEX*, 1990.

[42] Norman, Donald A. *The Psychology of Everyday Things.* Basic Books, Inc., 1988.

[43] Patashnik, Oren. *Designing BIBTEX Styles*, February 1988.
`CTAN:biblio/bibtex/distribs/doc/btxhak.tex`.

[44] Patashnik, Oren. *BIBTEXing*, February 1988.
`CTAN:biblio/bibtex/distribs/doc/btxdoc.tex`.

[45] Pickrell, Lee S. "Combining graphics with TEX on IBM PC-compatible systems with LaserJet printers". *TUGboat*, 11(1):26–31, April 1990.

[46] Pickrell, Lee S. "Combining graphics with TEX on PC systems with laser printers, part II". *TUGboat*, 11(2):200–206, June 1990.

[47] Quin, Liam R. E. *Definitive List of All Fonts Available for METAFONT*, September 1991.
`CTAN:info/metafonts.lst`.

[48] Schrod, Joachim. *The Components of TEX*, March 1991.
`CTAN:info/components-of-TeX/*`.

[49] Schwer, Len. "Including Macintosh graphics in LATEX documents". *TUGboat*, 11(2):194–200, June 1990.

[50] Sowa, Friedhelm. "Bitmaps and halftones with BM2FONT". *TUGboat*, 12(3):534–539, December 1991.

[51] Sowa, Friedhelm. "Integration of graphics into TEX". *TUGboat*, 12(1):58–63, March 1991.

[52] Spivak, Michel. *The Joy of TEX—A Gourmet Guide to Typesetting with the $\mathcal{A}_{\mathcal{M}}\mathcal{S}$-TEX Macro Package*. Addison Wesley, 1986.

[53] The TUG DVI Driver Standards Committee. *The DVI Driver Standard, Level 0 Version 0.05*, August 1991.
`jasper.ora.com:/pub/docs/DVI-Standard-level0/*`.

[54] Tobin, Geoffrey. *METAFONT for Beginners*, December 1992.
`CTAN:info/metafont-for-beginners.tex`.

[55] University of Chicago. *The Chicago Manual of Style*, fourteenth edition, 1993.

[56] Uren, Emmanual et al. *Software Internationalization and Localization: An Introduction*. Van Nostrand Reinhold, 1993.

[57] Vulis, Michael. "VTEX enhancements to the TEX language". *TUGboat*, 11(3):429–435, September 1990.

[58] Wagner, Zdeněk. *Simple Drawings in METAFONT*, 1993.
`CTAN:info/wagner-drawing.tex`.

[59] Wall, Larry and Randal L. Schwartz. *Programming Perl*. O'Reilly & Associates, 1992.

[60] Walsh, Norman. *The comp.fonts Frequently Asked Questions List*, December 1992.
`rtfm.mit.edu:/pub/usenet/comp.fonts/FAQ.*`.

[61] Walsh, Norman. *Font Samples of Internet-Available PostScript Type1 Fonts*, December 1992.
`jasper.ora.com:/pub/fontbook/*`.

[62] Wichura, Michael J. *The PICTEX Manual*, March 1992.

# *Index*

# About the Author

Norm Walsh is a Production Tools Specialist at O'Reilly and Associates' Cambridge office. Before Norm joined ORA, he was a research assistant at University of Massachusetts, Amherst where he earned his master's degree in computer science.

Besides maintaining a number of TEX and font-related resources on the Net, Norm enjoys bicycling, herpetology, prestidigitation, and browsing record and book stores. Norm lives in Boxborough, MA with his wife Deborah, two cats, a box turtle, two toads, and two frogs.

# Colophon

Our look is the result of reader comments, our own experimentation, and feedback from distribution channels.

Distinctive covers complement our distinctive approach to technical topics, breathing personality and life into potentially dry subjects. UNIX and its attendant programs can be unruly beasts. Nutshell Handbooks® help you tame them.

The animal featured on the cover of *Making TEX Work* is the European garden spider. Garden spiders are orb weavers, known for their intricate orb-shaped webs. Web building is a complex process: support lines are constructed first; then the radial lines; and finally the spiraling strands are spun from the center outward. Without training from adults, even the tiniest just-hatched spiderlings are able to spin silk and weave webs. Another orb weaver, *nephila*, builds an extremely thick and strong web, up to eight feet in diameter. People in Southeast Asia have found an interesting use for this spider's web—they bend a pliable stick into a loop and pass it through the large web, resulting in a surprisingly strong and effective fishing net!

Spiders produce silk from glands called spinnerets. Orb weavers can have three or four pairs of these glands, each producing different textures of silk: non-stick silk for the radial web lines, and sticky silk for the spiraling strands. Some spiders even produce an ultraviolet silk to attract insects. Spider silk, a super protein that hardens as it is stretched from the spinnerets, may look delicate but it is unbelievably tough. The relative tension necessary to break it is far greater than for steel.

When finished with the construction of its web, the garden spider will often go to the center, hang upside down, and wait for a flying or jumping insect to become ensnared. Having poor eyesight, orb weavers rely on a highly-developed sense of touch. When an insect becomes caught in the web and struggles, the spider is alerted by the vibrations. It rushes out to secure its prey, usually wrapping it in silk. A poison is injected into the victim, paralyzing it and converting the contents of its body to liquid. The spider returns later to insert its tube-like fangs and suck up its meal.

The garden spider's profound sense of touch has another purpose: it provides male spiders with a channel to communicate with females. Before climbing onto the female's web, the male taps out a special message. Then he cautiously crawls toward his mate—a perilous task, for he is always in danger of being mistaken for prey. It is commonly thought that the female spider kills and eats the male after mating, but this is an exaggeration. The male, who stops eating during his mate-hunting ordeal, generally dies of malnourishment and exhaustion.

Spiders are similar to, but not the same as insects. They belong to the class *Arachnida*, named after Arachne, a maiden in Greek mythology. She defeated the goddess Athena in a weaving contest. In a fury of anger, Athena destroyed Arachne's weaving and beat the girl about the head. In utter disgrace, Arachne hanged herself. A regretful Athena changed Arachne into a spider so that she could weave forever.

While they are certainly not going to win any popularity contests, spiders' insect-eating habits are extremely helpful to humans. Every year, billions of spiders do away with a large number of disease-carrying and crop-destroying insects. If every spider ate just one a day for a year, those insects, piled in one spot, would weigh as much as 50 million people. Spiders are, by far, the most important predator of insects in our world.

Edie Freedman designed this cover and the entire UNIX bestiary that appears on other Nutshell Handbooks. The beasts themselves are adapted from nineteenth century engravings from the Dover Pictorial Archive. The cover layout was produced with QuarkXPress 3.1 using the ITC Garamond font.

The inside layout was designed by Edie Freedman and implemented by Norm Walsh in TEX using the ITC Garamond font family. The figures (except those in chapter 6) were created in Aldus Freehand 3.1 by Chris Reilley. The colophon was written by Elaine and Michael Kalantarian.

# USING UNIX AND X

*Books from O'Reilly & Associates, Inc.*

## –Basics–

*Our* UNIX in a Nutshell *guides are the most comprehensive quick reference on the market—a must for every* UNIX *user. No matter what system you use, we've got a version to cover your needs.*

### UNIX in a Nutshell: System V Edition

*By Daniel Gilly & the staff of O'Reilly & Associates*
*2nd Edition June 1992*
*444 pages, ISBN 1-56592-001-5*

You may have seen UNIX quick-reference guides, but you've never seen anything like *UNIX in a Nutshell*. Not a scaled-down quick reference of common commands, *UNIX in a Nutshell* is a complete reference containing all commands and options, along with generous descriptions and examples that put the commands in context. For all but the thorniest UNIX problems, this one reference should be all the documentation you need. Covers System V, Releases 3 and 4, and Solaris 2.0.

"This book is the perfect desktop reference.... The authors have presented a clear and concisely written book which would make an excellent addition to any UNIX user's library."
—*SysAdmin*

"Whether you are setting up your first UNIX system or adding your fiftieth user, these books can ease you through learning the fundamentals of the UNIX system."
—Michael J. O'Brien, Hardware Editor,
  *ABA/Unix/group Newsletter*

### SCO UNIX in a Nutshell

*By Ellie Cutler & the staff of O'Reilly & Associates*
*1st Edition February 1994*
*590 pages, ISBN 1-56592-037-6*

*The* desktop reference to SCO UNIX and Open Desktop®, this version of *UNIX in a Nutshell* shows you what's under the hood of your SCO system. It isn't a scaled-down quick reference of common commands, but a complete reference containing all user, programming, administration, and networking commands.

Contents include:

- All commands and options
- Shell syntax for the Bourne, Korn, C, and SCO shells
- Pattern matching, with *vi, ex, sed*, and *aw*k commands
- Compiler and debugging commands for software development
- Networking with email, TCP/IP, NFS, and UUCP
- System administration commands and the SCO sysadmsh shell

This edition of *UNIX in a Nutshell* is the most comprehensive SCO quick reference on the market, a must for any SCO user. You'll want to keep *SCO UNIX in a Nutshell* close by as you use your computer: it'll become a handy, indispensible reference for working with your SCO system.

## Learning the UNIX Operating System

*By Grace Todino, John Strang & Jerry Peek*
*3rd Edition August 1993*
*108 pages, ISBN 1-56592-060-0*

If you are new to UNIX, this concise introduction will tell you just what you need to get started and no more. Why wade through a 600-page book when you can begin working productively in a matter of minutes? It's an ideal primer for Mac and PC users of the Internet who need to know a little bit about UNIX on the systems they visit.

*Topics covered include:*

- Logging in and logging out
- Window systems (especially X/Motif)
- Managing UNIX files and directories
- Sending and receiving mail
- Redirecting input/output
- Pipes and filters
- Background processing
- Basic network commands

This book is the most effective introduction to UNIX in print. The third edition has been updated and expanded to provide increased coverage of window systems and networking. It's a handy book for someone just starting with UNIX, as well as someone who encounters a UNIX system as a visitor via remote login over the Internet.

"Once you've established a connection with the network, there's often a secondary obstacle to surmount.... *Learning the UNIX Operating System* helps you figure out what to do next by presenting in a nutshell the basics of how to deal with the 'U-word.' Obviously a 92-page book isn't going to make you an instant UNIX guru, but it does an excellent job of introducing basic operations in a concise nontechnical way, including how to navigate through the file system, send and receive E-mail and—most importantly—get to the online help...."
—Michael L. Porter, Associate Editor, *Personal Engineering & Instrumentation News*

"Whether you are setting up your first UNIX system or adding your fiftieth user, [this book] can ease you through learning the fundamentals of the UNIX system."
—Michael J. O'Brien, *ABA/Unix/group Newsletter*

## Learning the vi Editor

*By Linda Lamb*
*5th Edition October 1990*
*192 pages, ISBN 0-937175-67-6*

A complete guide to text editing with *vi*, the editor available on nearly every UNIX system. Early chapters cover the basics; later chapters explain more advanced editing tools, such as *ex* commands and global search and replacement.

"For those who are looking for an introductory book to give to new staff members who have no acquaintance with either screen editing or with UNIX screen editing, this is it: a book on *vi* that is neither designed for the UNIX in-crowd, nor so imbecilic that one is ashamed to use it."
—*;login*

## Learning the Korn Shell

*By Bill Rosenblatt*
*1st Edition June 1993*
*363 pages, ISBN 1-56592-054-6*

A thorough introduction to the Korn shell, both as a user interface and as a programming language. This book provides a clear explanation of the Korn shell's features, including *ksh* string operations, co-processes, signals and signal handling, and command-line interpretation. *Learning the Korn Shell* also includes real-life programming examples and a Korn shell debugger (*kshdb*).

"Readers still bending back the pages of Korn-shell manuals will find relief in...*Learning the Korn Shell*...a gentle introduction to the shell. Rather than focusing on syntax issues, the book quickly takes on the task of solving day-to-day problems with Korn-shell scripts. Application scripts are also shown and explained in detail. In fact, the book even presents a script debugger written for *ksh*. This is a good book for improving your knowledge of the shell."
—*Unix Review*

### MH & xmh: E-mail for Users & Programmers

*By Jerry Peek*
*2nd Edition September 1992*
*728 pages, ISBN 1-56592-027-9*

Customizing your email environment can save time and make communicating more enjoyable. *MH & xmh: E-Mail for Users & Programmers* explains how to use, customize, and program with the MH electronic mail commands available on virtually any UNIX system. The handbook also covers *xmh*, an X Window System client that runs MH programs.

The second edition added a chapter on *mhook*, sections explaining under-appreciated small commands and features, and more examples showing how to use MH to handle common situations.

"The MH bible is irrefutably Jerry Peek's *MH & xmh: E-mail for Users & Programmers*. This book covers just about everything that is known about MH and *xmh* (the X Windows front end to MH), presented in a clear and easy-to-read format. I strongly recommend that anybody serious about MH get a copy."
—James Hamilton, *UnixWorld*

### Learning the GNU Emacs

*By Debra Cameron & Bill Rosenblatt*
*1st Edition October 1991*
*442 pages, ISBN 0-937175-84-6*

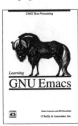

An introduction to the GNU Emacs editor, one of the most widely used and powerful editors available under UNIX. Provides a solid introduction to basic editing, a look at several important editing modes (special Emacs features for editing specific types of documents), and a brief introduction to customization and Emacs LISP programming. The book is aimed at new Emacs users, whether or not they are programmers.

"Authors Debra Cameron and Bill Rosenblatt do a particularly admirable job presenting the extensive functionality of GNU Emacs in well-organized, easily digested chapters.... Despite its title, *Learning GNU Emacs* could easily serve as a reference for the experienced Emacs user."
—Linda Branagan, Convex Computer Corporation

### The USENET Handbook

*By Mark Harrison*
*1st Edition Winter 1994-95 (est.)*
*250 pages (est.), ISBN 1-56592-101-1*

*The USENET Handbook* describes how to get the most out of the USENET news network, a worldwide network of cooperating computer sites that exchange public user messages known as "articles" or "postings." These postings are an electric mix of questions, commentary, hints, and ideas of all kinds, expressing the views of the thousands of participants at these sites.

Tutorials show you how to read news using the most popular newsreaders—*tin* and Trumpet for Windows and *nn*, *emacs* and *gnus* for UNIX. It also explains how to post articles to the Net.

The book discusses things you can do to increase your productivity by using the resources mentioned on USENET, such as anonymous FTP (file transfer protocol), mail servers, FAQs, and mailing lists. It covers network etiquette, processing encoded and compressed files (i.e., software, pictures, etc.), and lots of historical information.

### Using UUCP and Usenet

*By Grace Todino & Dale Dougherty*
*1st Edition February 1986 (latest update October 1991)*
*210 pages, ISBN 0-937175-10-2*

Shows users how to communicate with both UNIX and non-UNIX systems using UUCP and *cu* or *tip* and how to read news and post articles. This handbook assumes that UUCP is already running at your site.

"Are you having trouble with UUCP? Have you torn out your hair trying to set the Dialers file? *Managing UUCP and Usenet* and *Using UUCP and Usenet* will give you the information you need to become an accomplished net user. The companion book is *!%@:: A Directory of Electronic Mail Addressing & Networks*, a compendium of world networks and how to address and read them. All of these books are well written, and I urge you to take a look at them."
—*Root Journal*

## X User Tools

By Linda Mui & Valerie Quercia
1st Edition October 1994 (est.)
750 pages (est.) (CD-ROM included)
ISBN 1-56592-019-8

*X User Tools* provides for X users what *UNIX Power Tools* provides for UNIX users: hundreds of tips, tricks, scripts, techniques, and programs—plus a CD-ROM—to make the X Windowing System more enjoyable, more powerful, and easier to use.

This browser's book emphasizes useful programs, culled from the network and contributed by X programmers worldwide. Programs range from fun (games, screensavers, and a variety of online clocks) to business tools (calendar, memo, and mailer programs) to graphics (programs for drawing, displaying, and converting images). You'll also find a number of tips and techniques for configuring both individual and systemwide environments, as well as a glossary of common X and UNIX terms.

The browser style of organization—pioneered by *UNIX Power Tools*—encourages readers to leaf through the book at will, focusing on what appeals at the time. Each article stands on its own, many containing cross-references to related articles. Before you know it, you'll have covered the entire book, simply by scanning what's of interest and following cross-references to more detailed information.

The enclosed CD-ROM contains source files for all and binary files for some of the programs—for a number of platforms, including Sun 4, Solaris, HP 700, Alpha/OSF, and AIX. Note that the CD-ROM contains software for both *emacs* and *tcl/tk*.

## Volume 3: X Window System User's Guide

Standard Edition
By Valerie Quercia & Tim O'Reilly
4th Edition May 1993
836 pages, ISBN 1-56592-014-7

*The X Window System User's Guide* orients the new user to window system concepts and provides detailed tutorials for many client programs, including the *xterm* terminal emulator and window managers. Building on this basic knowledge, later chapters explain how to customize the X environment and provide sample configurations. The *Standard Edition* uses the *twm* manager in most examples and illustrations. Revised for X11 Release 5. This popular manual is available in two editions, one for users of the MIT software, and one for users of Motif. (see below).

"For the novice, this is the best introduction to X available. It will also be a convenient reference for experienced users and X applications developers."
—*Computing Reviews*

## Volume 3M: X Window System User's Guide

Motif Edition
By Valerie Quercia & Tim O'Reilly
2nd Edition January 1993
956 pages, ISBN 1-56592-015-5

This alternative edition of the *User's Guide* highlights the Motif window manager for users of the Motif graphical user interface. Revised for Motif 1.2 and X11 Release 5.

Material covered in this second edition includes:

- Overview of the X Color Management System (Xcms)

- Creating your own Xcms color database

- Tutorials for two "color editors": *xcoloredit* and *xtici*

- Using the X font server

- Tutorial for *editres*, a resource editor

- Extensive coverage of the new implementations of *bitmap* and *xmag*

- Overview of internationalization features

- Features common to Motif 1.2 applications: tear-off menus and drag-and-drop

# –Advanced–

## UNIX Power Tools

*By Jerry Peek, Mike Loukides, Tim O'Reilly, et al.*
*1st Edition March 1993*
*1162 pages (includes CD-ROM)*
*Random House ISBN 0-679-79073-X*

Ideal for UNIX users who hunger for technical—yet accessible—information, *UNIX Power Tools* consists of tips, tricks, concepts, and freeware (CD-ROM included). It also covers add-on utilities and how to take advantage of clever features in the most popular UNIX utilities.

This is a browser's book... like a magazine that you don't read from start to finish, but leaf through repeatedly until you realize that you've read it all. You'll find articles abstracted from O'Reilly Nutshell Handbooks®, new information that highlights program "tricks" and "gotchas," tips posted to the net over the years, and other accumulated wisdom. The goal of *UNIX Power Tools* is to help you think creatively about UNIX and get you to the point where you can analyze your own problems. Your own solutions won't be far behind.

The CD-ROM includes all of the scripts and aliases from the book, plus *perl*, GNU *emacs*, *pbmplus* (manipulation utilities), *ispell*, *screen*, the *sc*spreadsheet, and about 60 other freeware programs. In addition to the source code, all the software is precompiled for Sun3, Sun4, DECstation, IBM RS/6000, HP 9000 (700 series), SCO Xenix, and SCO UNIX. (SCO UNIX binaries will likely also run on other Intel UNIX platforms, including Univel's new UNIXware.)

"Chockful of ideas on how to get the most from UNIX, this book is aimed at those who want to improve their proficiency with this versatile operating system. Best of all, you don't have to be a computer scientist to understand it. If you use UNIX, this book belongs on your desk."
—Book Reviews, *Compuserve Magazine*

"*Unix Power Tools* is an encyclopedic work that belongs next to every serious UNIX user's terminal. If you're already a UNIX wizard, keep this book tucked under your desk for late-night reference when solving those difficult problems."
—Raymond GA Côté, *Byte*

## Making TₑX Work

*By Norman Walsh*
*1st Edition April 1994*
*522 pages, ISBN 1-56592-051-1*

TeX is a powerful tool for creating professional-quality typeset text and is unsurpassed at typesetting mathematical equations, scientific text, and multiple languages. Many books describe how you use TeX to construct sentences, paragraphs, and chapters. Until now, no book has described all the software that actually lets you build, run, and use TeX to best advantage on your platform. Because creating a TeX document requires the use of many tools, this lack of information is a serious problem for TeX users.

*Making TₑX Work* guides you through the maze of tools available in the TeX system. Beyond the core TeX program there are myriad drivers, macro packages, previewers, printing programs, online documentation facilities, graphics programs, and much more. This book describes them all.

## The Frame Handbook

*By Linda Branagan & Mike Sierra*
*1st Edition October 1994 (est.)*
*500 pages (est.), ISBN 1-56592-009-0*

A thorough, single-volume guide to using the UNIX version of FrameMaker 4.0, a sophisticated document production system. This book is for everyone who creates technical manuals and reports, from technical writers and editors who will become power users to administrative assistants and engineers. The book contains a thorough introduction to Frame and covers creating document templates, assembling books, and Frame tips and tricks. It begins by discussing the basic features of any text-formatting system: how it handles text and text-based tools (like spell-checking). It quickly gets into areas that benefit from a sophisticated tool like Frame: cross-references and footnotes; styles, master pages, and templates; tables and graphics; tables of contents and indexes; and, for those interested in online access, hypertext. Once you've finished this book, you'll be able to use Frame to create and produce a book or even a series of books.

## Exploring Expect

By Don Libes
1st Edition Winter 1994-95 (est.)
500 pages (est.), ISBN 1-56592-090-2

Written by the author of Expect, this is the first book to explain how this new part of the UNIX toolbox can be used to automate *telnet*, *ftp*, *passwd*, *rlogin*, and hundreds of other interactive applications. Based on *Tcl* (Tool Control Language), Expect lets you automate interactive applications that have previously been extremely difficult to handle with any scripting language.

The book briefly describes *Tcl* and how Expect relates to it. It then describes the *Tcl* language, using a combination of reference material and specific, useful examples of its features. It shows how to use Expect in background, in multiple processes, and with standard languages and tools like C, C++, and *Tk*, the X-based extension to *Tcl*. The strength in the book is in its scripts, conveniently listed in a separate index.

"Expect was the first widely used *Tcl* application, and it is still one of the most popular. This is a must-know tool for system administrators and many others."
—John Ousterhout, John.Ousterhout@Eng.Sun.COM

## sed & awk

By Dale Dougherty
1st Edition November 1990
414 pages, ISBN 0-937175-59-5

For people who create and modify text files, *sed* and *awk* are power tools for editing. Most of the things that you can do with these programs can be done interactively with a text editor; however, using *sed* and *awk* can save many hours of repetitive work in achieving the same result.

"*sed & awk* is a must for UNIX system programmers and administrators, and even general UNIX readers will benefit. I have over a hundred UNIX and C books in my personal library at home, but only a dozen are duplicated on the shelf where I work. This one just became number twelve."
—*Root Journal*

## Learning Perl

By Randal L. Schwartz, Foreword by Larry Wall
1st Edition November 1993
274 pages, ISBN 1-56592-042-2

*Learning Perl* is ideal for system administrators, programmers, and anyone else wanting a down-to-earth introduction to this useful language. Written by a Perl trainer, its aim is to make a competent, hands-on Perl programmer out of the reader as quickly as possible. The book takes a tutorial approach and includes hundreds of short code examples, along with some lengthy ones. The relatively inexperienced programmer will find *Learning Perl* easily accessible. Each chapter of the book includes practical programming exercises. Solutions are presented for all exercises.

For a comprehensive and detailed guide to advanced programming with Perl, read O'Reilly's companion book, *Programming perl*.

"All-in-all, *Learning Perl* is a fine introductory text that can dramatically ease moving into the world of *perl*. It fills a niche previously filled only by tutorials taught by a small number of *perl* experts.... The UNIX community too often lacks the kind of tutorial that this book offers."
—Rob Kolstad, *;login*

## Programming perl

By Larry Wall & Randal L. Schwartz
1st Edition January 1991
482 pages, ISBN 0-937175-64-1

This is the authoritative guide to the hottest new UNIX utility in years, coauthored by its creator, Larry Wall. Perl is a language for easily manipulating text, files, and processes. Perl provides a more concise and readable way to do many jobs that were formerly accomplished (with difficulty) by programming in the C language or one of the shells.

*Programming perl* covers Perl syntax, functions, debugging, efficiency, the Perl library, and more, including real-world Perl programs dealing with such issues as system administration and text manipulation. Also includes a pull-out quick-reference card (designed and created by Johan Vromans).

# O'Reilly & Associates—
# GLOBAL NETWORK NAVIGATOR

The Global Network Navigator (GNN)™ is a unique kind of information service that makes the Internet easy and enjoyable to use. We organize access to the vast information resources of the Internet so that you can find what you want. We also help you understand the Internet and the many ways you can explore it.

*In GNN you'll find:*

## Navigating the Net with GNN

 The *Whole Internet Catalog* contains a descriptive listing of the most useful Net resources and services with live links to those resources.

 The *GNN Business Pages* are where you'll learn about companies who have established a presence on the Internet and use its worldwide reach to help educate consumers.

 The *Internet Help Desk* helps folks who are new to the Net orient themselves and gets them started on the road to Internet exploration.

## News

 *NetNews* is a weekly publication that reports on the news of the Internet, with weekly feature articles that focus on Internet trends and special events. The Sports, Weather, and Comix Pages round out the news.

## Special Interest Publications

 Whether you're planning a trip or are just interested in reading about the journeys of others, you'll find that the *Travelers' Center* contains a rich collection of feature articles and ongoing columns about travel. In the *Travelers' Center*, you can link to many helpful and informative travel-related Internet resources.

 The *Personal Finance Center* is the place to go for information about money management and investment on the Internet. Whether you're an old pro at playing the market or are thinking about investing for the first time, you'll read articles and discover Internet resources that will help you to think of the Internet as a personal finance information tool.

*All in all, GNN helps you get more value for the time you spend on the Internet.*

 **The Best of the Web**

*GNN* received "Honorable Mention" for **"Best Overall Site," "Best Entertainment Service,"** and **"Most Important Service Concept."**

The *GNN NetNews* received "Honorable Mention" for **"Best Document Design."**

## Subscribe Today

GNN is available over the Internet as a subscription service. To get complete information about subscribing to GNN, send email to **info@gnn.com**. If you have access to a World Wide Web browser such as Mosaic or Lynx, you can use the following URL to register online: **http://gnn.com/**

If you use a browser that does not support online forms, you can retrieve an email version of the registration form automatically by sending email to **form@gnn.com**. Fill this form out and send it back to us by email, and we will confirm your registration.

## O'Reilly on the Net—
# ONLINE PROGRAM GUIDE

O'Reilly & Associates offers extensive information through our online resources. If you've got Internet access, we invite you to come and explore our little neck-of-the-woods.

### Online Resource Center

Most comprehensive among our online offerings is the O'Reilly Resource Center. Here, you'll find detailed information and descriptions on all O'Reilly products: titles, prices, tables of contents, indexes, author bios, CD-ROM directory listings, reviews... you can even view images of the products themselves. We also supply helpful ordering information: how to contact us, how to order online, distributors and bookstores around the world, discounts, upgrades, etc. In addition, we provide informative literature in the field, featuring articles, interviews, bibliographies, and columns that help you stay informed and abreast.

 **The Best of the Web**

The *O'Reilly Resource Center* was voted "**Best Commercial Site**" by users participating in "Best of the Web '94."

### To access ORA's Online Resource Center:

Point your Web browser (e.g., `mosaic` or `lynx`) to:

`http://gnn.com/ora/`

For the plaintext version, `telnet` or `gopher` to:

`gopher.ora.com`

(telnetters login: `gopher`)

### FTP

The example files and programs in many of our books are available electronically via FTP.

### To obtain example files and programs from O'Reilly texts:

`ftp` to:

`ftp.uu.net`

`cd published/oreilly`

or
`ftp.ora.com`

### Ora-news

An easy way to stay informed of the latest projects and products from O'Reilly & Associates is to subscribe to "ora-news," our electronic news service. Subscribers receive email as soon as the information breaks.

### To subscribe to "ora-news":

Send email to:
**listproc@online.ora.com**

and put the following information on the first line of your message (not in "Subject"):
**subscribe ora-news** "your name" **of** "your company"

For example:
**subscribe ora-news Jim Dandy of Mighty Fine Enterprises**

### Email

Many other helpful customer services are provided via email. Here's a few of the most popular and useful.

### Useful email addresses

**nuts@ora.com**
> For general questions and information.

**bookquestions@ora.com**
> For technical questions, or corrections, concerning book contents.

**order@ora.com**
> To order books online and for ordering questions.

**catalog@ora.com**
> To receive a free copy of our magazine/catalog, "ora.com" (please include a snailmail address).

### Snailmail and phones

**O'Reilly & Associates, Inc.**
**103A Morris Street, Sebastopol, CA 95472**
Inquiries: **707-829-0515, 800-998-9938**
Credit card orders: **800-889-8969**
FAX: **707-829-0104**

# O'Reilly & Associates—
# LISTING OF TITLES

## INTERNET

!%@:: A Directory of Electronic Mail
    Addressing & Networks
Connecting to the Internet: An O'Reilly Buyer's Guide
Internet In A Box
MH & xmh: E-mail for Users & Programmers
The Mosaic Handbook for Microsoft Windows
The Mosaic Handbook for the Macintosh
The Mosaic Handbook for the X Window System
Smileys
The Whole Internet User's Guide & Catalog

## SYSTEM ADMINISTRATION

Computer Security Basics
DNS and BIND
Essential System Administration
Linux Network Administrator's Guide (Fall 94 est.)
Managing Internet Information Services (Fall 94 est.)
Managing NFS and NIS
Managing UUCP and Usenet
sendmail
Practical UNIX Security
PGP: Pretty Good Privacy (Winter 94/95 est.)
System Performance Tuning
TCP/IP Network Administration
termcap & terminfo
X Window System Administrator's Guide: Volume 8
X Window System ,R6, Companion CD (Fall 94 est.)

## USING UNIX AND X

### BASICS

Learning GNU Emacs
Learning the Korn Shell
Learning the UNIX Operating System
Learning the vi Editor
SCO UNIX in a Nutshell
The USENET Handbook (Winter 94/95 est.)
Using UUCP and Usenet
UNIX in a Nutshell: System V Edition
The X Window System in a Nutshell
X Window System User's Guide: Volume 3
X Window System User's Guide, Motif Ed.: Vol. 3M
X User Tools (with CD-ROM) (10/94 est.)

### ADVANCED

Exploring Expect (Winter 94/95 est.)
The Frame Handbook (10/94 est.)
Making TeX Work
Learning Perl
Programming perl
sed & awk
UNIX Power Tools (with CD-ROM)

## PROGRAMMING UNIX, C, AND MULTI-PLATFORM

### FORTRAN/SCIENTIFIC COMPUTING

High Performance Computing
Migrating to Fortran 90
UNIX for FORTRAN Programmers

### C PROGRAMMING LIBRARIES

Practical C Programming
POSIX Programmer's Guide
POSIX.4: Programming for the Real World
    (Fall 94 est.)
Programming with curses
Understanding and Using COFF
Using C on the UNIX System

### C PROGRAMMING TOOLS

Checking C Programs with lint
lex & yacc
Managing Projects with make
Power Programming with RPC
Software Portability with imake

### MULTI-PLATFORM PROGRAMMING

Encyclopedia of Graphics File Formats
Distributing Applications Across DCE and
    Windows NT
Guide to Writing DCE Applications
Multi-Platform Code Management
Understanding DCE
Understanding Japanese Information Processing
ORACLE Performance Tuning

## BERKELEY 4.4 SOFTWARE DISTRIBUTION

4.4BSD System Manager's Manual
4.4BSD User's Reference Manual
4.4BSD User's Supplementary Documents
4.4BSD Programmer's Reference Manual
4.4BSD Programmer's Supplementary Documents
4.4BSD-Lite CD Companion
4.4BSD-Lite CD Companion: International Version

## X PROGRAMMING

Motif Programming Manual: Volume 6A
Motif Reference Manual: Volume 6B
Motif Tools
PEXlib Programming Manual
PEXlib Reference Manual
PHIGS Programming Manual (soft or hard cover)
PHIGS Reference Manual
Programmer's Supplement for R6 (Winter 94/95 est.)
Xlib Programming Manual: Volume 1
Xlib Reference Manual: Volume 2
X Protocol Reference Manual, R5: Volume 0
X Protocol Reference Manual, R6: Volume 0 (11/94 est.)
X Toolkit Intrinsics Programming Manual: Vol. 4
X Toolkit Intrinsics Programming Manual,
    Motif Edition: Volume 4M
X Toolkit Intrinsics Reference Manual: Volume 5
XView Programming Manual: Volume 7A
XView Reference Manual: Volume 7B

## THE X RESOURCE

### A QUARTERLY WORKING JOURNAL FOR X PROGRAMMERS

The X Resource: Issues 0 through 12
    (Issue 12 available 10/94)

## BUSINESS/CAREER

Building a Successful Software Business
Love Your Job!

## TRAVEL

Travelers' Tales Thailand
Travelers' Tales Mexico
Travelers' Tales India (Winter 94/95 est.)

## AUDIOTAPES

### INTERNET TALK RADIO'S "GEEK OF THE WEEK" INTERVIEWS

The Future of the Internet Protocol, 4 hours
Global Network Operations, 2 hours
Mobile IP Networking, 1 hour
Networked Information and
    Online Libraries, 1 hour
Security and Networks, 1 hour
European Networking, 1 hour

### NOTABLE SPEECHES OF THE INFORMATION AGE

John Perry Barlow, 1.5 hours

# O'Reilly & Associates—
# INTERNATIONAL DISTRIBUTORS

Customers outside North America can now order O'Reilly & Associates books through the following distributors. They offer our international customers faster order processing, more bookstores, increased representation at tradeshows worldwide, and the high quality, responsive service our customers have come to expect.

## EUROPE, MIDDLE EAST, AND AFRICA
*(except Germany, Switzerland, and Austria)*

### INQUIRIES
International Thomson Publishing Europe
Berkshire House
168-173 High Holborn
London WC1V 7AA
United Kingdom
Telephone: 44-71-497-1422
Fax: 44-71-497-1426
Email: danni.dolbear@itpuk.co.uk

### ORDERS
International Thomson Publishing Services, Ltd.
Cheriton House, North Way
Andover, Hampshire SP10 5BE
United Kingdom
Telephone: 44-264-342-832 (UK orders)
Telephone: 44-264-342-806 (outside UK)
Fax: 44-264-364418 (UK orders)
Fax: 44-264-342761 (outside UK)

## GERMANY, SWITZERLAND, AND AUSTRIA
International Thomson Publishing GmbH
O'Reilly-International Thomson Verlag
Attn: Mr. G. Miske
Königswinterer Strasse 418
53227 Bonn
Germany
Telephone: 49-228-970240
Fax: 49-228-441342
Email: gerd@orade.ora.com

## THE AMERICAS, JAPAN, AND OCEANIA
O'Reilly & Associates, Inc.
103A Morris Street
Sebastopol, CA 95472 U.S.A.
Telephone: 707-829-0515
Telephone: 800-998-9938 (U.S. & Canada)
Fax: 707-829-0104
Email: order@ora.com

## ASIA
*(except Japan)*

### INQUIRIES
International Thomson Publishing Asia
221 Henderson Road
#05 10 Henderson Building
Singapore 0315
Telephone: 65-272-6496
Fax: 65-272-6498

### ORDERS
Telephone: 65-268-7867
Fax: 65-268-6727

## AUSTRALIA
WoodsLane Pty. Ltd.
Unit 8, 101 Darley Street (P.O. Box 935)
Mona Vale NSW 2103
Australia
Telephone: 61-2-979-5944
Fax: 61-2-997-3348
Email: woods@tmx.mhs.oz.au

## NEW ZEALAND
WoodsLane New Zealand Ltd.
21 Cooks Street (P.O. Box 575)
Wanganui, New Zealand
Telephone: 64-6-347-6543
Fax: 64-6-345-4840
Email: woods@tmx.mhs.oz.au